THE SCIENCE OF MAN
IN THE WORLD CRISIS

THE SCIENCE OF
MAN
IN THE
WORLD CRISIS

EDITED BY
RALPH LINTON
Professor of Anthropology
Columbia University

COLUMBIA UNIVERSITY PRESS
NEW YORK · MORNINGSIDE HEIGHTS · 1945

THIS SYMPOSIUM and its publication were made possible by funds granted by the Viking Fund, Inc., a foundation created and endowed at the instance of A. L. Wenner-Gren for scientific, educational, and charitable purposes. The Viking Fund, Inc., is not, however, the author or publisher of this publication, and is not to be understood as approving, by virtue of its grant, any of the statements made, or views expressed, therein.

COPYRIGHT 1945 BY COLUMBIA UNIVERSITY PRESS, NEW YORK
Foreign agent: OXFORD UNIVERSITY PRESS, Humphrey Milford, Amen House, London, E.C., 4, England, AND B. I. Building, Nicol Road, Bombay, India

MANUFACTURED IN THE UNITED STATES OF AMERICA

*TO ALL WHO HAVE APPLIED
THE TECHNIQUES OF SCIENCE
TO THE SOLVING OF
HUMAN PROBLEMS*

Preface

THE PRESENT CRISIS in world affairs has resulted in a flood of books. Most of these are concerned with plans for world reorganization. The purpose of the present volume is much less ambitious. Everyone recognizes that such planning will require all the aid which science can give. At the same time, the problems involved are complex and many sided and can only be solved by collaboration between workers in many different fields of scientific research. It has been observed that it usually takes about a generation for the new discoveries and techniques of one science to become a part of the regular working equipment of other sciences. It takes considerably longer for such findings to become familiar to the layman and to exert any significant influence upon his thinking. The present book is an attempt to shorten this time interval. It is directed both to scientists and planners and to the general public without whose coöperation no plan can succeed.

The science of man is so new and its fund of knowledge has been increasing so rapidly that many of its findings have not yet reached scientific workers in other fields, let alone the man in the street. At the same time, some of these findings are of the utmost importance both for the intelligent planning of the new world order which now appears inevitable and for the implementation of any plans which may be made. The builders of such an order are foredoomed to failure unless they understand the potentialities and limitations of their human material. Scarcely less important is a knowledge of those trends which operate over long periods of time and of the problems which the specialist can foresee before they arise or can recognize before they become acute enough to call for drastic action. Lastly, even plans which take all these factors into account cannot succeed without the use of adequate techniques. At all these points the science of man can provide some aid.

In the preparation of the present volume the editor has been confronted with certain wartime limitations with regard to both space and personnel. A very large proportion of the younger scientists in this field are engaged in government service, many of them with the armed forces. After due consideration it was decided to make this book a report from the frontiers of research, the outposts of science rather than its settled hinterland. This has resulted in the exclusion of various subjects which might well have been included under other circumstances. Facts which are all ready well known have been passed over lightly and various problems which are already widely recognized and discussed have been omitted. Thus it has been taken for granted that the average reader knows and accepts the basic facts of man's origin and evolution and no space has been devoted to them. However, since much of our most recent knowledge of race has not reached the layman, this has been dealt with at some length. Again, the problems of Jewish and Negro minorities have not been dealt with specifically. Everyone is conscious of the existence of these problems and the literature dealing with them is already voluminous. They have been passed over in favor of a presentation of our new knowledge regarding the problems of minority groups in general. On the other hand, the looming problem of how to deal with the American Indian has been given considerable space since most laymen scarcely realize that such a problem exists. While such selectivity is sure to arouse criticism in certain quarters it is hoped that the present book will be judged on the basis of what it includes, not what it omits.

The editor wishes to express his gratitude to the numerous contributors who have collaborated to make available the results of recent research in their special fields. He feels that particular thanks are due them for their willingness to coöperate in terms of the all-over plan of the volume and to assume the added work involved by their collaboration, especially at this time. Thanks are also due to Dr. Paul Fejos, Director of Research of the Viking Fund, with whom the idea of this symposium originated and to the President and Directors of the Viking Fund, whose generosity has made possible its preparation and publication.

RALPH LINTON

Department of Anthropology
Columbia University
New York, N.Y.
August, 1944

Contents

THE SCOPE AND AIMS OF ANTHROPOLOGY 3
  Ralph Linton

SOCIETY AND BIOLOGICAL MAN 19
  H. L. Shapiro

THE CONCEPT OF RACE 38
  Wilton Marion Krogman

RACIAL PSYCHOLOGY 63
  Otto Klineberg

THE CONCEPT OF CULTURE 78
  Clyde Kluckhohn and William H. Kelly

THE CONCEPT OF BASIC PERSONALITY STRUCTURE AS AN OPERATIONAL TOOL IN THE SOCIAL SCIENCES 107
  Abram Kardiner

THE COMMON DENOMINATOR OF CULTURES 123
  George Peter Murdock

THE PROCESSES OF CULTURAL CHANGE 143
  Melville J. Herskovits

SOCIOPSYCHOLOGICAL ASPECTS OF ACCULTURATION 171
  A. Irving Hallowell

PRESENT WORLD CONDITIONS IN CULTURAL PERSPECTIVE 201
  Ralph Linton

THE PRESENT STATE OF WORLD RESOURCES 222
  Howard A. Meyerhoff

CONTENTS

POPULATION PROBLEMS   258
   Karl Sax

THE CHANGING AMERICAN INDIAN   282
   Julian H. Steward

THE COLONIAL CRISIS AND THE FUTURE   306
   Raymond Kennedy

THE PROBLEM OF MINORITY GROUPS   347
   Louis Wirth

APPLIED ANTHROPOLOGY IN COLONIAL ADMINISTRATION   373
   Felix M. Keesing

SOME CONSIDERATIONS OF INDIANIST POLICY   399
   Manuel Gamio

TECHNIQUES OF COMMUNITY STUDY AND ANALYSIS AS APPLIED TO MODERN CIVILIZED SOCIETIES   416
   Carl C. Taylor

THE ACQUISITION OF NEW SOCIAL HABITS   442
   John Dollard

COMMUNICATIONS RESEARCH AND INTERNATIONAL COÖPERATION   465
   Paul F. Lazarsfeld and Genevieve Knupfer

NATIONALISM, INTERNATIONALISM, AND THE WAR   496
   Grayson Kirk

INDEX   521

The Authors

JOHN DOLLARD is Professor of Social Anthropology and research worker in the Institute of Human Relations at Yale University. Since 1942 he has been Expert Consultant to the Secretary of War. His publications include: *Criteria for the Life History*, 1933; *Cast and Class in a Southern Town*, 1937; *Frustration and Aggression* (with L. W. Doob and others), 1939; *Children of Bondage* (with Allison Davis), 1940; *Victory over Fear*, 1942; *Fear in Battle*, 1943.

MANUEL GAMIO is Director of the Inter-American Indian Institute of Mexico and former Under Secretary of Education and Director of the Department of Rural Populations in the Ministry of Agriculture, Republic of Mexico. His most important publications are: *El Gobierno, el territorio, la poblacion*, 1917; *La Poblacion del Valle de Teotihuacan* (en colaboracion), 1921; *Mexican Immigration to the United States*, 1930; *Hacia un Mexico Nuevo, Problemas Sociales*, 1935.

A. IRVING HALLOWELL is Professor of Anthropology at Northwestern University. His publications include: *Bear Ceremonialism in the Northern Hemisphere*, 1926; *The Role of Conjuring in Saulteaux Society*, 1942; and numerous contributions to anthropological, psychological, and psychiatric journals.

MELVILLE J. HERSKOVITS is Professor of Anthropology at Northwestern University. His publications include: *The American Negro, a Study in Racial Crossing*, 1928; *Life in a Haitian Valley*, 1937; *Dahomey*, 1938; *Acculturation*, 1938; *The Economic Life of Primitive Peoples*, 1940; *The Myth of the Negro Past*, 1941.

ABRAM KARDINER is Assistant Professor in the Columbia University School of Medicine, Collaborator in the Department of Anthropology, Columbia University, and a practicing Psychoanalyst of long experience. His publications include: *The Individual and His Society*, 1939; *The Traumatic Neuroses of War*, 1941; *The Psychological Frontiers of Society* (in press).

FELIX M. KEESING is Professor of Anthropology at Stanford University. His publications include: *The Changing Maori*, 1928; *Modern*

Samoa, 1934; *Taming Philippine Headhunters*, 1934; *Education in Pacific Countries*, 1937; *The Menominee Indians of Wisconsin*, 1939; *The South Seas in the Modern World*, 1941.

WILLIAM H. KELLY is Instructor in Anthropology at Harvard University. His publications include articles in various anthropological journals.

RAYMOND KENNEDY is Associate Professor of Sociology at Yale University. His publications include: *The Ageless Indies*, 1942; *Islands and Peoples of the Indies*, 1943.

GRAYSON L. KIRK is Professor of Government at Columbia University, Research Associate in the Yale Institute of International Studies, and Research Secretary, Council of Foreign Relations. His publications include: *Philippine Independence*, 1936; *Contemporary International Politics* (with W. R. Sharp), 1940; *War and National Policy, a Syllabus* (with R. P. Stebbins), 1942.

OTTO L. KLINEBERG is Assistant Professor of Psychology at Columbia University. His publications include: *Experimental Study of Speed and Other Factors in "Racial" Differences*, 1928; *Race Differences*, 1935; *Social Psychology*, 1940.

CLYDE KLUCKHOHN is Associate Professor of Anthropology at Harvard University. His publications include: *Navaho Witchcraft*, 1943; *The Use of Personal Documents in Anthropological Science*, 1944; and numerous contributions to anthropological, psychological, and sociological journals.

GENEVIEVE KNUPFER is Research Analyst, Overseas Division OWI, and author of *The Measurement of Social Economic Status* (in press).

WILTON MARION KROGMAN is Associate Professor of Anatomy and Physical Anthropology at the University of Chicago and Research Associate in Physical Anthropology at the Chicago Natural History Museum. His publications include: *The Physical Anthropology of the Seminole Indians of Oklahoma*, 1935; *Bibliography of Human Morphology, 1914–1939*, 1941; *The Growth of Man*, 1941.

PAUL F. LAZARSFELD is Associate Professor of Sociology, at Columbia University, Director of Bureau of Applied Social Research. His publications include: *The Family in the Depression* (with S. Stouffer) 1937; *Radio and the Printed Page*, 1940; *The Daily Newspaper and Its Competitors*, 1942; *Radio Research*, 1941, 1942, 1943; *Votes in the Making* (with Bernard Berelson and Hazel Guadet), 1944.

RALPH LINTON is Professor of Anthropology at Columbia University and Associate at the American Museum of Natural History. His publications include: *The Material Culture of the Marquesas Islands*, 1924; *The Tanala, a Hill Tribe of Madagascar*, 1933; *The Study of Man*, 1936.

HOWARD A. MEYERHOFF is Professor of Geology at Smith College. His publications include: *Geology of Puerto Rico* (with George W. Bain) 1933; *The Flow of Time in the Connecticut Valley*, 1942; and numerous contributions to scientific journals.

GEORGE PETER MURDOCK, now serving as Lieutenant Commander USNR, is in peacetimes Professor of Anthropology at Yale University. His publications include: *Our Primitive Contemporaries*, 1934; *Outline of Cultural Materials*, 1938; *Ethnographic Bibliography of North America*, 1941.

KARL SAX is Professor of Botany, Arnold Arboretum, Harvard University. His publications include: *Chromosome Relations in Wheat*, 1921; *The Nature of Size Inheritance*, 1924; *An Analysis of X-Ray Induced Chromosomal Aberrations in Tradescantia*, 1940.

HARRY L. SHAPIRO is Curator of Anthropology at the American Museum of Natural History and Professor of Anthropology at Columbia University. His publications include: *The Heritage of Bounty*, 1936; *Migrations and Environment*, 1939; and numerous articles in scientific journals.

JULIAN H. STEWARD is Director of the Institute of Social Anthropology in the Smithsonian Institution, and Editor of the Handbook of South American Indians. He is the author of papers and monographs on the Shoshonean Indians of the Western United States, the Carrier of British Columbia, and various South American tribes.

CARL C. TAYLOR is Head of the Division of Farm Population and Rural Welfare, Bureau of Agricultural Economics, U.S. Department of Agriculture. His publications include: *The Social Survey*, 1919; *Rural Sociology*, 1926; *Human Relations*, 1927; and numerous articles in sociological journals and agricultural periodicals.

THE AUTHORS

LOUIS WIRTH is Professor of Sociology at the University of Chicago. His publications include: *The City* (with R. E. Park and others), 1925; *The Ghetto*, 1928; *Our Cities, Their Role in the National Economy* (with others), 1937; *Urban Planning and Land Policies* (with others), 1939.

THE SCIENCE OF MAN
IN THE WORLD CRISIS

The Scope and Aims of Anthropology
By RALPH LINTON

THE PRESENT period is the first in the world's history in which men have turned to science for aid rather than to the supernatural. Unfortunately those who seek such aid too often find themselves in the position of a sick man shifted from specialist to specialist without obtaining any over-all picture of his illness or any one plan for its cure. Science began as natural philosophy, a particular way of looking at the world with particular techniques for studying it. At its inception it had a universality comparable to that of the Church. However, no sooner had it won its right to live than it began to propagate itself by an amoebalike process of fission. It ceased to be one science and became instead a series of sciences each of which had its own interests and its own rigidly delimited subject matter. Even the amoeba has learned the advantage of occasional conjugations from which both parties emerge invigorated, but it seems that many scientists have still to learn it. During the last hundred years the tendency has been for each science to hold the others at a safe distance, browsing on its own selected pastures and learning more and more about less and less. Although this is undoubtedly due in part to the vast accumulation of factual knowledge which this period has seen, it also represents a definite attitude whose effects have been stultifying. It is true that no one scientist can possibly acquaint himself with the whole range of scientific knowledge as it exists today, yet it is quite possible for any man to know the conclusions which have been arrived at in several sciences other than his own and to apply these to his own problems. Most of these conclusions are relatively simple and the time would seem to be ripe for a new synthesis of science, especially of those sciences which deal with human beings and their problems.

By its very definition, the science of anthropology makes a bid for this position. In all English-speaking countries the term is taken to mean "the science of man and his works." In Europe the term has been given a somewhat different meaning, being limited to the study of man's physical characteristics, but we will adhere to the broader definition. Throughout its entire history, anthropology has differed from such familiar sciences as zoology or physiology or genetics in one important respect. Where these sciences have concentrated upon phenomena of certain limited sorts wherever they occurred in nature, anthropology has concentrated its interest upon a single organism, man, and has tried to understand all sorts of phenomena as they affected him. It has attempted to find out all that there was to be known about this curious biped and his still more curious behavior. This has not improved its standing among the sciences. Followers of the natural and physical sciences have tended to regard the anthropologist as an anachronism, the last survivor of that class of pleasant gentlemen who, in the eighteenth century, knew something about almost everything but not much about anything. However, it is equally possible to regard anthropology as the first of a series of synthesizing sciences the need for which is becoming ever more apparent. The writer feels that it is to the credit rather than the discredit of anthropologists that most of them have been willing to employ the techniques and conclusions of other sciences and to follow problems wherever they led without paying much attention to scientific borders and "No Trespassing" signs.

Even with the best intentions, anthropology has not been able to avoid the atomistic tendencies which have characterized science in general. The field which anthropology has attempted to cover is so vast and involves phenomena of so many different sorts that no one individual can be intimately acquainted with the whole of it. It has, therefore, followed the familiar pattern of fission and split into a number of subsciences each of which has developed its own group of specialists. It has even had its minor civil wars over the exact limits of such subsciences and their relative importance. However, the modern tendency is to pay less and less attention to these limits and to recognize that all these subsciences are parts of a whole, some useful for solving one problem and some useful for another, but all necessary to the understanding of human existence.

The sharpest split within anthropology has been that along the line laid down in the very definition of the science, the distinction between man and his works. The study of man as an animal, one of many mammalian species, leans almost exclusively upon the techniques and conclusions developed by the natural sciences. Actually, it can use only a small part of the techniques, since human beings do not take kindly to being made the subject of experiment. Again and again it has had to wait for the natural sciences to clear up some point by animal experiment. Thus the controlled breeding of human beings presents great difficulties even in a totalitarian state. The understanding of human heredity and the clearing up of various problems connected with the human varieties which we call races was impossible until the geneticist's work with fruit flies and rats had provided the necessary information. On the other hand, the study of human behavior can receive little help from the findings of natural science. Although some of the simplest behavioral phenomena, such as learning processes, can be studied in animals and by experimental techniques most of them have no close parallel at the animal level. This is especially true with respect to the complex phenomena involved in organized social life. Although in this field anthropologists have been able to use some of the techniques developed by the social sciences, they have rarely had to wait upon the development of such techniques. In fact they have been able to contribute quite as much to the development of these sciences as they have received from them.

The two great divisions of anthropology which deal respectively with man and with his works are known as physical anthropology and cultural anthropology. This division dates back to the very beginnings of anthropology and each branch of the science has followed its own line of development and produced its own group of specialists. Very few individuals have been active in and familiar with both fields, with the result that the two have largely lost touch with each other. It seemed for a time that the separation might be a permanent one, with physical anthropology becoming completely aligned with the natural sciences and cultural anthropology with the social sciences. However, they are now beginning to be drawn together again as we become increasingly conscious of the influence of certain physiological factors upon culture and vice versa. This process is being reinforced by a sort of renaissance in the field of physical anthropology itself. After generations of preoccupation with bones, bodily measurements, and systems of racial classification, the physical anthropologists are beginning to turn to studies of a more dynamic sort and to recognize that in these cultural factors have to be taken into account.

Each of the main divisions of anthropology has undergone further differentiation. Physical anthropology has split into human paleontology and somatology; cultural anthropology into archeology, ethnology, and linguistics. The names of these subsciences are daunting, but the sciences themselves, or at least their more spectacular findings, will be familiar to most readers. Human paleontology deals with the origins and evolution of our species, especially as these are revealed by fossils. Every time one reads of the finding of another fragment of some ancient half-human form, with a discussion of its relations to modern man, he is coming into contact with this branch of anthropology. This is, or was before the present war, one of the most rapidly developing areas in the science. Every year brought forth new finds and new disputes as to where even the old ones belonged in the human family tree. What the investigators in this field have lacked in numbers they have more than compensated for in enthusiasm. The exceedingly fragmentary nature of the finds, and the fact that many of them were one of a kind, have simply given the human paleontologists more room for maneuver on the field of battle. The only undisputed facts which have emerged from this work so far are that there were a number of ancient species which were more or less intermediate between men and apes and that one or more of these must have been the ancestors of modern man. Which one has the proud distinction is still an unsettled question. Since even the final establishment of the "missing link" will not be of much aid to his descendants in their present difficulties, the results of this branch of anthropology have been excluded from the present symposium.

Somatology deals with modern man in all his physical aspects. The general characteristics of our species as vertebrates and mammals are well taken care of by such general sciences as anatomy and physiology. The somatologists have, therefore, concentrated upon the study of human varieties, their differences and the probable causes of these differences. Until very recent times, most of their attention has been concentrated upon the classification of the various human varieties—that is, races—and their possible relationships. The classifications which they have developed still depend mainly upon simple, superficial characteristics such as skin color and hair form. In recent years attention has been turned to less obvious but intrinsically more important differences such as blood types, differences in musculature, and so on. Still more recently, somatologists have begun to study group differences in growth rates, time of sexual maturation, metabolic rates, and disease immunities. Here many of their findings may be of immediate practical value. The head shape of a particular human variety has little importance except in cases where it has been given social significance, but the adjustment of a particular variety to certain conditions of altitude and temperature, or its inherited resistance to malaria, may be of great importance for any resettlement program.

The whole concept of race, so vigorously misused in certain quarters, lies within the field of somatology and we must look to it for the final settlement of those problems which are connected with race at the physiological as distinct from the social level. Unfortunately, such problems are in the minority. Aside from the demonstrable fact that certain races do better than others in certain environments, the main significance of racial differences in a modern world lies in the social values attached to them. Our present frictions arise not from anything inherent in racial differences but from the fact that such differences have come to be used as indicators of social status. The average individual in our own society is quite unable to say which of the various European racial types most of his friends belong to, since this is a matter of no social importance. At the same time he will be conscious of very small differences in physical type when these indicate that the individual belongs to some socially differentiated group such as the Jew or the Negro.

Turning to the field of cultural anthropology and its subsciences, we find that the subscience of linguistics is, at present, the most isolated and self-contained. The study of languages can be and largely has been carried on with little relation to other aspects of human activity. The great diversity of languages, especially among the so-called primitive peoples, and their curious and complex structures affords the investigator unlimited material for research. When presented with the results of such research the layman is likely to be reminded of Abe Martin's dictum: "It takes years to become a champeen checker player and what then?" However, the analysis and classification of languages, like the classification of human varieties, is only a first step. In language and its diversities the scientist has a tool which should ultimately prove of great value for understanding the deeper levels of both individual and group psychology. Although we are taught to regard language as primarily a means of communication, it is equally important as a tool for thinking. This is the area in which the wide range of existing linguistic forms is most significant. Any idea can be communicated in any language if the speaker will take time enough, but the concepts which are an integral part of all linguistic forms have a subtle influence upon the individual's ways of thinking. These concepts are even more compulsive because they are totally unconscious.

An example may help to make this clear. The lack of an inanimate gender in English gives an animistic slant to all our thinking. An inanimate gender is not to be confused with a neuter one. *It* in English can refer to inanimate objects, but it can also refer to animate ones such as ghosts or, at some risk of the parents' displeasure, babies. *He* and *She*, with their implicit ascription of sex, always imply animation. The result of this linguistic accident is that we cannot refer to anything, even the most abstract concept, without unconsciously endowing it with life and capacity for volition. We have to personify everything we talk or even think about. Those who try to work with abstractions find themselves in a constant battle with this tendency toward personification and no matter how careful they are it slips through occasionally to interfere with their clarity of thought. If English had an inanimate gender, as many other languages do, the words used for abstractions would, in themselves, provide a constant corrective for such a tendency.

Finally, it should be noted that the study of linguistics is not to be confused with the trick of learning languages. Understanding of the structure of a language may be an aid in learning it but it is by no means necessary. Note the experience of children and of those who "pick up" a foreign language without any knowledge of its grammar. There are plenty of people who can speak several languages while remaining blissfully unconscious of the structure of any of them. That linguistics ultimately will be of great value for the understanding of human behavior and especially of human thought processes can hardly be doubted. However, work along these lines has barely begun and linguistics is still unable to make any great contribution toward the solution of our current problems. For that reason it has been ignored in the present volume.

The two other subsciences in the field of cultural anthropology, namely archeology and ethnology, bear somewhat the same relation to each other that human paleontology bears to somatology in the field of physical anthropology. Archeology deals with the beginnings of culture and with those cultures or phases of culture which are now extinct. Ethnology deals with the living cultures of mankind in all their variety. Archeology is, perhaps, the most popular branch of anthropology and the one whose findings are best known to the average layman. The results of various "digs" are constantly noted in the newspapers so that, to cite a single case, the name of an obscure Egyptian king, Tut-ank-amen, has become almost a household word. In general, archeologists try to discover and interpret that part of our past which is not revealed by written records. The study of the recorded past is assigned to the field of history. Since men have been writing for, at most, 6,000 years while our species has been in existence for at least 100,000 years, the archeologist has plenty of room for his operations. Moreover, it is only under exceptional conditions that written records tell us much about the life of the common man in any society. Ancient scribes usually wrote for and about kings and priests. Even our knowledge of such a well-documented civilization as that of the Romans has been tremendously enlarged by such excavations as those at Pompeii.

For the archeologist himself this science provides a happy combination of the thrills of research with those of treasure hunting, plus the added advantage of salary and expenses. For the wealthy backer it provides tangible, visible returns for the money invested, plus a complete absence of anything which might disturb the social *status quo*. It is not surprising, therefore, that archeological studies are usually easy to finance and that the science has progressed by leaps and bounds. The war has brought some interruption, but in spite of this it seems probable that another fifty years will give us a fairly clear picture of man's past in most parts of the world. This applies, of course, to those aspects of the past which are reflected in imperishable objects. We can discover what sort of tools an ancient society used, what its members ate, what sort of houses they lived in and how they disposed of their dead, but archeology cannot tell us whether they were addicted to wife beating.

Although the immediate and obvious purpose of archeological work is to fill out our factual knowledge of man's past, its ultimate purpose is to give us an understanding of the processes involved in the growth, flowering and collapse of civilizations and the factors which may be responsible for these. This is also the ultimate aim of history, but in the absence of written records the archeologist has developed new techniques, borrowing from other sciences in the process. He can deduce the opening of new trade routes from the chemical analysis of fragments of metal or pottery and, with the aid of dendrochronology, date the sack of a city from a few bits of charred timber. Moreover, the vast periods with which he deals make it possible for him to discern the working of trends and cycles which operate in terms of millennia. He can trace the effects of climatic change or soil exhaustion in a way impossible to the historian and map the path of civilization on a wider field. Although the specific findings of archeology are not dealt with in the present volume, its conclusions with regard to process have become part of the common knowledge of all anthropologists working with phenomena of culture change. As such they are reflected in several of the contributions.

Ethnology deals with the ways of life of societies which are still extant or, at most, so recently extinct that fairly complete records are available. Every society has its own way of life, called its "culture" by anthropologists. The concept of culture is one of the most important tools of the anthropological investigator. Since one of the papers in this symposium is devoted to it, we need not deal with it here. At the same time, culture is such a convenient label for designating the organized collection of habits, ideas, and attitudes shared by the members of any society that it is almost impossible for any anthropologist to discuss these without using it. The task of the ethnologist is to study and compare cultures which are still going concerns and, from this, to develop conclusions which will hold good for culture in general. As in any other scientific work, the first step is the collection of facts about these cultures, and the work of the ethnologist takes him into all sorts of out-of-the-way places and among all sorts of people. Until very recent times, ethnologists have limited their fact-finding activities to the so-called "primitive" peoples, those living outside the scope of the few rich and complex cultures which we call civilizations. The more isolated such groups and the more widely their cultures differed from our own, the greater has been the interest in them. The old line ethnologist is in the seventh heaven if he can find a group which has never seen a white man before and he views the current opening up of the far corners of the earth with all the alarm of any craftsman whose livelihood is threatened. Ethnologists of the younger generation are less worried by the march of events. The study of cultures widely different from our own has led to the development of techniques for fact finding and, above all, of attitudes of detachment, which lose none of their value when they are applied to civilized societies and cultures in transition. It is more romantic to study the natives of a South Sea island than a community of Iowa farmers, but the same scientific methods can be used with both and both can yield significant results. As long as human beings continue to live in communities and to develop special ways of life to meet special conditions the ethnologist will not be threatened with technological unemployment.

It might be questioned why the ethnologist should try to work with "primitive" peoples at all. It would seem that the culture of some dwindling tribe of Australian aborigines or American Indians, doomed to certain extinction, could give us little information which would be of use to us in meeting our own urgent problems. Actually, the study of one such tribe is of little practical value, but the study of a series of tribes, with later comparisons and analyses, may be exceedingly valuable. The social sciences are, by the very nature of their materials, debarred from using the techniques of controlled experiment which are the main stock in trade of the physical and even the natural sciences. No one can put a human society in a laboratory and see how it responds to various stimuli. The only substitute is to study and record societies as we find them and the more diverse the conditions under which they can be observed, the better the opportunity for arriving at conclusions which will hold good for all societies everywhere.

The ultimate aims of the ethnologist are essentially the same as those of the sociologist, economist and, in part, the historian. All four are trying to understand how societies and cultures operate and why and how cultures change. They are attempting to arrive at certain generalizations, "laws" in common parlance, which will make it possible to predict the course of events and ultimately to control it. The main difference between ethnology on the one hand and sociology and economics on the other is that the latter have carried on their investigations almost entirely within the narrow frame of reference provided by our own society and culture. They have thus taken for granted many factors which have been characteristic of our own way of life during the last two or three hundred years but which are not an invariable accompaniment of social living. This might be well enough for the prediction and control of events in our own society if we lived in a period when most elements in our culture could be counted on to persist over long periods with little change. However, generalizations based upon such a narrow frame of reference have little value when the conditions which they take for granted are changing rapidly. The rise of new culture patterns and the disappearance of old ones robs such generalizations of most of their significance. Thus it would be an exceedingly optimistic economist who would try to use the generalizations based on our own business cycles of the past fifty years to predict what would happen in a totalitarian state. To be of value under the current conditions of rapid and basic change, generalizations about cultural and social phenomena will have to be based on the comparison of a much wider range of societies than the established social sciences have so far attempted to deal with. Such generalizations will have to get back to the basic principles on which all societies and cultures operate; the common denominators of human existence.

In the search for such common denominators the ethnologist has certain initial advantages. The "primitive" societies which have been, until very recent times, the center of his interest are, for the most part, small and compact and their cultures both simpler and better integrated than our own. There are thus fewer variables to be dealt with and a better chance of ascertaining how such societies and cultures really work. It is a general rule of science that research should proceed, when possible, from the simple to the complex and the ethnologist has been doing just this in his social and cultural investigations. He hopes and believes that his findings in the simpler societies will help us to understand the more complicated ones, including our own. Still another factor which has worked to his advantage is that the investigator of an alien society can approach his work with a measure of detachment quite impossible in dealing with his own. Although no human being can approach the study of his own species in the same completely impersonal terms which he might apply to a study of ants, he can come closest to it when the society in question is completely different from that in which he was reared. After the initial shock of discovering that wives in a polygynous society are strongly in favor of the institution or that old people ask their children to kill them when their rheumatism gets too troublesome, the ethnologist soon develops the attitude summed up in the familiar phrase: "Well, some do and some don't." The attitude is fatal to any reforming ardor, but it is a great help in acquiring the sort of accurate information needed for comparative studies. A high moral purpose has its uses in many situations but not in scientific research.

The various subsciences just discussed represent the content of anthropology as a formal discipline and as it is embalmed in the course announcements of most universities. However, there are important developments under way in various areas marginal to this long-established nucleus. The most important of these, at least from the point of view of furthering the development of pure science, is the emergence of a new field of research dealing with the interrelations of personality and culture. Until very recent times, ethnologists have deliberately limited their investigations to the mass phenomena of society and culture. They have regarded the individual as a mere culture carrier, one of a series of identical and interchangeable units. They have not troubled to enquire how he became a culture carrier or why, under certain circumstances, he departed from this passive role and initiated culture change. However, as time has gone on and as a better understanding of cultural phenomena has been achieved, the importance of these problems has become increasingly apparent. Lacking any techniques of his own for dealing with the individual, the ethnologist has turned to the personality psychologist for aid.

Personality psychology has followed a somewhat similar course in its development. It concentrated upon the individual and at first, under the influence of the natural sciences, tried to explain all individual similarities and differences on a physiological basis. Although the importance of environment in personality formation soon became apparent, this was used, at first, simply to explain individual differences. Lacking familiarity with the concept of culture and of any culture other than that of Europeans, the psychologists overlooked the importance of those experiences common to all individuals reared in our own civilization. In fact they took these results so much for granted that they posited various universal instincts to account for them. The discovery that personality norms differed for different societies and cultures came as a shock and one which necessitated a basic reorganization of many of their concepts. Since most of the personality psychologists were not in a position to obtain firsthand data on societies other than their own and since they had developed no techniques for recording or organizing cultural material, they have turned to the ethnologists for help.

The result of these convergent developments has been the emergence of a new area of concentration. It is too early to say whether the study of personality and culture will become a distinct subscience, but it certainly manifests a high degree of hybrid vigor. Although barely twenty years old it has already exerted considerable influence upon both of the parent sciences. It is giving the psychologists a much better understanding of the principles underlying personality formation and especially of the wide range of forms which the personalities of "normal" individuals may assume. Conversely, it has drawn the attention of the ethnologist to the differences in basic personality type for various societies; something which he had previously recognized without attempting to deal with or explain. Through this it is pointing the way toward the solution of one of the most difficult problems with which the ethnologist has to deal. Since the very beginning of his research he has sought to discover why certain societies develop particular foci of interest, why they accept or reject various innovations when no factors of utility seem to be involved, and why various cultures manifest different but consistent trends in their development. These things have so far been ascribed to historic accident, a manifest begging of the question. With the recognition of the existence of basic personality types and an understanding of how they are produced, such "accidents" become comprehensible and even, in certain cases, predictable. The importance of this for the planning and direction of culture change cannot be overestimated.

Although coöperation of anthropology with psychology has been, perhaps, the most fertile in results, anthropology has also worked with other disciplines toward the solution of common problems. There has been a steady exchange of ideas and techniques between ethnology and sociology. Sociology, as the older and also the more philosophic science, has far surpassed ethnology in the number and elaboration of its concepts and theories. It has also developed statistical techniques to a point far beyond anything ordinarily known to the ethnologist. However, it has limited itself almost exclusively to the study of our own institutions, so that many of its conclusions have not been applicable to mankind as a whole or even to our own society under conditions of rapid change. Contact with ethnology has provided sociology with new research techniques which are proving of especial value in the study of the smaller modern communities. It has also greatly expanded sociology's frame of reference, with consequent changes in certain of its theoretical formulations. In fact, at the level of theory the two sciences are converging so rapidly that it seems probable that within a few years there will be no important differences.

Another significant field of collaboration is that of somatology, physiology, and ethnology in the study of diet. This work, which has been carried on primarily under the direction of Dr. Margaret Mead and the sponsorship of the National Research Council, has been directed toward practical rather than theoretical ends. Its purpose has been to provide information on the basis of which nutritional standards in the United States might be improved and the feeding of foreign populations during the immediate post-war period carried out more effectively. The main contribution of ethnology in this work has been the recognition that food habits may be almost as important as food supply in determining whether a particular group is adequately nourished. However, such studies would seem to have important implications in connection with the possible physiological adjustment of various human groups to various diets, a field in which research has barely begun.

In addition to these coöperative activities in connection with adjoining sciences, anthropology has, in recent years, begun to invade the field of applied science. Its first excursions in this direction were, quite understandably, in connection with colonial administration. The more progressive colonial powers, notably England and Holland, learned by painful experience that an understanding of native institutions is a prerequisite for successful colonial government. They also discovered that it took years for the average individual to acquire such an understanding and that he was likely to make costly mistakes in the meanwhile. The trained ethnologist, on the other hand, could ascertain the nature of native institutions rapidly and accurately and pass on this knowledge in concise, usable form. Before the present war the use of ethnologists as colonial advisers was increasing rapidly. Under the progressive leadership of Commissioner John Collier they have even been introduced into our own Indian service. However, with few exceptions, such specialists have been used to devise ways and means for implementing policies rather than in the development of policies. The contributions which they have been able to make to the well-being of subject peoples has thus depended largely upon the intentions of their superiors. The very knowledge which makes it possible to control a native people with a minimum of friction can become a deadly weapon in the hands of those who wish to destroy a native society or to break down its culture for their own selfish ends.

More recently, a number of individuals who have been trained in ethnological theories and techniques have begun to employ these in the study of industrial relations, race relations, and the work of various social agencies. It is still too early to predict what the final outcome of this work will be. The main contribution to date seems to have been that of bringing to such studies improved methods for the diagnosis of the social situations involved.

Although most of the current applications of anthropology use the data and techniques of ethnology, somatology also has numerous practical possibilities. To cite only a few of these, one anthropologist, Dr. M. R. Stein, has made an extensive study of racial differences in teeth and in the size and shape of the dental arch. On the basis of these studies an American firm has developed special dentures designed to meet the needs of various populations and these have proved highly profitable. An upper plate with jet black teeth, made for the Thailand trade, is one of the writer's treasured possessions. Somatologists can provide data on local and racial differences in size and body build which will be exceedingly useful to firms competing for foreign markets. They have also been employed during the present war in connection with the designing of better airplane cockpits and seats for paratroops, and they may well play their part in the post-war development of new furniture designs.

Such contributions are after all of minor importance, contributing to comfort rather than survival. Much more important is the knowledge which anthropologists are obtaining of the differing disease resistances of different human groups and the conditions of temperature, humidity, and altitude which are optimum for them. In the extensive movements of populations which will probably follow the war, this material should be taken into account. Thus it is an established fact that West African Negroes have a high tolerance for malignant malaria and are, with few exceptions, carriers of this disease. Racial groups who lack such immunity cannot be settled successfully in West Africa. Conversely, the introduction of West Africans into regions where there are suitable vectors for the disease but where it has not existed previously will cause great injury to the local populations. Many other examples of this sort could be cited.

This survey of the various areas of research and applied science in which anthropologists are at work should suffice to give some idea of the scope of formal anthropology. It naturally raises the question of where the limits of this science should be placed, but it seems to the writer that this is largely an academic one. Every science can contribute to the development of several others and receive corresponding aid from them. The present lines between disciplines are rarely inherent in the phenomena with which they have elected to deal and, as time goes on, such lines seem to be maintained more by inertia and by the vested interests of university departments than by anything else. Anthropology is by no means the only discipline which has concerned itself with the study of man. Sociology, economics, history, psychology and even the newer geography are all primarily concerned with him. Anthropology has differed from these mainly in the wider scope of its interests and in its greater willingness to borrow and integrate data from any source. The increasing coöperation between anthropologists and workers in other disciplines has filled some of the older anthropologists with fears that their science may cease to exist as a distinct discipline. They believe that if the present trends continue it may be torn limb from limb and the bleeding fragments distributed among its older and stronger neighbors. The writer believes such fears to be groundless. It seems much more probable that it will become the nucleus of a new Science of Man which will be broad enough in its scope to include all aspects of human existence, civilized as well as primitive. While there will always be need for specialists the crying need of the present is for a synthesis of the knowledge which such specialists have been able to accumulate.

Actually, such a generalized Science of Man is already taking shape through the coöperation of members of the various specialized disciplines. The aim of this science is the same as that of all sciences. It seeks to ascertain the processes and continuities involved in the phenomena with which it deals with a view to the prediction of events and ultimately to their control. The phenomena of human existence and especially of human behavior are exceedingly complex and the work of reducing them to intelligible order has only begun. Anthropologists of the past generation, dazed by the variety of the cultures with which they were becoming acquainted, doubted the possibility of arriving at valid generalizations with respect to them. It must be admitted at once that it is almost impossible to make any generalizations about the behavior of human beings in groups, that is, social and cultural phenomena, to which there will not be a few apparent exceptions. However, this does not mean that such phenomena are without order. Every generalization must begin with the assumption of a particular frame of reference; a set of conditions under which it will hold good. Thus, to cite a familiar example, the law of falling bodies as it is stated in elementary physics books begins with the assumption that the bodies are falling in a vacuum, a condition never encountered in real life. The conditions under which societies and cultures have to operate are exceedingly complex and involve a great number of variable factors. In spite of this it is possible to arrive at a considerable number of generalizations which hold good for nearly all the cases which have been observed. Such generalizations can be made both with respect to the normal coexistence and functional interrelations of particular phenomena and with respect to various processes. Although they lack the absolute quality associated in our thinking with the term "law" and embody a lower factor of probability than do the laws of the physical or natural sciences, such generalizations are still valuable guides to the prediction of events. They will become even more so as the frames of reference within which they may be expected to hold good are more clearly delimited.

All the sciences which deal with man have developed a considerable number of such generalizations and have proved the worth of these by simple, pragmatic tests. Even when the generalizations have not been formally stated, they are implicit in the techniques and conceptual systems of such sciences. The principle task of the emergent Science of Man will be to draw these generalizations together and to develop new ones of wider scope and greater accuracy. Since this unification has barely begun, we must still turn to each of the specialized sciences concerned for its particular contributions—and each of them can contribute toward the solution of our current problems. It is for this reason that no attempt has been made to confine the contributions included in the present volume to the field of formal anthropology or the contributors to those who would call themselves anthropologists. It is enough that they are all coworkers in the Science of Man, attempting in one way or another to understand him and the phenomena which affect him and to find solutions for his problems.

Society and Biological Man
By H. L. SHAPIRO

HUMAN society, which sometimes seems to possess a life of its own, following its own laws and molding man in its own image, arises in fact out of the needs and the functions of the human organism. Social organization must contribute to or at least sustain the basic necessities of man, or be rejected. But having fulfilled its essential requirements, society may and often does elaborate itself in a multiplicity of fashions and enjoy something like an independent existence. It may develop the graces and accomplishments of civilization, it may evolve complex rituals and patterns of behavior, it may set up restrictions, encourage excesses or cultivate moderation. Of these patterns of living, man, as a biological phenomenon, is remarkably tolerant. The variety of societies in which man can live is enormous. But all of them in greater or lesser degree reflect the biological man.

It is, therefore, of great importance that we possess some understanding of this aspect of man, for as society becomes more complex and ramified the danger increases of fatally divorcing society from its biological origins. The study of man from this point of view has never had a greater significance, and its neglect, comparatively speaking, is therefore all the more astonishing. For society in subtle and sometimes in not so subtle fashion may exert dysgenic effects upon its population even though it respects the primary needs for survival. It may destroy or hamper desirable elements. It may fail to provide the most favorable conditions for biological quality. Whether or not these undesirable tendencies develop through ignorance, neglect, or active but erroneous attitudes, it is unforgivable in an era of science that man himself be a kind of afterthought, a stepchild of scientific investigation. It is essential that we begin to acquire at last a sound body of knowledge about the basic biological characteristics of the men who make up our social units.

Moreover, the knowledge of these things by a handful of specialists, even if we possessed it, would hardly suffice in a world unusually conscious of certain phases of biological differentiation in man. For perhaps the first time in human history vast numbers of men from opposite corners of the earth, men of the most diverse aspects, are within easy access of one another. The expansion of horizons which began half a millennium ago is approaching its culmination with all mankind open to the contacts and the traffic of the world. This alone would be sufficient reason for a sound approach to human biology. It is, however, only one of many reasons.

In the following discussion I propose to deal with only a limited portion of the vast field which human biology presents. To cover it completely within the present compass is manifestly impossible. The topics I have elected to touch upon represent not necessarily the most significant but all of them seem to me of pertinence in the world we face. Nor will it be my aim to lay out blueprints for biological man in a future society. We do not know enough, at present, for such a godlike undertaking. I shall be content if I clarify some of the problems that face human biology even though the answers are lacking.

The biological characteristic of man which above all others seems to exercise a special attraction for the world of today is his racial differentiation. Although there perhaps never was a time when men were completely unaware of the physical differences between themselves and all others or between their own group and of some neighboring one, it may with equal justice be said that men have never been so intensely and generally sensitive to these differences as they are today. It is interesting to note that the first attempts in the seventeenth and eighteenth centuries to classify the races of man were still so unsophisticated that they made no distinction between American Indians and Europeans. Up to the early nineteenth century all Europeans with the exception of the Lapps were racially one in the eyes of the Europeans themselves. The breakdown of Europeans into an increasing number of racial entities has evolved *pari passu* with an intensification of racial self-consciousness that in some degree reflects the rise of European nationalism. Although I do not propose to discuss the history of race or its zoological concept, there is one aspect of it which serves to introduce a subject I do wish to explore.

Man, like all other organisms, tends to conform to a pattern. Yet no two individuals are ever absolutely identical in every detail. This failure of the individual to reach a perfect coincidence with any specific type gives rise to the equally characteristic phenomenon of variation. It is perhaps open to debate whether the variations should be regarded as deviations from a pattern, or the sequence be reversed and the pattern derived from the distribution of the variates. But by whichever end one grasps this apparent duality, the inevitable association of a central tendency with the deviations from it constitutes a fixed attribute of organic life. Indeed, in a highly generalized sense, the exposition of the central tendency and the understanding of individual variation furnish the several biological, and possibly all the natural, sciences with their basic problem. So pervasive is the phenomenon, it is difficult to conjure up any aspect of biological research that cannot ultimately be resolved into these fundamental terms.

It is perhaps because one of these complementary aspects of the human organism tends to be emphasized at the expense of the other that we find at present something of a dichotomy among the students of human biology. The conflict is nowhere more explicit than in the problem of race. There are those who, following the traditional line, zealously continue to seek an all-embracing system of races which will accommodate the complexities of human morphology and at the same time explain the stubborn contradictions that confront the necessarily arbitrary categories of such a classification. Opposed to them, in part or in whole, are those students who deny the existence of race altogether, deprecate its conceptual usefulness in terms of the realities or substitute other phrases to exorcise the evil which has come to dwell within its name. To a large extent, the attitude of the extremists of the second group represents a revulsion against the oversimplification of an extraordinarily complicated situation and a reaction to the extraneous and nonzoological accretions that have grown up around the notion of race. Here may be found those who quite legitimately have been profoundly shocked by the monstrous abuse, for political ends, of a highly tentative scheme of human classification and who, concerned by the dangerous and unjustifiable extensions of these concepts into other realms, have sought to combat the part by denying the whole. They would like to throw the baby out with the bath water.

The persistence, however, of the racial taxonomists in the pursuit of the ideal racial classification, attributed perhaps unjustly to inertia and conservatism, may more reasonably be accounted for by the existence of anatomical differences which race seems best, if incompletely, to explain. The disparity between these views, more apparent than real when the problems are strictly restated in the light of recent knowledge, seems to arise from the overemphasis of one or the other of the dual aspects of man.

One consequence of the preoccupation of physical anthropology with race has been to give the concept of type or race a fixity that has hampered our thinking about the human organism. The races of mankind have until quite recently been regarded as relatively unchanging entities, impervious to milieu or to innate forces of change. The apotheosis of race has also fastened upon the infinite variety of mankind a limited number of rigid categories into which the individual is firmly pressed, thus obscuring his own intrinsic character. If classification were pursued for its convenience, for the light it might shed on the evolution of man, at the same time recognizing its somewhat arbitrary nature, its consequences might be confined to legitimate scientific uses. But unfortunately the process carries its own proclivity to exaggeration, for it is in the very nature of classification to regard exceptions and deviates as undesirable and a nuisance.

It is, however, precisely these variations that have come to have special significance in recent developments of human biology. The tendency previously was to disregard the deviate altogether as unimportant, or, if its presence was inescapable, to dismiss it as an anomaly, an atavism or simply as a natural expression of the organic tendency to variation. Darwin's observation that all forms of life varied, and by their variations furnished the materials upon which evolution might work, seemed by its universality to explain somehow the inevitability of variation in man without in fact providing any causal explanation of the phenomenon itself. Physical anthropology, which in the last century had alone staked out any claim in human biology, was preoccupied with classifying racial types. Variations were recognized, to be sure, but only to extract from them the archetype around which they distributed themselves. When discussion was explicit, and mostly it was not, the assumption was that the racial type and its concomitant variation represented a more or less fixed expression. The growing body of general biological observation and experiment on the plasticity of organic life was itself neutralized, at least on the human level, by Weismannean interpretations and consequently had little effect on the accepted dogma on the fixity of human type.

It was, therefore, with something of a shock that Boas's publication on the changing bodily form of the descendants of immigrants to the United States was received by students of man. For the first time a full-dress, documented investigation attempted to show that at least some groups of mankind do not maintain a rigid fixity within the ranges of normal environmental changes but on the contrary reveal a perceptible tendency to vary with the environment. The organic expression of man, therefore, seemed to be plastic and subject to the influence of the milieu in which the organism developed. Moreover, the effect of the environment seemed to increase with time and generation. Although Boas's results were often magnified beyond his own interpretation, they were sufficiently disturbing to elicit wide comment and intense reaction. A number of scholia appeared in an attempt to explain away his conclusions and to prove that his observations were attributable to innocuous causes, undisturbing to the *status quo*. But succeeding studies along similar and extended lines have apparently confirmed Boas's major contention that the human organism is plastic and subject to environmental conditioning. Pointing to the same interpretation of organic plasticity in man are the data gathered by Bowles from the physical records of Harvard students over three generations. From his array of successive generations he was enabled to demonstrate a very real and progressive increase in size together with alterations in bodily proportion. A parallel examination of the records of students in women's colleges turned up similar results. Generally overlooked in the discussion of organic plasticity in man is the remarkable record published by Martin of the average stature of army recruits in the Ligurian canton of St. Marie Vesubie. During the period from 1792 to 1872 the average stature increased 9.5 cm. from 155.5 cm. to 165.0 cm. Everywhere in Europe and America where physical examinations have been maintained over a period of years—in schools, colleges, military establishments, and other institutions—a consistent accretion to the average stature is evident. Nor is the phenomenon exclusively linked with the white stocks, since similar results have been reported for Chinese and Japanese.

It is evident, therefore, that the former conception of a human organism rigidly held to fixed standards of development by the germ plasm must be modified. Instead we must conceive of a genetic control which is flexible enough to permit the organism a considerable range in its development. This does not mean that the human organism may be modified in any direction or to any extent. It does not mean that an individual subjected to appropriate environmental stimuli may be altered from one racial type to another. It may perhaps best be expressed by saying that a given genotype or genetic combination has an orbit of plasticity within which it may develop normally. The extent of the orbit however is unknown.

Although such a conclusion from the evidence seems fair enough, our understanding of the causes of organic plasticity still lack specific determination. Various aspects of the environment such as nutrition, climate, economic level, and ecology have been adduced to explain the observed modifications of bodily form. Ameliorating circumstances of life, rising standards of living, improved medical knowledge also have been suggested as causative factors. While it is possible that all these and more may individually influence the development of the human organism, it is, however, rather more likely that many of them on analysis will prove to have common elements and that the significant environmental stimuli will be reduced to relatively few in number with an interlocking tie-up.

Despite the overwhelming tendency to attribute the various manifestations of bodily plasticity to environment as a whole or to some special aspect of it, there are some who see in them a cyclic phenomenon, operating more or less independently of the milieu. The increase in body size might then, according to this view, have its origin in some genetic fluctuation. Although it is at present difficult to rule out this explanation completely, it is not adequate to satisfy the observations. Data collected on the growth of children reveal significant differences at various nutritional levels. The famine years during and after the last war had a markedly deteriorating effect upon the growth of children observed in Germany and Russia. Not only was stature and weight reduced below previous norms, but the cephalic index as well was altered. My own studies on the Japanese in Hawaii, controlled by parallel investigations on their relatives in Japan, revealed considerable changes in the body size and proportions.

One of the most striking claims for environment affecting bodily development has been put forth by Professor Mills. His work on man, checked by laboratory experiments on rats and other experimental animals, seems to indicate that climate, temperature, and humidity influence the regulation of body heat, with consequent and important modifications in food intake and activity. He claims an elaborate interlocking of body growth, feeding habits, onset of maturity, aging, physical activity, and susceptibility to disease correlated with differences in climatic conditions. Certainly if his own and other laboratory results may be transferred to man, the claims are at least impressive. They together with the abundant collateral evidence available on physical differentiation associated with geography, socioeconomic level, nutrition, climate, health, and a host of other environmental elements leave little room to doubt the ability of the human organism to respond to differences in milieu within its genetic possibilities.

Thus far, I have cited only a small part of the evidence to indicate the role of milieu in guiding and shaping the genetic tendencies of the human organism. Presumably, the diverse variations produced by such environmental factors do not touch the basic genotype, which preserves its integrity and plasticity for other modifications in the environment with which it may need to cope. Important as these environmentally induced variations are, they are not adequate, however, to account for all the complexities and ramifications of human diversity. Variations of a purely genetic origin also play a significant part in producing the full range of human difference. It is, of course, well known that the genes in their diverse expressions and combinations determine many of the varied forms of normal and abnormal characteristics in man. Indeed some features seem largely genetic in their variations and impervious to environment. Eye color, for example, as far as we know is not susceptible to environmental influence, but owes its shades of pigmentation to genetic causes. Brachydactyly, an abnormal shortening of the digits, to cite another kind of deviation, also arises only from specific genetic factors.

The ultimate origin of gene differences is still obscure. Whether or not alterations in the genes may occur as a result of external influences from such sources as radioactive substances does not alter the essential distinction between variations arising from the environment acting upon but not changing the genotype and those variations which spring directly from gene changes or from the countless permutations of gene combinations.

One of the most fruitful sources of genetic variation in man is race mixture. Although the term is something of a misnomer, its usage is firmly established. Actually anything from the latest international marriage of an American heiress with a British peer to the miscegenation of Australian aborigines with Europeans is called race mixture. In no case does race mixture in man represent the crossing of pure-line races such as might be possible in the laboratory, for pure-line human races do not exist. The very fact that pure human races are not to be found in nature—a situation which, paradoxically, "race mixture" has done much to bring about—makes it impossible to draw a hard and fast line between miscegenation of related peoples and the crossing of genetically distinct populations. The process of mixture, however, whether or not between closely related or widely diverse stocks is one that tends to create new gene combinations and therefore increased variation. The gene distributions which are known, the geographic continuities of physical variation and the prehistoric as well as the historic records are abundant evidence for the belief that mixture has always been a significant factor in man's past. That it will involve a larger proportion of the world's population in the future is not unlikely in view of the increasing contacts between the peoples of the earth. In the New World great areas are even now inhabited by populations of mixed blood. In the colonial empires of European nations, half-caste groups quickly become established. The migrations and resettlements of the past which brought millions of diverse Europeans to the United States, the dislocations of the present war, the opening up of Asiatic Russia, also provide fertile opportunities for reshuffling the genes of mankind. Up to the present only a handful of students have concerned themselves with the biological consequences of race mixture. Propagandists and Nordophiles like Madison Grant, echoing the racist literature of Germany, see nothing but evil in the process. At least, the evil was inevitable as far as the Nordics were concerned, for in the view of the racists the manifest supremacy of the Nordics could only suffer deterioration by miscegenation since they had no peer with which to mingle in equality. Although this extreme view was characteristic mainly of certain popular writers distinguished by their zeal rather than their scientific attainments, several geneticists have suggested that in crossing divergent races serious disharmonies were likely to develop. Castle among others has effectively disproved these claims, but there still lingers a common belief that the mulatto, for example, is inferior, at least physically, to either Negro or white. The high rate of tuberculosis among mulattoes is sometimes cited as evidence of this. Careful studies of the environment, however, usually reveals that in this condition other factors than race are determinants.

Contrary to belief that race mixture leads to deterioration, an actual superiority in some instances may characterize the half-caste population. Fischer's study of the Rehobother Bastards, a cross between South African Boers and Hottentots (certainly as divergent a pair of stocks as might be expected to mate) disclosed evidence of a hybrid vigor which in fertility surpassed the performances of either Boers or Hottentots. In a study of the Polynesian-English descendants of the Mutineers of the *Bounty*, I found in the early generations a marked superiority over the parental stocks not only in physical size but also in the birth rate. Boas's investigations on half-breed Indians indicated something of the same order. Such a phenomenon as hybrid vigor or heterosis is well known in biology and is now commercially applied in the propagation of hybrid corn, whose increased yields over pure-line strains has led to its wide adoption in agriculture. Experimental animals display the same results in certain crosses. There is then every reason to suppose that the increase of size, vigor, and fertility which is sometimes found in human hybrids is part of the same general biological principle. While it would be erroneous to assume that race mixture in every case leads to an enhanced biological status, it is worth considering as one of the possible explanations of the recurrent epochs of outstanding intellectual activity that mark European history. The intermingling of various strains that preceded the classic development of Greece and the miscegenation that accompanied the "Völkerwanderung" of the millennium before the Renaissance suggest that an unusually active reshuffling of genes produces a heightened vitality that finds expression in high peaks of civilization. This is not a novel construction of European history, but it does receive added credence from recent observations on race mixture.

But whether or not the shining epochs of human history can be traced to an active mingling of related stocks, it does seem clear that such a process, by introducing new genes to each other or by increasing the opportunities for those of small acquaintance to enlarge their contacts, does make possible an increased variety of phenotypes. Thus by miscegenation mankind increases its variation and widens the possibilities for superior as well as inferior combinations of genes.

Although theoretically such an expanded range offers a more abundant field for selection and evolution, it is doubtful whether any major advances in human evolution may be achieved by this route. Selection alone can produce only a more perfect example of existing genetic possibilities, it cannot evoke a new and advanced type. Without mutations animal breeders would have made much less progress than they have. Only by seizing upon new genetic developments can they fundamentally alter the type. For that reason progress by selection alone slows down rapidly after the first stages of selection are passed. Similarly in man, improvement based upon the selection of existing genes can lead only to a refinement and purity of type. Basic modifications must await actual genic mutation.

Selection alone, however, has possibilities not to be despised for improving the general run of humankind. But, however desirable such a program may be, its operation is inevitably linked with social factors which are as important to solve as are the biological problems involved.

It has frequently been advanced that race mixture in itself might well solve the racial problems which confront us. If reducing the population of the world to a common racial heritage could do so, it might have merits. However, certain obvious considerations of international antagonisms reveal the frailty of such a hope. European history is full of wars between closely related peoples. Moreover, the history of various nations themselves bear witness to the intense pitch to which parochial disharmonies between people of the same stock will rise. Our own civil war, while in fact fought on a racial question, was carried on by members of a common strain. In other words, the antagonisms and schisms of mankind are more frequently religious, or social than they are racial. Race prejudices are apt to be convenient handles for emotional outlet rather than determining causes. It seems, therefore, that race mixture is an unreliable panacea for the conflicts arising out of international competition.

Within a nation, however, where common language, traditions, government, and other unifying forces seek to create a common interest and loyalty, pronounced racial differences between diverse segments of the population either geographically or socially erect an impediment of serious proportions. Physical differences that are patent and easy to observe become a convenient nucleus around which a variety of prejudices may crystallize. Thus although race may not be a cause, it may easily become an excuse; and biological differences become lines of cleavage that may split a nation into unbridgeable units. It may, therefore, be argued with some cogency that the elimination of racial differentiation by miscegenation within the nation releases the accumulated conventions that divide one section from another. With the foci dissolved the infecting prejudices disintegrate. This is a solution which can only be achieved if the social attitudes are modified to permit it. If, indeed, such tolerance were developed, one might foresee that the very need itself would disappear.

SOCIETY AND BIOLOGICAL MAN

This discussion of race mixture raises the question whether or not such a process aside from its social implication has any biological consequences on a population. It is obvious that if races or populations are distinguished from each other not only by the color of their skins, the character of their hair, or the color of their eyes, but also by the way they function and by the capabilities or vices they possess, their hybridization offers possibilities for good, indifferent, or undesirable recombinations of vital importance for society. It should be restated, of course, that racial classification is essentially a zoological concept and is primarily based upon physical criteria. The traits that set off a Negro from a white man or a Chinese from an Australian aboriginal are first of all purely physical ones. Only after the racial divisions are established and diverse groups are rendered recognizable anatomical aggregations, does the problem of associated differences come into being. The extension of racial differences into the realms of personality, intelligence, and physiology represents a tendency that somehow seems an inevitable process of the human mind. The justification, however, of such a ramification is still at this late date far from clear.

The flurry of racial mental testing that followed Brigham's publication on Army Intelligence seemed at first to yield differences in mental ability that coincided with conventional racial lines. Various segments of the population of the United States assumed rankings according to national and presumably racial origins. The Northwest Europeans and Jews topped the lists while Italians were near the bottom. Garth's early work seemed to place the American Indian in a lower category than the average white. Portellus, working on the polyglot population of Hawaii, published results that confirmed these racial values in intelligence.

This line of investigation, however, was fated to suffer a severe reaction. Critics arose who pointed out the influence of educational, social, and other environmental factors upon intellectual performance. They showed how great was the effect upon the Negroes' I.Q. of a migration from the oppressive conditions in the South to the greater opportunities to be found in the North. Moreover the environment was shown to effect the white ratings as well. Studies on twins, especially identical twins who had been reared apart, revealed according to Newman's data some modification in I.Q. according to the milieu in which the twins were raised. Klineberg particularly has been the protagonist of these critics who sought to repudiate the whole school of racial psychology. His own investigations on the American Negro and on various populations in Europe did much to place in disrepute the thesis that races differ significantly in innate capacity as measured by an I.Q.

Even the indirect evidence of capacity offered by a people's progress in civilization has been discounted by most anthropologists. Impressed by the progress that the diffusion of culture encourages and the so-called "accidents" that guide its development, they are more inclined to write the history of civilization in terms of environment, ecology, happy chance or fortunate concatenation of events than in terms of the innate abilities of the peoples of the world. It is perhaps doubtful if a categorical and dogmatic answer can be given to this problem, and for this reason cultures and civilizations are difficult to equate and subjective judgment of their merits vary. If one points to the low scale of native Australian culture, the social anthropologist responds by extolling the complexity of their marriage system, implying that the capacities of the aborigines have merely specialized in a certain direction but are capable of fuller expression in a more favorable environment. If the African cultures and civilizations are compared unfavorably with Western Europe, the sculpture, dance, music, material and other arts of Africa are cited in rebuttal. To refer to a contemporary people as deficient in innate ability because the culture they bear is on a low level elicits the comparison of the uncivilized Britons of Roman times with the preëminent British people of today. Thus no objective scale exists for rating civilizations, and the progress of one people in the arts of civilization is assumed to be possible for all.

Thus, while all the arguments for racial correlations with innate capacity may be explained away, a tantalizing but elusive conviction that races or peoples are in some degree differentiated by their inherited abilities lingers on. My own inclination is to regard the extreme, all or nothing, hypothesis as eventually unsatisfactory in clarifying the relationship of race, capacity, and civilization. Just as the racist explanation of every minutia of culture behavior and capacity is obviously maleficent and untenable before the facts, so the tendency to interpret all aspects of civilization and society as based on factors outside and beyond the genes seems only a partial explanation of an extraordinarily complex interrelationship.

On physiological grounds, too, the demonstration of racial differences is far from satisfactory. In certain respects the problem here is simpler, because bodily functions lend themselves in some instances at least to precise and objective recording, nevertheless the data are meager and largely uncontrolled against environmental influences. Claims have been made that races differ, among other physiological functions, in metabolic rates, energy output, susceptibility to disease, in the balance of hormones and activity of the ductless glands, in nervous excitability, and in sense perceptions.

Some years ago, physiologists seemed on the verge of accumulating evidence to prove that various racial groups could be distinguished by their metabolism. The Chinese were reported with an average rate appreciably lower than the standard for Americans. Similarly, the Maya Indians, another Mongoloid people, yielded rates divergent from European norms. The significance of these results from a racial point of view faded as it became obvious that the metabolic rate is susceptible to climatic conditions and that individual rates fluctuated with the environment.

Mills has insisted on the effect of climate upon metabolism and the energy quotient. The lethargy characteristic of tropic dwellers and the dynamic quality of inhabitants of cool and stormy belts he correlates with weather. The close association of weather and function has recently been meticulously analyzed by Dr. William Petersen in connection with the progress of patients. The fluctuations recorded by barometric pressure and the condition of the sick follow a similar pattern as though the former were directly influencing the latter.

The disease rate, even the susceptibility to certain organic and infectious disturbances has been frequently reported to be different in diverse races and peoples. As an objective fact there seems to be little doubt that these distinctions do indeed exist. To any one familiar with the history of European contact with primitive people the evidence of it is all too tragic. Tuberculosis and measles decimated, for example, the Polynesians. These people isolated from the world had little or no resistance to diseases introduced by Europeans and consequently perished from them in such numbers that whole villages were depopulated and human habitations collapsed into ruins. Similarly the American Indian fell victim to diseases brought to his shores by European settlers. Europeans, in their turn are easy prey to malaria in areas where the natives are less prone to its ravages. If some medical historians are correct, susceptibility to syphilis was once highly characteristic of Old World populations as compared with the inhabitants of the New,

Similar examples might easily be piled up. The high rate of tuberculosis among Negroes, the relative infrequency of tuberculosis and the high rate of diabetes among Jews are also well known in medical statistics. Recent investigations in South Africa report characteristic disease rates among the Negroes of that part of the continent.

Leaving aside the occupational and environmental diseases which may temporarily flourish among certain groups because they engage in activities or dwell in localities that predispose them to a higher incidence—such phenomena for example as goitre and cretinism in Switzerland—there still remains a pattern of disease rates that differ among various peoples. It is, however, doubtful that all these diverse patterns are primarily racial. Some, it is true, appear to arise directly from specialized racial characters such as the relative immunity of the Negro to certain skin diseases provided for him by his heavy concentration of skin pigmentation. In other instances, such as the presence of sickle cell anemia in Negroes and its absence in whites, the distinction also appears to be a racial one, even though a causal relationship is not evident. The high fatality of measles among the newly discovered Polynesians, on the contrary, cannot be primarily laid to race. Such associations are more logically explained on other grounds. The Polynesians through the accident of geographic isolation lacked or never developed an immunity to measles, so that its virulence fortuitously therefore became characteristic among them. Conversely, various other associations of disease incidence and group might arise through intense selection. The relative infrequency of tuberculosis among Jews is often attributed to their long urbanization and the consequent elimination of the susceptible. In some instances it is possible that organic disturbances of a hereditary nature might come into existence through a mutation. Disease patterns originating in this manner, however, are not racial, even if they may be hereditary, unless they are equally characteristic of the race as a whole. It may be concluded, therefore, that the distribution of disease rates, like various other phenomena, requires for its explanation more than a single factor. Environment, selection, mutation, and race all contribute to form the existing patterns.

The hormones or secretions of the endocrine glands have, ever since Keith's essay on the endocrine origin of racial differences, been suspected of having racial patterns in regard to secretion and balance. As our knowledge of these once mysterious structures advanced, it became clearer that they played an important role in the growth and development of the individual. Excessive stature was shown to be linked with an active anterior lobe of the pituitary, one type of adiposity with a sluggish pituitary and another with an inactive thyroid. Certain forms of dwarfism were produced experimentally by removing the pituitary. Thus size, bodily proportions, rate of growth, onset of maturity, and various other features could be traced to specific hormones or hormone balances. The implications of this revolutionary advance were tremendous. The temptation to explain most, if not all, the individual differences of anatomy and personality by reference to the endocrine system was alluring and a few popular writers did, indeed, succumb to it. Although some of this excessive enthusiasm has receded, the evidence that the hormones are in large measure involved in shaping the individual cannot be avoided, whether or not the ultimate influence of heredity, environment, nutrition, and other factors, on the functioning of the endocrine system prove to be basic determinants. To seek what governs the endocrine governors simply brings us back again to the fundamental question of heredity and environment.

It was, then, a logical speculation to assume that if the hormones could explain individual differences, they could also account for racial ones, which are after all extensions and elaborations of individual variations. Keith, seeing in the hormones the possibility of a mechanism for explaining racial patterns, even if not at its ultimate terms, elaborated an hypothesis which, with our present more detailed knowledge, is easy to criticize in its applications. Perhaps rashly, he attempted to suggest the specific glands responsible for the differences between whites, Negroes, and Mongoloids. The line of speculation he broached has never been intensively pursued. I have myself attempted at one time to investigate the racial aspects of endocrine patterns, but the techniques then available were inadequate to overcome the clinical uncertainties. It is, therefore, impossible to assess this aspect of human biology beyond the statement that it offers an attractive field of research.

Travelers frequently remark on the greater insensitivity to pain among primitive people and upon their finer sense perceptions. These and other aspects of the nervous system and the sensory organs have been investigated among various people in a rather desultory fashion without unequivocal results. It may be said that in these functions, too, the effects of training, conditioning, and environment play an important role. Urban populations, for example, are notoriously more excitable than their country cousins.

The admittedly inadequate evidence on racial physiology as far as it goes offers no clear-cut case of differentiation along strictly racial lines. Physiological distinctions seem more a matter of local adaptation than a concomitant of anatomical differentiation. It is, however, hazardous to be dogmatic on this point since the entire field of racial physiology is practically untouched. Especially is it necessary to remain open-minded on this score when one realizes the great question mark that the functioning of the endocrine system represents in explaining the diversities of mankind. Yet if plasticity, the ability to adapt to environmental circumstances, is inherent in the anatomical structure of man, we might anticipate that human physiology as well would exhibit an equal if not a greater capacity to adjust itself to milieu. The enormous range of circumstances to which the individual will happily accustom himself suggests strongly that whole populations might do likewise with comparable ease. In fact, one of the most impressive aspects of the functioning of the human organism is its flexibility, its nicely organized margins of safety, and its various devices to see the individual through the stresses of environmental fluctuation.

The fact, however, that man's physiological functioning is adaptable enough to permit him to occupy almost every known type of environment from the arctic to the tropics or from the rarefied elevations of the Andes to the humid deltas of the Amazon, does not mean that he will thrive well in all of them. Huntington some time ago began a series of books in which he stressed the importance to human welfare of optimal environments. He contended that human energy was at its highest in temperate regions that were subjected to stimulating climatic changes and storms. In such areas, Huntington maintained, civilization rose to its greatest peaks, since, presumably, activity and enterprise were greatest here. In this view progress and energy are associated, not because energy in itself had any mysterious power to create civilization, but because energy provided the power for creative imagination. Almost at once, critics pointed out that the first civilizations in human history, such as those of the Nile and the Tigris-Euphrates valleys, evolved in areas quite unlike the storm-driven belts of the temperate zones where civilization now flourishes. Nevertheless, despite this easy rejoinder Huntington's contention makes sense. If we modify his thesis sufficiently to admit that circumstance alters cases, we may reconcile the facts of history with his fundamental proposition.

At certain stages in cultural evolution it is conceivable that some aspects of ecology may have relatively greater significance than others. The fertility of the flood plains of the Nile, the Tigris, and the Euphrates and their ready adaptability to agriculture possessed for man struggling through to an agriculturally based civilization a transcendent importance, overweighing, at least temporarily, the value of climate. The first agriculturists were probably unaware that they were revolutionizing human existence and forging a way of life that permitted developments impossible to a hunting or a grazing people. The start which their favorable ecology gave them permitted them to forge ahead of other people and for millennia to surpass all competitors. In the paleolithic period before they discovered how to till the soil they were undistinguished and were probably inferior to the peoples of western France. As the arts of agriculture spread and men in less propitious regions learned to accommodate them to their own fields, as industry advanced and the dwellers in unfavorable areas found or made resources in their own countries, the quotient of energy and enterprise available became a determining factor in shifting the seat of civilization. From this point of view and with these modifications we may consider the existence of optimum environments. On the scale of energy production alone, climatic conditions are unquestionably of prime importance. The precise energy rating of various climatic combinations are yet to be established, although some beginnings in this direction have been undertaken and more may be expected from the research carried on in connection with the war. The problem, however, is complicated by individual differences in reaction. It is possible, also, that racial differences may exist. But, in general, it appears that cool climates by facilitating the loss of body heat stimulate the metabolism and are productive of energy. Where storms break up the monotony of unchanging weather they serve to enhance activity. For the European, at least, such regions provide his most favorable milieu.

This question of optimal climates has played a decisive role in the colonization of large areas of the earth. Although some students have contended that the white man may settle the tropics and thrive if certain precautions as to sanitation and regime are followed, the fact remains that most Europeans prefer to settle in cooler climates. The distribution of European settlement in the New World demonstrates how effective an agent climate can be. The preference of Europeans for temperate regions does not of course mean that other stocks may not do well in other climatic zones. The Eskimo, for example, appear to maintain themselves better in cold, arctic areas than in the moderated regions to the south of them. I have seen them complain of the heat with the thermometer at 60° F. It is, moreover, no accident that the Negroes have flourished in the Caribbean world and along the hot coastline of northern South America. Although they were introduced originally by Spanish and Portuguese planters, they have themselves actively spread their settlements and in a number of places displaced Indians who had successfully survived Spanish domination. Africa, too, exhibits a pattern of European settlement that follows climatic lines.

It is, therefore, hardly likely that in the post-war world we shall see any mass movements of displaced Europeans toward the tropical areas of the earth; the still unexploited and vast stretches of a region like Siberia conform more closely to the climatic conditions under which they thrive. The extent to which this area may be opened to migration is, of course, a matter for the Soviet Republic to determine. Indeed, the entire problem of population movement can no longer be a matter of individual choice as it once was. There are few empty stretches left suitable for mass European settlement and these together with the remaining areas of thin concentration are under strict governmental control. Wholesale migration therefore, is no longer the simple solution for population pressure, social and religious dissatisfactions, or economic depression.

In a world distraught by war, with its people decimated, uprooted or starved, the effects of these violences upon its future population cannot be denied. Here is a field which human biology should be encouraged to explore. It is deplorable that in a crisis so pregnant for our future our knowledge should be so inadequate. Although it is frequently asserted that wars exert a dysgenic influence upon the populations engaged in them, the data is lacking upon which to base an accurate assessment of the damage suffered. The argument goes that the most highly selected youth of a nation, its potential breeders of future replacements, are destroyed first and most completely and that the less desirable elements consequently breed a larger proportion of the future population than they normally would. Such a disruption of the balance tends then to lower the standards and increase the disabilities inherent in the nation. That some such process, in fact, takes place seems reasonable if not susceptible to exact measurement. There are, however, some extenuating circumstances that should not be overlooked even through the major contention be correct. It should not be assumed that the rejects

Racial Psychology
By OTTO KLINEBERG

AMONG the problems which concern anthropology and related sciences probably none has aroused more popular interest or has had more far-reaching practical implications than that of psychological differences between races. The uncritical belief in the innate superiority of one's own group over others has helped to explain, or at least to rationalize, a substantial proportion of the world's organized aggression. It is a fundamental aspect of the ideology of the Nazis and of the Japanese militarists, and plays its part in our own attitudes toward, and treatment of, American minority groups. It may not be the primary cause of such aggression, but it has certainly contributed a portion of the psychological ammunition with which the aggression has been implemented.

The belief in inherited psychological differences between groups is widespread. In September, 1939, a *Fortune* survey (conducted at the request of the Carnegie Corporation Study of the Negro in America) asked the question: "Do you think Negroes now generally have higher intelligence than white people, lower, or about the same?" In all sections of the country the majority of those interviewed regarded the Negroes as inferior, the figures for different regions varying from 60.0 to 76.9 percent. Those who believed Negroes to be inferior were then asked the further question: "Do you think this is because: (1) they have lacked opportunities, or (2) they are born less intelligent, or (3) both?" The percentages attributing the inferiority to innate factors alone ranged from 28.7 to 54.8 percent. The percentages of those, however, who regarded the difference as due at least in part to heredity (that is, those checking the second or third answers) ranged from 55.5 to 79.2 percent.[1] These last figures should not be misunderstood; they are percentages not of the total population but of those who regard the Negro as inferior. They do at the same time give some indication of the extent of popular belief in the biological inequality of racial groups.

The present position of American scientists, on the other hand, ap-

---

[1] From E. L. Horowitz, "Race Attitudes," in *Characteristics of the American Negro*, ed. Otto Klineberg (New York, 1944).

pears to be overwhelmingly on the side of those who believe that the differences in the behavior of various racial or national groups have not been demonstrated to be of biological origin. With few exceptions, such differences as exist can be and have been explained on the basis of historical and cultural conditions, variations in opportunity, in education and experience. It is perhaps worth noting that, as Gunnar Myrdal puts it: "Hardly anywhere else or on any other issue is there —in spite of intensive and laudable efforts to popularize the new results of research—such a wide gap between scientific thought and popular belief." [2] In the following pages the attempt will be made to provide some of the evidence on which the present anthropological viewpoint is based.

The emphasis on the word "present" in this context should not be interpreted as meaning that the position here adopted is a temporary one, or that it is likely to be superseded in the near future; it is meant rather to indicate the contrast with the past. In a significant summary of the "errors of sociology," Odum includes "the assumption that races are inherently different rather than group products of differentials due to the cumulative power of folk-regional and cultural environment." [3] This error, it may be added, was not confined to sociologists but was shared by many psychologists and some anthropologists as well. In several instances writers who, in their earlier works, had more or less accepted the popular opinion concerning racial differences in psychology later renounced that opinion completely; this fact is perhaps the best evidence of the change which has occurred in this whole area of investigation.

One final word of introduction. The words "race" and "racial" have been popularly employed in a very loose manner. In an earlier chapter of this volume, some of the difficulties and complexities in the concept have been discussed. Perhaps the only point that need be made here is that races are biological groups, and should not be confused with nations (English, American, Russian, Japanese) or with families of languages (Aryan, Latin, Semitic). In what follows the attempt will be made to specify with some exactness the nature of the groups whose "psychology" is being considered.

The problem of racial psychology has been approached from a number of different directions, and with the application of several distinct

[2] Myrdal, *An American Dilemma* (New York, 1944), p. 93.
[3] H. W. Odum, "The Errors of Sociology," *Social Forces*, XV (1936–37), 327–42.

criteria or principles of evaluation. A study of the physical characteristics of racial groups, for example, led some of the earlier investigators to the conclusion that such groups differed in their degree of evolutionary development; some were more "primitive," others more advanced. The inference was that as a consequence the psychological level of these groups would differ correspondingly. It has been repeatedly demonstrated, however (see Dr. Krogman's discussion), that the alleged hierarchy in the morphological structure of living races rests upon a one-sided and incomplete reading of the evidence and that, when all the available data are considered, no such hierarchy emerges. The data on differences in racial physiology, also pertinent to a decision concerning the problem of racial psychology, are analyzed elsewhere (see the preceding chapter). In the present context it may be sufficient to point out that most of the observed physiological differences appear to be secondary to other factors. To take only one example, variations in basal metabolism apparently occur under the influence of variations in climate, occupation, tempo of activity, emotional experiences, and the like, and cannot be used convincingly as explanations of differences in behavior.

Another approach to the problem is represented by the attempt to deduce differences in racial psychology from the contributions made by different racial groups to the sum-total of the world's culture or civilization. Perhaps the outstanding historical example of such an attempt is represented by de Gobineau in his *Essay on the Inequality of Human Races*, which appeared in the middle of the last century and which helped to develop a vogue in racial theorizing, the effects of which have by no means disappeared. Apart from the fact that the "race" glorified by Gobineau consisted of the "Aryans," that is to say, no race at all, this whole type of approach is unconvincing for many reasons. For one thing, there is no satisfactory criterion as to what constitutes a superior culture, and the decision as to which contributions point to biological superiority will vary according to the prejudices and preferences of the individual writer. For another, the same group may vary so much throughout its history that the judgment concerning its abilities will depend not only upon bias but also upon the particular moment at which the judgment is made; the unflattering description of North European peoples by Aristotle provides a striking contrast to the assumption of Houston Stewart Chamberlain, in his *Foundations of the Nineteenth Century*, that North Europeans, and specifically Teutons, are superior to all others. In addition, the fact that two different samples of the same racial group may present such divergent cultures adds to the difficulty of relating culture to race. Some of the simplest tribes of the Burmese jungle are similar in physical type to the Chinese, who built one of the most complex of the world's civilizations; and the warlike Apache of our own Southwest are of the same "race" as the much more peaceful Pueblos.

From still another direction, the belief has been expressed (and rather widely accepted by laymen and even by some scientists) that the very fact that groups differ physically makes it exceedingly probable that they should differ psychologically as well. Even Franz Boas wrote, in the first edition of *The Mind of Primitive Man:*

It does not seem probable that the minds of races which show variations in their anatomical structure should act in exactly the same way. Differences of structure must be accompanied by differences of function, physiological as well as psychological; and, as we found clear evidence of difference in structure between the races, so we must anticipate that differences in mental characteristics will be found.[4]

It is significant that this passage does not appear in the 1938 edition of the book, and it seems highly probable that Boas changed his opinion on this point. In any case, the inference from physical to psychological differences is a highly dubious one. In the first place, there has been no acceptable demonstration of any relationship between physique and personality within the normal range of individual variations. The correlations between traits of intelligence or temperament, on the one hand, and anatomical characteristics (stature, skin color, shape of head, size of head, height of forehead, and so on), on the other, have almost invariably yielded results of no predictive value. Even the approach in terms of constitutional type, as represented by the work of Kretschmer [5] has failed to fulfill its earlier promise and in its application to normal personalities has proved quite unconvincing. A still more recent attempt to link constitution with psychology has been made by Shelden and his collaborators.[6] This investigation marks a definite advance as far as the description of human constitutional types is concerned, but the alleged relationship between such types and the varieties of temperament remains a matter of controversy and cannot

[4] New York, 1911, pp. 114–15.
[5] Ernst Kretschmer, *Physique and Character*, trans. W. J. H. Sprott (New York, 1925).
[6] W. H. Shelden, S. S. Stevens, and W. B. Tucker, *The Varieties of Human Physique* (New York, 1940).

as yet be regarded as established. In other words the statement that "differences of structure must be accompanied by differences of function" remains an unproved assumption with regard to the normal range of human physical characteristics.

Under certain rather specialized conditions, on the other hand, there may be a relationship of the type suggested. Among the members of relatively small, isolated, and therefore inbred communities, we may expect a marked degree of homogeneity in physical features and an accompanying "typical" psychology, genetically determined. A group of this kind represents a sort of enlarged family, and the individuals in it may actually resemble one another, both physically and psychologically, even more than do the members of a typical family, if the inbreeding has been practiced for a number of generations. In this sense, and in this sense alone, there is a kind of "racial psychology." Very much the same considerations would apply to the observed "psychological" differences between various "breeds" of dogs. The genetic make-up of a "pure breed" is relatively homogeneous, since no outside genes are permitted to mix with those of the "pure" cocker spaniel or the Scotch terrier, and it would not be surprising, therefore, if one type of dog showed a native predilection for one particular type of behavior. (Even in such "pure breeds" there is still considerable individual variability.) It should be clear, however, that it is impossible to argue from the concomitance of physique and psychology, either in such isolated human communities or in homogeneous breeds of animals, to a similar concomitance in the much larger and much more variable human populations that constitute the so-called "races of mankind."

One final consideration in this connection. If the anatomical variations that constitute the basis of racial classification have taken place in relation to conditions in the geographic environment, there is no reason to assume that such variations must have psychological significance. To take a specific example, it has been suggested that variations in skin color may be due to certain processes of differential selection related to the effects of the actinic rays of the sun. In northern Europe a relatively unpigmented skin would be an advantage for survival, since such a skin would aid in the absorption of the comparatively weak actinic rays. Conversely, in the tropics a dark skin would have survival value, since the pigment would act as a preventive against too large an amount of such absorption. Given enough time, we would expect those with fairer skins to survive in the north and those with darker skins in the tropics. Under these conditions (or similar selective influences) there would be no reason to assume that psychological factors played any significant part in the development of these anatomical variations. There would be no reason to anticipate any relationship between traits of personality and the amount of melanin or other pigment in the skin.

This description of various approaches to racial psychology is far from exhaustive, but it may perhaps give some idea of the complexities of the problem and some justification for the unwillingness of so many social and biological scientists to accept the popular view that races differ in their inherited mentality. There is one further method of investigation in this area which has attracted a great deal of attention in recent years, and which requires somewhat more extensive consideration.

The use of mental tests in this controversial field appears to have certain advantages over most, if not all, of the other methods suggested. A test does have a certain objectivity. It yields results which can be checked by another investigator who can repeat the study, using similar tests on more or less similar groups. It furnishes a quantitative score permitting statistical analysis, so that differences between any two samples of races or nations can be judged in relation to whether they satisfy the statistical criteria of significance. It gives some indication not only of average performance, but also of the range and variability of the scores of the individuals who comprise the group. It has, however, one serious if not insurmountable drawback; namely, it furnishes individual and group variations which can safely be attributed to heredity only if the individuals and groups concerned have had, in the broadest sense, similar environmental opportunities. In the case of a relatively homogeneous group, the wide range of scores obtained by the application of mental tests almost certainly points to a wide range of inherited mental abilities. In the case of the comparison of two distinct racial or national populations, such a degree of homogeneity is almost impossible to find, and the differences in test scores will therefore always be subject to the widest differences in interpretation.

Differences occur in the average test scores reported for various ethnic groups studied in the United States. In comparison with the results obtained on American control groups, the results show that subjects of English, Scotch, German, Jewish, Chinese, and Japanese origin test at or near the American norm. Other groups fall, on the average, definitely below. In twenty-seven different studies of American Negroes, for example, the median result was an intelligence quotient of 86 (the norm, of course, being 100); it should be noted, however, that the range of the average scores reported in these studies was from an I.Q. of 58 (in Tennessee) to 105 (for Negro children tested in Los Angeles). Other groups which also rank, on the average, below the American norms are Americans of Italian origin, among whom sixteen different studies yielded a median I.Q. of 85, the results of the individual studies ranging from 79 to 96; Portuguese, with six studies, a median I.Q. of 84 and a range from 83 to 96; Mexicans, with nine studies, a median I.Q. of 83.4 and a range from 78 to 101; and American Indians, with eleven studies, a median I.Q. of 80.5 and a range from 65 to 100.

The wide range in the averages reported for various American Negro groups—from an I.Q. of 58 to one of 105—raises the problem of variations within the same "racial" group living under different conditions. It has, of course, long been recognized that Northern Negroes obtain, on the average, better test scores than do Negroes from the South. The examination of army recruits in the last war, for example, demonstrated this superiority unequivocally.[7] At the same time there was evidence to indicate that Negroes from some of the Northern states obtained average scores superior to those of the white recruits from some of the Southern states. This was at least true for those who took the Army Alpha examination. Frequent mention has been made of the fact that Negro recruits from Ohio, Illinois, and New York obtained higher scores on this test than did the whites, for example, from Mississippi, Kentucky, and Arkansas. In previous discussions of this comparison (including those by the present writer) it was not made sufficiently clear that these comparisons referred only to the Army Alpha. Since this is a "language" test which was not taken by all the recruits, a fairer statement would run somewhat as follows: that the literate Negroes from certain Northern states who took the Army Alpha obtained higher average scores than the literate whites from certain Southern states who were examined by the same test.

A more complete basis for comparison would be possible if the scores on all the tests used during the last war could be combined. This is

---

[7] See R. M. Yerkes, ed., "Psychological Examining in the U.S. Army," *Memoirs of the National Academy of Science*, XV (1921).

difficult to do in any satisfactory manner, since the other tests (for example, the Army Beta, a non-language test) undoubtedly measure abilities which are not quite the same as those which enter into the Army Alpha. In his *Study of American Intelligence* (1922) C. C. Brigham used a combination of these various test scores in analyzing the army results, but later concluded [8] that there was so much inconsistency even within the Army Alpha itself, that "it is absurd to go beyond this point and combine Alpha, Beta, the Stanford-Binet and the individual performance tests in the so-called 'combined scale.'" On the basis of these and similar difficulties, Brigham completely repudiated the "racial hierarchy" which he had attempted to demonstrate in his earlier work; this repudiation, incidentally, may be regarded, like Odum's description of "the errors of sociology," as still one more example of the change in the attitude of American social scientists in this field.

In view of Brigham's strictures, it seems preferable not to attempt a combination of the scores obtained in the separate tests. It is possible, however, to arrive at the same result by seeing whether any Northern Negro groups obtain average scores superior to those of any Southern whites, in *both* Army Alpha and Beta. An inspection of the original results in Tables 200, 201, 247, and 250 of the Yerkes *Memoir* does indeed show this to be the case. Negroes from Ohio and Indiana, for example, are superior in both tests to whites from Kentucky and Mississippi. The conclusion is therefore justified that the Negro recruits in some of the Northern states did obtain higher scores on the army intelligence tests than the whites in some of the Southern states.

The most probable interpretation of this finding is that when American Negroes live under relatively favorable environmental conditions their test scores are correspondingly high, and when whites live under relatively poor conditions their tests scores are correspondingly low. It is apparently not "race" but environment which is the crucial variable. As for the factors in the environment which are mainly responsible for these and similar results, it is likely that the nature of the available schooling plays a major role. A glance at the figures for per capita expenditures for Negro and white children in the segregated school system of the South brings into sharp focus the handicaps of the Negro children; the figures also reveal that Southern white children suffer

---

[8] Brigham, "Intelligence Tests of Immigrant Groups," *Psychological Review*, XXXVII (1930), 158–65.

similar, though not such extreme, handicaps. For the year 1935–36, the average per capita expenditure for all public-school children in the country was $74. The range between different states was great. New York, Nevada, and California spent more than $115; Alabama, Mississippi, and Arkansas, less than $30. As for the Negro children, the average expenditure in ten Southern states was $17.04; the average for white children in these same states was $49.30. In Mississippi and Georgia, only about $9 was spent in one year for the education of a Negro child.[9] In the light of the known relationship between good schooling and performance on tests of intelligence, it is hardly surprising that Southern whites obtain lower scores than those from the north or that Southern Negroes usually make such a poor showing.

There remains the possibility that the superiority of Northern over Southern Negroes is due not so much to differences in schooling as to "selective migration"—a movement of the most intelligent Negroes away from the South. This explanation has been offered, for example, by Peterson and Lanier [10] to account for the fact that in their investigation, whereas Nashville whites were markedly superior to Nashville Negroes, Chicago whites were only slightly superior to Chicago Negroes, and in New York City there were no significant differences between the two racial groups. They write: "There is apparently developing in New York, under the more severe struggle for existence, a highly selected Negro population which represents the best genes in the race." This remains an hypothesis, however, for which there is little concrete evidence. People migrate for many different reasons, and it has never been demonstrated that it is always the brightest ones who leave and the least intelligent who stay behind. A series of studies directed at this problem [11] failed to discover any evidence that the migration of Southern Negroes was "selective" with regard to intelligence. It was, on the other hand, possible to demonstrate that among Negro children now living in New York but born in the South there was, on the average, a close correspondence between their test scores and the length of time they had lived in the superior Northern environment. To put it in other words, those Negro children who migrated from the South to the North gave no evidence of being superior in "intelligence" (as measured by the tests) when they first came North;

[9] Myrdal, *An American Dilemma*.
[10] J. Peterson and L. H. Lanier, "Studies in the Comparative Abilities of Whites and Negroes," *Mental Measurement Monographs*, V (1929), 1–156.
[11] Otto Klineberg, *Negro Intelligence and Selective Migration* (New York, 1935).

rather, they became superior under the influence of the better schooling and wider opportunities for learning provided them in the new environment.

There is nothing surprising about this conclusion. A large amount of evidence has accumulated which indicates the extent to which test scores vary with environmental changes. Perhaps the best-known studies in this field, and the ones which have aroused the greatest controversy, are those of B. L. Wellman and her collaborators at Iowa University.[12] Some of the changes reported for individual subjects are so great as to suggest that other factors—possibly variations in the emotional state or the bodily health of the individual at the time of different examinations—may have played a part, but on the average the amount of change as the result of nursery-school attendance seems well within the expected limits. In any case, this general result is so completely consonant with the results reported in many other studies that any argument concerning it seems justified only in relation to the amount of change reported, and not to the fact that environmental changes may have a significant influence on test scores.

Since these environmental effects can be demonstrated even in the case of white children of native white American parentage, it is perhaps unnecessary to labor the point that interracial comparisons by means of intelligence tests will always be suspect as long as discrepancies exist in the environmental opportunities of the various groups tested. Reference has already been made to the discrepancy in schooling, most marked in the case of the Southern Negro. This is only one of a number of factors which have some effect on the test scores. For example, many studies have demonstrated a hierarchy in the intelligence quotients of children living under different economic conditions; children of farmers and of day laborers do not do so well on the tests as children of doctors or bankers. There is of course the possibility (not as yet established) that genetic factors contribute to these differences. For present purposes, it is sufficient to point out that whether or not heredity enters here, environment certainly plays a part. This comes out clearly in the studies of foster children, whose test scores rise when they are adopted by well-to-do families. That being the case, the inferior economic position of the Negroes, Italians, Poles, Portu-

---

[12] A summary of these studies, as well as some of the criticisms leveled against them, may be found in *Intelligence: Its Nature and Nurture*, the 39th Yearbook of the National Society for the Study of Education, published in 1940.

guese, and other groups who fail on the average to meet the test norms, cannot be disregarded in any interpretation of the results.

The fact that many of these groups are bilingual also has the effect of handicapping them in test comparisons.[13] To cite one representative study, it was found that a group of Ontario Indians, all of whom spoke English but usually with some difficulty, obtained much lower I.Q.'s on the linguistic than on the performance (nonlanguage) tests. In addition, the monoglot Indian children, who spoke only English, were superior to the bilingual children on all tests except the Pintner-Paterson performance scale.[14] This result has been repeated with many other groups. Children who are bilingual are at a definite disadvantage, in most cases, when the usual type of intelligence test is used. On performance tests their inferiority is much less noticeable and often disappears entirely.

This raises the question as to whether it might be possible to devise tests of intelligence which would be entirely free of cultural or environmental influences. There have been many attempts to devise such "culture-free" tests, but it appears unlikely that they will ever be successful. Even if the specific content is equally familiar (or unfamiliar) to the groups concerned, it would still be impossible to equate the groups for other, more indirect factors. One group may be more strongly motivated, more anxious to succeed; one group may have a friendlier attitude to the tester; one group may be more at home in the testing situation; one group may be more accustomed to tasks involving competition between individuals; one group may have a stronger pattern of getting things done quickly. Differences of this kind are familiar to all ethnologists, but it is doubtful whether their influence could be adequately measured—or even estimated—so as to allow the proper weight for their contribution to the final test score. Until that is done for these and other factors, present and potential, the prospect of constructing a truly "culture-free" test seems almost to be a contradiction in terms.

There is another problem which runs through all of these test comparisons, namely, that of obtaining a representative sample. Suppose tests are given to a group of Italian children in one of the schools in

---

[13] A review of studies in this field is found in S. Arsenian, *Bilingualism and Mental Development*, "Teachers College Contributions to Education," No. 712 (New York, 1937).

[14] E. Jamieson and P. Sandiford, "The Mental Capacity of Southern Ontario Indians," *Journal of Educational Psychology*, XIX (1928), 536-51.

New York City. The question arises as to whether this group is representative of all Italian children; or of all Italian children living in the United States; or of all Italian children in New York; or even of all Italian children in that particular school. There is evidence to show that one Italian group in the United States may differ markedly from another; that Italian girls tested in Rome, Italy, obtain superior scores to those tested in New York City, and so on. It has already been pointed out that groups of Negro children varied in average I.Q. from 58 in Tennessee to 105 in Los Angeles. Some of the methods used in obtaining samples for Public Opinion polls might profitably be applied here. The mere increase in the number of cases would not be sufficient—as was demonstrated by the failure of the *Literary Digest* political poll of 1936 when two million ballots were received. It should be pointed out, however, that even the use of a truly representative sample would not eliminate the other difficulties discussed here.

If the samples can be demonstrated to be adequate and representative, the test scores may be very useful as a measure of present achievement in the particular abilities involved (though not as a measure of inherited capacity). As such, they may serve as indications of the extent to which individuals and groups fall below the standards set by one particular culture. They may uncover weak points and indicate the directions in which remedial measures may profitably and effectively be applied. In the case of the Southern Negro, for example, the low test scores may legitimately be used to demonstrate a present inferiority based in large measure upon inadequate schooling—and such schooling may then be regarded as the first line of attack directed to the more complete incorporation of the Negro in the American community as a whole. Only when the Negro has been given the same opportunities for learning will the test scores serve as an indication of possible limitations in learning capacity.

In any interpretation of group differences in test scores it must not be forgotten that the difference is one of averages, and that the overlapping is great. There are always some Negroes who do better than some whites, no matter how unfavorable to the Negro the environmental factors may be. As a matter of fact, there are some Negroes who do better than almost all whites. The upper and lower limits of achievement, even under present testing conditions, are the same for the two groups. There are some Negroes and some whites who are so feeble-minded that they cannot do anything with the problems presented by the tests. At the other extreme, there are Negro children who obtain an I.Q. equal to that of the most successful white children. There is one report [15] of a Negro girl who at the age of nine years and four months obtained a Standford-Binet I.Q. of 200. This child was apparently of unmixed Negro origin; there is no record of any white admixture on either side of the family. Her background was superior; her father was a former college teacher who later became a practicing electrical engineer, and her mother formerly taught school in a large city. This case is of course exceptional, and would be so in any group, but it at least indicates that the upper limit of abilities as measured by the tests is just as high for Negroes as for whites.

The criticisms that have been leveled against the use of intelligence tests in the field of racial psychology apply even more strongly in the case of most tests of personality. Such tests are so deeply impregnated with the culture in which they have originated that their direct application to other groups and other cultures yields results that may be very misleading. To mention one specific example, the Pressey X-O test, which is designed to measure emotional responses, was administered to Indians of varying tribal origin, now living in Nebraska, Montana, California, New Mexico, and Oklahoma.[16] The investigators report that the Indians were less mature emotionally than the whites with whom they were compared. "The Indian tends to remain immature; either he is incapable of a more mature adjustment or else his environment has been so simplified that adjustment on a childish level is good enough." In view of the cultural relativity of the concept of emotional maturity, this statement does not seem especially meaningful. Even if we grant that this particular test has validity in a more or less homogeneous American community, its use "cross-culturally" will always be suspect. The investigators themselves realize this at least in part, for in a subsequent study [17] they point out that the tribes with the greatest degree of white contacts (like the Crow) are "less retarded emotionally" than those which have remained relatively isolated (like the Hopi). This conclusion closely parallels the finding in the case of intelligence tests: that the more similar the environments

[15] P. A. Witty and M. A. Jenkins, "The Case of 'B'—a Gifted Negro Girl," *Journal of Social Psychology*, VI (1935), 117–24.
[16] S. L. Pressey and L. C. Pressey, "A Comparative Study of the Emotional Attitudes and Interests of Indian and White Children," *Journal of Applied Psychology*, XVII (1933), 227–38.
[17] "A Comparison of the Emotional Development of Indians Belonging to Different Tribes," *Journal of Applied Psychology*, XVII (1933), 535–41.

of the groups compared, the smaller the difference in their average test scores.

One more example of the effect of cultural background on personality test scores may be mentioned. When a Chinese translation of the Thurstone Neurotic Inventory was administered in various Chinese universities, the results showed much more "neuroticism" among those students than among the American students with whom they were compared.[18] The investigators apparently accept this result at its face value, since they express some concern over the "lack of adjustment" among Chinese students, and advocate a mental hygiene program in their universities as a corrective. Such an interpretation is warranted only if the items in the Inventory have the same significance and fit into a similar "frame of reference" in China as in the United States. That this is not the case is recognized by other investigators [19] who obtained results similar to those of Chou and Mi, but who point out that the answers are in many cases affected not by "neuroticism" but by specific viewpoints resulting from Chinese (Confucian) precepts and principles.

These and similar considerations apply so widely in the field of personality tests, that, as measures of "racial psychology," the results must be dismissed. As indications of group differences in culturally determined attitudes, however, they may have considerable interest. Findings such as those of Pressey and of Chou and Mi, when combined with an adequate ethnological picture of the groups concerned, may be valuable in bringing out such differences in greater detail, as well as in demonstrating the amount of variation among individuals within any one culture.

There is some evidence to the effect that the Rorschach test may be somewhat more "culture-free" in its application to personality than the other tests so far considered. Even if this should turn out to be true, however, it would probably mean that the Rorschach could be used to discover the personality organization of an individual apart from the impact of his culture upon him; it would not mean that cultural differences would be irrelevant to the group comparisons. Nor would it mean that "racial"—that is, hereditary—group differences could be discovered by this method, since even within our own culture Ror-

[18] S. K. Chou and C. Y. Mi, "Relative Neurotic Tendency of Chinese and American Students," *Journal of Social Psychology*, VIII (1937), 155–84.
[19] T. Pai, S. M. Sung, and E. H. Hsü, "The Application of Thurstone's Personality Schedule to Chinese Students," *Journal of Social Psychology*, VIII (1937), 47–72.

schach specialists do not claim that their method is capable of differentiating between genetic and environmental influences upon personality organization.

The conclusion is therefore justified that mental tests, whether of personality or of intelligence, cannot be used as a foundation for a racial psychology. This method, like the others previously discussed, is open to so much criticism that in this case also the conclusion must be that racial differences in psychology have not been—and perhaps cannot be—demonstrated.

At the same time, it can hardly be denied that there are significant psychological differences between ethnic groups. The rich and varied material collected by ethnologists, the life histories of individuals of minority status (for example, Negroes) in this country, the descriptions of variations in "national character," all point in that direction, though these approaches raise methodological problems of a controversial nature. They do not, however, constitute a "racial" psychology. They indicate differences, but these are differences which are almost certainly the product of historical and environmental factors rather than genetic or racial. Only in the case of relatively small isolated and inbred communities, as indicated above, can one speak with any degree of probability of a racial psychology. For the larger, more heterogeneous populations with which we are familiar, "race" and psychology appear, in the present stage of our knowledge, to be unrelated.

This conclusion has certain important practical implications. If there is no racial psychology, discrimination against minority groups on the basis of their alleged hereditary inferiority is completely unjustified. If there is no racial psychology, the behavior of large national communities is to be ascribed to environmental factors (in the largest sense) and not to the germ plasm, which means that it may change with time and with new conditions. And if there is no racial psychology, any hope that we may have of making our own democracy broader and more efficient rests not so much on an improvement in our "stock" as on making available to the whole community the educational and economic opportunities which pave the way for fuller and richer living.

The Concept of Culture

By CLYDE KLUCKHOHN and WILLIAM H. KELLY [1]

THE LAWYER: At the last meeting of this little discussion group of ours, we got into quite an argument about "culture" as a technical term in anthropology—exactly what anthropologists mean by it and whether it is any use or not. The big dictionaries and even the anthropological books here in the club library didn't help us out very much. We did gather that the anthropological conception, like all the other scientific and popular usages, carries with it an implication of human interference, of something being added to, or altered from, a state of nature. But we found ourselves wishing that we could ask questions which might clear up points which were sidestepped or simply not discussed by these formal statements. We therefore prevailed upon you gentlemen to come here and let us put you on the spot.

THE HISTORIAN: Was I right in insisting last time that the anthropologist's conception of culture is much more inclusive than the historian's?

FIRST ANTHROPOLOGIST: Yes, to anthropologists a humble cooking pot is as much a cultural product as is a Beethoven sonata.

THE BUSINESSMAN: I am relieved to hear that. For my wife a person who has culture is a person who can talk about Debussy, T. S. Eliot, Picasso, and those people.

THE LAWYER: Do anthropologists apply the term "culture" to our civilization? Isn't there a difference between "culture" and "civilization"?

SECOND ANTHROPOLOGIST: To most anthropologists, a civilization is simply a special type of a culture, namely, a complex or "high" culture. More specifically, a civilization is—as the derivation of the word itself suggests—the culture of a people who live in cities. People who have lived in cities have invariably possessed a somewhat complex way of life, and have almost always had a written language.

THIRD ANTHROPOLOGIST: Perhaps it would also be well to state for the record that anthropologists have never followed another distinction

[1] We are grateful to Dr. Florence Kluckhohn for critical suggestions and other help.

which certain sociologists have made between culture and civilization. This usage discriminates between "civilization" as comprising the sum total of human "means" and "culture" as constituting the collectivity of human "ends."

FIRST ANTHROPOLOGIST: Many educated people seem to have the notion that "culture" applies only to exotic ways of life or to societies where relative simplicity and relative homogeneity prevail. Some sophisticated missionaries, for example, will use the anthropological conception in discussing the special modes of living of South Sea Islanders, but seem amazed at the idea that it could be applied equally to the inhabitants of New York City. And social workers in New York City will talk about the "culture" of a colorful and well-knit immigrant group, but boggle at utilizing the concept toward understanding the behavior of staff members in the social service agency itself.

THE ECONOMIST: A moment ago you used the term "society." This brings me to a point which I have found confusing in certain recent more or less popular writings of anthropologists. Sometimes the terms "culture" and "society" seem to have been used almost as synonyms.

FIRST ANTHROPOLOGIST: There would be fairly general agreement in our profession that this is undesirable. The usage which has attained almost complete acceptance among us can be put simply, though not altogether precisely, as follows: A "society" refers to a group of people who have learned to work together; a "culture" refers to the distinctive ways of life of such a group of people.

THE PHILOSOPHER: In my language, then, "a culture" is an abstraction, whereas "a society" is not?

THIRD ANTHROPOLOGIST: That is certainly correct in the sense that you can see the individuals who make up a society, while you never see "culture." However, the statement must not be made to imply that the processes of inference and abstraction are not involved in many of the specific problems of deciding where one society leaves off and another begins. Some anthropologists assert that such problems can always be resolved by sufficiently detailed observation of the frequencies with which human beings in a defined territory interact. This is doubtless a valid operation by which to decide what individuals constitute "a society," but we should be deluding ourselves if we pretended that reasoning were not as necessary as observation to the delimitation of a society.

SECOND ANTHROPOLOGIST: I can't agree with your first statement that culture is never observed directly. What does an anthropologist actually do when he is working in the field? Yes, he sees the human organisms who make up a society. He sees not only them, but also their behavior. He likewise sees the objects they have made and all of the alterations which they produced in their natural environment. What the anthropologist does is to record the distinctive ways of behaving which he sees and those results of behavior which are also characteristic. These constitute the culture of the group.

THIRD ANTHROPOLOGIST: There is no doubt that you have rightly described what anthropologists actually do in the field. But those recordings which you have mentioned I would prefer to consider as the anthropologist's raw data. Both "society" and "culture" are conceptual constructs. In each case, although in importantly different ways, the anthropologist has added to or subtracted from what he actually saw. Both the society and the culture which he portrays are conceptual models—not firsthand recordings of all he observed.

THE PSYCHOLOGIST: Let me see if I can translate into my own lingo. Culture means the totality of social habits.

FIRST ANTHROPOLOGIST: "Habit" is too neutral a term. It would be more exact to say "socially valued habits," for a group is never affectively indifferent to its culture.

THE PSYCHOLOGIST: I suppose that branch of psychology which is most intimately related to "culture" is what we today call "learning theory." Wouldn't you agree that the transmission of culture can be understood only in so far as learning and teaching are understood?

FIRST ANTHROPOLOGIST: Yes, inasmuch as all human beings of whatever "races" seem to have about the same nervous systems and biological equipment generally, we would anticipate that the basic processes of learning are very similar if not identical among all groups. We therefore look to the psychologist to inform us about the laws of learning. On the other hand, we can show that *what* is learned, from whom learning takes place, and when the learning of certain skills usually occurs, varies according to culture. Also, I should like to point out that there is one danger in speaking of culture as being "taught." "Teaching" is not limited, as in the popular sense, to conscious instruction. Individuals learn—"absorb" more nearly suggests, in nontechnical language, the process—much of their culture through imitation of both the "matched-dependent" and "copying" types. Take, for example, those gestures and expressive movements ("motor habits") which are observed as characteristic of certain groups. Every anthropologist regards these as cultural phenomena, and yet only in dancing schools, armies, and the like is explicit instruction as to posture, and so forth, given.

THE PSYCHOLOGIST: If I am not mistaken, C. S. Ford has defined culture as consisting of "traditional ways of solving problems" or "learned problem solutions."

THIRD ANTHROPOLOGIST: It is true that any culture is, among other things, a set of techniques for adjusting both to the external environment and to other men. In so far as Ford's statement points to this fact, it is helpful, but it will not do as a synoptic definition. For cultures create problems as well as solving them. If the lore of a people states that frogs are dangerous creatures, or that it is not safe to go about at night because of were-animals or ghosts, threats are posed which do not arise out of the inexorable facts of the external world. This is why all "functional" definitions of culture tend to be unsatisfactory: they disregard the fact that cultures create needs as well as provide a means of fulfilling them.

THE PSYCHIATRIST: In fact, my profession has always tended to think of culture as something which was repressive to the "natural" nature of man, as something which produced needless neuroses by demands and thwartings during the process of molding individuals into shapes uncongenial to their native temperament.

THIRD ANTHROPOLOGIST: This seems to us to be another half-truth. Culture is *both* fulfilling and frustrating.

FOURTH ANTHROPOLOGIST: I have held my peace, but at this point I really must protest. Where is this "culture" which you talk about as doing this and that? If anthropology is to become a natural science, it must deal only in empirical and observable entities. In spite of the fact that most archeologists, ethnologists, and social anthropologists still feel that "culture" is their master concept, I maintain we would get further if we stuck to human interaction with other humans and with the natural environment. You can see those things, but has any of you ever seen "culture"?

FIRST ANTHROPOLOGIST: I freely admit that to say "culture" does something is an inexact or metaphorical way of speaking. But this is merely a convenient shorthand expression in place of the long-winded though admittedly more precise "the human representatives of the group which share this culture do thus and so." As for "seeing": your admired natural scientists have never seen "gravity" or "evolution." And yet they find the introduction of these concepts indispensable for making the facts intelligible and for predicting them. "Culture" is an abstract generalizing concept, as essential to the understanding and prediction of events in the human world as is gravity to the understanding and prediction of events in the physical world.

SECOND ANTHROPOLOGIST: I accept and use the concept "culture," but I shy away from these high abstractions. I think it is better to stick to a more traditional definition, such as: "Culture is that complex whole which includes artifacts, beliefs, art, all the other habits acquired by man as a member of society, and all products of human activity as determined by these habits."

FIRST ANTHROPOLOGIST: That is all right as a descriptive statement of what students of culture investigate. But as a definition I find it awkward. The enumeration is incomplete, and experience shows that in definitions by enumeration those elements which are not explicitly stated tend to be forgotten even though they be implied. You, for example, have not even mentioned language.

THIRD ANTHROPOLOGIST: I would file two other objections. First, the definition is too intellectualistic. One gets no hint that people are other than affectively neutral toward their culture. This is just a list of culture content. Except, possibly, for the single word "whole," there is no indication that culture has organization as well as content.

THE ECONOMIST: How about "social heredity" as a brief abstract definition of culture?

THIRD ANTHROPOLOGIST: This definition has been widely current and has been of much utility in drawing attention to the fact that human beings have a social as well as a biological heritage. The principal drawbacks to this conception of culture are that it implies too great stability of culture and too passive a role on the part of man. It suggests that man gets his culture as he gets his genes—without effort and without resistance. It tends too much to make us think of the human being as what Dollard has called "the passive porter of a cultural tradition." Men are, as Simmons has recently reminded us, not only the carriers and the creatures of culture—they are also creators and manipulators of culture. "Social heredity" suggests too much of the dead weight of tradition.

THE PSYCHIATRIST: Yes, culture is not merely a "given." Really, in a strictly literal sense, it is not a "given" at all—it is only available. Indeed, Ortega y Gasset has defined culture as "that which is sought." The phrase "social legacy" perhaps avoids some of these difficulties, but even this is hardly satisfactory. One wants a definition which points to the fact that the irreducible datum of the social scientist is the individual and his behavior. From the angle of individual psychology, no definition of culture is adequate which does not make us aware of the active role of the individual as regards his culture and of the fact that he has an impulse life.

THE BUSINESSMAN: Much of what has been said was mildly diverting as an exhibition in logical adroitness, but frankly I still don't altogether see why anybody bothers about "culture" at all.

FIRST ANTHROPOLOGIST: Well, one of the interesting things about human beings is that they try to understand themselves and their own behavior. While this has been particularly true of Europeans in recent times, there is no group which has not developed a scheme or schemes to explain man's actions. I would claim that the concept of culture is essential to such understanding.

SECOND ANTHROPOLOGIST: I would phrase the case a little differently. Science is concerned with all observable phenomena, including man himself and his behavior. "Culture" is a convenient descriptive category for organizing our objective reports on human behavior.

THE PHILOSOPHER: It strikes me that the last two statements contain the key to much of our apparent disagreement. For some anthropologists "culture" is primarily a descriptive concept; for others it is primarily an explanatory concept. So-called "definitions" are always constructed from a point of view—which is all too often left unstated. Not all definitions are substantive (that is, "descriptive"). Nor is "explanatory" the only other alternative. Some of the definitions which have been partially stated or implied have been "functional"; others may be characterized as epistemological—that is, they have been intended to point toward the type of phenomena from which we gain our knowledge of "culture." There is also the point that some definitions look toward the actions of the individual as the starting point of all assertions, whereas others, while perhaps admitting these as ultimate referents, depart from abstractions attributable to groups. However, the distinction between "explanatory" and "descriptive" seems to be most central.

"CULTURE" AS AN EXPLANATORY CONCEPT

THIRD ANTHROPOLOGIST: By *"culture"* we mean those historically created selective processes which channel men's reactions both to internal and to external stimuli.

SECOND ANTHROPOLOGIST: That is certainly an "analytical abstraction" all right.

THIRD ANTHROPOLOGIST: That is precisely the idea: that with this concept certain aspects of the concrete phenomena may be analyzed out, and thus whole events may be better "explained" and predicted.

FIRST ANTHROPOLOGIST: Very neat. And it seems to me to cover the ground. It avoids the difficulty lurking in those many definitions of culture which employ the phrase "acquired by man as a member of society." That phrase seems to suggest that "culture" as an explanatory concept refers *only* to dimensions of the behavior of individuals resultant upon their membership in a particular society (either through birth or through later affiliation). But "culture" also helps us to understand such processes as "diffusion," "culture contact," "acculturation."

THIRD ANTHROPOLOGIST: Yes, culture as an explanatory concept is useful alike in analyzing actions of individuals (whether treated as individuals or as groups) and in elucidating geographical distributions of artifacts or forms of behavior and historical sequences.

FIRST ANTHROPOLOGIST: One could perhaps rephrase your definition along substantive lines by saying that by culture we mean those historically created definitions of the situation which individuals tend to acquire by virtue of participation in or contact with groups which tend to share ways of life which are in some respects distinctive.

FOURTH ANTHROPOLOGIST: Even I find some merit in the explanatory definition proposed. You at least make some concession to a behavioristic approach when you speak of "reactions" and "stimuli."

THIRD ANTHROPOLOGIST: Naturally I would agree that any concept or proposition in social science must be ultimately referable back to human behavior. Even when we deal with distribution of "culture traits," we must not forget that we are dealing with products of human hands, with traces left by human activity.

FOURTH ANTHROPOLOGIST: But why did you find it necessary to include *"internal* stimuli"?

THIRD ANTHROPOLOGIST: When a man eats, he is reacting to an internal "drive," namely, hunger contractions consequent upon the lowering of blood sugar and so forth, but his precise reaction to these internal stimuli cannot be predicted by physiological knowledge alone. Whether a healthy adult tends to "feel hungry" twice, three times, or four times a day and the hours at which these "feelings" tend to recur is a question of culture. *What* he eats is of course limited by sheer objective availability, but is also partly regulated by culture. It is a biological fact that some types of berries are poisonous, but it is a cultural fact that, a few generations ago, most Americans considered tomatoes to be poisonous and refused to eat them. On the other hand, milk, which we regard as a healthful and pleasing food, is regarded by certain peoples of the earth as either dangerous or disgusting. Such selective, discriminative use of the environment is characteristically cultural. In a still more general sense, too, the process of eating is channeled by culture. Whether a man eats to live, lives to eat, or eats and lives is partly individual idiosyncrasy, but there are also marked correlations of individual tendencies along these lines with cultural groups.

SECOND ANTHROPOLOGIST: Why do you use the word "reaction" instead of more straightforward "action"?

THIRD ANTHROPOLOGIST: Because "reaction" comes nearer to conveying the feeling tone which is associated with all selective designs for living.

FOURTH ANTHROPOLOGIST: I am partially convinced, but I must once more come back to my question: Why did you introduce this unseen "culture"?

THIRD ANTHROPOLOGIST: There is no human being, if he be even a few weeks old, who reacts completely freshly to any stimulus situation. Very few human responses indeed can be explained entirely through even the most complete knowledge of the individual biological equipment, private experience up to that point, and the objective facts of the given situation.

FOURTH ANTHROPOLOGIST: But where does "culture" come from? You seem to invoke it as a kind of *deus ex machina*.

THIRD ANTHROPOLOGIST: Culture is, as it were, the precipitate of history. It includes those aspects of the past which, usually in altered form, live on in the present. In more than one sense "history is a sieve."

BIOLOGIST: Do you mean that culture consists of those ways of meeting situations which prove to have survival value?

THIRD ANTHROPOLOGIST: This is a large and important part of the truth.

The process of culture may well be regarded as something added to man's innate biological capacities; it provides instruments which enlarge or may even substitute for biological functions and which to a limited degree compensate for biological limitations—as in insuring that the biological fact of death does not always mean that what the dead individual has learned is lost to humanity.

Nevertheless, I believe this to be a dangerously misleading formulation unless it is properly explained and qualified. In the first place, as Linton and others have documented, it is an observed fact that most groups elaborate certain aspects of their culture far beyond maximal relative utility or survival value. In other words, not all culture is adaptive—in the sense of promoting sheer physical survival. At times indeed it does exactly the opposite. We must bring in the concept of adjustment (that is, lowering of tension) as well as that of adaptation. In the second place, aspects of culture which once directly promoted survival may persist even after they have ceased to have survival value. An analysis of contemporary Navaho culture will disclose many features which cannot possibly be construed as adaptations to the total environment in which Navahos now find themselves. However, it is altogether likely that these represent survivals, with modifications which have occurred during the centuries, of cultural forms which were adaptive in one or another environment in which certain ancestors of the contemporary Navaho lived prior to entering the Southwest.

FIRST ANTHROPOLOGIST: In other words, you are saying that no way of reacting is taken over by the group unless it has direct adaptive or adjustive value for individuals as such (or as constituting a group) at the time the design for living becomes cultural.

THIRD ANTHROPOLOGIST: Right. The main point is that, as Boas so often insisted, we cannot account for complex historical changes by any simple formula. While many patterned ways of reacting unquestionably represent almost inevitable responses to an external environment in which the group lives or once lived, there are certainly also many cases where the inexorable conditions of action merely limit the possibility of response rather than eventually compelling one and only one mode of adaptation. These "choices" are probably themselves determined—if we make our theoretical system wide enough to encompass all possible types of factors. But, within the more usual frame of reference, they are the "accidents of history."

Let me give an example or two. In a society where the chief really has great power, one particular chief happens to be born with an endocrine imbalance which brings about certain (to that group) unusual idiosyncrasies in personality. By virtue of his position, he is able to bring about certain modifications in the way of life of his group (say, in religion) which are congenial to his "temperament." It may be argued, and it may be true, that no amount of authority could insure the persistence of such alterations unless they somehow had adjustive or adaptive value for more than a single individual. I do not believe that the empirical evidence bearing on this problem has been sufficiently analyzed to permit a definite answer to the question. But what is certain is that such a circumstance has been known to be followed by relatively temporary or relatively enduring changes in group designs for living—sometimes primarily in the form of strong "reaction formations." The fact of the chief's position and all that was consequent upon it is not an accident from the point of view of the theoretical systems usually employed in analyzing such steps. The unusual temperament is, however, due to an "accident of the genetic process."

Or, suppose that in the same group a chief dies as a relatively young man, leaving an infant as his heir. This has been observed to result in a marked crystallization of two factions around two rival older relatives, each of whom has about an equally valid claim to act as "regent." Through these circumstances a complete and lasting splitting off of two groups has been observed to take place. Each group thereafter has pursued its own separate destiny, and the end result is the formation of two distinguishable variants of what was at one time a more or less homogeneous culture. Now, to be sure, it is likely that the original factional lines had their bases in "economic," demographic, or other "external" conditions. Yet, had it not been for the "accidental" death of the one chief in his early maturity, the society might have indefinitely continued intact as an equilibrium of opposed tendencies. In short, the form and the mesh of the "sieve which is history" must be seen and shaped not only by the total "environment" at any given point in time but also by individual "psychological" and "accidental" factors.

FIRST ANTHROPOLOGIST: Could we then say that culture includes all those ways of feeling, thinking, and acting which are not inevitable as a result of human biological equipment and process and (or) objective external situations?

THIRD ANTHROPOLOGIST: My objection to that definition would be: first, that this defines culture as a "residual category"—which is logically undesirable; second, I believe it is better to mention explicitly the time dimension as indicated by the phrase "historically created."

FIRST ANTHROPOLOGIST: This suggests also the cumulative nature of culture.

THIRD ANTHROPOLOGIST: Yes, provided we remember that in another sense culture is not exactly "cumulative." Culture at any given time-point has likewise the property of uniqueness. That is why it is absolutely essential to include the word "selective" in any definition.

THE LAWYER: I can see that there has been a selection of possible modes of behavior and that these selections then may become established in a group, but aren't you overemphasizing this aspect? It seems to me that in common sense terms if we understand human nature, and if we then make our interpretation in the light of the concrete situation at hand, we get along very well.

FIRST ANTHROPOLOGIST: No, if you will look beyond the records of our own time and place you will find that the matter is not so simple. There are certain recurrent and inevitable human problems, and the ways in which man can meet them are limited by his biological equipment and by certain facts of the external world. Anthropologists have perhaps in recent years been too much preoccupied with the diversity found upon the earth and have neglected the basic similarities. But apart from these important but very general resemblances, the conception of one single, unchanging "human nature" is a reassuring fiction of folklore. When it comes to details, there are "human natures." For example, old age is a situation to which all human beings who live long enough must adjust. But we find that in some human societies the old, regardless of their particular achievements, are entitled to respect and even to authority. In other societies, we find that the old, again regardless of individual differences, are ordinarily treated with relative indifference or active contempt. In still other societies, whether or not an aged person is treated with deference or with neglect seems to depend on his own past history rather than upon his period of life. Thus we see that though age is a biological fact it is always culturally defined. This fact of the plasticity of "human nature" is the widest and the most certain induction which anthropologists can derive from the cross-cultural record.

The precise *forms* which biological and social processes take are myriad, and these *forms* are cultural. Let us take an instance where, as

THE CONCEPT OF CULTURE

so often, biological and social facts are intertwined. In many human groups which have been described, the physically weak have been, almost without qualification, at a disadvantage. In some groups, however, it has been observed that there have been effective deterrents against the strong taking advantage of the weak. Bullying has been punished by social disapproval and hence has actually been relatively rare. In a few societies, there is a tendency to give privileged positions to the physically weak or to certain types of the physically weak.

Just as sociobiological situations or purely social situations can be stylized, so also some purely biological situations may be stylized. Take vomiting, for example. Vomiting is a biological event and it can be produced by causes which are solely biological. But in other cases, although individual differences in neurological equipment and in previous experience play their part, the event sequence which would lead up to vomiting could never be predicted purely on the basis of biological knowledge. For instance, Americans who have eaten rattlesnake have been known to vomit upon being told what they had been fed. Since rattlesnake meat is perfectly nutritious, the vomiting is produced by some extrabiological factor.

Similar illustrations could be given for other biological processes, such as weeping and fainting. These biological processes are also caught in a cultural web, as it were. Here is a particularly telling example. The newborn infant excretes whenever tensions in bladder and colon reach a certain level of intensity. Before long, however, biological rhythms have surrendered to superimposed designs which are not directly derived from the facts of biology. Most adult human beings in normal health defecate only once or at most twice during a day. This tends to occur within rather fixed hours and, in many human groups, only at certain designated places and under defined conditions as to who else may (should) or may (should) not be present. So interesting and so vital is the interrelation of the biological and the cultural dimensions of human behavior that some anthropologists feel the study of these connections to be the differential feature of anthropology.

THE PSYCHOLOGIST: Isn't this just a kind of "conditioning"?

THE BIOLOGIST: Yes, couldn't we call it simply "environmental conditioning"?

FIRST ANTHROPOLOGIST: A very special sort of conditioning. No group deliberately sets out to train its children to vomit under certain circumstances. This result, rather, is a kind of incidental by-product of a style of life or of some aspect of such a style of life.

THIRD ANTHROPOLOGIST: The naïve—and very powerful—view is that we have individual organisms (they can be seen) and that they exist in an external world (which can also be seen and described). This is the view which "common-sense" takes, and it is very hard to shake oneself out of this apparently sensible formula. But it simply won't cover the facts, the awareness of the external environment is too highly selective for that. Put down various groups of adults who have been trained in different social traditions in the same desert island. What they see in their surroundings will not be identical at all. Nor will, of course, the techniques by which they endeavor to adjust themselves to the surroundings. Between culturalized men and their environment there exists, as it were, a screen which is intangible and invisible but none the less real. This screen is "culture."

THE PSYCHOLOGIST: In trying to understand a single concrete act on the part of an individual I have found it helpful to ask these questions:

1. What are the innate endowments and limitations of the individual?
2. What has his total experience been prior to the act we are studying?
3. What is his immediate situation?

FIRST ANTHROPOLOGIST: No one of these variables can be elucidated in a completely satisfactory manner without introducing the concept "culture."

1. Except in the case of newborn babies and of individuals born with clear-cut structural or functional abnormalities we can observe "innate endowments" only as modified by cultural training. In a hospital in New Mexico where Zuni Indian, Navaho Indian, and white American babies are born it is possible to classify the newly arrived infants as hyperactive, average, and hypoactive. Some babies from each "racial" group will fall into each category, though a higher proportion of the white babies will fall into the hyperactive class. But if a Navaho baby, a Zuni baby, and a white baby—all classified as about equally hyperactive at birth—are again observed at the age of two years, the Zuni baby—*as compared with the white child*—will no longer seem given to quick and restless activity, though he may seem

so as compared with other Zunis of the same age. The Navaho child is likely to fall in between as contrasted with the Zuni and the white though he will probably still seem hyperactive if seen against the standard of a series of Navaho youngsters.

2. The sheer factual description of the individual's experience doesn't get us very far. His interpretation of these events is indispensable, and this will be made, at least in part, in terms of norms current in his group. Losing a mother tends to mean one thing in one society, quite a different thing in another society.

3. Naturally, the immediate situation as well as past experience is reacted to, not in purely rational or objective fashion but in terms of the situation as meaningfully defined by the participant. Almost no human situations are viewed in ways which are altogether a consequence of the individual's experience. Culture is—among other things—a set of ready-made definitions of the situation which each participant only slightly retailors in his own idiomatic way.

THE BIOLOGIST: May we get back to some examples?

THIRD ANTHROPOLOGIST: If we are to begin at the beginning we start off, I suppose, with the basic observation of the diversity of human behavior.

A few years ago a young man of American parentage but who had been reared in a Chinese family from infancy on, paid his first visit to America. Reporters commented not only upon his apparently complete bewilderment in the American way of life, but also upon the fact that his walk, arm and hand movements, and facial expression were "Chinese—not American." They insisted that one had to fix one's attention upon his blond hair and blue eyes to convince oneself that he was of white stock at all. Here the point is that an individual's acts and attitudes not only failed to resemble those of his own close relatives in this country but that they resembled those of all members of an alien physical group and contrasted with those of all members of his own physical group.

To take a less dramatic but better-known illustration, a third generation Italian, unless he has been reared in the Italian colony of a large American city, shows "social habits" which resemble those of "Old Americans" much more closely than they do those of residents of Italy. The influence of the various domestic and geographical environments in which these Italian-Americans grew up was not so powerful but that we can recognize common tendencies in all of them which ally them to other "Americans."

The variations and similarities which obtain between groups of human beings must also both be clarified. Groups of the same strain of physical heredity show great differences in behavioral norms and groups of unquestionably different strains show great similarities. It has been remarked by many observers in the Japanese relocation centers that Japanese who have been born and brought up in this country, especially those who were reared apart from any large colony of Japanese, resemble their white neighbors in all behavioral characteristics much more closely than they do their own Japanese relatives who had been educated in Japan and then immigrated to this country.

THE PSYCHOLOGIST: This proves that human beings can learn from each other—and we knew that already. What proof is there that if all white Americans were wiped out the Japanese-American wouldn't eventually revert to designs for living highly similar to those characteristic of the Japanese of Japan?

THIRD ANTHROPOLOGIST: Obviously, there can be no certain answer to such a hypothetical question. But note carefully that the concept of culture as I have phrased it in no way denies the possible importance of innate factors. It does not assert the patent absurdity that the behavior of all Japanese (of Japan) or the behavior of all white Americans is minutely identical. It says merely that the behavior of each group though showing much individual variation still shows certain common tendencies within the one group which contrast sharply with those within the other group. Since the common tendencies of the American group are also to a perceptible degree exhibited by large numbers of individuals of Japanese racial stock—although it is not claimed that their behavior shows precisely the same modalities as the white Americans—it is argued that these shared trends may be attributed to the presence and influence of communicable designs for living.

THE ECONOMIST: Perhaps if Japan were depopulated and colonized by white Americans these would, within a certain number of generations, develop social definitions of the situation which would hardly be distinguishable from those characteristic of the Japanese today.

THIRD ANTHROPOLOGIST: The natural environments of the United States are very various, and yet the Americans of the arid Southwest and of rainy Oregon still behave in ways which are easily distinguishable from inhabitants of the Australian desert on the one hand and from those of verdant England on the other.

Tribes like the Pueblo and Navaho, living in substantially identical natural and biological environments, still manifest very different ways of life. The English who live in the Hudson Bay region and those who live in British Somaliland still share common designs for living. It is true, of course, that the different natural environments are responsible for observable alterations. But the striking fact is that, in spite of the tremendous environmental differences, shared designs for living still persist.

The inhabitants of two not widely separated villages in New Mexico, Ramah and Fence Lake, are both of the so-called "Old American" physical stock. Almost certainly a physical anthropologist would say they represented random samples from the same physical population. The rocky tablelands, the annual rainfall and its distribution, the flora and fauna surrounding the two villages hardly show perceptible variations. The density of population and the distance from a main highway is almost exactly the same in the two cases. Nevertheless, even the casual visitor immediately notices distinctions. There are characteristic differences in dress; the style of the houses is different; there is a saloon in one town and not in the other. A completion of this catalog would conclusively demonstrate that very different patterns of life prevail in the two settlements. Why? Primarily because the two villages represent variants of the general Anglo-American social traditions. They have slightly different cultures.

THE PHILOSOPHER: There are two questions upon which I must pin you down. The first is: where is the locus of culture—in society or in the individual?

THIRD ANTHROPOLOGIST: Asking the question that way poses a false dilemma. Remember that "culture" is an abstraction. Hence culture as a concrete, observable entity does not exist anywhere—unless you wish to say that it exists in the "minds" of the men who make the abstractions. The objects and events from which we make our abstractions do have an observable existence. But culture is like a map. Just as a map isn't the territory but an abstract representation of the territory so also a culture is an abstract description of trends toward uniformity in the words, acts, and artifacts of human groups. The data, then, from which we come to know culture are not derived from an abstraction such as "society" but from direct observable behavior and behavioral products. Note, however, that "culture" may be said to be "supraindividual" in at least two nonmystical, perfectly empirical senses:

1. Objects as well as individuals manifest culture.
2. The continuity of culture never depends upon the continued existence of any particular individuals.

THE PHILOSOPHER: Very good. Now my second question: Can "culture" ever be said to be the cause of anything?

THIRD ANTHROPOLOGIST: Not in any very strict or exact way of speaking. In the first place, I would always question the advisability of using the term "cause" in any social science theory. Too much of a unidirectional force is implied. Rather I should use "determinant" with its connotation of interdependence of the relevant forces. But even to say "culture determines" is a very inexact and elliptical way of speaking, justified perhaps in certain circumstances by the convenience of brevity. Inexact, however, it is, because no concrete phenomenon is ever completely and solely determined by culture. Sometimes, to be sure, culture may be the "strategic factor"—that is, the crucial element that determines that a given act tends to be differently carried out in one group than in another or that the act is somehow not what we would anticipate from a knowledge of the physical and biological forces operative. But "cultural determinism" in any simple or literal sense is as objectionable as any other class of unilateral determinism such as "geographical determinism" or "economic determinism."

Although, in the concrete, the influence of culture is always mediated by men or artifacts, one is nevertheless justified in speaking of culture as *a* determinant of events when a discussion is being carried on at a high level of abstraction—provided the degree of abstraction is not lost sight of. The point may become clearer from an analogy—though all analogies (including this one!) are dangerous. Suppose a man who has a plague which is thought to be due to a postulated but unseen virus enters a city and infects the population. What "causes" the epidemic—the man or the virus? Clearly, either answer is equally correct depending upon the conceptual system within which one is working. We should be too close to reifying an abstraction if we said that, in similar fashion, either men or things can become "hosts" to culture. Also, this metaphor, like the definition of culture as "social heredity" implies too passive a relationship between men and culture —as if culture were a bacteria acquired entirely casually and unknowingly by contact. And yet the simile remains tantalizing. One may even point out that it is less misleading than "social heredity," for genes are acquired in fixed and immutable form—once and for all—at birth, whereas bacteria change with the host and in time, though a given species remains recognizable in spite of this variation according to different hosts.

THE PHILOSOPHER: Could you relate what you have just said to the arguments over the proposition of Spengler, Sorokin, and others that cultures have their own independent laws of growth and decay?

THIRD ANTHROPOLOGIST: If what I have said is correct, anthropologists have probably been too hasty in their rejections of these theories. The theories you mention have, to greater or lesser degree, been phrased unfortunately so that condemnations of them as "mystical" or "metaphysical" can be given superficial plausibility. But an anthropologist who really wishes to understand these interpretations can "translate" them into his own conceptual scheme so that, if the levels of abstraction be kept straight, they seem to merit partial acceptance or at least careful reëxamination.

For, while no culture is "superorganic" in the sense that it would continue to "exist" after all the human beings who shared it had died and all the nonhuman manifestations of that culture had been destroyed, still a culture that is a going concern has properties which exhibit some independence from the other forces with which the culture is in interaction. One of the diagnostic features of a culture is its selectivity. Most specific needs can be satisfied in a wide variety of ways but "the culture selects" only one or a very few of the organically and physically possible modes. "The culture selects" is, to be sure, a metaphorical way of speaking. The *original* choice was necessarily made by an individual and then followed by other individuals (or it wouldn't have become culture). But from the angle of those individuals who later learn this bit of culture the existence of this element in a design for living has the *effect* of a selection which was not made by these human beings as a reaction to their own particular situation but was rather a choice made by individuals long gone but which still tends to bind our contemporary actors.

Such a selective awareness of the natural environment, such a stereotyped interpretation of man's place in the world is not merely inclusive; by implication it also excludes other possible alternatives. Because of the "strain toward consistency" in cultures such inclusions and exclusions are meaningful far beyond the specific activity which is overtly involved. Just as the "choice" of an individual at a crucial epoch commits him in certain directions for the rest of his life, so the original bents, trends, "interests" which become established in the designs for living of a newly formed society tend to channel a culture in some directions as opposed to others. Subsequent variations in the culture—both those which arise internally and those which are a response to contact with other cultures or to changes in the natural environment—are not random. In some sense, at least, there is probably "cultural orthogenesis" as well as biological orthogenesis.

THE LAWYER: Now I only wonder how you are going to make the transition from "culture" to "a culture." No physicist speaks of "a gravity."

FIRST ANTHROPOLOGIST: Surely when the physicist "explains" the falling of certain concrete bodies at a given time and place he must—if he is to be precise as to details—get beyond the general principle of "gravity." He must describe the particular field of gravity which affected those bodies at just that time. Similarly "a culture" is just a convenient short expression for "a special field of that force known as culture."

"CULTURE" AS A DESCRIPTIVE CONCEPT

THE PHYSICIAN: Can we say that culture in general as a descriptive concept means the accumulated treasury of human creation: books, paintings, buildings, and the like; the knowledge of ways of adjusting to our surroundings, both human and physical; language, customs, and systems of etiquette, ethics, religion, and morals that have been built up through the ages?

FIRST ANTHROPOLOGIST: In referring to culture as "a storehouse of adjustive responses" and as a human creation you strike notes upon which we would all now agree. But the objections to an enumerative definition and to a definition which lists, in part, concrete phenomena are serious.

SECOND ANTHROPOLOGIST: Yes, I also now fully share the view that, even at a descriptive level, culture must be considered as an abstraction. Even a "culture trait" is, in a sense, an "ideal type." Take, for instance, the alarm clock. No two are ever exactly alike: some are large, some are small; some work perfectly and others don't; some are shiny and some are painted in soft colors. If we examine minutely enough several which have just been produced by the same factory, we should find that even these show small differences.

THE BUSINESSMAN: Let me take this idea a little further. A bank is a general term applying to all the specific institutions that conduct certain types of financial transactions. Doesn't culture, then, as a descriptive concept mean the sum of all such generalizations?

FIRST ANTHROPOLOGIST: I would prefer to say "a summation of all the ideas for standardized types of behavior."

THIRD ANTHROPOLOGIST: The notion of defining culture, in a descriptive sense, as a set of blueprints for action in the widest sense (including feeling, of course) is very attractive. And it is probably perfectly sound, provided that it is clearly realized that such a statement is made from the standpoint of the observer, the student of culture, rather than from that of the participant in culture. For the participant much of culture is unverbalized and probably in a still wider sense implicit.

THE PSYCHIATRIST: I agree. I have always protested against such statements as "culture consists of ideas" because we know well from comparative psychiatry that there is also such a thing as "culturally standardized unreason."

FIRST ANTHROPOLOGIST: Yes, while a great deal of culture is cognitive and is cognitively transmitted, the place of feeling bulks enormously.

THE ECONOMIST: Perhaps we need three categories: rational, irrational, and nonrational.

THIRD ANTHROPOLOGIST: Quite. In Pareto's jargon, some of culture is "logical," some is "illogical," but probably the highest proportion is "nonlogical."

FOURTH ANTHROPOLOGIST: May we then give the following substantive definition: *By culture we mean all those historically created designs for living, explicit and implicit, rational, irrational, and nonrational, which exist at any given time as potential guides for the behavior of men.*

THE LAWYER: I have only one question: Why is it necessary to say "at any given time"?

FOURTH ANTHROPOLOGIST: Because culture is constantly being created and lost. No definition must suggest that culture is static or completely stable.

SECOND ANTHROPOLOGIST: Does "designs for living" mean that you intend the concept to include only "theory"—that is, the ways in which things ought to be done or felt?

FOURTH ANTHROPOLOGIST: No, "design" denotes both "theory" and "practice." In our own professional jargon "design" is meant to designate both "behavioral patterns" and "ideal patterns." Remember that culture is always a conceptual construct. The anthropologist not only observes that people say (or otherwise indicate) that they have certain standards for behavior, violations of which are punished by great or small sanctions; he equally notes that even disapproved behavior systems tend to fall into certain modalities. From the observer's standpoint it is as if people were unconsciously adhering to certain "blueprints" or "designs" also for conduct which is prohibited or indifferent from the standpoint of shared "moral" norms.

THE LAWYER: May we have a definition of "a culture," in the descriptive sense?

FIRST ANTHROPOLOGIST: *A culture is a historically derived system of explicit and implicit designs for living, which tends to be shared by all or specially designated members of a group.*

THIRD ANTHROPOLOGIST: That satisfies me. The word "system" does a lot of work in that definition. It suggests abstraction. It directly implies that a culture is organized, that it is selective.

THE PSYCHOLOGIST: I like the word "tends." Some of us have in the past felt cheated because we have been assured that studying a culture would give us the common ground against which various personality figures emerged. Our own investigations along this line seem to indicate that it was misleading to depict any single background as being in any literal sense "common" to all members of any group.

FIRST ANTHROPOLOGIST: Yes, just as "tends" reminds us that no individual thinks, feels, or acts precisely as the "design" indicates that he will or should, so also "specially designated" is a reminder that not all of the "blueprints" which constitute a culture are meant to apply to each and every individual. There are sex differentials, age differentials, class differentials, prestige differentials, and so on.

THIRD ANTHROPOLOGIST: It seems to me that you have enunciated two related but separate propositions. It is important that we should not mix them. First, there is the proposition that the sharing is tendency rather than fact. As L. K. Frank puts it, what we can actually observe is the "idiomatic version of each personality's utilization of cultural patterns." And he goes on to make a useful analogy something along these lines:

We can abstract the regularities and uniformities and likewise observe the personality distortions and skewings, as we have learned to observe the statistical regularities of a gas but also recognize and acknowledge the irregular and non-conforming behavior of individual molecules of that gas.

Second, there is the proposition of the compartmentalization and segmentation of a culture. While each individual's utilization of pattern is idiomatic, some sets of patterns are always felt as appropriate for certain categories of individuals. A background of culture is to be regarded as approximately constant—not for every individual in all groups which have some continuity and functional wholeness, but rather for those who occupy the same set of statuses or perform about the same roles within the total group.

FIRST ANTHROPOLOGIST: Correct. But this important fact must not obscure another fact of equal or greater significance. At least in those groups which have some historical continuity and which are generally designated as "societies," all individuals tend to share common interpretations of the external world and man's place in it. To some degree every individual is affected by this common "view of life." A culture is made up of overt patterned ways of behaving, feeling, and reacting. But it also includes a characteristic set of unstated premises or hypotheses which vary greatly in different societies. Thus one group unconsciously assumes that every chain of actions has a goal and that when this goal is reached tension will be reduced or disappear. To another group, thinking based upon this assumption is meaningless: they see life not as a series of purposive sequences but as made up of experiences which are satisfying in and of themselves, rather than as means to ends.

THE PHILOSOPHER: Are you saying that each culture is integrated about certain dominant interests and in accord with certain postulates and assumptions?

THIRD ANTHROPOLOGIST: Probably very few cultures indeed can be regarded as completely integrated systems. Most cultures, like most personalities, can be regarded as equilibria of opposed tendencies. But even in cultures which do not approach complete integration one may detect certain recurrent themes in a variety of specific contexts.

THE PSYCHOLOGIST: Are you talking about what some anthropologists have called the "absolute logics," of a people or about what others refer to as "the logic of the sentiments."

THIRD ANTHROPOLOGIST: Both. Every people not only has a sentiment structure which is to some degree unique but also a more or less coherent body of distinctive presuppositions about the world. This last is really a borderland between reason and feeling. Perhaps in a certain ultimate sense the "logic" of all peoples is the same. But their premises are certainly different.

THE PHILOSOPHER: Do you mean the conscious, the stated premises—what a logician would call the "postulates"—or the unstated premises or "assumptions"?

THIRD ANTHROPOLOGIST: Both. Certainly some of the most critical premises of any culture are often unstated, even by the intellectuals of the group. Likewise the basic categories of "thinking" are implicit, save, perhaps, to a tiny minority in rationally sophisticated societies like our own.

FOURTH ANTHROPOLOGIST: If the premises and the system of categories are unconscious, how are they transmitted?

FIRST ANTHROPOLOGIST: Mainly, probably, through the language. Especially the morphology of a language preserves the unformulated philosophy of the group. For example, Dorothy Lee has shown that among the Trobriand Islanders "the sequence of events does not automatically fall into the mold of causal or telic relationship." Because of the mold which grammar imposes upon their "thinking" these people find certain types of communication with Europeans difficult since Europeans almost inevitably talk in causal terms.

The very morphology of any language inevitably begs far-reaching questions of metaphysics and of values. A language is not merely an instrument for communication and for rousing the emotions. Every language is also a device for categorizing experience. The continuum of experience can be sliced very differently. We tend all too easily to assume that the distinctions which Indo-European languages (or our own particular language) force us to make are given by the world of nature. As a matter of fact, comparative linguistics shows very plainly that any speech demands unconscious conceptual selection on the part of its speaker. No human organism can respond to all the kaleidoscopic stimuli which impinge upon it from the external world. What we notice, what we talk about, what we feel as important is in some part a function of our linguistic patterns. Because these linguistic habits tend to remain as unquestioned "background phenomena," each people tends to take its fundamental categories, its unstated basic premises for granted. It is assumed that others will "think the same way," for "it's only human nature." When others face the same body of data but come to different conclusions, it is seldom thought that they might be proceeding from different premises. Rather, it is inferred that they are "stupid" or "illogical" or "obstinate."

FOURTH ANTHROPOLOGIST: How does it happen that different people have different systems of categories?

FIRST ANTHROPOLOGIST: A language is one aspect of a culture. Therefore, we must refer to the "accidents of history" and to all the other forces which we mentioned as producing the forms of culture. Each individual tends to classify his experiences along the lines laid down by the grammar to which he is habituated, but the grammar itself is a cultural product. Dorothy Lee has made this point very well:

True enough, the thought of the individual must run along its grooves; but these grooves, themselves, are a heritage from individuals who laid them down in an unconscious effort to express their attitudes toward the world. Grammar contains in crystalized form the accumulated and accumulating experience, the Weltanschauung of a people.

THIRD ANTHROPOLOGIST: There is perhaps also another angle to the perpetuation of cultural organization, particularly at the implicit level. This is the culturally prescribed system of child training. If all adults have been subjected to about the same deprivations and frustrations during socialization, they tend to see life in somewhat the same terms. Roheim says, "The dominant idea of a culture may be an addiction but it is always a system formation that can be explained on the basis of the infantile situation." Margaret Mead deals with the relation of "infantile traumas" to the one or more focal points in each culture under the conception of "plot in culture."

FOURTH ANTHROPOLOGIST: Although partially won over, I am still unhappy about this term "implicit culture."

THIRD ANTHROPOLOGIST: A conception of this order is made necessary by certain eminently practical considerations. It is well documented that programs of the British Colonial services or of our own Indian service which have been carefully thought through for their continuity with the cultural inventory and with the overt cultural patterns, nevertheless fail to work out. Intensive investigation also does not reveal any flaws in the set-up at the technological level. The program is sabotaged by resistance which must be imputed to the manner in which the members of the group have been conditioned by *implicit* designs for living to think and feel in ways which were unexpected to the administrator.

FIRST ANTHROPOLOGIST: Students of culture change are also agreed that the way in which a group accepts, rejects, or readapts borrowed elements cannot be fully understood in terms of direct and explicit functions. The process is also related to the cultural structure, including those portions of it which are implicit. Even after the content of the culture of a group of American Indians has become completely European, its way of life still somehow retains a distinctive flavor, as if the "container" remained "aboriginal."

THIRD ANTHROPOLOGIST: We would freely admit that conceptual instruments which are objective enough and precise enough to deal with the patterning of implicit culture are only beginning to be evolved. The importance of tacit cultural premises and categories is probably obvious enough. But the sheer statement of the presence and absence of these (and of all other features of culture, whether implicit or explicit) is not enough. The full significance of any single element in a cultural design will be seen only when that element is viewed in the total matrix of its relationship to other elements and indeed to other designs. Naturally, this includes accent or emphasis, as well as position. Accent is manifested sometimes through frequency, sometimes through intensity. The indispensable importance of these questions of arrangement and emphasis may be driven home by an analogy. Take a musical chord made up of three notes. If we are told that the three notes in question are A, B, and G, we receive information which is fundamental. But it alone will not enable us to predict the type of sensation which the playing of this chord is likely to evoke in us or in other specified visitors. We need many different sorts of relationship data. Are the notes to be played in that or some other order? What duration will each receive? How will the emphasis, if any, be distributed? We also need, of course, to know whether the chord will be played in the key of C or in the key of B-flat minor, and whether the instrument is to be a piano or an accordion.[2]

---

[2] Limitations of space necessitated shortening the final typescript draft of this paper by one third. In addition to the elimination of certain technical refinements, the authors were obliged to omit two topics which they consider essential to a complete treatment of the subject: The distinction between the "social" and the "cultural" and the place of symbols in a consideration of culture theory.

THE UTILITY OF THE CONCEPT "CULTURE" IN ITS VARIOUS SENSES

THE BUSINESSMAN. I'd like to interject a practical question: What good is this concept so far as the contemporary world is concerned? What can you do with it?

FIRST ANTHROPOLOGIST: First and foremost I would insist that its use lies in the aid the concept gives to man's endless quest to understand himself and his own behavior. For example, this relatively new idea makes some of the questions which trouble one of the most learned and acute thinkers of our age, Reinhold Niebuhr, seem pseudo-problems. In his recent book *The Nature and Destiny of Man* he argues that the universally human sense of guilt or shame and man's capacity for self-judgment necessitates the assumption of supernatural forces. But these facts are susceptible of self-consistent and relatively simple "explanation" in purely naturalistic terms through the concept of culture. Social life among humans never occurs without a system of "conventional understandings" which are transmitted more or less intact from generation to generation. Any individual is familiar with some of these and they constitute a set of standards against which he judges himself. To the extent that he fails to conform he experiences discomfort, because the intimate conditioning of infancy and childhood put great pressure on him to internalize these norms, and his unconscious tendency is to associate withdrawal of love and protection or active punishment with deviation.

This and other issues which have puzzled philosophers and scientists for countless generations become fully or partially understandable by means of this fresh conceptual instrument. But if your interest is in action rather than thought, the principal claim which can be made for culture is that it helps us enormously toward predicting human behavior. One of the reasons that such prediction has not been very successful thus far has been that it has been carried out, for the most part, on the naïve assumption of a minutely homogeneous "human nature." In the framework of this assumption all human thinking proceeds from the same premises; all human beings are motivated by the same needs and goals. But in the cultural framework we see that, while the ultimate logic of all peoples may be the same (and thus communication and understanding are possible), the thought processes depart from radically different premises—especially unconscious or unstated premises. But those who have the cultural outlook are more likely to look beneath the surface and bring the culturally determined premises to the light of day. This may well not bring about immediate agreement and harmony, but it will at least facilitate a more rational approach to the problem of "international understanding" and to diminishing friction between groups within a nation.

The conception of culture also encourages paying attention to the more concrete aspects of ways of life other than our own. It suggests, for example, the usefulness of knowledge of alien "customs" if we wish to predict how a foreign people will behave in a certain situation and of respect for these same customs if we wish to get along with that foreign people.

A culture is not only a reticulum of patterned means for satisfying needs but equally a network of stylized goals for individual and group achievement. If we need to predict human action we must not assume that the effective motivations in all human groups are the same. Even the primary drives, like hunger and sex, though biological "givens," are subtly modified and channeled by culture. What kind of food, what type of sexual experience will be most striven after cannot be predicted through biological knowledge alone. There exists for every human group "secondary drives." Among us, for example, the "need" for cars or radios often goads individuals even harder than that for sexual satisfaction.

Every culture is also a structure of expectancies. If we know a culture, we know what various classes of individuals within it expect from each other—and from outsiders of various categories. We know what types of activity are held to be inherently gratifying.

SECOND ANTHROPOLOGIST: One great contribution is that of providing some persons with some detachment from the conscious and unconscious emotional values of their own culture. The phrase "some detachment" must be emphasized. An individual who viewed the designs for living of his group with complete detachment would almost certainly be disoriented and unhappy. But I can prefer (that is, feel affectively attached to) American manners while at the same time perceiving certain graces in English manners which are lacking or more grossly expressed in ours. Thus while unwilling to forget that I am an American and hence with no desire to ape English drawing room behaviors, I can still derive a lively pleasure from association with English people on "social" occasions. Whereas if I have no detachment, if I am utterly provincial, I am likely to regard English manners as utterly ridiculous, uncouth, perhaps even immoral. With that attitude I shall certainly not get on well with the English and I am likely to resent bitterly any modification of our manners in the English or any other direction. Such attitudes clearly do not make for international understanding, friendship, and coöperation. They equally make for a too rigid social structure. Anthropological documents and anthropological teachings are valuable, therefore, in that they tend to emancipate individuals from a too perfervid allegiance to every item in the cultural inventory. The person who has been exposed to the anthropological perspective by incongruity is more likely, on the one hand, to "live and let live" both within his own society and in his dealings with members of other societies; on the other hand, he will probably be more flexible in regard to needful changes in social organization to meet changed technological structure and changed economies.

THIRD ANTHROPOLOGIST: In a way, I would say that the most important implication of "culture" for action is the profound truth (so frequently overlooked by every sort of "social planners") that you can never start with a clean slate so far as human beings are concerned. No human being or group of human beings can ever freshly see the world in which they move. Every human is born into a world defined by already existing cultural patterns. Just as an individual who has lost his memory is no longer "normal," so the idea that at any point in its history a society can become completely emancipated from its past culture is inconceivable. This is the source of the tragic failure of the Weimar constitution in Germany. Seen in detached context, it was an admirable document. But it failed miserably in actual life, partly because it provided for no continuity with existent designs for acting, feeling, and thinking.

Finally, as the word "design" in our definitions implies, every culture has organization as well as content. This fact carries with it the highly practical warning to administrators and lawmakers that a "custom" which it is desired to abolish or modify cannot be isolated. Any change may have repercussions in areas of behavior where they are least expected.

While serious anthropologists disavow all messianic pretensions and make no claim that "culture" is any "philosopher's stone" which will end all problems, nevertheless the explanatory concept does carry an overtone of legitimate hope to troubled men. If the Germans and the

Japanese are as they have been mainly because of their genes, the outlook is an almost hopeless one, but if their propensities for cruelty and aggrandizement are primarily the result of situational factors ("economic" pressures and so on) and their cultures, then something can be done about it.

BIBLIOGRAPHIC NOTE

WE HAVE THOUGHT it inappropriate to burden this paper with detailed documentation. But the principal sources which have directly influenced our thinking follow.

Bidney, David, "On the Philosophy of Culture in the Social Sciences," *Journal of Philosophy*, XXXIX (1942), 449–57; "On the Concept of Culture and Some Cultural Fallacies," *American Anthropologist*, XLVI (1944), 30–45.

Blumenthal, Albert, "A New Definition of Culture," *American Anthropologist*, XLII (1940), 571–86.

Dollard, John, "Culture, Society, Impulse and Socialization," *American Journal of Sociology*, XLV (1939), 50–63.

Ford, C. S., "Culture and Human Behavior," *Scientific Monthly*, LV (1942), 546–57.

Frank, L. K., "Man's Multidimensional Environment," *Scientific Monthly*, LVI (1943), 344–57.

Lee, Dorothy, "Conceptual Implications of an Indian Language," *Philosophy of Science*, V, No. 1 (Jan., 1938); "A Primitive System of Values," *Philosophy of Science*, VII, No. 3 (July, 1940).

Linton, Ralph, *The Study of Man* (New York, 1936); "Culture, Society and the Individual," *Journal of Abnormal and Social Psychology*, XXXV (1938), 425–36; *Acculturation in Seven American Indian Tribes* (New York, 1940).

Malinowski, B., "Culture," *Encyclopedia of the Social Sciences*, IV (1931), 621–45; "Man's Culture and Man's Behavior," *Sigma Xi Quarterly*, XXIX (1941), 182–96; XXX (1942), 66–78.

Miller, Neal E., and John Dollard, *Social Learning and Imitation* (New Haven, Conn., 1941).

Murdock, G. P., "The Science of Culture," *American Anthropologist*, XXXIV (1932), 200–215.

Redfield, Robert, *The Folk Culture of Yucatan* (Chicago, 1941).

Roheim, Geza, *The Origin and Function of Culture* (Nervous and Mental Disease Monograph Series, No. 69, New York, 1943).

Sapir, Edward, "Culture, Genuine and Spurious," *American Journal of Sociology*, XXIX (1924), 401–29.

Simmons, Leo, *Sun Chief* (New Haven, Conn., 1942).

The Concept of Basic Personality Structure as an Operational Tool in the Social Sciences   By ABRAM KARDINER

THE PROCESSES of adaptation in man have been treated in various ways. The biologist limits the meaning of the term to those autoplastic changes in bodily structure which take place presumably to accommodate the organism to its physical environment. On this basis he can describe certain long-term phases of human adjustment, but he has to treat his subject with bold strokes and in relation to long periods of time. Morphological criteria cannot be used to describe the adaptive maneuvers of man covering short periods of time. Morphological adaptation in our species seems to have become almost stabilized, in spite of a long series of minor variations which now form the basis for the concept of race. Moreover, such adaptations record only the response of man to his external physical environment. What has become more important in the thinking of the past century is the adaptation of man to his human environment, the behavioral adjustments which he has had to make to the conditions imposed by social living.

While the morphological adjustments of our species could be studied and described in the familiar terms of biology, new techniques had to be devised for the description of behavioral and psychological adjustments. The concept which showed the greatest usefulness and viability in this connection was that of culture. This concept was purely descriptive, but it furnished a definite way of identifying at least the end products of the processes of adaptation and hence laid a basis for the comparison of various types of adaptive maneuvers.

The culture concept was first used with relation to the culture trait, an item of behavior common to the members of a particular society. Such a culture trait was presumably isolated and idiosyncratic. Later, the sociologists developed the concept of institutions—configurations of functionally interrelated culture traits, which are the dynamic units within culture. Although comparative studies of the forms of the institutions within various cultures could now be made, no significant conclusions concerning the relations of institutions within the same culture were possible without the aid of new techniques. Up to now only one technique has been able to yield decisive results in the interpretation of the variations in institutional combinations—and this technique is a psychological one. This psychological technique has shown itself capable of investigating the minutiae of those adaptive processes which cover short spans of time and represent reactions to both the natural and the human environment.

Preliminary attempts to establish relationships between institutions within the same culture had to draw heavily upon our knowledge of psychopathology. From this contact there emerged the concept of the psychological culture pattern.[1] However, early attempts based on too close analogies between society and the individual did not furnish a basis for a dynamic concept of society. The culture pattern merely gave recognition to the fact that personality and institutions were always to be found in some persistent relationship. It remained a difficult technical problem to demonstrate this relationship in an empirically verifiable manner without merely referring in a descriptive way to certain pathological configurations of frequent occurrence in individuals.

The study of "primitive" societies offered the best opportunity for the working out of such a technique. It could be legitimately anticipated that "primitive" societies would prove simpler in structure than our own and that the psychological constellations there found would be more consistent and more naïve in character. By far the most difficult problem was that of selecting a psychological technique suited to this particular assignment. Neither the classical psychologies, behaviorism, nor Gestalt psychology had made more than sporadic attempts to apply themselves to this problem. Psychoanalysis seemed the technique best suited to the task; yet Freud himself, in spite of his application of psychoanalysis to sociology, did not develop an empirically verifiable technique. On the whole, his efforts were dedicated to the verification in primitive society of those constellations found in modern man. This endeavor was consistent with the evolutionary hypothesis regarding the development of society and culture which was in vogue at the end of the nineteenth century. Among the most valuable

[1] Ruth Benedict, *Patterns of Culture* (New York, 1934).

suggestions made by Freud was that of an analogy between the practices of primitive people and neurotic symptoms. Some rather unproductive hypotheses resulted from the pursuit of this analogy to too great lengths; nevertheless, the study of the origin of neurotic symptoms in the individual laid a basis for the understanding of the minimal adaptive tools of man. Thus, even though the neurotic symptom is a special case, the principles upon which symptom formation are based cannot be very different from those involved in the development of any of the habitual modes of behavior which we identify in the character of the individual.

The integration of the two techniques, anthropological and psychological, was later facilitated by the abandonment of the evolutionary hypothesis exploited by the early anthropologists. For this was substituted the concept of cultures as functional wholes and the study of primitive societies as entities, a point of view of which Malinowski was the earliest exponent. All that was gained by the application of the concept of psychological culture pattern to primitive societies was the impression that institutions within a society were in large measure consistent with each other and that this consistency could be described in terms of analogies with entities found in psychopathology. This was a definite gain, but it was not a technique.

The most obvious approach to the problem of devising a definite technique was to utilize the known fact that cultures are transmitted within a society from generation to generation. It was natural, therefore, to attempt to develop such a technique with the aid of learning-theory formulations. However, what we know about acculturation and diffusion indicates that there is a limit to the sort of culture content which can be transmitted by direct learning processes. Though no one can deny the role of direct learning in culture transmission, qualified of course by the age of the individual who is exposed to culture change, there seems to be a high degree of selection in the acceptance of elements from any culture by individuals reared in another. Moreover, if learning process alone could account for the transmission of culture, it is difficult to see how culture change without borrowing from other cultures could ever take place. The point is that learning processes do not account for the integrative character of the human mind in so far as the emotional relationships of the individual to his environment are concerned. There is another factor at work, a factor upon which psychoanalytic technique can throw much light. In addition to direct learning processes, the individual builds up a highly complicated series of integrative systems which are not a result of direct learning. The concept of basic personality structure was established on the basis of a recognition of these factors.

The purely descriptive use of very similar concepts is an exceedingly old one. One can easily find it, by implication, in the writings of Herodotus and Caesar. Both of these authors recognize that the various peoples they described not only had unique customs and practices but were also unique in temperament, disposition, and character. Caesar took this factor into account and used it to the advantage of Rome in his dealings with the various barbarian tribes. However, the recognition that there are different basic personality structures for different societies really takes us no farther than did the concept of psychological culture pattern. It can acquire an operational significance only when the formation of this basic personality structure can be tracked down to identifiable causes and if significant generalizations can be made concerning the relation between the formation of basic personality structure and the individual's specific potentialities for adaptation.

The realization that the concept of basic personality structure was a dynamic instrument of sociological research was not an a priori judgment. It was a conclusion reached after two cultures described by Linton—the Tanala and the Marquesan—had been analyzed with the objective of correlating personality with institutions. In the analysis of these two cultures the potentialities of psychoanalytic principles were first shown. The analyses began with the study of the integrational systems formed in the child by the direct experiences during the process of growth. In other words, the approach was a genetic one. It followed two standards: (1) that integrative processes were at work, and (2) that the end results of these integrative processes could be identified. A technique which follows this line is, however, bound to have limitations. The first limitation is that, if the investigator is a citizen of Western society, and if he is moreover a psychopathologist, he will usually be able to identify only those end products which have significance in the neurotic and psychotic disturbances in his own society. But it must be recognized that, simultaneously, other end products were formed which we in our society could not possibly identify. Notwithstanding these limitations, some significant results were obtained in the first few attempts. The first correlation to be observed was that, in any given culture, religious systems were replicas of the experiences of the child with parental disciplines. It was noted that the concept of deity was universal, but that the technique for soliciting divine aid varied according to the specific experiences of the child and the particular life goals defined by the society. In one culture this technique for solicitation was merely to demonstrate endurance; in another it was to punish oneself in order to be reinstated in the good graces of the deity, a position that had been lost by some transgression clearly defined in the actual life practices sanctioned by the community. These variations in the technique of soliciting divine aid pointed, therefore, to different influences which shaped the personality in each specific culture.

From this first correlation several important conclusions could be drawn. The first of these was that certain culturally established techniques of child treatment had the effect of shaping basic attitudes toward parents and that these attitudes enjoyed a permanent existence in the mental equipment of the individual. The institutions from which the growing child received the experience responsible for the production of these basic constellations were, therefore, called primary institutions. The religious ideologies and methods of solicitation were, for the most part, consistent with these basic constellations and had presumably been derived from them by a process known as projection. In other words, primary institutions laid the basis for the projective system which was subsequently reflected in the development of other institutions. Institutions developed as a result of the projective systems were, therefore, called secondary institutions. If this correlation proved to be correct, it followed that between the primary experiences and the end results, identifiable through their projective manifestations, there stood this entity which could now be called the basic personality structure. Primary institutions were responsible for the basic personality structure which, in turn, was responsible for the secondary institutions. It must be emphasized that the important feature of this concept is not its name—although a good many investigators have since attempted variations in the name without any effort to modify or criticize the technique by which it was derived. This name stands for a special technique. Its importance depends upon the fact that it is possible to demonstrate that certain practices are significant for the individual during his period of growth and that the constellations thus formed remain as a continuity in the personality. This technique is an achievement of psychodynamics.

Although the development of these correlations began with a demonstration of the relation of religion to childhood experiences, as time went on, the technique was extended to include more and more factors. When all the institutions of a culture had been described, it became possible to classify them and to point out many which were instrumental in the creation of specific disposition, temperament, and values. Furthermore, many of the institutions proved to be oriented toward specific conditions in the life of a particular society as, for example, food supply. It was shown conclusively that in the Marquesas Islands anxiety about food created within the individual a specific series of integrative systems from which were derived special value systems, as well as certain religious practices.

Because of its many strange contrasts with the conditions of life and the value systems of our society, the Marquesans [2] furnished the first opportunity to establish the influence of early constellations. In this culture the ratio of men to women was 2½ to 1. It was a society much occupied with the threat of periodic starvation. Accordingly, its folktales showed that the relationship of men to women was strikingly different from that in our society. The initiative seemed to be decidedly in the hands of the women, and in many of the tales the young boy occupied precisely the same position that the innocent girl in our culture occupies in relation to the sex-hungry, brutal male. It was the woman who appeared in the place of the bad man of our society. The boy was subject to the sexual wishes of the woman. It was clear to see from these folktales that certain processes not present in our society were at work. It was the woman who was desired and hated, yet there was little overt hostility of the men toward each other in their competition for women. In other words, here was another evidence of areas of repression that differ from those in our culture.

In Tanala, as described by Linton,[3] another important aspect of basic personality structure was uncovered. There the important lesson was the demonstration of the confusion created by social changes when the basic personality remained intact. The old Tanala society had as its economic basis the cultivation of dry rice. This technique permitted a certain type of social organization, based on communal ownership of

[2] See A. Kardiner, *The Individual and His Society* (New York, 1939).
[3] *Ibid.*

land, in which produce was divided under the extremely authoritarian rule of the father. The basic needs of the individual (that is, particularly of the younger sons upon whose labor the economy chiefly depended) were completely satisfied, nothwithstanding what we should call in our society submission to despotic rule. Passive adaptation to a father was perfectly satisfactory as long as the basic needs of the individual were met. When the wet method of rice cultivation was introduced, communal ownership of land had to be abandoned. The individual suddenly became important, and his rights were threatened by the competitive needs of other individuals for the same means of subsistence. In other words, private property was introduced. The mad scramble for the favored valleys led to the disruption of the whole family organization. This resulted in a great increase in crime, homosexuality, magic, and hysterical illnesses. These social phenomena indicated quite clearly that when the personality, as shaped by the customs suited to the old method of economy, encountered, in the new economy, psychological tasks it was in no way prepared to meet, the result was an enormous outbreak of anxiety with various manifestations. Defensive measures had to be introduced by both the "haves" and the "have-nots."

Still another facet of basic personality structure was clearly demonstrated in Linton's description of the Comanche. These were a predatory people. Enterprise, courage, and initiative were the attributes needed in the individual to perpetuate the society. It was a society in which the young and able-bodied male bore all the burdens. Moreover it was a society which demanded a high degree of coöperation between the young males. It is clearly predictable from these demands that the greatest anxiety for the individual would come at that period in life when his powers, endurance, and courage were on the wane. Since there were no vested interests in this society, the individual could not accumulate any emblems of social value to perpetuate a status once achieved. Perforce, the society was a democracy in which status must be constantly validated. The discipline to which the individual must conform in childhood could not therefore be of a kind that would impede development and growth, especially along those lines most valuable to the society. Accordingly we find that no impediments were placed in the path of development; the self-esteem, courage and enterprise of the individual were fostered by every possible device, and the qualifications he had to meet in later life were consistent with the constellations created in childhood. It is therefore not surprising to find that the projective systems in Comanche were extremely uncomplicated. In their religion there was no concept of sin and no complicated ritual for reinstatement in the good graces of the deity. A Comanche who wanted "power" simply asked for it, or demonstrated his fortitude. In other words, the practical religion was merely a replica of those conventions which guaranteed the fullest coöperation between the males for their common enterprise.

Up to this point we have been using source material of a limited kind. We have used only the institutional set-up of a given society and have established a relationship between the various institutions by demonstrating their consistency with the basic experiences of the individual during the process of growth. Even if our conclusions are valid, no more can be said for the result obtained than that it is a good guess. But thus far we have no way of checking the validity of our conclusions. New data are imperative. If there is such a thing as a basic personality, we should be able to identify it in the individuals composing a particular society. However, we are obliged to reckon with the fact that all individuals are different, that is, each has a different character. Therefore, how is it possible to reconcile the idea of basic personality with the known fact that each individual in a given culture has his own individual character?

This question is readily answered when we examine the structure of the personalities of one hundred individuals in our own society. Each of them will have a specific character-structure shaped partly by potentialities at birth and by innate predispositions, but also by those specific influences encountered during the process of growth. Were it not for the fact that there is a basic personality among these one hundred people, we could never identify such specific constellations as Oedipus complex, castration complex, and so on, which were made so noteworthy by Freud. Freud, however, did not know that these constellations, which were so universal in the people in our society, were specific to our culture. He believed that they were universal to all mankind, and therefore that many of them were of phylogenetic origin. One can define such a thing as a basic personality among these one hundred individuals in our society by the fact that they all have been shaped by situations which have their origin in institutional practices. Each individual handles the specific influences in a characteristic way, but this notwithstanding, the character-structure is formed

BASIC PERSONALITY STRUCTURE

within an ambit of a certain range of potentialities, and within this latter the basic personality is to be found.

A study of biographies therefore became imperative for the further development of our work. It was important also that there should be a series of biographies for each society—in fact, the more the better. But the study of a dozen biographies including both sexes and representing variations in status and age could give us not only those features which all had in common but could also indicate for us those places at which the variations occurred. It might be mentioned parenthetically that the technique of taking such a biography is not an easy task, because when individuals are invited to recount the story of their lives they take for granted all the background of value systems and socially approved objectives and therefore all one gets is a *curriculum vitae*. Such a record is of no value. What is needed is a cross-section of the individual which embraces the influences of his childhood, the history of his entire development, and a cross-section of his adaptation at the time the history is taken.

The opportunity for such an experiment presented itself in the description of Alorese culture by Dr. Cora DuBois. She brought back from this culture not only a description of the institutional set-up, but a series of eight biographies together with Porteus intelligence tests, children's drawings, and a series of thirty-seven Rorschach tests. The study of this culture revealed the following: The conclusions already reached in the study of Marquesans, Tanala, and Comanche were corroborated. From the institutional description of Alor it was not difficult to reconstruct the basic personality. The influences to which the child was subjected in this society were of a unique character. Owing to the peculiar division of function between the males and the females, the woman bore the brunt of the vegetable food economy. She worked in the fields all day and could take care of her children only before she went out to the fields and after she returned. Maternal neglect was therefore the rule, and by that is meant that the supportive influences of the mother in establishing the structure of the ego were in default. Tensions from hunger, the need for support, for emotional response, were therefore greatly neglected, and the child was left in the care of older siblings, relatives, or other persons. The consistency of the disciplines was therefore destroyed; the image of the parent as a persistent and solicitous helper in case of need was not built up. The ego was feeble in development and filled with anxiety. The patterns of aggression remained amorphous. Accordingly, although we find in the projective systems the concept of a deity, there is no effort at idealization of the divine image and the Alorese perform their religious rituals only under the pressure of urgent circumstances, and then in a reluctant manner. The interpersonal tensions within the society run high, distrust is universal, and the emotional development retarded and filled with anxiety.

We then turned our attention to the study of the individual biographers. Fortunately they were documented in such a way that the basic requirements for our specific needs were fully met, notwithstanding the fact that many of them were faulty from the point of view of a fully documented life history. Many things concerning the character structure of the individuals were picked up by observing these subjects in the actual process of living from day to day, and moreover by observing their reactions to the ethnographer and by studying their dream life. In connection with the studies of these individuals certain new features concerning basic personality were unraveled. It was an extraordinary fact to find in half a dozen of these biographies that, whenever the subject of hunger was touched upon, the associations led to some form of natural catastrophe, such as earthquake or flood. This was quite in accordance with what we would expect and what we predicted from the study of the basic personality structure. Each of these eight people had an individual character, but nevertheless all had certain features in common, not because they followed certain conventions in common but because the deeper fabric of their personalities was molded on similar lines. Furthermore, the points at which the individuals differed in character structure could be clearly tracked down to variations in the influences at work during the period of growth. Where the parental care was good, specific variations in character appeared. For example, one of the men proved to have a conscience molded upon lines similar to those found in our society. He had moreover a patent Oedipus complex. But all these factors were clearly traceable to the influence of a powerful father who had more than the usual amount of solicitude for his son. Conscience was a rare phenomenon among the Alorese, and the relation of conscience to the absence of good parental care was therefore clearly demonstrated. Moreover all the individuals showed similar sequences in aggression patterns and in the absence of specific constellations that are found in our society.

But we still had, in addition to these biographical studies, a new series of data which could be used to corroborate, amplify, or refute the findings up to this point. These were the conclusions of the Rorschach tests, which were made by Dr. Emil Oberholzer "blind," that is, without knowledge either of the personalities or of the specific features of the culture. Dr. Oberholzer's report concerning these Rorschach findings was to me the most astonishing confirmation of the validity of the concept of basic personality. First of all, he identified certain features which all Alorese had in common. Secondly, the specific individuals all showed individual variations from this basic pattern. But to me these findings were less important than another order of data revealed by the Rorschach tests. As previously stated, the psychologist who operates only within the knowledge of the psychopathological entities found in our society has an insuperable handicap—he is capable of identifying only those entities found in our society. It is at this point that the Rorschach test adds a new series of data. Whereas the Rorschach test can give no information concerning the genesis of distinctive traits in the individual or in the group, the test nevertheless demonstrates emotional combinations which are not identifiable in the psychopathological entities common in our society. With the aid of those features, revealed by the Rorschach but which do not appear either in the basic personality or in the study of biographies, it is now possible to rework the original genetic picture so as to describe how the new entities came into existence. The Rorschach test therefore is an instrument not only for checking conclusions already reached but for discovering new entities inaccessible to the other techniques. It may be objected that, after all, the Rorschach is a projective test and therefore its utility may be limited by the fact that its norm has been based upon the study of our society, or, to be more specific, upon the citizens of Switzerland. In actual operation this limitation proves to be unimportant.

In studies undertaken after the Alorese only three yielded significant results: a description by Mr. James West of a community in the United States called Plainville; a study of Sikh culture, described by Dr. Marian W. Smith; and a study of the Ojibwa, described by Miss Ernestine Friedl.

The first study showed that Plainville, a small, rural community in the Middle West, had distinctive features which deviated in a considerable number of respects from urban communities. Furthermore, it precipitated the entire question of whether one can study such large groups as nations with the aid of the concept of basic personality. The answer seems to be in the affirmative, since the Plainville variations from the norm established in urban centers are not very wide. The study of Plainville also precipitated the issue of whether or not the concept of basic personality may be profitably applied to the history of Western society. This is a problem yet to be resolved.

In the study of Sikh we again found some unique features. Here we worked largely with a description of the institutions and with Rorschach tests. The consistency of the two kinds of data was again quite remarkable. The same was true of Ojibwa. It was clearly demonstrated that the Rorschach was indispensable in checking up essential features of basic personality which could not be identified from the genetic picture alone. For example, it was noted in Ojibwa that the disciplines of childhood and the folktales concerning Wenebojo (the Ojibwa culture hero) all pointed to the fact that the claims the child made upon the parent were definitely limited. He was discouraged from believing that the parent had magical powers which could be used for the benefit of the child. The tenor of the early disciplines was all in the direction of informing the child that he could make but limited claims upon the parent, all this notwithstanding the fact that the child was given excellent care. We had here, therefore, a combination not to be found in our society: the personality was given a good foundation, but emotional development was limited in a manner very different from anything we find in our society. This limitation could not be completely identified from the genetic picture of the development of the child. It required the Rorschach test to demonstrate quite conclusively the peculiar limitations of the Ojibwa in his emotional contact with others. A second feature of Ojibwa was that it afforded an excellent opportunity for the study of the acculturation processes and the specific manner in which acculturation took place. It was very clear from the Rorschach picture that these processes introduced factors into the emotional life of the individual which were common in our society but unknown to Ojibwa, who had not been exposed to the ways of white men or to Catholicism.

The technique of deriving the basic personality as it has been described up to this point is open to some serious objections. One may say that people are what they are because they grow up under certain conditions; we have known that for some thousands of years. Quite true. But the technique as described furnishes a specific bill of particulars as to what conditions give rise to precisely what results in the personality; moreover, because of the integrational processes at work and the unforeseen combinations, it is able to derive some indirect results. But so far the technique is open to a still more serious objection: It gives no answer to the question of why one people finds it necessary to institute certain disciplines, impulse controls, and so on, while others do not. This objection finally reduces the technique to a refinement of the old saw that some people do one thing and some do another, a position not far removed from that furnished by the use of the culture pattern.

The crucial question then becomes: What determines the parental attitude toward children and hence the specific influences to which the child is subject? In general, one can say that these parental attitudes are determined by the social organization and the subsistence techniques. Whereas this statement is, strictly speaking, true, we are likely to get many surprises unless we qualify it with several conditions. And these conditions are of the highest importance in relation to cultural change.

If we attempt to define those conditions which qualify the socioeconomic determinants of parental attitudes, apparently we immediately run into the problem of social origins. This is a hopeless task, and theories at this point are no substitute for demonstrable evidence. An excellent case in point is Comanche culture. As we compare the institutions of the old Plateau culture from which the Comanche derived, we notice that some institutions are the same in both, some are modified, and some disappear in the new conditions. Hunting medicine, though common in the old culture, disappears in the new. The reason is obvious. In the new environment game was plentiful, which meant no anxiety and no need for supernatural aid, skill being the only requirement. The raising of the young, especially the young male, was not the same in the new culture as in the old. But there was an *Anlage* in the old culture for the new development; and the new economy could not be aided in any way by impulse control over the young. On the contrary, everything was to be gained from an unobstructed development of the young male.

In old Tanala the parental attitudes were likewise consistent with the economy of communal ownership of land; but when private property was introduced, chaos resulted because the disciplines in the old culture qualified the individual for a very passive adaptation to an economy devoid of opportunities for competition. The new economy demanded strong competitive attitudes; the result was only an increase in anxiety, symptomatic of the absence of executive capacities to deal with the situation.

One would be inclined to generalize from the illustration of Comanche and to conclude that, of course, when economic and social conditions change, attitudes to children and hence the conditions for growth change. This might be true if the parental attitude were determined by factors which were perfectly well known to the parents. They are not. And hence one cannot generalize from Comanche, which is the exception and not the rule. We have long since heard of the "cultural lag," which some attempt to account for on the basis of an inertia principle. Such philosophical formulae, even if true, do not explain the facts.

The case of Alor is one in which the rearing of the child and the influences to which it is exposed are in keeping with the socioeconomic conditions. But we do not know the origins of the particular type of economy, nor does it appear to make any sense to us. In Alor the division of labor is such that the female carries the entire burden—with sporadic help—of the main diet of vegetable food. She is thus taken away from the children all day, caring for them before she leaves for the fields and after she returns. The fields are not contiguous and are sometimes quite far from the village. The effects of the absent mother we have already described, but we cannot answer the question of why labor is so unevenly and capriciously divided. The remote effects of this single institution on the culture as a whole is surely not known to the Alorese. If we say that this institution is not rationally determined, or that it is an illustration of cultural lag, we are not saying much. This cultural lag is no abstract principle of inertia; it is caused by the accumulation of vested emotional interests, which in this instance accrue on the side of the males. To discontinue these interests would cause enormous resistance and discomfort, even if the women had imagination enough to demand that some of the burden of the food economy be lifted from their shoulders. This is an illustration of how "rights" of a certain group in a society (in this instance the males) are established and maintained. To alter the economy would be to alter the entire psychological adaptation of both males and females. This is precisely the point at which anxiety and defensive maneuvers became necessary to retain a system of adaptation and to resist change.

We must pause to make a parenthetical observation on the relative usefulness of a descriptive versus an operational concept. To call the phenomena described in the preceding paragraph a principle of inertia is not incorrect—even though it calls to mind the physical phenomena on which the principle of inertia was based and is hence a false analogy. The real objection to it is that the concept does not reach the facts. Moreover, to a law of inertia one can only bow with humility. But if we point out that this inertia is localized in specific emotional factors, we can mobilize some specific antidotes at these points.

What we have been saying is that the operational value of the concept of basic personality is not only to diagnose the factors which mold the personality but also to furnish some clues about why these influences are what they are. The concept therefore implies a technique which will explore with some degree of accuracy the widest ramifications between culture and personality.

It remains a question whether this technique can be used to describe the dynamics of Western society and to attempt an analysis of the dynamics of culture change over long spans of time. Such an attempt would really be the proof of the technique. But this problem is not as simple as the one in "primitive society." "Western" society is not a single culture but a conglomeration of cultures in which the socio-economic order has gone through a host of vicissitudes. The number of factors which must be brought into correlation is much greater than any we have encountered in primitive society. Whether the attempt at such correlation can succeed remains to be seen; meanwhile there have been enough efforts to solve the problem by other techniques to show us what to avoid. We cannot work on the basis of physiological analogies as did Spengler. One can tell a good story by comparing the rise and fall of civilizations with the physiological life cycle of individuals, but societies are organisms of a quite different order. Following the fate of elites, as does Pareto, leaves many questions unanswered. We can get no real guidance from Toynbee, who tries to follow the process of adaptation of large groups according to various ideas—successful or unsuccessful struggle with the external environment, and soon—without benefit of a psychology to track down the minutiae of adaptation. Least of all can we extract much benefit from a long series of correlations such as Mumford [4] marshals and then proceeds to evaluate on the basis of a highly personal system of value judgments. Endeavors like these give no empirical basis for action

---

[4] Lewis Mumford, *The Condition of Man* (New York, 1944).

based on rational principles. They must degenerate into doctrines which one may endorse or reject according to personal predilection or in defense of interests, whether conscious or unconscious.

The outline for a plan of research derived from our present knowledge of basic personality type is given elsewhere.[5] Here we can only make a few suggestions about technique. One can determine the basic personality for a few communities, both urban and rural. There are appreciable differences between the two. One can then see where the points of difference lie and try to ascertain their causes. The same procedure can be used for communities in other countries as, for example, England and France. Once a dozen such studies have been made, accompanied by biographies, Rorschachs and other projective tests, we can tell what clues to follow in our historical researches. We have already done enough of this to know that there are three systems whose vicissitudes we must follow historically: (1) the projective systems, (2) the empirically derived rational systems, such as technologies, and (3) the endless labyrinths or rationalizations whereby actions are justified but the sources of which lie in projective systems of which man is not aware. One cannot follow the reactions of man to his physical and human environment without the aid of these psychological guides.

The promise which this new technique offers lies in a direction quite different from the current condition of decisions by force or the defense of personal or class interests. It offers a greater insight into personal and social motivations and points the way toward the introduction of controls over the anxieties of men and the defenses mobilized by these anxieties. Any plan for social action based on these principles must, however, compete with powerful forces lined up on the side of simpler principles, such as race theories of superiority, of eugenic selection of elites, of the "rights" of certain classes, and so on, which derive from the projective systems of contemporary man. These forces are all polarized toward the dominance-submission principle. The triumph of empirically derived directives for social action can only follow in the wake of a triumph for greater democracy and of an increased desire to gain insight into the psychological fabric of the forces that can either hold society together or tear it apart and destroy it.

[5] A. Kardiner, *The Psychological Frontiers of Society* (New York, in press).

The Common Denominator of Cultures
By GEORGE PETER MURDOCK

MOST of anthropological theory has revolved about the interpretation of the similarities and differences between the various cultures of mankind. Cultural differences, perhaps because they are more immediately obvious, have received especially close attention. They have been variously explained in terms of distinct stages of postulated evolutionary series, of allegedly disparate racial endowments, of diverse geographic or economic conditions, of nonrepetitive historical accidents, of endlessly varying social contexts, of unique configurations of like or unlike elements, of divergent personality characteristics created by differential childhood training, and so on. Cross-cultural similarities have received theoretical consideration, in the main, only when they have been confined to a limited number of particular cultures, in other words, when they could be regarded as exceptions in a universe of cultural diversity. Such instances of similarity have been explained in terms of the transplantation of culture through migration, of cultural diffusion through contact and borrowing, of parallel development from similar cultural backgrounds, of convergent development from unlike backgrounds, of the independent burgeoning of hereditary potentialities, or of the allegedly determining influence of like geographical factors. In comparison, universal similarities in culture, the respects in which all known cultures resemble each other, have received relatively little theoretical treatment. It is this subject—the common denominator of cultures—with which the present paper will be exclusively concerned.[1]

Early reports of peoples lacking language or fire, morals or religion, marriage or government, have been proved erroneous in every in-

[1] The views of the author have been significantly influenced by John Dollard, Clellan S. Ford, Clark Hull, Albert G. Keller, Ralph Linton, Bronislaw Malinowski, John Whiting, Earl Zinn, and others of his present and past colleagues of the departments of Anthropology and Sociology and the Institute of Human Relations at Yale University. So great is the personal interdependence in scientific endeavor that he is incapable of isolating those portions of the present contribution which are independently his own from those which he has acquired from others, much less of distributing adequately the credit for the latter. Since he is writing from his post in the naval service he is unable even to cite supporting bibliographical references.

stance. Nevertheless, even today it is not generally recognized how numerous and diverse are the elements common to all known cultures. The following is a partial list of items, arranged in alphabetical order to emphasize their variety, which occur, so far as the author's knowledge goes, in every culture known to history or ethnography: age-grading, athletic sports, bodily adornment, calendar, cleanliness training, community organization, cooking, coöperative labor, cosmology, courtship, dancing, decorative art, divination, division of labor, dream interpretation, education, eschatology, ethics, ethnobotany, etiquette, faith healing, family, feasting, fire making, folklore, food taboos, funeral rites, games, gestures, gift giving, government, greetings, hair styles, hospitality, housing, hygiene, incest taboos, inheritance rules, joking, kin-groups, kinship nomenclature, language, law, luck superstitions, magic, marriage, mealtimes, medicine, modesty concerning natural functions, mourning, music, mythology, numerals, obstetrics, penal sanctions, personal names, population policy, postnatal care, pregnancy usages, property rights, propitiation of supernatural beings, puberty customs, religious ritual, residence rules, sexual restrictions, soul concepts, status differentiation, surgery, tool making, trade, visiting, weaning, and weather control.

Cross-cultural similarities appear even more far-reaching when individual items in such a list are subjected to further analysis. For example, not only does every culture have a language, but all languages are resolvable into identical kinds of components, such as phonemes or conventional sound units, words or meaningful combinations of phonemes, grammar or standard rules for combining words into sentences. Similarly funeral rites always include expressions of grief, a means of disposing of the corpse, rituals designed to protect the participants from supernatural harm, and the like. When thus analyzed in detail, the resemblances between all cultures are found to be exceedingly numerous.

Rarely if ever, however, do these universal similarities represent identities in specific cultural content. The actual components of any culture are elements of behavior—motor, verbal, or implicit—which are habitual, in the appropriate context, either to all the members of a social group or to those who occupy particular statuses within it. Each such component, whether called a folkway or a cultural trait or item, can be described with precision in terms of the responses of the behaving individuals and of the stimulus situations in which the responses are evoked. Eating rice with chopsticks, tipping the hat to a woman, scalping a slain enemy, and attributing colic to the evil eye are random examples. Any such specifically defined unit of customary behavior may be found in a particular society or in a number of societies which have had sufficient contact to permit acculturative modifications in behavior. It is highly doubtful, however, whether any specific element of behavior has ever attained genuinely universal distribution.

The true universals of culture, then, are not identities in habit, in definable behavior. They are similarities in classification, not in content. They represent categories of historically and behaviorally diverse elements which nevertheless have so much in common that competent observers feel compelled to classify them together. There can be no question, for example, that the actual behavior exhibited in acquiring a spouse, teaching a child, or treating a sick person differs enormously from society to society. Few would hesitate, however, to group such divergent acts under the unifying categories of marriage, education, and medicine. All of the genuinely widespread or universal resemblances between cultures resolve themselves upon analysis into a series of such generally recognized categories. What cultures are found to have in common is a uniform system of classification, not a fund of identical elements. Despite immense diversity in behavioristic detail, all cultures are constructed according to a single fundamental plan— the "universal culture pattern" as Wissler has so aptly termed it.

The essential unanimity with which the universal culture pattern is accepted by competent authorities, irrespective of theoretical divergences on other issues, suggests that it is not a mere artifact of classificatory ingenuity but rests upon some substantial foundation. This basis cannot be sought in history, or geography, or race, or any other factor limited in time or space, since the universal pattern links all known cultures, simple and complex, ancient and modern. It can only be sought, therefore, in the fundamental biological and psychological nature of man and in the universal conditions of human existence.

The fact that all cultures conform in structure to a single basic plan was already recognized by anthropologists of the nineteenth century. Morgan, Spencer, and Tylor not only established the broad outlines of the universal culture pattern but also filled in many of the details. No adequate understanding of the phenomenon was available, however, until a reasonably satisfactory integration of sociological and psychological theory with anthropological science was at last achieved during the third and fourth decades of the twentieth century.

Most attempts to explain the universal culture pattern have started with the "psychic unity of mankind"—with the assumption, now firmly grounded in social science, that all peoples now living or of whom we possess substantial historical records, irrespective of differences in geography and physique, are essentially alike in their basic psychological equipment and mechanism, and that the cultural differences between them reflect only the differential responses of essentially similar organisms to unlike stimuli or conditions. In its broader aspects this position is probably not open to serious challenge. However, the great majority of theorists have sought the unifying factor in a single facet of man's fundamentally similar psychology, namely, in the common impulse factors in behavior. All cultures are said to resemble one another because men everywhere are driven to action by an identical set of inborn impulses which direct their behavior along parallel lines.

Until some two decades ago these common impulses were widely regarded as instincts. The success and prestige of the biological sciences since Darwin's day led many, if not most, social scientists to equate human behavior with that of the lower animals and to explain social institutions as the expression of a series of universal instincts. Marriage was equated with animal mating, housebuilding with nesting behavior, government with the rule of the herd by the strongest male. The marked parallels between the social behavior of ants, bees, wasps, and termites and the cultural behavior of man appeared especially convincing. However, the progress of science began to show increasingly the importance of learning and habit, even among the lower animals, and anthropological research, in particular, demonstrated beyond possibility of rebuttal that human behavior shows infinite variation from society to society and perpetual change in any one society as it exists through time, instead of the identity and persistency demanded by an instinct theory. It became abundantly clear that the invariable association of a particular series of responses with a specific stimulus, which always characterizes an instinct, is not only not the rule in man's social behavior but is actually so rare as to be practically undiscoverable. Culture is in no respect instinctive; it is exclusively learned. Since the publication of Bernard's *Instinct* in 1924, it has been impossible to accept any theory of instincts as an explanation of the universal culture pattern, or indeed as a solution of any cultural problem.

As instinct theories lost scientific respectability, strenuous efforts at salvage were made. Admitting the importance of the habit-forming mechanism and recognizing that different forms of behavior may be associated, through learning, with an identical stimulus, many authorities clung to the impulse factor in instinct and compiled various lists of "drives," "wishes," "needs," "dispositions," or "prepotent reflexes" which were asserted to underlie cultural behavior in much the same way as instincts had previously been invoked. The principal distinction lay in the divorce of impulses from invariable behavioral expressions and in the recognition that different and even diverse forms of behavior may be evoked by the same impulse in consequence of learning under differential conditions. It was maintained nevertheless that the impulses, being fundamentally physiological in nature, could be allayed only by behavior which relieved the conditions which gave rise to them, so that various responses to the same impulse, however else they might differ, would resemble each other in this vital respect. Responses to the hunger drive, for example, must have the ingesting of food in common.

Many attempts have been made to interpret the universal culture pattern along these lines, explaining cross-cultural similarities in the basic plan, structure, or organization of cultures in terms of a series of fundamental drives or impulses. Among the best known are the division of all social institutions, by Sumner and Keller, into those of self-maintenance, self-perpetuation, self-gratification, and religion on the basis of the four "socializing forces" of hunger, love, vanity, and fear, and the somewhat more complex functional analysis of institutions, by Malinowski, in terms of the satisfaction of certain basic "needs." Comparable but on the whole less satisfactory efforts are legion.

It is not the purpose of this paper to discredit such interpretations. On the contrary, the author believes them to be suggestive and, within limits, sound. Modern psychology and physiology have established the existence of a number of basic impulses—those of ingestion (hunger, thirst, inhalation), of excretion (urination, defecation, exhalation, sexual emission, lactation), and of avoidance (pain, heat, cold). To these must certainly be added anger or aggression, induced by frustration of the expression of other drives, and anxiety or fear, induced apparently by situations resembling those in which pain or deprivation have been experienced. There can be little question but that these impulses or drives represent a common factor in the experience of all human beings, that they are aroused from time to time in all individuals of all societies, that the kinds of behavior that will allay them are universally limited by the fundamental biological and psychological nature of man, and that they consequently operate to channelize cultural as well as individual behavior. They certainly serve as a partial explanation of the universal culture pattern. There are, however, substantial grounds for believing that they do not provide a complete explanation.

In the first place, the impulses or drives that have been scientifically established do not account for all parts of the universal pattern in an equally satisfactory manner. It seems reasonably safe to attribute the food quest to the hunger drive, shelter to heat and cold avoidance, war to aggression, and marriage to the sex impulse. To what recognized impulses, however, can we assign such equally universal cultural phenomena as the arts and crafts, family organization, and religion? Defenders of the interpretation in question are prone to invent hypothetical impulses to meet such cases, postulating, for example, an instinct of workmanship, a parental drive, or a religious thrill. Such inventions, however, find no shred of support in physiological or psychological science. On the contrary, a fully satisfactory alternative explanation of the underlying motivations is available in the psychological theory of acquired or derived drives.

It is common knowledge that only a small proportion of men's actions in any society spring directly from any of the demonstrable basic drives. In most human behavior the motivation is exceedingly complex and derivative. Even in the case of eating, the widespread prevalence of food preferences and taboos reveals the importance of acquired appetites as contrasted with the inborn drive of hunger. We eat what we like, at hours to which we are habituated, in surroundings which we enjoy. Daily in our habitual eating behavior we satisfy appetitive cravings, but rarely in adult life are we driven by actual hunger pangs. In obeying the dictates of an acquired appetite we incidentally satisfy, of course, the hunger drive, and thereby reinforce the appetite, but the actual incentive is the derived and not the basic impulse.

What is true of eating is even more characteristic of other forms of behavior. Many of our sexual responses, for example, are also appetitive in character; acquired drives impel us to seek the company of persons of opposite sex on the basis of age, appearance and garb, social congeniality, and other factors irrelevant to physical sex, and to engage in conversation, dancing, and divers other activities short of copulation. In still other aspects of social behavior—for example, in religious ritual and the fine arts—the factor of basic-drive reduction shrinks to relative insignificance by comparison with derivative motivations, and may even become impossible to identify. In the case of those elements of the universal culture pattern which cannot readily be attributed, at least in part, to some recognized basic drive, it seems more scientific to ascribe them to derived or acquired drives, which naturally vary from society to society, than to invent hypothetical new drives for which no factual evidence can be advanced.

A second substantial reason for rejecting the impulse factor in behavior as the sole explanation of the universal culture pattern is the fact that most social institutions or culture complexes actually give satisfaction to several basic impulses as well as to a variety of derived drives. To attribute marriage to sex alone, for example, is greatly to oversimplify a complex social phenomenon. As Lippert was the first to point out clearly, the economic factor in marriage is at least as important as the sex factor. The latter can really account only for copulation; it is the conjunction of the former that produces an enduring marital association. The relation of the hunger drive to marriage is seen, for example, in the division of labor by sex, which characterizes marital unions in all societies and, in most of them, demonstrably increases, diversifies, and stabilizes the food supply available to each spouse. Even our own society, which emphasizes the sex factor in marriage to an exceptional degree, has enshrined the hunger factor in a proverb about the most direct way to a man's heart. Marriage gives expression to still another basic impulse in various forms of relief from anxiety; for example, escape from the social disapproval commonly encountered by celibates, economic security gained through union with a wealthy spouse or a good provider, and the personal solace achievable in an intimate relationship.

Similarly, war is motivated not alone by aggression but often in large measure by fear, by the desire for feminine approbation (derivative in part from the sex impulse), and by greed for gain (in which the hunger drive may be significantly involved). Religious behavior is often rooted in anxiety—in fear of the unknown and unpredictable, in dread of what the future may bring, or in a sense of personal inadequacy. In addition, it frequently has a strong erotic component, as psychiatrists have pointed out; or it expresses aggression as in sorcery or religious intolerance; or it reflects the need for food or material comforts, as in magic or prayer. Analysis of almost any other large segment of cultural behavior would reveal a similar conjunction of diverse motives. This interlacing of basic drives, which is, of course, rendered infinitely more complex by the intervention of acquired motivations, makes it exceedingly difficult to segregate cultural phenomena according to their impulse components.

It must be conceded, therefore, that the analysis of collective behavior from the point of view of underlying motives, although suggestive, does not yield a fully satisfactory explanation of the universal culture pattern. Its principal defect seems to lie in the fact that it does not take into account the complete psychological mechanism involved in habitual behavior. Derived as it is from earlier instinct theory, it considers exclusively the impulse factor in behavior and ignores all else. When other aspects of the mechanism of habit formation and perpetuation are taken into account, a more adequate interpretation of the universal culture pattern emerges.

Fundamentally, all behavior is designed to mediate between two types of situations in which organisms find themselves, namely, those in which impulses are aroused and those in which they are satisfied. An organism encountering a situation of the first type is stimulated to activity; encountering a situation of the second type, it experiences a reduction in drive, and its activity ceases or is replaced by behavior in response to other stimulation. Once initiated by a drive, behavior in response thereto continues until satisfaction has been achieved, or a stronger drive intervenes to impel behavior in another direction, or unsuccessful responses have brought exhaustion or fatigue. In the last case, the drive-impelled behavior will recommence after an interval, and continue to appear until satisfaction is achieved or, if success is essential to life, until the organism dies.

Living organisms have evolved two distinctive means of adapting their behavior so as to transform situations evoking drives into those bringing about their reduction. The first, shared by all forms of life, is instinct, a precise organization of behavior developed through natural selection and transmitted through heredity. An instinct enables an organism to respond automatically to a drive-arousing situation by specific forms of behavior which have been established by the evolutionary process because they normally result in drive reduction. In cases where this does not happen, however, the individual organism is helpless; it is incapable of producing alternative forms of behavior. This defect is corrected by the second mechanism, that of habit formation, which is well developed in all the higher forms of life, including man. Through this mechanism, an individual can meet a drive-evoking situation for which the species has evolved no suitable instinctive response, by varying his behavior and by acquiring as a habit any new response which happens to lead to reduction of the drive. It is this second psychological mechanism upon which all cultural behavior depends.

Now it is significant that, in the process of establishing and maintaining habits, the crucial factor is not the source of the behavior in impulse or stimulus but its effect in drive reduction. It is the latter which fixes, reinforces, or perpetuates the responses that have occurred. Whenever a drive is reduced, the probability of the recurrence of the same behavior in a similar situation is increased. Mere repetition of the stimulation, in the absence of drive reduction, does not strengthen the ensuing behavior. On the contrary, it leads to its extinction and to the appearance of random responses of other kinds, that is, to trial-and-error behavior.

Whenever behavior results in the allaying of a drive, even though by sheerest accident, its effect is to connect that behavior not only with the impulse which produced it but with all the stimuli concurrently impinging upon the organism. With repetition, not only of the behavior but of its drive-reducing effect, certain of the concurrent stimuli, singly or in combination, gain the power to evoke the now habitual responses even though the original impulse is not present. Such stimuli which have gained the force of drives are essentially what is meant by "acquired drives." They are the product of learning as much as are the responses they evoke. It is in this way, for example, that the appetite for food can be aroused, in the absence of perceptible hunger, by the sight, the odor, or even the verbal description of a juicy steak.

The fact that the crucial factor in habitual behavior is its effect rather than its origin suggests that an explanation of widespread cultural similarities might more profitably be sought in an examination of cultural forms from the point of view of their relation to drive reduction or reward than in an analysis of their impulse components. The interplay of different motives in the same behavior and the problem of differentiating acquired from basic drives offer no obstacles to this type of interpretation. If a particular kind of behavior regularly results in drive reduction, any or every motive which may evoke it will be reinforced, and complex and derivative motivations are to be expected.

Since cultural behavior is always habitual in character, and since habits are maintained only so long as they bring rewards, every established element of culture is necessarily accompanied and supported by impulse satisfaction. The insistence of the "functionalists" in anthropology on this point has the full backing of psychological science. When traditional forms of behavior cease to gratify impulses, random responses supervene and cultural change is in the making. The present paper is not concerned, however, with cultural change. It takes cognizance only of cultural forms which are firmly entrenched and of widespread occurrence, and which consequently are regularly bulwarked by rewards.

Cultural behavior may be related to rewards in various ways. In some instances it leads directly and almost exclusively to the reduction of a basic drive. Thus the food quest leads directly to hunger satisfaction, the use of fire and clothing in northern latitudes to cold avoidance, and various sex practices to sexual gratification. The behavior must conform to conditions set by human physiology and psychology for the reduction of the drive in question, and the variant customs of different societies have in common the fact that they all meet these conditions. They can be regarded as alternative solutions to identical problems posed by original human nature. If this were the only relation of cultural behavior to rewards, analysis in terms of underlying impulse factors would provide an adequate explanation of the universal culture pattern.

Many cultural habits, however, instead of gratifying basic drives directly, serve only to facilitate their eventual satisfaction. Cultures contain an immense number of so-called "instrumental responses" which of themselves reduce no basic drives but merely pave the way for other acts which have rewarding results. Instrumental acts acquire in time, of course, the support of learned or derived drives, but they are seldom innately rewarding in themselves. Making a spear or a pot, for instance, gratifies no basic impulse, although at some future time the result may serve to lessen the interval or the expended effort between the onset of the hunger drive and its reduction. The reciprocal habits embodied in social and economic organization represent another outstanding example of instrumental behavior. Through interpersonal relationships and organization, individuals are enabled to use other individuals as instruments to facilitate eventual impulse gratification in much the same way as technology enables them to use artifacts.

Instrumental responses do not become established because they themselves bring gratification but because of a particular characteristic of the learning mechanism. Any response which reduces the elapsed time or the expended effort intervening between drive and reward is reinforced and strengthened, and thus tends to be repeated under similar conditions until it becomes fixed as a habit. Such responses become as readily associated with attendant external stimuli as with whatever drives are operative, and in this way they tend to become supported by derivative rather than primary motivations. Since acquired drives can differ widely from society to society, it is unsafe to attribute cross-cultural similarities in instrumental responses to identical basic impulses. Resemblances are more likely to be due to the particular characteristics of the instrument, whether artifact or social arrangement, or to similarities in the conditions under which reward occurs.

A like situation prevails with respect to a third and very large category of cultural habits, namely, those in which behavior is followed by rewards that bear no relation, or only an incidental one, to the impulses prompting the behavior. A gambling spell may be followed by a lucky fall of the dice, or rain-making magic by a providential thunderstorm, and thus become entrenched as a habit. Neither action, however, either produced the rewarding situation or facilitated it in instrumental fashion. Such cultural responses can survive frequent nonsuccess because of the psychological fact that a habit is commonly strengthened by a single successful exercise more than it is weakened by several failures.

Another example is seen in instances where behavior motivated by one drive results in the gratification of other drives not actually involved in the particular response. A superstitious fear of blood may motivate a tribe to isolate its women after childbirth, but this action may incidentally achieve the fortunate results of assuring postparturient mothers of a needed rest period and of preventing the spread of puerperal fever or other infections, and these may be at least as rewarding as the effect in relieving anxiety. Similarly, even though marriage may often be prompted in large measure by the sex drive, the matrimonial relationship brings other rewards—food, physical comforts, and security—without which, as we have seen, the institution would be difficult to explain.

All cultures, moreover, exhibit numerous adaptive responses which are not directly supported by primary impulse satisfactions. Some authors have attributed these to "social needs," which are defined as depending not upon drives but upon requirements which must be met if groups of individuals and the cultures they bear are to survive in competition with other societies bearing other cultures. One example is the so-called need of education. A culture cannot persist unless it is transmitted from generation to generation, and a society cannot survive without culture, which embodies in the form of collective habits the successful experience of past generations in meeting the problems of living. Hence every society is said to be characterized by the need of educating its young. Unlike reproduction, which is assured in large measure by the sex impulse, education is supported by no primary drive. The immense effort which must be expended by parents and teachers over so many years to inculcate in the young the full cultural equipment of adults is not in itself rewarding but must be bulwarked with auxiliary rewards.

Similarly every society is said to have a "need" for government—for a political organization sufficiently developed to provide for effective common action against potential enemies, to maintain internal order against dangerous interferences with the routine of social living, and to furnish necessary social services not achievable in other ways. Public service is not self-rewarding. Men cannot be depended upon to devote themselves to the common weal through altruism alone. Every society consequently surrounds the holders of political positions with prerogatives and dignities.

The concept of social needs, though useful as a first approximation, is a loose and not wholly satisfactory solution of the scientific problem presented by the universality of certain social institutions or culture complexes which are not directly maintained by specific primary impulse gratifications. It seems preferable to state rather that they have their origin in the ordinary processes of cultural change and their support in the gratification of complex and derivative impulses. Under the pressure of frustration and nonsuccess, behavior is altered. Certain responses, either random in their origin or borrowed from contiguous societies which appear to have achieved greater success, are tried out. If they chance to be followed by rewards of any sort, or even by a lesser degree of discomfort than attends alternative responses, they tend to be repeated and to become established as habits. The situations under which they arise acquire increasing power to evoke them. Learned or derivative impulses develop in support of them, and primary impulses which chance to be satisfied incidentally are pressed into their service, until they are amply fortified with auxiliary rewards.

In the case of education, acquired drives such as pride, prestige, identification, and parental love spring to the support of instruction. The primary drives of pain and anxiety are mobilized in the form of social sanctions for nonconformity. The children themselves, as they become socialized and acquire skills, reciprocate with materially rewarding behavior in ever increasing measure, and in many societies become actual economic assets at an early age. In divers ways an adjustment is evolved whereby the effort expended in education is balanced by a complex system of commensurate rewards.

In the case of government, through a similar process of adaptive cultural change, chiefs are induced to assume war leadership, maintain public order, and perform other social services by according them deference, the right to exact tribute, the privilege of polygyny, or other rewards. Feudal lords receive rents and services, municipal officials enrich themselves by graft, legislators secure jobs for their relatives or special favors for themselves and their business associates, and so on. Actually, of course, the power and pelf of political office are usually sufficiently great to attract a plethora of applicants, and the social problem is more commonly that of keeping exploitation within moderate limits—by revolution or "voting the rascals out"—rather than that of finding somebody who will assume the responsibilities. Only the naïve expect good government at no cost.

The process by which adaptive behavior that is not obviously expressive of basic drives or rewarded by their gratification becomes established in human cultures has been likened by some authors to the process of organic evolution in biology. Human societies enter into competition, it is alleged, as do subcultural organisms, and as they succeed or fail in the competition for life their customs are perpetuated or eliminated. The chances of success are enhanced to the extent that the customs are adaptive, irrespective of whether or not they are rationally devised. Within the same society, moreover, alternative customs—old and new, native and borrowed—compete with one another, as it were, and over time the fitter tend to survive. There is thus operative in cultures, it is asserted, a selective process analogous to natural selection on the biological plane by which adaptations in culture are brought into being and perpetuated.

This theory has been received with scant respect by American anthropologists, who have dismissed it as an unwarranted analogy from biology. In the opinion of the present writer the dismissal was not wholly warranted. Despite certain deficiencies, the theory represented a distinct advance over the crude invention-diffusion hypothesis inherited by the critics via Boas from the French sociologist, Tarde. Its real defect is not its derivation from biological science, for a scientist may legitimately seek his hypotheses anywhere, and it in no way confused the cultural and the organic. Nor is it necessarily invalidated by the epistemological criticism of circular reasoning, namely, that adaptation and survival are defined in terms of each other. Its principal fault appears to be that it attempts to explain too much.

It is difficult to escape the conclusion that cultural change depends upon conflict and survival in certain extreme instances. Thus Carthaginian culture certainly disappeared and Roman culture spread as a consequence of the extirpation of the Carthaginians in the Punic Wars. Since the Discoveries Period, moreover, native cultures have been exterminated with their bearers in various parts of America and Oceania, and replaced by European civilization. It is also probable that cultures have occasionally disappeared from the stage of history in consequence of maladaptive practices pursued until the entire society became extinct, much as numerous animal species have failed to survive because they were unable to produce adaptive mutations when needed.

On the other hand, the obliteration of a culture through the elimination of the entire society that bears it is by no means the rule in human history. If defeat in war or depopulation from maladaptive practices leaves any survivors, cultural change comes about through another and far less drastic mechanism. Prompted by discomfort and frustration, the survivors try out innovations in behavior, invented or borrowed, and through successful trial and error arrive at new cultural adjustments. They may end up, to be sure, with a culture much like that of their more successful neighbors. However, this result has not been produced by a pseudo-biological process of selective elimination and replacement of culture bearers, but through the ordinary psychological process of learning, undergone on a mass scale. All normal cultural change proceeds in precisely the same manner. The usual adaptive mechanism in human history, then, is neither that of biological evolution nor yet one that it unique to man. Instead of a new phenomenon in nature, that of social or cultural evolution, there is simply the age-old phenomenon of habit formation, operating under the distinctive conditions of human society and culture.

The essentially psychological character of the processes and products of culture change suggests that we look into the principles of learning for an interpretation of the universal culture pattern. One factor, that of basic drive or impulse, has already been isolated and found helpful, though not sufficient in itself to provide a complete explanation. A second factor is that of stimulus or cue. Any recurrent element or pattern of elements in the situations in which particular responses occur and are rewarded may acquire the power to evoke those responses, even in the absence of the original impulse. Any prominent stimuli that are of worldwide occurrence might thus be expected to be associated with cultural responses in numerous societies. Among the stimuli of this type are night and day, the heavenly bodies, widespread meteorological and geographical phenomena, certain animals and plants, and the features of human anatomy and physiology. As a matter of fact, nearly all peoples have cultural beliefs about, and cultural responses to, such phenomena as the sun and moon, darkness, rain, thunder, the ocean, mountains, streams, blood, hair, the heart, the genitals, sneezing, breathing, menstruation, childbirth, sickness, and death. Although these cultural forms need have nothing in common save their stimuli, the principle of limited possibilities and the psychological factor of generalization, not to mention cultural diffusion, often result in striking similarities among different populations. In any event, widely occurring natural stimuli provide a useful auxiliary basis for classifying and interpreting cultural universals.

A third important factor in learning is that of prior habit. Since preëxisting habits greatly affect behavior in a learning situation, experimenters in animal learning always use naïve subjects, that is, those as free as possible from unknown prior habits that might predetermine their behavior. It is perhaps for this reason that the psychologists themselves have been so uniformly unsuccessful in their attempts to interpret cultural behavior, for no adult human being in any society ever enters naïve into a situation of cultural learning; on the contrary, men carry into every learning situation a battery of cultural habits in comparison with which the prior conditioning of the most maze-wise experimental rat appears infinitesimal.

From the point of view of the universal culture pattern, prior habit becomes important especially in connection with the psychological factor of generalization, by which is meant the tendency of any learned response to be repeated under similar conditions of drive and stimulus. In consequence of generalization, a response adapted to one situation will tend to reappear in another in proportion to the elements of similarity between the two. Cultures provide innumerable examples. Supernatural beings are regularly anthropomorphized and dealt with in ways that have proved successful in human relations—by supplication (prayer), gift (sacrifice), aggression (exorcism), flattery (laudation), self-abasement (asceticism), or etiquette (ritual). Political organization commonly follows the model of the family, with which it has an authoritarian element in common. Departed spirits are often assimilated to the breath, which also leaves the body in death. Menstrual and lunar phenomena are frequently equated because of their similar periodicity. Numerous indeed are the cross-cultural similarities which result from generalization.

A final important factor in learning is that of limitation in the range of potential responses. In any learning situation the number of possible responses an organism can make is always limited. No animal can respond with an act for which it is not physically adapted. A man cannot jump or fly to the top of a tree to gather its fruits; his responses are limited to such acts as climbing, cutting down the tree, or employing a pole or a missile. Prior habits or their lack sharply limit the range of possible behavior. Familiar situations tend to evoke familiar responses and inhibit novel ones, and complex responses, like speaking a new language or making an important invention, are impossible until a whole series of prerequisite habits has been acquired. Limitations are also set by the structure of the situation in which behavior occurs. Under identical conditions of drive, reward, and prior conditioning, an experimental rat will behave differently in two mazes of different shape, and a human being in two differing social situations: The limiting conditions of geographical environment have often been pointed out; a Samoan cannot build an igloo or an Eskimo prepare kava.

The most important of limitations on the possibilities of response are probably those set by the nature of man himself and of the world in which he lives, as these are known to science. Technological activities must conform to the physical and chemical properties of the materials with which men work. There are relatively few ways, for example, in which fire can be generated or a pot constructed. Customs in hunting and animal husbandry must conform not only to the physical but also to the biological and behavioral characteristics of the animals concerned. Human physiology and psychology set limits to the ways in which disease can be cured or a child brought into the world. Habit and custom must be observed in social relations. Successful responses—and all established cultural responses are successful, that is, normally rewarded—must cope with all the conditions under which they take place. These conditions introduce into culture the principle of limited possibilities, which is of extreme importance in determining the universal culture patterns.

Where the limitations on potential responses are slight, the variation in detail between unrelated cultures may be immense, even though traits be fundamentally related through a common drive, stimulus, or other universal factor. Thus, though every society has a language with a vocabulary, the words for any universal phenomenon, such as water, walk, or woman, may be and are formed by an almost infinite variety of phonetic combinations among the different peoples of the earth. Folktales, taboos, and ceremonials reveal a similar variety in detail. In nearly all such cases, specific similarities are reasonably attributable to a historical connection.

In other instances the limitations are greater and the possible responses can be exhausted in a short list. Every society affiliates a child with a group of relatives through a rule of descent. Only three alternatives are known, namely, patrilineal, matrilineal, or bilateral descent, and every culture incorporates one of these rules or some combination thereof, such as optional, alternating, or double descent. Again all societies have to deal with the corpses of the dead, and face therein a limitation in practicable possibilities. Among these the most prominent are abandonment of the place of death, feeding the corpse to carnivorous animals or birds, inhumation, rock burial, water disposition, tree or scaffold burial, cremation, mummification, and embalming. In such cases it is to be expected that different and even historically unconnected peoples will frequently chance upon the identical solution to the same problem.

The extreme situation is encountered in those instances where the number of practicable or satisfying responses is limited to one. When this happens, cultural uniformities are not of pattern or structure only but of content as well. Disparities in actual behavior become minimal. Perhaps the most striking example is seen in family organization.

Complex family forms, such as polygynous and extended families, are variable, but all known societies have the same fundamental form, the nuclear family of father, mother, and children.[2] This may stand alone, as in our own society; it may be complicated in particular cases by the inclusion of other relatives; or it may exist as a distinguishable unit within a more complex social grouping. Extended families, for example, normally consist of a number of nuclear families united by a common line of descent, and polygynous families typically include several nuclear families in which the same man plays the role of father in each. In contrast to many lower animals, the father is always a member of the human family—presumably because education is one of the family's universal functions and only a man is capable of training a male child in masculine cultural skills.

In all societies the nuclear family is established by marriage, and the relationship between its adult members is characterized by a division of labor according to sex. Sexual intercourse is always permitted between father and mother, but invariably prohibited as incestuous between father and daughter, mother and son, brother and sister. Seeming exceptions, such as dynastic incest, pertain only to small groups of peculiar status, never to an entire society. The nuclear family is always an economic unit, and it is universally charged with the functions of child rearing, socialization, and early education. The family may gather to itself other functions in particular societies, but throughout history and ethnography it is invariably the focus of the sexual, economic, reproductive, and educational relationships indicated above. This coincidence of behavior is truly remarkable in view of the diversity of responses in other departments of culture.

The explanation is not far to seek. The sex drive accounts for cohabitation, and indirectly for reproduction. Its satisfaction tends to give at least some permanence to sexual association, during which the ad-

---

[2] The propositions with respect to the family stated herewith are inductions from a careful analysis of 220 societies made in a study of the relationship between sex behavior and social structure, the completion of which was interrupted by the outbreak of war. In no case is a statement of fact made to which there is a single exception either in the sample of 220 or in any other society known to the author from his general anthropological reading.

vantages inherent in a division of labor have an opportunity to manifest themselves. Primary sex differences channelize economic pursuits, and economic rewards fortify the sexual association. Children make their appearance in this context, and are bound to the mother through lactation. Their care and training are more naturally assigned to the mother and her sexual and economic partner than to anyone else. In so far as derivative motivations are required to support the parents in these tasks, they will be supplied in the manner previously outlined.

At no point in this development are the initial responses so difficult as to lie outside the range of probable occurrence in any society. Factors of drive, stimulus, and circumstances sharply limit alternative possibilities. Finally, the particular constellation of relationships provides individuals with such powerful rewards and solves at once so many problems of vital importance to society that, once made, the responses are certain to be fixed and perpetuated. Man has never discovered an adequate substitute for the family, and all Utopian attempts at its abolition have spectacularly failed.

The only universal characteristics of the family that have proved difficult to explain are its associated incest taboos. Freudian psychology offers the most hopeful lead, but the problem is too complex for consideration here. It is of interest to note, however, that Freud chose this particular cultural universal, the family, as the keystone of his entire theoretical system. Reversing the usual scientific practice of making psychology an underlying discipline in relation to the social sciences, Freud founded his psychology on a cultural fact, though he used the terminology of instinct. Whereas behaviorists look primarily to the inherited mechanism of learning for the interpretation of behavior, Freudians look to the conditions of learning, and in particular to the structure of family relationships under which the earliest human learning occurs in all societies. Both approaches are presumably sound, and the psychology of the future will doubtless result from their amalgamation.[3]

[3] The author, whose acquaintance with Freudian psychology stems from experience in analysis as well as from books and discussion, predicts that behaviorism will prevail in the synthesis because of its far more rigorous scientific methodology. It must, however, take full account of the conditions of human learning, not only as these have been illuminated in Freud's momentous contributions but also as they are established by anthropological science with its unique cross-cultural orientation. The peculiar Freudian mechanisms—repression, regression, identification, and projection—have already been reasonably well translated into behavioristic terms. The therapeutic technique and clinical value of psychoanalysis will, of course, survive. Freud's attempts at cultural interpretation, however, deserve the oblivion they have already achieved.

An attempt to present a complete analysis of the universal culture pattern, with a full consideration of the factors underlying each category, would far exceed the limits of the present paper. The author's primary purpose has been to indicate the general lines along which such an analysis might be undertaken and to present a few illustrative examples. The principal conclusion has been that the common denominator of cultures is to be sought in the factors governing the acquisition of all habitual behavior, including that which is socially shared. Among these the most important are those which bear directly upon the incidence of reward. To the extent that these conclusions prove valid, one brick will have been added to the scientific edifice of the future, in which anthropological and psychological theory will be united in a broader science of human behavior.

The Processes of Cultural Change
By MELVILLE J. HERSKOVITS

A SOCIETY may be never so small, never so isolated; its technological equipment may be of the simplest, its devotion to its own way of life expressed in extreme conservatism; yet changes constantly take place as generation succeeds generation, and new ideas, new alignments, new techniques come into the thinking of its members. For no living culture is static.

The evidence for the universality of cultural change is massive. It takes various forms, such as the objective analysis of local variations in custom among societies representing a single cultural stream demonstrates, or the utterances of the elders of any society about the past. Testimony of the second type has been gathered by many students of non-literate, remote groups, to whom older people have confided their dissatisfaction with the conduct of younger members. "When we were young," runs the widespread, oft-repeated plaint, "things were different. Our generation respected their elders, and knew how to worship the gods. Today everything is changed; the young are unwilling to learn and to follow." Yet to the outsider, the changes seem slight indeed—a new dance, an altered formula, a new version of an accepted tribal style of clothing, perhaps.

Comparison of local groups belonging to the same people similarly demonstrates the ubiquity of cultural change. One such study, published many years ago by Franz Boas,[1] though concerned with quite a different theoretical problem, tellingly makes the point. In this study Boas treated variations in the designs on Eskimo needlecases, tubular containers made of fossil ivory, near the top of which are two protuberances to assure that the sinew cord by which a case is fastened to its owner's belt will hold. The designs vary from one local Eskimo group to another, in addition to the differences that arise within each group out of the fact that individual makers follow their own conceptions of how most agreeably to embellish the cases they carve. Nevertheless, in the varieties of aesthetic expression encountered in such

[1] "Decorative Designs of Alaskan Needle-Cases," *Proceedings, U.S. National Museum,* XXXIV (1905), 321-44.

small, isolated, but historically related groups, the differences in these minute elements of culture are different only in degree from those found in areas of lesser conservatism. In this instance, the evidence is rendered more weighty by the fact that the harshness of the Arctic setting combines with other factors to encourage the closest conformity to all aspects of a way of life of proved efficacy.

But in recognizing the ubiquity of cultural change and the importance of its analysis, it must not be forgotten that, as in any aspect of the study of culture, the phenomenon exists in terms of setting and background, and not by and of itself. This is why a discussion of change in culture has meaning only as part of the problem of cultural stability. Both terms are relative, and in any specific culture are relative not only to one another but are dependent as well on the degree of detachment of the observer who evaluates the stability of a given body of custom or the changes occurring within it. Just as with the elders whose distaste for minor changes brings forth expressions of dire forebodings, so also does intimate or too prolonged association within a culture tend to induce an especially limited perspective. This is why it is so difficult for members of a society to assess significant change in it. Conversely, it follows equally that it is no simple task, even for the trained student, on first contact with a culture foreign to one's own to sense those differences in individual behavior that at a given moment are the expressions of change in process.

Thus it is that one of the most perplexing aspects of the study of culture is the contemplation of the factors that make for permanence and change in human institutions. Viewed at a given moment, the cultures of men present a range of infinite variety. On the closest scrutiny, however, they prove to be but intricate variations on a number of basic themes, which compose the unities of human culture and human experience. These unities encompass the satisfaction of the demands made by the physical organism, the perpetuation of the group, the achievement of a sanctioned order of living, adjustment to the universe, and the fulfillment of aesthetic impulses—all carried on by a system of communication that constitutes the language of a people.

Whatever the forms of the institutions by which a society lives, or of the cultural and social forces that play on the individual and mold his endowments, they take shape within the limits set by these universal aspects of culture. For, as has been asserted with considerable insight, these aspects can be thought of as a kind of table of contents of any work dealing with a specific civilization. Certainly the omission of any of them makes the description less complete, and to that degree blunts comprehension. It follows, therefore, that though our concern here is with the processes that have operated to achieve the varieties of cultures existing on earth today, perspective will be awry and conclusions warped unless the significance of the institutional and psychological background against which cultural change occurs is continuously held in mind.

The controversy over the historical and nonhistorical approaches to the study of social life has arisen largely, we may say, out of the somewhat paradoxical nature of the problem of conservatism and change in culture. As Bennett [2] has recently shown, this stresses the importance of an eclectic point of view, perhaps in the manner of the categories for the study of society suggested by Goldenweiser.[3] It is apparent that every normal culture is an integral whole, possessing a stability which causes its patterns to continue in recognizable form despite the changing personnel of its carriers in successive generations. But this integration does not prevent the constant addition of some new elements to a given set of traditions, or the discarding of others. For every society that is a going concern has a culture tightly enough knit so that only under conditions of the greatest stress does it yield sufficiently to blur its identity; and when this occurs, demoralization ensues and continues until such time as reintegration is achieved, or the group, as such, disappears.

The importance of taking the past into full account in the study of culture has come in for fresh examination in recent years. The essential problem is one of method—particularly where it is necessary to devise a technique whereby significant aspects of the history of nonliterate and therefore nonhistorical peoples can be recovered. This problem must be approached in terms of the type of question that is posed about a given historical past, for the analysis must be suited to each individual question. In some instances, we know in advance that the answers are not discoverable. To take an extreme example, it is evident that to recover such historical facts as the absolute origin of the family, or of language, is futile. A single beginning for a phenomenon of this

---

[2] J. Bennett, "The Development of Ethnological Theory as Illustrated by Studies of the Plains Sun Dance," *American Anthropologist*, XLVI (1944), 162-81.
[3] A. A. Goldenweiser, "History, Psychology and Culture: a Set of Categories for an Introduction to Social Science," *History, Psychology and Culture* (New York, 1933), pp. 5-32.

order—or even a series of multiple origins, if there were several independent beginnings—was an event specific in time and place of which no record, even archeological, can in the nature of the case be recovered. We can merely record that these institutions must have originated early in the childhood of man on earth, that they are universals in human experience, and are to be studied in terms of their present variation and, historically, in such truncated form as the records permit.

This is likewise true, though to a lesser degree, of less remote events in the development of human culture. The origin of agriculture, or the discovery of ironworking, or the initial appearance of pottery can be localized in a general way, though in these instances it should also be observed that any attempt at precision in time or place leads to controversy. Where we extend the inquiry and seek to ascertain the circumstances under which these events occurred, or even what people were responsible for them, we again meet with no more than hypotheses which, it is granted, are not susceptible of objective proof, since our yield consists of data that give no more than a few clues of the effect these happenings may have had on the way of life of those to whom they came. Nonetheless, viewed down the long perspective of elapsed time, we can perceive, even if we cannot give in detail, the processes of change set in motion as a result of their introduction into the repertory of human cultural resources.

The essential historical approach to the study of living nonliterate folk is based on the assumption that culture is dynamic, and thus in process of continuous change. The changes that have occurred are discernible in the differing forms which the same element in the material culture of tribes in a given area take, or the variations on a type of social structure, or in a ritual complex, or an art style. Peoples in contact, we now recognize, borrow liberally from each other. The careful student, therefore, who compares what is actually found in such cultures as they exist today achieves two ends. He establishes first the fact of historic contact through establishing resemblances which, on the basis of the probabilities involved, could not have originated independently of each other. In addition, he throws light on the processes of cultural change by considering the manner in which the common element has been variously molded in form and meaning, in conformity with the body of conventions of which it has become a part.

During the first quarter of the present century students devoted themselves to the task of amassing the documentation needed to establish the fact of borrowing. From the point of view of the history of anthropological method, it is interesting to note that even in establishing diffusion as a primary result of contact between peoples the historical factor was held to the forefront, and there was full awareness of the importance of the data for an understanding of cultural dynamics. Diffusion studies associated with the names of Boas,[4] Nordenskiöld,[5] Kroeber,[6] Spier,[7] and others have become classic. They took varied forms. The Jessup North Pacific Expedition, a series of field studies along the west coast of North America and in Siberia, showed the historical relationships across the Bering Straits. Nordenskiöld's comparative ethnographic studies demonstrated the widespread contacts between peoples inhabiting South America. Kroeber's continuing intensive researches in the California area, Spier's synthesis of the Sun Dance in the Plains region, all established the fact of diffusion; but more than that, they gave us much excellent data bearing on the processes through which the borrowing occurred.

It is, however, necessary to distinguish the theory and method of these men from the approach and techniques of others to whom the term "historical" is also applied. Distributional studies of the type mentioned are marked off from these others by two characteristics. They are empirical, moving from data to conclusions; and they are concerned with distributions of specific cultural phenomena in restricted areas. They are thus quite different from the German and English distributional schools, whose effort has been world-wide reconstruction of the contacts of peoples and the spread of culture, based on certain a priori assumptions. Both these schools take for granted an extreme degree of conservatism in culture. Fundamental to their approach is the hypothesis that a given cultural element, or a complex of traits, can retain its identity while being passed from one people to another over the principal parts of the earth's inhabited surface. Without this assumption, even though it is rarely stated explicitly in their writings, the systems of analyses they have devised fail of a logical foundation.

Let us indicate briefly the position of each of these schools. The

---

[4] F. Boas, "The Jessup North Pacific Expedition," *Verh. des VII. Int. Geographen-Kongresses in Berlin* (1899), pp. 678–85.
[5] E. Nordenskiöld, *Comparative Ethnographic Studies*, Nos. 1–6 (Gothenburg, 1919–26).
[6] A. L. Kroeber, *Anthropology* (New York, 1923).
[7] L. Spier, "The Sun Dance of the Plains Indians, Its Development and Diffusion," *Anthropological Papers, Am. Mus. Nat. History*, XVI (1921).

English diffusionist school, headed by G. Elliot-Smith and W. J. Perry,[8] which achieved considerable prominence in the twenties, did not weather the many criticisms lodged against it and today rests as a kind of curiosity in the study of culture. Its founder, Elliot-Smith, was a great anatomist who made classic studies of the brains of Egyptian mummies and was so impressed with the quality of Egyptian culture that to it he ascribed the derivation of all the "civilizations" of mankind. From Egypt, this complex—that is, rulers considered as "children of the sun," megalithic monuments, the importance of gold and pearls, mummification, and pyramidal structures, to name but a few of its items—was held to have spread to India, to the Far East, and across the Pacific into the Americas; into Africa, and thence north and northwest as far as Britain and Scandinavia. The *stelae* of the Mexican Maya and their temples atop pyramids, the mummified remains found in Peru, the mounds of the Ohio and Mississippi valleys—all these were described as expressions of the high culture which, once devised in Egypt, traveled around the world in identifiable form, raising the pre-existing food gatherers to the status of civilized folk.

The naïveté of this approach is not difficult to discern; but the attack of the "cultural-historical" school of Germany and Austria is anything but naïve. Based on the original hypotheses developed by Fritz Graebner[9] and his associate W. Foy, it was taken up by Father W. Schmidt[10] and is today one of the outstanding points of view in central European ethnology. No single source of origin is envisaged. Rather, a series of "cultural circles" is postulated which represent both spatial and temporal conceptions. Each "circle" is characterized by a cultural complex which, because it is a series of unrelated traits, can be submitted to certain criteria of "form" and "quantity," as they are termed, in order to establish presumed historical relationships in various parts of the earth. While it is held desirable to establish a path whereby diffusion could have occurred, this is not deemed indispensable; so that the same cultural complex found in areas remote from each other is assumed a priori to give evidence of historic contact.

Reconstructions of presumed history on a world-wide basis of this sort can be criticized from many points of view. For one thing, the only technique whereby proofs can be amassed is by means of a comparative

---

[8] G. Elliot-Smith, *The Migrations of Early Culture* (Manchester, 1915); W. J. Perry, *The Children of the Sun* (New York, 1923).
[9] *Methode der Ethnologie* (Heidelberg, 1911).
[10] *The Culture Historical Method of Ethnology* (New York, 1939).

method which neglects the psychological factor whose importance in shaping culture is today recognized as essential. The "complexes" of these systems, again, are conglomerates of traits related only in the mind of the student, not in the thinking and behavior of the peoples in whose cultures they are found. This assumption that aspects of culture are diffused in little changed form over vast areas differentiates most importantly both the British diffusionists and the culture-historical school from those whose diffusion studies are pointed toward the understanding of cultural processes as evidenced in the cultural history of a limited area.

A reaction against these schools of thought brought to the fore a nonhistorical approach. The reconstruction of history on any level, world-wide or limited, came to be regarded by some as impossible to achieve and therefore undesirable to attempt. From this it was but a step to an obliviousness of the problems of dynamics in the study of culture; and, on the positive side, to a heightened awareness of inner structure and forms of organization, and of the relationship between a culture and its carriers.

The chief point of attack on the problems of culture by those who took this position was through the study of the interrelationship of the various aspects of a given culture and their reaction to each other. Research in Melanesia or the South Pacific by such students as Malinowski [11] or Firth [12] or Fortune [13] was characterized by intensive analysis of the particular culture of their concern; or of a single aspect of this culture, showing in great detail how it integrated with certain other aspects. The fact of cultural change was not denied, nor that life is not lived on a single time-plane; problems of this kind were merely ignored. Essentially, work was carried on without reference to the past; without anything of that sense of historicity that makes the historically minded student of culture cognizant of the facts of time-depth and historic change even when analyzing a culture of which no written record is at hand. The rule in such research was rather concentration on the study of a given culture, to the end that the functioning of each phase of that culture in relation to other phases might be discerned—whence was derived the term functionalist, customarily applied to those who make studies of this type.

[11] B. Malinowski, *Coral Gardens and Their Magic* (New York, 1935).
[12] R. Firth, *We, the Tikopia: a Sociological Study of Kinship in Primitive Polynesia* (London, 1936).
[13] R. Fortune, *Sorcerers of Dobu* (London, 1932).

Consideration of cultural change was, however, forcibly brought to the attention of members of this group as they moved from the analysis of relatively isolated, stable cultures to research in areas where societies exist in contact with European communities, or have been influenced to an appreciable extent by European custom. For when studies having this essentially static attack were attempted in Africa, or Australia, or in some parts of Melanesia where European influence has been significant, the historic past was found to be of too great importance to be disregarded. Once change incident upon historically known contact was encountered, the need for a more dynamic approach could on no account be side-stepped, inasmuch as where integration between cultural elements had broken down the historical process became inescapable. To understand what had occurred in such societies, moreover, it was found essential to establish a base line from which change began. The need to reconstruct the life of earlier days consequently became imperative, and to the problem of cultural integration was added that of cultural change.

This orientation toward the study of a culture on a timeless plane, in order to understand how its various aspects are integrated, has had several beneficial effects on the study of culture in general. It has sharpened the awareness of many students to the need of reëxamining the validity of all historical reconstructions, in restricted areas no less than for the world at large. Its analytic approach has corrected a tendency to fix too exclusively on the problems of cultural dynamics, by calling attention to the fact that a culture, though intangible, is to the individual living under it of durable texture. It has stressed the fact that the unity of a culture affords the means whereby the psychological integration of its carriers is achieved, and thus has underscored the fact that a culture is something to which men and women can hold fast and in its conventions find the directives and values necessary for coherent behavior.

In essence, however, the principal distinction between the two positions is that those who emphasize the historical quality of culture are concerned primarily with cultural change, while those who hold the nonhistorical point of view frame their investigations in terms of cultural stability.

Changes in a culture are effected by innovations introduced from within and from without. Changes initiated from within take the form of inventions or discoveries; those from without are due to borrowing. In either case, the critical problem is whether or not the element newly presented will be accepted or rejected. If rejected, it of course disappears; but if accepted, it is then important to determine, as far as possible, the mechanisms by which it was incorporated into the existing body of custom that accepted it, particularly whether it was taken over in its entirety or partially accepted, and how it was changed while being integrated into the accepting culture.

To the present, it has not been possible to isolate the principles which control this process. In part, this is to be explained by the fact that, outside our own culture, and perhaps in a few instances in other literate societies, adequate data on which to base generalizations are lacking. Diffusion in process, invention or discovery being achieved are not readily encountered in the primitive societies which serve the student of culture as sources of comparative data. The unique contribution of the study of culture-contact is that it does take the student to the localities where different cultural streams are in the act of exerting an influence on each other. Yet even here the problem of controlling enough variables looms prominently, since so large a part of the cross-cultural contacts of the present day are between varied native cultures and Euro-American traditions. The analysis of contact between two non-European cultures which involves the task of dissecting two series of unfamiliar strands understandably presents great methodological difficulty. Where nonhistoric, primitive folk have borrowed from one another, recourse must be had to the techniques of diffusion studies, wherein the cultures of a given area are assessed in terms of how a series of institutions common to them, and therefore presumably borrowed from each other, vary from tribe to tribe.

When considering the mechanisms of cultural change, the meanings of certain terms that recur must be kept well in mind, and especially such words as discovery and invention. Dixon,[14] who has discussed at some length the problem presented by these phenomena, considers the element of purpose crucial in differentiating the two terms. That is, he regards it as discovery when one stumbles, so to speak, on some phenomenon already existing in unrecognized form; invention, he says, is "purposeful discovery." The making of a discovery to him implies three conditions—opportunity, observation, and "appreciation

[14] R. B. Dixon, *The Building of Cultures* (New York, 1928).

plus imagination, in other words a measure of genius." On the other hand, he holds need to be essential to invention. As with all those who have discussed the problem, he acknowledges that these categories are by no means mutually exclusive. Like other cultural phenomena, they are difficult to delimit accurately, but instead often merge into each other, while instances occur where inventions are what Harrison [15] has termed "directional," that is to say, they involve improvements whose deviations in form or structure serve to make an object more effective in performance or function.

At this point, it is of value to reëxamine the meaning of the word "invention," since its current use must be differentiated from its technical connotation. In everyday speech, an invention is the formulation of some new object, some hitherto unknown thing. The entire weighting of the word is toward the domain of material culture, so preponderantly, in fact, that as astute a thinker as Dixon failed to sense the logical fallacy inherent in differentiating invention of a material good from the "invention" of a new conception of the universe, or a new kinship term, or a new value system. Dixon's discussion of invention, which is based solely on data from the study of material objects, completely overlooks the role of the inventor of new ideas and new concepts in contributing toward the changes which occur in a society. Yet it will be readily granted that ideas are surely no less potent than things in shaping the lives lived in terms of them. The inventors who devised the method of counting descent on one side of the family, and those who later developed classificatory systems of relationship terminology, had no less influence on the course of human culture than the inventor of the skin tent, or of the canoe, or of snowshoes.

One other question must be raised in connection with the problem of internal cultural change, and that is to what extent invention is a response to recognized need. "Necessity is the mother of invention," is an aphorism that has gained wider acceptance than it perhaps deserves. Thorstein Veblen, humorously but with equal cogency, was fond of turning it about: "Invention is the mother of necessity." In science, no less than in life, the truth is probably somewhat between these two extremes. Discoveries are accidental—they are so by current definition. Yet it is likewise conceivable that random manipulations have in many instances brought objects or ideas together in relationships

[15] H. S. Harrison, "Inventions; Obtrusive, Directional, and Independent," *Man*, XXVI (1926), 74, 117–21.

hitherto unexperienced—relationships so advantageous to the individual or the group that recognition has followed and indispensability has come to be taken for granted.

The conditions antecedent to a discovery or an invention have been phrased only in the most general terms, largely because of the difficulties inherent in more specific analysis of the question. It has been stated, for example, that an innovation cannot be made if the culture is not prepared for it—if the existing "cultural base" is insufficiently broad to permit its application. In other words, one who has only studied arithmetic cannot be expected to master the calculus. This follows almost in the nature of the case, for even the most creative imagination cannot function in fields of which there is no awareness. This is important in that it gives us clues to an understanding of why cultural change is orderly, why the changes that take place seem, in retrospect, to flow out of antecedent conditions.

There are those who maintain that the influence of the cultural setting is so strong that it itself inevitably generates the situations from which discoveries and inventions derive. This is the cultural deterministic position. It holds that a given culture, developing out of its own historic past, contains the germs of a future that unrolls with but little regard for the will of its carriers. This statement of the position may be regarded as extreme, yet it follows from such a study as that of Ogburn and Thomas,[16] who have documented their hypothesis of the inevitability of cultural change with an impressive list of discoveries and inventions in many fields—technological, scientific, artistic. Others who take a similar position have made detailed analyses of the reception of innovations in special fields of our own culture—as Stern [17] has done concerning certain medical discoveries and Gilfillan [18] has done concerning the ship. The data of all these studies point the same conclusions—that if a given invention or discovery had not been made by the person or persons who actually did make it, the logic of the developing culture would have caused someone else to achieve the same end.

This point of view, it is to be noted, reduces the role of the individual in culture to a minimum. It makes of culture an independent force whose carriers are its creatures rather than its masters. The evidence brought forward by those who support the cultural deterministic po-

[16] W. F. Ogburn and D. Thomas, "Are Inventions Inevitable? a Note on Social Evolution," *Political Science Quarterly*, XXXVII (1922), 83–99.
[17] B. Stern, *Social Factors in Medical Progress* (New York, 1927).
[18] S. C. Gilfillan, *The Sociology of Invention* (Chicago, 1935).

sition may profitably be subjected to reëxamination when sufficient documentation from cultures other than our own are at hand, but it cannot be ignored, for they have given objective proofs from our own culture, at least, of how innovations in accord with the cultural base were so much in the approved stream of logic that they occurred to more than one individual at the time they were introduced. And at the same time, they have shown how these innovations, even though they were initially and at each step in their development resisted, by the same cultural logic forced their eventual acceptance and became an integral part of the culture. Today one can but wonder to what extent, in primitive societies, the same compulsions are operative. It is regrettable that we can but speculate concerning the logic of innovation in stable cultures, where change is neither valued highly nor unduly resisted.

Some aid is given our quest when the problem of acceptance or rejection of a discovery or an invention, once made, is considered. As customarily phrased, the formula of explanation holds that acceptance or rejection depends on the degree to which the innovation is aligned with preëxisting orientations. This seems self-evident when approached a priori, and there is some documentation that bears upon this point, as for example the steam turbine, which was discovered many centuries ago in Alexandria. It could have been quite possible, from a mechanical point of view, to harness and use power generated by this device, but since in this nonindustrial society there was no background in the culture to which it might be referred, it remained a curiosity, a toy.

Let us see if in the fields of mythology or art we can come upon some clues to help clarify this difficult topic. Storytellers and artists, in any culture, are those in whom the creative imagination is strong, and they might therefore be expected to be the instruments of far-reaching innovations. When we study that which their genius has created over countless generations, what impresses us, however, is not evidences of innovation, but rather the unity of the total achievement. The maker of a myth may be highly resourceful in creating supernatural beings and the events that befall them, yet the counterpart of setting and motivation will be found in the culture of which these are a part, while the situations are resolved in accord with solutions that derive from the everyday life of the society where they are told, and the values they reflect are the values of the people who tell and hear them.

The will of the artist who works in graphic and plastic arts to devise new ways of handling his materials is a commonplace. The artist is above all an inventor, and is conscious of the fact, as is attested by various studies from various cultures of the lines along which artistic innovations are devised. But again, innovation of itself becomes a convention, and experiment is well within sanctioned limits. This is why art styles, not only of tribes but of groups within tribes, are so readily recognizable, despite the wide variety of expressions of a local style found in the individual examples of it. In historic societies, the variations in local differences can be translated into differences that distinguish the art of one period from that of another. In changes in art styles of any kind, however, we find reflected the inventiveness of the individual artists, who developed their styles through the play of their imagination on the tradition they found and within the limits set by the conventions of their culture and their time.

Much of what has been asserted for discovery and invention holds true of diffusion. As concerns nonliterate folk, it is rarely possible to distinguish that which has been diffused from without from that which has been devised inside the group. From an empirical point of view, it is apparent that much more of any single culture has been borrowed than has been invented. This is evidenced by the wide distribution of quite complicated cultural elements, technological, folkloristic, religious, sociological. Each manifestation of a specific diffused element or complex, as Spier's analysis of the Plains Sun Dance demonstrated, differs from every other. Yet in each locale the manifestation has enough interrelated parts, with specific enough assignment of values and functions, to make unthinkable the separate origin of the complex everywhere it is found.

However rich the documentation of diffusion, the unsolved problem, as in the case of inventions and discoveries, is why, in given instances, one innovation presented by a foreign culture is accepted and another rejected; why one is taken over entirely and another only partially, why some are accepted with little change and others changed radically. Wissler's [19] description of the manner in which the early American colonists took over the maize complex from the Indians in its entirety need not be repeated here. Nor need the further tale of its partial acceptance and almost complete transformation when brought

---

[19] C. Wissler, "The Aboriginal Maize Culture as a Typical Culture-Complex," *American Journal of Sociology*, XXI (1916), 656–61.

to Europe be given, except perhaps to indicate the point that the colonists were faced with the task of accommodating themselves to a new environment for which they found this instrument ready to hand, while the established agricultural practices and food economy of Europe had little place for the newcomer.

What is less well known is the acceptance of the maize complex in West Africa. Here yams had always been planted in rows, so that the substitution of maize was a simple matter. It is not so clear why maize, which was regarded in Europe as food for animals rather than human beings, should have encountered no such resistance in Africa. But boiled ears of corn, to be eaten on the cob, are a favorite African food today, a staple that can be bought out of the pot in the native markets. Moreover, so completely has maize been accepted into the culture that corn meal is a standard offering to West African gods.

Fundamental in the diffusion process is the manner in which cultural borowings are reworked as they move from people to people. Such an instance is had in Hallowell's account of the variations in bear ceremonialism in the Northern Hemisphere.[20] Here each element is considered in its many forms—the hunting of the animal, the mode of addressing it, techniques of slaying it, propitiation of its spirit, the disposal of the remains. It is possible to abstract from the mass of data a type of least common denominator of customary usage as regards the bear, about which the complex centers. But in form and presumably in significance, one finds, in no two cultures, identity in the complex of practices or interpretations.

Many examples of this reworking under diffusion are to be found in the realm of folklore. For example, folk tales of the Old World tend to be moralizing tales, while those of the Indians are not. The adventures of such a European fable as "The Ant and the Grasshopper" may be followed to advantage. This tale found its way to the Saushwap of western Canada, who retained it intact, except for its moral which, as we know, points the importance of providing in times of plenty for times of want. The Indians, however, appended an equally cogent point, one as valid artistically as it is logically; that is, for the Saushwap, the story explains why grasshoppers are not found in the wintertime! To follow the numberless variations on such American Indian tales as "Sky Husband," or "The Sharing of the Sun," or "The Ladder of Ar-

---

[20] A. I. Hallowell, "Bear Ceremonialism in the Northern Hemisphere," *American Anthropologist* XXVIII (1926), 1-175.

rows," is to obtain a vivid sense of what happens to cultural elements in transmission. This can be paralleled by following, in the same way, the permutations among peoples of Europe and Africa, or in Asia as far as the land of the Siberian nomads, of the story called "Mother Holle" by the Grimm brothers who recorded it in Germany, or of other tales of this collection.

That diffusion has occurred to so considerable a degree is indicative of the hospitality of cultures to outside influences. As with invention and discovery, it illustrates the propensity of culture to change. Nevertheless, the fact that the acceptance of what comes from the outside is never a total acceptance, that reworking is the rule and reinterpretation inevitable, shows how stubbornly a consistent body of custom maintains its unifying pattern. Understandably, the closer two peoples are in contact, the less resistance to borrowing, and the less need of marked reinterpretation. This is but another way of stating that the more restricted the area in which the varieties of a specific cultural element is studied, the less the degree of variation there will be in common elements of the cultures of the region; that the closer a people live to a "cross-roads" of humanity, the more varied their cultural resources will be. Yet whether isolated or of wide contact, whether inordinately conservative or willing to accept innovations from within and without, changes in the customary habits of life will manifest themselves.

Any investigation into cultural change must consider its institutional and its psychological aspects. From the institutional point of view, cultures are analyzed in what may be called behavioristic terms; that is to say, the sanctioned forms of conduct, gathered into institutions capable of objective description, are studied in terms of the variation they show in outer form. The psychological approach seeks to understand the interaction between these institutions and the individuals who order their lives in terms of them. On the one hand, it attempts to gain insight into the reasons why human beings hold tenaciously to what they know, to what they have been taught; on the other, it seeks to understand why they come to accept new ways of achieving the ends hitherto accomplished by the custom and usage of past generations. In the preceding sections both the institutional and psychological aspects have entered into our discussion. We may now give separate attention to each, in terms of their relevance to the problem of our concern.

The most important concept in the objective analysis of cultural change, from the institutional point of view, is the concept of cultural pattern. A thing without material form—except in so far as material objects enter into culture—it has the reality of any abstraction drawn from a many-sided, complicated phenomenon. It stems from a behavioristic base, since it is to be thought of as a kind of consensus of the individual behavior patterns of those whose lives are lived according to its requirements. Yet, like culture as a whole, it is more than the totality of the behavior of its carriers, for it represents a continuum that existed before any given generation was born, that will outlive the longest-lived member of this generation.

To think in terms of a single pattern for a single culture is to distort reality and make competent analysis more difficult, for no culture is too simple to have various patterns. We may conceive of them as a series of interlocking behavior and thought and value systems, some of wider applicability than others, some even in conflict with others. The patterns of fundamental values in a society, for example, will be effective over the entire group; but there will be subpatterns by which men order their lives differently from women, young and middle-aged folk from their elders, members of lower from those of higher socioeconomic status. It is the multiplicity of patterns which together make up the culture as a whole; it is the particular patterns that impinge on the life of an individual member of society that will shape his behavior. But all must be taken into account when an understanding of the mutations of culture in change is the end of analysis.

Viewed objectively, these patterns can—and have been—further divided into subunits, composed of elements called traits which merge into larger subdivisions called complexes. One point, however, must be stressed in connection with this type of breakdown of patterns into smaller components. For the person who lives in a culture, these subdivisions are nonexistent. Behavior is largely automatic, so that attitudes and the sanctions that validate them are accepted implicitly. Where the reasons for behavior in terms of convention rise into consciousness and become the subject for thought, reasoning is cast in terms of the total patterns of conduct applicable. It is here, indeed, that the *gestalt* principle of the psychologists finds its more apt reference.

The most carefully documented analysis of change in a specific pattern is the study of women's fashions during the past three centuries made by Richardson and Kroeber [21] as an extension of earlier research into the problem by Kroeber.[22] Though theoretically the investigation examines the validity of the principle of order in cultural change, the study is equally applicable to a consideration of change in terms of the pattern phenomenon. From various fashion guides, these students made measurements and calculated ratios for certain traits in the female dress pattern year by year from 1787 to 1936; for the period 1605 to 1787 they gathered the same information for the years for which data were available. The traits thus followed were length and width of the skirt, position and diameter of the waist, and length and width of the decolletage.

In these traits they found changes in regular sequence, exhibiting a periodicity in the swings from large measurements to small that would seem to transcend any operation of factors due solely to chance. Yet within this dress-complex, individual items were found to vary differently. Dress length, for example, seemed to demand the closest conformity to the style-dictates of the day, while in such traits as fullness of the skirt or decolletage greater exercise of individual preference was possible. Such swings, these students show, represent the ebb and flow of fashion about an ideal pattern which acts as a stabilizing force in the movement of the entire complex. It is the backdrop against which the cyclical alterations find their points of reference, the ideal pattern that sets the limits within which this variation in detail occurs.

Most available studies of the patterning phenomenon approach the problem from another point of view. That is, in place of historical variations of the units comprising a pattern followed over a period of years—something manifestly impossible in a nonliterate culture—the pattern is described and differing elements within it are detailed as these occur from tribe to tribe in a single area, or within different groups in the same society. The result is the same. The differences found at a given moment represent the end achieved by a process of change which took place in the area, or in the society, antecedent to the investigation. The time of original introduction of the cultural element may be unknown, the rate of speed with which changes occurred impossible to obtain. Yet the varying manifestations of a basic pattern, comparatively studied, point to conclusions as to how each

[21] J. Richardson and A. L. Kroeber, "Three Centuries of Women's Dress Fashions; a Quantitative Analysis," *Anthropological Records*, V (1940), 111-53.
[22] A. L. Kroeber, "On the Principle of Order in Civilization as Exemplified by Changes of Fashion," *American Anthropologist*, XXI (1919), 235-63.

group in a society or each society in an area of distribution shaped the common over-all conventions in terms of its own ways of life.

Analysis of this type can profitably be made in the field of associations, that is, of secret and nonsecret societies of all kinds, perhaps for the very reason that membership in them derives from voluntary affiliation rather than birth. Gist [23] has shown how sharply drawn is the pattern of the fraternal order in the United States, yet how, at the same time, in terms of this pattern, variations in names, in rituals, in organization, in objectives are to be found. This suggests that the pattern, however firmly held to in outline, is made flexible in detail by the tendency of groups to deviate even while following the conventional forms.

The same sort of analysis is possible for other kinds of societies in our culture, though it is apparent that all varieties of groupings partake of a more general form, which not only mark them off as a whole from the societies of the Plains Indians, or of West Africa, or of Melanesia, but even of Europe. One detail of this general American pattern of associations will make the point—the convention of publicly marking one's allegiance, even to secret societies. The member of a society is known by his badges, and since "joining" is general, there are few Americans who do not wear insignia marking them as members of at least one lodge, order, fraternity, association or brotherhood. In Europe, similar and even the same societies are found, but membership is something to be kept to oneself—especially in the case of secret orders. Europeans tend to react strongly to the openness with which Americans indicate their affiliation, in violation of the European pattern.

If we turn to the emblem itself, we can even describe subpatterns in this minute element of the total complex. Thus, fraternal orders employing the names of animals tend to incorporate their eponymous symbols in their badges. Lodge emblems and those of other adult male organizations not associated with institutions of higher learning are, furthermore, worn in the lapel button, or as a ring on the finger. They may be contrasted in various ways with college secret societies and honorary groups. The former, whether for men or women, are called by Greek letters, which are incorporated into or marked on the enameled surface of a pin. Men wear them on their waistcoats, women

---

[23] N. Gist, "Secret Societies; a Cultural Study of Fraternalism in the United States," *University of Missouri Studies*, XV, No. 4 (1940).

on their dresses on the left side. Honorific societies, on the other hand, while also designated by Greek initials, shape their identifying badges in the form of "keys."

Now this is in our own society, where the population mass is so great that the regional differentiation of cultural patterns which characterizes the areas inhabited by nonliterate folk gives way to group differentiation. In this case diffusion becomes two-directional. For in large societies, in addition to what has been received from other cultures by diffusion in the common sense of the term, there is the further diffusion of patterns, subpatterns, and all their components between the groups within the total population. This fact of the existence of subgroups, each having its distinctive subpatterns, is to a considerable degree related to the class structure of these societies; and this opens further facets of the problem of incentives to cultural change within the society that can only be mentioned here.

Studies of the distribution of varying expressions of specific patterns in regions inhabited by primitive societies indicate how the processes of cultural change have operated in the instance of these groups, wherein subcultures are relatively few. Analyses of this kind have been made often enough, and in enough different parts of the world, to prove that the mechanisms of change are effective among human societies everywhere. The studies of the Plains Indian sun dance and of bear ceremonialism are of this type. In both instances, we find an over-all regional pattern comparable to that which shapes the subpatterns of a society having a large population, one in which adaptations congenial to the borrowing folk have been made during the process of diffusion from one tribe to another. Whether the entire institution is diffused as a unit, with subsequent local alterations, or whether elements of the total complex are diffused independently, cannot be discovered in researches of this kind. It is reasonable to assume, however, that once the basic pattern had spread over a region, innovations and changes made in one tribe would at least be something to which the others would give consideration.

The variations in the complex of custom which centers about cattle in East Africa afford an instance of how change occurs as tribe after tribe takes over a patterned institution.[24] Cattle, in all this region, are central in the culture. They are symbols of value, not in the subsistence

---

[24] M. J. Herskovits, "The Cattle Complex in East Africa," *American Anthropologist*, XXVIII (1926), 230–72, 361–88, 494–528, 633–64.

economy of the people but in their prestige system. For a man of position not to have cattle is unthinkable, and wealth in terms of other goods receives no social recognition. The importance of cattle is reflected in linguistic patterns, for in these tribes the concept "cow" is sometimes refined until, as among the Nuer, over fifty different terms specify color, or size, or the shape of an animal's horns, or other characteristics.[25] Cattle are essential if one is to be married, since only when they pass from groom to bride's father is a mating recognized. In many tribes the social position of a child depends on where the cattle given for his mother came from, and a woman for whom many animals pass has high status and her children benefit from the fact.

This is the over-all pattern, of which there are endless variants. In some tribes cattle enter the cult of the dead, so that a man's favorite ox is slaughtered at his death, its skin is used to cover his body, its meat to provide the funeral feast. Among some folk the association may be with birth rites, as where the umbilical cord and the afterbirth are buried in the cattle pen, the thong used to tether the animals is tied about the mother's waist, a post from the kraal furnishes the wood for the fire inside the hut, and mother and child are forbidden to go outside until the wood is consumed. In some areas milk, drunk fresh, must not be taken after eating vegetables until a certain time has elapsed; elsewhere milk is soured and eaten as a kind of clabber.

These instances of subpatterns found in restricted parts of the total area could be multiplied indefinitely, while more detailed description would reveal more minute differences in the character and relationship of components in the individual tribes of each subarea. Yet all the tribes of the entire area are in agreement as to the importance of cattle, and this importance finds expression in terms of the over-all pattern which regulates their place in the life of the people. Thus, in space, we find expressed in terms of their end results the changes that have occurred in time as the general pattern was taken over, modified, and fitted to the total culture of each local, tribal group.

It is apparent, therefore, that in approaching the problem of cultural change from the behavioristic, institutional point of view, much insight is to be gained through the study of the variations in custom found to exist between historically related peoples, or within subgroups of a populous society, or through the alternations that can be established as having taken place over a given period of time. The general pat-

[25] E. E. Evans-Pritchard, *The Nuer* (Oxford, 1940).

tern gives direction to change and limits the degree of deviation from accepted custom. But its limits are broad enough so that it does not stand in the way of local or subgroup variations; broad enough so that individual variation is allowed for. It is this that makes it possible to consider a pattern in culture as a consensus of the individual behavior patterns of those who live in accordance with it; a fact that, when the complexity of overlapping patterns within a culture is taken into account, provides an important tool for the understanding of the nature of culture and the processes of cultural change.

It has been claimed, and with some justice, that preoccupation with the outer forms of culture has militated against adequate search for its psychological significance. We know that the ultimate reality of culture is psychological; that only in so far as there are people to carry on the institutions of a culture can that culture exist. In this psychological reality of culture lies the mechanism of cultural stability, the reason why human beings find greatest ease living their lives under a known, a predictable routine. But by the same token, this is also the mechanism of cultural change, since in a given society differing aptitudes, incentives, interests, and abilities of individual members operate within the limits set by the matrix of their culture to make for continuous revisions and refinements in existing custom.

The psychological approach to cultural change, moreover, gives us clues toward understanding the baffling problems of acceptance and rejection of innovation, and of differential rates of change. The phenomenon of innovation has been touched upon in preceding sections, where it was pointed out that new elements made available to a body of custom are accepted only if they are congenial to preëxisting patterns. Differential rates of change are implied in analyses of the distribution of elements in a given pattern over an area of the primitive world, or in our own culture in such a complex as that studied by Richardson and Kroeber, of the changes that actually took place over a fixed period of time. But such studies tell us only what happened, not why they had happened. If we wish to understand the reasons for change, if we seek to decipher the "why" in culture, we must probe for these in the psychology of change.

We may begin our analysis with the well-recognized principle that in any culture much more will be taken for granted than is given purposeful thought or articulate expression. The learning process, which leads to the mastery of custom, is so thorough, so pervasive, that the members of a society can be thought of as reacting automatically to their culture rather than reflecting upon it. Born into a society where an accepted way of life prevails, an individual performing the round of everyday behavior may be likened to the trained musician who does not need to pause and give thought to the playing of each successive note in the score before him.

One illustration of how culture is, so to speak, taken for granted is to be had in the reasons men and women assign for their behavior when queried about some particular act. Their answers, when they can be controlled, are rarely found to be objectively correct. Just as the answers to questions concerning language are usually given in terms of folk etymology, so, in the field of custom, the answers given are usually what may be termed "folk-rationalizations." Man, indeed, may well be characterized as a rationalizing animal, rather than a rational one. Why do we not convey food to the mouth with a knife? Because, the answer runs, we might cut ourselves—an answer that quite ignores the fact that our table knives are not sharp, and that in cultures where sharp knives are used for the purpose, the dexterity of experience takes care of possible injury. Of a similar nature is the explanation of the taboo on the eating of pork by Arabs and Jews, that the danger of trichinosis was sensed and, in consequence, the tradition of avoidance established. A totemistic explanation of the origin of the custom, which seems historically more reasonable, is not only not offered, but is commonly rejected when its possibility is pointed out.

Not every musician is a virtuoso, nor does he control the full range of orchestral instruments; and in the same manner no one individual controls his culture or is even conscious of its total resources, and no group, as a group, places the same emphases on all facets of the entire body of custom of which its members are the carriers. Thus as we examine different cultures, we perceive that they differ not alone in their outer form, but also in the dominant concerns of their carriers. This factor is of the greatest importance in cultural change. For of the many aspects of culture by which men live it is those which, in a given culture at a given period, hold greatest sway that are the least prone to be taken for granted, that will be most discussed, and that will therefore be farthest removed from unthinking response. Looked at in structural terms, these aspects of culture will exhibit the most variable patterns. Or, as we may say, a people's dominant concern may be thought of as the focus of their culture; that area of activity or belief where the greatest awareness of form exists, the most discussion of values is heard, the widest difference in structure is to be discerned.

Let us now examine in somewhat greater detail this point of focus in culture. Just because among all groups certain aspects of life are emphasized and these are more discussed, alternate possibilities, such as Linton [26] describes, are the more readily granted a hearing. This is to be contrasted with the case of elements in culture taken for granted, for here the suggestion of change, even of relatively slight change, falls on unprepared ground and reactions are commonly negative. It thus appears that a psychological basis for differential rates of change accounts for the wider acceptance of innovations in one aspect of a culture than in others.

This may be illustrated by an example drawn from the cultures of West Africa and their New World derivatives. West African societies are among the most populous in the nonliterate world. Their technology is advanced, their economic and political systems sophisticated; their social structures are complex, and their art and folklore and music have had the attention of many students. The focus of these cultures, however, rests in the religious life of the people. Here is lodged the greatest stimulus to thought and creative expression, the greatest proliferation of institutional forms.

The student conducting field research in these cultures is made immediately aware of this psychological emphasis on supernatural validating agencies. Again and again, it is the supernatural aspects of a given body of data that are crucial to understanding. The importance of the nonsecular sanctions for one engaged in trade, or the need to propitiate the spirits of the earth before agricultural operations can commence, or the duty of the ironworker to care for the sensibilities of the god of iron appears early in any discussion of these aspects of everyday secular life. The controls of social structure lie in the ancestral cult; and, since this cult also functioned in the life of the royal family, it was a preponderant influence in the political order. Much of the woodcarving and a large proportion of the songs of the people are of a religious character. The most important body of folk literature treats of the supernatural beings who rule the universe and their adventures in the world of men.

The focal character of this aspect of culture becomes even more fixed when their ways of life are discussed with the natives. Economics

[26] R. Linton, *The Study of Man* (New York, 1936).

has a certain hold on them, for the tradition of the importance of wealth is a strong one. But kinship, as a subject for conversation, they find boresome, and the talk soon turns to the ancestors, and from this to the gods and the other forces that rule the universe. Reactions to folk tales are enlightening. Animal stories are for the young; grownups like to recount nonesoteric tales of the adventures of creatures who have certain supernatural endowments, such as hunters who understand magic, or twins, or the monsters, or little folk of the forest. This focal concern with religion is likewise manifest in the New World, even where the life about these people of African descent is that of the thoroughly secular modern city, as in Brazil, or in certain West Indian towns, or in Northern and Southern urban centers of the United States.

The testimony of members of these societies supports the objective data in revealing the function of this focus in cultural change. In West Africa the various deities have been freely borrowed, and tribal provenience of many of the gods worshiped by a people is often ascribed by them to these borrowings. A native explanation of the process may be mentioned. When one tribe conquered another, the superior power of the gods of the conquerors was patent, and it was, therefore, to the advantage of the conquered to appease them. But the conquerors also took over the gods of their foes, for, it was reasoned, a defeated, frustrated god is one especially to be feared, and, furthermore, as indigenous gods they had power over earth and stream and forest. It was for them, too, the part of wisdom to adopt the deities of the conquered enemy, and conquest thus became a mechanism for an interchange of gods on the basis of a concept which, it is obvious, accelerated the process of diffusion of this particular cultural element. The significant point is that one does not hear of conscious diffusion of this kind in fields which lie outside the cultural focus.

This phenomenon of focus can be seen to have operated as a factor of importance in making for the adjustment of the New World descendants of Africans. Because recognition of the value of taking over the gods of other folk inhered in the patterned reactions to situations of the type encountered by Africans in the New World, the adaptations, institutional and psychological, without which survival would have been impossible were achieved. But the changes made in aboriginal African custom did not come about only in deference to the superior power of the European's deity. Where Africans had contact with Indians, as in Brazil and Guiana, and the African cults survived in recognizable form, full attention was given the autochthonous spirits of the land who ruled the new environment. This is the derivation of the Caboclo cult in Brazil, or of the "Indian spirit" (*Ingi winti*) of the Dutch Guiana Negroes, or the Creole spirits in Haiti.

Where the Africans were converted, the operation of the focal areas of tradition was particularly manifest. In Catholic countries they developed the syncretisms between African gods and Catholic saints found in Cuba, Haiti, Brazil, and Louisiana; or they retained certain ritual forms, such as possession and baptism and curing in connection with worship, where retention of the aboriginal deities was not possible. Change was relatively simple because tradition ruled that adaptations in supernatural worship were not to be resisted, and hence they fitted their religion to the new setting. And it is worth emphasizing that, in the situations of deprivation and demoralization experienced today as a result of living the life of an underprivileged group, the Negro continues to make an adjustment in his religion that stands in notable contrast to the lack of adjustment found in his social institutions.

In modern American life, the same mechanism functions in another field. There is little doubt that the cultural focus of our modern society lies in the field of technology. It is interesting to compare our readiness to accept technological changes with our resistance to changes in economic theory (to take a field closely related to the cultural focus), or in religion, or the family. It is said that language is an index to culture, and the semantics of our use of the word "inventor" reflects the orientation of our culture. It has been necessary in an earlier page to phrase a definition which differed from the common one, wherein an inventor is characterized as one who effects a reorientation in the field of material culture alone. That the inventor of intangibles is rather termed a revolutionist gives further insight, particularly when the invidious connotation attached to the latter term is considered.

The fact of the existence of manifest focal orientations has given plausibility to various kinds of typological approaches to the study of culture, whether couched in terms of the genius of a culture, or its soul, or through all-inclusive definitions of a spiritual or moral character derived from these overemphasized focal aspects of culture. The concept of cultural focus is, however, not of this static nature. It is an element making for the dynamic drives which bring about greater ease in change, and consequently greater diversity of manifestation in some aspects of a culture than in others.

Essentially, the concept is an historical one, for a focus is no less subject to realignment over the years than any other aspect of human experience. How these focal orientations shift and how the cultural focus changes—as in the movement of the past five hundred years of our culture from a focus on the other world reflected in the belief in supernatural forces, to one on technology wherein miracles are performed by science—we do not as yet know. Explanation in terms of the cumulative effect of small changes over the years—of a kind of cultural "drift" somewhat like the linguistic "drift" demonstrated by Sapir [27]—may give us the answer we seek. The fact of differing dominant concerns in different cultures is apparent to any firsthand student of society, and implicit in most ethnographic reports which reflect in their emphasis the emphases of the cultures they describe. But it is again to be stressed that the phenomenon of focus, as reflected in the relatively large number of variants in the institutions which lie in the field of principal orientation of a people, points a significant mechanism operative in inducing and encouraging, but also in regulating, cultural change.

One of the principal aims of the study of cultural dynamics is the prediction of cultural change. At the present time we are far from achieving this end. Certain very general principles, it is true, have been formulated. One such is the self-evident principle that peoples in contact will borrow the customs of each other. Another principle is that cultures found closer together will, in overwhelming proportion, have more in common than those removed from each other. Even in such a simple formulation as the latter, however, reservations must be made, since in this connection nearness is an historical as well as a spatial concept. Thus, the culture of modern Australia is much like that of England, which is geographically distant from it but close historically; in contrast, it has little in common with that of the aboriginal inhabitants who are geographically near at hand.

The problem becomes much more complicated when changes in particular forms of culture are examined. Not so long ago we accounted it almost a truism that material culture changes more readily than nonmaterial; that under diffusion things are taken over with less

[27] E. Sapir, *Language, an Introduction to the Study of Speech* (New York, 1921).

resistance than are ideas. Yet the findings of recent investigation, often pointed toward other problems, raise serious doubts as to the validity of such an hypothesis. How, if this were true, could the Indians of southwestern United States, of Mexico, and of Central America have been as hospitable as they were to Catholicism and as resistant to the material culture of the Europeans who exposed them to this aspect of their culture as well as to their religion? A similar phenomenon is found in Africa, where the pagans have accepted Mohammedanism but have retained intact other aspects of their indigenous culture. Elements of compulsion, of prestige, of adjustment to a stable natural environment undoubtedly enter; and they are not too difficult to isolate. But to know, when dealing with a new situation, what the selective adaptation of the cultures in contact will be is quite another matter—one that is increased in difficulty if to the problem of change induced by external stimulus is added that of change from within.

There are several factors that challenge the student who would generalize concerning the kinds of change that occur in culture, or would predict the future course of a given culture. Foremost among these is the factor of cultural accident. The word accident as used here does not in any sense denote happenings outside the line of causation. It is used, somewhat after the matter of Goldenweiser,[28] to signify the unexpected in culture; an event which, in its historical and cultural context, could not have been foreseen. It is, in short, employed to explain—if explain is the word for it—those chains of events which result when some happening from outside a culture impinges on that culture. An illustration, arresting despite its obviousness, will make the point. The wisest Japanese who lived two centuries ago could not have predicted the history of his country after the visit of Commodore Perry. A student of world history, it is true, might have sensed that sooner or later an expanding western culture would reach Japan, but to have explained the resulting sequence of events would have been no more than a guess.

Another factor is the individual, whose role in cultural change is likewise obscure—especially when we attempt to ascertain the influence an individual may exert on his group in particular situations. A traveler brings an idea, a tool, a custom from a visit to a foreign people. Such may be his personality, his prestige, his power, that the innovation will be accepted. But it is equally possible that, for all his

---

[28] A. A. Goldenweiser, *History, Psychology and Culture*, pp. 5–32.

position, what he introduces will fail to be taken over; while a humbler voyager will come home with a usage from outside the group that gains a favorable reception. Schapera [29] tells of the role of the Kgatla chief in the conversion of his people to Christianity, and this can be paralleled in the history of the spread of Christianity in Europe. Yet other rulers have been themselves converted, as in the kingdom of Congo, and the people have retained the beliefs of their forefathers. The same uncertainty is true in this instance of the individual who, through discovery or invention, introduces a new element to his culture. Even in our own society, with its pecuniary organization attuned to the importance of predicting success for a novelty, the results are negligible—as any book or music publisher can attest.

The situations which make for differing rates of change also constitute a factor of no small moment. Opportunities for new developments are enlarged where populations are dense and contacts with the outside world numerous. Yet what, for example, does the element of writing contribute to the equation? It is perhaps true that nonliterate societies know less change over a given period than literate ones. But primitive groups are also smaller and live in a greater isolation than those having writing. Nor can one speak of whole cultures in discussing the problem. There are not a few groups in literate societies, composed of individuals themselves literate, whose resistance to change is quite comparable to that found in primitive societies, as for example, the persistence of certain traditional forms of behavior among European nobility.

Despite these difficulties, the need to press toward an understanding of the processes of cultural change is at the present time of particular urgency. The question can advantageously be reëxamined in the light of concepts currently held by students of culture, while from a wider point of view, it is imperative that the deepest probing be brought to bear on it because consciousness of changing conditions is abroad in the world as perhaps never before in the experience of mankind. What occasions change and what discourages it; the scope of change, whether extensive or minute, and its rate; selectivity in the acceptance of changes in prospect—these are all matters to which must be brought the finest perceptions of the range of cultures and the fullest historical study if situations which many regard as already beyond control are to be shaped to the well-being of mankind.

[29] I. Schapera, "Cultural Changes in Tribal Life," in *The Bantu-Speaking Tribes of South Africa* (London, 1937), pp. 368–69.

Sociopsychological Aspects of Acculturation   By A. IRVING HALLOWELL

ONE OF the most impressive events in the recent history of mankind has been the global expansion of European peoples. The Greek and Roman expansion in the ancient Mediterranean world, the migration of the Arabs across North Africa and into the Iberian Peninsula, the Mohammedan expansion into Northern India, are hardly to be compared with it. For our time the subsequent economic, political, and military repercussions of this movement of European peoples and the influence of their culture have created the modern world as we know it and the world crisis in which we live.

Among other things, this invasion, conquest, and colonization of various parts of the world by Europeans stimulated an interest in the aboriginal peoples who were discovered in Africa, Asia, Australia, the islands of the Pacific and the New World. Collections were made of native manufacturers, very strange at the time to European eyes, and ultimately the systematic study of the mode of life of these peoples was begun. Before the end of the nineteenth century cultural anthropology had been born.

At first, anthropologists were primarily interested in speculating upon possible stages of cultural evolution. They became engaged in salvaging all possible information about the life that aboriginal peoples had lived prior to the influence of European culture. There was also a tendency to identify nonliterate peoples with the different stages through which it was believed mankind as a whole had passed. The fact that various aboriginal peoples had been undergoing cultural changes and readaptation in mode of life ever since Europeans had come in contact with them aroused scarcely a casual interest. Even after the pseudo-historical theories of unilinear cultural evolution were given up, native peoples with a "living" or "functioning" culture were chosen for study in preference to those having a "broken down" or "disorganized" culture. When the latter were investigated at all it was with the intention of "reconstructing" the aboriginal culture of the past from the memories of individuals, rather than of obtaining information about the conditions which had promoted changes, the aspects of the native culture that had changed, the processes by which these changes had come about, or the results.

In recent years, however, the study of the influence of the culture of one people upon that of another has emerged as one of the major interests of anthropologists. There is no doubt that, to some extent, this interest has been stimulated by the inescapable magnitude of the problems created by racial and cultural contacts in the modern world and, in particular, by the practical administrative problems faced by all governments which now have to deal with aboriginal peoples who have come within the domain of their political control. But the scientific stimulus to the study of the contacts between peoples with different modes of life lies in the contribution it can make to our understanding of the dynamics of human behavior and adaptation. The culture of a human population cannot change unless the people themselves show changes in their habits, attitudes, motivations and, ultimately, their personality organization. This means that individuals have undergone a process of readjustment. Hence, anthropologists are making careful inquiry into the concrete events, specific circumstances and processes involved in cases where cultural changes are resulting from the interaction of peoples with different cultural backgrounds, because the more that is known about the actual dynamics of human adaptation and readaptation under observed conditions, the sounder will be the foundations for a study of the general principles involved in these processes.

One is reminded here of the doctrine of uniformitarianism enunciated by Lyell when he wrote his *Principles of Geology* over a century ago. Whereas earlier geologists had sometimes invoked specific explanations (for example, catastrophes) for certain past events, Lyell emphasized the fact that the same processes must be assumed to be operating in the past as at present. By carefully observing the effects of contemporary processes we will be in a better position, he said, to understand the events of past epochs. This principle has become well established in the natural sciences and is just as applicable in the scientific study of man.

There is no reason to assume, for instance, that the societies of nonliterate peoples whether past or present are intrinsically more static or conservative than the literate, historic, or so-called "advanced" peoples. Neither can we assume the operation of an automatic law of progressive unilinear stages in human adaptation or that there were some mysterious or "X" factors at work in the past. The scientific problem consists in the discovery of the actual factors that create stability in human culture as well as the necessary and sufficient conditions under which modifications in the mode of life of a people take place.

So far as the distant past is concerned, it is obvious that we can never know very much about the actual processes and conditions of adaptation and readaptation that took place. We do know that there was a revolutionary change in man's subsistence economy, in more than one area, when a transition was made from a food-gathering to a food-producing economy. But the details escape us; we are only acquainted with the results produced. Archeologists have also supplied us with a great deal of information about the tools, weapons, utensils and other objects that man used in the past and the changes that occurred in the forms of these. And while we assume that some of these changes must have been the results of indigenous inventions and discoveries in particular societies we can know nothing about the concrete events that led up to them. We do not even know whether such inventions and discoveries resulted from a conscious attempt to solve certain practical problems, or how far they were the result of fumbling trial and error methods or the accumulative trend of small changes. Hence, it is practically impossible to deal with the dynamics of inventions and discoveries in early human societies except in a relatively few instances. We have to be satisfied with a knowledge of the end-products. We have some notion of *what* occurred but not *how* it occurred.

Some kind of contact of different peoples can also be considered to be as old in human history as differentiated modes of adaptation themselves. While it is true that, after man had reached his maximum expansion, peoples in certain parts of the world never knew of each other's existence, to say nothing of coming into contact with each other, yet it would be difficult to demonstrate a case in which any particular people has been completely isolated from all other peoples throughout its entire history. All our present knowledge of human migrations and racial mixture precludes this. Besides, how many culture traits of any human society can be demonstrated to be locally invented and completely unconnected with those of any other people whatsoever? Indeed, the resemblances between cultural items of peoples widely separated in space, and sometimes in time, has presented a major problem to the anthropologist. In the history of anthropology the interpretation of such data has resolved itself again and again into weighing the possibility of local or independent origin and development against the possibility of the diffusion or spread of such traits or complexes from one people to another.

Studies of cultural diffusion usually have begun, however, with an inventory of the geographical distribution of particular traits or assemblages of them, rather than with a study of the contact of specific peoples in a concrete historical setting. While the possible origin and presumed spread of such cultural items may be considered an historical question in the broadcast sense of the term, it is history devoid of real knowledge of any specific events, conditions, or personalities. When considered at all, the actual processes that mediated diffusion and the conditions of cultural change have to be inferred. The consequence has been that in such studies culture traits and complexes often undergo a kind of reification, in so far as they are treated as if they had a life of their own, quite unconnected with human beings of flesh and blood. The most extreme example is typified by members of the German "historical" school. They have abstracted assemblages of culture traits which are asserted to be highly integrated and of great stability. These "culture circles" are then manipulated in time and space as reified units which meet, blend, or overlie each other so that certain new combinations are produced. There is no attempt to deal with the complex details of actual historical events or the processes of interaction that follow contacts between actual human beings.

While American anthropologists have been more cautious, on the whole, the conceptualization of culture as a "superorganic" or "sui generis" level of phenomena does lend itself to unconscious reification in unskilled hands. There are also difficulties encountered when the dynamics of culture are dealt with. For it is hard to see how culture —an abstract summation of the mode of life of a people—can exert an influence except as it is a definable constituent of the activities of human individuals in interaction with each other. In the last analysis it is individuals who respond to and influence one another. Culture as Bidney [1] has pointed out "is not an efficient cause and does not develop

[1] David Bidney, "On the Concept of Culture and Some Cultural Fallacies," *American Anthropologist*, XLVI (1944), 30–44.

itself, hence it is not capable of interacting with any other entity." To argue otherwise leads to what he calls the "culturalistic fallacy" "which is based on the assumption that culture is a force that may make and develop itself and that individuals are but its passive vehicles or instruments."

Actually, human beings always are the active agents to be considered. Considered biologically, and from a long range point of view, man derives his unique significance among all other living creatures as the creator of culture, not as a mere creature of it. Man is only a creature of culture in so far as he learns and uses the traditional cultural instrumentalities of his society. But even so he is far from a passive instrument since he uses cultural means for attaining satisfying individual ends. What is more important, readaptation is always possible if some new cultural means can be invented or new ways of doing things learned from people with a different cultural heritage.

Although anthropologists often speak of the "movements" of culture or the "meeting" of cultural traits or complexes, this manner of speaking must be understood as an economical mode of abstract speech. In a literal sense cultures never have met nor will ever meet. What is meant is that peoples meet and that, as a result of the processes of social interaction, acculturation [2]—modifications in the mode of life of one or both peoples—may take place. Individuals are the dynamic centers of this process of interaction. If perceptible differences in the mode of life of either people result it means that new ways of acting, thinking, and feeling have been learned by individuals.

All this implies that readaptation has taken place because some rewarding experience or new satisfaction was gained. For learning never takes place without some drive or motivation. In such a process individuals hardly can be viewed as passive carriers of culture; they appear rather as striving organisms engaged in adopting new means to achieve their ends. This is typical of human behavior at large. For human adaptation is adaptation in terms of unique means, and the readaptation that anthropologists have come to characterize as acculturation is an illustration of the flexibility of man's characteristic tools of adaptation.

Organisms are said by the biologist to be adapted to their environ-

---

[2] For a formal definition of acculturation and the history of this term, see Melville J. Herskovits, *Acculturation* (New York, 1938), and Ralph Linton, ed., *Acculturation in Seven American Indian Tribes* (New York, 1940), particularly Chap. VIII.

ment when they exhibit a structure and behave in a manner that enables them to survive in a healthy state and propagate their kind. Now one of the peculiarities of our species, as compared with other animals, is that we are not equipped with phylogenetically fixed mechanisms for adaptation. The characteristic mode of human adaptation was achieved through instrumentalities that depended on man's capacities for invention, learning, and the manipulation of symbols. When an anthropologist gives an account of the mode of life of a people in terms of cultural forms and patterns he is, at the same time, describing the tested and traditionally established means they employ in solving the fundamental problems of human living. In other words, the unique instrument of human adaptation is what the anthropologist calls culture, when viewed in its basic functional aspects. Human adaptation is adaptation in cultural terms. The life of human beings both in relation to each other and to their geographic environment is always mediated and organized in terms of cultural instrumentalities of various orders. For social and economic institutions, ideas, values and beliefs are tools of human adaptation quite as much as material devices. And John Dewey has called speech "the tool of tools."

By capitalizing on his capacity for invention and learning, by making the experience of the individual available to other individuals and the experience of others available to him, man created a new world, a human world, one that depended upon the character and efficiency of the cultural instrumentalities that man himself invented and learned to use. It was a world that functioned and possessed meaning in terms of cultural achievement. And because achievements could be added to, discarded or modified, as circumstances demanded, man found himself in the possession of an adaptive instrument of remarkable flexibility. On the one hand, it was possible to reap the security afforded by tested instruments of living by incorporating them into a mode of life that was transferable from one generation to another; while, on the other hand, should circumstances demand it, readjustment was always possible. As compared with adaptation dependent upon germinal changes where stability is overweighted and relatively rapid readaptation impossible, cultural adaptation has proved of high survival value in the human species.

In fact, adaptation mediated in cultural terms permitted so much latitude that, in time, man created many quite different worlds for himself. All of them had adaptive value under given conditions. Each of them was an experiment in social living, ecological adjustment, and psychological orientation, that is, a culture. The many and varied cultures of the nonliterate peoples of the world described by anthropologists may be considered arresting samples of the immense range in the cultural means employed by members of a single organic species in achieving adaptation. We can only conclude that it is possible for many widely different cultural forms to serve basic adaptive ends. The significance of acculturation as a process of readaptation lies in this fact.

The human individual, however, because of the spatial and temporal accident of birth is always faced with the necessity of learning to live his life in terms of the traditional cultural forms of his society, despite the fact that he is potentially capable of social and ecological adjustment in terms of any system of cultural instrumentalities. So far as our empirical data go, some set of cultural forms is always prior to the individual. Through a process of learning or socialization (motivated by biologically rooted as well as acquired drives which are reinforced by a system of rewards and punishments), specific beliefs, attitudes, and values are acquired, technological processes are mastered, roles are learned, and a personality structure is built up that prepares the individual for meeting the problems of life in the provincial terms characteristic of his society. The basic function of the socialization process, therefore, is to prepare individuals for participation in a specific behavioral world.

Such a process is also one of the fundamental stabilizing agencies in all human societies, since it tends to produce the regularities in patterns of behavior that lend themselves to abstract summarization as culture. But socialization does not produce robots. The persistence of cultural forms is only a function of the expected or predictable behavior of individuals in social interaction. Idiosyncratic or deviant behavior occurs in all societies. It may or may not become accumulative and take a socially significant trend. Imaginative and fantasy processes are also a constant factor in the psychic life of individuals so that new solutions to old problems may be found, or a novel situation may be met in a novel way. In short, readjustment on the part of individuals may influence the thinking, feeling, or behavior of other individuals and perhaps lead to readaptation in the mode of life of the group.

In other words, the analysis of cultural changes always leads us from our initial descriptive abstractions of stabilized cultural forms, through a series of processes involving conditions that have led to readjustments on the part of individuals, and then back again to the socially discernible effects of such readaptation which can once more be described as new or modified cultural forms. The problem of cultural change hinges, therefore, on the conditions and processes that bring about socially significant readjustments of individual behavior.

One of the generic conditions of culture change lies in the fact that the specific cultural equipment of any single society does not provide its members with the means of adjusting themselves to all possible circumstances or for the solution of every possible problem that may arise. Every mode of cultural adaptation has its own peculiar limitations. Just as organic adaptation implies structured types of responses that have phylogenetic roots, so cultural adaptation implies structured responses with ontogenetic roots in the training and experience of individuals. This is the price that must be paid for any kind of stabilized form of adaptation, whether organic or cultural. Otherwise, new and untried means would have to be improvised by the individual to meet each situation. Difficulties may arise, however, when conditions occur which expose the inadequacy of traditional means. The bow and arrow may be a highly adaptive device in the food quest of a given people under certain conditions but utterly inadequate as a weapon against another people in possession of firearms.

We in Western civilization and people in nonliterate cultures alike must accept the intrinsic limitations of techniques or institutions until new ones can be invented. But we are aware of this fact. In the technological sphere we even encourage the invention of novel mechanical devices. We are less conscious of the instrumental nature of our social and economic institutions and their limitations. In times of crisis we, too, tend to solve our problems in traditional ways instead of devising novel means. Consider, for instance, the situation which arose in the depression when the market was glutted with certain commodities which it was unprofitable to sell. In Western society the market constitutes our established social mechanism for the distribution of goods. Commodities, that is, are produced for sale at a certain price. Consequently, when they cannot be sold profitably there is no way to distribute them to consumers. Thus some unsalable commodities were destroyed in the depression despite the fact that there were consumers who could have used them. In other societies where goods are not produced for sale in a market but are distributed in other ways, the destruction of consumable goods when potential consumers exist would be unthinkable.

To human beings whose whole behavioral world has been built up in culturally provincial terms, however, it only becomes apparent under special circumstances that their native language, social and economic institutions, their system of beliefs, or any other aspect of their traditional mode of life have any intrinsic limitations. This is because different cultural forms share basic instrumental functions whatever their specific limitations may be. The Iroquois and English languages may be considered functionally equivalent as means of communication despite their differences as linguistic structures. Similarly, the polygynous family as well as the monogamous family may serve basic familial functions. If individuals never have to adjust to situations they are not fully prepared to meet in terms of their own traditional beliefs and institutions, if they never feel frustrated in their conventional roles, if there is no intellectual awareness of any other than their own scheme of values or technological equipment, if there is never any external threat to the continuance of established cultural forms, or any internal conflicts that suggest modifications in them, conditions that might serve as a fulcrum for cultural changes would seemingly be reduced to a minimum. Consequently, it is true, as has often been pointed out, that relatively isolated or marginal societies incline to conservatism and stability in their cultural forms. So long as cultural change is dependent upon some impetus from within, such changes may be relatively insignificant and the rate of change extremely slow. The problem in such cases is to define the conditions and to seek out the possible motivations which impel individuals to develop modifications of their institutions without any stimulus from outside their own group.

Our concern here, however, is with the antithetical case. How do changes result from the contact of peoples with different modes of life? The problem of central scientific importance here is not the *fact* of culture borrowing or the reality of the process of culture diffusion—there are hundreds of thousands of historically verifiable facts that could be marshaled—the problem is to understand the conditions and processes involved in borrowing and the effects upon the mode of life of the people concerned.

When peoples with different modes of life come into contact, this event does not necessarily precipitate any radical modifications in the culture of either group, even though they may remain in continuous social interaction with each other. That is, such contacts are a necessary but not a sufficient condition of acculturation. One should expect to find some instances, therefore, wherein, instead of leading to radical changes in the cultural mode of adaptation, social interaction between groups with different cultural systems is limited to securing the benefits of specialized goods or services which members of either group can offer.

Such a situation is concretely exemplified in the relationship that existed among four tribal groups, neighbors for years, in the Nilgiri Hills (India). Culturally and linguistically distinct, they "lived in economic and social symbiosis," says Mandelbaum.[3] The economic life of the Toda was centered on their sacred buffalo, the Badaga were agriculturalists; the Kota smiths; while the Kurumba were food gatherers of the jungle and noted for their sorcerers. The latter were often called in by the Kota and Badaga. But on such occasions the transactions usually took place outside the village limits and the women and children always disappeared immediately into their houses. Kota musicians, on the other hand, were called upon to serve in all major Toda ceremonies, but were never allowed near the dairies for fear of pollution. The Badaga wore turbans, the Kota did not. Once when some Kotas took to wearing the prized headdress they were ambushed by Badagas and beaten up. The Kotas had borrowed a prestige symbol and the Badagas resented it.

"Although contact was frequent," says Mandelbaum," social intercourse was confined to a fixed number of narrowly defined activities. Any intimate contact, of a kind which would allow members of one group to mingle freely with another, was stringently tabooed." Consequently, these people retained their cultural uniqueness until recent years when Hindu and European influences have intruded themselves with varied results.

Thus contact situations may sometimes produce negative responses so far as any fundamental readaptation is concerned. For why, indeed, should any people whose own way of life is satisfactory to them learn new skills or remodel their institutions if they can supplement the

[3] David G. Mandelbaum, "Cultural Changes among the Nilgiri Tribes," *American Anthropologist*, XLIII (1941), 19–26.

services that are lacking in their own society by hiring specialists from neighboring groups?

In principle, such a relationship may become the basis of mutual benefits, the social interaction of the two peoples much less channelized and more positively friendly than that of the Indian groups mentioned, with the result that only a minimum of acculturation occurs. This is essentially the situation pictured by Lindgren in her characterization of the relations that have persisted for almost a century between Russian Cossacks and Reindeer Tungus in northwestern Manchuria as "culture contact without conflict." [4] Markets, encounters in the woods, and sometimes even protracted residence of members of one group in the communities of the other group are the main channels of social interaction. There is practically no intermarriage, it may be added. Regular trade relations are the most active mode of contact mentioned and "when these brief meetings are over," she says, "the routine of their daily life proceeds quite independently." While the Cossacks enjoy a higher degree of literacy than the Tungus "all Tungus men, the older boys, and most of the women understand Russian, often expressing themselves fluently in that language, which is used exclusively in trade." Although nominally Christian, shamans play an important role in Tungus society and the Cossacks, while they may feign skepticism, often give genuine credence to these shaman prophecies.

Lingren stresses the friendly nature of the contacts between the two groups, the reciprocal benefits of trade, and the interchange of a few cultural traits. By and large any demand for readaptation in mode of life is absent and what readjustment has taken place is on a purely voluntary basis. Although Lingren presents her data as an uncommon situation, Redfield [5] points out certain analogies with "the situation that prevails between the lower-class agricultural *ladinos* of the Lake Atitlan region of the midwestern highlands of Guatemala and the Indians of that region," although the cultural differences between these latter groups is less marked. The common factors in both situations which seem to be productive of "benign ethnic relations" says Redfield are:

[4] Ethel J. Lindgren, "An Example of Culture Contact without Conflict; the Reindeer Tungus and Russian Cossacks of Northwest Manchuria," *American Anthropologist*, XL (1938), 305–621.
[5] Robert Redfield, "Culture Contact without Conflict," *American Anthropologist*, XLI (1939), 514–17.

The absence of recent attempts by one group to dominate the other; the fact that there is little or no economic competition along ethnic lines; the circumstance that natural resources are plentiful; the individualistic character of the economy and the social organization; and the fact that both groups carry on some of the same prevailing means of livelihood. It is also no doubt important that neither Cossack nor Spaniard brought into the area of the new contacts any very strong tradition of prejudice against people of other skin color or physical type.

Moreover, in Guatemala there is a "prevailing cultural pluralism" which, "combined with the widespread commercialism, tends to free differences in custom from depreciative sentiments and to make them clear of emotional attachments." Guatemalan communities, Tax points out,[6] may be viewed as "separate local societies, and it may be said that as such they merely recognize in each other groups which appropriately have different cultures."

A plant or technique or custom appears to be considered as belonging to a particular community, its people and its soil. Thus, there is a fairly strong belief in Panajachel that if a crop that grows well in one town is planted in another where it has not been grown, the "spirit" of the plant might shift its locale and the plant consequently prosper in its new habitat and fail in its old. (Hence the Indians are disturbed when Indians of another town begin to cultivate a local crop.)

Viewed in broad sociopsychological terms it can readily be seen that, in the situations just referred to, relatively little acculturation occurs because of the limited incentives on the part of the individuals of the groups in social interaction to learn the ways of their neighbors, for learning is the psychological crux of acculturation. Just as it is the basic process in the original socialization process that prepares individuals for participation in some particular manner of life, it is equally central in the readaptation of individuals to another manner of life.

When peoples with different cultural systems come into contact with one another, an examination of the barriers to learning, on the one hand, and the incentives to learning on the other, afford us direct insight into the dynamics of acculturation, although this angle of approach has not yet been systematically explored. The essential questions are the specific conditions under which individuals of either group gain an opportunity to learn about the ways of the other group, how far such learning is promoted or discouraged, what is learned and the

[6] Sol Tax, "World View and Social Relations in Guatemala," *American Anthropologist*, XLIII (1941), 37–42.

various incentives to learning, the kind of people who have taken the initiative in learning, and the results of the process with respect to the subsequent relations of both groups and their cultural systems.

While it will be unnecessary to go into the technical aspects of the learning process here, contemporary learning theory does provide a fruitful frame of reference in terms of which the sociopsychological aspects of acculturation may be conceptualized and may also be used as a guide for empirical research.[7]

For learning to take place at all there must be adequate motivation. That is to say, primary or secondary drives must be aroused that elicit responses (any activity of the organism—muscular, glandular, verbal, ideational) to certain cues which, in turn, determine when, where, and how we act. Whether or not these responses will be repeated depends on whether the drives that impelled them are "rewarded," that is, whether they are reduced in intensity; in which case the particular responses are said to be reinforced. In other words, "the learner must be driven to make the response and rewarded for having responded in the presence of the cue. This may be expressed in a homely way by saying that in order to learn one must want something, notice something, do something, and get something."[8] If, on the other hand, drives are not rewarded or even are punished, as may happen, some particular response, lacking reinforcement, will be avoided in the future so that learning will not take place.

Hunger, thirst, and sex are primary drives. In human behavior it is the secondary drives that are of major concern. These are acquired drives that depend on the past experience of the individual and are themselves inculcated through social interaction with other individuals in the learning process. Fears and anxieties, desires for prestige, appetites for particular foods are examples of acquired drives. And, since all secondary drives are built up as part of the training an individual receives in order to participate in a society dominated by a particular cultural system, the kinds of responses elicited and the cues responded to, as well as the rewards which serve to reduce the various drives, are all colored by this original adaptation. While a new mode of life may demand the same primary drives and perhaps some of the secondary ones also, acculturation on a major scale implies radically significant

[7] Neal E. Miller and John Dollard, *Social Learning and Imitation* (New Haven, Conn., 1941); Chap. XVI is devoted to "Copying in the Diffusion of Culture."
[8] *Ibid.*, p. 2.

readaptation in an individual's behavior. New responses, new cues, and new drives are all involved. Obviously, the incentives to such readaptation must be well rewarded.

All such processes offer an extremely important field for study. Food habits are a pertinent example. In human beings food habits have been overlaid with so many acquired drives that they are never a simple function of the primary hunger drive. There are definite food preferences in all human groups. This means that appetite is only rewarded by certain kinds of food and not by others. When a strange kind of food is presented to an individual or eaten by him, his reaction may be one of disgust or nausea. Instead of being rewarded, the food drive is punished, thereby prompting rejection on subsequent occasions so that the individual may never learn to eat the new food.

Once I offered an old Indian and his wife some oatmeal with milk on it. They refused it, although I know they were hungry. The Saulteaux Indians that I know do not like milk, but they will eat oatmeal without it. To adapt themselves to milk as a food would require a very strong incentive indeed. On the other hand, the same Indians love strawberry jam, but then they have always been very fond of wild strawberries. They are also very fond of fat, so it is no hardship for them to eat pure lard instead of butter with their bannock, a habit I could not adopt with relish. Another example which illustrates in a more subtle fashion the difficulties presented by readaptation in food habits comes from modern Hawaii.[9] The old Hawaiians preferred cool or even cold foods. It has been very difficult for them to learn to like hot foods, despite a long period of acculturation. One woman, for example, found it impossible to enjoy the cup of "nice hot tea" presented to her by her hostess. It was not the tea that was distasteful but the temperature of the drink. The American father of this same woman was accustomed to eat his meals separately from the other members of his family because he preferred his food hot.

The kind of social learning that is typical of the acculturation process is imitative learning in the technical sense of the term. This is because the behavior that occurs always involves some kind of model as a stimulus. Whether the newly learned responses only approximate the model or whether a close matching is achieved depends upon a number of variables which require technical distinctions that it will be

---

[9] Ernest Beaglehole, *Some Modern Hawaiians* (University of Hawaii Research Publication No. 19), p. 39.

unnecessary to go into here (they can be found in any detailed analysis of concrete situations). Imitation is not necessarily a conscious process, and inexactness in "copying" and its determinants provide some of the most interesting problems for analysis in the acculturation process. Then, too, copying may itself become a drive that is rewarded in some situations. So we are always brought back to the drives that have motivated individuals toward readaptation and how these drives are rewarded.

It may be assumed that, if individuals with one cultural background are brought into social interaction with those of a different cultural heritage and are allowed to respond freely to the differences encountered, they will only imitate food habits, skills, attitudes or other items that, for one reason or another, satisfy their own culturally acquired drives. There is also no demand for exactness of imitation if approximate imitation is rewarding. One old Indian I know used to wear a hat he obtained from the missionary box. It happened to be a woman's hat but he did not know this. Neither did the other Indians. Consequently, his adoption of this headgear was just as rewarding to him as if it had been a man's hat. What was imitated was the wearing of a hat, not a particular style of hat. Thus in this case only part of our pattern of hat-wearing was copied. There was no incentive to great exactness. In fact, there was no one to teach him what the precise pattern among white men was. A contrary case is the one where missionaries have motivated natives to copy European forms of dress instead of letting them choose freely or modify the items of dress congenial to them.

The study of acculturation processes, then, involves not only an examination of drive and reward, but the details of the process of imitative learning in the transfer of habit patterns. In the social interaction of Cossacks and Tungus, for example, it undoubtedly was a rewarding experience for the Tungus to learn Russian for trading purposes. But it would be interesting to know how much Russian they learned and what the peculiarities were of the Russian they spoke. Another interesting aspect of this case is the fact, recorded by Lindgren, that the women as well as the men understood Russian. On the basis of our knowledge of trade relations between other groups where a language is learned without systematic instruction, one might have predicted that the Tungus men but not the women would have become bilingual. The question arises why the learning of a new language was a rewarding experience to Tungus women. One might also ask whether the Russian spoken by them differed at all from that spoken by the men and whether such differences might be linked to diverse motivations. A still broader problem would be an investigation of the conditions that have determined sexual differences in the acquisition of new languages when people meet.

The kind of foodstuffs obtained in trade by the Tungus (flour, tea, salt, sugar) indicate a change in their food habits; the same articles, incidentally, being primary trade commodities among the Indians of Canada today. The demand for them, in both cases, probably lies in the manner in which these foods supplement and enhance the native diet which consists mainly of fish and meat. Like the northern Algonkians, the Tungus obtain firearms, axes, iron pots and frying pans, copper kettles, enamel dishes, forks, knives, needles, thimbles, scissors, and so on, the utilitarian values of which to a people with no metallurgical techniques of their own is obvious. Nevertheless, the fact that the Tungus have learned to use such articles does not mean that they have imitated the complete pattern of their usage found among the Cossacks. Lindgren does not discuss this point, but among the northern Algonkian I have seen thimbles used decoratively and as jingles. Indians have also bought alarm clocks, not as timepieces but just to hear them ring, and one man whom I knew carried a watch, although it was doubtful whether he could tell time. In East Africa safety pins have been worn as hair ornaments.[10]

The fact that imitative learning can take place without exact copying enhances the reward values of trade objects far beyond their obvious utilitarian values. It means that various secondary drives may be satisfied in new ways. In terms of trait analysis it explains the latitude permitted in fitting borrowed items into the culture pattern of the borrowers and the necessity for considering the form, meaning, and function of traits as interrelated but independently variable attributes.[11]

Where there is freedom for imitative learning to take place in the social interaction between two peoples, it is hardly conceivable that acculturation can be in any sense a disruptive process, since the cultural features of one society that are imitated by members of another become functionally connected with established drives or with new ones

[10] Richard C. Thurnwald, *Black and White in East Africa: the Fabric of a New Civilization; a Study in Social Contact and Adaptation of Life in East Africa* (London, 1935), p. 174.
[11] H. G. Barnett, "Culture Processes," *American Anthropologist*, XLII (1940), 21-48.

that are in harmony with the cultural system of the borrowers. Learning a new linguistic medium of communication, learning to prepare and eat new types of food or condiments that have positive nutritional value but are only obtainable in trade, learning to use more efficient types of tools, or supplementing objects of local manufacture with trade objects that reward some drive, are no more disruptive than a new invention or discovery when considered from the standpoint of a cultural system as a whole. In other words, it is possible for acculturation to take place on a modest scale through selective processes of voluntary imitative learning without radical readaptation in the behavior of individuals or a reshaping of the total mode of life of the society in which they function.

In most of our case studies of acculturation, however, the situation is scarcely so simple as this. There are other complex variables that act as determinants. Instead of one group permitting the individuals of another to imitate freely any aspect of their culture, we encounter situations in which there is active discouragement of any such behavior. This may be expressed by some penalty meted out to individuals who attempt to adopt a certain habit or custom, or a similar result may be achieved by setting up barriers to imitative learning. The penalization of the Kota who started wearing the headdress of the Badaga has already been referred to. In sociopsychological terms, their behavior was punished instead of being rewarded. So far as the relations of these peoples of the Nilgiri Hills are concerned, it seems likely that the ubiquitous institution of caste in India may have had something to do with the maintenance of their cultural autonomy. For one of the distinctive features of caste is the nontransferable character of activities or services caste members everywhere perform. This might account for the barriers to acculturation and might explain why, for example, the Todas always hire Kota musicians for their ceremonies.

Another example is the attempt on the part of the Spaniards of the colonial period to prevent some of the Indians from possessing firearms or riding horseback.[12] The Dutch administration of the East Indies offers a large-scale and highly organized attempt to erect barriers against acculturation of the native peoples. Kennedy characterizes it as an anti-acculturation policy. The idea was to discourage acculturation by fostering the persistence of certain native institutions. Native forms of government were kept intact wherever possible, missionary

[12] H. J. Priestly, *The Coming of the White Man, 1492–1848* (New York, 1930), p. 89.

zeal was rigidly controlled, and the communalistic system of landholding was upheld. Kennedy says that the effect of this has been "intact and flourishing native cultures, a just and comprehensible legal system, a basically sound native agricultural economy—and an Indonesia so far behind the times that it is helpless unless protected by some strong, modern, outside power." [13]

Aside from institutionalized attitudes or policies on the part of one group that offer barriers to members of another group who desire to imitate certain aspects of their way of life, there are also intrinsic barriers which may make it impossible for one people to adopt the cultural instrumentalities of another people even if they should desire to do so. While many aboriginal peoples with whom Europeans came into contact almost immediately appreciated the metal implements and utensils of the latter and soon learned to use them, there was no attempt to learn the processes of their manufacture. This was impossible because of the enormous gap between the level of knowledge and technology of these stone-age peoples and that of European peoples. The Japanese, on the other hand, who had previously drawn so heavily on the resources of Chinese culture, were prepared by the middle of the nineteenth century to assimilate and use for their own autonomous ends the technology of Western culture, while rejecting certain other aspects of it.[14] The nonliterate peoples of the world, on the other hand, were merely drawn into the world market of a rapidly expanding capitalism as consumers of commodities which they never aspired to produce themselves.

This brings us to one of the most important, as well as characteristic, features of the process by which the expansion of European peoples came to exert such a profound influence upon the lives of the nonliterate peoples with whom they came into contact. From the very beginning of this movement two classes of European people, traders and missionaries, immediately began to play a promotional role in the contact situation. They made it their special business to persuade aboriginal peoples to adopt new tools, implements, skills, beliefs, and moral attitudes. The traders were essentially salesmen of material objects; the missionaries, salesmen of immaterial values. The presence of these two groups of peoples as agents in promoting the accultura-

[13] Raymond Kennedy, "Acculturation and Administration in Indonesia," *American Anthropologist*, XLV (1943), 185-90.
[14] George Devereux and E. M. Loeb, "Antagonistic Acculturation," *American Sociological Review*, VIII (1943), 133-47.

tion process must, therefore, be considered as one of the differential features of the contact of Europeans with non-Europeans, rather than as typical of acculturation wherever we find it in human history.

The role of the trader has been to offer the natives goods that quickly rewarded already existent primary and secondary drives (although he would not understand these terms) and to foster the acquisition of new secondary drives. It is no concern of his whether the natives accept or reject Christianity or in what ways learning the use of new objects or techniques may affect the traditional pattern of native life. As a practical psychologist he will soon learn the objects that are the most rewarding.

Primitive man [says Reed] was once believed to have so few needs that the only trade-articles he desired at first were those which gratified his love for ostentation. This has never been the case in New Guinea, where tribe after tribe of new, previously unknown peoples have been encountered, from the time of Finsch's explorations [1880–1882 and 1884] down to the present. Always they have first demanded iron tools; only after these most highly desired articles are in their hands will they show interest in beads, face paint, and calico. If one enters the uncontrolled area of the upper Sepik River today he is surrounded by natives who literally howl for iron knives, axes, and fishhooks. In all except the most remote regions, however, the simpler type of European tools and artifacts have almost entirely replaced aboriginal implements.[15]

In the Canadian north the process has gone much further. There is a steady demand for canvas canoes (the designs based, of course, on Indian models) in an area which is the home of the aboriginal birch-bark canoe. The trade canoe, however, will stand much rougher usage, carries a bulkier and heavier load, lasts longer that the birch-bark canoe, and is equipped so that oarlocks may be attached for rowing. The Indian is no sentimentalist; it is not he who bemoans the passing of the more picturesque craft and the extinction in many places of the skills required for its manufacture. Thus the trader has been able to meet an old-established and continuing demand by marketing a variety of canoe that meets contemporay needs better than the aboriginal article. This is good business, and what has proved good business in the contact of nonliterate peoples with Europeans has promoted acculturation. In the north, too, the fur traders have promoted the use of the outboard motor, a distinct labor-saving device so long as gaso-

[15] Stephen W. Reed, "The Making of New Guinea," *Memoirs of the American Philosophical Society*, XVIII (1942), 254.

line is available. Unlike the canoe itself, the outboard motor is far from a necessity in this part of the world. It is also expensive and unless the individual running it knows something about machinery, it may delay rather than aid ease and speed of travel. The traders, however, have been willing to give the Indians some of the necessary instruction, and up until the outbreak of the war the number of sales was multiplying rapidly. A great deal of prestige satisfaction was involved in the possession of a motor: all the best hunters had them. A parallel situation is to be found in South Africa where "the art of iron work, formerly in the hands of special craftsmen, has completely disappeared. Iron goods are now obtained from the traders, while such work as repairs to wagons and plows is done exclusively by European blacksmiths." [16]

Missionaries were faced with a more complicated and difficult task than the traders. The system of beliefs and values they endeavored to "sell" were more intangible instruments of living than the commodities of the trader and, at first, had a less obvious appeal. The existence of gods or other supernatural powers was not unfamiliar to primitive peoples, nor were techniques for obtaining benefits from them. The discovery of certain analogies, not sensed at first by the missionaries, undoubtedly helped to bridge the gap between native beliefs and practices and Christianity. The northern Algonkian soon identified their own Supreme Being with the Christian God, despite the fact that some missionaries resisted this idea. Indians who have spoken to me about this cannot understand why the identification was not an obvious one. Beaglehole, referring to the Hawaiians, remarks that

a religion based on ten tapus was easily understandable by a mind nurtured in a way of life where the multitudinous observances of tapus gave one secular and religious satisfaction and success. The very dogmatism with which Calvinistic Puritanism was preached to the natives was without doubt a point in its favor. The native was used to gods that were all-powerful, and all-dreadful, sometimes benign, sometimes ruthless.[17]

Syncretisms, too, have arisen out of the awareness of analogous attributes of native gods and the saints of the Catholic Church.[18] Verbal techniques (prayers) for influencing supernaturals may become identi-

---

[16] I. Schapera, ed., *Western Civilization and the Natives of South Africa; Studies in Culture Contact* (George Routledge and Sons, Ltd., London, 1934), p. 42. Reprinted by permission of the publisher.
[17] Beaglehole, *Some Modern Hawaiians*, p. 14.
[18] Melville J. Herskovits, "African Gods and Catholic Saints in New World Negro Belief," *American Anthropologist*, XXXIX (1932), 635-43.

fied with verbal magic (spells) since both may be used for similar ends.[19]

Learning new religious beliefs and practices, however, had to be motivated. Man is essentially a pragmatist and a belief in the existence of supernatural beings and powers cannot be dissociated from his drives. The reality of the supernatural realm must meet the test of experience. When conditions arose which seemed to indicate that activities carried out in accordance with the native belief system were unrewarding, an opportunity was presented that the missionary could exploit. That is to say, there was the possibility that the anxieties that had arisen could be reduced by encouraging individuals to learn new articles of faith. Some natives joined one of the Solomon Island missions, says Hogbin, "after a run of extraordinary bad luck. The *akalo* (ancestral spirits), they point out, did not live up to their part of the bargain and they determined in consequence to make no more sacrifices." [20] Eiselen points out that the success of the early missionaries in certain South African tribes probably can be explained by the synchronization of their arrival with "singular events."

Petty intertribal wars, with little bloodshed, had been common enough among the Bantu, but when the missionaries came to this country it was just one great battlefield. The tribes of the Free State and the Transvaal had been reduced to terrible straits by the wars of Tshaka and his emulators and by the ensuing years of famine. Starving remnants of once powerful tribes were wandering aimlessly about the country in constant fear of attack by some band of cannibals, or they were eking out a miserable existence in some mountain refuge. To these harassed people the missionaries came like so many Good Samaritans. Their faith in the ancestral gods had been badly shaken and they were ready to open their ears to the message of love and hope.[21]

On the other hand, "all those tribes which emerged with flying colours from the chaos of the Zulu wars of the early nineteenth century—the Zulus, the Swazi, and the Amandebele of Mapoch—did not in the beginning befriend the missionaries."

There were, of course, other rewards than a reduction in anxiety drives which missionaries could make use of, some of them being

---

[19] H. Ian Hogbin, *Experiments in Civilization: the Effects of European Culture on a Native Community of the Solomon Islands* (London, 1939), p. 156; and also Chap. VIII, "Native Christianity."
[20] *Ibid.*, pp. 181–82.
[21] Schapera, ed., *Western Civilization and the Natives of South Africa*, p. 68. Reprinted by permission of the publishers.

of a definitely material sort. A systematic study of the various methods the missionaries used and the measure of their successes and failures when viewed from the standpoint of learning theory would constitute a valuable study. The local conditions and events that they exploited, the kind of people they attempted to influence, the motives they appealed to, the acquired drives they fostered, the types of reward they emphasized, and the rewards that the natives themselves found in adopting Christianity, would all throw a great deal of important light on the acculturation process.

Although the activities of both traders and missionaries were aimed at introducing new objects, beliefs, or usages, they were in the vanguard of European expansion and, at first, were not in a position to force changes in the lives of the peoples with whom they came into contact. At times their lives were even endangered if the people among whom they lived and worked found their presence uncongenial, so that they were almost compelled to adopt persuasive methods. Their clientele could take or leave the objects or doctrines offered them.

As the expansion of European peoples continued to gain momentum, however, conditions were created that directly or indirectly forced native peoples to make all kinds of cultural readaptations for which they were totally unprepared. This was inevitable since the ultimate aim of European expansion was the colonization and economic exploitation of new regions, and the extension of sovereignty over the aboriginal peoples who lived in them. Furthermore, this expansionist movement was carried on by military conquests or the threat of force; it was prepared to meet and overcome all opposition. In short, it was a movement fraught with conflict and patterns of social interaction that always resulted in the subordination of native groups to the power exercised by the intruders. Whole populations were decimated or displaced in the process; new diseases were carried to regions where they had not existed before and were followed by epidemics of great destructiveness; and well-established ecological adjustments of native peoples were disturbed. Consequently, new problems were created which native peoples had to solve either in terms of their own cultural means or by learning some new mode of adaptation.

The culmination of enforced readaptation was reached with the establishment of more and more local settlements, the dispersal of native people beyond the frontiers occupied by Europeans, or the settlement of them upon reservations and the extension of sovereignty over them by formal means. In this way they were brought within the jurisdiction of various European nations and made subject to their penal sanctions. This resulted in the deliberate suppression in some regions of certain tribal usages (cannibalism, head-hunting, intertribal warfare, sorcery), the passage of new rules and regulations, and in some cases the presence of officials (native or otherwise) appointed by the government. As some natives of the Solomon Islands put it,

You white men give us orders; we no longer give orders to ourselves. . . . The white man has come and tells us we must behave like *his* father. Our own fathers, we must forget them. . . . In the olden days we did this thing, we did that thing. We did not stop and say to ourselves first, "This thing I want to do, is it right?" We always knew. Now we have to say, "This thing I want to do, will the white man tell me it is wrong and punish me?" [22]

The negative effects of the impact of Western culture upon that of the nonliterate peoples has frequently been described. In many cases their mode of life has been so completely transformed that they have become almost completely Europeanized and little of their old manner of life remains. While this result is negative in so far as it involves the disappearance of a once flourishing cultural system, nevertheless it is positive in so far as various peoples have met the challenge of new conditions through the acculturation process. Much less is known, however, of the detailed steps involved. What characteristic rewards reinforced the learning process and led to the adoption of new cultural instrumentalities under conditions of enforced readaptation and the coercive power of a dominant group? This problem is a complex one. It needs charting and systematic exploration before any adequate answer can be given.

But the fact that European encroachment upon the domain of the nonliterate peoples everywhere created such a large variety of anxiety-arousing situations suggests that an examination of the role that anxiety drives of all kinds play as motivating factors in readaptation may be especially valuable. Of all acquired drives those keyed to what is probably a primary drive toward avoidance of pain or the threat of pain are among the strongest motivating forces in human behavior. This is the reason anxiety drives are important in the socialization process as well as in the operation of many social sanctions. Through a conditioning process and personal experience, the human being learns what is physically and psychically painful to him, and which events

[22] Hogbin, *Experiments in Civilization*, pp. 153–54.

may bring threatening or punishing effects—sickness and death, for example, may be interpreted as punishments, mediated by supernatural beings or other persons, for wrong conduct. Thus certain anxieties may be inculcated in individuals in order to motivate them in the performance of patterns of behavior that are socially approved. In stabilized societies the range of socially acquired anxiety drives is limited; they are functionally important in the maintenance of the social order. There are characteristic dangers and threatening situations in the behavioral world of the individual—there is pain and trouble that he has to face—but traditional instrumentalities are provided for dealing with them. The individual has been taught how to get relief from the expected anxieties which may arise. In terms of learning theory this relief is rewarding. It helps provide the individual with a basic sense of security. If conditions arise, therefore, which threaten a people through death or disease, which compel them to seek new homes, which menace their livelihood or force them into new economic tasks, which compel them to give up old, traditional usages and ultimately threatens their whole manner of life, it is obvious that many new anxiety drives will arise that cannot be rewarded in their own cultural ways.

But anxiety drives of all kinds are very strong motives to action; they demand relief. How have the nonliterate peoples acted under such pressures, and how has their behavior affected the acculturation process? Only a few examples can be given here. The realistic way to meet any danger is to combat it as best one can. So the hostile reactions provoked by Europeans need no documentation. The fact that whole populations were in some cases soon wiped out (Haiti, Tasmania) is evidence of the reality of the dangers faced and is justification for the anxieties that must have been aroused. On the other hand, native peoples were given the strongest kind of incentives to acquire and learn to use firearms as quickly as possible in order to be able to defend themselves. This can be interpreted as rewarding their anxiety drives. In the United States some Indian tribes who became excellent fighters successfully resisted the further encroachment of the whites for a long period. But it should also be noted that in certain areas such drives must have been heightened rather than relieved by local governments, as, for instance, when the English High Commissioner for the Western Pacific forbade British subjects to supply guns to the natives under his control.[23] Where in the same area (Melanesia) guns were secured by some native peoples and not by others, intertribal tensions were greatly increased, because the former could more easily rout their enemies. How acute such a situation could become is vividly illustrated by a casual remark of Keesing's that "even up to a few years ago, for a native to be without a gun in some parts of Melanesia meant certain death."[24] It is easily understandable why in New Guinea "two or three years work [at indentured labor] was not considered too high a price to pay for a weapon which would bring not only prestige to its possessor, but also great advantages to the clan or village in native warfare."[25]

Another source of anxiety created by European expansion was the spread of such diseases as smallpox, scarlet fever, measles, and diphtheria, familiar enough to Europeans but unknown to the peoples of North America or the South Seas. There were no native remedies for these diseases, which frequently took a more virulent form in populations that had built up no resistance to them. Since there was no way for these people to learn to apply the medical techniques of Western culture, their anxieties could not be alleviated through acculturative means. The only resort was to apply their own remedies or to invent new ones. To this day the northern Indians are in great fear of syphilis, yet modern procedures known to us are still unavailable to them. Some of their own medicine men are said to have a cure. The Mohave in the old days had a "cure" for arrow wounds. "After the introduction of firearms," says Devereux, "they felt helpless, since arrow-wound magic could not cure gunshot wounds. The situation remained unsolved until a native shaman claimed to have received special power to cure gunshot wounds."[26] In other words, there was no more realistic means of relieving this anxiety than magic could provide. The introduction of new sources of disease, therefore, in view of the limitations of the native methods for combating them, may be considered a continuing cause of unrelieved anxiety, except as relieved by what Devereux calls "cultural bromides."

Any disturbances that influence traditional sources of food supply

---

[23] Reed, "The Making of New Guinea," p. 103.
[24] Felix M. Keesing, *The South Seas in the Modern World* (New York, 1941), p. 130.
[25] Reed, *op. cit.*, p. 102.
[26] George Devereux, "The Mental Hygiene of the American Indian," *Mental Hygiene*, XXVI (1942), 71–84.

are a serious threat and are bound to result in anxieties. It is not merely a matter of hunger or deprivation, but of acquired appetites for the particular kinds of food which are an integral and satisfying part of existence. This is why the food habits of human groups or individuals have a deep psychological significance. Even though some new sources of food are discovered or the balance redressed by rations issued by some government agency, the food that may be nutritionally adequate may not be psychologically rewarding. Even under the stress of hunger, as I have already mentioned, certain foods may be refused. Disturbances in the food supply may also demand a change in occupation—new techniques for earning a living may have to be learned. The history of the Indians of the Plains subsequent to the disappearance of the buffalo is a classic illustration of the difficulties of enforced readaptation in food habits and occupation. Despite pressures of all kinds, men who had been hunters and warriors could not be motivated for a generation or more to find farming or cattle-raising rewarding occupations. Undoubtedly there is a deep conflict here between various drives, so that inhibitions to learning were at first operative despite what must have been a heavy burden of anxiety connected with food and status. The opportunities for readaptation, however, were not of a rewarding kind in the eyes of the Plains Indians. This is a striking example of the highly structured relations that can exist between acquired drives and their specific rewards in a culture.

Where social interaction involves marked differences in power between the members of two groups, one type of response that may result from anxieties arising from feelings of insecurity in members of the subordinate group is identification, in one way or another, with the dominant group. In this case anxiety may function as an important stimulus to learning. Easily adopted symbols of the powerful group—for example articles of clothing—may be sufficiently rewarding, or there may be deeper or more comprehensive imitation. Native opportunists who, for one reason or another, feel insecure in their own social hierarchy may hasten to embrace Christianity and then influence others in the same direction, thus gaining the support of the whites for the enhancement of their personal prestige. There have been several examples of this in the South Seas. (Pomare of Tahiti was a lesser chief who managed to have himself elevated over his native superiors.) Thus new leaders arose in some regions who were equipped with symbols of the white man's power—guns, clothing, household furnishings, and so on. But in turn this threat to the status and power of traditional leaders caused further tensions and anxieties in other quarters.[27]

Furthermore, to the natives the power of the white man sometimes seems explicable only in magical terms. Reading books may furnish the key and thus learning to read becomes the chief desire. A Solomon Island lad said to Hogbin, "You white men are like us. You have only two eyes, two hands, two feet. How are you different? Because you can read books. That is why you can buy axes, knives, clothing, ships and motorcars. . . . If we could read your books we would have money and possessions." [28]

For those in a social or power hierarchy to seek reassurance consciously or unconsciously for their insecurities by imitating those higher in the same social scale is not an unknown phenomenon in Western culture, where it is also a factor in learning.[29] Possibly, therefore, the tendency of the younger generation in many nonliterate societies to imitate the more powerful whites instead of their elders belongs in a comparable category. But this leads to a decline in the authority of their elders over them, a fact that has been commented upon in almost every region where there has been more or less continuous social contact between whites and natives. This behavior may be interpreted as an unconscious search for a new basis of personal security which, since it is not always found, may give rise to further anxieties. Imitation of the dominant group may offer only temporary rewards. An extremely important factor in the outcome is the total configuration of relations that crystallize between Europeans and native peoples. Where a caste structure has developed or is developing, the limited nature of the participation in Western culture to which individuals may aspire naturally creates problems of sociopsychological adjustment different from those where such a structure is absent. In New Guinea, says Reed,

so long as European domination avowedly rested upon armed guards and European weapons of war, there could be no threat to the white man's position. But now that rights have been freely parceled out to the natives and the use of armed force is condemned, the white man resorts to caste rules—taboos, prescription, and juridical sanctions—to assure his continuing superiority.[30]

Even where no well-defined caste lines have crystallized, native peoples who continue to speak their own language, wear their own tradi-

[27] Keesing, *op. cit.*, pp. 66, 149. [28] Hogbin, *op. cit.*, pp. 180–81.
[29] Miller and Dollard, *Social Learning and Imitation*, pp. 188 et seq.
[30] Reed, *op. cit.*, p. 245.

tional dress, or observe certain customs, may discover that the retention of these is punishing rather than rewarding in social intercourse with whites. They may be made the subject of ridicule or invidious comparisons, or they may find themselves underpriviliged in certain situations as compared with the dominant group. Gillen has called this "status anxiety."[31] Although the subject needs further study in other areas, on the basis of Tsimshian material from the Northwest Coast, Barnett maintains the thesis that the "socially unadjusted or maladjusted, the suppressed and frustrated and those who have suffered a social displacement" in their own society, more especially "half-breeds, widows, orphans, invalids, rebels, and chronic trouble-makers have been in the vanguard of those accepting newly introduced patterns,"[32] rather than those persons of real eminence who have a vested interest in native institutions. From the standpoint of anxiety drives and the possible rewards that may accrue to such persons from readaptation in new cultural terms this seems entirely plausible.

In some cases, however, instead of turning toward acculturation as a way out, the confusions, frustrations, and social inequalities that have accompanied contacts with Europeans have created nativistic movements, consciously organized attempts to revive or perpetuate certain aspects of the aboriginal culture. Linton has presented a tentative typology of these [33] which distinguishes magical and rational forms. Both arise in times of stress, but in the magical varieties

moribund elements of culture are not revived for their own sake or in anticipation of practical advantages from the elements themselves. Their revival is part of a magical formula designed to modify the society's environment in ways which will be favorable to it. . . . The society's members feel that by behaving as their ancestors did they will, in some usually undefined way, help to recreate the total situation in which the ancestors lived.

In the more rationalistic movements, on the other hand, the "culture elements selected for symbolic use are chosen realistically and with regard to the possibility of perpetuating them under current conditions" in order to maintain social solidarity and to "help reëstablish

[31] John Gillen, "Acquired Drives in Culture Contact," *American Anthropologist*, LXIV (1942), 550–51.
[32] H. G. Barnett, *Year Book of the American Philosophical Society* (1941), p. 216; also, "Personal Conflicts and Cultural Changes," *Social Forces*, XX (1941), 160–71.
[33] Ralph Linton, "Nativistic Movements," *American Anthropologist*, LXV (1943), 230–40. See also B. Barber, "Acculturation and Messianic Movements," *American Sociological Review*, VI (1941), 662–67.

and maintain the self respect of the group's members in the face of adverse conditions."

The literature on nativistic movements is extensive, but here it must suffice to point out that while those of the magical type may reward the anxiety drives of those that participate in them, there is no ultimate readaptation possible that will prove satisfactory in such terms. The old manner of life can never be revived. On the other hand, as Linton observes, rational revivalistic or perpetuative movements may provide a mechanism of adjustment that may compensate in a more positive way for the feelings of inferiority that have been aroused.

All these processes of readaptation are still going on and, so far as the nonliterate peoples are concerned, the global scale of the second World War will only serve to accentuate them, since the domain of such peoples is in some instances the actual theater of military operations. The revolutionary changes in their lives since the expansion of European peoples began cannot be viewed in adequate perspective, however, without considering the radical transformations that have occurred in Western culture itself during the same period. It is well within this period that our scientific tradition arose, that our technology has been revolutionized through all sorts of mechanical inventions, that a world economy has come into existence, that nationalism in its modern form has arisen, and that wars on a momentous and enormously destructive scale have been fought. As a result, the capacity of Western man to readapt has also been put to the test. Again and again in our society, too, there has been expressed a nostalgia for "the good old days," whether those of yesterday or many centuries ago. The question whether nonliterate peoples' assimilation of our culture, or certain aspects of it, has proved more satisfying to them than their native ways may be paralleled by the question how far we are fully satisfied with the mode of life that is our own traditional one. Furthermore, those of us in the democracies have recently experienced the anxiety of having our way of life disrupted by the threatened imposition of another manner of life. But we are in a better position than the nonliterate peoples to meet the challenge and to help mold our future.

If man's life is one of continual adaptation and readaptation through cultural instrumentalities, a large part of the efforts of students of man must be devoted to understanding as thoroughly as possible the nature of these instrumentalities and their relation to the healthy functioning of the human organism. When the application of our knowledge becomes possible, man in his role of the creator of cultural instrumentalities should be able to devise cultural forms that will bring to human beings the maximum rewards in living. Further study of the sociopsychological aspects of acculturation may contribute valuable knowledge to this end.

Present World Conditions in Cultural Perspective   By RALPH LINTON

PERIODS of stress are no new thing in human history. All civilizations have experienced them and every generation which has been confronted by them has felt that its own emergency was the worst. The only unique thing about the present period is the large number of people who believe that such periods are not inevitable and that they can be avoided by intelligent planning for the future. This attitude seems to be something new in human history. It could not arise as long as men regarded themselves as playthings of the gods or pieces moved by blind fate. It reflects our increasing realization that man has made and can make himself. With it there has come an increasing unwillingness to accept the old facile explanations of disaster and a desire to understand the underlying causes. Only the naïve believe that our present troubles are due to Fascist aggression and that, once it has been stamped out, everything will automatically return to the good old days. The thoughtful recognize Fascism for what it is, a symptom of a deeper disorder, and are eager to know what this disorder may be and how it can be cured. Behind the immediate uncertainties of war they feel a deeper uncertainty which makes them dread what may come after more than they dread war itself.

Although man is beginning to learn to stand on his own feet and to accept responsibility for the working out of his own destiny, this does not diminish his need for immediate reassurance. In the past he has always turned to his gods for the explanation of present calamity and for advice on how to mitigate it. These two are equally necessary to his peace of mind. Discomforts become somehow more bearable if their causes are understood. Today he turns with the same blind faith to the new god, Science, and expects from it everything that the old gods provided. This has made the present a field day for charlatans, especially those who volunteer to foretell the future. However, the true scientists find such faith embarrassing. No one knows the shortcomings of a God as well as his own priests and those who devote their lives to the search for scientific truth realize better than anyone else how little they know. The social scientists, in particular, are reluctant to assume the role of the ancient oracles. They realize that they have only begun to understand the behavior of human beings, whether as individuals or in groups. There is a fine irony in the fact that those sciences whose services are most urgently needed in the present crisis are the youngest and least developed of all. Science gave man new weapons in his age-old battle with nature and in the first flush of victory he pushed his advantage against the ancient enemy, ignoring everything else. The application of scientific methods to the study of man and society is barely a century old, and even at the present rate of progress it will require many years to bring the social sciences abreast of the others.

In spite of this lag the social scientist can point to certain important results. He knows that the future of any society and culture cannot be predicted in the exact terms which the man in the street demands of him. The future is determined by the interaction of innumerable factors many of which the scientist cannot ascertain, still less control. Not the least important of these determinants are the personalities of the individuals whom chance places in commanding positions. No one could have predicted a Hitler, although many could see that in Germany the time was ripe for a Fuehrer of some sort. At the same time, the social scientist is beginning to recognize that these seemingly chance-determined events conform to some sort of order. Although no two events are ever exactly the same, the same patterns of organization and the same processes of growth and change repeat themselves again and again. In this respect at least, social phenomena parallel biological ones. Thus in living forms the pattern of bilateral symmetry is repeated in organisms ranging from worms to men. Similarly, many of the same physiological processes can be recognized in all animals. Again the processes of evolution have produced forms as diverse as the ant and the elephant, the fin, the leg, and the wing, yet the processes themselves can still be recognized. In the same way we can recognize, behind the tremendous diversity of existing cultures and the innumerable episodes of history, certain basic principles of organization and growth. These are repeated again and again although the results will vary with the materials with which such principles operate.

The importance of these principles for the understanding of cultural phenomena can hardly be overestimated. Each society with its associated culture is a continuum. It persists through time, and at each point in time it has a limited number of possible futures. In this again societies parallel living organisms. A species which has reached a certain point in its evolution can go on developing along certain lines but not along others. A generalized species of elephant can evolve into several specialized species but it can never evolve into a horse. Similarly, a particular culture can evolve in any one of several directions but it cannot evolve in certain other directions. Chance may determine which of the possible lines of evolution it will take, but the choice is limited. In other words, the stream of history runs between banks. There are many points at which it may shift from one channel to another but it cannot wander at will. Above all, neither chance nor deliberate intent can turn the stream backward nor make it retrace the course which it has already covered. Civilizations may collapse, but they can never return to the good old days. Instead they have to go forward and create good new ones. Plans which ignore this fact are foredoomed to failure, as are those which ignore the other principles of culture growth and integration. On the other hand, plans which are based upon an understanding of these principles have a chance of success.

To set the stage for a discussion of these principles it is necessary to point out briefly what all cultures have to do, that is, their basic functions. Since much of the present section of this book has been devoted to a discussion of various aspects of culture, it is taken for granted that the reader understands the general meaning of the term. The culture of a society is the way of life of its members; the collection of ideas and habits which they learn, share, and transmit from generation to generation. Culture provides the members of each new generation with effective, ready-made answers to most of the problems with which they are likely to be confronted. These problems, in turn, stem from the needs of individuals living as members of organized groups. Such needs fall into two classes, which we may call practical needs and psychological needs. The former are those which must be met to insure the physical survival of a society's members and the perpetuation of the society as a going concern. The latter are those which must be met to keep these members happy and contented. No society can survive for any length of time unless its culture provides satisfaction for the needs of both orders. However, there is considerable difference in the number of forms required to satisfy the needs of each order in any particular society.

Satisfaction of what we have called the practical needs is intimately bound up with the hard realities imposed by the general characteristics of our species and by the environments in which societies have to operate. Thus all human beings need food, shelter, opportunities for sexual satisfaction, and protection from sudden death. These, with the possible exception of sex, have to be met in terms of the society's environment and the techniques which the society has developed for exploiting it. The importance of the latter has often been overlooked by strict environmentalists, but the potentialities of any environment for a society depend both upon what is there and upon what the society has learned to do with it. Deposits of coal and iron ore mean nothing for a society which has not learned to smelt iron. All normal societies include individuals of both sexes and all ages, and this fact has to be taken into account in the development of any workable system of social organization. In addition, the mere fact of social living sets certain problems of control, direction, division of labor, and distribution of products which have to be solved if the society is to survive but which can only be solved in a limited number of ways. The meeting of practical needs is a strictly down-to-earth matter in which the possibilities are limited by factors over which the society has no control. At the same time, these needs must be met if the society is to survive even briefly, and in times of stress they take precedence over all others.

Most of the practical needs can be met by exceedingly simple patterns of behavior. In fact few people can realize how simple such patterns can be until they find themselves in a situation in which the elaborate cultural responses which they have learned in childhood prove useless. We share these needs with the other species of gregarious primates and if these had been our only needs our method of life would probably have remained much like theirs. However, we are also endowed with other needs, which derive from the peculiar qualities of the human mind and personality. Exploration of these is only beginning, but we must recognize that all normal individuals require certain things over and above those which would suffice to insure physical survival. After all, the inmates of a modern prison are better assured of survival than most of those on the outside, but they are far from happy about it. We need the ego satisfaction that comes from the favorable response of others; we need reassurance when the outcome of our efforts is in doubt; and we need at least some measure of novelty and variety of experience. The genesis of such needs is still in dispute among psychologists and it is unnecessary to discuss the problem here. Suffice it to say that their connection with the physiological tensions cannot be proved. They seem to originate in the mind and can only be satisfied in the mind. Nevertheless, their satisfaction, if not as pressing as that of the practical needs, is quite as necessary to the long term well-being of both individuals and societies.

The role of these needs with respect to culture is complex and still very imperfectly understood. They seem to be the main reason for the instability of cultures, their tendency toward constant change and elaboration. Such changes go on even when a good adjustment to environment has been achieved. The old saying that necessity is the mother of invention holds only for immediate, specific inventions. It seems that the enrichment of culture goes forward most briskly under conditions of peace, security, and economic surplus, when people have time to become bored. It is then that the craftsman plays with his art, inventing new techniques in the process, and curiosity points the way to new discoveries. The psychological needs must also be held responsible for the perpetuation of those elaborations of behavior which, in all societies, go far beyond the level of complexity which would suffice to insure survival. The outsider who looks at any culture with a coldly practical eye cannot fail to be impressed by how much of it appears unnecessary. Almost every culture pattern is a mixture of useful and seemingly useless acts, yet it is practiced and transmitted as a whole. It is only when one gains an intimate knowledge of the culture that the function of such "useless" acts in terms of the psychological needs of the group becomes clear.

In spite of their dynamic quality, the psychological needs of individuals are not too hard to satisfy. All the needs of the individual are shaped by his experience into drives toward specific goals. Thus the need for food becomes a desire for certain specific foods and is reflected in the behavior which will get these. Similarly, the psychological needs are shaped by experience into desires for the attainment of certain goals. Every society trains its members to work toward and find satisfaction in certain goals and not in others. Under normal conditions these goals are of a sort which will further the well-being of the group or, at the very least, will not interfere with the meeting of its practical needs. Thus the craftsman works all the better because he knows that a good product will bring him the admiration which he craves. The task of meeting psychological needs is made still easier by the fact that the mind often fails to distinguish between shadow and substance. Everyone learns quite unconsciously to attach value to various symbols and to operate with them. Men will work as hard and fight even harder for a medal than they will for money. A high-sounding title which is no more than a symbol for power or authority still has the ability to satisfy ambition. The really successful society is the one which trains its members to be content with harmless symbols and to strive toward goals which it can award them without inconvenience.

Although the practical and psychological needs together provide the motive power which keeps cultures operating and are also responsible for their growth and change, knowledge of them does not help much in the understanding of the structure of cultures. Most of the patterns of behavior which a society transmits to its members are of such a sort that they contribute to the satisfaction of several needs simultaneously and may be touched off by any one of these. Thus, the practical reason for wearing clothes is to keep warm. At the same time, people in all societies derive a high degree of ego satisfaction from the feeling that they are well dressed, whether this involves a Hattie Carnegie model or a coat of paint. People dress to keep warm but also to make a good impression, and which of these motives is the dominant one depends upon the circumstances. Culture as a whole satisfies the society's needs as a whole, but the interrelations are so complex as to defy analysis.

The organization of culture is such that it is difficult to find similes that will explain it in terms of everyday experience. Actually, this organization is much closer to that of the combined ideas and habits of the individual—his personality—than to anything else. Cultures, like personalities, are flexible, loosely organized wholes. All their parts are in some degree interrelated and have to be more or less adjusted to each other if the culture is to function successfully. At the same time, they do not mesh with the accuracy of the cogs in a machine. Up to a certain point cultures, like personalities, can continue to operate in the face of internal maladjustments and inconsistencies. However, just as in the personality, there is a point beyond which maladjustments have a paralyzing effect and lead to an eventual breakdown. Since the society itself is usually conscious of such maladjustments only in terms of a vague discomfort, such breakdowns are not infrequent. When they occur in complex cultures, such as those recorded in history, we call them the fall of civilizations.

In spite of these ultimate limits, it is always possible for a culture to acquire new elements and discard old ones without interrupting its operation. In this it is, again, comparable to the personality of the growing individual who can learn and forget all sorts of things without too serious inconvenience. At the same time, every new element which is introduced into a culture sets in train a series of changes in certain of the elements which were there before. These changes are designed to bring the culture into adjustment again. An easy way to picture what happens is to think of a still pool filled with floating rubbish. When some new object, say a block of wood, is dropped into the pool, ripples are set up which shift the positions of the other float-objects and bring them into new relationships with each other. In time the ripples die down and one sees the contents of the pool arranged in a new pattern. This simile is not too accurate, for the changes set in train by the introduction of a new element into culture are not of such a simple, mechanical sort. Many of the old elements of culture may be changed in the course of adjusting to the new pattern and some of them may even be lost. Also, the movements set up in culture by the processes of change never cease. As soon as those produced by one new element begin to die down some other new element is introduced and the process of reorganization begins again. Cultures are always moving toward a stable integration but never reach it.

Perhaps the simplest way to illustrate these processes is by taking the familiar example of what happened when the automobile was introduced into our own culture. When it first appeared we already had what seemed then quite adequate means of transportation in the wagon and the railroad. Most people regarded the auto as an amusing toy, limited in its possibilities for use by its unreliability and by the bad roads and lack of service facilities one encountered as soon as one left metropolitan areas. As time went on the machines themselves were improved and all sorts of new uses were found for them. Hard roads crept out over the countryside and the filling station and small-town garage became regular features of the American landscape. However, the changes which had been set in train did not end with these obvious, practical adjustments. The little towns which had been rural trading centers withered and died, while the middle-sized ones became larger.

Auto camps and road houses sprang up, and the standardized tea shoppe, catering to the auto trade, strewed its parsley from coast to coast. Motorized crime developed with equal rapidity, making the town constable and even the county sheriff anachronisms. Even sex mores and family organization were changed as the institution of chaperonage proved soluble in gasoline and the question of who gets the car tonight became another point of stress between parents and children. These changes are little more than a random sample of those which have followed in the auto's train and the reader is left to fill out the list for himself. Moreover, while we are still struggling with the aftermath of the auto, we can see the shadow of the helicopter poised above us ready to swoop.

Such cultural changes with their resulting disintegration and reintegration are in progress always and everywhere. Their effects upon the societies which are subjected to them depend upon two things: the sort of new elements which are being introduced and the number of new elements which the society has to contend with at any point in time. It is obvious that certain new things will be more disruptive in their effects than others. Thus the introduction of the auto has called for much wider readjustments than that of, say, the electric toaster. It is also obvious that the more new elements a society has to cope with at any given time, the more widespread the maladjustments within its culture. It is quite possible for a society to suffer from a sort of cultural indigestion due to its having accepted more new things than it can absorb at once. In our own case factors of both sorts are working to our disadvantage. We are getting too many new things and too many of these are of a sort whose integration entails fundamental changes in our established way of living and thinking. However, we will return to this later.

One other significant feature of culture remains to be pointed out. Cultures are rarely if ever what one might term well rounded. It seems that societies, like individuals, tend to be much more interested in some things than in others. As a result, their cultures grow and expand in the direction of their interests. Some particular activity catches their attention and they proceed to amplify this at the expense of the rest. The process by which this is accomplished is obvious enough. Societies per se do not invent or borrow but their members do. Inventions which are along the lines in which the society is primarily interested at the time are the ones which bring the largest rewards. Contrast the rewards which our own society bestows upon a man who invents a new rhyme form with that it gives to the inventor of a new and more effective type of radio receiver. Moreover, inventions which are along the lines of a society's dominant interests have a much better chance of being accepted and incorporated into the culture than those which are not. People feel that even a slight improvement along these lines is worth the trouble of readjusting other parts of the culture. The same things holds for borrowing from other societies, one of the most important processes of culture growth. People will borrow things that they are interested in while blandly ignoring other things seemingly of much greater obvious advantage.

Since cultures tend to grow irregularly, pushing out in certain directions and lagging in others, it follows that when we study a culture at any one point in time it almost always seems disharmonic. Cultures are like growing children, disproportionately long in the body at one stage of their development, disproportionately long in the legs at another. Anthropologists can cite innumerable examples of this from their studies of primitive cultures but a few will suffice to illustrate the point. The Australian blackfellows have been satisfied with the simplest sort of technological equipment and live happily at what we would regard as a level of extreme discomfort and insecurity. At the same time they have elaborated their social organization and rules governing marriage until these have reached a complexity beyond those of any other known society. The Polynesians of the western islands have developed an amazingly complicated system of rank and etiquette, but display a polite well-bred indifference toward religion. We ourselves have concentrated upon technological development until the average middle-class American home is a mass of mechanical gadgets of questionable utility. At the same time we have, until very recently at least, been blandly indifferent to the social problems which this very development was creating.

Two things limit the distance to which such one-sided developments can be carried. The first of these is the increasing disharmony produced within the culture by extending one aspect farther and farther while failing to use thought and ingenuity in developing other aspects to the point where they will work under the conditions created by the overextension. Our own indifference toward developing techniques of distribution to match rapidly improving techniques of production is a case in point. The second factor, which is in some ways only a special aspect of the first, is that the techniques of production which are known to any society set definite limits to the development of its culture in other directions. The most pressing needs of any society are for food and shelter. The ways in which these needs are met lie at the foundation of every culture. It is through them that the society discovers the realities and inescapable limitations of its natural environment. Such technical processes are potentially no more stable than any other part of culture. In fact much of human history could be written in terms of technological growth and improvement. However, interest in technology is no more a constant feature of human life than is interest in any other special sort of activity. From the point of view of the societies which practice them, all technologies are adequate as long as they provide for the society's material needs. Difficult as it may be for the modern American to understand this, there are innumerable societies which are not interested in material progress. They accept their long-established methods of getting food and making objects quite as unquestioningly as we accept our particular patterns of family life. This attitude is by no means limited to the so-called primitive cultures. Even such a complex civilization as that of India existed for thousands of years with no important changes in its technology. Even today the Indian peasant goes on raising his crops by methods which have not altered since the dawn of history and the Indian craftsman practices his art by methods of immemorial antiquity.

Such stabilized technologies set the limits within which all other aspects of a culture can develop and operate. I say "set the limits" since no technological system pins a society down to a single possible line of further cultural development. Any particular technological foundation is capable of supporting any one of several different cultural superstructures. The nature of the foundation merely limits the range of possibilities. Thus a society which lives by hunting may develop either an elaborate clan or a simple family organization, it may be warlike or peaceful, worship a single great deity or a host of individual guardian spirits. However, it cannot develop a slave economy, or strong patterns of centralized political control or even a class of skilled artisans who make their living by their crafts. Whenever, as not infrequently happens, some part of the cultural superstructure begins to develop beyond the limits set by the basic technological equipment, its further development is halted. Sometimes, if the interest of the group in this sort of activity is intense, it may be pushed too far in spite of the increasing disharmonies which its development creates. In such cases there will be a collapse in this part of the cultural superstructure followed by a period of confusion and the final emergence of a new set of culture patterns designed along more modest lines. Thus a society may go on developing its religious rituals and holy days to the point where its members have not enough time left to provide for their ordinary wants. The resulting stresses make them feel that the supernatural is not doing its part, devotion wanes and presently sundry priests find themselves out of jobs.

Since men are never content to leave well enough alone, societies tend to swing from one interest to another, testing the cultural limits set by their technologies. Moreover, they return to try the same limits again and again. The Greeks perceived this without understanding its underlying cause. They saw that the political organization of their small city states went through a dreary round from democratic institutions to tyrannies and back to democratic institutions again and repeated the process over and over. The thing that they did not perceive was that the rest of their culture, and especially their simple technological development, set limits which made other developments impossible. They might have come to rest at either end of the scale if their interests had been diverted elsewhere so that they were content to leave politics alone. Failing this, they paced their cultural cage like a tiger returning again and again to try the strength of the same bars. It never occurred to the Greek philosopher to concern himself with technology. This was left to the common people and slaves, and the Greek aristocrat accepted as something in the nature of things a degree of physical discomfort which we would find intolerable.

Out of his experience, the Greek philosopher evolved a theory of the cyclical nature of history. This was a sound theory as long as the technological background against which the cycles repeating themselves remained unchanged. However, it is unfortunate that it should have been espoused by certain modern philosophers and historians who have tried to apply it to current conditions. As we shall see, there has only been one other period in the world's history to which it was less applicable. The significant feature of the present period is that the cultural changes which are in train are not only rapid and numerous but are also taking place in that very aspect of culture which is most fundamental. When men discovered how to produce power and how to apply the scientific method to the solution of technical problems, they dug a tunnel under the bars which have confined the possible development of cultures throughout most of recorded history. This does not mean that we are completely free, but it does mean that the limitations with which we have to deal are new and provide us with new possibilities for growth. If history repeats itself under these conditions it will be mainly because we choose to try to model the future on the past.

It has already been said that, in the last analysis, it is technology which sets the ultimate limits within which cultures can develop. The term technology is used in a very broad sense to refer to the methods which any society has developed for dealing with its natural environment. The most important of these, from the point of view of cultural limitation, are techniques for producing food and other necessities. All other aspects of a culture must be of a sort which will not interfere with the successful operation of these. It should be pointed out that such technological determinism is not to be confused with the classical theories of economic determinism. The latter fail to distinguish in most cases between the actual techniques of production and a society's regulations covering ownership and distribution. A particular set of productive techniques may be linked with any one of several systems of ownership and distribution. In the modern world our own system and the Russian one would be a case in point. Both use the same technological equipment and production methods, although the patterns of ownership and distribution differ profoundly. Among primitive peoples we find that essentially the same productive techniques may be linked in different groups with individual ownership or group ownership of resources, with a money economy, a system of gift exchange, or a system in which all surplus is concentrated in the hands of chiefs who then disburse it downward to the rest of the tribe as needed. Each of these systems appears to work well enough as long as there are sanctions which assure everyone of the necessities of life.

If we use technology in this broad sense, ignoring minor changes and improvements in specific processes, the fundamental changes which have occurred in the course of human history have been surprisingly few. It is a curious and still quite unexplained fact that very much the same fundamental inventions seem to have been made quite independently at different times by societies living in different parts of the world. Thus the development of civilization in the Old and in the New World shows a great number of similarities which certainly were not due to contact. In every case where such fundamental changes in technology have occurred, they have been followed by exceedingly rapid and far-reaching changes in other aspects of the culture. In the evolution of culture such basic technological advances seem to play very much the same role as the fundamental mutations which occur from time to time in the evolution of living forms. They provide a new starting point for development and variation and these result in the production of new forms vastly different from any which have existed before. There seem to have been only three of these fundamental mutations in human history, but each of them had far-reaching and long-enduring consequences.

The first mutation came at a period so remote that we can only conjecture what its immediate results were. It consisted in the development of tools and the use of fire. These gave man a control of his environment which, slight as it may seem to us, was vastly greater than anything which the world had seen before. Many animals make use of natural objects when these are both available and needed. Thus even some species of wasps have been seen to use pebbles to tamp the earth in their burrows. However, the essence of tool using is that objects are made for a specific purpose and kept for repeated use. Man is the only animal which has progressed to this point. That man is the only fire-using animal is too well known to require discussion. Our ancestors tamed and kept this tricky element long before they learned how to make it and it had an enormous influence upon the development of culture. We are accustomed to think of the contribution of fire mainly in terms of light, warmth, and protection from animal enemies. Actually, it had even more important effects in connection with the human food supply. Almost any sort of animal food that can be eaten cooked can also be eaten raw. However, most vegetable foods require cooking. This is universally true of the hard seeds which became the mainstay of man's diet in most regions where game was scarce and which are still his basic food in most parts of the world. We still pray for our daily bread but there can be no bread without fire.

Armed with tools and fire, man was able to push out into regions which he had been unable to occupy before and greatly to increase his numbers. However, these first steps only enabled him to make a better use of the resources which his environment provided. He could not increase these resources. Neither could he, except in a few favored localities, live in groups of more than a few families or remain in one place more than a few days at a time. These conditions continued for hundreds of thousands of years. Within the limits which they set, various societies developed a wide range of social institutions and an amazing skill in exploiting what their various environments had to offer. Such a group as the Eskimo, for instance, have developed an adjustment to the harsh region in which they live that the modern European, with all his science, can scarcely better. However, as long as men remained dependent upon the supply of wild foods, there were well-marked limits to the development of culture and especially to the size of human populations.

The second basic mutation came with the invention of food raising. This mutation took place independently a number of times, as the varying domestic plants and animals of various regions attest. The idea that man became first a herdsman and then a farmer has become a part of our mythology. It was first advanced by scientists who were attempting to arrange the history of all cultures in a single evolutionary sequence and was based more upon logic than upon evidence. Actually, the development of food raising did not progress in any such regular fashion. Here and there some tribe of big game hunters may have begun to guard and eventually to tend the herds which they followed, but there are few parts of the world in which this could have happened. Even today most primitive food-gathering groups depend more upon plants than animals. Meat, being a scarce and preferred food, looms larger in their talk than in their diet. In most regions food raising seems to have begun with the domestication of plants. Animals came later, and in many cases their domestication would have been impossible without the at least semisettled life which crops make possible. Thus anyone who has tried to drive pigs knows that they could not have been domesticated by any group who spent most of its time on the move.

Although the ultimate consequences of food raising were almost as far-reaching as those of the use of tools and fire, they took some time to make themselves felt. The earliest agriculture seems to have been little more than a supplement to hunting and wild-food gathering. Even within the historic period there have been many tribes who planted a crop and then wandered off to live on the country, returning at harvest to gather anything which had survived weeds, blight, and insects. With the improvement of agricultural techniques and the greater assurance of a yield, men stayed closer to their fields and spent more time on them, but for many generations they must have relied upon wild foods for certain important elements in their diet. The real shift of human existence from a food-gathering to a food-raising basis came only when food raising had been developed to a point where it could provide a balanced ration; one containing all the elements necessary to life and health. In that part of the Old World from which most of our own civilization is derived, this was accomplished by a combination of plant and animal raising plus the truly revolutionary invention of milking. By milking, herds could be made to yield a steady supply of most of the food elements lacking in the grains which were here the basis of agriculture. The lack of vitamin B in the grain-milk diet was taken care of by making a large portion of the grain into beer, a yeasty home brew much like that with which many of us became acquainted during the dark days of prohibition. In the New World, milking was never invented and the balanced ration was provided by various combinations of crops, notably one consisting of corn, beans, and chili peppers.

The ability to raise a balanced ration opened up a whole new range of possibilities for cultural development. Over a large part of the world men could now settle down and live in the same place generation after generation. Nomads have to be jacks-of-all-trades since they can never tell when a particular skill will be needed or be sure that there will be a specialist at hand who knows it. Now specialists of all sorts grew and multiplied, with a corresponding improvement in the various crafts. The stable village lent itself to the development of more rigid forms of social organization, while the farmer's constant worry about crops and weather made him more religious than his predecessors. Temples appeared and the primitive medicine man developed into a priest. In those areas where the soil was rich enough to support large populations and where adequate techniques of transportation had been developed, a new phenomenon appeared, namely, the city. Here specialized manufacture and trade was centered, while the crowding together of great numbers of people set new problems of rule and organization. City dwelling is so new in human history that our species still has not been able to adapt to it physiological terms. Men do not breed well in cities and each city has to depend upon its countryside for the upkeep of its population, just as it depends upon it for food and raw materials. The constant influx of strangers who have broken their home ties and achieved a sort of social anonymity poses a whole set of new problems of control which have never been perfectly solved. These problems are complicated by the fact that cities tend to draw to them the maladjusted members of the rural community. The contented peasant stays at home and cultivates his fields as his fathers did; the discontented one, whether knave or genius, moves to the town where his abilities will be given wider scope.

Perhaps the most important feature of the new situation was the creation of a steady predictable economic surplus which was available year after year. On the one hand this provided a strong incentive for vigorous and warlike groups to conquer others which were less warlike and to take this surplus for themselves. On the other, it became the basis for the development of a class structure within the agricultural societies themselves. Under the new conditions, ruling and fighting also became professions practiced by specialists, and these could use their power to draw off the surplus produced by the peasants and artisans. This was made easier by the fact that in most cases the peasants accepted such a division of activities as a matter of course. They tilled the land and left ruling and fighting to their betters. Even when they were goaded into revolt by unbearable conditions their revolts proved abortive since they did not know how to rule and would not trust anyone of their own sort who attempted to rule.

Recent archeological discoveries have shown the speed with which men adapted themselves to the new conditions provided by successful food raising. While the initial adaptations were going on, there must have been a time of internal confusion and cultural reorganization much like the present, but of this we have little knowledge. One wonders what a food-gathering people thought when they discovered that the land, something previously of no value in itself, now was something possession of which gave a man power over his fellows. The only thing that we know with certainty is that a great number of changes in culture took place in a very short time. In the Near East, from which our own civilization mainly stems, a thousand years witnessed the whole shift from a primitive method of life on a par with that of modern hunting tribes to full-blown civilization. In this brief period men learned to smelt metals, to write, to govern themselves by formal law codes, to deal with banking and credit and in general to live on very much the terms that our own ancestors lived on only two hundred years ago. Much the same thing seems to have happened in the New World, although present indications are that here the speed was even greater. Thus in our own Southwest the establishment of a balanced ration on an agricultural basis resulted in a shift from a very simple wandering pattern of life to the complex culture of the Pueblos in only three hundred years.

Once the limits to cultural development established by the new food-raising basis had been explored and successful adjustments worked out, the various civilizations settled down once more. Further developments became a matter of swings within these limits which left the basic patterns of life largely unaffected. In the Near East these have persisted down to the present time. Here for nearly eight thousand years the peasant with his ox plowing the land and the artisan working in the front of his little shop have gone on unchanged while empires rose and fell, and gods were born and died. In Europe civilization was established much later but here also there was the same continuity, once it had been established. It has been said quite truthfully that George Washington would have felt more at home in Athens of the time of Pericles, or even at the court of Hammurabi, King of Babylon in 2200 B.C., than in any modern American city. Ignoring the obvious point of language, he would have seen far fewer things which were unfamiliar and would have understood better the life which was going on around him. Many of these long-enduring patterns are still a part of our culture, but it is an open question which and how many of them will survive in the new culture configuration which is now coming into being as a result of the third mutation, now under way.

The third mutation is so recent that even the basic changes in technology which are responsible for it have not yet run their course. It springs from two fundamental inventions, that of how to produce power and that of the scientific method. The use of natural power, as in the water wheel, goes back to almost the beginnings of civilization as does the use of animal power. However, both of these were strictly limited in quantity, while water power was only available in a few favored places. The discovery of how to get power from fuel released it from these limitations and made it possible to employ it everywhere and in quantity. This in turn inaugurated the search for new sources of power which is still going on briskly. Our attempts to tap the tremendous resources of solar energy and atomic energy are still in their infancy, but the problems involved may not be insoluble. What the results of success might be we can only conjecture, but one of the first results would certainly be a shifting of the value of various territories. Thus if we learn how to tap solar energy, our production centers will automatically shift from regions of mineral fuel to those of intense sunlight, leaving Europe stranded under its low-cloud ceiling. Even the further development of the recently announced methods for synthesizing oil products from vegetable matter may result in an ultimate shift of many industries to tropical regions where crops for this purpose can be grown most advantageously.

The invention of the scientific method may prove even more revolutionary in the long run than that of getting power from fuel. It must be emphasized that this was an invention. Man has dealt with the qualities and potentialities of inanimate objects ever since he chipped the first flint and fed the first fire. However, what he learned about them he learned more or less by accident and his knowledge was transmitted unquestioningly. He learned that certain techniques produced certain results but he did not bother to inquire how they produced them or how many of the things included in the technique really contributed to the outcome. Even today techniques which have not been touched by science include a great amount of ritual and unnecessary movement, as may be observed even in the workings of our own kitchens. The essence of the scientific method lies in two things, the repeated experiment and the accurate record of its results measured by methods which are, as far as possible, divorced from the conclusions of the individual observer. These two things are equally important and it was their combination which produced science. The modern scientist does not trust the evidence of his own senses or the workings of his own mind unless these can be checked either by mechanical means or by the observations of others. In this he differs from the Greeks. Their lively and universal curiosity carried them to the point of experiment, but they did not understand the fallibility of the intellect. In fact they regarded it as the court of last resort in all questionable cases. It was not until man became suspicious of his own mind that he could become a true scientist. Ironically enough it was probably the Christian Church, with its insistence on the fallibility of the mind as contrasted with the infallibility of authority, which laid the groundwork for this new attitude. The suspicion which this engendered extended at last to authority also and the awakening intelligence of the Renaissance turned toward measurements, mathematics, and machines in its search for certainty. As these were refined and extended, modern science was born.

We have only begun to explore the potentialities of the scientific method even in the field of technological advance. However, it seems probable that we will eventually be able to create out of other substances anything which is to be found in nature. The possibilities for improvement in technology, and consequently in standards of living, which this opens up are so vast that we can hardly perceive their limits. Even without the development of such synthetics our techniques of mass production have given us, at least in times of peace, an *embarras de riches*. We can produce much more than we can contrive to distribute to the people who still need it. That this should be so stems in large part from the particular fixation of interest which we have already mentioned as characteristic of our current culture. While the scientific method had been applied wholeheartedly to everything which has to do with material advance, it has only been applied haltingly and tentatively to the social and psychological problems which that advance has brought to the fore. Moreover, while even the most conservative manufacturer is quick to take the advice of the chemist or engineer, the legislator rarely pays any attention to the findings of the social scientist. Someone has said that in this age of wireless and airplanes the legislator typically keeps his ear to the ground.

It is true that the social scientist often does not have too much to offer. He is only beginning to develop the special techniques necessary for the study of the particular order of phenomena with which he deals. However, even the slender guidance which he can provide is of value under present conditions. The forces which the third mutation has unleashed are so vast that they cannot be left to work themselves out without conscious direction. If they are so left the most probable result will be a collapse of the cultures which have experienced their first impact—those of western Europe and America.

In recognizing this fact the social scientist is no more a prophet of doom than is the physician who predicts that there will be an epidemic unless proper steps are taken to avert it. There are two factors involved in the present situation which are distinctly encouraging. One of them is the tremendous productive power of modern industry and scientific agriculture. Some idea of how great this is can be drawn from the fact that the United States has been able to carry on a war of unprecedented magnitude and at the same time feed and clothe its population better than many of them were fed and clothed in peacetime. A society which has such an economic margin can survive a great deal of cultural maladjustment and muddling through without exposing its members to actual physical deprivation. The other encouraging feature of the present situation is that there are a larger number of individuals in all Western societies who recognize the need for conscious planning and direction in the development of a new social order and know that there must be a new social order, planned or otherwise. Although such recognition is by no means general, it is steadily gaining ground and its ultimate effects must be tremendous.

It is an important sign of the times that the last twenty years have witnessed two attempts to reorganize European society and culture, one in Russia, the other in the various Fascist countries. Each of these attempts, while denying religion, has assumed many of the aspects of an organized religion, including swift punishment for all heretics who questioned the creeds on which the movements were based. Each of them has also, in the absence of supernatural sanctions, sought to justify itself in terms of inevitability. They have advertised such new orders as the next predestined stages in the evolution of civilization, stages whose arrival may be delayed but cannot be prevented. If our present knowledge of the principles underlying the growth and organization of culture indicates anything, it indicates that there is no such thing as cultural predestination. The present technological advance, like those of the past, has opened up a wide range of possibilities for social and cultural reorganization and neither Communism nor Fascism has exploited more than a few of these. As has already been pointed out, any successful, in the sense of enduring, culture must provide satisfactions for man's psychological needs as well as his physiological ones. Both the Communist and Fascist systems include numerous features inacceptable to those reared in the Western traditions of individual freedom of thought and action and of tolerance. These traditions are deeply ingrained in most of us and no planned culture which refuses to recognize and provide for them can satisfy our needs. Even though such a culture may be temporarily advantageous to a small ruling group, it carries within it the seeds of so many discontents and psychological deprivations that it is hard to see how it could survive for long. It seems highly improbable, therefore, that either Fascism or Communism will become permanently established in Western Europe, still less in America. Certain aspects of both may be incorporated into the new civilization which is emerging, but these movements, in their present form, will find their place in history as little more than initial experiments in social planning, the first halting and unsuccessful attempts at a conscious rebuilding of civilization in the face of new conditions.

One last word should be said. Even if the Western peoples remain so entranced with their new mechanical and scientific toys that they fail to make the necessary adjustments in time, this will not mean the end of the world. In spite of airplanes and factories the bulk of the world's population still lives under the relatively stable, integrated cultures which have been erected on the basis of the second mutation. The impact of Western civilization upon these has been disturbing but not, as yet, disintegrating. Most of these "backward" peoples do not share our own fixation on technological improvement for its own sake. If the pressures which the Western nations are now able to exert are removed, it seems highly probable that these people will profit by our errors, take over the new technology at a slower rate and exercise much greater selectivity. Their aim, conscious or otherwise, will be to adapt the machine to man rather than man to the machine. Stable and enduring civilizations can be established on no other basis.

The Present State of World Resources
By HOWARD A. MEYERHOFF

NATURAL resources have long been appraised from a nationalistic point of view which has made the physical possession or political control of basic raw materials a primary objective of governments. No major power has wholly escaped the philosophy of self-sufficiency, but the Nazi approach to the problem illustrates the type of orthogenetic thinking inspired by uncompromising nationalism. One of Hitler's earliest objectives was to make Germany self-sufficient. Where this end could not be achieved by use of available domestic resources, German ingenuity and technological skill were directed to the creation of *ersatz* products. When ingenuity failed either quantitatively or qualitatively, the mania for self-sufficiency expressed itself in the political philosophy of the "haves" and the "have-nots." Germany's possession of coal, the most critical of all raw materials, was waved aside as inconsequential in comparison with her deficiencies. The fact that no other nation, great or small, has a complete assortment of natural products—that only the world as a whole is reasonably self-sufficient—seemed immaterial. Military and ultimate political control of all essential materials for industrial production assumed the status of an imperative goal, and the war which ultimately came, quickly lost the initial aspect of petulant insistence on the rights of German minorities and assumed the stature of a drive for permament industrial might—to determine the destiny of the Reich "for a thousand years."

Shrewdly the Nazi concept coupled manpower with the products of the earth, and there is no question that, in the New Order in Europe, as in the New Order in Asia, regimented populations were as integral a part of the planned economy as were politically controlled crops, animals, and minerals. Repugnant though the regimentation of peoples may be to us, the conjunction of people and products in Nazi *Geopolitik* is a fundamental concept. It recognizes that inventories of raw materials are merely indices of potential strength, whereas the use to which these raw materials are put is the only measure of actual progress among nations and races. The Nazi attitude recalls the old philosophical question—does the falling tree in the wilderness make a sound? The Nazi answer was pragmatic: No, unless there is a human ear to hear it; for the fall of the tree sets up atmospheric waves which are translated into sound only upon impact against an ear drum.

So, in a study of natural resources the distinction between reserves and production is important, and in any country the ratio between the two assumes the role of a vital economic statistic, with a range as great as the spread between zero and infinity. It is inevitable that the thoughts of industrialists and ultimately the fancy of statesmen should stray to those parts of the earth where the ratio of inventories to use is infinity. The history of the Hudson's Bay Company or of the growth of the British Empire reveals how action may evolve from this kind of thinking. And if it was believed that dreams of empire had run their course when the First World War ended, the Fascists, followed by the bolder Nazis and the still more daring Japanese, have shattered the belief beyond repair. It behooves the democratic peoples to learn all they can from the more constructive lessons which the dictators can teach. One of these lessons is the international significance of the earth's riches.

In totalitarian codes, the world's raw materials acquire importance solely as instruments of nationalistic aggrandizement. Original political ownership is regarded as immaterial, for under "national socialism," socialization extends to the owners as well as to the property owned. The code of the democracies needs clarification in a number of particulars, but it appears definite enough on one important point: though it insists on freedom of access to natural resources for all nations, this freedom applies to surpluses produced in excess of domestic needs in the country of origin. There is no implication of internationalization of raw materials in a political sense, but economic internationalization is a well-defined objective of the Atlantic Charter. It will be profitable to approach the problem of the world's natural wealth from this special economic viewpoint.

Since the industrial revolution, there has been a steady trend toward economic specialization. Prior to the development of efficient transportation, national or regional self-sufficiency was fundamental, and the first demands which had to be met in any economy were the requirements for food, clothing, and shelter. Once these needs were satisfied, attention could be turned to trade in regional specialties. Now the situation is all but reversed. Ordinarily the United Kingdom can neglect the soil and depend upon the value of its manufactures to bring food to its industrial population. Argentinians can depend upon the value of their grains and animals in industrial countries to bring them the products of industry. The revival of nationalism following the last war upset the trend somewhat, but it conclusively demonstrated that self-sufficiency is an expensive and uneconomic luxury if it is not based on native resources. The Fascist effort to raise wheat—"the battle of grain"—on land that was better for olives or grapes succeeded only in lowering the Italian standard of living. If there is a lesson to be learned from nationalistic philosophies of the past twenty-five years, surely it is the uneconomic futility of artificially induced self-sufficiency.

In its characteristic and theoretical way, the Union of Soviet Socialist Republics explored the trend of specialization to the opposite extreme. Afflicted with a mania for bigness, it built the largest of everything—tractor plant, shoe factory, locomotive works, and so on and on. It was not long before the severe geographic limitations of distribution became painfully apparent. The theoretical efficiency of specialization was nullified by the problems of supply and distribution. Here, too, if there is a lesson to be learned, it is the fallacy of overspecialization. In combination, the two lessons indicate that there is an optimum in the wise use of domestic resources for purposes of specialization, and the economic penalties are immediate when the optimum is disregarded.

The examples of Britain, Argentina, and the U.S.S.R. suggest several generalizations which may serve as premises for an analysis of the world's natural wealth: Although there is scientific system in the distribution of the soils, climates, vegetation, animals, rocks and minerals which comprise the world's natural wealth, the political distribution is fortuitous. A few nations like the U.S.S.R. have achieved a large measure of relative self-sufficiency, but the vast majority of countries are dependent on outside sources of supply for several basic raw materials that are critical even for the maintenance of a balanced peacetime economy.

It follows from the fortuitous distribution of natural resources that nature is as often prodigal as it is niggardly. Thus Germany was the recipient of the best industrial coal of Europe, but has little metallic wealth to complement it. Italy has rich reserves of aluminum, mercury, and sulphur, modest supplies of lead, zinc, and manganese, but no coal or oil. Uruguay could feed most of South America with her wheat, corn, beef; but, lacking coal and iron ore, she could not manufacture a ton of steel from native raw materials.

From such considerations as the contributions of specific nations to the world's economy, two fundamental conclusions can be drawn. First, the natural wealth of nations tends to be complementary, and proper use calls for some redistribution through the medium of international trade. Second, the nations which most nearly approach self-sufficiency do so more by virtue of size, abetted by chance, than by any element of design. The United States, the British Empire, and the Soviet Union are the only countries which can lay a valid claim to comparative self-sufficiency. Of the earth's 55,885,000 square miles of land surface, Great Britain controls 13,355,000, or 24 percent; the U.S.S.R. controls 8,348,000 square miles, or approximately 15 percent. It is inevitable that the British holdings, with their remarkable geographic range in the several continents, should encompass virtually every kind of natural region and must therefore, by the mere law of averages, possess a maximum amount and a maximum variety of resources. The U.S.S.R., on the other hand, is "all of a piece," and what it gains in unity is offset by more limited diversification of natural regions and natural wealth. But even so, its territory embraces many regions whose separate resources make an impressive total. But it must be noted that it is the sum of the raw materials in many natural regions within each of these vast political units that creates relative self-sufficiency. The separate regions are themselves economically dependent; and both in their size and dependence they are individually comparable with the smaller nations of the earth.

The United States differs from the British Empire and the U.S.S.R. in its small size. Its 3,734,000 square miles makes it comparable with China (3,756,000), Canada (3,695,000), Brazil (3,285,000), Australia (2,975,000), or the whole of Europe (3,773,000). Yet, in regard to natural wealth, the United States ranks with the British Empire and with the U.S.S.R. This phenomenon requires brief examination, and upon analysis it will be found to require qualification. The United States and its possessions support 150,000,000 people, in contrast with 540,000,000 in Europe and 422,000,000 in China. Even if liberal allowance be made for differences in standards of living, it follows that Europe and China have achieved a higher degree of agricultural production and hence of agricultural wealth than the United States, and that the high rating which this country has earned is based chiefly on its mineral production, supplemented by adequate farm, forest, and animal economies. In comparison with Canada, Brazil, and Australia, the United States has a much denser population, which reflects its climatic advantages more than any other single factor. Brazil has a large area of tropical rain forest which can never be densely settled; Australia has an immense area of low-latitude desert with equally rigorous limitations; whereas a large section of Canada suffers the handicap of an arctic or subarctic climate. And from a climatic standpoint the United States enjoys distinct advantages over the British Empire and the U.S.S.R.: whereas most of the United States lies within the 30th and 50th parallels, most of the U.S.S.R. is situated north of 50° North Latitude, and most of the Empire lies outside the limits of these two parallels.

In one most important particular, the U.S.S.R. and the United States are comparable: they occupy geologically analogous positions within the continents of Eurasia and North America. Although Eurasia's tremendous size gives the Russians a great deal more land, the similarity of continental structure in North America provides the United States with comparable diversity of landforms and resources within 40 percent of the area. There are no other countries anywhere in the world which enjoy the unique advantage of possessing every genetic type of geologic structure, although both Australia and Canada approximate, without quite achieving, it. The diversity of resources in the British Empire as a whole depends upon the aggregate of wealth in isolated dominions and colonies scattered widely over the earth; and even though the known and probable natural wealth of this vast domain is great, its value is partially offset because it lacks the geographic and political integration which is being achieved in the U.S.S.R. and which has been achieved in the more compact United States. When it is further considered that no other nations in the world have the same or comparable relationships to the geological structures of the several continents, it is easy to understand why these three allies stand preëminent, and why the compact and climatically favored United States, despite its relatively small size, has most fully utilized its natural wealth.

The preëminent ratings assigned to the British Empire, the United States, and the U.S.S.R. are not strictly comparable; and, indeed, it is difficult to agree upon a common denominator which will serve as a basis for rating the natural wealth of nations. No one can attempt a direct comparison of the agricultural and pastoral wealth of the Argentine and the mineral wealth of Chile. Yet an analysis of the flow of trade instantly reveals that raw materials, regardless of their nature, are drawn irresistibly to power. And even if it be recognized that producer and consumer are mutually dependent, monetary wealth and industrial strength—and commonly, political power—increase most rapidly in those regions where energy is available for application to raw materials. For this reason an examination of the world's natural resources may profitably start with the energy resources. Herein will be found the best index for a classification of nations, and for a rating, of a kind.

ENERGY RESOURCES

Coal, oil, natural gas, and water are the chief sources of industrial energy. In the United States coal meets 50 percent of the needs for heat, power, and metallurgy; oil satisfies approximately 30 percent of the demand, whereas natural gas and hydroelectric energy account for 10 percent apiece. In other parts of the world and within the several sections of the United States the proportions vary; and if recast for the world as a whole in 1937,[1] the ratios of these four sources of energy were

	Percent
Coal	62
Oil	21
Water Power	12
Natural Gas	5
	100

Although coal leads by a wide margin, its relative position has changed considerably since the last war. In 1910 it supplied about 86 percent of the energy requirements in the United States, and roughly 90 percent of the world's needs. The rapid rise of petroleum as a source of energy has coincided with revolutionary changes in transportation, but its use has spread beyond the fields of optimum utility to the point where it has replaced coal under stationary boilers and other installa-

[1] The year 1937 has been selected as the last pre-war year for which a full set of figures is available, and in which industrial operations were relatively normal and well balanced. War industries tend to increase the consumption of coal without proportionate increases in the other energy producers, partly because of expansion in the metallurgical industries but chiefly because coal is the only fuel the production of which can respond immediately to increased demand.

tions in which the sole function of fuel is the generation of heat. Optimistically it was predicted that oil would replace coal in most phases of industry except metallurgy, but this prediction failed to consider the efficiency that could be achieved by the more effective use of coal and the quantitative limitations on petroleum reserves. It now appears doubtful whether new drilling in oil fields can more than keep pace with essential requirements. It has further been learned that oil is a more expensive fuel than coal for heating except in regions where coal deposits are remote, and that there are rigid economic limitations on the substitution of oil for coal. And finally, coincident with the discovery that the world's supply of petroleum is finite has come the synthesis of oil products from coal, crude oil, and hydrogen.

The invention of synthetic processes of manufacture for oil products makes it easier to appraise the several sources of industrial energy more calmly and accurately. In the United States coal production was no lower in 1937 than it was in 1910, and the tremendous increase in the yields of petroleum, natural gas, and hydroelectric energy has merely sufficed to meet the accelerated demand for heat and power. In the rest of the world, where oil-field technology has developed more slowly, coal production has steadily increased since 1910. Further, even the most superficial survey of recent industrial history reveals that the nations which possess large coal reserves consume most of the oil. Mexico has gone through a fortune in petroleum, reaching second place in world production but dropping to sixth place in 1941; yet Mexico's industrialization has been only mildly accelerated by the fluid energy which has been withdrawn from its rocks. Even now, Venezuela, Colombia, Iran, Iraq, and Rumania are pouring their oil into the holds of tankers which sail for the highly industrialized countries of North America and Europe—for the most part, the countries generously endowed with coal.

The basic raw material in synthetic oil is lignite, a low-grade member of the coal series. The synthetic product costs $2\frac{1}{2}$ to 5 times as much to make as the products of refining, hence it is not likely to replace fluid petroleum until the latter becomes much scarcer. But even so, when that day comes, possession of coal will be critical, for the world's oil supply will be coextensive with the coal reserves.

In the past, in the present, and as far into the future as the time when atomic energy becomes available, coal is the fundamental source of heat and power. Individual regions may erect a limited industrial economy on oil, or natural gas, or water power. But in so far as economic and military strength depends upon heavy industry, and heavy industry leans upon coking coal, a nation's potentialities can be gauged from its coal reserves; its actual power, from the ratio of use to reserves. Other forms of energy may find important uses in a few countries lacking coal, but this is true primarily of water power. For the most part, however, per capita consumption of the other energy resources is highest in the countries most richly supplied with coal.

Coal is carbonized and lithified vegetation, and as such it is found in beds or seams in sedimentary rocks. The quality of coal depends upon the degree of carbonization it has achieved, and as carbonization is in part a function of geologic age, the best coals are ordinarily the oldest, geologically speaking. Most of the world's coke is made from these older coals, and up to the present time Japan and Italy are the only nations which have assayed heavy industry without ready access to large supplies of high quality industrial fuel. Although there are substantial deposits of these good coals in Australia and western Siberia, most of the reserves are situated in eastern North America and in Europe. The younger coals of subbituminous and lignitic grades are more widely scattered over the earth, yet North America has the largest reserves, with Asia ranking second. Some of the younger coals have acquired coking characteristics and can be used metallurgically; and within the past two or three decades, they have found increasing utility in industry, thanks to technological developments in Germany and in Soviet Russia.

In the accompanying tables, the figures for reserves and production include all grades of coal, from lignite to anthracite. The figures are eloquent without subdivision according to quality, for they reveal how lavish nature was in the Northern Hemisphere and how parsimonious she was in the Southern. They further show the firm foundation on which the preëminence of the United States rests, as well as the important position occupied by the U.S.S.R., by several political units in the British Empire, by Germany, and by China. They inspire the conviction that industrial strength will continue to reside, or to develop, in these several countries; and even though substantial progress is by no means precluded in other parts of the earth, the deficiency of coal reserves is a limiting circumstance which cannot be ignored in predicting or in planning the future.

Not all of the countries which possess rich coal reserves have put them to equal use, and the statistics of production also reveal that several of the 52 nations which mine coal are maintaining a relatively

The World's Coal Reserve

Continent	Metric Tons (in billions)	Percentage of Total
North America	4,500	57.5
Asia	2,250	28.8
Europe	800	10.2
Australasia	170	2.2
Africa	70 [a]	0.9
South America	30 [a]	0.4

National Coal Reserves

Country	Metric Tons (in billions)	Percentage of Total
United States	3,150	40.1
U.S.S.R.	1,650	21.2
Canada	1,200	15.3
China	800 [b]	10.1
Germany	425	5.4
United Kingdom	190	2.4
Australia	117	1.5
All others	288	3.7

[a] Recent exploratory work has disclosed a few new deposits in Africa and South America. Although some upward revision of these figures may be in order, the relative positions of the continents will remain unchanged, and the percentages will not be materially altered.
[b] Estimates for China are high and may be subject to downward revision.

high output at the expense of rapid depletion of their reserves. Japan, for example, is mining 41,900,000 tons a year against a reserve of 8 billion. The penalty paid for such an abnormally rapid rate of use is not simply the remote and intangible threat of exhaustion of the deposits within 200 years, but is rather the practical penalty of high operating costs and a higher price per ton. In most coal fields only a fraction of the deposits are cheaply accessible, and rapid use will soon require mining at greater depth, or extraction of thinner seams, or utilization of inferior grades, or some combination of these expensive possibilities. Costs may be kept down at the expense of labor, and this dubious economy is practiced in Japan; but in general, industry cannot flourish long when it is based upon high-cost energy. Although the ratio of production to reserves is not an accurate index of unit cost, it offers a fairly satisfactory means of approximating relative costs, notwithstanding contrasts in wages and in standards of living among the coal-producing countries.

One way in which the relative positions of the several nations may be visualized may be termed the "life expectancy" of other respective reserves, which is merely the number of years their individual deposits will last at the current rate of use. Such a picture is instructive but altogether too simple, for it does not reflect the adequacy of current production. It ignores very significant facts; for example, that, if Italy's coal, which will last 75 years at the normal rate of production, were

COAL PRODUCTION—1937

Country	Metric Tons (in millions)	Percentage
United States	450	29.0
Germany	380	24.5
United Kingdom	244	15.7
U.S.S.R.	127	8.2
France	45	2.9
Japan	42	2.7
Poland	36	2.3
Czechoslovakia	34	2.2
Belgium	29	1.9
China	27	1.7
British India	26	1.7
All others	110	7.1
World	1,550	100

mined at the same rate as coal in Great Britain, the entire Italian reserve would be exhausted in 31 weeks. If reserves are figured on a per capita basis rather than on life expectancy, the United States ranks second to Canada, and the relative positions of the countries included in the list will change considerably.

LIFE EXPECTANCY OF COAL RESERVES

Country	Years
Canada	85,000
China	30,000
U.S.S.R.	13,000
Australia	8,000
United States	7,000
Germany	1,000
United Kingdom	800
Japan	200
France	190
Italy	75

At this particular moment in the history of the human race, the gross tonnages which are commercially available in the several parts of the world are more significant than any absolute measure of the relative ranks of individual nations. Without appeal to the size of populations or to the stage of industrialization that has been attained by any particular people, these figures in themselves spell out the kind of economy which can be developed or maintained. It is obvious Italy's future does not lie in the direction of heavy industry, and the sooner her population is guided into more productive fields of activity the sooner she will evolve a normal place in European and world economy. It is equally clear that the industrialization of Soviet Russia and of Canada has infinite possibilities, which are circumscribed only by climatic and physiographic handicaps and, in the case of Canada, by the low (lignitic) grade of most of her reserves. Above all, the unique preëminence of the United States is so evident as to require but one cautionary comment: The estimate of reserves is an accurate measure of the coal which can be recovered, but not necessarily of the amount which will be. Careless mining, especially in the coal fields of the Appalachians and of Illinois, where seams are superimposed, can greatly reduce the quantity of our best industrial grades. Actually, we have but 40 to 50 years supply of anthracite; possibly 1,000 years of bituminous; and limitless supplies only of lignite and subbituminous coal. It is none too early to introduce conservational practices if we are to have the full benefits of the greatest and most valuable of our own natural resources.

The world's oil reserves cannot be estimated with the same precision as the coal deposits, for coal seams are solid and measurable, whereas fluid petroleum can be measured only in production. Unless an oil pool has actually been drilled, there is little basis for confidence that oil is present; and unless there has been a measured flow from a number of wells there is no accurate method of approximating the amount of oil which a pool may be expected to yield. For this reason estimates of reserves must be made on an accrual basis, and the only country in which drilling has determined the approximate total of future production is the United States. It is probable that similar limits can be set for Mexico and Rumania, and comparable information is rapidly being obtained for Venezuela. But elsewhere the word "guesstimate," which has been given currency in *Time*, is the kindest term which can be used for figures on reserves.

STATE OF WORLD RESOURCES

A few facts stand out clearly. As an oil producer, the United States has led the world for many decades and will continue to do so for some years to come. Thanks to the full knowledge of our oil fields, it is possible to approximate the assured future production fairly accurately at 18 to 20 billion barrels. Theoretically, at the current rate of production (1,505 million bbl. in 1943), this country has but a twelve- to fourteen-year supply left. But oil fields are characterized by a declining yield, and the rate of decline is a determinable constant for each component horizon or pool within the field. Hence, even if it be pessimistically assumed that no more pools will be discovered in the United States, some wells will continue to yield for 30 years more; but the gap between demand and supply will steadily widen.

The predicament of this country as the world's most insatiable consumer of petroleum has drawn attention to other parts of the earth as potential sources of supply. The nearest source of any significance is the Gulf-Caribbean basin, where Venezuela, Colombia, Mexico, and Trinidad are producers of some importance. Their combined output, however, is a scant 20 percent of the yield in the United States. The prospect for a substantial increase, large enough to fill the anticipated gap between production and consumption in the United States, is remote. Mexico seems to have passed its peak. The Maracaibo basin of Venezuela and Colombia has been intensively exploited with highly satisfactory results but with little prospect of marked increases in the yield. Work elsewhere in these two countries, though not unproductive, has failed to meet expectations. Trinidad has good prospects, but they possess severe geographic limitations. Only new discoveries farther inland in South America can greatly enlarge that continent's role in the problem of petroleum supply; and although there is no reason to dismiss the possibility of encountering more oil, there is certainly no basis for predicting discoveries of great importance. Current information regarding Caribbean and South American reserves suggest that five to eight billion barrels may be counted on, but this is not enough greatly to prolong the world's supply.

In the Eastern Hemisphere the continents of Africa and Australia contribute little to the world's supply of oil. Egypt has a small but increasing production in the country marginal to the Red Sea and may, in consequence of the location of its oil pools, be appropriately included in the Near East. The rest of Africa reported only 27,000 barrels in 1940, and all of Australia and New Zealand reported 4,000.

Japan has a meager production estimated at 3,400,000 barrels in 1942, and Sakhalin yields only a little more (3,900,000). In all of the Far East, only the East Indies can boast of a high petroleum yield, and from the steady increase which had been registered over a long period of years, up until the islands were invaded by the Japanese, two conclusions can be drawn: first, that by careful exploitation, the East Indies, both Dutch and British, may be counted on to occupy a significant position for many years to come; and second, the reserves are modest—probably under three billion barrels—and will not constitute a major source of supply, except for southern and eastern Asia and for Australia.

Scattered but disappointing oil pools have been encountered in Europe, and a full roster of producing countries includes Rumania, Germany, Poland, Hungary, Albania, France, Czechoslovakia, and Italy. Only Rumania has acquired any importance, and her wells at Ploesti have been characterized by a declining yield for several years. Neither Germany's technologists nor dire needs have been able to reverse the trend since 1939, and it looks as if Rumania's one big field, like Mexico's, has entered the final phase of gradual exhaustion. It is unsafe to say that the rest of Europe offers no more possibilities than those which have been thus far developed. American geologists have pointed out that American methods of exploration have never been applied; that it is possible Europe may be as richly endowed as the American mid-continent. Although the plausibility of this assumption may be granted, it provides no basis for estimating resources, notwithstanding some promising pre-war developments in the province of Perm, on the west slope of the Ural Mountains in Russia. Here, in its characteristic way, the Soviet Government drilled wells, installed pipelines, constructed storage facilities, and erected refineries to handle production in a new field which had never produced. The outbreak of war on June 22, 1941, either arrested development or imposed an impenetrable censorship, and what potentialities the new field possesses are unknown. If they are like those of the American mid-continent, the whole of Europe may have undreamed of prospects.

There is but one section of the Eastern Hemisphere which will rival the output and the historical record of the United States, and that is the Near East. Starting in Egypt on the western margin of the Red Sea and stretching across the Arabian peninsula to the Persian Gulf and thence northward through Iraq and Iran to the Caucasus Mountains, this region is currently regarded by the ever-optimistic oil industry as a vast reservoir of liquid wealth. Conservative estimates place the proved reserves at 16 to 20 billion barrels, but thereafter conservatism is cast to the winds. "Probable reserves" are claimed to be in the neighborhood of 50 to 55 billion barrels, and "possible reserves" are reckoned at an astronomical 80 to 90 billion. True, this section of the earth embraces 2,000,000 square miles, and its geological history is favorable for the origin and accumulation of low-grade oil. Ninety percent or more of Soviet production (240,000,000 bbl. in 1941) and all the production in Iran (78,000,000), Iraq (15,000,000), Egypt (8,000,000), Bahrein Island (8,000,000), and Saudi Arabia (6,000,000) come from this petroliferous region and furnish eloquent testimony of its wealth. But it still seems probable that, when the heat of the desert becomes more evident than its glamor, and when producing wells and dry holes supplant the visions of airplane reconnaissance, the oil profession will be happy to settle for something short of the "probable reserve." India and Burma lie within an extension of the Near Eastern province and may further bolster its output, but even if all the wildest hopest are realized, the Near East, the Middle East, and the Far East can add but forty years of life to the earth's oil supply.

With an over-all limit of 75 years' supply of oil available to the human race, the industrial nations are living from hand to mouth on annual yields that barely keep pace with growing demands. Offhand this situation sounds alarming, and it has featured in power politics and in military strategy since 1914, and especially since 1939, notwithstanding the fact that the discovery of synthetic methods of making petroleum products has robbed the oil problem of its political significance. Oil can be obtained from oil shales and tar sands in quantities that equal the probable fluid oil supply. Through the German development of hydrogenation, petroleum products can now be made from coal, particularly from the lowest grade of coal—lignite. True, oil obtained from these sources is much more costly than liquid petroleum, but the important fact is that, thanks to synthesis, the world's reserves are coextensive with the reserves of coal. From the standpoint of world prices and international stabilization, it will be desirable to utilize the low-cost liquid petroleum, wherever found, until the annual yield is no longer adequate to satisfy the annual demand. Then the higher-cost petroleum from distilled oil shales and tar sands and from hydrogenated coal can be developed without working premature economic hardships on any nation or group of nations.

It is difficult to appraise the significance of natural gas as a prospective source of energy, and its reserves are speculative in the extreme. Although it is put to some use in almost every oil field, its commercial utilization is a unique American institution. Produced in 22 states, it makes its way by pipeline to urban centers in 34 states. Distribution by pipeline can be undertaken only where large consuming centers justify the investment. Substantial amounts of the world's oil and gas are produced in regions which lack the population or the technological development or the individual and collective wealth to use natural gas; hence, of the oil- and gas-producing areas outside the United States, only the U.S.S.R. has reached a stage of population density and technological evolution adequate for effective use of natural gas. Indeed, the Russians have worked out and are utilizing an American suggestion for the gasification of thin, unworkable coal seams, and this development may broaden the entire base of natural gas production and at the same time enlarge the world's energy reserves by making hitherto unusable deposits available. The Soviet innovation is so recent that it is not yet possible to gauge its potentialities. Certainly America's example of obtaining 10 percent of its energy requirements from natural gas from oil fields, coupled with Soviet pioneering in coal gasification by controlled underground combustion of thin coal seams, materially expands the industrial horizon, chiefly for those nations which have oil or coal, but also for a few countries which lack commercial seams of coal but which have deposits that will meet the requirements of gasification. To this extent, small-scale industrialization may be achieved where it has been nonexistent in the past; but in general, the countries which have the best commercial coal deposits are most likely to have the noncommercial seams which can be gasified. Hence, however much the harnessing of gas from petroleum and coal fields may extend the world's energy reserves, the development of supplies of natural gas is not likely to alter the major geographic and political features of the industrial pattern.

In the United States there is a tendency to overrate the importance of water as a source of power, primarily because water power has been injected into politics. A succession of court decisions has made most of the nation's power sites public property, and our public servants are convinced that hydroelectric energy can, and must, be generated on such sites by the investment of public funds for the public good. Regardless of the merits of contemporary argument on this problem, there are four significant facts which may well be kept in mind in dealing with water power as a source of energy: first, it is perennially renewed, hence indestructible; second, it is available only within the narrow limits imposed by economic transmission; third, if all the power in the United States were harnessed, it would supply a scant 20 percent of our normal energy requirements; fourth, its industrial utility is limited, and in many situations it cannot compete on a cost basis with other forms of energy. It is not intended to underrate the importance of hydroelectric energy, but a review of its limitations will assist in placing it in better perspective.

It is a major misfortune that human habitation is least adaptable to the climatic and topographic situations which favor a high water-power potential. It rains most in the tropical rain forest, where the white race is unable to live or to carry on industrial pursuits, and for this reason the greatest sources of potential energy in Africa, Asia, and South America are unused. Of an estimated world total of 675,000,000 horse power, African streams would yield 275,000,000, or 35 percent, if harnessed; Asiatic streams, 150,000,000, or 22 percent; South American rivers, 75,000,000, or 11 percent. Not all of this 68 percent of the world's water-power reserve is situated in the rain forest, but the small amount which has a more favorable climatic location is found in almost equally inhospitable mountains. Only in such overcrowded countries as Japan has it proved feasible to make extended use of the streams which descend the mountain slopes, and it is significant that 77 percent of the installed generator capacity in all of Asia is in Japan.

Elsewhere in the world, streams have their greatest fall in relatively inaccessible mountains, and it is a most fortunate circumstance when a river like the Niagara plunges 168 feet in a comparatively flat plain, or the Dnepr rushes through an easily damned rock gorge and thus provides a ready-made site for a dam and reservoir. In some mountainous regions power sites are located within economic transmission distance of industrially inclined populations. This is the case in Italy, where Alpine streams supply electricity to the cities of the Po valley, and in eastern Canada, where streams drop from the Laurentian upland into the habitable Ottawa and Saint Lawrence lowlands. But in many parts of the earth, there is a vast reserve of power just beyond the pale of economic use, and its development depends upon the willingness of private capital or public agencies to anticipate demand and to gamble on the possibility that cheap power will attract a market and the basic transportational requirements of a market. Installations of this kind are pioneering ventures which involve more risk or a longer period of low returns than private utility companies can normally face. Governmental agencies, on the other hand, are not under comparable obligations to stockholders, and the judicious investment of public funds in power projects has unquestionably aided Canada, the U.S.S.R., and the United States in promoting settlement and regional development, just as it has assisted Italy, Germany, and Japan in providing more power for industries that give employment to rapidly growing populations.

As in the case of coal and oil, water power is haphazardly distributed with reference to political boundaries, and genetically the greatest potential reserves tend to be concentrated in regions of minimum accessibility. Utilization of the available power, however, exhibits a familiar pattern: With all due allowance for its fortuitous distribution, it is being harnessed by those nations which have undergone industrialization chiefly through the initial application of other forms of energy.

DISTRIBUTION OF HYDROELECTRIC ENERGY

	HORSE POWER	
	Potential	*Developed*
Africa	275,000,000	175,000
Asia	150,000,000	6,000,000
North America	77,000,000	29,000,000
South America	75,000,000	1,300,000
Europe	74,000,000	27,500,000
Australasia	24,000,000	600,000
World	675,000,000	64,000,000

In certain of them—notably Italy, Norway, and Switzerland—present-day industrial activity leans heavily upon domestic power, but in most of the other nations which have put their streams to work, economic strength is founded upon coal. There is, therefore, nothing fortuitous about the fact that 85 percent of the generator capacity has been installed in nine countries which, among them, have only 25 percent of the world's reserves of water power. Six of those nine nations also possess 80 percent of the world's coal reserves and are responsible for

STATE OF WORLD RESOURCES

two thirds of the world's coal production. Two of them can take credit for producing two thirds of the annual yield of oil, as well as for the entire yield of natural gas.

Power Utilization

	Horse Power	
	Developed	*Potential*
United States	19,000,000	33,000,000
Canada	8,000,000	25,000,000
Italy	6,000,000	6,000,000
France	5,250,000	6,000,000
Japan	4,250,000	7,000,000
U.S.S.R.	3,000,000	70,000,000
Norway	3,000,000	16,000,000
Switzerland	2,800,000	3,600,000
Germany	2,500,000	2,500,000

It is altogether too easy to make sweeping generalizations from a survey of the energy resources, but even with the exercise of self-restraint, several conclusions are inescapable:

1. Industrialization has progressed farthest among the few nations that possess an abundance of coal, although it has spread to a few neighboring countries which can import coal without undue economic hardship.

2. These same nations are also consuming most of the world's petroleum, regardless of its geographic origin.

3. They are producing most of the hydroelectric energy and all of the natural gas.

4. Outside these ten or twelve favored nations, only China has any serious prospect of evolving an industrial economy; all other countries lack coal; their oil and gas will probably be exhausted within a century; only water power will remain—barring the discovery of new forms of industrial energy.

5. With the possible exception of China, the industrial nations are even now firmly established; and though relative positions may change, there is little prospect of any major alteration in the general politico-economic pattern. The role of other nations need not be subordinate, but it will remain fundamentally agricultural, pastoral or extractive.

6. Of the ten or twelve industrial nations, only the United Kingdom has devoted itself to manufacturing, trade, and transportation to

the virtual exclusion of agriculture. In all of the others, the industries are regionalized, and a large fraction of the population is engaged in extractive, agricultural and pastoral occupations. Conservatively it is safe to say that a scant 20 percent of the world's workers make, sell, and deliver the world's manufactured goods. But a large segment of the world's peoples has not yet entered the market for the products of industry.

THE MINERAL SUPPLY

Although coal and the other energy resources have sired our modern industrialization, it is the application of heat and energy to metals which provides the products of industry. Initially, possession of the metals was as vital as the possession of fuel, but modern transportation has altered the geographic and political significance of mineral supplies, and the exploitation of ores is governed rigidly by costs. Thus, we witness the phenomenon of iron ore moving from Chile to Baltimore to be converted into steel; of copper mined in the heart of Africa underselling in the United States copper mined in northern Michigan. As in the case of oil, efficient transportation has placed the world's ore bodies at the disposal of the industrial nations. Although the factor of accessibility is still a fundamental consideration in the exploitation of certain mineral deposits, the location of specific industries is primarily a function of the geography of fuel and transportation.

Accompanying improvements in transportation there has also been a phenomenal increase in the consumption of metals. Mineral statisticians have demonstrated that more metal has been mined since 1900 than in all the earlier history of man. Mining operations have shifted from small enterprises on high-grade deposits to vast extractive projects involving deposits of any grade, so long as they are large. Milling and metallurgy have focused attention upon the recovery of metal from low-grade ores, in a successful effort to keep the known reserves abreast of the insatiable demand. Exploration has extended not merely to the corners of the earth but to the depths, as well. For geophysical equipment is being employed to an increasing extent to peer beneath the inscrutable surface and to determine what lies hidden at depths within reach of the drill and the shaft.

For the most part, the search for raw materials or for economic methods of recovery has been successful. A few things, like beryllium and radium, have not been found in sufficient concentrations to meet the potential demand. Other minerals have been found in superabundance—for example, the phosphates of Wyoming and Idaho. But there has usually been enough ore of the common metals in sight to insure a continuous supply, notwithstanding obvious vagaries and inequities in geographic distribution. Even the war has not overtaxed the capacity of existing mines, except for a few strategic minerals like mica. But the accelerated tempo of war use has forced the industrial nations of the earth, and especially the United States, to reassess the mineral wealth available for post-war industry. Intensive exploration has made practically all pre-war estimates of reserves obsolete, and in the absence of revised computations, it seems wise to make limited use of figures in the ensuing discussion.

From the standpoint of tonnage, the iron and steel industry not only yields the highest metal output but also draws most heavily on reserves of raw materials. Notwithstanding the growing competition between steel products and the light metals and plastics, there is little prospect that steel will be eclipsed by lighter substitutes. The latter will find their way into many new situations and will displace steel in some; but the displacement is not likely to alter the magnitude of steel production. The flow of iron ore, scrap, and alloys is, therefore, a matter of major concern to all the larger industrial nations.

At the start of the present war, nearly 90 percent of the world's iron ore came from seven districts:

1. Lake Superior district (Minnesota, Michigan, Wisconsin)
2. Lorraine (France)
3. Krivoi Rog (Ukraine)
4. Kiruna district (northern Sweden)
5. Midlands (England)
6. Magnitogorsk district (southern Ural Mountains)
7. Birmingham district (Alabama)

The districts are listed in the order of their production, and hence in the order of current importance. Their present importance is not, however, a measure of the reserves which they contain, but rather of their convenient location with respect to large consuming centers. It is significant that neither Germany nor the United Kingdom can operate their large steel industries solely on the basis of domestic ore production. The United Kingdom has made liberal use of beneficiating or high grade ores from northern Sweden and from the Bilbao district of northern Spain. Germany has combined Swedish and Lorraine ores with her own meager supply of domestic ore. The U.S.S.R. is entirely self-sufficient, even for a considerably enlarged steel industry. Soviet estimates of high-grade ore in the southern Ural Mountains require some revision downward, but even so, the magnetic iron of Magnitogorsk was ample to keep Soviet furnaces operating with only a fractional decline in output when German armies overran the Krivoi Rog district in the Dnepr bend of the Ukraine.

Although the United States has regularly imported some foreign ore, it has been able to supply its own needs. It still is; but known reserves, especially of high grade ores, have been seriously depleted, and concern is now felt regarding future supplies. It is difficult to appraise the situation accurately, because in the Lake Superior district, which yields over 85 percent of United States iron ore, the states have the stupid policy of taxing reserves. Hence, there is little incentive either to know how large the reserve may be, or to conserve the reserves which have been determined by exploration. As of 1940, the known reserves in the Lake Superior district were 1,342,000,000 tons. At the 1940 rate of exploitation, the quantity of good ore (about 50 percent metallic iron) will last only 20 years; at the 1943 rate, it would be good for a scant 14 years. For many years, however, the rate of decline in reserves has been substantially less than the annual production, and it is reasonably safe to conclude that reserves of 50 percent ore in the Lake Superior district are probably adequate for another 40 years of peak exploitation, and for 60 years of normal drain. Lower-grade ores are even more abundant, but there is understandable reluctance to include in an inventory raw materials whose quality and location make them marginal or submarginal under current economic conditions.

The cautious estimates of reserves in our major ore-producing district have occasioned some alarm over the future of the American steel industry. Although there is reason to take the situation seriously and to institute conservational practices and new exploration, there is no cause for panic. Viewed broadly, American reserves, though not the greatest domestic supply in the world, are still impressive:

	Million Tons
Lake Superior district	2,600
Southeastern States (chiefly Alabama)	1,900
Northeastern States (chiefly New York)	600
Scattered	100
Total	5,200

To this total may be added at least another 40 million tons of Canadian high-grade ore in the Lake Superior district, and the estimate may be raised by 40 percent, or more, if one is willing to hazard the opinion that submarginal ores will ultimately yield to new milling and metallurgical techniques.

The horizon expands still farther when foreign ores within economic shipping distances of the United States are taken into account: Newfoundland has estimated reserves of four billion tons at tidewater, although for some time the tonnage mined has been limited to the comparatively modest requirements of the steel industry at Sydney, N.S. For many years the Bethlehem Steel Company's plant at Sparrow Point, Maryland, has drawn extensively upon the iron ores near Coquimbo, Chile; moderately upon ores in Oriente Providence, Cuba; and it is ready to utilize iron deposits in Venezuela. In consequence of developments which have accompanied the war, the 7.5 billion-ton reserve in Brazil is now available not only for a small Brazilian steel industry, but also for any American mills which can economically use raw material from the largest single reserve in the world. The total additional supply within commercial reach of the United States steel industry is no less than 16 billion tons, and with more exhaustive exploration it may prove to be substantially more. Utilization of these foreign supplies will inevitably be accompanied by the erection of more blast furnaces on the Atlantic and Gulf coasts within easy reach of Appalachian coal; but there is no prospect of mass migration of the industry.

Western Europe is also well endowed with iron ore, and the largest reserves are in the Lorraine district of France, which is believed to contain as much ore as all the districts in the United States combined. The metallic content of the raw material is low, and it is only the proximity of metallurgical coal in the Ruhr-Sambre-Meuse basin that makes its use profitable. The United Kingdom has another 1.3 billion tons of similar low-grade iron ore, and it has been found expedient to mix high-grade Swedish or Spanish ore with the leaner material from the Midlands in British furnaces. Germany, too, depends upon Swedish ores for "beneficiation." Thus, in a sense, the steel industries of Germany, Britain, France, Belgium, and Luxembourg depend upon four productive areas:

	Million Tons
Lorraine (low grade)	5,600
Midlands (low grade)	1,300
Sweden (high grade)	1,500
Spain (high grade)	700
Total	8,100

North Africa contributes some beneficiating ore, and minor amounts of medium- to high-grade iron are taken from small reserves in Czechoslovakia, Germany, Austria, and Poland. Though these countries feature modestly in the statistics of production, they scarcely rate serious consideration in an estimate of reserves.

In the U.S.R.R. the reserves are at least equal to the total in western Europe, but the claim that proven Soviet reserves are as large as those in all the rest of the world combined may be regarded with some skepticism. Ore of Lake Superior type and quality has long been mined in the Krivoi Rog district, lying in the bend of the Dnepr River, about 240 miles west of the coking coals in the Donets Basin. Iron of Swedish type and quality occurs in scattered but large deposits through the Ural Mountains, particularly in the area between Sverdlovsk and Magnitogorsk. Good coking coal, unfortunately, is not at hand, and the steel industry has been founded on a coal-ore shuttle system between the Ural heavy industrial cities and the Kuznetsk Basin, 1,200 miles to the east, near Novo Sibirsk.

Although the iron deposits elsewhere in the Eastern Hemisphere have been underrated until recent years, it is safe to say that, in the aggregate, they contain less ore than any of the major districts of Europe. Japan has pieced together a marginal steel industry which found Manchukuoan iron ore none too satisfactory. Ore from the Philippines helped raise its quality, but even so, greater dependence was placed upon the purchase and use of scrap. The war has seen local iron-ore deposits exploited for the manufacture of steel in Australia, in northeastern India, and in the Union of South Africa. There is evidently adequate raw material of commercial grade to sustain iron and steel industries commensurate with the needs of these three divisions of the British Empire, but the ore reserves now known are not likely to alter the geographic pattern of heavy industry at any time in the future. That pattern is geared to the deposits of coking coal in the eastern United States, western Europe, and the U.S.S.R. The industry can still use conveniently situated bodies of iron ore, but it no longer hesitates to assemble the iron, as well as the ferrous alloys, from distant sources. Only one requirement must be met: the over-all cost of raw materials must be at competitive levels.

Ever since bauxite, the ore of aluminum, was discovered at, and named from, Baux, France, that country has featured in bauxite production, but not in the reduction of the ore to metallic aluminum. The ore is exceedingly refractory, and the elimination of chemically combined water requires heat, whereas the elimination of the oxygen is accomplished by an electrochemical process which puts a premium on cheap and abundant hydroelectric power. At no time in the comparatively brief history of the aluminum industry has the geography of bauxite been more than a secondary factor. Ore from Arkansas and ore from Surinam ultimately arrive in electrochemical plants in northern and western New York; French, Hungarian, Yugoslavian, and Italian ores gravitate to the hydroelectric facilities of the Alps and the Scandinavian mountains; and British aluminum reaches the mother country circuitously—starting perhaps, in British Guiana and undergoing reduction in southeastern Canada, where the power available has greatly exceeded the industrial and domestic demand.

Accessibility is not, however, a negligible factor, as the distribution of bauxite mining reveals upon closer scrutiny. Remote deposits in India, Africa, and Brazil are neglected in favor of ores that are closer to the power sites nearest the consuming markets. Indeed, when it was discovered that magnesium can be effectively alloyed with aluminum and that it can be commercially recovered and reduced from salts, brines, and certain rocks which are widespread, it was a definite relief to the industry to have a new commercial metal that could be recovered from domestic raw materials.

In consequence of the war there has been a heavy drain on the world's more accessible bauxite deposits. A vigorous search is being made for new supplies, not so much to sustain war production as to provide the raw materials for post-war industry, which anticipates a vigorous demand for light metal products. There is no reason to believe that the well-defined geographic pattern of the industry will change; on the contrary, it is likely that every effort will be made to commercialize the recovery of aluminum from deposits with a lower metal content than bauxite, in preference to the extension of mining operations into still more distant corners of the globe. Aluminum is the most abundant of the metals; every clay soil and nearly every common rock contain it in tantalizing quantities. War needs have prompted a lot of expensive experimentation with the low-grade aluminous materials, and it may ultimately take only a small differential in shipping costs to inspire the recovery of aluminum from the commonest of local raw materials.

Unlike iron and aluminum, the base metals are rare substances, and only under special geological circumstances has nature concentrated even the more abundant of them—copper, lead, and zinc—in deposits that can be exploited profitably. Mines producing one or more of these metals have been opened on rich concentrations in such relatively remote regions as Katanga in central Africa, Yunnan in southern China, and Chuquicamata in the Andes of Chile. Yet a study of the geography, the history and the economics of the base-metal industry reveals the same general trend as in the recovery of iron and aluminum: Cost is the governing factor, and remote deposits can be utilized only when, by virtue of extraordinary quality or quantity, or the availability of cheap labor, the cost of transportation can be completely neutralized. Mining operations are thus more numerous near the world's industrial centers, and the phenomenon of exhausted mines, like the old lead-zinc workings of the Galena district in Illinois, Iowa, and Wisconsin, reveals the exacting penalty of intensive use. It is rare that any single metallic deposit can long stand the wear and tear of exploitation, although Rio Tinto in Spain seems to have supplied as much copper to Mussolini as to his Roman precursors, and to the Carthaginians and Phoenicians before them.

Old and long-worked deposits are being exhausted. Indeed, mines that were important sources of supply in central Europe at the time of Agricola (1490–1555), who described them picturesquely in *De re metallica*, were depleted before the modern industrial era began. The fabulous wealth in the copper mines of the Keweenaw Peninsula in northern Michigan is nearly gone; the mining profession anticipates early exhaustion of the lead and zinc deposits of the Missouri-Tri-state districts, of Belgium, and of Germany. To replace the deposits which are going, the mining profession will have to extend the geographic radius of its operations, but the important fact about geographic extension is this: It will go no farther than it must for iron, aluminum, copper, lead and zinc. It may go far afield for higher priced raw materials like tin, tungsten, gold, platinum, and radium. But only the rarest or the most precious of metals can draw men much beyond the limit of cheap and quick access to the world's few industrial centers. Although accessibility is relative, the industrial centers are fixed by the presence of coal. They may grow or undergo other changes; new transportation lines may bring them closer in time or in cost. But the geographic handicaps of distance, climate and topography are immutable, and they must still be regarded this way in viewing the world's resources. When supplies of metals run low, new deposits will be sought and worked, but their locations are likely to fall within the same economic range—hence the same geographic range—as the mines now in operation. Only the optimist can see immense possibilities for the immediate future in reported mineral wealth in the Siberian Arctic or in the inner plateaus of the Himalayas; for the hardheaded industrialist would sooner turn to substitutes than pay the profitless cost of acquiring such remote supplies.

In viewing the mineral resources available for use in the post-war period, therefore, one must take a coldly practical view. The war has taken a terrific toll of supplies which are conveniently located with respect to the industrial centers. With regard to every metal, the United States has suffered most, and it is fortunate that stocks aboveground and limitless quantities of scrap will enable her to coast along on current facilities until her industries become reoriented to other hemispheric sources of supply. More iron will come from Newfoundland, Alabama, the Caribbean, and northern South America; proportionately and progressively less from Lake Superior. More aluminum will be imported from the Caribbean countries; the Guianas will hold their own, but Arkansas will become an incidental source of supply. American copper will not relinquish its primary place to African and South American sources of supply without a bitter struggle. Survival depends entirely on the American consumer's willingness to pay a premium of four cents a pound on the domestic product.

Europe's supply problems are somewhat less urgent, thanks to nature's generosity in dispensing iron ore and bauxite. African copper is the answer to a critical deficiency of that metal; and even though the per capita consumption of lead and zinc is far below that of the United States, most of the European deposits of these two metals are in an even more advanced state of depletion. In the U.S.S.R. the development of three centers of heavy industry—in the Donets Basin, the Urals, and the Kuznetsk Basin—is being followed by local and peripheral developments in the extraction of other minerals. Except for the manganese at Nikopol, European Russia is not mineralogically rich, though small mines are numerous. In the Urals, the mineralogy is somewhat specialized, but copper is important, and platinum is worthy of mention. It is in the headwater reaches of the Ob-Irtish and Yenesei rivers, along the Sinkiang border and in the Balkhash Lake district that Soviet industry is finding its principal supplies of the base metals. In the rest of the world, desultory mining activities have sprung up to supply smaller regional industrial centers, like those of Honshu-Shanghai, Sydney-Melbourne, Calcutta, and Johannesburg-Pretoria; or to exploit a phenomenally rich strike which would be a profitable venture anywhere, like the gold of the Witwatersrand, or the lead-zinc-silver ore of Broken Hill, Australia, or the silver-pitchblende deposits of Great Bear Lake.

If our knowledge of metallic reserves other than iron seems to lie outside the category of exact science, vagueness does not imply deficiency. On the contrary, unconcern regarding inventories is an indication of their adequacy. In fact, in normal times the world is troubled with too much of many things, while individual nations are troubled about the lack of certain critical raw materials. There is no discernible scientific reason why nature should have placed 80 percent of the world's tin in Malaysia, about as much of its antimony in China, approximately the same proportion of its nickel in Ontario, and perhaps 85 percent of its molybdenum in Colorado. The need for such metals as these is no less urgent for being quantitatively small, and its urgency makes it certain that no nation will ever be mineralogically self-sufficient. Indeed, there is only approximate self-sufficiency within the broad industrial regions.

THE FOOD SUPPLY

The space devoted to the mineral raw materials of industry may seem out of proportion to their relative importance, especially as a scant 20 percent of the world's population depends upon direct participation in industry for a livelihood. But it is this 20 percent, regimented by the inexorable requirements of mills, motors, and machines, which is steadily shaping the economy, the habits, and even the psychology of the other 80 percent. For food the industrial populations of North America and Europe depend upon a comparatively modern type of agricultural and pastoral specialization. Subsistence farming has been gradually relegated to remote regions, and in the Western Hemisphere

STATE OF WORLD RESOURCES

it is vanishing. Land use has acquired a rigid pattern in which the farmer or the rancher may think that he retains his individualism; but agricultural and pastoral self-expression attain approximately the degree of individualism which one finds in male attire at a Chamber of Commerce banquet. This is not to reflect on conformance in either group; but in the case of the farmer nonconformance with the requirements of growing season, precipitation, topography, and soil would inevitably result in bankruptcy. True, he has some latitude in the selection of secondary or minor crops, but he has little choice among the major commercial crops. Despite the suspicion that, like Topsy, the specialized farming and grazing of the United States just grew, its systematization is remarkable, and it is serving as a model which has been widely adopted in the best agricultural lands of the Southern Hemisphere. It was forceably introduced, also, in the richest farmlands of Eurasia, in the program of collectivization which Stalin applied in the Ukraine, in eastern European Russia, and in western Siberia. The raising of crops and animals is thus taking on certain of the attributes of industry.

A mineral economist must approach the subject of land use with trepidation, for this field of study is still too new to have escaped the mixed blessing and curse of highly partisan theory. A few fundamentals are beyond argument. No academician can argue about the lengths of growing seasons in specific regions, which approximate latitudinal zones but which shift somewhat in latitudinal position and in width as they pass from the Mediterranean and marine west-coast climates of the continental margins to the continental climates of the interiors and of the east coasts. No one can argue about the minimum moisture requirements of specific crops, although available moisture may vary not only with the amount of precipitation, but also with the seasonal distribution of rainfall, the evaporation rate, the texture of the soil, the nature of the landforms, the texture of the topography, the position of the water table, the character and structure of the underlying rocks.

With due allowance for these important variables, it is possible to plot the land-use pattern, especially within the temperate zone. Toward the Arctic, not only are there limitations on the growing season, but there are no available soils in the true agronomic sense. Frost action is the only weathering process in operation, and the fragmentation of the rocks which it causes cannot be said to produce soils. Although the raising of reindeer has been undertaken in the tundra, the

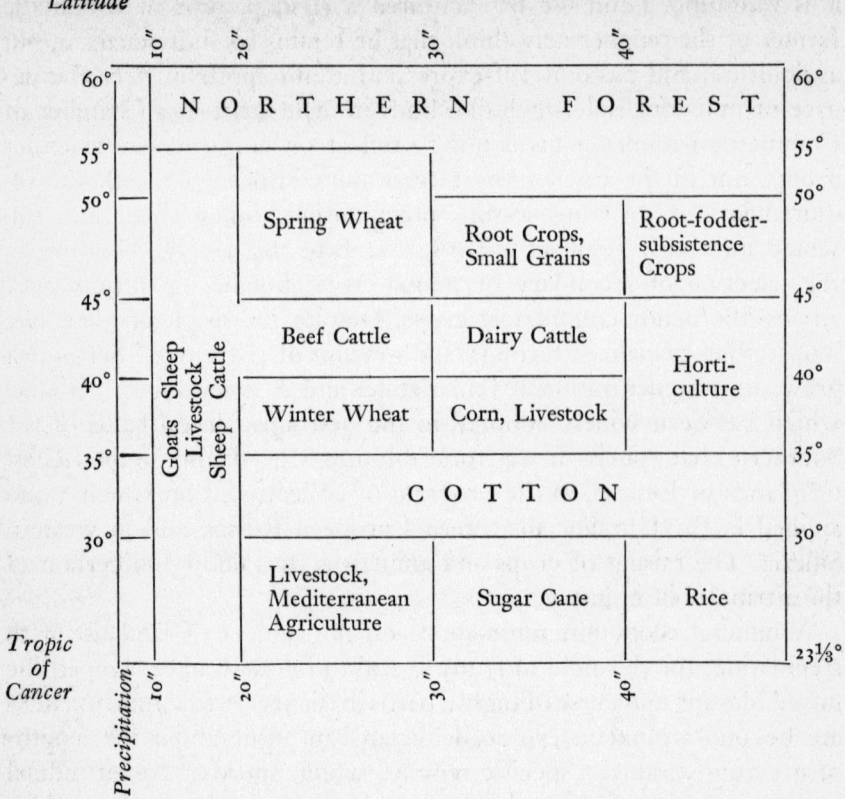

LAND-USE PATTERN IN THE TEMPERATE ZONE

projects have been experimental, and no final conclusion has been reached as to whether this kind of grazing can assume commercial importance. Obviously such an enterprise might be of more concern to a country like the U.S.S.R., where the land is under greater pressure, than it would be to Canada, which is so seriously underpopulated.

Commercial agriculture starts with the taiga or northern forest zone close to the Arctic Circle, and from the forest southward, wherever the rainfall exceeds ten inches, there is no major area which does not lend itself to the raising of crops or animals on a commercial basis. In North America, land use has taken on a pattern which is ideally systematic, and which is repeated, with or without modification, in other sections of the world. The presence of mountains or of highlands and plateaus may break the continuity of the pattern; such regional modifications of temperature as are caused by the Gulf Stream along the west coast of Europe may shift the agricultural belts as much as five degrees farther north; the vicissitudes of political boundaries and national habits, or programs designed to achieve national self-sufficiency may warp the pattern without invalidating it. For long and hard experience has demonstrated that this is the most efficient way in which the land may be used, though it does not represent natural limitations of crop cultivation. Corn can be grown in the cotton belt, but cotton offers the highest cash return; wheat can be raised in the corn belt, and it is a minor crop in still other situations; the limits of cotton culture have not yet been fully explored. But as a general rule, the optimum product for each latitude-precipitation zone provides the soundest investment for the landowner.

In the Tropics, commercial agriculture has not yet claimed so much of the land, and where the climate encourages or permits settlement, there is still a great deal of subsistence farming. For the most part, commercialization has been synonymous with foreign investment and exploitation, and in different parts of the world, plantation agriculture has been responsible for incidental land reclamation, social improvement, and economic stabilization. The system, however, has its vicious aspects, and it has been blamed for many evils, such as peonage, destruction of forests, exhaustion of soils. It is not the purpose of this article to condemn or to defend the system. It does regiment the people and the countries in which it is introduced, and too often it leaves nothing of value behind. But many plantation projects have brought permanent employment and improvement, and all of them have wrested a greater return from the land. Only in the Far East has the native landowner and laborer obtained maximum value from every acre of land without benefit of plantation technique; for here the pressure of population, coupled with the copious rainfall, has led to intensive rice culture. Neither the topography nor the natural vegetation has been a bar to complete land utilization, for the available manpower is so enormous as to have accomplished prodigious feats—the terracing of mountains, the annihilation and elimination of the irrepressible rain forest, the conservation of virtually every drop of water and nearly every particle of soil. The price in human labor which must be paid for overpopulation comes high, and the reward to those who pay it is small. But they have demonstrated to an unbelieving white race that even the tropical rain forest can be controlled and can be made habitable if the pressure on the land becomes sufficiently great.

No attempt will be made to chart tropical agriculture in the systematic way which was tried for temperate zone products. Except in the highest mountain ranges the growing season is perpetual throughout the Torrid Zone, and variations in altitude provide the minor modifications in temperature which individual crops, such as coffee, may require. Precipitation varies with latitude: the world's largest deserts coincide with the tropics of Cancer and Capricorn. Toward the equator the seasonal rainfall increases, initially to the point at which it will support the mixed grassland-forest vegetation of the tropical savannas. The lands beneath the equator are so thoroughly drenched that a dense forest growth covers the earth with incredible speed, usually to the exclusion of cultivated crops, unless the latter are protected from encroachment by unremitting labor.

As a consequence of the distribution of rainfall, the Torrid Zone acquires maximum utility for the human race in two zones that roughly parallel the equator, and in which there is sufficient rain for grass or savanna but not so much as to create a jungle. The deserts which lie poleward are utterly useless; but the grasslands support a pastoral economy, and the tropical savannas make satisfactory sites for sugar cane or, at higher elevations, for coffee, and for other specialized crops. The rain forest normally defies widespread settlement and human use, yet part of the Malay-East Indian region, which lies in the equatorial rain belt, supports dense populations. In some of the Dutch and British islands, plantation agriculture has so successfully commercialized the growing of rubber, cinchona, and coconut trees as to have cornered the rubber, quinine, and copra production of the world. Elsewhere in these islands and nearby mainland areas, the rain forest has been literally up-rooted, and the land is used for the intensive cultivation of rice on mountainous topography which would defy conversion to machine agriculture.

The phenomenon of dense settlement in the East Indies has not been duplicated elsewhere in the tropical rain belt. The sparsely inhabited coastal lands along the Caribbean, chiefly in Central America, have kept the United States market supplied with bananas, but on the basis of shifting sites of cultivation, as disease claims the older plantations. Brazil lost its rubber industry, and the strenuous war effort to resuscitate the cultivation of rubber in Brazil and in Liberia has been inconclusive save on one point: Wild rubber cannot compete with plantation rubber from the standpoint of efficiency in gathering the latex. And whether wild or cultivated, the rubber tree yields a profit only where labor is abundant, intelligent, and cheap. Locale seems to be of minor importance so long as transportation is available. At the moment, the weight of evidence suggests that, in contrast with every other climatic region, the rain forest can most effectively be utilized where it is well drained. Hill lands and mountain slopes are better adapted both to subsistence and to commercial agriculture, for in such situations the superabundant water can be drained or controlled. On the plains it gets beyond control and inhibits tillage and at the same time takes a heavy toll of human, animal, and vegetable life through the media of bacterial and fungal diseases and insect-borne plagues.

Except in the rain forest, agricultural and pastoral peoples have placed a premium on plains. Whether they be in the Danubian basin, the Ukraine or the Po; the Mississippi, the Missouri, or the Red River valleys; Patagonia or Australia; the valleys of the Indus, the Ganges, Yangtze-Kiang or Hwang-ho—so long as there is water and a growing season, the world's peoples have consistently found their efforts to earn a living most successful on the world's plains. Within limits, the antiquity of settlement is reflected in the density of settlement, with the flood plains of China and of India reaching appalling acmes, followed closely by the narrow valley of the Nile, which supports most of Egypt's population. The plains of the Po, of the central Danube valley, and of the Ukraine illustrate the same trend in Europe. In all of these Old World localities, the presence of crowded populations and the hereditary subdivision of farms have led to development of small holdings which must be managed on an intensive subsistence basis. The demand made upon every acre is very nearly as great as in the rice lands of South China or Java; and high yields per acre, if obtained at all, are wrested from the soil only at the expense of soil enrichment, careful soil management, and back-breaking labor.

Only in the U.S.S.R. has there been any movement to modernize the agriculture of the plains. Through collectivization the individual has been "relieved" of the burdens of private ownership, and large farm units have been created out of the hopeless welter of minuscule private holdings. Both the principle and the method of collectivization generated a storm of criticism and applause; but without holding any brief for the principle or for the method of implementing it, the geographer may well ponder the result: From the impartial viewpoint of agricultural economics, the farm program has benefited greatly. The small farmer was unable to manage the soil, and acreage yields were pitifully low. Under collectivization the fertility of the soil has been preserved or improved, yields have been increased, and mechanization has augmented production and income with a fraction of the farm labor formerly employed. On the other hand, the livestock program has been a dismal failure, and the one part of the farm program which has been successful is patterned closely upon the system of private ownership of large farm units which characterizes the plains of the United States, Argentina, and Uruguay.

The Soviet experiment has quite clearly demonstrated the superiority of modernized, extensive farming over antiquated, intensive cultivation of small individual holdings. But whether conversion may be wisely attempted in the plains of Europe, and northern India and North China is problematical. Mechanization releases labor, and where would the technologically unemployed of the Danubian Basin, the Po valley, North China, and northern India find a substitute means of livelihood? Stalin had new mines and mills available to reëmploy his dispossessed peasants; and until similar possibilities of reëmployment are available elsewhere in the Old World, it seems necessary to retain the present vicious system, in which the crowded, poverty-stricken peasant toils to give his family a meager living, that it may reproduce to provide abundant and cheap labor to repeat the cycle.

The Dutch and British have likewise demonstrated the economy of systematization and modernization in the rubber industry. But thanks partly to the nature of the industry, they have also provided an ideal illustration of rural employment for teeming millions. The Dutch and the British have not modernized the raising of the main food crop of these peoples—rice; and one may take some comfort in the thought that food for half the world must still be raised the hard way, by the expenditure of almost limitless human effort. American ingenuity has discovered that the exacting demands of rice can be met mechanically on the alluvial plains of Louisiana, but the American system is not applicable to the rugged terrane of southeastern Asia, nor can it compete with the cheap manual labor available in that part of the world.

CONCLUSION

The foregoing review of the natural resources may seem too optimistic in its insistence that there is no impending failure of any major raw material. Among the energy resources the supply of coal is adequate for centuries to come, and the life of the scattered reserves will be prolonged by the utilization of self-renewing hydroelectric energy. Fluid petroleum is good for at least two generations. The known supply will probably be stretched by improvements in combustion-efficiency; the reserves themselves may be extended; and even with impending exhaustion, oil shales, tar sands, lignite, and fast-growing tropical vegetation offer proven possibilities of conversion to petroleum and its products. Among the metals, only the adequacy of the most conveniently located deposits is in doubt or in jeopardy. For the United States the main sources of supply for iron and aluminum are likely to shift—aluminum, quickly; iron, more gradually and over a period of two or three generations. The United States is likely to face comparable adjustments in meeting its huge demands for copper, lead, and zinc. It is no longer the self-sufficient nation of 1938 and ante, but its tremendous coal reserve and its unrivaled technological facilities leave no doubt as to its leadership in the century ahead.

Specialization in industry and commerce on the part of certain nations and regions has called for comparable specialization in agriculture, livestock raising and forestry in other areas. And specialization has led steadily to commercialization, one phase of which is mechanization. This trend has achieved its most advanced development in the parts of the earth that are "new," from the standpoint of human history. Throughout the temperate zones and, to a growing degree, in the Torrid Zone, the adaptability of plains and low, but flat, plateaus and uplands to machine agriculture has placed a premium on this kind of topography. Mountainous areas, which commonly rise along the margins of the continents, have been partially abandoned or completely avoided, save as sources of supply for water or for minerals. In the plains of the United States, mechanization permits roughly 40 percent of the population to feed the other 60 percent, and to supply half the world's needs for cotton. In the more humid sections of the Russian steppes, the food requirements of 180,000,000 people are now being met with a steadily diminishing supply of farm labor.

In both the United States and the U.S.S.R., the primary concern is to satisfy large domestic populations. In the sparsely-settled Southern Hemisphere, on the other hand, the small domestic demands are easily met; large surpluses of wheat, cattle, sheep (and wool), and even cotton and corn are grown for export. The Argentine, Uruguay, and Paraguay; Australia and New Zealand; and, to less degree, South Africa—together with Canada in the Northern Hemisphere—are the world's underpopulated countries; and in this role they have undertaken to supply the deficiencies of overpopulated Europe and, to some extent, of overpopulated Asia. Their ability to do so clearly bespeaks their capacity to support larger domestic populations, and from an historical standpoint it will not take long for these countries to fill up. As they fill, they will absorb a higher percentage of their food production, and it is inevitable that they will soon cease to supply the densely populated sections of the earth. Under these circumstances, it seems likely that mechanized agriculture is due to spread steadily to all the plains of Europe and ultimately to those of Asia and of the tropics. For it is the paradox of agriculture that the few, with mechanical aids, can more effectively feed the many than the many can feed themselves.

If this prophecy is valid, there may be good reason to ponder the threat of technological unemployment—the problem of plenty of everything except work. This was the dilemma of the thirties, when the philosophy of defeatism lamented the loss of the American frontier—the refuge of the unemployed. If the frontier's function was the absorption of the unemployed—an assumption which was never proved—it has not vanished. It has merely shifted from the United States to other lands. It has also changed character, for the problem is no longer that of transforming the wilderness into self-sustaining farmland, but of supplying a hungry world with food and an industrial civilization with raw materials. The U.S.S.R. and Canada are just discovering the possibilities of their subarctic terrane. Brazil, Paraguay, and Argentina are beginning to utilize their subtropical savannas and steppes. The eyes of American and European industry are shifting to more distant sources for their raw materials and to foreign populations for expanded markets to absorb the products of their mills. As the horizon expands beyond national boundaries, individual opportunities expand in the same direction—not in competition with the nationals of foreign countries, for post-war needs will require products and services which they have never supplied.

There may be serious domestic dislocations among the industrial nations as the sights are raised and refocused on foreign raw materials and markets. Among self-centered and self-satisfied peoples, like Americans, psychological adjustment to foreign service may come slowly. But with post-war demands to be met and with post-war reconstruction and rehabilitation to be achieved, there is no dearth of work, though it will take some organizing genius to effect a union of workers and the jobs to be done.

Population Problems
By KARL SAX

ACCORDING to Archbishop Usher, man was created in 4004 B.C. Let us assume that the Bishop was correct, that Pandora had not released the host of evils to plague mankind, that Ceres had provided an unlimited food supply, and that man was able to move freely to all parts of the world. Under such conditions the descendants of Adam and Eve could have doubled the population of the world every twenty-five years. But let us assume a population growth rate equal to that maintained by modern man in the nineteenth century, when, in spite of disease, famine and war, the world population was doubled in one hundred years. Even this relatively moderate growth rate would have resulted in a population of more than 2,100 million—the present figure—by 1000 B.C. Four hundred years later the population density of the entire world would have been nearly 700 per square mile, or about equal to that of the most densely populated countries of Europe. By the beginning of the Christian era the world population would have grown so large that there would have been 43,000 people for every square mile of land surface of the world, and by 800 A.D. there would not have been standing room for all on the entire surface of the earth.

We now know that the genus *Homo* has lived on this earth for several hundred thousand years and that the species *sapiens* has existed for at least 40,000 years. Obviously man's early existence was precarious and the human population grew very slowly. Disease, starvation, and sudden death took a heavy toll. Presumably man multiplied as rapidly as biological and environmental circumstances would permit, but not until about 1825 did world population reach a billion souls. In one additional century it had nearly doubled. This rapid increase has been made possible by the application of scientific methods to agriculture, industry, transportation and medicine. The rate of growth has declined in many parts of the world during the past fifty years, but for the world as a whole the population has been increasing at the rate of about one percent per year—a rate which doubles the population every 70 years.[1] In some areas the population growth is rapid and in other regions it is declining. This differential growth rate and population density in various parts of the world creates problems which lead to economic and military strife.

I

The fundamental laws which determine population growth were formulated by Malthus almost 150 years ago.[2] "I think I may fairly make two postulates," said Malthus. "First that food is necessary to the existence of man, secondly that the passion between sexes is necessary, and will remain nearly in its present state. These two laws," he continued, "ever since we have had any knowledge of mankind, appear to have been fixed laws of nature; and, as we have not hitherto seen any alteration in them, we have no right to conclude that they will ever cease to be what they were."

Malthus then proceeded to show that the tendency for all living things, including man, is to increase in numbers beyond the means of subsistence, and that everywhere "checks" are operating to restrict the growth of populations. The human population has been held in check by famine, disease, war, and infanticide, and these checks continue to operate to a considerable extent in all parts of the world even at the present time. Science has made great advances in control of disease, and the span of human life in many countries is nearly double that which prevailed in the Middle Ages. Wars may be eliminated when we realize how completely futile they have become. Infanticide is no longer tolerated in civilized societies. Preventive checks to population growth are becoming widespread in many parts of the world, but are not prevalent in some of the most overpopulated areas. Of the positive checks to population growth, the food supply is the most basic factor.

Of the 51 million square miles of land surface of the earth, only about 20 percent is suitable for cultivation or effective pasture.[3] These 6,500 million acres must support the future population of the world if man is to be dependent on agriculture for his food supply. We now use about 4,000 million acres of arable land to support a world population of 2,100 million people, or two acres per person. Even with this amount of land available, about half of the people of the world live little above

---

[1] R. Pearl, *The Natural History of Population* (New York, 1939).
[2] T. R. Malthus, *An Essay on the Principle of Population* (1809).
[3] "Two Billion People," *Fortune*, February, 1944.

the subsistence level, and many suffer from recurrent famines. Estimates based on average crop yields and a reasonable standard of living show that about 2.5 acres of arable land are needed to provide a person with food, clothing, and other necessities.[4] If all of the good potentially arable land were brought into cultivation we would have for our present world population a little more than 3 acres of arable land per capita. It is possible that the utilization of marginal land and the extension of agriculture into colder regions of the world might bring the total acreage of arable land to 10,000 million acres or nearly 5 acres per capita,[5] but, obviously, much of the additional land would be much less productive than that now in use. It is clear that the growth of the human population cannot long continue, even at the present rate, if a reasonably high standard of living is to be enjoyed by all people of all nations.

So long as man is dependent on agriculture for his food supply, the population will be limited by the amount and productivity of the arable land. There is the possibility that the chemist can produce food from air, coal and sawdust, or that the physiologist may be able to develop photosynthetic production of food independently of the living plant, but for the immediate future at least, we must rely on agriculture. New technical processes and new and better crops will aid agriculture, but many of the new innovations have been greatly over-rated. The production of yeast as a source of both protein and vitamins in the human diet is a promising development, but the sugar or molasses used in its production still has to be synthesized by living green plants. The prediction that yeast may be produced to sell at ten cents per pound seems unduly optimistic in view of present retail prices of nearly a dollar a pound for bakers' yeast, and nearly two dollars a pound for brewers' yeast prepared for human consumption. Journalists write assuringly of increased production by hydroponics and vernalization. Crop production by soilless agriculture has decided limitations, both biological and economic; while vernalization, although discovered in the United States before the Civil War, is used only in Russia and is of doubtful economic value.

Any calculation of the land necessary to produce the food and clothing for a given population involves two variables—soil productivity and the standard of living. These two factors vary enormously in dif-

[4] P. E. Brown, "Land and Land Use," *Science*, LXXXIII (1936).
[5] W. S. Thompson, *Population Problems* (New York, 1935).

ferent parts of the world. In Japan and parts of China, one acre of arable land supports two or three persons, but the yields per acre are high and the level of living is low. The more productive countries of Europe—England, Germany, and France—are able to support about one person per acre of arable land after allowing for food imports.[6] A favorable climate, intensive cultivation and good soil enables these farmers to produce yields per acre nearly 50 percent above the world average. In Italy there is also about one acre of crop land per person, but the soil is poor and the dietary standards are low. In the United States we have more than three acres of arable land per capita and our crop yields per acre are only slightly above the world average. The dietary standards of this country, Canada, Australia, and New Zealand are the highest in the world. Populations of more than two persons per acre are now supported only in regions where two crops per year can be grown and where the standard of living is little above subsistence levels.

Since the population density of the United States is almost exactly that of the world as a whole and since our crop yields per acre are but little above the world average, an analysis of our agricultural production and consumption is of particular interest. We have been using about 3 acres of arable land per person, yet we do not have adequate nutritional standards for many of our people. According to the Department of Agriculture *Yearbook* for 1940, a good nutritional standard for all families in the United States would require at least 70 percent more tomatoes and citrus fruits, 100 percent more green leafy and yellow vegetables, and perhaps double the present consumption of dairy products. Brigadier General Hershey, of the Selective Service, reports that of the first million men examined one third were rejected because of ailments traceable to nutritional deficiencies. These dietary deficiencies are primarily due to economic factors, but the protective foods require relatively high labor costs in production and distribution. We cannot increase farm acreage appreciably because the total arable land which can be used safely and economically amounts to about 3.3 acres per person. According to the Department of Agriculture *Yearbook* for 1938, the best agricultural practices would permit the cultivation of about 340,000,000 acres of our present crop land, but another 108,000,000 acres could be added by using pasture, brush, or timber land, and other areas which could be drained or irrigated. Much

[6] J. D. Black, *Food Enough* (Lancaster, Pa., 1943).

of this additional land could be made available only at the expense of considerable time and labor.

Some increase in crop yields per acre can be expected, but in the recent past the potential increase in yields of as much as 50 percent from improved crop plants and farm practices have been largely offset by the decline in soil productivity from erosion and depletion of soil fertility.[7] Dr. Charles E. Kellogg, Chief of the Division of Soil Survey of the Department of Agriculture, estimates that proper fertilization, combined with best farm practices, might result in a 25 percent increase in crop yields.[8] We must realize, however, that any great intensification of cultivation may increase costs out of all proportion to increased yields. Much of our agriculture has been exploitative in nature, and proper soil conservation practices, which have to be adopted in any system of permanent agriculture, must necessarily reduce the acreage of cultivated crops and add to the cost of production.

If we continue our normal dietary habits of pre-war years, we shall use nearly 3 acres of arable land per person to provide our food supply. Since it requires from four to ten times as much land to produce food in the form of meat as it does to produce the basic food crops, we can reduce our meat consumption and still produce an adequate and satisfactory diet on 2 acres of land per capita.[9] A reduction of dietary standards to the level of the average European would permit a reduction of required land to about 1.5 acres. If we wished to rely on a cereal and vegetable diet, comparable to that of the Asiatics, we could provide the necessary calories and proteins from half an acre of land at present levels of production. Moreover, it is possible that such a diet, supplemented with synthetic vitamins and added minerals, would be nutritionally adequate. But the use of only half an acre per person would demand complete utilization of all food grown, there would be no reserves for poor years, and this limited acreage could not adequately provide the plant and animal products needed for clothing and other necessities. However, there is little probability that we shall have to reduce our diet to a lower level.

Another factor should be considered. In the United States, where large scale mechanized farming is prevalent, about 20 percent of the working population is engaged in agriculture and 16 percent could

[7] United States Department of Agriculture, *Yearbook* (1938).
[8] Black, *op. cit.*
[9] R. P. Christensen, *Using Resources to Meet Food Needs* (Bureau of Agricultural Economics, Washington, D.C., 1943).

do the job of producing the American food supplies; in Europe about a third of the population is engaged in agriculture even though considerable food is imported, while in Asia about 75 percent of the working population is required to provide the meager and inadequate food supply.[10]

Here is one of the most important factors in the future of world civilization and one which has all too frequently been overlooked by those optimists who see no limit to the world's capacity to produce food. The history of mankind shows that civilization advanced in direct proportion to man's release from the inevitable task of feeding himself. In a primitive hunting and fishing or other food-gathering culture, man devotes himself largely to the constant search for his next meal. The invention of agriculture is usually the greatest single step in the march from savagery to civilization, because the practice of agriculture enables a fraction of the population to produce food for all. A part of the population is released from food-gathering and food-producing activities and can devote itself to the arts, the crafts, and the sciences—the building stones from which civilizations are fashioned. However, if the population increases without restriction in an agricultural civilization, less fertile lands must be brought into cultivation, less efficient methods (in terms of human labor) must be employed and an ever-increasing proportion of the population must return to the age-old task of providing food. Ultimately an overpopulated agricultural society fares no better and contributes no more to the advance of civilization than a primitive hunting and fishing culture.

II

A survey of the population problems of the major geographic areas of the world shows that they correspond rather closely to the population problems of the major racial stocks of the human race—the Whites, Yellow-Browns, and Negroid. During the past three hundred years the white population has increased about 700 percent, the Yellow-Brown races a little more than 200 percent, while the pure Negroid population has increased only about 100 percent.[11]

As the people of Europe emerged from the Dark Ages, the population grew rapidly and by 1800 numbered nearly 200 million. Under the existing conditions it appeared that the population was increasing faster than the food supply, and could be held in check only by

[10] Thompson, *Population Problems*.   [11] *Ibid*.

starvation, disease or war. The population continued to grow and yet Europe was able to avoid most of the consequences of the Malthusian Law. This has been done by following three paths of escape. The food supply has been increased by improvements in farm machinery and better agricultural methods. Industrialization has not only greatly increased the production of goods and means of transportation, but has permitted the importation of food in exchange for manufactured products. Population pressure also has been relieved by the migration of large numbers of Europeans to the Americas and other parts of the world; of the people of European origin there are nearly half as many in other parts of the world as there are now in Europe.

The third and most important factor in the solution of Europe's population problem has been the artificial reduction in birth rate. Most of the countries of western Europe have reduced their birth rates during the past sixty years from over 30 per thousand to less than 20 per thousand. Primitive contraceptive methods have been known for at least several thousand years, but not until about 1880 were effective methods available and more generally known. The practice of contraception became general in both Catholic and Protestant countries in spite of legal restrictions, religious bans, primitive taboos, and the exhortations of priests and politicians. In England, France, Germany, Austria, and Sweden, birth control has reduced birth rates to below replacement levels, and in most other countries the population growth rate is fast approaching unity. Of all the countries of Europe, only the Slavic nations have anything even approaching a natural birth rate of 40 per thousand, and only Russia has resources to support a much larger population. Even in Russia the birth rates in some of the larger cities are beginning to follow the trend of those in western Europe, and as socio-economic conditions improve in the Soviet Union, the birth rate will decline.

The Americas face no immediate problems of population pressure. Both Canada and the United States have adequate resources for larger populations. If recent trends in growth continue, the United States will have a maximum population of perhaps 150 to 160 million by 1975, after which the population will remain almost stable or begin to decrease. Canada can expect a proportionally greater population growth, but in neither country is it likely that the population density will ever require much greater intensification of agriculture or a lower standard of living. The countries of Central America are growing rapidly and, if present trends continue, most of them will double their populations in 25 to 35 years. Unless the standard of living can be raised in some of these countries, population pressure may become acute in several generations. In South America, where populations are also growing rapidly, there is ample land for agricultural expansion, although settlement of the Amazon river basin will present some difficult climatic and public health problems.

The population problem for the white race in Australia is unique. Growth is nearly stationary in a country capable of supporting much larger numbers.

The white races have acquired a large part of the world's territory and either occupy or control most of the undeveloped and sparsely populated areas of the earth. In the overpopulated countries the birth rate is low and the population is declining or approaching a stationary level, while in most of the sparsely populated countries the birth rates are high and the populations are growing rapidly. There should be no serious problem for the Western nations unless political or religious leaders can persuade them to engage in a population race with each other or with Asia. In fact the population problem of the future for many of these countries may be the maintenance of population size at optimum levels.

Although Africa was the site of early white civilizations, it is still relatively undeveloped and sparsely populated; the majority of its inhabitants belong to the Negroid races. The native Negroid population has grown slowly, although ample natural resources exist in Central Africa. The slow growth rate has been due to various causes including the involuntary emigration of millions of Negroes during the eighteenth and nineteenth centuries, exploitation of the remaining population by the white races, and inability to solve the climatic problems of Central Africa. The population problems of the Negroids are primarily those related to social and economic improvement.

More than half of the world population lives in Asia, with little relief from population pressure by migration, industrialization, or birth control. The population density varies—nearly four per acre of arable land in Japan, two in China, and about one in India. Some reserve land is available for development in parts of Asia, but not enough to relieve the pressure. Food production cannot be increased greatly. Production per acre is already high because of intensive cultivation, but production per man is very low. The Chinese farmer expends 80 days of labor to grow an acre of rice yielding an average of 2 million calories.[12] The American farmer can produce 2 million calories in the form of corn with the expenditure of 4 days of labor, in the form of wheat with 2 days labor, and of soy beans with 3 days labor.[13] In terms of human labor expended the American farmer produces about 20 times as much food as does the Asiatic. The greater efficiency of the American farmer is due to the use of modern farm machinery. Actually he may use as much or more energy to grow an acre of farm produce as does the Oriental farmer, but the American obtains most of the required energy from gasoline and oil. Modern farming methods in Asia would not increase crop yields appreciably, although they would release many people for industrial work.

Industrialization can increase the food supply of Asia only to the extent that industrial products can be exchanged for food from nations now producing a surplus of agricultural products. Most countries which are able to produce surplus food, including Russia, Canada, and Argentina, are growing rapidly and in a few generations will require all the food they can efficiently grow. Moreover, these countries already have, or are developing, their own industries and will need to import only the products which cannot be manufactured economically by local industries.

Emigration offers little hope for Asia since the white races occupy or control most of the rest of the world territory. It is improbable that Australia, Canada, the United States, or the countries of South America will in the future welcome large numbers of Asiatics with any greater enthusiasm than they have in the past. Nor is there any moral reason why the nations which control their birth rates in order to maintain a high standard of living should provide for the surplus populations of other countries which breed without consideration of economic and social consequences.

The only rational solution of Asia's population problem is the reduction of the birth rate. The entire world could not support the population of Asia for more than several generations if birth rate remains at about 40 per thousand, and if the death rate were reduced to European levels. Either the Orientals must adopt birth control or the population must continue to be held in check by infanticide, starvation, and disease, or war. But the very low levels of living standards would seem

[12] Pei-sung Tang, *Helios and Prometheus: a Philosophy of Agriculture* (1944).
[13] Christensen, *Using Resources to Meet Food Needs*.

to preclude any extensive use of birth control, for voluntary birth control does not begin to operate until a certain standard of living is attained. When man lives too close to a bare subsistence level, he remains indifferent to the consequences of uncontrolled procreation. However, the Orientals are not conditioned by the Christian dogma that "man is conceived in sin, and born in iniquity" and their attitude towards contraception may be more rational than that of Occidentals of comparable economic status. The Japanese have adopted contraception to some extent, and birth rates in Japan have been as low as 28 per thousand before the war. The practice of contraception may spread throughout Asia if cheap and effective contraceptives are made available, and if living standards can be temporarily raised by the development of industry.

III

The white races have been able to escape the more serious consequences of the Malthusian law, but the control of the birth rate has led to other problems which threaten the welfare of the Western nations. In all countries where the practice of birth control is prevalent, the poorer economic and educational classes reproduce much faster than do those in the upper socio-economic groups. The situation in the United States is typical of the trend in most Occidental countries. A survey of birth rates in urban communities in 1935 showed that the white families with annual incomes of more than $3,000 had a reproductive index of 0.46—only half enough children to maintain a stationary population. Those with incomes of $1,500 to $2,000 had a reproductive index of 0.70, while those with earned incomes of less than $1,000 had a reproductive index of 0.93. But the only urban groups which exceeded replacement levels were those on relief; their reproductive index was 1.43.[14] The same trend was found in relation to education. College graduates had a reproductive index of 0.57, high school graduates 0.77, and those with less than a 7th grade education 1.18. Even in normal times the third of our population least able economically to feed, clothe, and educate children, produces two thirds of the next generation. Rural birth rates are still well above replacement levels, but the same relation between economic status and size of family is found in rural communities.

[14] F. Lorimer, E. Winston, and L. K. Kiser, *Foundations of American Population Policy* (New York, 1940).

The dependence upon the poorer and more ignorant members of society for the major portion of the future generation is not conducive to the best interests of the individual or the nation. If poverty and ignorance are the result of bad heredity, the excessive birth rate of this group will lower the average capacity of the nation. If, on the other hand, environmental and social conditions account for the high birth rate, the consequences remain equally undesirable, because poor and ignorant parents cannot provide favorable conditions in which to rear their children. Both heredity and environment are responsible for variation in man's physical and mental development, but since these two factors are so interdependent it is difficult to determine their relative roles. There is some evidence that inherent ability bears some relation to socioeconomic status,[15] but the correlation is not high and is based largely on the extreme variants. For the great majority of the population, an individual's attainments seem to be determined largely by environmental factors, including the subtle influence of family, racial, and religious mores.

The most serious aspect of the differential birth rate of the various socioeconomic classes at present is the environmental factor. In many cases poverty and ignorance are associated with a lack of individual and social responsibility which is passed on as a family tradition to the future generation. Under such circumstances, even children of average or superior intelligence start life under serious handicaps, and only a few are able to overcome the effects of such an environment. Since the family environment is one of the most important factors in the development of the child, there can be no real equality of opportunity, as the intelligence, and the social and economic status of parents can never be equalized. The only means of providing a moderately uniform environment would be to raise all children in institutions, and most people agree that the elimination of the family system would be too high a price to pay for a greater uniformity in environment.[16]

Even if a uniform and favorable environment could be provided for all, men would continue to vary in intelligence and ability because of differences in genetic constitution. No amount of factual knowledge and training in the most favorable environment can fully compensate for mental and physical defects which are genetic in their origin. It must be realized also that the effects of a superior environ-

[15] G. Schweizinger, *Heredity and Environment* (New York, 1933).
[16] S. J. Holmes, *Human Genetics and Its Social Import* (New York, 1936).

ment are not hereditary and cannot be transmitted directly to following generations. If economic success and cultural advancement are to be correlated with inherent abilities, the poor and the ignorant will be with us always. Dreams of a high standard of living for all seem rather remote and to be attained only by a Utopian society operating on the Marxian principle of "from each according to his ability, to each according to his needs." It seems improbable that this Christian ideal can be attained in man's present state of social evolution. Any social or religious ideology which must be maintained by force or fear cannot long endure in an educated population.

Any permanent improvement of the human race must depend upon the genetic constitution of the individual. In primitive societies the mental defectives and morons did not survive very long because nature had many efficient fool-killing devices. In man's later civilization, such defectives were luxuries which society could not afford to keep. But morons continued to be produced. Under modern conditions of differential birth rates and a more humanitarian civilization their production is increasing. There is no truth in the statement by an "eminent psychologist," that "moronity has a biological trend to eliminate itself," [17] either in a primitive society or in a modern civilization. Haldane, a strong advocate of environmental effects on man, concedes that the average intelligence quotient may be expected to decline at the rate of 1 or 2 percent per generation so long as the present differential birth rate of social classes continues.[18] The mentally deficient and defective will continue to be produced. Sterilization of all mental defectives might reduce their number by about 10 percent in the next generation with smaller proportional reductions in subsequent generations, but they could not be eliminated because many normal individuals carry genes for mental defects, and random mating will continue to produce some individuals who are mentally deficient or defective. We are not yet in a position, either scientifically or socially, to do very much to improve the genetic constitution of the human race. Those who are inherently so mentally or physically defective as to be socially inadequate under the most favorable existing environment should be sterilized or otherwise prevented from reproducing. Such action, it is true, would prevent the birth of many normal, or at least socially adequate, individuals. But defective parents cannot provide a

[17] *A Holy War* (National Catholic Welfare Conference, Washington, D.C., 1942).
[18] J. B. S. Haldane, *Heredity and Politics* (New York, 1938).

proper environment for these children, and we should not have to rely on such sources for our future generations under any social system. Any real progress in the genetic improvement of the human race must, however, involve more than the prevention of genetic deterioration of the population. Eventually it should be quite possible to raise the genetic capacity of the human race, but we first need more knowledge of heredity in man and a more rational attitude towards sex and reproduction.

In nature a reproductive rate far in excess of possible survival is prevalent and, through natural selection, is of evolutionary value. Those who believe that high human birth rates are of evolutionary value seem to imply that natural selection will eliminate all but the toughest and most aggressive individuals. In a civilized and modern society, such elimination has no moral justification and might be socially deleterious in the artificial environment of modern times. Biological fitness in our modern world is of a different order than that which prevailed in a natural primitive environment. Most of our economic crop plants and many of our domestic animals could not survive in nature, yet they are far better adapted for their purpose in an artificial environment than are their wild relatives. Survival value in the modern world is not a valid measure for human values.

A somewhat broader aspect of the effect of differential fertility, and its effect upon the racial and ethnic components of populations, is evident in certain areas of the world. In Europe the proportion of the population of Slavic origin was 34 percent in 1810, 46 percent in 1930,[19] and will continue to increase because Russia alone has the resources to support a much larger population. The countries of Western Europe now have a declining population with an average reproductive index of less than 1.0, while Russia maintained a reproductive index of at least 1.5 before the war.[20] If these trends continue the population of Western Europe will decline while the population of Russia will double in less than two generations. Biologically, it makes little difference which racial group dominates Europe, and the effect of probable Russian dominion may be of importance only in relation to social philosophy and religion.

In Canada also, the differential birth rates of ethnic groups may have social consequences. The reproductive index for the English speaking

[19] Holmes, *op. cit.*
[20] A. M. Carr-Saunders, *World Population* (Oxford, 1936).

population is less than 1.0, while for the French Canadians, it is above 1.5. Within relatively few years the French stock will outnumber the English.

Puerto Rico has a population of nearly 2 million people living on a island approximately 100 miles long and 35 miles wide. Natural resources are limited and the agricultural resources are hardly adequate to support the existing population. Yet the population is increasing at the rate of 2.3 percent per year and would increase still faster if adequate food and medical service were provided. Even at the present rate the population would double in 30 years. During the depression years nearly 90,000 Puerto Ricans emigrated to New York; in 1938 about 60,000 were on relief.[21] Economists have been busy trying to solve Puerto Rico's population problems, but none has suggested the only rational and obvious solution.

IV

Why do those who are least able to feed, clothe, and educate their children have the largest families? The late Dr. Pearl, in a survey of 30,000 women in urban maternity hospitals in the United States, has shown that there is little or no difference in the natural fertility of the various major racial, religious, educational, or economic classes.[22] The differences in actual birth rates of the various classes is due largely to the differences in the prevalence and effectiveness of artificial contraception, and to a minor extent to age of marriage and the practice of criminal abortion. Dr. Pearl found that among the white women with more than one child, contraception was practiced by 83 percent of the rich or well-to-do mothers and that their average birth rate per 100 years opportunity for pregnancy was 66. Of those in moderate economic circumstances, 62 percent practiced contraception and had a relative birth rate of 109. About half of those in the lower-income group practiced contraception and the corresponding birth rate was 132, while only 35 percent of the very poor practiced, or attempted to practice, contraception and their corresponding birth rate was 153. The same trend was found in relation to education. Less than half of those with an elementary education used birth control methods, while 76 percent of the college graduates practiced contraception.

There are differences in the birth rates of the major religious and

[21] Lee, Hager, *Too Many People* (Houston, Texas, 1943).
[22] Pearl, *The Natural History of Population*.

racial groups, but the differences can be attributed largely to the corresponding differences in economic and educational levels of these classes. Dr. Pearl's survey showed that contraception was practiced by 67 percent of the Jews, 45 percent of the Protestants, 33 percent of the Catholics and 17 percent of the Negroes.[23] The educational status of these groups was shown by the percentage of high school and college graduates—Protestants 48 percent, Jews 44 percent, Negroes 30 percent, and Catholics 24 percent. No data were presented on the economic status of these groups, but one might expect a higher economic status for the Jews and a lower one for the Negroes, in relation to their relative educational attainments. The relatively high incidence of contraception among the Jews and the low incidence among the Negroes may also be due, in part, to racial tradition—the sense of family responsibility and the strong desire for personal advancement among the Jews, and the irresponsibility of the Negro conditioned by past and present economic factors. There can be little doubt that Catholics practice contraception to about the same extent as do Protestants of similar economic and educational status. The higher birth rate of Catholics, and of the members of the more orthodox Protestant denominations, can be attributed largely to the lower educational and economic standards of these groups. The Church is not a factor in the differential birth rate except as it may effect lower socio-economic standards by glorifying ignorance and poverty.

Although the practice of contraception is prevalent in Europe and America, it is not used extensively or effectively by the poor and the ignorant. The reasons for this are several. Ignorance of contraceptive methods is one, although anyone really interested in obtaining the information should be able to do so, even in the United States where the Comstock law classes such information as obscene literature and proscribes it from the mails. Another factor is the superstitious attitude towards sex and reproduction resulting from the Christian dogma that "man is conceived in sin." The most important factor probably is the lack of a sense of responsibility, and an indifference to the future consequences of uncontrolled procreation. The philosophy of this group seems to be that God or the government will provide their needs, regardless of their own efforts.

The paradox of this Age of Science is the present status of contraceptive knowledge. The great majority of Europeans and Ameri-

[23] Pearl, "Contraception and Fertility," *Human Biology*, VI (1943), 355-401.

cans recognize the necessity for the control of the birth rate and approve of the proper dissemination of contraception information, but many countries still have restrictive laws and primitive taboos. In the United States less than 5 percent of the contraceptors use the most reliable methods recommended by birth control clinics, and about 20 percent get their birth control information from the Bible (Genesis 38:8, 9).[24] This situation was emphasized by the late Dr. Pearl, who wrote: "What these women, taken as a group, know about contraception is mainly what has been passed on to them by mothers, husbands, friends, or drug-store attendants, who in turn derived it from precisely the same kind of sources, back to the debarkation at Ararat." Even the medical profession has been reluctant to consider contraceptive techniques; it was not until 1943 that the *Journal of the American Medical Association* accepted an article dealing with them.

The only important opposition to effective birth control now comes from the Catholic Church, although the Church has modified its traditional attitude by permitting natural birth control based upon the "circumstances of time." Just why "artificial" birth control is considered immoral and the "rhythm" method moral and permissible is beyond the comprehension of a biologist, or even of a secular student of morals. Perhaps the real reason is that the rhythm method is not very reliable. Although the Church has permitted natural birth control since 1932,[25] some Church officials and representatives still maintain that "birth control is against God's Law." [26] Fortunately many Catholics do not agree with their leaders. Contraception has long been practiced in France and Austria and is prevalent in Italy, Spain, Portugal, and Belgium. In this country 70 percent of the Catholic women between the ages of 20 and 35 believe that birth control information should be made available to all married women, according to a recent public opinion survey published by *Fortune* magazine.[27] Pearl's data show that Catholics practice artificial contraception to about the same extent as do Protestants of comparable socio-economic status. Although more than 80 percent of the people in the United States believe in the proper dissemination of contraceptive information our

[24] Pearl, "Contraception and Fertility."
[25] Editors of *Fortune*, *The Accident of Birth* (New York, 1938).
[26] See the works of Haldane and Holmes, referred to above, and see also F. W. Mansfield, *Birth Control Is Against God's Law* (Boston, 1942); "Knights of Columbus Resolution," *Boston Globe*, May 13, 1942.
[27] *The Accident of Birth*.

archaic laws and primitive taboos restrict such information and keep the contraceptive industry on a quasi bootleg status.

V

Man has made little concious effort to solve the problems of population growth and distribution. The white races are now in a position to regulate population in accord with their resources, but this progress has been attained by individual initiative and action and not as the result of any planned population policy. Political, religious, and business leaders have been in favor of a large and growing population. Such an attitude is justified in a newly settled or sparsely populated country, but excessive populations are not conducive to the best interests of government, religion, or business. Nationalistic and racial pride also have been responsible for the attitude that a nation which was not expanding in numbers and territory was degenerate and senescent.

There is some justification for populations in excess of the optimum number if wars are to continue. But even in a world at war a large population does not imply military might: India and China together have about ten times as many men as has Japan. Education and technical skill for both civilians and soldiers are essential in modern war.

In the past, nations have resorted to war in order to acquire additional territory and resources, but in modern times such action is futile. Occupation of a country already overpopulated can result in no more *Lebensraum* unless the people of the invaded country are exterminated. If the people are not exterminated, the invaded territory can produce no more for itself or its conquerors than would be possible in times of peace; occupied by subjugated people it would probably produce less.

The greatest paradox in national policies is the demand for larger populations in countries already overpopulated. Hitler, Mussolini and Tojo have called for higher birth rates, while at the same time complaining of overpopulation and the need for territorial expansion. Even when Germany, Italy, and Japan had an opportunity to expand into colonial possessions, relatively few people left the homeland. Before emigration to other countries was checked by either the home or foreign governments, only Japan made any considerable effort to aid and finance her emigrants.

Prime Minister Churchill's appeal for a higher birth rate in England is justified only if he is looking forward to establishing a stabilized population in England not greatly below the present level, or if he wishes to increase the populations of Canada, Australia, and New Zealand by emigration from England. These colonies can support, and really need, larger populations. But if Churchill succeeds in his plans for a larger population in England that country will suffer. England is able to support her present population in reasonable comfort only because she has a highly industrialized society and the British Empire provides both raw materials and markets. England has no monopoly on industrialization or technical skill, and eventually the colonies and the other countries will develop their own industries. When that time comes, England may have a larger population than her agriculture will support, and she will possess no industrial advantages that will insure an ample supply of imported food. This eventual situation was realized by Malthus nearly one hundred and fifty years ago, and another Prime Minister, William Pitt, had the perspicacity to see that Malthus was right. Pitt, who once believed that every man who fathered many children "enriched his country," changed his views after reading Malthus's *Essay on Population* and withdrew his Poor Bill of 1800, stating in the House of Commons that he did so in deference to the views of "those whose opinions he was bound to respect."

National and racial pride has always been a factor in war and aggression. The peoples of the various nations would be less than human if they did not believe that their nation or their race was especially chosen by God to carry the torch of civilization. Most of us believe that the rapid growth and expansion of the white races has been desirable, but many Japanese are just as sure that their civilization and their race is destined to lead the world. There is, however, no biological justification for the myth of racial superiority. All races have contributed to the cultural and economic development of civilization. The rise and fall of empires and civilizations during the course of history cannot be attributed to any corresponding rise and fall in the average inherent ability of the populations. The excessive loss of the stronger and more aggressive men in the recurrent wars of the world has weakened many nations, and there may be truth in the quatrain published in the London *Spectator:*

> Science finds out ingenious ways to kill
> Strong men, and keep alive the weak and ill—
> That these a sickly progeny may breed
> Too poor to tax, too numerous to feed.

But in view of the genetic constitution of a human population it seems improbable that war or other vices have resulted in any very appreciable decrease in the inherent intellectual capacity of past generations. The rise and fall of empires must be attributed to other factors.

The major races of man do differ in morphological characters and psychological traits just as the different breeds of domestic animals vary in physical proportions and temperament, but in neither case can we be sure that there are inherent differences in intelligence. In one respect this comparison is not justified because the races of men are far more heterozygous than are the breeds of domestic animals which have been developed by severe selection and inbreeding. There are genetic grounds for assuming that racial differences in intelligence could occur even though all races were originally derived from a common stock. If at any time in human history a racial group became isolated and greatly reduced in numbers, the frequency of certain genes in the limited population might fall so low that they would be lost. The effect would be essentially similar to the effects of artificial inbreeding and would tend to stabilize the race for better or worse— usually worse—depending on the genetic nature of the surviving stocks. The great physical variation within the major races of man is adequate evidence that no such genetic limitations have occurred. It is possible, however, that small isolated communities within this and other countries have been subjected to the unfavorable effects of limited gene frequencies. As Haldane has suggested, the introduction of modern means of transportation, with its consequent effect on population movement and mixture, should be of considerable value in suppressing the effects of deleterious genes.[28]

Various human groups do vary in intelligence as measured by tests or by performance. The relative intelligence in turn depends upon heredity and environment. Tests made in the United States show low scores for those of recent southern European origin, as well as for Mexicans and Negroes.[29] Obviously, these people do not have the educational background and other environmental conditions to compete with native-born Americans or those from the more advanced socio-economic environment of western Europe, who are accepted on a more nearly equal social status. In the Southern states, native whites

[28] Haldane, *Heredity and Politics*.
[29] E. M. East, *Mankind at the Crossroads* (New York, 1923).

score higher than Negroes, but Negroes in the Northern cities outscore native whites of certain regions of the South.

We must realize that several generations under a favorable external environment may be necessary to compensate for racial attitudes that may become traditional. But the problem is complex. In this country the Negro's inferior economic position is attributed to racial discrimination which denies him equal economic or educational opportunities. But in Brazil, where racial discrimination is largely absent, the Negro still occupies an inferior economic position, and here, paradoxically, the situation is attributed to the fact that, having achieved relative equality in social status, the Negro feels under no compulsion to exert himself in improving his economic status.[30] The French in Canada are of the same ethnic stocks and have had the same cultural background as the natives of France, but as a group their social, educational, and cultural development has not kept pace with that of their cousins in Europe. Yet the Canadians of English origin have maintained the British cultural and economic traditions in the New World. The Chinese and Japanese in the United States rate as high in mental tests, on the average, as native-born white Americans,[31] although they have been subjected to about as much social and economic discrimination as have the Italians, Mexicans, and Negroes. It is possible that severe natural selection in Asia has raised the inherent intellectual level of the population, but it is more probable that all of these racial differences can be attributed to differences in reactions to environment, nonrandom selection of population samples, and traditions and mores of the various races. Certainly there is no biological justification for the myth of racial superiority which Hitler has used as an excuse for exterminating peoples of other nations or other racial elements of Germany's own population.

If man's primary function in this world is to provide souls for the next, there might be some justification for religious leaders to appeal for unrestricted birth rates. We are told that "God sends children" and that all must be welcomed regardless of the genetic or economic status of the family. In discussing God's decree on this subject, the late Cardinal Hayes wrote

"Even though some little angels in the flesh, through the moral, mental or physical deformity of the parents, may appear to the eye hideous, mis-

[30] E. Pierson, "The Brazilian Racial Situation," *Scientific Monthly*, March, 1944.
[31] Holmes, *Human Genetics and Its Social Import*.

shaped, a blot on civilized society, we must not lose sight of this Christian thought, that under and within this visible malformation there lives an immortal soul to be saved and glorified for all eternity among the blessed in Heaven." [32]

An even more amazing statement was made by the late Cardinal O'Connell in 1942—ten years after Pope Pius XI permitted Catholics to use the "rhythm" method of birth control. According to the Cardinal, "The Church teaches and history proves that the practice of artificial birth control inevitably brings in its train woeful consequences to the individual, the family, and the nation." [33] Compare, for example, the people of western Europe with those of India, China, and Japan in times of either peace or war. France is usually cited as the horrible example of the consequences of birth control, and Italy is praised for her expanding population. True, France was not prepared for war, but in times of peace she led the world in the average cultural and social development of her population. As Pearl remarked of pre-war France, "He who thinks France an unhappy or wretched country is both ignorant and stupid." If the other countries of Europe had reduced their birth rates when France did there would have been no excuse for aggression by other nations. In a pamphlet entitled "A Holy War," published in 1942 by the National Catholic Welfare Conference, much emphasis is placed on the necessity for a large population on the grounds of military expediency. It is indeed strange for the self-appointed spokesmen for the Prince of Peace to lay so much emphasis on the needs of Mars.

Certain religious leaders are inclined to associate poverty and ignorance with spiritual development, and wealth and education with a materialistic civilization, thus justifying large populations in excess of family or national resources. The facts do not support such a philosophy. Those who must work from dawn to dark for a mere subsistence have little opportunity or inclination for the development of the spirit. They may take refuge in the religion of defeatism, but as Hu Shih remarks, "That very self-hypnotizing philosophy is more materialistic than the dirty houses they live in, the scanty food they eat, and the clay and wood with which they make images of their gods." [34] Man's

[32] J. H. Dietrich, *The Ethics of Birth Control* (First Unitarian Society, Minneapolis, 1930).
[33] Cardinal O'Connell in the Boston *Herald*, Oct. 22, 1942.
[34] Hu Shih, "The Civilizations of the East and the West," in *Whither Mankind*, ed. Charles A. Beard (New York, 1928).

spiritual development can best be developed by a greater knowledge and control of nature, and a greater appreciation and understanding of his fellow man, and not by abandoning rational thought and reverting to mysticism.

Industrial leaders in the past have favored large populations to provide both labor and markets. A surplus of labor meant lower wages and higher profits. Businessmen are now beginning to realize that the welfare of the entire population must be considered in industrial development. Modern industry requires healthy and intelligent workers and good health and education can be attained only by raising the standards of living. The increased efficiency of labor should more than compensate for higher wages, and at the same time the purchasing power of the population would be increased. But it must be realized that increased production is the only road to prosperity. Both business and labor must abandon the creed "produce as little as you can for as much as you can get."

Political and religious leaders have met with little success in their appeals for higher birth rates, yet infallible methods of attaining this end are at their disposal. The political or religious dictator of the future who demands a higher birth rate needs only to keep his people poor and ignorant. Poverty and ignorance have never failed to result in high birth rates. To insure an increase in the total population the standard of living would have to be kept high enough to prevent excessive death rates, but Japan has proved that this standard need not be very high. A certain degree of technical training could be maintained for the masses of the workers. An effective propaganda or religious organization would be needed to keep the people subservient to the new order, but both political and religious propaganda is effective even in an educated society.

The maintenance of birth rates sufficient to maintain optimum populations may be a serious problem in the near future in many parts of the world. Within relatively few years the decline of birth rates should be checked in most European countries and in the United States. But it is probable that birth rates will continue to decline in these countries. If we can look forward to improved socio-economic conditions for the average citizen, this factor alone would reduce the birth rate. Public opinion is so overwhelmingly in favor of the spread of contraceptive information that it is sure to increase the prevalence of birth control among all but the most ignorant and irresponsible members of the population. The increasing economic independence of women is also bound to have some effect. Two or three children are sufficient to satisfy the maternal instincts and few modern women want more. *Fortune's* recent survey of young American women between the ages of 20 and 35 showed that the average number of children desired was 2.6. With present marriage and death rates, an average of 2.6 children per mother would maintain a stationary population. But there is no assurance that even a stationary population can be maintained by voluntary parenthood unless some of the economic penalties of parenthood are removed. Attempts to increase the birth rate have been tried in Europe by providing family allowances, marriage loans, and maternity aids of various sorts, but with relatively little success.

VI

The population problems of the world are complex and paradoxical. If birth rates are not restricted the population can be held in check only by a high death rate. This condition prevailed until modern times and still persists in most of Asia. But if birth rates depend upon voluntary parenthood it may be difficult to maintain an optimum population for either peace or war. Many countries are faced with this situation now and the problem may become more acute before it is solved.

There is room for a larger world population—how much room depends upon the standard of living which the majority wish to enjoy. A high standard of living could be provided for 3 billion people, but perhaps 8 billion could exist at a bare subsistence level on the present and potentially available agricultural resources of the world.

The white races now occupy or control all of the continents of the world with the exception of Asia. They have plenty of room for expansion, but their birth rates are declining and in some regions are below replacement levels. The Yellow-Brown races are confined to Asia; they exhibit excessive populations, high birth rates and high death rates, and no opportunity for expansion. The population problem of the Negroid races are conditioned by the white races with whom they are associated as fellow citizens or who have established colonial control.

Attempts to solve the problems of population pressure by invasion of neighboring territory already overpopulated cannot be justified. If the peoples of the invaded areas are not exterminated, there can be no release of population pressure. Nor is there any biological justification for such action on the grounds of racial superiority. Races differ in physical traits and educational status, but there is no evidence that they differ in inherent intelligence and ability. The cultural, economic and intellectual differences which now exist can be largely attributed to differences in environment.

Control of the birth rate is essential in most parts of the world, and is prevalent in all countries which have attained a high standard of living. But in these countries the practice of contraception is correlated with the economic and educational status of the individuals. Those who are economically most able to have children do not have enough and those who are poor have more than they can provide for. The consequences of these differential birth rates are unfavorable for individual or national development regardless of the causal factors responsible for the differential economic and educational status of the parents. At present, environmental factors are of the most importance in human development and attainments, but eventually we must rely on genetic principles for any permanent improvement of the human race.

The Changing American Indian
By JULIAN H. STEWARD

TODAY, there are some 15,000,000 persons in the Western Hemisphere who are classed as Indians—somewhat more than in 1492. Throughout most of Ibero-America, however, the definition of an Indian is a cultural rather than biological one. When Indians have adopted the Spanish language, European clothing, and other national traits, so that they are no longer conspicuously different from other people, they are classed as mestizos, though racially they may be pure Indian. Consequently, America has far more than 15,000,000 persons of Indian descent.

The numerical and cultural importance of the Indians in the different American Republics is extremely varied. In the United States, at one extreme, they constitute about one third of one percent of the total population and are largely isolated on reservations. In Bolivia, at the other extreme, Indians and mestizos make up over 90 percent of the population, so that the nation may be said to be Indian. Because of differing aboriginal backgrounds and varying degrees of assimilation to European civilization, present-day Indians are culturally so heterogeneous that at least five major areas must be distinguished, each with its peculiar combination of forces and trends.

1. The Indian is virtually extinct in the eastern United States, Uruguay, eastern Brazil, and the pampas of Argentina. It is solely a question of a few years before the last survivors disappear without leaving any important cultural or racial mark on the national population.

2. The Indian has nearly vanished, having been swallowed up by the large Negro population, in the Antilles and on much of the coast and along the great rivers of tropical Central and South America.

3. Indians now survive in small numbers as a national minority in the western United States, much of Canada, portions of Brazil, northwestern Argentina, Chile, and Colombia, Many of the tribes live on reservations, which constitute worlds in themselves. The people have some contact with the national population through the sale of agricultural or other reservation products, but do not participate directly in the white man's life. Indians not on reservations in these countries

have usually found their niche in white society as a laboring class, most often as agricultural workers but sometimes as artisans. In Ibero-America, they come to be considered mestizos, but in the United States and Canada, where Indians are racially defined, they tend to remain apart from the whites until their physical characteristics disappear through miscegenation.

4. About four hundred thousand primitive Indians, who have scarcely been in contact with civilization, still live in the remote tropical forests around the Amazon basin—in Matto Grosso, the eastern portions of Bolivia, Peru, Ecuador, and Colombia, and the area between the Orinoco and Amazon rivers in northern Brazil and southern Venezuela. Certain isolated sections of Central America, especially Panama and Costa Rica, also shelter a few primitive tribes.

5. Nine tenths of all American Indians live in the highland countries—Mexico, Central America, Ecuador, Peru, and Bolivia. The aboriginal cultural heritage of these countries is so great that it has given a strong Indian flavor to national life, and Indian problems are to a very large extent synonymous with national problems.

Before discussing these major areas in greater detail, it is necessary to consider some of the general factors and trends which, in varying combination, have contributed to each local situation. Following sections, therefore, will deal with general trends of Indian acculturation under European influence; the differing European economico-political patterns imposed on the Indians; manifestations of solidarity among Indians and the recent Indianist movement; population trends; and racial attitudes affecting the Indian's role in national life.

SOME GENERAL CULTURAL TRENDS

Certain general processes of acculturation have been at work on the Indian since the Conquest, and account for his partial or complete assimilation in Euro-American national cultures. These operate largely without special plan or political design.

European influences are usually felt by Indians before the white man comes into direct contact with them. Almost universally, their initial effect is to bring an efflorescence of, and often a profound change in, native culture, so that what the white man finds among the Indians is rarely a pure pre-Columbian culture. New crops, domesticated animals, steel tools, rifles, traps, improved fish gear and other items acquired through trade may radically alter economic life by providing a more abundant and stable food supply, which in turn permits larger population aggregates with concomitant social and political developments. Similarly, increased intertribal contacts, often initiated by dislocation of tribes on the frontier of European settlement, may bring about alliances and warfare with a large number of political and social rearrangements consequent to them. Before the white man arrived in important numbers, the Indians of the Great Plains and the Pampas, for example, developed large bands of warrior horsemen, the Indians of the Northwest Coast intensified their potlatch-class-totemic system, and the Indians of the tropical forests drew together in larger settlements.

When contact with the white man becomes direct, new factors are introduced. The Indian not only borrows more material items from the European's cultural inventory but the very pattern of his own society is liable to change if not to destruction.

In areas of low population density, the Indian is soon outnumbered by the white and, unless he is segregated on reservations, he usually clusters around white settlements, working for wages so as to purchase the material goods he covets. The tribal economy is immediately disrupted and the tribal villages are abandoned, removing all basis for aboriginal social life. Unsanitary houses and clothing, new foods, intoxicating liquors, diseases to which no native immunity exists, unaccustomed work habits, and other factors lower the birth rate and raise the death rate. The survivors eventually live more or less on European terms, and, except where there is race prejudice, they cease to be regarded as Indian. Missions also generally hasten the disappearance of the Indian, for they not only encourage his adoption of European customs but the large mission villages facilitate the spread of disease with its fearful toll.

In areas of dense aboriginal Indian population the reaction to direct European contact was quite different. Here the Indians so outnumbered the whites that it was necessary for the latter to adapt their settlements somewhat to the native communities. Even the reducciones, or reductions, which placed the Indians in fewer and larger villages, were more or less within preëxisting patterns in the Andes and Mexico. Moreover, the Indians from Mexico to Bolivia had so rich a native culture that European civilization was not particularly revolutionary in terms of content. European domesticated plants supplemented, but did not supplant, the large number of excellent native crops, and even steel farm tools and draft animals did not entirely overthrow aboriginal farm methods. European clothing was mainly a matter of new styles for an already well-clad people. European tools and household equipment were useful but not strikingly novel where there was a great native proficiency in ceramics, weaving, stonework, building, and, in some areas, metallurgy. Even the introduction of Christianity often meant essentially the enrichment of an already complex set of rituals and religious beliefs.

It was the socio-economic patterns which the Europeans brought to these areas of dense population and aboriginal high cultures which were fundamentally upsetting, not the cultural content of European living. The local community had been fundamental to aboriginal life. It had been the essential element of which aboriginal social and political systems were constructed, and today it constitutes the least common denominator to the practical problems. It was a typically agricultural community, in which lands were held communally and allotted to individuals. Communal aid in planting and harvesting and a series of village agricultural rites were outstanding among a large number of community activities that reinforced group cohesion. Ties beyond the village were extremely tenuous, for the basis of life was subsistence farming, cash crops being unknown. Houses, clothing, utensils, and art products were all made in the home, and the number of specialized products that were obtained through barter was limited. Although aboriginal empires, such as those of the Inca, Aztec, and Maya, had brought about trade or tribute involving the community in a wider sphere or had fostered nationalistic religious cults drawing many peoples to great religious centers, they had not done so at the expense of the local community.

The Spanish economic system destroyed the very core of the community, however, for it was incompatible with communal lands. At least half the Indians lost their lands to the Spaniards and either went to work on the haciendas or formed a general mestizo proletariat. The latter became rapidly Europeanized through service in the army, in mines, and in domestic situations, through some schooling, and through greatly increased contacts with whites in the growing urban centers that characterize European culture. Even the Indians who retained their lands were subject to influences tending to destroy their Indian characteristics. The introduction of a cash crop system along with other factors making for individual land ownership weakened the family by leaving many members landless and weakened the community by eliminating many of its communal activities. Present-day Indians who have acquired sufficient knowledge of European culture to function successfully in its economic and political patterns, usually drift into the class of mestizos; for the ability to read, write, and speak Spanish, to grasp and utilize national laws, and to farm or carry on commerce successfully in a cash and credit system are not Indian traits.

There are, however, still millions of Indians, and most of them are subject to great cultural stress and strain. There are those who cling to the community but have insufficient lands; those who retain native family and community customs but, having no lands, live in communities on the haciendas; and those who own land individually and perhaps cultivate cash crops but attempt to retain the old pattern of local life. The transitional situations take many local forms, but in general they are marked by a loss of agricultural productivity, destruction of native work habits, weakening of family and community structure, and abandonment of many religious beliefs and festivals. It may be said, therefore, that one of the most striking characteristics of the Indian is his economic and cultural maladjustment. His inability to contend with national patterns and to solve his own problems requires paternalistic governmental intervention and has stimulated certain groups of white men to work on his behalf.

EUROPEAN PATTERNS AFFECTING INDIANS

The present national differences in Indian problems are in part the direct heritage of patterns of colonization and land settlement brought from Europe. In Anglo-America, colonization tended to be by whole families, often refugees, who settled the land and worked it themselves. In Ibero-America, people steeped in the great landlord traditions of the Old World sought vast domains with masses of cheap labor. The conquistadors were more interested in amassing fortunes befitting noblemen than in obtaining lands on which to colonize their families. Even the lowliest soldiers, who had been mere laborers in the Old World, saw the Conquest as an opportunity to rise to the status of landlord and caballero.

White land-settlement in North America was imposed on an area of low native population density and brought early extermination of many tribes. As landholders, the Indians were competitors of the colonists. They could not be readily absorbed through intermarriage because the settlers had their own families. They were consequently dispossessed and pushed westward, disease and warfare rapidly wiping out the weakened remnants of the dislocated tribes. This course of events was checked only in the far north and in the mountains and deserts of the far west, where the colonists and settlers encountered submarginal lands that did not seem worth more broken treaties, such as those which had marked the history of European settlement. The pattern of large estates based on mass labor was not unknown in North America, but, lacking a dense native population, it relied on imported Negro slaves.

Increased industrialization in North America finally produced a large urban class which could view Indian problems disinterestedly. First, spoliation was stopped, later many broken treaty obligations were fulfilled, and finally, within the past two decades, a strong, humanitarian attitude has reversed previous policies and permitted Indianism to become effective.

The Spanish and Portuguese conquistadors were favored by local circumstances in implanting powerful landlordism in America. The Spaniards found a dense native population in Mexico, the Central American republics, highland Colombia, Ecuador, Peru, and Bolivia. Initial grants gave the conquerors rights to control vast tracts of land and the Indians on them, an arrangement that ultimately led to the establishment of huge estates (haciendas) of which abundant cheap labor formed an essential part. These estates still flourish.

Ibero-America has also differed from Anglo-America in remaining essentially agrarian. The urban and industrial classes that could play an impartial role in the struggle between the Indian and the landlord were always outweighed politically by the dominant agrarian interests. Reforms in Indian laws, therefore, which started in the colonial period and have been enacted from time to time up to the present, have been ineffective for want of a potent, disinterested element to enforce them. A liberal tendency is growing in these countries, however, and the recent organization of the forces of Indianism will doubtless further it. Many countries now have governmental departments charged with the Indian's welfare—Argentina, Brazil, Bolivia, Chile, Colombia, and Ecuador, for example, where the function of the departments is protective, and Peru, Mexico, the United States, and Canada, where it is intended to effect fundamental improvements. It is questionable, however, whether anything far-reaching will be accomplished until the potentially powerful Indian element has gained sufficient national consciousness to lend its weight to efforts on its own behalf.

The tropical and subtropical portions of Ibero-America had too sparse a population to meet the demands of the landlord pattern. In the tropics, the need was remedied by Negro slave labor, which hastened the disappearance of the Indian. In Argentina, as in North America, the Indian was dispossessed and soon disappeared throughout much of the country.

INDIAN MOVEMENTS AND INDIANISM

It has been argued that the millions of present-day Indians represent a vast potential of political strength which, with proper education and organization, will develop into pan-Indian movements dedicated to self-help. It may seem somewhat paradoxical that historical trends have in reality brought a narrowing of the Indian's political horizon and that the possibility for effective solidarity is more remote now than ever before, unless the definition of Indian be broadened to include those who are generally considered mestizos.

The early violent clashes between Indians and whites produced strong native movements. To protect their lands and economic resources, the Indians resorted to open warfare at first. But sooner or later European influences caused a disastrous breakup of Indian culture, not only severely damaging the basic economy but also disrupting the customary patterns of behavior by which the individual had guided his life. When insecurity brought the natives to the point of desperation, a religious leader—a prophet or messiah—frequently arose among them and promised supernatural help in the elimination of the white man and the restoration of aboriginal conditions or at least the reëstablishment of an Indian-dominated world. Messianic movements, though intensely Indian, could never be pan-Indian because of the differences between tribal cultures. Tribes might form military alliances to drive out the intruder, but the very heterogeneity of the aboriginal tribal cultures they sought to restore precluded a unified movement to this end.

The progressive narrowing of the Indian's outlook has been most extreme in the areas of dense Indian population from Mexico to Bolivia. Here the conquerors found several large political units based on considerable cultural homogeneity and common interests. The Inca empire, extending from southern Colombia to northern Chile, was the largest. Other important examples were the Chibcha realm in central Colombia and the Aztec state in Mexico. Once the military power of these empires was broken, dissolution into small political units began. Peru experienced messianic movements long after Inca resistance had been crushed, but when it became obvious that a true aboriginal life could not be recaptured, the Indians began adapting themselves as best they could to the white man's patterns. Their struggle became essentially one for economic self-preservation and their principal adversary was the local landlord. Their allies were their fellow villagers, members of the local community which has had such great stability throughout all periods. If they coöperated on a broader scale, it was in the capacity of mestizos, not Indians, for the processes that gave them a national outlook were now directing them toward the European and away from native culture. Any national efforts made on behalf of those still designated Indian rather than mestizo had to be made by friendly whites.

In the United States and Canada, the Indian's self-consciousness is furthered through prevailing racial attitudes, combined in many places with the reservation system. As the Indian constitutes a politically unimportant minority which finds competition difficult in the national population, he seeks to satisfy his desires and achieve status within his own group. This tends to foster Indian self-consciousness and helps perpetuate Indian values. It may be questioned, however, whether it is not more a matter of Indian as against white than of true solidarity among Indians. There is often bitter antagonism where two tribes occupy the same reservation, while individual differences in assimilation are a further cause of discord.

The Araucanian Indians in Chile, also living on a reservation, have an extraordinarily strong tribal sense. They have always been remarkable for their indominable spirit, and today exhibit tremendous energy in developing coöperatives, schools, and other means to effect their adjustment to modern conditions. They are not groping for the past, as in a true nativistic movement, but are utilizing tribal solidarity for self-help.

Because the Indian's horizon has actually narrowed since the messianic attempts to recreate aboriginal conditions were given up, it is evident that leadership in pan-Indian movements and in efforts to win benefits for Indians will come from the white man. This leadership is found in the movement called Indigenismo or Indianism; it represents an effort not only to rehabilitate the Indian economically but to restore his cultural values. As such, it brings a sharp reversal in historic policy, for during both the colonial and republican periods, the Indian was regarded either as an obstacle or as an exploitable source of labor. If the course of his acculturation were not ignored, an effort was made to enforce his assimilation, for his native customs, beliefs, and languages prevented his effective integration in the European system of land tenure and land use.

The probable success of the Indigenista program would seem to depend upon local circumstances. Economic rehabilitation will be easier where the Indian is on reservations under strong paternalistic governmental control than where restoration of his lands is in direct conflict with nationally powerful agrarian interests. So far as the program seeks to restore the aboriginal communal land-ownership and land-use patterns, its success depends on the possibility of establishing such a system in the midst of nations whose economic structures are based on private property.

The Indianist's success in preserving distinctive customs, beliefs, and cultural values will involve definitions. Obviously, the Indian culture of 1492 cannot be restored, and probably no one holds that the course of acculturation can be stopped at any given date. Perhaps enough features of Indianhood can be retained to prevent vast numbers of Indians from slipping annually into the categories of mestizos or whites.

Anthropologists are in general agreement that it is purely a question of time before all Indians lose their identity. But this does not mean that the Indians will disappear in a national, cultural penoplane. Many Ibero-American nations now take great pride in certain folk cultures that have developed from the Indian-white blend—for example, the Guaraní of Paraguay, the Ladino of Central America, and the criollo of Argentina and Mexico. These peoples are an integral part of their countries but they retain distinctive local characteristics. It is from such groups that revolutionary reform movements in Mexico sprang, and it is conceivable that their broader outlook and greater self-consciousness will provide a basis for important movements elsewhere.

POPULATION TRENDS

Data on aboriginal American population figures are so inadequate that competent scientists have variously estimated the total at from

8,000,000 to 80,000,000. The figure of 13,000,000 carries a large margin of probable error but is the best guess.

The first European contact had devastating effects on the numbers of Indians, bringing a sharp decline everywhere and rapid extinction in some areas. During the first two centuries after the Conquest, the total number was at least halved. Many factors were involved in this decline, and some of them continue to operate today.

Epidemics repeatedly swept Indian communities, taking an enormous toll. As many of the diseases were of European origin, like smallpox, the Indians had no immunity and whole villages were wiped out. These diseases are still prevalent, but less ravaging. Larger Indian communities, however, have created conditions for greater spread and perhaps more virulent forms even of native diseases. This will continue to keep down Indian population until thorough health education has enormously improved sanitary conditions and until rudimentary knowledge of the nature and cause of disease is general.

The other factors which reduced the Indian population are less important today though not entirely eliminated. Warfare now affects only a few very isolated jungle people and those who, like the Chaco tribes, were disastrously caught in the midst of an international war. Cold-blooded extermination of Indians is not now a consideration. But a lack of fertility, which seemingly is a symptom of extreme cultural disequilibrium, is not entirely unknown. Infant mortality among primitives at best is tremendous. Extreme despair brought on by cultural conflict has led to extensive abortion, infanticide, and even failure to conceive. The factors involved in the last are not fully understood, but appear to be both physiological, including general health and diet, and emotional, arising from the traumatic experience of extreme cultural shock. The combination of these factors has led to a sharp decline in the birth rate among many of the maladjusted surviving tribal fragments in Venezuela, Brazil, the Gran Chaco, and elsewhere. This, coupled with racial mixing and rapid acculturation, seems to doom many marginal tribes as Indian groups.

On the other hand, once adjustment was achieved, many Indians showed a remarkable increase, despite the difficulties just mentioned, and some multiplied beyond all expectation. The Navajo, for example, increased in a century from some 8,000 to more than 50,000. Mexico, Guatemala, Honduras, and the Andean countries have almost certainly more than regained their aboriginal number. In fact, if mestizos are included they have doubled it. Unquestionably, improved diets and health practices together with the usual vigor and fertility of hybrids will cause the proportion of Americans who have Indian ancestry to increase in the future.

The accompanying table is based on available census data, which are none too good. More significant than the absolute numbers are the differences in population distribution between 1492 and the present day. In general, the Indians have diminished or disappeared in the areas of low aboriginal density and have increased where the native density was greatest.

American Indian Population

	1500 (in thousands)	1940 (in thousands)	Percent of Total 1940 Population
Northern Nations			
Canada	230	108	1.0
United States	770	395	0.3
Southern Nations			
Chile	750	290	9.0
Argentina	300	120	1.0
Uruguay	20	...	0.0
Tropical and Subtropical Nations			
Antilles	300	...	0.0
Venezuela	350	103	3.7
Guianas	90	11	2.4
Brazil	1,200	500	11.0
Paraguay	100	60	6.0
Panama	70	42	9.0
Costa Rica	40	3	0.6
Tropical Colombia	350	105	...
Highland Nations			
Mexico	3,200 [a]	6,000	33.0
Guatemala		1,820	55.0
Nicaragua, Honduras, and El Salvador	100	85	9.0
Highland Colombia	800	60	3.2
Ecuador	1,090	960	50.0
Peru	3,500 [b]	2,800	40.0
Bolivia		1,800	51.0
Total	13,170	15,262	

[a] This estimate includes Guatemala.
[b] This estimate includes Bolivia.

RACIAL ATTITUDES

The role of race in determining social status and opportunities for Indians is fundamentally different in the Anglo-American and Ibero-American countries. In the former, especially in the United States, society tends to be caste-structured, each race having a fairly unalterable place within it. The pattern of the Ibero-American countries, by contrast, is characterized more by a class system, race tending to coincide with but not to be unalterably linked with class position. Moreover, although the whites are in the dominant position in both kinds of society, Negroes tend to outrank Indians in Ibero-America but to rank definitely below them in the United States wherever the two are in contact.

The Anglo-American race-caste system in the United States is exceptional for its rigidity and for the fervor which underlies it, especially in those sections of the country where the races are in closest contact. The three races are socially segregated in such a way that each contains in large measure within itself the entire range of occupations and social statuses. A Negro or Indian may rise to the top occupationally or socially only within his own group. He may rarely enter the dominant white group, and almost never successfully competes with its members. Ordinarily, he enters the white man's world only in the lowest occupational levels, largely as unskilled labor.

The Indian is not always clearly bracketed in this scheme, largely because his physical isolation on reservations usually averts the necessity of pigeonholing him socially. There is even some glamor attached to the Indian, and people feel pride in possessing a small amount of Indian blood though too much places them at a disadvantage. Where the Indian participates to a significant degree in local economic affairs, he is held pretty strictly to the levels of laboring groups, though he ranks definitely above the Negro, whom he in turn regards as inferior.

Ibero-American countries, although far more rigidly class-structured than the United States, tend to lack its race attitudes. A person is judged and classed by his culture, not his race. An Indian is a person with an Indian culture; a Negro is a member of the lower, laboring class or a person with an African culture. This permits great social and racial fluidity. It is literally possible that of two full-blood Indian brothers, one may be regarded as an Indian, the other as a mestizo or white man, and that an individual may be born an Indian and later become a white. If Indians and Negroes tend to constitute the lower classes of these countries and carry the disabilities of their class, it is for purely historical reasons. They were the conquered, preliterate populations who furnished labor from the earliest colonial days, and they still earn their living predominantly by unskilled labor and spring from a cultural background that fails to equip them for competition with the white man. Nonetheless, if anyone has exceptional ability and is favored by circumstances, he may realize his aspirations within the national culture. Consequently, many Indians and Negroes have attained the highest professional, social, and political positions. They have become prominent artists, writers, lawyers, doctors, and legislators; many have even become the presidents of their republics.

So far as the class system of Ibero-America has produced a hierarchy of races, the Indian tends to rank below the Negro. Many countries, of course, have an insignificant Negro population, but where slaves were brought from Africa in large numbers, they have overwhelmed the Indian. Replacement of the Indian by the Negro was most rapid and most complete in the island republics of the Antilles. On the tropical lowlands of the South American coast and along the major rivers, the Negro has also absorbed all but a vestige of the Indian, or driven him into remoter territory. This area includes the lowlands of Brazil, the Guianas, Venezuela, Colombia, and portions of the Central American republics. In Brazil near the centers of civilization, for example, the Negro population is numerically far stronger and much more completely assimilated than the Indians, for the Indian is by definition the primitive jungle inhabitant and therefore is regarded as inferior to the Negro. Where these two races have had important contacts—for example, in the Amazon area during the days of the early rubber boom—it was the Negro who was made labor boss of the Indian.

PRESENT CONDITIONS

The present condition of the Indian and the factors which will influence his future are so unlike in different parts of America that each area requires separate consideration. As national policy is one of the most important factors, it is convenient to consider these areas largely under national headings.

Large portions of the United States fall into the area where the Indian, never numerous, has become extinct or survives in comparatively small groups on reservations. The total population, however, is some 395,000, which is roughly half that of pre-Columbian days.

It consists mainly of Indians on reservations in the Far West. Some were native to the area; others, like the Creek and Seminole of Oklahoma, were dislocated peoples who were moved west.

The tribes of the Southwest were in effective contact with Spanish civilization at an early date, and, like most of the tribes of Latin America, they absorbed many Spanish elements into their own comparatively advanced culture without extreme cultural disintegration. Most of the remainder, however, were first affected by Anglo-American civilization, which reached them so recently that many old men still live who remember the first real migration of white men into their country. This is one of the facts which gives the Indian problem in the United States its peculiar character. European civilization impinged on the tribes with such suddenness and force that every reservation today is extraordinarily heterogeneous culturally, individual variation ranging from old, illiterate, non-English-speaking persons, usually full-bloods, to young, educated, and largely assimilated persons, who are often mixed bloods. This, above all, is the difficulty which the modern Indian program faces in the United States.

Historical circumstances in the United States forced the Indians into more and more remote areas, reservations being set aside from time to time in fulfillment of treaties. As usual, the pivotal point of the problem has been land ownership. Although reservations and other benefits were guaranteed by treaties, only recently have the abrogated rights been compensated by juridical action. The historic policy was one of enforced assimilation and a step to this end was granting Indians individual title to their lands in 1887 with right to sell. The result was further expropriation of Indian lands and further demoralization of an already disorganized people.

Since 1934, with the Reorganization Act and other fundamental changes in policy, a more humanitarian attitude has prevailed in Indian affairs. According to a clearly stated policy, the aim is to restore an effective economy, to preserve lands, and to foster Indian values while introducing the benefits of European civilization. To a degree, this has meant entrenchment of the reservation system, for the Indians are not yet ready to manage their own affairs. Old land is protected and new land given to the reservation group, a charter governing the business transactions and loans from a revolving fund being among the benefits. Meanwhile, despite forward-looking health and education programs, native culture is not only tolerated but encouraged.

This program encounters certain obvious difficulties. The tribal council governing tribal affairs can with difficulty represent the disparate elements ranging from illiterate full-bloods to college graduates of mixed blood. Interest in preserving Indian custom varies tremendously between old and young. And the very tendency to segregate Indians and foster their Indianhood—a reversal of the previous policy of insisting on assimilation—while saving them from the friction of racial conflict stamps them as definitely Indian in a nation that has strong racial prejudices. These observations hold, however, with different force for different sections of the country. Among the Pueblo and Navajo Indians of the Southwest, the tribes are most homogeneous and native culture survives with greatest strength. The "New Deal" for the Indians here will certainly ease the process of their eventual assimilation, although it can hardly check it permanently. Where, however, the Indian is already nearly assimilated culturally and, in large measure, biologically, the disparity between old and young, Indian and American, and reservation and assimilation, presents the most serious difficulties.

Canadian Indian affairs do not differ essentially from those in the United States, except that in the far north, which has not yet been truly settled by the white man, there are a number of tribes which are only partially assimilated. The most numerous group is the Eskimo, which, including those of Danish Greenland, numbers about 36,000. The Eskimos are still a seacoast people, living substantially as in aboriginal days, except for some contact with trading posts and some missionary teaching at remote stations. A number of tribes carry on fur trapping in the north woods of the MacKenzie River basin and of Labrador, but seem destined to be absorbed as whites push northward to exploit these areas.

The remainder of Canada's Indians are largely on reservations, and their relationship to the national population is very similar to that of the tribes of the United States. Better protected in the past from expropriation of their lands, they are now subject to a less far-reaching and adequately financed program on their behalf than in the United States. It is difficult to see that any peculiar Indian cultural values survive even now in sufficient strength to make a lasting impression on Canadian national culture.

In Argentina the largest "Indian" element is in the Argentine Chaco. This area, long unexploited, is now being opened up and the tribes are experiencing a more or less violent impact of civilization. Because of the small number of Indians, Argentina has no strong Indianist movement. The Chaco Indians are attaching themselves in increasing numbers to white commercial enterprises—cattle ranches, lumber mills, sugar cane factories—and in time will unquestionably blend into the criollo population, which is also absorbing the thirty or forty thousand Argentine Araucanian Indians. The criollos form the great rural population of western and northwestern Argentina which is strongly Indian in blood but is largely assimilated culturally. The criollo rather than the Indian is a source of national pride and of literary and "folklorist" interest in that he has contributed to such picturesque local types as the gaucho.

Chile's 250,000 reservation Araucanians have already been mentioned in connection with Indian movements. In addition, the Andes of northern Chile have some 40,000 Aymara, who are very similar to the Indians of Peru and Bolivia.

The general trend in Ibero-America has been penetration by white and Negro of the more accessible areas, first along the coast and later up the larger rivers which provide thoroughfares to the inland regions. Today only the periphery of the Amazon basin remains in relative isolation, and it appears that the next few years will bring strong white influences to the Indian tribes in this area. The effect of this penetration has been almost complete cultural absorption of the Indian and the creation of every degree and combination of racial mixture of white, Indian, and Negro.

In the Antilles the Indian virtually disappeared within a few decades of the Conquest and a Negro slave population was imported. The handful of culturally hybridized and mixed-blood descendants of the natives can scarcely now be classed as Indians, and the most liberal definition of Indian could hardly be stretched to include such people as the Black Caribs, who are Negro in race and who speak French.

The tropical coast of South America is also now strongly Negro, the Indians having been either absorbed or pushed inland. The Guiana jungles have many Bush Negroes, whose culture is very similar to that of native tropical Africa and who have exerted some influence on the neighboring Indian tribes.

The absorption of the Indian into the national population, is well illustrated in the case of Venezuela. About 3 percent of the total population is Indian but in the remote jungle area of Amazonas Territory in

Southern Venezuela, 39,000 of a total population of 41,000 are Indians. As the frontier of civilization pushes deeper into the jungle, its Indians are destined to lose their identity. Even in the decade between 1926 and 1936 the total Indian population of Venezuela decreased from 136,000 to 103,000.

The Indian will probably not become extinct racially, and it is very possible that the various Indian-white-Negro mixtures will produce physical types better adapted to the tropics than any of the parent races. Certain elements of the Indian's cultural adaptation to the jungle have already proved valuable in the culture of such hybrid peoples as the Neo-Brazilians and may well contribute to the adjustment of colonists who are being brought into the Amazon basin to exploit its rubber, drugs, hardwoods, nuts and other resources. Ultimately, however, the Tropical Forest Indians seem destined to lose their ethnic identity, so that from a practical point of view the most important problem is to soften the impact of civilization upon them. Several countries have already created departments of Indian affairs for this purpose; Brazil's, created in 1910, for example, is designed to regulate and humanize treatment of the Indians, to further their education, and to improve their economic condition.

Paraguay, a subtropical country, deserves special mention, for it is not only strongly Indian but exemplifies many features in which Ibero-America differs from Anglo-America. The basic population is descended from the Spanish colonists and the Guaraní Indians. The people are predominantly Indian in race, Guaraní is as much the national language as Spanish, and there is a strong residue of Indian traits in modern life. Yet the Guaraní are not thought of as Indians. The term "Indian" is reserved for the primitive tribes of the Gran Chaco, people who hunt and farm in the bush, do not speak Spanish, and in general are not assimilated. Whereas Guaraní is a source of great national pride, the "Indians" are disdainfully regarded as heathen, and, in so far as the Indianist movement has become articulate in Paraguay, its attention is devoted exclusively to the Chaco tribes.

Peru has over 7,000,000 persons, 2,800,000 of whom are Indians, 3,000,000 mestizos. Contrast between coast and highland has marked the history of Peru. Today the coast is more Spanish and more susceptible to foreign influence. It is what makes Peru nationalistic, and Lima has always been the nation's capital. The highland is Indian. Virtually all its people, including whites, speak Quechua, whereas only 31 percent of the country as a whole speaks Quechua and another 16 percent both Quechua and Spanish. Education has reached 75 percent of the coastal people but only 30 percent of those in the highland. The highland strongly influences foreigners who live there, and conversely Indians who descend to the coast tend to lose their Indian characteristics.

The most important fact about the highland Indians is not their great uniformity in race, language, and general culture, but their organization in agricultural communities, some of which apparently go back to aboriginal ayllus and others to colonial reducciones. Communal agricultural lands and group agricultural activities underlie the structure and function of these communities. Community members own and work their lands in common, perform rituals to insure their fertility, and struggle jointly to protect them.

The community is not static, however, and its ideal form is being destroyed by various factors, some bringing economic disaster but retarding change and others aiding economic readjustment but destroying the community's Indian characteristics. The most important factor is encroaching haciendas, which gradually appropriate Indian lands. About half the Quechua now farm only hacienda lands, and pay for their use by straight rentals, by giving certain amounts of work to the hacienda, by sharecropping, and by a combination of these methods. These hacienda Indians are little exposed to forces making for assimilation, for they are uneducated, impoverished, and comparatively isolated. Their loss of lands has reduced them to an economic level that leaves neither time, energy, nor wealth to maintain characteristic community activities.

On the other hand, many communities have succeeded in protecting their lands, but in doing so have acquired features of mestizo communities. Their size has often increased through accretion of dispossessed people from elsewhere, and some have organized coöperatives, municipal power plants, schools, and other benefits. Another factor making for assimilation is participation in national commerce, both through community specialization in the manufacture of pottery, tiles, hats, textiles, shoes, and other products and through the growing of special cash crops or of salable crop surpluses. The individualization of land ownership likewise undermines the typical Indian community, for it splits the family and destroys many forms of communal work.

It appears inevitable that the Indian agricultural community as it is now defined will disappear and that the mestizo community will take its place, for the Indian's lack of national outlook and inability to participate in pan-Indian movements makes him unable to contend with the forces working toward the destruction of his typical community. At the same time, there seems little immediate chance that community lands can be restored to any important extent, for a country that is over 80 percent rural, with whites in control of the greater part of agrarian wealth, will not readily redistribute lands to the extent of sacrificing its own interests. As present trends continue, however, more and more Indians will enter the class of mestizos, which already outnumbers them. The mestizo proletariat will increase, especially on the coast where there is more industrialization and the haciendas are more modern. Successful and stable agricultural communities will acquire an increasing number of mestizo features, and many will grow in size and importance as specialized crafts and trades spring up in them. More widespread Indian education, which is now an important national policy, will eventually broaden the outlook of all Indians.

Many observers have thought that a pan-Indian movement is gathering force in Peru. The Apristas, a liberal political movement, made a bid for Indian support, but their effective membership was the mestizo proletariat. It is likely that any strong attempt to remedy the problem of insufficient lands through political means will come on a mestizo rather than an Indian level, as the latter is now defined. An effective mestizo movement may even bear the name Quechua, and the people will preserve many Indian features for years to come. But there will be little interest in restoring Indian culture as such—a culture that now has few characteristics of pre-Conquest culture.

Bolivia is fundamentally like Peru, but is more thoroughly Indian, for of its population of some 3,500,000 people, about 1,800,000 are Indians and 1,120,000 are mestizos. In addition to the Quechua, who form the highland population of Peru, it has about 500,000 Aymara-speaking Indians. Bolivia also differs from Peru in lacking a coastal lowland. Both its Indian and national life center in the highlands, and Indian problems are national problems.

The general nature of Bolivian Indian problems is similar to that of Peru and the ultimate outlook is probably the same. A more immediate difficulty, however, arises from the fact that a larger proportion of Bolivia's farm workers have been drawn into the mines, leaving a national food shortage. As at least a partial solution to this problem, it has been proposed to colonize the extensive, fertile, and fairly accessible but little exploited lands of the eastern Bolivian lowlands. Such a solution would require careful readaption of the highland Indians to this new environment and to its native peoples.

Meanwhile, the extreme economic maladjustment of many Bolivian Indians, together with mine work, service in the army, and other factors making for a sense of common interest and common cause, creates a general situation which many observers regard as potentially far more explosive than that in Peru.

The situation in Ecuador is also very similar to that in Peru, except that Ecuador's lowlands are largely tropical forests and had an aboriginal population very different from that of the highland. The coastal tribes were quickly crushed by the colonial encomiendas, and today only a handful of Cayapa and Colorado Indians survive; the basic population has become Negro. Highland Ecuador, on the other hand, is strongly Indian. About 50 percent of the national population is classed as Indian, and most of them speak Quechua. At least 80 percent have Indian ancestry.

The basis of Indian life is the community (here called the parcialidad or anejo), in which the Indians have their own lands, keep their own culture alive, and tend to be hostile to outsiders. But at least half the Indians are landless, and although some land is being made available to them, haciendas are at the same time encroaching on existing Indian holdings. Indians who lack lands either give labor on haciendas or sharecrop in return for the use of land, or work in towns, or devote themselves to crafts. Some communities have made considerable progress in developing local crafts, and have improved their economic and educational status. As in Peru, however, the spread of economic and educational reforms tends to destroy the Indian characteristics of the communities.

Mexico's present Indian population is about 6,000,000—about the same as that of the Andean countries. Like the Andean peoples, most Mexican Indians were intensive horticulturalists and possessed a society based on the local community. In contrast to the Andes, however, Mexico is characterized by great geographic and cultural heterogeneity. The mountain mass of the Andes is continuous and it harbors a uniform people, nearly all of whom speak Quechua and share the cultural heritage of the Inca. Mexico, on the other hand, is broken into several mountain masses; it also has both tropical forests and deserts, which are found on the coast as well as in the interior. Its native cultural variation was commensurate with geographical differences and no single political empire introduced a national language and a uniform culture to all its peoples. The conquerors found 20 linguistic stocks and 125 major tribal groups, each culturally distinctive. The Maya, Aztec, Tarascan, Otomi, and other realms never exercised a control over their subject peoples that was remotely comparable to the absolutism of the Inca empire.

The course of Spanish settlement of Mexico likewise differed from that of the Andes in its lack of uniformity. Many tribes were first brought into contact with European culture through missions, and subsequently lapsed into an independent existence that has largely persisted today. So far as these have a European culture, it is that of sixteenth- and seventeenth-century Spain. Some remote tribes have been effectively contacted only recently. Others quickly came under the encomienda system, and in the areas of dense settlement, such as the valley of Mexico, have been subject to continuous Europeanizing influence, so that the enormous mestizo population shares much of modern culture.

Mexico and the Andes are also unlike in that the former has already had an agrarian revolution, and now possesses a strong and effective Indigenista movement. That a popular movement should develop among the diversified population of Mexico sooner than among the very homogeneous Andean Indians is striking evidence of the insufficiency of common culture alone to supply a basis for pan-Indianism. The success of this movement in Mexico is probably explainable by two facts. First, about ten of Mexico's sixteen million people are mestizos and therefore possess the necessary education and national outlook to achieve solidarity. Second, so far as Indians participated in this movement, they brought to it a spirit of independence far greater than that of the Quechua. The latter had been thoroughly regimented under the absolutistic Inca regime, and white landlords merely represented new rulers who differed from the Inca mainly in the kind of their rule. In native Mexico, by contrast, defeated people had merely been forced to pay tribute; they had not been conquered socially and spiritually.

Change in Mexico has not yet run its course, but strong popular regard for Indian needs enables the Indigenistas to play an important role in formulating Indian policy. Restoration of lands in the pattern of the aboriginal communities is more likely to succeed than in the Andes. It remains to be seen, however, whether even in Mexico, part of the country can operate through collectives while the national economy is based on private ownership. Apart from economic problems, there are many Indian needs in the fields of diet and health, education (especially in view of the great linguistic diversity), and cultural readjustment. In these the Indigenistas' efforts hold great promise.

In Central America, all the republics except British Honduras, Costa Rica, and Panama have a large Indian population, whose development and problems have been somewhat similar to those of Mexico. The main difference has been a less vigorous Indigenista movement. It was only in 1934, for example, that Guatemala abolished debt peonage, lowered interest rates, and introduced measures to help Indians acquire lands.

Costa Rica and Panama really belong among the tropical countries; the native population here was sparse and comparatively primitive. Today only a few remote jungle tribes remain and their problem is that of an unassimilated national minority.

The Indigenista movement is now spreading through Central America and more liberal policies can be expected. Reforms of the depth of those already effected in Mexico, however, cannot be realized for some time because the proportion of Indians with a sense of solidarity is smaller in these countries than in Mexico.

The greater part of Colombia's Indian population is in the jungle areas, already mentioned. Its highland population was never comparable to that of Ecuador, Peru, and Bolivia, for the area is not a large, continuous highland, but is, rather, broken into mountain blocks. The native highland people probably did not number over 800,000. These were mainly Chibchan-speaking peoples whose terrain was almost wholly preëmpted and settled by the Spaniards. Most of these Indians fell before the conquistadors or were rapidly assimilated into a mestizo population. A few retreated to mountain fastnesses, where some 60,000 survivors still retain much of their aboriginal culture. Most of these are on reservations, and are slowly selling off their lands to the whites.

Appropriate governmental policies may help rehabilitate these peoples economically and ease their assimilation, but as a political minority their problems are very different from those of Ecuador, Peru, and Bolivia.

THE OUTLOOK

There is little doubt that biologically the Indian will increase, but whether this increase will more than offset cultural assimilation which removes people from the category of Indians into that of mestizos is doubtful.

The basic forces bringing national cultures to the Indian will unquestionably increase, regardless of political programs to further or hinder them. Improved transportation through a vast extension of highways and feeder roads, of air routes, and of new river travel will disseminate white influence in expanding volume. New demands for specialized local products will furnish a motive for opening up now isolated regions and for supplanting subsistence farming with cash crops. And greater national wealth, coupled with increased interest in education, will extend formal means for acculturation. Certain results will inevitably follow. Better material goods, especially when they can be purchased by a people who have learned a cash economy, will replace many native products. Individual land ownership and inheritance, so far as it advances, will undermine the family and comunidad. Education in health and sanitation will weaken the position of the native medicine man. And the introduction of scientific knowledge about weather, soils, crops, and cultivation will tend to destroy beliefs, ritual, and pageantry dedicated to success in agriculture.

The dividing line between the Indians and the mestizos will be established by the census taker with the help of the Indianists. Those on the Indian side will, in general, be those who have clung to aboriginal ways and are in need of paternalistic help. On the other side will be people more sophisticated in the national culture. The latter will not be homogeneous, for cultural regionalism will always exist, but localism will be in terms of what the Ibero-Americans call folklore—the folk culture of the varied rural populations. The local cultural values, then, will be found among such people as the criollo, Guaraní, or Ladino. To these, perhaps, will be added other groups, such as the Quechua or Aymara—not as Indians but as rural mestizo populations. These groups will be comparable to minor nationalities and other special segments of the population—the cowboy, the Swede, or the hillbilly. It is quite possible that much Indian culture may be perpetuated on new bases. Thus, distinctive arts and crafts may flourish for home consumption and, if they find a profitable market, for outside sale. Religious rites, festivals, and ceremonialism may survive for their social value. So, in fact, may dance, music, and costume where the people remain sufficiently integrated locally to retain cohesion and pride in the in-group.

From a political point of view, those who ethnically are still classed as Indians will be the object of the Indianists' concern, for it is they who most often are underprivileged and incompetent to fight their own battles. Many anthropologists have expressed some concern, however, whether the very efforts to develop a program for an exclusive group which is arbitrarily defined will not create race prejudice where it does not now exist, creating some opposition to the program and making national integration more difficult. Certainly strong efforts toward self-help will come from the more educated, which generally means more assimilated Indians, whether they have been acculturated through education or through more informal processes. The agrarian reforms in Mexico were brought about by this group and many observers believe that they see in the Andean countries similar potentialities when acculturation has given the Indians or mestizos a sense of common purpose. Whether the typical Indian agricultural community can be restored and mestizo agricultural collectives can thrive in nations of capitalist landlords or whether other forms will be instituted remains to be seen.

The Colonial Crisis and the Future
By RAYMOND KENNEDY

THE MAJOR and most well-marked division of the lands and peoples of the world is that between colonial and noncolonial areas, dependent and independent nations. Although there are several kinds of colonies, and a certain range in degree of dependence and independence among countries, there is no mistaking this primary line of division. The dependent or colonial areas lie almost entirely in Asia, Africa, and Oceania. The great zone of independent countries covers Europe and the Americas. Some overlapping is apparent, however. China and Japan, as well as Asiatic Russia, Thailand, Iraq, Iran, and a few smaller states, are exceptions in Asia. Ethiopia, Egypt, Liberia, and South Africa stand out as independent countries in Africa. Australia and New Zealand are the sole outposts of independence in Oceania. Contrariwise, a few small colonial possessions dot the great mass of free states in the Americas. Europe, of course, contains no colonies. The exceptions mentioned do not alter the general fact that virtually all the dependent peoples of the world live in Asia, Africa, and Oceania; while the vast majority of independent nations are found in Europe and the Americas.

Starting with this basic geographical pattern, we at once perceive that certain outstanding racial and cultural correlations accompany it. The colonial areas are those inhabited almost completely by the two darker races, Mongoloid and Negroid; the zone of independence is populated for the most part by the Caucasoid or white race. Correspondingly, the colonial peoples possess either Oriental or "primitive" cultures; while the independent nations have cultures of the Occidental type.

Geographically, culturally, and racially, therefore, the two great world areas split cleanly, the only major exceptions being China and Japan. The racial element explains most of the other aberrant instances: South Africa, Australia, and New Zealand being ruled by white colonists; and Siberia being an extension of European Russia. Moreover, where sizable concentrations of Negroes and Indians are found in the Americas, they frequently occupy a kind of dependent status not unlike that of their Negroid and Mongoloid racial brethren in colonial areas.

The present pattern of colonialism has an easily explainable historical origin, for it had its beginnings about four hundred years ago, when Europeans "discovered" the rest of the world. By a lucky combination of circumstances, the European powers had at that time developed their culture strongly in the direction of navigational skill, military organization, refinement of lethal weapons, and commercial efficiency. In all these particulars, the other cultures of the world were relatively inferior; and the record of the last four centuries has been one of steady conquest of the native peoples of the Americas, Africa, Asia, and Oceania—a conquest accompanied by political subjugation and economic exploitation. Where enough European settlers occupied the new lands—as in the Americas, South Africa, Australia, and New Zealand—the natives were either annihilated or driven back into the wild hinterland or completely subordinated. Elsewhere small populations of whites, backed by naval and military contingents quartered in the colonies, established political and economic control over the natives.

The long course of conquest ended during the last forty years with the seizure of a few remote scraps of still unappropriated soil in Oceania and Africa. The world assumed its present pattern, with all of the major nonwhite populations except the Chinese and Japanese brought into a dependent status under the rule of one or another European state. The period of colonial wars and conquests is now past, and coming struggles for power must be either between the independent nations, or between the subject peoples of the colonies and their masters.

About one third of the land area of the earth is colonial territory; and of the two billion population of the world approximately 700,000,000 fall in the category of subject peoples. The gigantic proportions of the colonial problem and the tremendous potentialities involved in the future of the colonial system can hardly be exaggerated. In terms of land and population the issue is one of absolute primary importance, and if it is not a part of the present world crisis, then it will certainly press irresistibly to the forefront in the immediate postwar future.

Seven Western nations hold the bulk of colonial territory. Great Britain stands out as the major possessing power, dominating a mass of 500,000,000 subject peoples, over 350,000,000 of them in India.

The Netherlands and France rank next, with about 70,000,000 population in each of their empires. Japan, at the outbreak of war, ruled 30,000,000 colonial subjects; the United States and Belgium about 15,000,000 each; and Portugal approximately 10,000,000.

While social, economic, and political conditions vary in the colonies of the different powers, and even between the colonies of the same empire in most cases, and although there is a variation in policies, all the dependent areas manifest certain common characteristics, which may be termed the universal traits of colonialism. The only marked instance of deviation from the general pattern is the Philippines, for here, during the forty-odd years of American control, a rapid evolution away from colonial status has occurred.

The first of the universal traits of colonialism is the color line. In every dependent territory a true caste division exists, with the resident white population separated from the native masses by a social barrier that is virtually impassible. The color line, indeed, is the foundation of the entire colonial system, for on it is built the whole social, economic, and political structure. All the relationships between the racial groups are those of superordination and subordination, of superiority and inferiority. There is no mistaking this pattern for one of mere segregation, or separation with equality. The color line is horizontal, so to speak, and cuts across every colonial society in such a way as to leave the natives in the lower stratum and the whites in the upper. Even in the case of the one nonwhite imperialistic power, Japan, the representatives of the ruling nation occupy an upper-caste position, which is supported by a concept of racial superiority, although for practical purposes the Japanese have played up solidarity of the darker races against white domination. Throughout the colonies, we find a system of group discrimination and subordination, and natives are judged and treated, not on the basis of individual worth or ability, but as members of an undifferentiated group. Although other elements are involved, the heart of the colonial problem is the native problem, and the native problem is a racial or caste problem.

A second common feature of all colonial systems is political control by the possessing power, leaving the natives little or no share in the government of their homelands. The administration is directed from the mother country, whose local representatives hold all the important governing positions in the dependency. Most colonies have advisory councils, and some even have legislatures, in which natives are represented; but in every instance the powers of such bodies are circumscribed in such a manner that ultimate decisions on all important matters are made by the home government or its agents in the colony. Natives almost never rise to the higher echelons of the administration. In many colonies, notably those of Great Britain and the Netherlands, a pretense of native self-government is kept up by the so-called "indirect rule" system, which retains local potentates in their hereditary offices and allows them to go through the motions of administration. Actually, these native rulers are mere creatures of the central administration, and the whole system is a transparent façade behind which the real governors exercise their will. In this case, as in that of colonial councils, the generalization holds true that native opinion and native aspirations influence the administration of dependent areas very little, if at all. Whenever natives do try to organize their people for political action, or even express opinions that run counter to official policy, they are branded as "radical agitators," closely watched, and, unless they cease their preachments, imprisoned or exiled. In most colonies, the administration operates a network of secret police, which, with the regular police and the armed garrisons, has a single major function: to detect and suppress independent native political action. Remote penal establishments, reserved mainly for exiled native "agitators," are a common appendage of colonies. In addition to having a very small part, if any, in the domestic administration, colonial peoples are completely deprived of any voice in the foreign affairs of their countries; and the primary right surrendered by native princes who submit to "indirect rule" status is control of the relations of their states with other powers. Likewise, the military defense of colonial areas and the selection and training of all armed forces are completely dictated by the ruling state. Internally and externally, therefore, colonial peoples are politically impotent. Even in cases where lip-service is paid to "extension of local self-government" in colonies, this means an increase in the political privileges of the resident members of the dominant nationality and not the natives. Finally, in almost all dependent countries, special codes of law apply to resident whites, even in so called "native states" under indirect rule.

A third universal trait of all colonial areas is economic dependence upon and control by the mother country. This general principle has wide and varied implications, all of them following the pattern of native subordination. The colonial areas are exploited as hinterlands of raw material production, the output being exported for industrial processing to the home state or to other Western countries. This standard procedure has relegated the dependent areas to nonindustrial economic activities, principally agriculture and mineral exploitation, and has kept the concentration of industries in the European and American continents. If the development of industries has not been deliberately discouraged in the colonies, at least it has not been actively encouraged by the controlling powers. Moreover, besides having little chance at industrial employment and enterprise, colonial natives have almost no share in the direction or ownership of the large-scale exploitative undertakings of their homelands, nor in the export and import trade. It happens that these are the major profit-bearing enterprises, and the natives therefore participate hardly at all in the yield of larger profits from their countries. Indeed, they are, almost to a man, either subsistence farmers or low-paid laborers in the employ of foreign businesses.

The colonial populations are typically peasants, coolies, and servants. A glance at the statistics of occupation, wealth, and income for all colonies, or any one of them, leaves no doubt about this matter. The discrepancy between the economic status of the small group of resident whites at the top and that of the native masses at the bottom is so tremendous that no Western nation can show even a remote similarity. And between the thin top layer and the abysmally low native bulk there is no middle class—or if there is one, few natives are found in it. The middle economic levels, where they exist at all, are typically occupied by other nonnatives, in most cases Oriental immigrants such as Chinese or Indians. When natives do step out of their local subsistence economy into paid occupations, their wages are invariably low, almost incredibly so by Western standards. A Javanese rubber coolie, for instance, is lucky to earn as much as the equivalent of ten dollars a month. This is sufficient for him to live, but only on a very low level of subsistence. And, again a characteristic of all colonies, a native has little or no chance to rise in the economic scale. Occupational barriers are set firmly at the racial or caste level, and mobility upward is almost impossible for the native. Virtually all the higher and better paid positions are reserved for the resident whites. There is no economic "ladder" in colonies for the subject peoples, since there are no rungs between them and the dominant caste. The rule is: no profits and no good jobs for natives. Indeed, the profits that go to the upper caste are derived largely from the cheap labor of the economically stagnant native masses.

Fourth among the common features of the colonial system in general is a very low stage of development of social services, especially education. Public health and sanitation, public works, agricultural and veterinary programs, and other more material services in some instances receive a fair degree of care and support; but native education is universally neglected in colonies. Deliberate or not, this lack of attention to education makes very good sense when considered in connection with the other elements in the colonial system. Education of natives would threaten the whole structure of political and economic superordination and subordination. Education would be dynamite for the rigid caste systems of colonies.

A fifth characteristic of colonialism that might be mentioned is the lack of social contact between natives and the ruling caste. The groups are mutually exclusive to an almost total degree except in such formal relationships as those of employer and employee or master and servant, which are stamped with the mark of obvious inequality. The upper caste has its own clubs, recreational functions, friendship circles, and the like, from all of which natives are rigidly excluded. When native and white families are placed in situations where some social contact is unavoidable, as in small and isolated outposts, a code of wary etiquette artificially formalizes the relationships and symbolizes the social distance between the races. The white person who associates freely with natives is sure to be regarded with suspicion and even scorn by his fellows; and marriage with a native brings outright ostracism. There are degrees of variation in this matter between colonies—the British maintaining the strictest lines and the Portuguese the loosest—but the general pattern holds throughout the colonial world.

These, then, are the outstanding universal characteristics of colonialism all over the dependent areas of the world: the color line; political and economic subordination of the native population; poor development of social services, especially education, for natives; and rigid social barriers between the ruling class and the subject people. These are the elements of which the colonial system is constructed.

Every institution of human society is supported by a code of rationalization. Men must have reasons for the rules they follow and the institutions by which they live. The reasons may be logically verifiable or purely irrational, but this makes little difference to those who believe in them. Colonialism, like other institutionalized systems, is supported by a set of rationalizations, firmly held and fiercely defended.

The color line is rationalized by the doctrine generally accepted among Europeans and Americans that the white race is innately superior to the darker races. It happens that all the evidence of scientific research in anthropology, sociology, and psychology tends to disprove this assumption. It is false, but it is believed. As previously intimated, this curious misconception was born about four hundred years ago, when the Europeans began to extend conquest over the entire "native" world. The darker peoples lacked the superior military equipment and organization of the whites and were either slaughtered or subjugated. The owners of guns came to believe that they were also the possessors of superior racial endowments, and attributed their success not to material advantages but to inborn mental and physical superiority. They were white, and the beaten peoples black and brown; consequently inferiority must be linked with color and race. This idea has passed into the cultural heritage of Europeans and Americans, and constitutes the basic principle in the charter of colonialism, just as it is the foundation of the entire colonial system. Nevertheless, the conviction that the Oriental and African races are inferior has been weakening steadily in recent years. Although small, the rising class of educated and able leaders among colonial peoples is demonstrating the falseness of the doctrine by living proof. The meteoric ascent of the Chinese in world estimation during the present war has also been a potent factor in shaking the old prejudice. Moreover, although it is a bitter thing to say, the obvious skill and phenomenal achievements of the Japanese in employing the white man's industrial inventions and military methods have given the concept of racial inferiority a stunning blow. Finally, on the positive side, the fact that racial prejudice and doctrines of innate superiority constitute the foundation stones of the ideological structure of Nazi Germany has tended to bring all racialistic dogmas into odious disrepute among the United Nations. The colonial powers among the latter would find themselves uncomfortably embarrassed if they continued to use the argument of inborn inferiority of the darker races as a justification for their subjugation. Still, although the old prejudice is declining because of these factors, it is by no means extinct.

Political subjugation of the natives is rationalized by the theory that they are unable to rule themselves properly. Sometimes the doctrine goes further, and holds that the subject peoples do not want to govern themselves, and even like to be dominated. The latter assumption is dubious, to say the least, and becomes more so every year, with the increasing tempo of nationalistic agitation among the dependent nations in all parts of the world. The idea that they are incapable of proper self-government is the key rationalization of the political aspect of colonialism, and judgment of it must center upon the standard of good government used. That the colonial peoples could govern themselves is undoubted, for their ancestors did so for thousands of years before the first European administrator arrived. Probably even now the great majority of natives who think of the matter at all are convinced that they could handle at least their domestic political affairs better than their present masters can. The latter doubt this, and support their denial with copious arguments. Certainly the kinds of governments the colonial nations would have under immediate self-rule would be different from those of the present administrations, and, judged by European and American standards, would be full of faults. In any case, whenever the question of independence is raised, every dominant power immediately presents evidence that its colonies would fall into this or that dire condition if set free. Not long ago, this would have been followed by the assertion that the subject peoples could never govern themselves properly. As late as 1927, Governor Hugh Clifford made this claim concerning Malaya. Nowadays, the usual line of argument is that some day, after proper training, the colonial peoples will be ready for self-rule. Thus the old rationalization of essential incapacity to govern has now been replaced by the notion that a long period of tutelage will be necessary before the time is ripe for freedom. In the meantime, no definite program of native education for self-government has been announced by any of the colonial powers except the United States, which has actually carried out such a program in the United States.

When specifying the dangers of self-rule, the dominant states concentrate upon three lines of prediction: that the native rulers, now held in check by the system of indirect rule, would reintroduce the old despotism; or that the present political leaders, a small elite in every colony, would form a dictatorial clique and shackle democratic progress in order to ensure their power; or that other independent states (for example, Japan, Russia, China) would plot to take over the fledgling nations just emerged from colonial status, imposing an imperialistic rule no better, and probably worse, than that of the present administration.

The first of these claims is probably justified in certain areas, but for most colonies it would not hold, as the present native princes are supported more by the official administrations than by their own subjects. Indian rajas, African emirs, and Malayan sultans might try to redespotize their people, but if they did they would probably be faced with either indifference and disregard or outright revolt. In many, if not most, dependent areas, the native nationalist leaders would exercise more influence than the hereditary princes, with whom they usually have no sympathy. They regard them as mere puppets of the imperialist regime, which in truth they are.

As for the danger that the educated and politically active native elite would stifle democratic evolution for their own advantage, this is indeed possible. The Latin American countries, after liberation from Spain and Portugal, passed under the rule of dictatorships, from which few of them have even yet emerged. The solution here would seem to be rapid education of the native masses in the democratic process, so that popular opinion and pressure might resist the dictatorial ambitions of the small elite. Thus far, instead of preparing this democratic counterforce, the colonial governments have spent little effort on education, realizing that enlightened natives would be a threat to all dictatorships, including the present imperialist variety. By their very argument of the danger of dictatorship of the native elite, therefore, the colonial powers work themselves into a dilemma, the only solution to which would endanger their own survival. Their recourse has been to suppress colonial nationalists, thus snapping off the bud of an enlightened native mass, meanwhile keeping education for their subjects down to an absolute minimum.

The third of the alleged dangers of colonial independence, the threat of alien aggression, links with general problems of world security. Under prewar conditions, freed colonies, weak in industrial and military power, would succumb readily to stronger aggressors. And unless international control of military aggrandizement were established after the war the danger would still exist. Here again the colonial powers have done little or nothing to remedy the weakness, since they have neither encouraged industrial development in the dependencies nor trained the natives in defense of their homelands. How to achieve a balance between national independence and collective security is, in any case, a problem all countries will face after the war. The colonial areas happen to be more vulnerable than the normally free countries, although many of the latter are in no better condition of self-defense than the dependencies. The Netherlands, for instance, fell and would fall as easily as the Netherlands East Indies. The problem of military defense of the colonies is part of the general question of security for the smaller and weaker independent nations.

Economic subordination of colonial peoples finds support in the rationalization that the natives are incompetent to operate the productive and distributive systems of their homelands. An additional reason given is that they would not be able to develop the natural resources of their countries to full potentiality. The essential causes of these deficiencies are explained in various ways, ranging from the claim that the natives are innately inferior in organizing and technical talents to the admission that they merely lack the proper training. The latter kind of explanation is becoming the more prevalent as the old ideas of racial inferiority have weakened. Besides lack of training, absence of native capital for investment and development is an obvious handicap. The former deficiency could be rectified by education and by opportunities for practical experience. But so far in colonial history the subject peoples have had almost no chance to acquire advanced technical and commercial education, since they do not possess the funds to go abroad for study and only inferior facilities are provided in the colonies. Even in the rare instance where a native does acquire proficiency fitting him for higher positions, he is shut off from advancement by a universal code of discrimination in favor of whites on the managerial levels. Aside from high salaries, the really big financial gains in colonies take the form of interest on financial investment. Here again the natives have no chance at wealth, for they neither possess capital nor have the opportunity to earn or save much money to invest. Foreign capital has always been needed for large-scale exploitative or commercial development in colonies because of the absence of local funds.

Some colonial administrations have prepared plans for aiding natives to share in the profits of export production through the establishment of coöperative enterprises, and actual beginnings have been made in a few places—the Gilbert Islands in Oceania and the Netherlands East Indies, for instance. Perhaps the encouragement and even initial subsidization of producing and selling coöperatives would offer a way out of the economic handicap of lack of native capital. But the problem of native economic immobility would be more easily solved by opening the paths of occupational and wage advance to them through increased opportunity for training and removal of discriminatory barriers. However this may be, the present truth is that every colonial area has a dual economy: one part being the small-scale subsistence economy, usually agricultural, of the natives; and the other the large export production and trade of the ruling group. Virtually all the cash profits of colonies are derived from the latter sector of the economy, and natives have almost no share in it. Those natives who do work for wages are extremely low-paid, and until recently labor conditions in most dependent areas were poor, often being little better than slavery or serfdom. Conditions of labor have improved recently, and the worst abuses, such as forced labor and long-term contracts with penal provisions for breach of agreement, have been eliminated in most dependencies. But wages have not risen, and organization of labor unions by natives is sternly suppressed throughout the colonial world. In short and in sum, the economic stagnation of native peoples has yet to be broken in any appreciable way, although the barriers are showing slight signs of weakening, particularly the traditional dogma of inherent economic incapability of the darker races.

The poor development of social services in colonial areas is rationalized by the plea of financial insufficiency. In the case of education, this general claim is substantiated by the old familiar assertion of racial incapacity to learn, by the argument that education would cause discontent and unhappiness through stimulating unrealizable ambitions, and sometimes by the allegation that natives do not want much education anyway. The fundamental financial rationalization is certainly justified in many colonies, which simply do not yield revenue sufficient to support adequate social service programs. But in others, particularly the larger and better developed dependencies, a tremendous increase in funds for public services could be realized by raising taxation on the higher incomes and large-scale business enterprises. The plea is often made that heavier taxation would drive out old and discourage new foreign capital investments. Although no thorough study has been made in any colony of the possibilities of raising taxes without driving away capital, there is a strong indication that fair analysis would reveal that the actual tax revenue is far below practical potentiality. However this may be, in the past great profits have flowed from the soil

COLONIAL CRISIS AND THE FUTURE

and from the cheap native labor of the colonies, while expenditure on public services for the local populations has been far from adequate as judged by Western standards. As mentioned before, more progress has been made in the technical fields of health, public works, and the like than in education. Indeed, the educational system in colonial areas receives only a small share of whatever public revenues are available. In the Netherlands East Indies, for instance, educational expenditures have never taken more than 10 percent of the total budget. Colonial administrations, indeed, are not merely disinterested in native education; they distrust and even fear it, and with reason, as remarked above. Particularly has liberal higher education been kept to an absolute minimum; and whatever small enthusiasm may appear is directed toward technical training in agriculture, animal husbandry, and similar politically innocuous subjects.

The claim that education, especially on the secondary and university levels, would produce discontent and frustration among natives who could find no positions commensurate with their training after graduation would seem to point toward reform in the occupational rules and customs of the colonies. It doubtless holds true under present conditions, and the better jobs would have to be opened up to natives as higher education expanded in order to avoid the difficulty. So desperate is the need for well-trained native teachers in all colonies, however, that an enlarging school system would by itself absorb the whole output of higher institutions of learning for years before reaching saturation. However this may be, the colonies are the only areas in the world where it is assumed that the development of educational facilities must be geared in with actual job possibilities, on a kind of supply and demand basis.

That natives are racially incapable of absorbing higher education, and that they do not want schooling anyway are claims that rest solely upon unverified preconceptions. The evidence shows that there is no general reluctance to attend schools where they are provided, and that, where special conditions do not impede their progress, natives display the same range of learning ability as whites. Proponents of contrary views would do well to ponder the words of Snouck Hurgronje, one of the most profound students of colonial peoples, written in 1910 concerning the East Indies: "The Indonesians are imploring us to give them instruction; by granting them their will we shall secure their loyalty for an unlimited time." Recent evidence from the Philippines, where the native educational program was unequaled, bears out this opinion.

The colonial code that dictates complete social segregation of the races is rationalized either by the commonplace assertion that natives are ignorant or unclean or uninteresting; or by the claim that they do not desire whites to become familiar with them; or by the argument that informality, camaraderie, and, most of all, intermarriage would weaken the prestige of the ruling caste in the estimation of their subjects. Anthropologists who have done field research among colonial peoples would dispute the opinion that natives are uninteresting, or that they are ignorant within the bounds of their own habitat and culture. Some tribes are certainly unsanitary by prevalent Western standards, for instance the Melanesians; but others, like the Indonesians and Polynesians, are meticulous with regard to cleanliness. Judgments to the contrary are generally based upon provincialism and lack of actual experience with the people concerned. Most Europeans and Americans merely assume that natives do not wish to associate with them, and have never put this idea to the test of experiment. That injury to prestige would be caused by free social intercourse and even intermarriage with colonial peoples is another largely unverified preconception. The individual instances of behavior contrary to the code on the part of whites would seem to indicate that no such consequence need be expected if the social barriers were to be relaxed completely. One of the Hollanders with the highest personal prestige among Javanese is famous for his free and easy ways with them. Unfortunately, the majority of whites who have associated most intimately with the darker peoples have not represented the better elements among their kind. The stiffest of all social codes with relation to natives is that of the British, and their general reputation among colonial peoples is unenviable. Indeed, one of the most constant complaints of subject groups against the British is their ineffable snobbishness and exclusiveness.

Here, then, we have an institutionalized system, firmly set in tradition, that covers almost half the area of the earth. Every one of its component features is supported by a set of rationalizations which are used to justify the existence and continuation of the system. On these common elements and their accompanying rationalizations are based the colonial policies of the world.

The foregoing analysis has shown that the ideological substructure of the colonial system is shifting at many points. Concomitantly with this alteration in ideas, the practices and policies are changing. Colonialism is undergoing an evolutionary variation so radical and so fundamental that the process has the marks of a basic mutation in the institution. The present world crisis may well appear in historical retrospect as a turning point in the evolution of human society and culture, and, like all revolutionary periods it is characterized by such rapid modifications in behavior and thought that mutation rather than mere variation would seem to be involved in many of them. Colonial policies are in a state of complete flux, just as the general system is, and in surveying the specific policies of the various powers trends are even more important than fixed patterns.

The four powers principally involved in colonial destiny are Great Britain, France, the Netherlands, and the United States. Inclusion of America, which has controlled only one truly dependent area, in the forefront of the problem may seem odd; but the Philippine policy is so crucial to the whole question of the future of colonies that it must rank high in the selection of cases for comparison. Japan, on the way to utter defeat and loss of her recently acquired colonies, has interest for the future only as an historical case. Belgium and Portugal, small states holding relatively inconsiderable territories, will play purely subsidiary roles in future developments. The Spanish colonies are even smaller and poorer, and are of significance only as examples of utterly antiquated policy.

Great Britain is by all odds the dominant colonial power of the world, controlling 500,000,000 subject peoples in dependencies that extend across the face of the earth from the outermost isles of the Pacific to the eastern shores of the Americas. This small island state has achieved the greatest record of conquest in history and came close to winning the entire land surface of the globe outside Europe. The conquered areas which drew large numbers of white colonists—all of them in the temperate zones—have now attained independence within the framework of the Commonwealth. But no tropical British dependency, no area inhabited by peoples of the darker races, has gained or been granted freedom. Whether deliberately so planned or not, the color line is the dividing line between free and dependent nations in the British Empire. The colonial areas under British rule—and India must be included by all the normal standards of colonialism

—show a considerable range of political and economic development, all the way from largely self-governing Ceylon and rapidly industrializing India to completely dominated and economically primitive African possessions.

The British colonial code draws the most rigid color line of all. Paradoxically, the greatest colonizers in the world are the most provincial people in their attitudes toward strange groups and cultures. The British have been in contact for a longer time with more dark peoples than any other Western nation, yet they hold aloof from their subjects to an unequaled degree. They refuse to associate freely or make friends with other races, and this exclusiveness has engendered a reciprocal feeling toward them on the part of their colonial peoples. The attitude of the latter varies from indifference to active dislike, but, except in isolated instances, it never approaches friendliness. Natives often express a grudging admiration for the moral rectitude, financial incorruptibility, and legalistic fairness of Britishers, especially government officials, in the colonies; but bonds of mutual friendship and affection are lacking. Worst of all from the viewpoint of practical policy, the mass of natives have no feeling of political loyalty to the British Empire. This is true of most colonial populations with respect to their ruling states, but the absolute social segregation between the upper white caste and the lower colored caste in British dependencies has inhibited the growth of any feeling of identification with the dominant people and state.

The British demonstrate by their attitudes and behavior that they do not wish the natives to develop any sense of belonging to British society, and the entire social ritual of the colonies symbolizes the separateness of rulers and ruled. Nowhere in the colonial world are the lines of caste drawn more rigidly: in clubs, residential areas, places of public accommodation, and informal cliques. Nowhere is the taboo on intermarriage stronger and the penalty for infraction more drastic. And whereas in other colonies the social barriers are relaxed for mixed bloods, in British dependencies the caste line applies to the crossbreed group as well as to pure natives. It must be repeated that there are exceptions to the rule as always. In the British West Indies, for instance, mulattoes occupy a somewhat favored position. In every colony, an occasional Englishman breaks over the bounds of race, and rare natives of high rank are at least partially accepted in upper-caste circles. But the generalization holds true that race and caste consciousness and social exclusiveness based upon race stand out more glaringly in British colonies than in any others.

In the economic and political spheres there is greater variation. More British colonial subjects are wealthy, and more of them attain positions of administrative importance, than ever penetrate the barriers of social exclusion. Still, the general rule applies that the great mass of natives stand far below the ruling class on the economic scale, that the hindrances to advancement in position are set firmly at the caste line, and that effective political participation is denied to the subject peoples. The governorships and all civil service posts except the lower ones never go to natives. The governmental rules are such that no official body in which native opinion prevails or is even voiced has final decision on really important questions. Veto powers and an "official majority" of Britishers in every influential council ensure the maintenance of policies desired by the home government and its representatives in the dependencies. In India, Malaya, and other colonial areas where native princes are kept in office they function as political puppets of the administration. Native chieftains, lower down the scale, exercise power only within the sphere of local custom, and their actions are carefully controlled. Expression of political opinions contrary to official policy is restricted, if not suppressed, by censorship and police action. The jailing of Gandhi and Nehru in India may have been carried out under the guise of wartime emergency, but they, and thousands like them—not only in India but in other colonial areas—had been imprisoned for independent political activity during peace. The most convinced apologist for British rule could not honestly claim that the subject peoples have anything but a minimum of political power and freedom of political expression.

The practical administration of British colonies, judged by prevailing colonial standards, ranks higher in the over-all picture than that of any other ruling power with the exception of the Netherlands. Here again the range of achievement is variable, some of the smaller and poorer African dependencies being most backward in the development of public services, and other colonies, such as Malaya and certain Pacific islands, having well-rounded and effective programs. In no instance, however, do expenditures per capita on social services approach even remotely those of the Western nations. Education, which in Europe and America receives a large share of the public revenues, is one of the minor items in the budgets of all British colonies. In almost no dependent area is the literacy rate among the native population, in either local languages or English, as high as 10 percent.

With all this, it must seem something of a surprise that the announced and reiterated goal of British colonial policy is self-rule for all dependent areas within the Empire. However, absolute independence, by complete severing of ties with Britain, is not granted as even a possibility. All that is envisioned for any colony is eventual local self-government within the framework of the British Commonwealth. The right to secede is withheld in perpetuity, according to all pronouncements of policy. During the period that will intervene between the present time and the declaration of freedom, the role of the mother country is characterized as one of "trusteeship." Great Britain would appear to be personified as a political mother, with a brood of dark children at various levels of growth from mere infancy to adolescence, who will one by one reach maturity and be allowed to handle their own affairs. But none of them may ever leave the maternal family to set up an independent home or transfer to some other family. They must always hold to the imperial apron strings. Within this limitation, which at the moment seems unbearably irksome to the leaders of India at least, the dependencies are to mature toward self-rule.

This dynamic policy was announced over twenty years ago, in a "White Paper" dealing specifically with the future of the East African colonies, and has been repeated on several occasions. Since it is a statement of goal, the only logical means of judging it is to examine what has been done and what is being done to bring it to realization. In the jargon of the day, How is the policy being implemented? Candor compels the admission that, in most of the British dependencies, movement in the direction of self-rule has been barely perceptible. Three outstanding exceptions are Burma, Ceylon, and India. Burma has undergone a transition during the past twenty years from the status of an Indian province with little or no native share in government to that of a crown colony with an unusual degree of local self-rule for a dependency in this class. Before the war, it was well on the way to becoming a full-fledged dominion. Ceylon, also a crown colony, has a largely native legislature which is elected by complete adult franchise and which exercises a considerable measure of control over local affairs. India, whose actual status within the British Empire has never been properly defined (it being an "empire" in itself!), was actually offered immediate dominion status in 1942 by the Cripps Mission. So mistrustful of all things British were the Indian leaders, so much did they suspect the intentions of the masters even when they came bearing gifts, that the offer was refused. When the preoccupation with war has passed, the full significance of this somberly dramatic gesture will be appreciated. The greatest of all British possessions symbolically expressed a hatred and resentment so bitter that only complete separation from the mother country would be acceptable. And the Burmese, for all the concessions granted them in the direction of home rule, displayed little or no loyalty to the Empire bond when the Japanese invasion came. Not only did they refrain from aiding the British; a goodly proportion of them turned against their retreating masters. In the other British possessions, there is little sign of advance toward self-rule, and no specific programs aimed at the goal have been formulated.

The British, like the Dutch and unlike the French, foster and encourage the retention of native culture in their colonies. They have no desire or intention to assimilate the subject peoples to British civilization, preferring to allow each colonial area to develop in its own way, on the foundation of local traditions. However British imperialism may be defined, it is not cultural imperialism. Native institutions are kept intact to the greatest practicable degree, and every innovation in administration is carefully calculated to avoid disturbance of native tradition. To the extent that this policy entails tolerance in the spheres of religion and personal and domestic custom, it has encountered no adverse criticism, from either natives or Europeans. Its application to economic and political matters, however, has met increasing opposition. Educated native leaders, especially, see in the "nativist" policy of Britain a device designed to keep subject peoples economically and politically primitive and unsophisticated, so that they may never be able to achieve equality among the modern states of the world. The system of indirect rule, in particular, is singled out for attack on the ground that the native potentates whom the British government supports in the dependencies represent an outmoded type of political organization holding no promise of evolution in the direction of democratic institutions. The very gradual and grudging acceptance of natives in the ranks of the official administration, and even then only in inferior capacities, has also aroused impatience. And above all, lack of educational facilities for natives, by which they might train themselves for taking over directorial positions in the business and government of their homelands produces general disillusionment with the entire program of colonial emancipation.

Even within the limitations set by British policy, therefore, the pace of development has been so slow, and the provision of means for the realization of the goal of self-rule so inadequate, that the colonial peoples have come to view their prospects under British domination as anything but encouraging. The policy of fostering the growth of self-government within the framework of the Commonwealth cannot make much of an appeal to the colonial peoples until it is vitalized by a realistic program of training and education on the one hand and a sweeping extension of economic and political opportunities to natives on the other. A goal is worthless unless there are are steps leading to it.

The overseas possessions of the Netherlands include two small dependencies in the Americas and the enormously large and rich East Indies. Only the latter area is significant in worldwide perspective. Therefore, whereas the scores of British possessions display a wide range of variety in status and development—and all shades of administrative nuance from colonies and colonial protectorates and protectorates to protected states and condominiums and mandates of different kinds—the Dutch empire contains just one important unit, to which none of these conventional terms is officially applied. The East Indies are merely termed a "part" of the Netherlands Kingdom. In all important respects, however, Indonesia is a colonial area, and is characterized by the common traits of colonialism.

The color line is quite apparent in the Indies, but it is not nearly so rigid here as in the British possessions. The Dutch suffer less from preconceptions of racial superiority and inferiority than most other Western peoples, and are unusually liberal in their attitude toward deviations from the colonial code of caste. Social relations between natives and whites are by no means free and equal, but by comparison with the colonies of other powers the Indies appear as a zone of exceptional racial tolerance. Intermarriage with natives has been quite common in the past, and, although such direct mixture has become much less frequent during recent times, the half-castes are assimilated legally, and in large degree socially, to the European population. Social acceptability is measured by individual worth and achievement rather than by racial grouping. The allegation of innate inferiority of the darker peoples, so often heard in British dependencies, is rarely encountered in the East Indies.

Nevertheless, despite the relative absence of racialistic rationalizations, economic and political control of the Indies is held firmly by the Dutch. Until recently the islands were administered as a purely commercial enterprise, long after the Netherlands East India Company had passed out of existence. Holland took no interest in native welfare or internal affairs except as these related to the flow of profits from the colony. Official recognition of a "civilizing mission" and the responsibilities of trusteeship first appeared at the beginning of the present century, with the inauguration of the so-called "ethical policy." In essence, this policy stipulated that the interests and welfare of the Indonesians would in future take precedence over all other considerations in the administration of the Indies. The era of regimented labor, forced delivery of products at set prices, and lack of concern with native domestic affairs came to an end. The negative effects of this change in policy were decisive, but positive action in elevating the economic and political status of the native population has lagged. The 68,000,000 Indonesians are an economically inert mass, occupying the lowest levels of income and occupation. The great majority of them stand completely outside the profit economy of export production and trade, living on their ancestral lands as small farmers. Those who work for wages are hired almost exclusively as coolies, servants, and other menial employees. And so, for all the lack of pure racial prejudice as exhibited in British colonies, a rich native, or a native with a really good job, is almost as rare in the Indies as in the British dependencies.

The political status of the East Indies, however, has undergone a rapid transformation during the past forty years. By 1940 the islands had attained a degree of local self-government comparable to that of the most advanced British colonies, such as Burma and Ceylon. The administration was dominated by Netherlanders, with very few natives in the higher official ranks; but the Peoples Council, or "Volksraad," which was established in 1916 as a purely advisory body, had acquired such prestige and power in the intervening years that it functioned practically as the law-making organ of the Indies. Its enactments were subject to veto by the central government, and it had no control over the foreign or military affairs of the Kingdom; but in all other respects it exercised full parliamentary powers. The native representation in the Council was as large as that of the resident Dutch and foreign Asiatics combined, and two thirds of the Indonesian delegates were elected. The composition of the body was such, however, that although the elected members—Indonesian, European and alien Asiatic—had a clear majority, the appointed members and the European delegation together could outvote the remainder of the elected group. Thus, while the "official majority" characteristic of most councils in British dependencies was not maintained in the Volksraad, its peculiar composition counteracted the voting weight of the elected native representatives. Moreover, the franchise for natives was so limited, and the method of election of delegates to the Council so indirect, that the Volksraad could be regarded as at best only partially representative of Indonesian mass opinion.

The essential truth of the matter is that poverty has held back the great majority of Indonesian natives from voting for delegates to the Volksraad and other lesser councils, because income and property qualifications have restricted the franchise; and lack of education and training has rendered them ineligible for positions in the superior ranks of the administration. To the extent that they have been able to overcome these practical handicaps, they have been allowed to participate effectively in the government of their islands. Whereas all except those of pure white ancestry are ineligible for the higher posts in the British colonial services, and are statutorily disfranchised in most British dependencies, the Dutch have drawn only economic and educational lines of discrimination. Within these limitations, natives, half-castes, and whites have all received approximately equal treatment. The removal of income and property prerequisites to voting would solve one aspect of this problem, but a vast increase in educational facilities for Indonesians will be necessary before the Indies can mature to true democratic government with full native representation in the councils and official posts.

From most points of view the practical administration of the East Indies has been superior to that of any other colonial area. The personnel has been carefully selected, highly trained, and extremely efficient. The social services of the more practical sort have received a liberal share of government funds, and the programs have kept pace with the development of the country. The only laggard service, as usual in colonies, has been that of education. By 1940, less than

10 percent of the natives were literate in any language. During recent years the elementary school system expanded rapidly, so that just before the war about 40 percent of the Indonesian children of school age were enrolled. But the average length of attendance was scarcely three years, and higher education for natives was neglected. The Indonesian educational program has emphasized a broad base of lower schooling for natives, and has been deficient in provision for the training of leaders. In its prewar form, it was well on the way to erasing mere illiteracy, but had scarcely begun on the task of developing a native intellectual elite.

The fundamental philosophy of Dutch colonial policy is, like that of the British, one of nonassimilation. Perhaps even more than the British, the Dutch have tried to protect native culture from foreign encroachment, and to build on the basis of the old traditions. They have sternly suppressed "radical" native agitation in the sphere of politics; and have labored mightily to retain local forms of government, all the way down the scale from the exalted potentates of Javanese and Malay principalities to village chiefs. Wherever possible, the system of indirect rule has been employed, to the extent that well over three hundred separate sultanates and regencies still exist in the East Indies. One of the native languages of the islands, Malay, has been adopted as the official lingua franca, and the Indonesians have never been encouraged to learn Dutch or any other Western language. Indonesian customary law and religion—whether Mohammedan, Hinduist, or pagan—have been actively preserved, even in their minutest local variations. The educational system has been devised and operated in full accord with the basic "nativist" policy, and "Westernization" has been kept to a minimum. Whatever pride the Dutch may take in their rigid abstention from "cultural imperialism," the net result of their policy has been the cultural insulation of the Indonesian masses from the outside world. And however laudable may be the Dutch regard for and preservation of traditional native culture, it is doubtful that the glass dome of protection can be laid over the islands again after the war. Indeed, the Japanese have already shattered the delicate globe.

The Dutch have issued a plan for the future disposition of their dependencies which follows the trend of their developing policy. Like the British, they offer self-rule within the framework of a commonwealth as the immediate postwar solution. The Dutch empire is to be a confederation of equal partners, each section—Holland, Indonesia, Surinam, and Curaçao—having its own local government for domestic affairs, but all acting together in matters of general concern to the commonwealth, such as foreign affairs and defense. Unlike the British, however, the Dutch impose no waiting period upon the dependencies before they shall be granted "dominion" status. Self-rule is to come first, and internal political maturation to follow. The plan as announced is a statement of broad policy and principles only, the Dutch insisting that details must wait upon the liberation of the people of Holland and the Indies, so that they may participate in formulating the complete program. The full significance of this declaration of immediate dominion status for the Dutch dependencies after the war can be appreciated only in the perspective of past Netherlands policy. Such a swift evolution from the dead level of almost complete domination in 1900 to virtual self-government forty years later has the mark of a social mutation. Nevertheless, as in the case of the British, the Dutch refuse to recognize the eventual possibility of complete independence for their colonies. Equal partnership in a commonwealth confederation is the ultimate goal of Dutch policy as formulated at present.

France has followed a policy of assimilation in her colonial dependencies. Whereas the British and the Dutch refrain as much as possible from interference with native culture, and foster an evolution based upon local tradition, the goal of French policy is assimilation of the subject peoples to French civilization, and eventual amalgamation of the dependent countries into "Greater France." The phrase *la France outremer*, commonly applied to the colonies, epitomizes the idea. The British and Dutch never talk of "Overseas Britain" or "Overzeesch Nederland." The ideal of the present colonial policies of these two states is "linked independence" of the various parts of the empires, while the French ideal would be a single, centralized state including the mother country and all the overseas possessions. Perhaps the shortest way of expressing the basic difference is to term the French goal one of federation, and the Dutch and British intention one of confederation. The process involved in the former is centralization; in the latter, decentralization. Thus the final product of French policy would be a federation of provinces with a single political capital and central administration in France, all the parts of "Greater France" being represented in the supreme government. If the Dutch and British policies allow no place for final and complete independence of colonial areas,

France goes even further and hopes to forge an ever closer bond between the home country and the colonies in the future.

The French resemble the Dutch in their relative freedom from racial prejudice. To the extent that the color line is drawn in French colonies, it is an incidental product of the low economic and educational status of the mass of natives rather than a determinative factor in itself, as in the British dependencies. Indeed, one of the principal aims of French policy is to develop an educated native elite, to act as a kind of spearhead of acculturation in carrying French civilization to the colonial masses. The social and cultural aspects of "Gallicization" are reinforced by a scheme of progressive grades of political standing, the final step being full French citizenship. In line with the gradual political assimilation of natives, French colonial policy lays much less stress upon indirect rule through hereditary native potentates than the British and the Dutch. Many native rulers still hold office in the French empire, but their tenure is regarded as temporary during the transitional period between colonialism and political assimilation. Eventually these encysted principalities are to be absorbed into the new provinces of Greater France.

The French show little interest in the perpetuation of native culture and languages, and the educational system in their dependencies, to the degree that it is developed, emphasizes the civilization and language of France, the more so the higher the level of schooling. Unfortunately, this experiment in "Westernizing" natives by education on the European model has never had a chance to prove itself widely, for the school system in most colonies is still rudimentary. The other social services, too, appear to disadvantage when compared with those of the Netherlands colonies and many of the British possessions. Inadequacy of funds may excuse such deficiencies in the poorer French territories, but mismanagement and inferior personnel are factors also.

The financial weakness of French dependencies is largely owing to lagging economic development. Foreign capital investment has not been overly welcome, and the French themselves do not invest heavily in colonial projects. Moreover, the official tendency is to encourage independent native production for the export market rather than large-scale European exploitation. This may represent a conscious imitation of the pattern of small peasant proprietorship in France. In any case, the coolie type of native is less numerous in French dependencies than in those of most other countries. To the extent that the colonies are less prosperous in terms of profit and revenue, French economic policy compares unfavorably with Dutch and British; but perhaps the fostering of small native enterprise compensates for the low monetary yield.

When described in terms of ideals and methods, French colonial policy would seem to offer many advantages that are lacking in the dependencies of other states. The subject peoples of France are recognized as potential equals; they can look forward to full French citizenship when properly qualified; they are not saddled indefinitely with a host of antiquated feudal rulers; and they are to share in one of the great civilizations of the Western world. Unfortunately, however, these are statements of ideals, which, although still incorporated in French colonial policy, have receded further and further from realization as the years have passed. Rather than improving, the economic and political situation in French dependencies has deteriorated steadily, collapsing in near-debacle in Indo-China during the past two decades. Here the nadir was reached in a series of mass strikes, riots, and nationalist uprisings which were countered savagely by military force, mass arrests, and exiling of the native leaders to the penal colony of Pulo Condore. It is doubtful that the goodwill of the Indo-Chinese, especially the Annamites, can be regained.

The fact is that the high ideals of French policy have been negated by political chaos in the mother country and mismanagement and poor administrative personnel in the dependencies. The *mission civilisatrice* of France in her Asiatic, African, and Oceanian colonies has been rendered abortive by the confusion and weakness of France herself. Unable to manage their own country properly, the French have failed even more miserably in their overseas possessions. With consistent planning and expert direction, backed by political stability in France, the French colonial policy might have proved a greater success than that of any other state. In the absence of these requisites, it has fallen far short of its intrinsic promise.

While France saw in the diffusion of French culture a means of eventually blending the colonial peoples into the body politic of the mother country, the American policy in the Philippines—likewise one of "Westernization"—was directed toward the opposite goal of complete independence. Actually, the United States is the only ruling power that has ever carried out the "trusteeship" principle to the letter. Other countries with dependencies have paid loud lip-service to the doctrine that the justification for domination is preparing the subject peoples for self-rule; but the sole instance of practical and thoroughgoing application of the theory is the Philippines. Probably the real reason for this difference is that Great Britain, France, the Netherlands, and the smaller colonial powers do not sincerely wish to relinquish their dependencies, while America has no desire to keep the Philippines. It is customary to classify the states of the world as "have" and "have-not" powers, in the sense of possessing or not possessing colonies. An appropriate additional classification would be in terms of "want" and "want-not." All of the dominant countries except America "have" and "want" their colonies; the United States alone is a "want-not" nation.

This singular lack of imperialistic acquisitiveness undoubtedly accounts for the high prestige of America throughout the subject lands of Asia, Africa, and Oceania. Deservedly or not, the United States has come to symbolize freedom to the colonial peoples of the world. And this reputation is substantiated by the unprecedented course of events in the Philippines. The Americans entered the islands with the promise that everything possible would be done to prepare the way for independence in the shortest practicable time. Despite intermittent deviations, this policy has been pressed forward steadily; and now, after a period of only forty years, the initial promise has been fulfilled. Indeed, many Filipinos feel that freedom is being forced upon them too quickly, an absolutely unique experience for a dependent people. In all honesty it must be admitted that the American desire for Philippine independence is not entirely the product of disinterested idealism. The islands have been a financial burden and a vulnerable military zone, and only a restricted group of Americans have ever derived much profit from them. Moreover, the tariff preferences accorded to exports from the Philippines to the United States have galled certain beet-sugar and vegetable-oil interests in America, whose political weight has been persistently applied in pressure for separation of the islands from the United States.

The American policy, then, has been one of acculturation for independence, in contradistinction to the French scheme of acculturation for assimilation. With perhaps pardonable ethnocentrism, the Americans have acted on the assumption that the best preparation for freedom is Americanization, and have labored diligently to train the Filipinos in American methods of education, business enterprise, and political administration. They have done what other colonial powers promise to do but have shown only half-hearted signs of really doing. They have built up a school system unequaled in the other dependencies of the world, and have spread knowledge of the English language all over the islands. Not satisfied with mere eradication of illiteracy, they have set up high schools and a great national university, graduating hundreds of students every year. Technical training in agriculture and mechanical trades has been included in the program, but liberal academic education has not been neglected, as in most other colonial areas. A special advantage of the scheme has been its "self-fertilizing" power. The graduates of the high schools and university have been "plowed back" into the system, so to speak, with the result that almost the entire teaching staff was finally composed of Filipinos. In short, the American school system in the Philippines came to grips with the central problem of education for independence: the training of native leaders. And as time passed, more and more of the positions in government were surrendered to Filipinos, so that by 1940 very few Americans still held posts in the administration. Concomitantly with this progression, the scheme of representative government developed to maturity; until finally, before the war, the whole structure was complete and the Commonwealth of the Philippines had a democratic political system patterned on the American model, with full adult suffrage and natives in control of nearly all important offices. Now the date of final independence has been set at 1946.

However the results of American policy may be judged, and allowing for obvious shortcomings in the Philippine political system as it operated before the war, the record shows what can be accomplished by determined and consistent effort in only a little more than a generation. The Philippine experiment offers a model for other powers to use in preparing their colonies for independence, or at least self-government. It does not furnish a universally applicable pattern, but with modifications for local differences the main lines of the program could be followed in most other dependencies.

The American policy combines the Westernizing theme of the French plan with the local self-determination inherent in the British and Dutch programs; and carries both tendencies to a point beyond the accomplishment of any of these powers. Interestingly enough, for all their political liberalism, the Americans maintained a rather strict color line in the Philippines. It was manifested especially in the social and economic spheres. The Americans did not mix freely with Filipinos, and imposed a strong taboo on intermarriage. This social code was an obvious reflection of the racial mores of the United States, and might be characterized as a kind of "informal Jim-Crowism." It was merely understood that only under certain circumstances were Filipinos or mestizos invited to white homes, and that certain clubs and schools admitted only Americans. The caste line was not so rigid as in British colonies, but not so loose as in Dutch and French dependencies. Economic discrimination on the basis of color appeared particularly in employment practices. American firms reserved the better positions for whites, and Filipinos seldom rose above clerical jobs. The one great resentment Filipinos harbor against Americans is their racial prejudice. Indeed, this is the worst handicap Americans bear in their dealings with people of other races, outside as well as inside the United States.

Whether the Philippines, for all the aid and encouragement of the United States, can safely embark upon absolutely independent statehood after the war is a moot question. If international power politics backed by armed force prevails in the future, this small nation will need military protection. But aside from such dangers, the independent Philippines would face desperate problems of internal economy. Tariff preferences have functioned as a virtual subsidy for export production and trade, and with independence these favors would end. Unlike the Indies, where the Dutch have insisted on preserving native rights to property in land, the Philippines under Spanish rule suffered from an agrarian system that resulted in the dispossession of the great mass of peasant farmers. Landless families form the bulk of the rural population of the islands, and they are afflicted with all the besetting ills of farm tenancy and sharecropping. The present Philippine government inaugurated a comprehensive program of land purchase, resale, and resettlement in the years just before the war; and with wise operation this may solve the problem eventually. But the Philippine people would enter upon a period of severe economic dislocation and strain as soon as indirect financial subsidization by way of tariff preferences on the American market were terminated with the advent of independence. The islands are not naturally rich, and if the helping hand of the United States should be withdrawn the general standard of living would be sure to decline. The Filipino leaders realize the magnitude of these problems, and it would not be surprising if they asked for reconsideration of the issue of independence before all ties are severed.

The colonial policies of Portugal, Belgium, Spain, and Japan require only summary discussion; the first three because the possessions are relatively small and unimportant, the last because the brief period of Japanese imperialism will end shortly. Portugal, in her rather sizable African dependencies and scattered minor colonies elsewhere, has followed a weak imitation of the French policy, which, to the extent that it admits of any concise characterization, may be described as assimilationist. The Portuguese have a vague goal of eventually making their dependencies "ultramarine provinces" of the mother country, and in line with this have shown indifference to the preservation of native cultures and languages. Although race prejudice is less prevalent than in any other colonial area, and intermarriage with natives quite common, little positive effort has been made to improve the status of the subject peoples. The dominant purpose is to make the natives work so that they can earn money to pay taxes. Labor standards are low, and the social services poorly developed. Economic exploitation has lagged because investment of foreign capital has not been encouraged. As in French colonies, expansion of small-scale native enterprise, mainly in agriculture, is the principal economic aim. Unstable home government, lack of consistent planning, inferior personnel, and inefficient administration have combined to make of the Portuguese possessions the most backward of all, with the sole exception of the Spanish.

Belgium, in her one dependency, the Congo, has been accused of following no definite policy at all. This is true to the extent that the question of final goal has never been raised. The Belgians show no interest in either cultural or political assimilation of the natives, nor do they hold out any hope of ultimate self-government for the Congo. Their entire concern is with the economic development of the colony. Improvement of the status of the native population stands secondary to this leading purpose, and all plans are judged by the standard of financial advantage. If the lot of the Africans is coincidentally bettered, all well and good; but it is not the primary consideration. The result of this singleness of purpose, combined with efficient administration, has been a "model" colony of the old-fashioned variety, where the resources are intensively exploited, the profits large and steady, and the social services well advanced. Aside from the static political policy which includes no measures for any future change in the *status quo*, other aspects of Belgian rule that may appear unfavorable are the strict maintenance of the color line and the almost complete concentration in education upon technical training. The natives are schooled and aided in improving their agricultural and mechanical proficiency, but nontechnical education is sadly neglected. This system of education, conjoined with encouragement of small-scale native enterprise, has produced a growing middle class of native cash-crop farmers and tradesmen, but few native industrial or political leaders. The central administration of the colony is run almost entirely by Belgian officials, and the traditional princes and chieftains retain a show of local power in the typical pattern of indirect rule. The whole system is paternalistic, practical, and completely undynamic except in its material aspects. The prediction may be ventured that the enlarging group of middle-class natives will some day strike for political privileges, but so far no strong movements in this direction have occurred.

The Spanish colonies in Africa have a total population of only a million, and, except for Morocco, are insignificant in worldwide perspective. Spain has no colonial policy, unless complete political subjugation and economic exploitation of the natives may be so termed. Particularly oppressive are conditions of native labor, which, under a system of contract peonage, are little advanced beyond slavery. The administration is antiquated, the official personnel inferior, and the social services less developed than in any other colonial area. To the extent that Morocco is exceptional, the better conditions are owing to Spanish rivalry against France in North Africa. Realizing that anti-French feeling is strong among Mohammedans there, Spain, especially during the Franco regime, has striven for popularity as a protector of Islam. Aside from this purely opportunistic deviation, the colonial policy of Spain is one of utter footlessness and lack of direction, and the Spanish dependencies are pathological specimens of abysmal backwardness.

The Japanese, relative newcomers in the imperialistic ranks, have one great advantage over the white ruling nations: they themselves are dark-skinned racial brothers of their subjects. This natural advantage has been capitalized intensively during the present war, with what results we have yet to discover. But the ethnic vanity of the Japanese, supported by religious rationalizations of divine descent, inhibits full exploitation of the racial brotherhood theme. Certainly their treatment of Koreans and Manchurians, who form the bulk of their dependent populations, has given the lie to their protestations of racial affinity and sympathy; and their activities in China amount to nothing less than racialistic hara-kiri. Their general policy in Korea, Manchukuo, Formosa, and Micronesia has been one of halfhearted efforts toward assimilation combined with intensive economic exploitation and political subordination of the natives. The color line is not drawn, because it cannot be, but national arrogance has aroused the same kind of resentment as racial prejudice has in colonies ruled by whites. Despite all the propaganda about "Greater East Asia," the record of the Japanese in their older dependencies shows little effort at elevating the political status of the natives. Local princes and chieftains have been retained in office, and the Japanese, occupying all the higher administrative positions, have operated a system of indirect rule no different from that of the British or the Dutch. Natives have been given little opportunity to attain positions of economic power, and the profits of large-scale exploitation have been reserved for Japanese. The social services in general are poorly developed, and education, although it stresses Japanese language and culture in typical "assimilationist" fashion, is so inadequately provided that it falls far short of its purpose. The Japanese had a unique opportunity to set themselves up as the leaders and "liberators" of the Asiatic peoples; but, by imitating most of the faults of their imperialist precursors and fumbling their special advantages, they have missed the possibility of heading a crusade of freedom. Their failure has given the Western powers one more chance to gain the goodwill of the Asiatics before another and wiser nation may arise to organize a new movement of the subject peoples.

In attempting prediction of the future of colonial policies, the trends to the present are the best guide. The most important trend of all has been the gradual granting of more and more self-government to subject peoples. Not only is it a perceptible trend; it has been officially announced as the intention of the British, Dutch, and French governments. But in no instance save that of America is complete independence, the severing of all political ties with the ruling state, conceded to be even a remote possibility. Clearly there must be practical advantages in control of colonial areas to account for the stubborn tenacity of dominant nations in holding their dependencies even against the will of the subject peoples. Violent argument has raged over this question, one side claiming that the tangible benefits to the mother country are very great and the other insisting that the material advantages of domination are doubtful, if existent at all. Oddly enough, the latter view prevails most widely among the advocates of continuation of the system. Most colonial governments eagerly present evidence that dependencies are mainly liabilities to the governing power, implying that imperialism is largely a labor of love and disinterested devotion. The crucial question then is, Why do they try so hard to keep these troublesome and profitless territories? Why not be rid of them?

The truth is that the advantages and profits to be gained from the possession of colonies still far outweigh the disadvantages and expense involved. Most dependencies pay for themselves in the sense that budgets for administration, public services, and the like are almost always kept within the limits of local revenue. Once in a while, during times of crisis and depression, the mother country may contribute a subsidy to tide the colony over; but the sum total of such grants is inconsiderable. As a general rule, each colony nowadays has its own budget, and the rare surpluses are retained as reserves. Thus, although a large number of officials receive good salaries and pensions from colonial funds, the home government itself draws no outright revenue from its dependencies. The financial benefits are derived more indirectly. Even though in most colonies an "open-door" policy allows equal access in the sphere of capital investment and commercial exploitation to citizens and corporations of all nations, the nationals of the ruling power obtain inevitable preferences. The invisible connections between business and government in every state operate to give the citizens of the mother country first access to information about exploitable resources and priority in concessions. In virtually every dependency, the commercial interests of the ruling state have acquired a preponderant share of the profitable enterprises. Importing companies often have the advantage of preferential tariffs, and certainly need not fear discriminatory imposts. The monetary system is geared in with that of the governing state, obviating difficulties of exchange; the business practices and legal system follow familiar rules; and the official language is that of the dominant nation. In addition, there are the advantages of cheap labor, control of export and import trade, and regulation of economic development in favor of home industry. In short, a candid acknowledgment of the intermeshing of modern governments with commercial interests leaves no doubt that the financial benefits of colonial possessions to the economy of the mother country are considerable.

The military advantages accruing from the possession of colonies include not only the ownership of strategically located fortresses and naval and air bases, but also the control over vital materials of war which may be denied to the enemy or the potential enemy. Only one imperialistic power, France, has ever imposed conscription for military duty on subject peoples; but Great Britain draws a fair proportion of her armed forces from her dependencies, especially India. The potential military manpower of colonial areas is vast, but, significantly enough, the ruling powers have avoided training many of their subjects in warfare. The simple truth would seem to be that they are afraid to do so, for fear that the natives might turn their arms upon their masters. Thus the colonial peoples are denied the means of defending themselves and their homelands. Even worse, this denial points directly to a major flaw in military strategy based upon colonies. The fortifications may be strong and well defended, but the restive populations are a constant threat. It is probable that the effectiveness of Britain's armed forces in India during the present war has been considerably weakened by the necessity of using a goodly proportion of them in policing the native population. The enemy in the rear is an ever present danger to armies operating on colonial soil.

The possession of colonies is generally regarded as an important factor in raising the international prestige of a nation. Germany, Italy, and Japan are striking examples of the "urge to empire." The economic and military advantages of overseas possessions have attracted them, of course; but the desire to overcome feelings of national inferiority caused by lack of colonial territory has been a dominant element in their aggressive behavior. Contrariwise, an obvious stimulus to the occupation of previously unconquered territories in the backlands of the world has been anxiety to prevent seizure of them by other powers. Prestige is a powerful imponderable in human motivation, individual and national, and the imperial urge has been a potent factor in the causation of wars.

With all these advantages of colonial possession, and with the elaborate substructure of rationalization that supports the colonial system, it is not surprising that most imperialist nations hold tenaciously to their dependencies. Nevertheless, the rationalizations, as we have seen, are shifting, and the advantages are being counteracted by new developments in the political and economic spheres. The ferment of change is working in the two great divisions of the world, in the mother countries and in the colonies. Among the ruling peoples and the subject populations a basic transformation of opinion is taking place. Traditional racial preconceptions are disintegrating rapidly, and the cultural superiority in technology and organization of the Western world is being swiftly neutralized by the diffusion of knowledge and skills to the Orient and Africa. The pressure to learn is so strong on the part of colonial peoples that it cannot be controlled much longer. With the spread of Western civilization to the dependencies, the old justification of domination on the ground of ignorance and incompetence of the subject populations must lose force. Already these peoples have recovered from the stunning shock of conquest, and are regaining their spirit and will to freedom. An ever-growing number of them are losing their awe of the rulers, and becoming impatient for self-government and economic self-realization. If concessions are not freely granted, they are coming to the point where they will fight for them.

Concomitantly with the changing attitude of the colonial peoples, public opinion in the ruling countries is undergoing a transformation with respect to the whole question of political and social freedom. The ideological conflict at the root of the present war has finally projected the basic issues of political liberty, economic opportunity, intellectual freedom, and social justice into the forefront of men's thoughts. The countries fighting for individual and national freedom are confronted by the glaring paradox that they deny the same things to millions of their colonial subjects. This is the crux of the issue, and it is inescapable.

The reaction has been to seek compromises. If the era of colonialism now ending is aptly termed that of domination, then the period just beginning would seem to be shaping into one of compromise. A logical conclusion is that it will be followed, sometime in the future, by the culminating epoch of freedom. So far, no colonial power except the United States has been willing to look ahead to this third stage. They all stick at the point of compromise.

Generally, the favored word used to characterize the role of the dominant states during the coming period of compromise is "trusteeship." It would appear that the restive conscience of the Western world is going to be satisfied with this solution. The Dutch and the British have already declared their dedication to the mission of trusteeship and have pledged themselves to carry out its duties. In all probability, France, Belgium, Portugal, and Spain will fall in line and subscribe to the same general program. And American public opinion is most likely to support the new plan. A minority in each of the ruling nations will refuse to be content with such partial measures, and press forward the cause of immediate liberation. On the other extreme, a rather larger and more powerful minority in the dominant states will try by all means to preserve as many of the features of the old system as possible. On the other side of the world, in the dependencies themselves, it is likely that the majority of native leaders will accept, grudgingly and suspiciously, the new regime. It may well be that the champions of immediate and complete liberation will gain the upper hand in certain of the colonial areas, and stir up revolt against all compromise. India is the most explosive of these danger spots, but Burma and Indo-China will also require careful treatment. There is a fair chance, however, that the latter two countries will accept self-government within the British and French empires, respectively. But India would appear to be a lost hope for Great Britain. The path of wisdom and discretion for Britain would probably be to yield gracefully, salvaging whatever good will she may from her greatest failure. Skillful statesmanship may persuade the Indians to accept full dominion status within the empire, but the debacle of the Cripps Mission presages disappointment.

The other dependencies will probably submit to compromise, and, with perhaps sporadic rebellions, accept their old masters in the new role of trustees. But they will be vigilant to detect use of the new guise as a mask to conceal a return to former conditions. They will demand proof of good intentions, and any power which attempts deceit will find itself caught in the hopeless circle of ruthless suppression followed by increased bitterness, from which there is no escape.

The principle of trusteeship, as formulated for postwar application, is directed at the goal of self-government but not self-determination. Since no colonial power has yet announced a practical program explaining in detail exactly how the principle is to be put into operation, it is difficult to prejudge its merits. The main problems involved are, first, How are the colonial peoples to be trained for self-government? and second, Who is going to decide whether the program is being properly forwarded and when the natives of any particular country are ready for self-rule? If each of the powers is to act independently, with no interference from any outside source, the only judge of these matters will be the most interested party in every case. This leads directly into the vexed question of whether third-party judgment should be applied in the future of the colonies. That other nations than the ruling powers and the colonies are involved is a growing realization.

COLONIAL CRISIS AND THE FUTURE 341

Aside from idealistic issues of justice and freedom, every country in the narrowing world has a purely practical stake in the colonial problem, because not only has it been a source of disturbance and war in the past but it looms as a potential cause of future wars. It could quite conceivably bring about a cataclysmic struggle between the races. Therefore, if the settlement of European problems is one prerequisite for enduring peace, the other is solution of the problem of colonial areas. It cannot be dodged, and the whole world is involved.

If the stake is international, all nations should have a hand in the game. Fortunately, two of the three most powerful states in the world, America and Russia, are themselves nonimperialist. But the third of the great powers, Britain, is the principal imperialist nation. When the Atlantic Charter was signed by Britain, hope rose high that its principles were to be applied to colonial as well as independent countries, only to be dashed almost immediately by Churchill's devastating declaration that the dependent areas of Britain were not to be involved. A change of government in Great Britain, or concerted pressure by Russia and the United States, may well force retraction of this stipulation. In any event, the trusteeship principle needs the guarantee of international supervision. The main obstacle to realization of the latter is the attitude of the present British government. Lord Hailey, the cautiously liberal spokesman for British colonial policy, goes only so far as to propose "regional councils" in the various colonial zones, which would meet to discuss mutual problems. Thus, for example, the British, Dutch, and French would participate in the regional council of Southeast Asia. Perhaps the most revealing insight into the conservative British conception of this anemic scheme is offered unwittingly by Lord Hailey himself when he says: "Place might be found for the representatives of the [native] peoples themselves on the advisory or other committees attached to the councils."

The success of all plans for international coöperation in solving the colonial problem depends largely upon the establishment of an effective system of international government. If no international league is set up, then the present hope may as well be abandoned of solving not only the colonial problem but the whole problem of future peace and security in the world as well. The colonial problem may, however, be temporarily eased without the support of a league of nations. Indeed, the trusteeship principle if carried out would result in the creation of several "leagues of nations": British, Dutch, French, and others. Perhaps that is as much as can be expected at the present stage of man's social evolution.

If international government is established after the war, quick action in drawing up a "colonial charter" would be advisable. This document, to be signed by all colonial powers and countersigned by all the other nations, should stipulate in as precise terms as possible how the dependent peoples are to be prepared for self-government, how faithful following of the program is to be guaranteed, and how the time of maturity for self-rule is to be decided. One department of the international administration should have general supervision of all colonial problems. In each of the dependent areas, the governing power should be responsible to a resident international commission, composed of representatives of several nations, which would carry out constant research and investigation, function as a board of complaints for native pleas, and report at intervals to the central department. The device of resident commissions would correct one of the main weaknesses of the League of Nations mandate system, namely, the lack of impartial local supervision and judgment.

Such a plan, as already stated, presupposes a world organization which may not emerge from the present crisis. If not, then each colonial power will have to work out its own destiny and guarantee its own integrity as a trustee of its subject peoples. In either case, the practical problems are the same: how to prepare the natives for self-government, and how to decide when they are ready for it. The latter problem would probably solve itself through gradual evolution, or perhaps through more hasty evolution urged on by native pressure. The problem of preparation is, as every section of this essay has indicated, one of education primarily and of opportunity secondarily. Perhaps the most frustrating feature of official publications by colonial administrations and their spokesmen is their consistent avoidance of this basic question. When it is not side-stepped completely, it is passed over with empty phrases. Indeed, perhaps the best test of the quality of any book or essay on the colonial problem is its treatment of native education.

The foregoing pages have described the deficiencies of native education in all colonies except the Philippines. The schools concentrate upon either elementary subjects or technical training. High schools are few, and universities almost completely absent. The so-called "liberal arts" are represented feebly if at all; and subjects such as economics, sociology, world history, and international politics—in other words, studies which would give the student perspective on the world and his country's place in it—are avoided. However the apologists for colonial education may try to explain away these glaring omissions, the brutal truth is that such subjects are deliberately avoided in order to hide from the native students their lowly status in comparison with free peoples and thus keep them from inevitable discontent and rebelliousness. These are the fields with which able political and social leaders must be familiar; and as long as they are closed to natives such leadership will not arise among them. The sole purpose of most colonial education is to train natives in bare literacy and manual trades. As one Malay remarked: "Malay boys are trained to stay at the bottom." Obviously, if the colonial peoples are to learn to govern themselves wisely and develop their own leaders, a thoroughgoing revolution in native education is the first step. Without it, they will never be able to take places of equality among the other nations of the modern world.

The traditional barrier of discrimination must next be removed, so that educated natives may obtain positions for which their training qualifies them. Official posts in the administration must be open to natives without any restriction because of race. The expanding school and college system should be staffed with native teachers to the extent that proper standards are maintained. A program of scholarship aid to enable superior students to study abroad would be an excellent feature. As for employment in private enterprise, the laws should be strict in their prohibition of discrimination on the basis of race, for traditional prejudice will probably die hard in the colonies.

One generation of such intensive development of education, combined with removal of racial discrimination, should advance many of the colonial peoples well along the path to ruling and running their own countries. Some colonies, starting from a dead level of backwardness, will require more time; and some, handicapped by restricted finances, may have to proceed more slowly than others.

Any over-all plan for the future of colonies should provide for the federation of small dependencies into larger and stronger units wherever feasible. All the islands of Oceania could well be linked in a federated unit; or, if national rivalries could not be overcome, three unions—American, British, and French—might be established. The entire Malaysian area—including the Philippines, the East Indies, and Malaya—would constitute a logical unit. Where traditional enmities are still bitter—as between Burma, Indo-China, and Thailand—tentatives in the direction of a loose confederation might be tried. British and French Africa offer the possibility of setting up two federations. In short, "Balkanization" of the colonial world should be avoided by combining small and weak territories wherever possible. This need not be done suddenly, but may be allowed to evolve according to flexible plan.

Another problem is that of basic economy. Most colonial areas are either underdeveloped or completely undeveloped industrially. Some colonial governments—the British and Dutch notably—have already begun to make plans for encouraging and aiding industrial production of such articles as textiles and agricultural tools for the local market. Initial processing of raw materials for export—such as petroleum, rubber, and coconuts—offers further possibilities. The rising interest in industrial development of colonial areas is in part an outgrowth of a general concern with elevating the income and standard of living of subject peoples. There is a growing uneasiness about wage and labor differentials between countries, for the nations with a high standard of living are coming to fear the possibility that competition with cheap labor may eventually force a lowering of their own wages and prices. The new idea is that continued and increasing prosperity requires raising the standard of living all over the world. It is an adaptation of Gresham's Law concerning cheap money to the field of wages. Whatever the possibilities may be for the development of light industry, most colonial areas are evidently unfitted for heavy industry, mainly because of lack of iron and coal. India is an outstanding exception, and, especially during the present war, has expanded tremendously in this direction. Elsewhere, the absence of heavy industry is a major handicap in the military defense of colonial areas, since modern armaments cannot be produced locally. The same thing is true of many independent states, however, as noted previously; and this deficiency should not be used as an argument for the need of permanent "protection" of colonies alone.

The anthropologist, viewing the colonial question in the full perspective of human history, sees the four-hundred-year era of conquest and subjugation which is now ending as a passing phase in the cultural evolution of man. It began with a great development of material culture in Europe, which gave the Western nations a tremendous superiority over the other peoples of the world in technological and military organization. For four centuries this advantage has been held, enabling the conquerors to dominate their beaten subjects and keep them in a state of economic, political, and social subordination. During this time the colonial system became institutionalized, evolving a general code of rules and customs, supported by an elaborate philosophy of rationalization based largely upon theories of the fundamental racial and cultural inferiority of the dependent peoples. The practical benefits of the system to the rulers acted as a constant stimulus to its preservation.

Slowly, but with increasing momentum, three counteracting developments have been weakening the institution and preparing the way for its dissolution. In the first place, the practical advantages of colonialism have been declining. The cheapness and tractability of native labor are being threatened by a growing discontent and insistence upon higher wages and better economic opportunities among the subject peoples. Political consciousness is rapidly increasing in the colonial populations, making the task of control and suppression constantly more difficult. The problem of defending colonies against rival powers becomes more and more formidable as hostility on the part of the natives themselves threatens the rear of the occupying forces. In short the balance is swinging to the point where colonial possessions administered under the traditional system are losing their asset value and becoming potential liabilities to the ruling powers.

A second development, also swiftly accelerating, is the diffusion of Western civilization to the colonial areas. Despite the efforts of the governing states to insulate their subjects from outside influence, the wall of cultural isolation has been breached in most dependencies. Not only material aspects of culture, but knowledge of political, economic, and social conditions and trends in the rest of the world, are spreading to the colonies. The natives, comparing their situation with that of free peoples and learning of the democratic ideals of the Western nations, become critical and restive, and determine to get these privileges for themselves. Denial merely increases their discontent and rebelliousness, and stern suppression of native movements sows dragon teeth of spreading revolt. The wildfire of democratic ideas has sprung up all over the colonial world, and extinguishing it is now a hopeless task.

Finally, the institution of colonialism is being weakened by the rising tide of democratic enthusiasm in the Western world, where the ideal of democracy is itself undergoing a change. The new concept of democracy is international, whereas formerly each nation was concerned only to preserve liberty within its own borders. The present war has aroused the conviction that enemies of democracy are dangerous wherever they may arise in the world. When this international standard of democracy is applied to colonial areas, their deficiencies stand out conspicuously. The peoples of the Western countries are coming to feel that a world half-slave and half-free is a constant danger to the survival of liberty everywhere. This powerful trend in public opinion among the ruling nations themselves will be a decisive factor in determining the future of colonial policies.

The Problem of Minority Groups
By LOUIS WIRTH

AS THE WAR approaches a climax and the nature of the peace becomes a matter of public discussion the minorities question again moves into the center of world attention. It is becoming clear that unless the problems involved, especially on the continent of Europe, are more adequately solved than they were upon the conclusion of the first World War, the prospects for an enduring peace are slim. The influence which the United States will exert in the solution of these problems abroad is contingent upon the national conscience and policy toward minorities at home, for it is unlikely that our leaders in their participation in making of the peace will be able to advocate a more enlightened course for others than we are able to pursue ourselves.

The minorities question in all parts of the world is coming to be more and more indivisible as internal disturbances in any one country become a threat to the peace of all and as the ideals and ideologies originating in one group are soon shared by others in remote corners of the earth. In this shrunken and interdependent world, social movements of all sorts assume a progressively universal character and recruit their supporters and adversaries among peoples near and far, irrespective of national boundaries. The implications of this trend are of special significance to the United States since, aside from its traditional championship of movements of liberation of oppressed peoples, virtually every minority group in the world has its representatives among our population. Our domestic and our foreign policies are thus closely bound up one with the other.

We may define a minority as a group of people who, because of their physical or cultural characteristics, are singled out from the others in the society in which they live for differential and unequal treatment, and who therefore regard themselves as objects of collective discrimination. The existence of a minority in a society implies the existence of a corresponding dominant group enjoying higher social status and greater privileges. Minority status carries with it the exclusion from full participation in the life of the society. Though not necessarily an alien group the minority is treated and regards itself as a people apart.

To understand the nature and significance of minorities it is necessary to take account of their objective as well as their subjective position. A minority must be distinguishable from the dominant group by physical or cultural marks. In the absence of such identifying characteristics it blends into the rest of the population in the course of time. Minorities objectively occupy a disadvantageous position in society. As contrasted with the dominant group they are debarred from certain opportunities—economic, social and political. These deprivations circumscribe the individual's freedom of choice and self-development. The members of minority groups are held in lower esteem and may even be objects of contempt, hatred, ridicule, and violence. They are generally socially isolated and frequently spatially segregated. Their subordinate position becomes manifest in their unequal access to educational opportunities and in their restricted scope of occupational and professional advancement. They are not as free as other members of society to join the voluntary associations that express their interests. They suffer from more than the ordinary amount of social and economic insecurity. Even as concerns public policy they are frequently singled out for special treatment; their property rights may be restricted; they may not enjoy the equal protection of the laws; they may be deprived of the right of suffrage and may be excluded from public office.

Aside from these objective characteristics by which they are distinguished from the dominant group and in large measure as a result of them, minorities tend to develop a set of attitudes, forms of behavior, and other subjective characteristics which tend further to set them apart. One cannot long discriminate against people without generating in them a sense of isolation and of persecution and without giving them a conception of themselves as more different from others than in fact they are. Whether, as a result of this differential treatment, the minority comes to suffer from a sense of its own inferiority or develops a feeling that it is unjustly treated—which may lead to a rebellious attitude—depends in part upon the length of time that its status has existed and in part upon the total social setting in which the differential treatment operates. Where a caste system has existed over many generations and is sanctioned by religious and other sentiments, the attitude of resignation is likely to be dominant over the spirit of rebellion. But in a secular society where class rather than caste pervades the stratification of people, and where the tradition of minority status is of recent origin, minorities, driven by a sense of frustration and unjustified subordination, are likely to refuse to accept their status and their deprivation without some effort to improve their lot.

When the sentiments and attitude of such a disadvantaged group become articulate, and when the members become conscious of their deprivations and conceive of themselves as persons having rights, and when they clamor for emancipation and equality, a minority becomes a political force to be reckoned with. To the individual members of such a group the most onerous circumstance under which they have to labor is that they are treated as members of a category, irrespective of their individual merits. Hence it is important to recognize that membership in a minority is involuntary; our own behavior is irrelevant. Many of us are identified with political, social, and intellectual groups which do not enjoy the favor of the dominant group in society, but as long as we are free to join and to leave such groups at will we do not by virtue of our membership in them belong to a minority. Since the racial stock from which we are descended is something over which we have perhaps least control and since racial marks are the most visible and permanent marks with which we are afflicted, racial minorities tend to be the most enduring minorities of all.

It should be noted further that a minority is not necessarily an alien group. Indeed, in many parts of the world it is the native peoples who constitute the minority, whereas the invaders, the conquerors, or the newcomers occupy the status of dominant groups. In the United States the indigenous Indians occupy the position of a minority. In Canada the earlier French settlers are a minority in relation to the more recent English migrants. In almost all colonial countries it is the "foreigners" who are dominant and the indigenous populations who are subordinate.

Nor should it be assumed that the concept is a statistical one. Although the size of the group may have some effect upon its status and upon its relationship to the dominant group, minorities are not to be judged in terms of numbers. The people whom we regard as a minority may actually, from a numerical standpoint, be a majority. Thus, there are many parts of the South in the United States where the Negroes are the overwhelming majority of the inhabitants but, nevertheless, are an unmistakable minority in the sense that they are socially, politically, and economically subordinate.

It may even be true that a people may attain the status of a minority even though it does not become the object of disesteem, discrimination, and persecution. If it considers itself the object of such inferior treatment, an oppression psychosis may develop. If a group sets itself apart from others by a distinctive culture and perpetuates itself in this isolated condition long enough, the social distances between itself and others may grow so great as to lead to the accumulation of suspicion and nonintercourse which will make it virtually impossible for members of these groups to carry on a truly collective life. Lack of intimate knowledge of and contact with others may in the course of time generate an incapacity for mutual understanding and appreciation which allows mental stereotypes to arise which the individual cannot escape. What matters, then, about minorities is not merely their objective position but the corresponding patterns of behavior they develop and the pictures they carry around in their heads of themselves and of others. While minorities more often than not stand in a relationship of conflict with the dominant group, it is their nonparticipation in the life of the larger society, or in certain aspects thereof, that more particularly marks them as a minority people and perpetuates their status as such.

It is easy enough to catalog the minority peoples in various parts of the world in accordance with a set of criteria such as race, national origin, language, religion, or other distinctive cultural traits. Thus it is possible to define the areas of the world where one or another racial, ethnic, linguistic, or religious group occupies a subordinate status with reference to some other group. In different parts of the world different groups are consigned to minority status. A given racial, ethnic, linguistic, or religious group may be dominant in one area and be the minority in another. Similar variations are found throughout history. Groups which in one epoch were dominant may in another be reduced to subordinate status. Because of the colonizing enterprises of some of the nation-states of Western Europe a large part of the rest of the world has been subordinated to their political rule, their economic control, and the technology and culture which the European settlers managed to superimpose upon the peoples and areas which they brought under their domain. On a world scale, therefore, there is an extraordinarily close association between the white Western Europeans as colonizers and conquerors and their status as dominant groups. Correspondingly, there is a close association between the nonwhite peoples of the world as the conquered and enslaved peoples and their status as minority groups. There are notable exceptions, however, both in time and in space. In an earlier period of European history the yellow peoples of the East overran vast stretches of the European continent and for a time at least reduced the natives to inferior status. There had been similar, though temporary, invasions of Europe from Africa in the course of which Negroid groups became dominant over the white Europeans. Similarly, the enterprise and military prowess of the Japanese has led to the subjugation of vast stretches of the Orient beyond their island empire which contain many areas and great populations of non-Japanese stock, including European whites. On the whole, however, the expansion of European civilization to the ends of the earth has been so irresistible that from a racial standpoint, virtually the world over, the whites constitute the dominant group and the colored peoples the minorities.

We are less concerned, however, in this analysis, with racial minorities than with ethnic minorities, and hence it will be well to examine in some detail the linguistic, religious, and national minorities within the white group in Europe and in America. The existence of such groups in virtually every European and American country calls attention to the fact that the modern nation-states into which we are accustomed to divide the world and to which we are wont to ascribe a high degree of ethnic homogeneity are far from being as closely knit by intermarriage, in-breeding, social intercourse, and freedom of opportunity for everyone as the stereotypes of national cultures appear to indicate.

In Europe and in America there are today vast differences between the status of different ethnic groups from country to country and from region to region. In pre-war Poland under the Czarist regime the Poles were a distinct ethnic minority. When they gained their independence at the end of the first World War, they lost their minority status but reduced their Jewish fellow Poles to the status of a minority. As immigrants to the United States the Poles again became themselves a minority. During the brief period of Nazi domination the Sudeten Germans of Czechoslovakia reveled in their position of dominance over the Czechs among whom they had only recently been a minority. The European immigrants to the United States from such dominantly Catholic countries as Italy and Poland, for instance, find themselves reduced from a dominant to a minority group in the course of their immigration. It is not the specific characteristics, therefore, whether racial or ethnic, that mark a people as a minority but the relationship of their group to some other group in the society in which they live. The same characteristics may at one time and under one set of circumstances serve as marks of dominant status and at another time and under another set of circumstances symbolize identification with a minority.

It is much more important, therefore, to understand the nature and the genesis of the relationship between dominant group and minority group than it is to know the marks by the possession of which people are identified as members of either. Once we know that almost any distinctive characteristics, whether it be the physical marks of race, or language, religion, and culture, can serve as criteria of membership in a minority we will not be inclined to construct a typology of minorities upon the marks by which they are identified. A fruitful typology must rather be useful in delineating the kinds of relationships between minorities and dominant groups and on the kinds of behavior characteristically associated with these types of relationships.

An adequate typology of minorities must, therefore, take account of the general types of situations in which minorities find themselves and must seek to comprehend the *modus vivendi* that has grown up between the segments of those societies in which minority problems exist. There are a number of axes alongside of which the problems of minorities range themselves. Among these are: (1) the number and size of distinct minorities in the society in question; (2) the degree to which minority status involves friction with the dominant group or exclusion from participation in the common life of the society; (3) the nature of the social arrangement governing the relationship between minority and dominant group; and, (4) the goals toward which the minority and dominant groups are striving in quest of a new and more satisfactory equilibrium. A survey of historical and contemporary minority problems along these lines will probably not cover the whole range of minority problems and to that extent the typology will be partial. At the same time it should be understood that as long as the relations between minority and dominant group are fluid—and wherever they do not rest upon long-accepted and settled premises—any rigid typology will prove unsatisfactory. Conversely where the minority's relationship to the dominant group is definitely structuralized and embedded in the mores, laws, and institutions a typological approach may be highly rewarding.

The number of minorities that a country has appears to have a significant effect upon minority-dominant group relations. Where there is just one minority the attitudes of the dominant group are molded by the unique characteristics of that particular minority. This tends to bisect the country into two contending groups. This happens to be the case in Belgium where the Flemings and Walloons stand in relationship of dominant and minority group, respectively, to each other. The situation is quite different in the United States, where aside from the Negro, the Indian, and the Oriental, who constitute our leading racial minorities, we have many ethnic minorities, consisting of our European immigrant groups and their descendants and such religious minorities as Catholics, Jews, and Mormons in a predominantly Protestant country. A singular and unique minority must absorb all of the anxieties, frustrations, fears, and antipathies of the dominant group. But if dominant group attitudes are directed toward a number of minorities, some of these may escape relatively easily and often at the expense of the others. There is little doubt but that the Negro in the United States has become the principal shock absorber of the antiminority sentiment of the dominant whites. The Negro in this country has been so clearly our leading minority that in comparison with his status the ethnic minorities have occupied a relatively dominant position. Indeed the attitude of the ethnic minorities toward the Negro differs little from the attitude of the long-established white Protestant settlers. Where there are several distinct minorities in a country the dominant group can allow itself the luxury of treating some of them generously and can at the same time entrench itself and secure its own dominance by playing one minority against another.

Similarly, the extent to which a minority differs from the dominant group conditions the relations between the two. Where the groups differ widely in race and culture and are thus easily distinguishable in appearance and behavior, the lines separating them tend to persist without much overt effort. Where the dominant group is the bearer of an advanced civilization and the subordinate group is without modern technology and is characterized by a folk culture, as is the case in colonial situations, the dominant group can maintain its superior position simply by manipulating the military and administrative machinery. Where, however, the respective groups are of the same racial stock but differ only as regards language, religion, or culture, the tension between them becomes more marked, and the attempts at domination of the minority become more evident. The segregation of minority groups may be relatively complete or only partial, and their debarment from rights and privileges may be negligible or severe. Much depends upon their relative numerical strength and the extent to which they are believed to constitute a threat to the existing order.

The nature of the social relationships existing between the dominants and the minorities comes closer than either of these factors to illuminating the problems that arise. When the relationship between the two groups is that of master and slave, of rulers and ruled, of exploiters and exploited, the conflicts that arise are those characteristic of situations of super- and subordination. They become essentially power relationships involving on the part of the dominant group resort to the sanctions of custom, law, and force, whenever persuasion, prestige, and the manipulation of economic controls do not suffice. Where the minority occupies the position of a caste the sanctions of religion and custom may be quite adequate, but in secular societies the perpetuation of a group in minority status requires the manipulation of public opinion and of economic and political power, and, if these fail, the resort to violence.

Thoroughgoing differences and incompatibilities between dominant and minority groups on *all* fronts—economic, political, social, and religious—or consistent and complete separation and exclusion of the minority from participation in the life of the larger society have tended toward more stable relationships between dominant and minority groups than similarity and compatibility on merely *some* points, and the mere segmental sharing of life on a few frontiers of contact. The granting of some political and civil rights to hitherto submerged groups has inevitably led to the claim for the full rights of citizenship and of equality of opportunity in other respects. Slavery as an institution in the Western World was moribund as soon as the religions of the white man invested the Negro with a soul.

While the above criteria might give us a basis for the classification of minorities, they do not come as close to the actual minority problems that plague the modern world as we can come by analyzing the major goals toward which the ideas, the sentiments, and the actions of minority groups are directed. Viewed in this way minorities may conveniently be typed into: (1) pluralistic; (2) assimilationist; (3) secessionist; and (4) militant.

A pluralistic minority is one which seeks toleration for its differences on the part of the dominant group. Implicit in the quest for toleration of one's group differences is the conception that variant cultures can flourish peacefully side by side in the same society. Indeed, cultural pluralism has been held out as one of the necessary preconditions of a rich and dynamic civilization under conditions of freedom. It has been said in jest that "tolerance is the suspicion that the other fellow might be right."

Toleration requires that the dominant group shall feel sufficiently secure in its position to allow dissenters a certain leeway. Those in control must be convinced either that the issues at stake are not too vital, or else they must be so thoroughly imbued with the ideal of freedom that they do not wish to deny to others some of the liberties which they themselves enjoy. If there is a great gulf between their own status and that of the minority group, if there is a wide difference between the two groups in race or origin, the toleration of minorities may go as far as virtually to perpetuate several subsocieties within the larger society.

Even in the "sacred" society of medieval Europe dominated by the Church, there were long periods when heretics were tolerated, although at other times they faced the alternatives of conformity or extermination. The history of the Jews in medieval Europe offers ample evidence of the ability of a minority to survive even under minimum conditions of toleration. It should be noted, however, that at times the margin of safety was very narrow and that their ultimate survival was facilitated by the fact that they formed an alien cultural island within the larger Christian world and performed useful functions such as trade and commerce in which the creed of the dominant group would not allow its own members to engage. The coexistence of the Jews and Christians in the same countries often did not transcend the degree of mutuality characteristic of the symbiotic relations existing between different species of plants and animals occupying the same habitat but which are forced by their differential structure to live off one another. It involved a minimum of consensus.

The range of toleration which a pluralistic minority seeks may at first be quite narrow. As in the case of the Jews in medieval Europe, or the Protestants in dominantly Catholic countries, it may be confined to freedom to practice a dissenting religion. Or, as in the case of the ethnic minorities of Czarist Russia and the Austro-Hungarian empire of the Hapsburgs, it may take the form of the demand for the recognition of a language as the official medium of expression for the minority and the right to have it taught in their schools. While on the one hand the pluralistic minority craves the toleration of one or more of its cultural idiosyncrasies, on the other hand it resents and seeks protection against coerced absorption by the dominant group. Above all it wishes to maintain its cultural identity.

The nationalities of Europe, which in the nineteenth and early twentieth centuries embarked upon a course of achieving national independence, began their careers as pluralistic minorities bent merely upon attaining cultural autonomy. Some of these minorities had enjoyed national independence at an earlier period and merely wished to recover and preserve their cultural heritage. This was the case in Poland, for instance, which sought to recover from Czarist Russia a measure of religious and linguistic autonomy. Czech and Irish nationalism was initiated under similar historic circumstances.

It would be an error, however, to infer that the claims for cultural autonomy are generally pursued independently of other interests. Coupled with the demand, and often precedent to it there proceeds the struggle for economic and political equality or at least equalization of opportunity. Although the pluralistic minority does not wish to merge its total life with the larger society, it does demand for its members a greater measure of economic and political freedom if not outright civic equality. Ever since the revolutionary epoch of the late eighteenth century the economic and political enfranchisement of minorities has been regarded not merely as inherent in the "rights of man" but as the necessary instrument in the struggle for cultural emancipation. Freedom of choice in occupations, rights of landownership, entry into the civil service, access to the universities and the professions, freedom of speech, assembly, and publication, access to the ballot with a view to representation of minority voices in parliament and government—these and other full privileges of citizenship are the foundation upon which cultural freedom rests and the instruments through which it must be achieved and secured.

Throughout the period of awakening of dominant ethnic minorities in Europe in the nineteenth century and subsequently in all parts of the world the first stages of minority movements have been characterized by cultural renaissances. The primary emphasis in this stage of development has been upon accentuating the religious, linguistic, and cultural heritage of the group and driving to obtain recognition and toleration for these differences. This movement goes hand in hand with the clamor for economic and political equality. In the course of such movements what at first are marks of inferiority—a homely folk tongue, an alien religion, an obscure lore, and eccentric costume—are transformed into objects of pride and positive group values in which the intellectuals among the minority take an especially avid interest and the promotion of which becomes the road to their leadership and power. The aim of the pluralistic minority is achieved when it has succeeded in wresting from the dominant group the fullest measure of equality in all things economic and political and the right to be left alone in all things cultural. The atmosphere of liberalism in which pluralistic minorities developed has emerged since the Renaissance and has found expression in the movements for religious toleration at the end of the sixteenth century; it was further elaborated by the constitutional bills of rights wrested from absolute rulers in the course of the English, American and French revolutions, and found formal acceptance on a world scale in the minorities clauses of the treaties at the conclusion of the first World War. If the legal provisions of the minorities clauses have not been fully observed in practice, they have at least furnished a standard by which the relations between minorities and dominant groups may be more universally appraised by enlightened world opinion. If formal resolutions on such matters are valid as signs of the trend of opinion, the Catholic, Jewish and Protestant Declaration on World Peace, of October 7, 1943, may be adduced. On the Rights of Minorities this declaration says:

National governments and international organizations must respect and guarantee the rights of ethnic, religious and cultural minorities to economic livelihood, to equal opportunity for educational and cultural development, and to political equality.

More important than such utterances however is the most advanced practice to be found among the nations of the world. Of these the practice of the Soviet Union with its minority peoples appears to be the outstanding example. There the recognition of pluralistic minorities has become the accepted national policy.

It should be recognized however that pluralistic minorities, like all structures expressive of dynamic social movements, are merely way-stations on the road to further developments. They move on inexorably to other stages where correspondingly new types of social structures emerge. Unlike the pluralistic minority, which is content with toleration and the upper limit of whose aspiration is cultural autonomy, the assimilationist minority craves the fullest opportunity for participation in the life of the larger society with a view to uncoerced incorporation in that society. It seeks to lose itself in the larger whole by opening up to its members the greatest possibilities for their individual self-development. Rather than toleration and autonomy, which is the goal of the pluralistic minority, the assimilationist minority works toward complete acceptance by the dominant group and a merger with the larger society.

Whereas a pluralistic minority, in order to maintain its group integrity, will generally discourage intermarriage and intimate social intercourse with the dominant group, the assimilationist minority puts no such obstacles in the path of its members but looks upon the crossing of stocks as well as the blending of cultures as wholesome end products. Since assimilation is a two-way process, however, in which there is give and take, the mergence of an assimilationist minority rests upon a willingness of the dominant group to absorb and of the minority group to be absorbed. The ethnic differences that exist between the minority and the dominant group are not necessarily an obstacle to assimilation as long as the cultural traits of each group are not regarded as incompatible with those of the other and as long as their blending is desired by both. The "melting pot" philosophy in the United States which applied to the ethnic minorities but excluded the racial minorities, notably the Negro, in so far as it was actually followed, tended to develop both among immigrants and natives an atmosphere conducive to the emergence of a crescive American culture to which both the dominant and minority groups contributed their share. This new culture, which is still in the process of formation, comprises cultural elements derived from all the ethnic groups constituting the American people, but integrates them into a new blend.

The success with which such an experiment proceeds depends in part upon the relative numbers involved and the period of time over which the process extends. Although since the beginning of the nineteenth century the United States absorbed some 38 million immigrants from abroad, the influx was relatively gradual and the vast spaces and resources of the continent facilitated the settlement and absorption of the newcomers. America was a relatively young country, dominated by the spirit of the frontier and by a set of laws and social ideals strongly influenced by the humanistic, liberalistic doctrines of religious toleration and the rights of man. This, together with the great need for labor to exploit the vast resources of the continent, contributed to keeping American culture fluid and its people hospitable to the newcomers and the heritages they brought with them. No one group in the United States had so much power and pride of ancestry as to be able to assert itself as superior to all others.

Nevertheless as the immigrants came in great waves, and as the wide margin of economic opportunity shrank periodically, outbursts of intolerant and sometimes violent nativism and antialien feeling became manifest here too. As newer immigrant groups followed older waves the latest comers increasingly became the objects of prejudice and discrimination on the part of natives and older immigrants alike. Moreover, as the various ethnic groups concentrated in specific areas and in large urban colonies and thus conspicuously unfolded their old world cultural heritages, their life became virtually autonomous and hence, by isolating themselves, their contact with the broad stream of American culture was retarded. In addition, their very success in competing with native and older settlers in occupations, professions, and business provoked antipathies which found expression in intolerance movements and in the imposition of official and unofficial restrictions and handicaps.

Although the ethnic minorities in the United States suffer mainly from private prejudices rather than restrictive public policies, their path of assimilation is not without its serious obstacles. The distinctive cultures of the various ethnic groups are not merely assemblages of separable traits but historically welded wholes. Each immigrant group not only has its own language or dialect which serves as a barrier to intergroup communication and to the sharing of common ideas and ideals, but also its own religious, social, and even political institutions which tend to perpetuate group solidarity and to inhibit social intercourse with members of the "out" group. Moreover, each ethnic group in the United States, especially in the early period after its arrival, tends to occupy a characteristic niche in the economy which generates certain definite similarities among its members in occupation, standard of living, place of residence, and mode of life. On the basis of such likenesses within the group and differences without, stereotypes are built up and fixed attitudes arise which inhibit contact and develop social distances and prejudices. Overanxiety about being accepted sometimes results in a pattern of conduct among minorities that provokes a defense reaction on the part of the dominant group; these defense reactions may take the form of rebuffs which are likely to accentuate minority consciousness and thus retard assimilation.

No ethnic group is ever unanimous in all of its attitudes and actions, and minority groups are no exception. They, too, have their internal differentiations, their factions and ideological currents and movements. It should be understood, therefore, that the difference between a pluralistic and an assimilationist minority must be sought in the characteristic orientation and directing social movement of these groups. The Jews furnish an excellent illustration of a minority which especially in modern times has vacillated between these two types. When the "out" group was favorably disposed toward the Jews, assimilation proceeded apace, even in the face of occasional rebuffs and persistent discrimination. When the dominant group made entry of the Jews difficult, when intolerance movements became powerful and widespread, and when persecution came to be the order of the day, the Jews as a minority group generally withdrew into themselves and by virtue of being excluded became clannish. The most conspicuous example of this transformation is to be found in the shift in the attitude of the German Jews who—before the anti-Semitic wave climaxed by the Hitler epic—could have been correctly characterized as an assimilationist minority and whose optimum longing upon the advent of Hitler was for even a modicum of toleration. Among Jews in this country a similar differentiation is contemporaneously found. The older settlers and those who have climbed the economic and social scale seek on the whole full incorporation into the larger society and may truly be regarded as an assimilationist minority; but the later comers and those whose hopes have been frustrated by prejudice, those who through generations of persecution in the Old World retain a more orthodox ritual and a more isolated and self-sufficient community life, generally do not seek full cultural identification with American society at large. To be sure they aspire to full social and economic equality with the rest of the population but they seek to retain a degree of cultural autonomy.

There is little doubt that the world-wide crisis of the Jewish people precipitated by Fascism and its accompanying wave of racism and anti-Semitism has forged a new bond of solidarity among hitherto disparate sections of Jewry and has given impetus to a deep pessimism concerning the prospect of ultimate assimilation. But the eventual resumption of the assimilationist trend among the Jewish minorities in the Western World appears to have favorable prospects once Nazism has been defeated and the cult of racism to which it has given official sanction declines.

The secessionist minority represents a third distinct type. It repudiates assimilation on the one hand, and is not content with mere toleration or cultural autonomy on the other. The principal and ultimate objective of such a minority is to achieve political as well as cultural independence from the dominant group. If such a group has had statehood at an earlier period in its career, the demand for recognition of its national sovereignty may be based upon the cultivation among its members of the romantic sentiments associated—even if only in the imagination—with its former freedom, power, and glory. In such a case the minority's cultural monuments and survivals, its language, lore, literature, and ceremonial institutions, no matter how archaic or reminiscent of the epoch of the group's independence, are revivified and built up into moving symbols of national grandeur.

In this task the intellectuals among the minority group play a crucial role. They can find expression for their talents by recovering, disseminating, and inspiring pride in the group's history and civilization and by pleading its case before world public opinion. Having been rejected by the dominant group for higher positions of leadership, and often having been denied equal opportunity and full participation in the intellectual, social, economic and political life of the larger society, the intellectuals of such minorities tend to be particularly susceptible to a psychic malady bordering on an oppression psychosis. They find their compensation by plunging into the life of the smaller but more hospitable world of their minority.

The Irish, Czech, Polish, Lithuanian, Esthonian, Latvian and Finnish nationalistic movements culminating in the achievement of independent statehood at the end of the first World War were examples of secessionist minority groups. The case of the Jews may also be used to illustrate this type of minority. Zionism in its political, as distinguished from its cultural variety, has acquired considerable support as a result of the resurgence of organized anti-Semitic movements. The forced wholesale migration out of the countries practicing violent persecution and extermination has changed the conception of Palestine from a haven of refuge in which Jews are tolerated to a homeland to which Jews lay official claim.

The protest against the dominant group, however, does not always take the form of separatism and secessionism. It may, under certain circumstances express itself in movements to get out from under the yoke of a dominant group in order to join a group with whom there exists a closer historical and cultural affinity. This is particularly true of minorities located near national frontiers. Wars, and the accompanying repeated redefinitions of international boundaries rarely fail to do violence to the traditions and wishes of some of the populations of border territories. It is generally true that these marginal ethnic groups exhibit more fervid nationalistic feelings than those who have not been buffeted about by treaty-makers.

Secessionist minorities occupying border positions, moreover, generally can count upon the country with which they seek reunion for stimulation of minority consciousness. When France lost Alsace and Lorraine at the end of the Franco-Prussian war in 1871, the French culture of these "lost provinces" became the object of special interest on the part of Frenchmen in and out of these territories. And when these same provinces were lost to Germany at the end of the first World War, a similar propaganda wave on the German side was set in motion. When the Nazis came to power and embarked upon their imperialistic adventures they made the "reunion with the Fatherland" of such territories as the Saar, Alsace, Lorraine, Eupen-et-Malmédy; Sudetenland and the Danzig Corridor an object of frenzied agitation. By every means at their command they revived the flagging or dormant secessionist spirit among these ethnic groups. They created incidents wherever the slightest pretext existed to provoke violent outbreaks so as to elicit from the neighboring governments countermeasures that could be exploited for the purpose of creating a world opinion that the German minorities in these territories were suffering from extreme persecution and were anxiously waiting to be rescued by the armed might of the Fatherland.

The solidarity of modern states is always subject to the danger of the undermining influence of secessionist minorities, but it becomes particularly vulnerable if the minorities are allied with neighboring states which claim them as their own. Out of such situations have arisen many of the tensions which have provoked numerous wars in recent times.

There is a fourth type of minority which may be designated as militant. Its goal reaches far beyond toleration, assimilation, and even cultural and political autonomy. The militant minority has set domination over others as its goal. Far from suffering from feelings of inferiority, it is convinced of its own superiority and inspired by the lust for conquest. While the initial claims of minority movements are generally modest, like all accessions of power, they feed upon their own success and often culminate in delusions of grandeur.

Thus, for instance, the Sudeten Germans, aided and abetted by the Nazi propaganda, diplomatic, and military machine, made claims on the Czecho-Slovak republic which, if granted, would have reduced the Czechs to a minority in their own country. The story, let us hope it is legendary, of the slave who upon his emancipation immediately proceeded to buy himself a slave, suggests a perverse human tendency which applies to minorities as well. No imperialism is as ruthless as that of a relatively small upstart nation. Scarcely had Italy escaped the humiliation of utter defeat in the first World War when she embarked upon the acquisition of *Italia Irredenta* far beyond her own borders across the Adriatic. In recent times, the rise of the relatively obscure Prussian state to a position of dominance in Central Europe is illustrative of the dynamics of a militant minority in quest not merely of a secure basis of national existence but of empire. The none too generous treatment accorded by the newly emancipated Poles between the two World Wars to the Ukrainian, White Russian, Lithuanian, Jewish, and other minorities allotted to the Polish state offers another case of the lack of moderation characteristic of militant minorities once they arrive at a position of power.

The problem of finding a suitable formula for self-government in India would probably have been solved long ago if the Hindu "majority," which considers itself a minority in relation to British imperial rule, could have been satisfied with an arrangement which stopped short of Hindu domination over Moslems. Similarly the problem of Palestine could be brought much nearer a sensible solution if certain elements among Jewish and Arab groups were less militant and did not threaten, in case either were given the opportunity, to reduce the other to the status of a minority.

The justification for singling out the four types of minorities described above for special delineation lies in the fact that each of them exhibits a characteristic set of collective goals among historical and contemporary minority groups and a corresponding set of motives activating the conduct of its members. These four types point to significant differences between actual minority movements. They may also be regarded as marking crucial successive stages in the life cycle of minorities generally.

The initial goal of an emerging minority group, as it becomes aware of its ethnic identity, is to seek toleration for its cultural differences. By virtue of this striving it constitutes a pluralistic minority. If sufficient toleration and autonomy is attained the pluralistic minority advances to the assimilationist stage, characterized by the desire for acceptance by and incorporation into the dominant group. Frustration of this desire for full participation is likely to produce (1) secessionist tendencies which may take the form either of the complete separation from the dominant group and the establishment of sovereign nationhood, or (2) the drive to become incorporated into another state with which there exists close cultural or historical identification. Progress in either of these directions may in turn lead to the goal of domination over others and the resort to militant methods of achieving that objective. If this goal is actually reached the group sheds the distinctive characteristics of a minority.

It should be emphasized, of course, that this typology of minorities is a theoretical construct, rather than a description of actually existing groups. We should not expect to find any one of these types to occur in pure form either in history or in the present. All minorities contain within themselves tendencies and movements in which we can discern the characteristic features of one or more of these types. Using such a typology as a tool we are in a better position to analyze the empirical problems of minority situations and to evaluate the proposed programs for their solution.

The basic fact accounting for the emergence of minorities is the lack of congruence between political and ethnic groups. Political boundaries are definite and almost always arbitrary. Cultural and ethnic areas are more difficult to delineate. Political areas can be gerrymandered, whereas cultural areas are the product of growth. Virtually every contest of power between nations, whether around the diplomatic conference table or on the battlefield, is followed by some redrawing of boundaries, leaving cultural pockets enveloped islandlike by an alien sea. Even in the absence of territorial revisions, the indeterminate fringes along the frontiers, where marginal groups are interspersed, tend to be chronic danger spots of ethnic friction.

A second factor causing minority groups to arise lies in the fact that culture and people are seldom coterminous. Every living culture must be carried by some people. But culture consists of many elements which may be carried in varying combinations by diverse groups of people. Thus, for instance, a group of people who speak the same language, have the same religion and have an ancient common cultural heritage, are capable of more effective collective action than a similar group with the same religion but different language, or the same language but an otherwise different cultural heritage. It is sufficient for the formation of minorities if merely a few of the ethnic characteristics that give them distinctiveness coincide, especially if these include such elements as language or religion. But if a group should by accident of history and geography find itself united on a great range of cultural characteristics and fairly densely concentrated in a compact area so that the contrast between its status and that of its neighbors stands out sharply, the emergence of that group as a minority is almost inevitable.

The genesis of minorities must therefore be sought in the fact that territory, political authority, people, and culture only rarely coincide. Since the disintegration of tribal society the human stocks occupying virtually every area of the world have become progressively diversified. Through the rise of the modern state the parochial principalities of earlier ages have disintegrated and heterogeneous groupings of people and diverse areas have been consolidated into vast political domains. Through conquest and migration formerly compact groups have become dispersed and split up among different political entities. Through modern transportation, communication, commerce and technology the surviving folk cultures are being increasingly drawn into the vortex of world civilization. There still remain, in various parts of the world, some relatively limited islands of homogeneity and stability in a sea of conglomerate and swiftly moving heterogeneity, but on the whole the civilizing process is leveling them. Minority problems are symptomatic of this profound world-wide transition.

In the long perspective of centuries, therefore, one might expect minority problems to solve themselves. But for the time being they are in need of the best solution we can invent if we would live in peace and promote human progress. Anyone who dispassionately surveys the background of the first and the second World War cannot fail to see that minority questions have played a considerable part in their genesis. Unless these questions are more adequately solved in the next peace than they were in the last we shall, by that failure, contribute to an eventual new world conflagration; for in the future even more than in the past these problems will take on cosmic scope, no matter how local their origin. This is not to assert that minority problems are the major causes of international conflict, but merely that in the absence of effective world organization to regulate the play of interdependent economic, social, political, and military forces, these problems will continue to produce frictions and to furnish pretexts that may again lead to war.

In modern times, besides the technological and social changes that have profoundly affected the nature and significance of minority problems, there have been set afoot certain ideological forces which bear even more directly upon them. Of these, nationalism, the democratic ideology as applied to persons and groups, and secularism and science seem the most relevant.

The nineteenth century, which has often been called "the age of nationalism," saw the birth of a series of movements of national awakening, liberation, and consolidation resulting in the formation of modern Italy and Germany. It also saw the rapid development of modern empires and the crystallization of such movements as Pan-Slavism and Pan-Germanism, which became formidable threats to a state system based upon the balance of power. The lesser ethnic groups which were involuntarily enveloped by the nascent nations were frustrated and retarded in realizing their national aspirations. There were thus kindled seething movements of unrest which threatened the stability of the newly established states and the peace of the world. Minorities, especially those of the secessionist and militant variety, are in large part by-products of the ideology of nationalism, whose fundamental tenet it was that every people ought to have its own state but which failed to take full cognizance of the fact that political and ethnic lines do not always neatly coincide.

The forces of democracy and of nationalism were closely allied throughout most of the nineteenth century. The coalescence of these two ideologies became the principal weapon of the nationalities which were aspiring to independence at the peace discussions following the first World War. At Versailles the principle of national self-determination was invoked. It was construed to mean the right of every nation to form an independent state. But the conception of "nation" was far from clear and failed to take account of the many lesser ethnic and cultural groups which were not far enough advanced in the life-cycle of minorities to be considered eligible for nationhood and hence statehood. Versailles heard the articulate voices of the secessionist and militant minorities of the time, but failed to hear the softer whispering and petulant pleading of the pluralistic and assimilationist minorities who were put at the mercy of the former without more protection than the pious enunciation of high principles of toleration and nondiscrimination.

Woodrow Wilson, in insisting upon the right of self-determination before America's entrance into the war, said: "Every people has the right to choose the sovereignty under which they shall live." [1] When he came to interpret this principle under the Fourteen Points, however, he associated the concept of self-determination not with the freely expressed will of the people but with the criteria of nationality. In the drafting of the peace settlement, as E. H. Carr puts it, "it was assumed without more ado that nationality and self-determination meant the same thing and that, if a man had the objective distinguishing marks of a Pole or a Southern Slav, he wanted to be a citizen of a Polish or Southern Slav state." [2] The peace settlements had as one of their principal objectives the solution of the minorities questions and no doubt did assuage the legitimate claims of a number of oppressed peoples; at the same time they raised a number of new minority problems which hitherto had been either nonexistent or dormant.

The problems and the very existence of minorities rest upon the recognition of the rights of peoples, notably the right of self-determination. Ever since the revolutionary era of the late eighteenth century the liberation of oppressed peoples has been a cause which has enlisted the support of liberal thinkers. Though some of its advocates thought of this principle—which was implicit in the democratic ideology—as a step toward cosmopolitanism, its immediate effect was to intensify nationalism. The general principle of the Versailles treaty in effect proclaimed that any group belonging to a minority, whether ethnic, cultural, or religious, was entitled to equal protection and opportunity with others. This principle was easier to proclaim than to put into practice, especially among some of the newly created states comprising former minorities. Having gained their freedom, these militant minorities not infrequently reduced their fellow nationals with differ-

[1] Woodrow Wilson: *Public Papers of Woodrow Wilson*, Vol. II: *The New Democracy* (New York, 1927), p. 187.
[2] Edward Hallett Carr, *Conditions of Peace* (New World, 1943), p. 44.

ent ethnic characteristics to a state of barely tolerated minorities, and sometimes even made them objects of violent persecution.

In retrospect one of the great shortcomings in the application of the democratic principle under the treaty of Versailles was the emphasis upon groups rather than individuals. Unless the right of self-determination is applied not merely to nations or ethnic groups but also to the individual men and women comprising the nation or ethnic group, it can easily degenerate into license to suppress others. If in the coming peace the arrangement for setting up new states and redefining the territories of old ones does not provide a personal bill of rights for all inhabitants and for the protection of the rights of citizenship by an international authority, one of the most tragic lessons of the last peace will have been lost.

Even such an international guarantee of a universal bill of rights will probably prove insufficient to prevent the development of new minorities and the persistence of existing ones. Ethnic, linguistic, and religious differences will continue to divide people, and the prejudices that go with them cannot suddenly be wiped out by fiat. But whereas personal prejudices and antipathies can probably be expected to yield only to the tedious process of education and assimilation, collective programs and policies can be altered considerably in advance of the time when they have unanimous group consent. Law and public policy can go far toward minimizing the adverse effect even of personal prejudices. Moreover, it is for their public policies that we can and must hold states responsible.

The strategy for equalizing the opportunities of minorities has in the past been based upon the doctrine of the rights of man, which presumably applied to majority and minority alike. Only recently, however, has it been recognized that the subordination of minority ethnic groups and racial groups results in great cost to the whole society. From a military point of view it is undesirable because it weakens national loyalties and solidarity. The stunting of minority development reacts unfavorably upon the entire economy. As long as minorities suffer from discrimination and the denial of civil liberties the dominant group also is not free.

Another ideological factor that has appeared upon the modern scene and has left its impact upon the minorities problem is secularism. The secular trend in the modern world, which manifests itself in the spread of rationalism, science, and the general skepticism toward ideas and beliefs inherited from the past, has already made substantial inroads on parochial cults, on the divine right of some to rule, and on superstitions concerning the innate inferiority of racial and ethnic groups. It promises even greater progress in the future. Rigid caste systems, supported by sacred sanctions, are fast disintegrating. The separation of church and state has advanced to a point where a state religion is already regarded in most countries as intolerable. Even a "holy war" is almost inconceivable in modern times. With the spread of the ideal of equality of opportunity for all men there has come in most countries of the West a greater access for the masses of men, irrespective of race, ethnic affiliation, religion, or even economic status, to educational and cultural possibilities. The findings and methods of science may consequently find greater acceptance. The symbol of "the common man," despite the ridicule to which it has been subjected in some quarters seems to be on the way to making its influence felt the world over.

From anthropological studies of the last half century we should have gained a recognition of the inapplicability of the concept "race" as applied to the hybrid stocks comprising the European and American peoples. It is not race but culture—that is, linguistic, religious, economic, and social habits and attitudes, institutions, and values—that mark these peoples off from one another. And if science has demonstrated anything, it has shown conclusively that these traits are subject to human intervention, that they can be changed. The possibility of the ultimate assimilability of ethnic groups is thus beyond doubt.

It is coming to be recognized, moreover, that varying religious beliefs and cultural traits need not be a threat to national solidarity and are not necessarily disruptive of national loyalty. The private life of the individual is considered to an ever greater degree inviolable. What is required of the individual and of minority groups is that there be an adjustment to the social order and not necessarily that there be complete assimilation. Isolation of the minority from the body politic and social, on whatever ground it may be based and by whatever means enforced is increasingly regarded as the road to the perpetuation and accentuation of previously existing differences and as contrary to civilized public policy.

Until recently the United States in her policy toward her ethnic as distinguished from her racial minorities was regarded as the great experimental proving ground where minority problems either did not become acute or were being solved satisfactorily. Millions of our immigrants wanted to become Americans. Consequently we assumed that ours was the pattern after which other peoples would, if they could, model themselves. We had a further favorable fact to commend us in that we had a body of traditions and of fundamental laws expressive of the most liberal thought of mankind. Despite occasional relapses and despite the great contrast between the enlightened treatment we accorded our ethnic minorities and the backward policy we followed in the case of the Negro, the Indian, and the Oriental, it could still be said that the United States was in the forefront of the nations of the world in the treatment of minorities.

In recent years, however, world attention has been shifting to Russia's attempt to deal with her minorities. The Russian experiment is regarded by many as not only at least as enlightened as our own, but as much more relevant to the minority problems of Europe and the backward regions of the world. It is generally agreed among students of the problem that the Soviet nationalities and minorities policy represents one of the most outstanding achievements of the revolution and the period of reconstruction and that it holds great promise for the settlement of minority problems in the coming peace.

Inheriting as it did from the Czarist regime a tradition of deliberate hampering of industrialization, restricting the use of native languages and discouraging and suppressing the free development of the cultural life of its many and highly varied minorities, the Soviet Government under Lenin's leadership and with Stalin as Commissar for Nationalities, proceeded immediately after the Bolshevik revolution to inaugurate a policy which accords with the best scientific knowledge and the most enlightened moral principles. The achievement of the Soviet Union is all the more remarkable when it is considered that besides having to undo the accumulated effects of decades of cruelty, stupidity, and national chauvinism, the new state had to work against aggressive secessionist groups as well as mutual hostility and suspicion among her many minorities and armed external intervention and civil war.

The Declaration of the Rights of Peoples of Russia issued by the new government on November 15, 1917, one week after the Bolshevik revolution, over the signatures of Lenin and Stalin proclaimed the following principles: (1) Equality and sovereignty for the peoples of Russia; (2) The right of the peoples of Russia to self-determination to the point of separation from the state and creation of a new independent government; (3) Abolition of national and religious privileges; (4)

Free development of national minorities and ethnographic groups inhabiting the territory of Russia.³ This declaration became the guiding principle for later constitutional provisions and public policy. The policy followed was not improvised in the course of the revolutionary crisis. It had been well thought out. Writing in 1913 concerning the minorities situation in the Caucasus, Stalin expressed himself as follows:

> The national problem in the Caucasus can be solved *only by drawing the backward nations and peoples into the common stream of a higher culture.* . . . Regional autonomy in the Caucasus is acceptable because it draws the backward nations into the common cultural development; it helps to cast off the shell of isolation peculiar to small nationalities, it impels them forward and facilitates access to the benefits of higher culture; whereas national cultural autonomy acts in a diametrically opposite direction because it shuts up the nations within their old shells, chains them to the lower rungs of cultural development and prevents them from rising to the higher rungs of culture.⁴

> A minority is discontented not because there is no national union, but because it does not enjoy liberty of conscience, liberty of movement, etc. Give it these liberties and it will cease to be discontented. Thus *national equality in all forms (language, schools, etc.) is an essential element* in the solution of the national problem. A state law based on complete democracy in the country is required, prohibiting all national privileges without exception and all kinds of disabilities and restrictions on the rights of national minorities.⁵

After thirteen years experience with this policy, he wrote in 1930:

> The national cultures must be permitted to develop and expand and reveal all their potential qualities, in order to create the conditions necessary for their fusion into a single, common culture with a single, common language.⁶

When it is remembered that in 1941 the Soviet Union had books published in ninety languages to meet the linguistic variations of its peoples, the implications of the above principle becomes obvious.

The provisions in the Soviet Constitution of 1936 might be cited as the final official indication of Russian minority policy. It reads:

Equality of rights of citizens of the U.S.S.R. irrespective of their nationality or race, in all spheres of economic, state, cultural, social and political life is an indefeasible law. Any direct or indirect restriction of the rights, or con-

---

³ Bernhard J. Stern, "Soviet Policy on National Minorities," *American Sociological Review*, IX (1944), 231.
⁴ Joseph Stalin, *Marxism and the National and Colonial Question* (New York, 1934), pp. 49–50. (Quoted from Stern, *op. cit.*, p. 231.)
⁵ *Ibid.*, pp. 58–59. (Quoted from Stern, *op. cit.*, p. 231.)
⁶ *Ibid.*, p. 235.

versely any establishment of direct or indirect privileges for citizens on account of their race or nationality, as well as any advocacy of racial or national exclusiveness or hatred and contempt is punishable by law.[7]

Besides the experience of the United States and the Soviet Union, there are other indications in recent times of minority policies which point to a brighter prospect. The peaceful dissolution of the personal union between Norway and Sweden in 1905 furnished an example of a successful separatist solution, which, however, is not likely to be followed widely. Once the rights of persons as persons are recognized and respected by the state, once security and opportunity for all is guaranteed so that no group has to invent a scapegoat, once people are no longer regarded as objects of exploitation, the foundation will have been laid for a solution of the minorities problem if not for the disappearance of minorities altogether. Meanwhile it will be wise in the forthcoming peace settlements to recognize the importance in the drawing of national boundaries of the distribution of ethnic groups and to be prepared for the transference of people to more congenial states in case ethnic boundaries must be violated. The fairly satisfactory exchange of Turkish, Bulgar, and Greek populations after the Graeco-Turkish war of 1919–23 offers a valuable precedent, and the enlightened policy announced by the Czecho-Slovak Government with reference to the Sudeten Germans promises an equally humane, realistic solution. In the light of these events, the minority question can no longer be considered insoluble.[8]

[7] Stern, *op. cit.*, p. 235.
[8] For a more detailed treatment of the problem in the United States see Louis Wirth, "The Present Position of Minorities in the United States" (University of Pennsylvania Bicentennial Conference on Political Science and Sociology), pp. 137–56.

Applied Anthropology in Colonial Administration By FELIX M. KEESING

A PACT signed between Australia and New Zealand early in 1944—the so-called "Canberra Agreement" of these nations on current and post-war problems—refers to "anthropological investigation" as one of the most important matters requiring collaboration among the powers with colonial interests in the Pacific area. It has become axiomatic in colonial regions that wise and efficient administration must be based upon careful study of local conditions and sympathetic understanding of the local peoples. Hence administrators, and also missionaries and those interested in economic development, have turned increasingly to the sciences for information and guidance.

Just as they have looked to geology, entomology, and the other physical and biological sciences in handling the resources of the territories concerned, and to tropical medicine in meeting health problems, so they have drawn upon anthropology to throw light on the exceedingly difficult problems of human relations especially the adjustment of the so-called "native" or indigenous populations to modern civilization. This is for the obvious reason that such peoples who are the major charge of administrators and others concerned with colonial welfare have also been the main focus for anthropological study. Whether by way of professional workers or otherwise, "applied anthropology"—the use of the viewpoint, knowledge, and techniques of the science as aids in solving practical problems—has been most fully developed and tested along the colonial frontiers of the world.

By no means all anthropologists have been happy about the idea of having their science used in this way. Many have had serious misgivings that their studies might be prostituted to the service of exploitation and "imperialism." More generally, too, they have been loath to risk having their science assume pretensions in the field of "social engineering," as some of their companion human sciences have done with sometimes dubious results, or to have it bandied about by enthusiastic amateurs who may think it a panacea for human ills, colonial and otherwise. In the same way, many administrators and other men of action have had their doubts that academic people could contribute much of real importance to their tasks. Yet the very acuteness of colonial questions, and the peculiar difficulties of dealing with so-called "backward" peoples, are inevitably making the anthropologist's stock in trade an essential adjunct of administrative practice.

Sir Apirana Ngata, Maori scholar, lawyer and parliamentarian, one of the most unique figures to emerge among "native" [1] peoples in modern times, has stated in a significant essay on anthropology and administration that most of the errors and misunderstandings that have marked the contacts of such peoples with Westerners have arisen from "the intolerance, the narrowness, the prejudice and intellectual contempt" evinced by the latter.[2] Unhappily it has not been only exploitation and other callous treatment that have produced disorganization and ill feeling in the course of the colonial story, but also too often the well-intentioned mistakes and misdirected philanthropy of persons of goodwill. The enthusiastic agricultural inspector who tries to force "lazy" natives to work, the doctor who joins forces with the missionary in attacking native "superstition," the teacher who educates the youth away from the "degrading conditions" of their home communities, can be as destructive to the life and morale of these peoples as the old-time "blackbirder" or rum runner.

Administrators, missionaries, and others concerned with colonial tasks would freely confess that much of the maladjustment, perplexity, and frustration that set the problems of today could have been avoided if their predecessors had understood better the peoples and conditions with which they were dealing. Now, complicating much further the skein of relationships, has come the cataclysm of the second World War. Some colonial territories became actual battlegrounds, and the historic continuity of imperial control was snapped by German and especially Japanese conquest. Other areas were mobilized as bases for Allied military operations. Even remote and sleepy corners of empire became galvanized by bullets and billets, and the local peoples have variously been wracked by want, overwhelmed by surfeit, played upon by propaganda, and swept along in a tide of newly disruptive events over which they have had little control. Rehabilitating these communities, and working out their political, economic and social

---

[1] The term "native," though unsatisfactory, is current in the literature of colonial administration and is used here for want of a better term.
[2] Sir A. T. Ngata, "Anthropology and the Government of Native Races in the Pacific," *Australasian Journal of Psychology and Philosophy*, VI, No. 1 (1928), p. 3.

future, is going to need the most expert and wise help available. What can the science of anthropology contribute toward these practical tasks? As a first step in answering this question, a brief glimpse may be taken at how far it has already been used in the colonial field.

Anthropologists in the United States have been drawn more slowly into this type of work than those of countries like Great Britain and the Netherlands, which have more extensive overseas territories. Nevertheless it may fairly be claimed that the pioneer step in this direction was made by the United States Government when in 1879 it established the Bureau of American Ethnology to study the Indian peoples, then in a quasi-colonial status. In the Philippines, too, one of the first moves of American authorities after taking control from Spain was to set up a Philippine Ethnological Survey to study the peoples of the archipelago, as a basis for governing them successfully.

Dutch colonial administrators have made the most comprehensive and systematic use of anthropology in administration. Faced by the great diversity of peoples in the Netherlands Indies, they have made the science an essential subject in their training programs for colonial personnel at Leiden and Utrecht universities. Anthropological research supplementary to administration has been carried forward vigorously in the colonial areas under both government and private auspices. During the main period of pacification in the outer provinces of the Indies, from about 1906 to 1914, expeditions penetrated to remote places collecting information on the peoples with whom the authorities had to deal. Voluminous studies have been made of the local languages and cultures, particularly of the so-called *adat* or Indonesian customary law—the body of local codes and usages which are still accepted by the Dutch as a primary basis for civil law. The classic compilations of *adat* by Professor C. van Vollenhoven deserve special mention here. The great Colonial Institute at Amsterdam, and other study and research centers in both the Netherlands and the colonial territories, sponsored practical as well as academic projects in the anthropological field.

In Great Britain the Colonial Office has for years made anthropology a required subject in its courses for colonial service "cadets" at Oxford and Cambridge. Anthropologists are included on various advisory committees of that Office, and also on committees for the development of colonial studies at various British universities. Applied anthropology with reference to colonial problems is taught at the London School of Economics and Political Science, the London Institute of Education, and several other centers, and the Royal Anthropological Institute has a special committee on the subject. The Anthropological Museum of the University of Aberdeen recently established a "Bureau of Missions and Colonial Planning," having as its special field the potential contribution of the science to mission work. In almost every British colonial territory, government-sponsored museums, scientific institutes, or other bodies exist to carry on both academic and practical research in anthropology and other subjects. In India, for example, anthropological survey work is counted a vital part of administration, as readers of the Indian Census and of Kipling's *Kim* well know.

Attention of British scholars has been centered particularly on Africa, locale of various modern experiments in administration to which anthropologists have contributed. London is the headquarters for an organization known as the International Institute of African Languages and Cultures, developed under both government and private auspices to carry forward anthropological and related studies on that continent. A number of younger anthropologists from various countries were trained under the guidance of the late Professor Malinowski and sent into the African field by this organization, and its journal *Africa* is a main sourcebook for studies in applied anthropology. Other recent moves include the formation of the Rhodes-Livingstone Institute of Central African Studies, financed by both government and private sources, to "bring scientific anthropology to bear" on problems of Rhodesia and the neighboring British jurisdictions. In South Africa, the Institute of Race Relations, various government Commissions, and a number of individual research workers such as Dr. I. Schapera have utilized the anthropological viewpoint in studying conditions on the native reserves, labor migration, and other problems of welfare. Some of the mission bodies working in Africa have given opportunity for picked mission workers to receive training in anthropology.

The South Pacific, too, has been for the last quarter century a vigorous center for experiment in applied anthropology. In 1923, the Pacific Science Congress, meeting in Australia, indicated in one of its general resolutions that

the scientific problem of the Pacific which stands first in order of urgency is the preservation of . . . the native races by the application of the principles of the sciences of preventive medicine and anthropology.

Even before this, the government in the Australian territory of Papua had appointed a "Government Anthropologist," a post which was occupied with special distinction by Mr. F. E. Williams from 1922 until his accidental death in 1943. The late Sir Hubert Murray, long time Lieutenant-Governor of this territory, often claimed that his administration was "built upon scientific principles of anthropology," and few if any territories have had more spectacular success in carrying Stone Age peoples through their first steps in civilization. In 1924 a Government Anthropologist was also appointed in the neighboring Australian mandate of New Guinea, and Mr. E. W. P. Chinnery, who held the post until recently, was also put in charge of all native administration for this territory. Cadets joining the staff of this jurisdiction have been sent back at the end of two years for a period of training in "social and administrative anthropology" at the University of Sydney in Australia, and even senior officers have attended such classes on special leaves or furloughs. This center has also accepted a number of missionaries for such training. The Australian National Research Council has sponsored research in the applied field, and the subject has been extensively discussed in meetings of the Australian and New Zealand Association for the Advancement of Science.

In nearby New Zealand, studies in anthropology along both practical and academic lines have received perhaps their strongest support from the Polynesian Maori people. Years back, Maori leaders, as part of a remarkable renaissance movement that has invigorated their people, drew upon funds from land sales to establish under government supervision a Maori Purposes Board, a Board of Maori Ethnological Research, and a Maori Arts and Crafts Board. Sir Apirana Ngata, the Maori leader quoted earlier, has given the main impetus to this anthropological interest, and has paid the science the compliment of calling any successful administrator among native peoples an "empirical anthropologist." Anthropology has been introduced as a subject in training institutes for teachers in New Zealand's native schools, but no systematic training for administrators going to its tropical island territories has yet been undertaken. In these South Pacific lands, the limits to applied anthropology have been less in enthusiasm than in finance which has kept personnel and study far below the minimum desired.

Comparable developments have taken place within other imperial jurisdictions. French colonial authorities include anthropology as a subject at their main training center for colonial personnel, *l'Ecole Coloniale*, in Paris, and various institutes, museums, university centers, and other organizations both in France and in the colonies have interested themselves in "colonial ethnology." Italian, Belgian, and other European powers possessing overseas territories have also taken some steps in this direction. Brussels has been the headquarters of an international body for the study of colonial problems, *l'Institut Colonial International*, which has taken into account the anthropological viewpoint in its inquiries and discussions. In the twenties, Japan sent anthropological workers into its newly acquired mandated islands in Micronesia to study the local peoples and problems. By no means to be forgotten, too, is the fact that Germany put scholarship to work in the days of its colonial empire before the first World War, and that a constant stream of publications continued to come out of that country right up to the second World War, revealing a vigorous official and private interest in this and other phases of colonial problems. Mention may also be made of the work of anthropologists in the Soviet Union, where the science has aided in the administration and welfare of quasi-colonial groups scattered through the outer zones of that country.

In the American territories, applied anthropology has had a less systematic yet increasing impact. In the Philippines, Professor H. O. Beyer and several other workers have made studies and influenced policies, especially as regards the "Non-Christian Tribes," and have also aided in census taking and interpretation. In American Samoa, an experimental school established by the Barstow Memorial Foundation in collaboration with the local naval authorities to train the sons of chiefs for future leadership was developed and headed in its early stages by an anthropologist, Dr. G. G. Brown. Naval authorities also helped to sponsor a recent study of education in the territory of Guam by Dr. L. Thompson. The Institute of Pacific Relations, a private study and research organization, has initiated a number of studies in applied anthropology in American and other territories. Yale University, the University of Hawaii, and several other American universities have fostered an interest in colonial matters, with anthropology as a contributing study, though no outstanding center has yet developed. The newly formed Society for Applied Anthropology has included colonial administration among its fields of interest. Collateral work by the Office of Indian Affairs and the Extension Division of the Department of Agriculture in developing applied anthropology has won important experience that could be used in the colonial field.

The present war has given tremendous impetus to the application of the anthropological viewpoint. Professional anthropologists have been drawn into direct war work under both government and university auspices, with their main attention focused on the colonial battle fronts. Training programs of the army and navy in military government and administration of occupied areas, in "area and language" studies, and in other fields, have included anthropology among the basic subjects.

One particularly interesting phase of war training has been the work of anthropologists in passing on the knowledge and skills of the native peoples as invaluable aids to survival and comfort in the coral-strewn seas and the islands and jungles of the Pacific war theaters. Since, too, "getting along well" with the local peoples, winning their coöperation and help, is a vital phase of military operations, anthropologists have prepared materials for the use of troops on native life and custom and on practical ways of winning friendship and avoiding trouble. As a result of experience gained with military training programs, a number of American universities are planning more permanent work in relation to overseas countries, including colonial areas, and anthropologists will continue to be called on to make their special contributions.

It needs little emphasis, after what has been said in previous chapters, that the study of human problems and especially of the life and thought of the more "primitive" peoples in the colonial areas represents a highly technical and difficult task, and calls for a trained and objective observer. This is especially so in some of the key matters with which administrators have to deal: for example, indigenous systems of property holding, or kinship usages—which are an important factor in native-style leadership and authority—or taboos, magic, and other elements of native belief which shape fundamentally their actions.

Only anthropological science has specialized in developing a suitable frame of reference and adequate techniques of inquiry to handle such materials. Then, too, such study takes time, measured at least in terms of months, for more than superficial understanding. The investigator must live among the people, learn their language, work and play and gossip with them, take part in their ceremonial and religious life, and in this way gradually win their confidence so as to get at their real thought and feeling.

Ideally speaking, the administrator or other practical worker who has close touch with colonial peoples should have at his fingertips all the relevant technical equipment of the trained anthropologist. Yet even if this should be so, he is necessarily enmeshed in his professional duties, and rarely has time to give to basic research. Furthermore, he is hardly in a position to take the role of a disinterested and objective observer. The local people will always react to him as a representative of government, a religious leader, or whatever else pertains to his status, and be correspondingly guarded in what they say and do. The great advantage enjoyed by an independent anthropological worker is that he does not fit into any of the conventional pigeonholes of colonial society. Today he may dine with the Governor-General and tomorrow with the lowliest native family. It is recognized as his professional job to break whatever social canons exist against "going native." For these reasons it is necessary to bring in the specialist in the science, under government auspices or otherwise, as well as to have the "man of action" sensitized to the anthropological approach.

What, then, can anthropology really give to the practical worker? The most immediate and spectacular contributions, perhaps, occur when anthropologists are called upon to make studies of specific troubles or problems that arise from native custom or from contact between natives and non-natives. Given, so to speak, the role of "troubleshooters," they have to undertake a narrowly focused study, often in minimum time. Anthropologists have been sent in this way into areas where killings have occurred or aggressive cults have sprung up, and the authorities have wanted to minimize guess work and haphazard action. In Papua, the government anthropologist has sometimes accompanied expeditions into unknown areas to help establish the first friendly contacts and introduce government control. The anthropologist is lucky if under such emergency circumstances he has a backlog of basic information about the people being dealt with; often he has to rest his judgments upon a quick survey and fullest use of his anthropological wits.

At the other extreme from such practical tasks, anthropology has in a real sense an "applied" contribution to make in colonial areas in terms of the general perspectives of understanding it gives on "race," "culture," and other fundamentals of human nature and relationships. Dr. E. Beaglehole summarizes this aspect of the anthropological contribution as follows:

The inoculation of administrators and officials with the anthropological point of view contributes immeasurably to a more efficient, tolerant, enlightened, and sympathetic government of the native peoples concerned. Applied anthropology in this sense means little more than that informed and wise understanding which derives from an appreciation of the inherent values to be found in personalities and cultures different from those to which we are accustomed. . . . The educator, the missionary, the administrator, need anthropological sophistication if their relations with native peoples are to be fruitful and friendly; the citizen needs the same informed knowledge if he is to be critically aware of the policies and methods that rule the relation of his state to the native peoples in its charge.[3]

The possibilities of such "anthropological sophistication" will grow as anthropologists carry forward their systematization of the science, and as such materials are made more accessible beyond the narrow range of the specialist.

Between these two extremes of the immediate practical task and the larger informed viewpoint, anthropology has much to contribute. The actual contacts between an administrator and the colonial peoples under his charge can be facilitated by awareness of the field-work methods of the science: for example, how to make proper contacts in a native community, how to assess the value of native evidence, and especially how to get to grips with the "covert" culture of any group. Again, the science can supply basic information of various types that the man of action can use in meeting problems as they arise.

A fundamental tenet of anthropology is that any specific topic or phase of cultural study can only be fully understood when it is set within the total context of life of the people concerned. This would hold for any practical issue just as much as for an orthodox academic problem. A domestic argument brought by a husband or wife before a district officer can only be adequately dealt with after being checked against the whole background of family and community custom, including economic, religious, and other elements that contribute vitally to the local system of social integration. In relation to such background knowledge, even materials that were gathered without any reference to practical needs may become useful. In a broad sense, even highly technical data of physical anthropology, archeology, linguistics and

---

[3] E. Beaglehole, "New Zealand Anthropology Today," *Journal of the Polynesian Society*, XLVI, No. 3, 166.

ethnography may be relevant, as affording greater knowledge and insight, hence fuller control.

Governments have generally recognized the need for building up background information of this scientific character, as indicated by their support of the various study and research organizations at the imperial capitals and in the colonial areas. Government anthropologists, where they have been employed, have spent most of their time on detailed investigation of the antiquities, languages, and cultures of the more significant groups.

In earlier years, the scope of such basic studies was limited almost wholly to the pre-white life of the indigenous peoples, reconstructing as necessary their customs and conditions from the memories of elders and from other available sources while this could still be done. The changes of modern days were disregarded, or noted only to be discounted. In the last two decades, however, interest has burgeoned in study of post-white changes too—what Americans usually call "acculturation," and the British "culture contact"—as part of a larger exploration of culture in its dynamic aspects. This trend was reinforced by the vigorous insistence of the "functional school" of anthropology that cultures should be studied as they exist today, as "functioning realities," with full account taken of modern changes.[4] Research of this kind bears much more direct relation to the practical needs of the administrator.

Only in the remote interior of New Guinea and a few other colonial enclaves are there groups still at the "zero point" of modern acculturation, untouched by the trader, the official, or the missionary. Even in isolated districts where external appearances give the impression that native life has changed little, study quickly reveals that revolutionary modifications have taken place with the coming of these type figures of the frontier. A former head-hunter may now be a taxpayer, government headman in his village, and a church elder, while his sons work for wages at the white man's plantations or mines, and his grandsons go to school. Studies in such communities involve problems not at all familiar to the older anthropological eye: the historic effects of the coming of trade goods; the impact of new theologies; indentured labor; rise of urban communities; and so on. They may also take within

[4] B. Malinowski, "Practical Anthropology," *Africa*, II, No. 1 (1929); A. R. Radcliffe-Brown, "Applied Anthropology," *Report of the Australian and New Zealand Association for the Advancement of Science* (May–June, 1930).

their scope not only the native peoples but also white groups of the frontier, Chinese and other Asiatic immigrants, and that new product, persons of mixed ancestry.[5]

Anthropological workers have been increasingly called upon, under government or private auspices, to study phases of the contemporary scene deliberately chosen because of their practical importance. Here the administrator or other man of action is served directly with background material relating to his work, and the focus is much like that mentioned earlier as "troubleshooting," except that the problem may not be so acute and immediate. An example is provided by a series of investigations and discussions on how administrators can best handle native practices of sorcery—a thorny issue in many areas. In tropical Africa, governments have set anthropologists to work on serious problems arising out of the migration of workers to urban areas. The Australian administration on little Nauru island recently commissioned an anthropologist to study welfare questions brought to the fore by the disorganizing effects of paying large royalties to the native people from the local phosphate workings.

Work of this kind—"applied anthropology" studies in the narrower sense—is undoubtedly going to increase greatly in the future. The fact that such topics are chosen with practical considerations in mind does not mean that the investigator treats them cursorily or sentimentally. Rather, he endeavors to bring to bear the same rigid standards and objective methods of research that he applies to more academic problems. Incidentally, the resulting materials are by no means void of significance for anthropological theory.

Out of studies made from both the more academic and the more applied viewpoints, a body of general principles is being garnered which in the long run is likely to prove the most useful contribution of all that the science can make in the colonial field. These are taking form

[5] Among significant studies are E. and P. Beaglehole, *Pangai, a Village in Tonga* (Wellington, 1940); G. G. Brown and A. M. B. Hutt, *Anthropology in Action* (London, 1935); H. I. Hogbin, *Experiments in Civilization* [Solomons] (London, 1939); M. Hunter, *Reaction to Conquest* [South Africa] (London, 1936); F. Keesing, *Modern Samoa* (1934) and *The South Seas in the Modern World* (New York, 1941); F. and M. Keesing, *Taming Philippine Headhunters* (London, 1934); L. P. Mair, *An African People in the Twentieth Century* (London, 1934); D. N. Majumbar, *An Indian Tribe in Transition* (London, 1934); S. Reed, *The Making of Modern New Guinea* (Philadelphia, 1943); I. Schapera, ed., *Western Civilization and the Natives of South Africa* (London, 1934); I. G. Sutherland, ed., *The Maori People Today* (New York, 1940); L. Thompson, *Fijian Frontier* (New York, 1940); *Guam and Its People* (Shanghai, 1941).

from the slow accumulation of trustworthy insights and predictable regularities that anthropology can discern about man and his culture, and especially about cultural dynamics and cultural control. Here professional anthropologists would feel most modest of all. Many of these ideas have already been embodied in earlier chapters of this work. Reference will be made later to their application in the colonial field. First a preliminary question should be considered; namely, how far it is scientifically valid for the anthropologist to "apply" his findings in a direct sense, and, especially, whether it is legitimate for him to make judgments on policy, or to prepare blueprints for the man of action.

All anthropologists would agree that the prime role of their science, in all the phases just reviewed, is to provide what the late Professor Malinowski called "technical information." The anthropological worker can give specific knowledge about any situation or problem faced by the administrator, missionary, or other practical worker, and also fit it into the larger context of relevant materials. Many would say, however, that this is as far as a scientist should go. It would then be up to the man of action to read its implications, and tie it into policies and programs.

Some enthusiasts for anthropology, and a few professional workers, have gone more or less to the other extreme. The man who investigates the facts, they would say, is in the best position to evaluate policies, to praise or condemn existing practice, and to draw up blueprints for action.

This may in many instances be true. But what has to be clarified here is that if the anthropologist makes judgments beyond the strictly scientific confines of his work, he is committing only himself, not anthropology. At most, in the scientific mood, he might apply general principles and hypotheses so far as they will carry him. In some situations he might venture to predict that, if a certain line of action is tried, such and such is likely to be the result, and if another, then something else. Again, if a definite goal or policy is set, he might try to anticipate what would or would not contribute toward its fulfillment. Here he would speak only of probabilities, and even this might be the acme of scientific foolhardiness because of the exceedingly limited ability of such a human science to predict as yet with any exactness.

Nevertheless the fact remains that evaluations have to be made, and factual knowledge translated into action. It seems justifiable, therefore, that if the anthropologist is asked for advice, or is moved to volunteer his judgments, he should feel free to do so provided he makes it clear how far his comments are personal only. The anthropologist must recognize, however, that policies and plans cannot always be fitted to the scientific facts. In the colonial world there are matters of high imperial policy, problems of administrative organization, limitations of finance, and other considerations that bear in upon lines of action. Furthermore, for many of the problems to which applied anthropology contributes, other technical knowledge enters in which can only be properly handled by collateral experts: medical men, dietitians, agronomists, and so on. If the anthropologist exposes himself to the accusation of being naïve or overopinionative he may undermine confidence in the worth of the legitimate contribution of his science. This of course does not rule out the rich possibilities that may accrue if the person concerned has made himself expert in other scientific fields besides anthropology, or in practical administrative work. But such individuals are as yet all too rare.

A real problem exists here, namely how the gap may be bridged between the technical information supplied by a scientific worker and the actual needs of the practical man when he is faced by a specific problem or decision. Even discounting the fact that anthropological writings are sometimes couched in formidable jargon, and colored by theoretical viewpoints of the schools, they can rarely be couched in directly usable form. Even the most precise study of native land tenure, for example, can hardly anticipate all the local details that will emerge in any one land court dispute or title registration case. Anthropologists can supply an increasing amount of material that is related directly to practical questions, and in doing so can become progressively more sensitive to what is really needed for its best application. Administrators and others interested will in turn need to prepare themselves with training in the anthropological viewpoint and technique so as to make the best use of this material in concrete instances.

Space does not permit any full recital of the situations and problems to which anthropological science can contribute in the colonial field, or of the materials which have been covered to date. A brief glimpse, however, may be ventured, both to make more specific the characteristics of applied anthropology as discussed to this point, and to prepare the way for a summary of general principles and viewpoints to follow.

A first set of problems in which the approach of the science has been proving useful is connected with what might be called "biological welfare." Studies have been made of depopulation, still serious in some colonial areas, and also of population pressure, now looming as a threat in an increasing number of places. This has required detailed investigation of the factors that affect fertility and mortality in the groups concerned, including sex, family, religious and other customs, and the complex changes and pressures of modern days. A beginning has been made, too, with studies of nutritional problems, especially serious today among urban and labor groups which have shifted most fully from the traditional diets and become dependent on store foods. The study of native diet is no easy matter because eating habits as well as foods are usually very different from those of Westerners. Investigations of infant diet, and more widely of pregnancy, birth, weaning, and child care, have also been significant in relation to biological welfare.

Offhand it might seem that health and hygiene in colonial areas would be wholly the concern of medical men. Actually the medical ideas and practices of such peoples, and also their beliefs and customs relating to sickness, accident, death, burial and the hereafter, are bound up with the religious fundamentals of their culture. In this highly conservative realm of myth, ritual, taboo, magic, and sorcery, of basic fears and anxieties, the anthropologist alone can move with certainty. With his guidance, indeed, what seems at first a drag on modern health work may possibly be made useful, as where native methods of treatment may have actual worth, and even exotic rituals serve as psychological aids comparable with those used by Western medicos on their patients. Preventive medicine may call for interference with native death and burial customs, or with cherished household and community social arrangements, that must be understood before changes are pressed. Anthropological and medical workers can obviously team together with the greatest profit.

Another set of problems are those concerned with economic welfare. Anthropologists have shown the strongly conservative elements in native subsistence customs, especially among peoples living in highly specialized environments such as jungle and mountain regions, or coral atolls, where indeed the white man's technology contributes little toward better economic adjustment. They have also studied how selectively the native uses the modern trading store: what he has come to want from outside markets, and what he is willing to produce commercially in return. Only the anthropological approach can document in such societies the subtle concept of "standard of living," the local value systems which govern what is to be counted as "wealth" and provide the incentive to effort. The anthropologist can help the extension agent or his equivalent to appreciate how far and how fast he can go in promoting development schemes; for example, introducing new crops, changing work habits, building up surpluses to give greater economic security, or relieving population pressure through colonization projects.

White settlers migrating to the colonial territories have wanted good accessible land and cheap labor, and numerous troubles and misunderstandings stem from this element in the colonial story. Problems of land tenure continue high in the list of administrative difficulties, not only in relation to sales and leases, but also to registering titles and settling property disputes in the native communities. Where the local peoples were willing to work for wages, or were virtually forced to work to pay taxes, such use of native labor brought a train of problems. Anthropologists have studied to some extent conditions among labor groups, but still more they have reported upon the frequently disorganizing effects on village life of having any large proportion of young men away for months or years. Where the local natives refused to work, Asiatic or other cheap labor was usually brought in, with other complicating results. Labor matters in such colonial areas are obviously among the most delicate and emotionally charged problems which the anthropologist has to face.

The viewpoint of the science has run to earth a number of myths regarding native character and capacity which unfortunately are still widely current in colonial areas. Included are stereotypes of the "lazy" native, the "improvident" native, the "dishonest" native, and the "communal" native. Study of indigenous work methods, consumption habits, property customs, and other aspects of economic and social organization show such ideas to be the product of inadequate or myopic observation. Native peoples work hard, but according to their own rhythms and only when moved by incentives they count worth while. Allied troops on the South Pacific battle fronts are well aware of this. Again, many groups count prestige in terms of ostentatious giving rather than accumulating, and their "wasteful" feasts are likely to be bound up with religious as well as gastronomic satisfactions. A native judged as "dishonest" by Western codes may be doing what his own custom defines as the strait-laced thing. Again, vague terms like "communal" hardly do justice to the meticulous definitions of individual property rights, even where more than one person or possibly a large group may have interests and equities in the same object.

Wise administrators have been able to enlist native economic philosophies and methods to the service of their enterprises. This is notably so with coöperative usages which are emphasized among many colonial peoples, as where group effort has been invoked on construction work, or multi-ownership of resources has been modernized into something like a joint stock company. Yet Western-style individualism is also making headway in these societies, bringing at once a new degree of personal initiative and a great deal of disorganization. Here again, anthropological studies can help the administrator in the delicate task of balancing one against the other. In recent years colonial economies have been in an uncertain and vulnerable position because of glutted world markets and strictures of economic nationalism, and several economists have suggested on the basis of anthropological evidence that the traditional habits of coöperation may be of great importance in helping such peoples to achieve maximum security in the face of a not very promising commercial future.

In the political sphere, the first tendency of the imperial powers was to establish a highly centralized government structure, staffed by officials from the governing country. Away from the few main centers, however, government representatives found it politic and necessary to work through native authorities, and to take account of local codes and institutions of judicial control. Anthropologists have described for a number of areas the indigenous political and legal systems, discounting in the process popular ideas as to their "simplicity." They have also documented modern political changes, such as the metamorphosis of native leaders into salaried government agents, the dislocation and frequent decadence of traditional forms of authority, and the uncertain results of superimposing alien systems of justice upon local rules and sanctions.

In recent years, new yardsticks of colonial responsibility have been coming on the scene, summed up in terms like "trusteeship," "tutelage," "guardianship," and most recently, "partnership." Policies have swung toward decentralization of control, and toward training colonial peoples in self-government as measured by Western standards. Native and other local personnel have been replacing those coming from the governing country, at least in the lower rungs of the administrative services. So-called "indirect rule" has placed greater authority for local affairs upon native political leaders and institutions, where necessary bolstering or even re-creating the latter. Anthropologists in the British African jurisdictions have paid most attention to the results of such a policy. They have helped administrators to see the strengths of this method of government, as developing self-responsibility, but also its possible weaknesses, as perpetuating obsolete hierarchies in native society, thereby opening the way to irresponsible use of power by leaders and bolstering the imperial system to the detriment of advance in real self-government.

As another phase of these policies, the local peoples, native and otherwise, have usually been given a greater voice in the general government through representation on legislative or advisory bodies. Anthropologists are here enmeshed in another highly explosive series of problems, usually summed up in the term "nationalism." This sometimes takes the form of demands for greater self-government within the familiar imperial framework, but in the larger more developed territories it usually involves highly vocal and more or less organized sentiment for full independence. Colonial units almost without exception are artificial political constructs, and political integration tends to move slowly in the face of deep-rooted local self-sufficiency and "in-group" sentiment. At the same time, educated and sophisticated intelligentsias emerge under the influence of modern civilization—it is of course an old story in human political experience. A great range of difference exists between the warlike uprisings and "prophet" movements of the early colonial frontiers, in which natives tried to throw out the white man or find compensations for their inability to do so, and the noncoöperation movement of a Gandhi or the burning zeal of an Annamese or Javanese nationalist party. But anthropologists have shown that they are broadly of the same psychological and social texture. The post-war period will seemingly be marked by increasing strains between rulers and ruled in the colonial world. Anthropologists may feel that whatever work they are called upon to do on political questions subjects them to the dilemma posed by a sister science—that of an irresistible force meeting an immovable body.

Only passing mention can be made of problems of social welfare. Many native societies are in difficult stages of adjustment, marked by changes in kin and community organization, strains between youth and elders, and between "progressives" and "conservatives," and in the case of urban and laboring groups more or less extensive "detribalization." Leisure and recreational opportunities, too, may be inadequate as a result of the breakdown or suppression of former ceremonial and other activities and the decadence of traditional arts and crafts. On the other side of the picture, many groups have taken to Western sports and amusements, and some have consciously revived old arts and other expression forms. Anthropologists have made administrators and missionaries aware of the great importance of these less imperative aspects of life to morale and happiness, and have also revealed them to be among the most vulnerable points in the armor of conservatism.

Administrators have usually learned the hard way that the religion of such peoples—the fundamental assumptions and interpretations on which they rest their thought and action—must be handled with anthropological gloves. Many colonial groups hold conservatively to their traditional faiths, and even if they have become adherents of Buddhism, Islam, or Christianity, old beliefs still remain as an active residue. Anthropologists have documented to some extent the process of native "conversion" and especially the way in which a new faith such as Christianity becomes indigenized. They have also shown the driving forces back of the frequently exotic nativistic cults or movements which tend to mushroom in such areas: the attempt to reconcile old and new concepts of truth, to "escape from reality," and the search for spiritual certainty under conditions of alien pressure. The informed administrator, besides minimizing conflict and hostility on religious grounds, may at times be able to rally the powerful religious drives and sanctions to the support of his enterprises.

The subject of religion raises the question of how anthropology may be of service to mission work. This, again, is a delicate field, in which by no means all anthropologists would be comfortable. Yet already the viewpoint of the science is being brought to bear to some extent. Not all missionaries have been wholly alarmed at the indigenization of native Christianity. Furthermore, since mission work makes an impact upon the whole context of native life, what anthropologists are revealing in many fields other than those narrowly spiritual or theological is being seen by missionaries as highly relevant. An increasing number of mission workers have realized that an unnecessarily heavy swathe has been cut through native custom in the name of religion, and that some of the familiar mission techniques, such as bringing to bear "shame sanctions" or concentrating upon the young people, are particularly disorganizing and destructive in native life. In Africa, some mission workers influenced by findings of the science have been willing to accept even such native institutions as polygamy and "bride-price" as at least way stations on the road to Christian ethics. Coöperation between anthropologists and missionaries is made easier by the fact that many members of the latter group have been keen students of native cultures and languages, and indeed have contributed greatly to the development of anthropological science itself.

A final set of problems may be summarized under the category of "education," both in the narrower sense of schooling and the larger sense of giving guidance and control to the directions of change. Education is now counted as one of the principal yardsticks of enlightened colonial policy. Yet even where generations of native youth may already have passed through the schoolhouse, educational goals and methods are usually uncertain and surrounded with controversy. Toward what objectives should education of the colonial peoples be directed? What should be taught? What should be the languages of instruction? How much advanced schooling should be given? How far should governments control mission education? Is the school too destructive an influence, or is it the key to future welfare?

Anthropological study has made educators aware of indigenous methods of education by which the traditional heritages are transmitted, and also of the extensive "auto-education" by which such peoples have taught themselves new languages and customs in relation to the needs of modern days. It has also documented to some extent the influence of the Western-style schoolhouse as a new institution winning its way, not always smoothly and effectively as yet, into native community life. Language problems, including the rise and spread of common languages such as pidgins, and also the potent influence of higher education, have been studied in some areas. In these and other ways, the science can aid the educator to fit his program realistically to local conditions and needs, and to set adequate goals through which the educational process can be made purposeful and coherent.

Out of such topical studies, and from the larger viewpoints of their science, anthropologists have been slowly accumulating wider insights and principles that can be of use to the administrator. Scattered through the literature of applied anthropology, these bear a provisional stamp of scientific validity, and at least point the way toward greater control in matters of administration and welfare. A brief summary may now be given of some of the ideas thus in the process of crystallization.

Anthropologists have sometimes been falsely accused of favoring a "museum" or "zoo" policy by which colonial peoples should be left alone and their indigenous customs deliberately preserved. At times, perhaps, they have become a little sentimental about their primitives and critical of the agents of civilization. Yet all would agree that processes of cultural change cannot be stopped or reversed, and that these peoples for their own self-respect and protection must adjust their lives progressively to modern world conditions.

What anthropologists have really emphasized is the principle or viewpoint that the existing culture of a people must be made the constant point of reference if administrative and welfare work is to be intelligently planned and effective. Obvious as this seems to be, it is too often forgotten, and the colonial planner thinks rather in terms of his own cultural standards, or some distant goal of future improvement, or some over-all policy which will apply to every group in a colonial area regardless of local differences. To the anthropological eye, the administrator, missionary, or other man of action is too often like a bull in a China shop, crashing hither and yon through the delicate materials of native life and thought. Certainly if the ideal of colonial administration is to be what Dr. L. Mair, lecturer in this subject at the London School of Economics, has called "scientifically controlled adaptation," every projected activity must be measured against the actual life and needs of the people concerned.

The practical worker who follows this principle will be in a better position to give due weight to native cultural institutions and values, products of a rich cumulative experience and experiment in the local setting. He will be able to give them "selective support" in terms of informed judgments as to their strengths and weaknesses. He may also appreciate better what can be of use to the people out of the larger heritage of human experience. He is not likely, as is too often done, to bring school texts on icebergs to children in tropical jungles, or expect coöperative groups to be enthusiastic about building up individual bank accounts. He may also anticipate more fully what the cultural consequences of any proposed policy may be.

To the administrator who adopts such a realistic focus, anthropologists can contribute a growing "tool chest" of understandings and principles that are being wrought from their studies, especially from the field of cultural dynamics. As shown in earlier papers, they hold that the colonial groups, like other humans, have the capacity to change and adapt in the face of new experience. This, indeed, is already demonstrated in the lives of individuals who have had special opportunities and incentives, as with an educated Filipino, Hawaiian, or African. But they also know that cultural conditioning runs deep into human personality and society, so that people do not discard their traditional ways, or take on new ways, without good cause and real effort. Again, their growing awareness of "cultural integration" gives them insight into the strains and stresses that accompany change.

Aided by such general viewpoints, the administrator is able to move with increasing certainty in his tasks of control and direction. He will have a sense of the points at which conservatism is likely to be most rooted—as in matters pertaining to basic securities such as physical survival, social prestige and spiritual welfare. He may also get leads as to where a given culture should be most malleable, where there is more liberty for the individual to elect and choose—hence, where changes can be promoted with least shock to cultural integrity and morale. Among many other matters he will appreciate why some colonial peoples are adjusting much more readily than others to the impact of "civilization," and will interpret their responses not in short-cut judgments as to relative biological or racial capacities but rather in terms of the degree of local specialization of the cultures concerned, and their compatibility with Western institutions and values. The administrator thus sensitized should be particularly alive to the welfare problems of isolated peoples like the pygmy, the bushman, and the aboriginal, whose systems of life are most remote from those of the man of civilization, and whose efforts to cross the intervening gulf have so far usually led to extinction.

A somewhat more specific principle or viewpoint which has been put forward by a number of anthropologists from their studies of cultural dynamics is that adaptation is best fostered by allowing a people to elect as far as possible what they want to retain of existing custom, and what they want to take from outside. This principle of "cultural self-determination" or "cultural independence" is put forward not just as a moral right but as a demonstrated fact. Studies have shown that groups which have had in large measure such freedom of choice—as colonial groups off the main pathways of alien settlement

—have been able to fuse together old and new elements into reasonably integrated systems of life, and have experienced much less disorganization than those which have been under arbitrary direction and pressure.

Indeed, studies of cultural processes would seem to indicate that only as change is self-motivated is it really effective. Groups and individuals cannot be compelled by law or by force to modify their customary ways of life and thought. Conversely, they cannot be held back when they want to change. At most, attempts to direct behavior in these arbitrary ways will produce overt conformity to the demanded forms of conduct—when someone is checking up. They also generate psychological and social reactions which may be exceedingly difficult for the alien authority to handle—insecurity, resentment and hostility, frustration to the point of hopelessness, revulsion and retreat, and outcroppings of compensatory behavior, aggressive or escapist, such as have already been noted. Colonial domination has been especially provocative of these manifestations, as with "nativistic" movements, religious cults, noncoöperation, boycotts, "revolts," and the gathering forces of nationalism. The violence of such repercussions seems to be in proportion to the impact of compulsion upon the basic securities. The degree of disruption and maladjustment that comes from outside pressure also seems to depend on how far these cultural foundations are disturbed.

What has been said here does not rule out a positive role for the administrator or other worker. But the task of control and direction becomes the less arbitrary and more subtle one of developing incentives, of evoking and guiding the drives which will lead to self-motivated choice by the people concerned. Here wide scope exists for the man of action to open out new opportunities, to advise and persuade, to educate, and to knowingly manipulate a situation so that the native himself will want to adopt a desired policy or program. The colonial task becomes primarily one of encouraging and assisting these peoples to remodel and developing their own ways of living, rather than imposing alien forms upon them.

Anthropologists have suggested many leads here, and the experienced administrator could add more. The practical worker will need, for example, to keep as open as possible the channels of public information and understanding—a conspicuously weak phase of most colonial administrations to date. Even the wisest planning must seem arbitrary to the peoples concerned, so long as they are not informed as to its significance, and do not get the chance to pass fair judgment upon it. Again, the practical worker will learn how to influence a group by way of its accepted leaders, winning them to the support of his projects. He will devolve responsibilities upon the people commensurate with their capacity to bear them, and leave a margin, too, where they can experiment and even make mistakes that will be vital to learning. Since, also, intelligent leadership is an obvious key to future development, he will press forward the training of suitable persons from among the colonial peoples to handle the tasks of administration and welfare —medical practitioners, teachers, extension agents, and others. Native doctors, for example, can indigenize modern health and medical ideas to an extent no white doctor could do.

In emphasizing cultural self-determination, anthropologists recognize that no peoples can be left entirely free to choose for themselves. Emergency matters may leave no time for suasion, or larger considerations may make native wishes unacceptable. The practical worker will then have to use compulsion. Obviously head-hunting and cannibalism, whatever cherished functions they serve in the little local groups which practice them, must be suppressed. A health officer coping with an epidemic may have to enforce a quarantine order. Where such action involves "expurgating" any element of the existing culture, anthropologists stress the importance of using a positive principle of "substitution." In Papua, for example, footballs given out by the authorities now provide very effective substitutes for the old-time spears and bows in settling intergroup rivalries, and a pig may now replace a human body in some fertility rite which the people believe is essential to produce a good harvest. By applying this principle, the breakdown of cultural integration is minimized, and the people concerned are not left culturally impoverished. Correspondingly, when new elements have to be forced upon a people, every effort should be made to reduce their alien character by linking them to valued aspects of existing native life.

One last example of how anthropological principles and viewpoints may bear upon the tasks of the practical worker is the importance of getting proper "timing" for action. The ingrained habit of Westerners is to measure the effectiveness of their work against clock and calendar, and to want to marshal a people from Stone Age to civilization by a five-year plan. But cultural processes often move slowly, especially as the tempo of native action frequently calls for long ceremonious parleying, polite waiting, tossing ideas back and forth for the pleasure and prestige values involved. The administrator must have the patience to await the psychologically favorable moment for action, and in some matters he must think in terms of decades or generations. In the South Pacific, the Maoris have contributed a word to administration, epitomizing this idea: "*taihoa* policy," perhaps best translated "purposeful inactivity." It is of course also possible to err on the side of delay, through red tape or otherwise, with equally wasteful and disorganizing results.

What has been said so far is not intended as a eulogy of anthropological achievements to date in the colonial field, but rather to show how the science can make a valid contribution. In terms of the needs and opportunities, the work already done is merely a small if significant beginning. Basic research has touched only a tiny fraction of the colonial peoples, and current problems have been examined only sporadically. Studies of cultural dynamics and of the possibilities of prediction and control are in their infancy.

A number of writers interested in the applied field have made specific proposals as to future work in colonial areas. Professor A. P. Elkin of the University of Sydney and Mr. W. C. Groves, also of Australia, have discussed the staff arrangements that might be made in a colonial territory to meet the needs for anthropological work under government auspices.[6] They visualize a special unit of the "Department of Native Affairs" or its equivalent within the government structure to handle such responsibilities, with an experienced anthropologist as central officer, and a mobile field staff. They rightly emphasize the point that such personnel would have to be given the freedom of action necessary to achieve an objective approach and to mediate between the native society and the government. Other professional anthropologists, and specialists such as psychologists and educators with collateral training in anthropology, could be drawn in under government or private auspices as needed. Elkin has gone further in proposing that the various mission bodies working in a common area should pool their resources to employ one or more "mission anthropologists" to handle their special problems.

[6] A. P. Elkin, "Anthropology and the Peoples of the South-West Pacific," *Oceania*, XIV, No. 1 (1943), 1–19; W. C. Groves, "Anthropology and Native Administration in New Guinea," *Oceania*, VI, No. 1 (1935), 94–104. See also H. I. Hogbin and C. Wedgwood, "Development and Welfare in the Western Pacific," *Pacific Affairs* (June, 1944).

The obvious stumbling block to such planning is likely to be, as in the past, financial. Any large-scale study will be costly, because of the time element and the great ethnic heterogeneity in most colonial areas. Furthermore, those territories most in need of adequate welfare policies and skilled aid are the least in a position to pay for them, being undeveloped and backward. Apparently the answer must lie in special grants or subsidies from the imperial governments, perhaps augmented in the earlier stages by some of the large private foundations interested in the application of scientific knowledge to welfare. If the means were to be found for expanding and stabilizing such work, suitable anthropologists from the professional ranks and prospective recruits from the graduate schools could be given special training to meet "applied" tasks. They could also supplement their anthropological knowledge with the study of such useful subjects as tropical medicine, tropical agriculture and animal husbandry, and others that will easily come to mind.

An important responsibility for such an anthropological staff would be to train other government personnel, including native helpers, especially through practical demonstration in the field. In addition, instruction in the science would be included as part of the required preparation for colonial service recruits as is already the case under some administrations, and refresher courses and seminars should be available for officials in service. Centers for such training would have to be developed where they do not now exist. Plentiful room is available for experiment in developing more sharply focused teaching materials and methods to meet the needs in applied anthropology as well as in the relevant fundamentals of the science. An effort should also be made to build up technical libraries in the colonial territories so as to make materials more available than they are now to officials and others on the spot.

Solution of colonial problems awaits not only the response of the native peoples to more intelligent policies and enlarging opportunities, but also the further education of the guardian peoples in relation to their responsibilities. The dead weight of myths and inadequate observations referred to earlier, the racial and cultural prejudices, and other dark corners in "civilized" thought must have cast upon them the spotlight of truth. A man from Mars would indeed count it incongruous that nations or persons upholding a white-supremacy or master-race concept should be entrusted with the guardianship and development of dark-skinned peoples, and that the guardians should stigmatize their charges for not achieving precisely what is denied them to achieve. In these phases the colonial problem merges with the larger world problem of building understanding and tolerance.

Some Considerations of Indianist Policy
By MANUEL GAMIO

ALTHOUGH there is nothing to be gained by taking a pessimistic attitude toward the Indian problem of America, it is even less fruitful to regard it with self-deceptive optimism. If those who are familiar with the historical antecedents of the American aboriginal populations and who understand, through long years of contact, the social structure and function of these groups will examine the problem, they will see that now, four centuries after the conquest, various social phenomena have been produced by the periods of colonization and the subsequent independent regimes. The impact of races, ideas, habits, customs, and speech have synthesized the various elements that have been in conflict. In the matter of language, the invaders have triumphed. They have submerged the autochthonous languages and dialects and made their own tongue the official language of the country. But the blood of the conquered has maintained itself, in pure or mixed form, in the physical characteristics. The majority of the inhabitants of those countries which were densely populated in pre-Columbian times remain Indian in physical type, although they may have become Europeanized culturally. The European and aboriginal elements have been so fused, have undergone so much of substitution and elimination, that there is now a wide diversity of new culture elements which are more European, or more aboriginal, depending on the strength of the original trait.

But more important than an ethnological appreciation of these facts is the question of whether or not the Indian, ancient inheritor of the American soil, is well adjusted. How does his condition today compare with that of the white man who came from beyond the seas to conquer him? The answer is a bitter one. The processes of acculturation, although in many cases bringing apparent progress, are almost without exception laden with sadness for the Indian. He remains the lowest in the economic scale; he has the highest death rate; within the framework of the superimposed white culture it is impossible for him to compete on a par with white and mestizo minorities; he has no true nationality; his diet is nutritionally deficient; and he must make his living by hard physical labor. Thus handicapped, it is impossible for the Indian to better his position and achieve his aspirations. A comparison of the condition of the Indian with that of groups of European origin on this continent demonstrates incontrovertibly how inferior and unsatisfactory has been the development of the aboriginal populations.

It is true that during and after the colonial period, some legislation beneficial to the Indian was drafted; and, more recently, the intense Indianist movement has resulted in the formation of the First Inter-American Indianist Congress, held in Pátzcuaro, Mexico, in 1940; and the creation of the Inter-American Indianist Institute and the National Indianist Institute. These have been set up in conjunction with the International Convention,[1] which has brought these groups into contact with other institutions such as the Indian Council Fire of Canada and the Grupo "Amerindia" of Argentine. It is also true that present-day governments are becoming increasingly interested in the Indian problem. The establishment of many important government agencies attests this interest: the Office of Indian Affairs, United States; Departamento de Asunto Indígenas, Bolivia; Departamento de Asuntos Indígenas, Mexico; Procuraduría Gratuita de Indígenas, Peru; and Serviço de Proteção aos Indios, Brazil. However, with few exceptions, the majority of the Indians of the continent live in conditions of material and intellectual inferiority which are a disgrace to humanity. Until the people of America come to a realization of the magnitude and importance of the Indian problem, the thirty or more millions of aboriginal population will continue to live as pariahs, resentful of their condition and constituting a potential threat of revolution. The importance of making the Indians an integrated part of the Americas was recently emphasized when it was necessary for the United States Government to take measures to convince the Indians that the present war in Europe is our war and that they also have a direct part in it.

We do not believe that the present world situation will awaken the people of America to the importance of the Indian problem, nor that that problem can be solved during the present world conflict. However, when victory is won, we shall still be confronted with this problem, the solution of which demands the resources of will and sacrifice and calls for a struggle, not against foreign enemies, but against the misery and neglect to which our autochthonous populations are rele-

[1] National Institutes have been founded in Ecuador, Nicaragua, El Salvador, and the United States, and others are about to be established.

gated. The extraordinarily high agricultural and industrial production of wartime, the rapid progress in the fields of physics, chemistry and medicine, which absorb millions of dollars, must be diverted, when peace comes, to the task of rehabilitating and providing a better life for the hungry and retarded Indians. By improving their condition, we will increase their power of consumption and thereby create new markets. To be sure, the United States and Canada, which have made outstanding contributions to the winning of the war, have very small Indian minorities. Nevertheless, it will be to their advantage to eliminate the possibility of revolution which may spring from the bad conditions which exist among the great Indian masses to the south and which threaten the peace and well-being of post-war America. At the present time we can prepare for the future campaign by explaining and disseminating those aspects of the Indian problem which require most urgent attention. The published materials which have been issued by various governments and institutions and individuals should be resurveyed and made available. The most important subjects for the study and evaluation of this problem are: the laws with relation to the Indians; the conditions of their incorporation into the nationalities of the country in which they live; and the concepts by which they are, or are not, classified as Indians.

When laws are framed with a view to the needs and aspirations of the people who are to be governed by them, the group prospers and develops normally; but if the laws have been conceived by men whose culture and values differ completely from those of the group for whom the laws are designed, such laws must be enforced upon an unwilling population; they do not help the people to satisfy their needs and aspirations and consequently the development of the population is abnormal and at a low level. The latter case is true in almost all the countries of America where the populations include a large proportion of aboriginal peoples.

Diverse considerations, some noble and humanitarian but for the most part directed only toward the best utilization of Indian labor for the benefit of the foreign colonizer, led the Spanish crown to formulate the famous "Laws of the Indies." These were originally devised to provide for the well-being of both Indian and white; but, in practice, they were generally interpreted and exercised in such a way that they worked out to the exclusive benefit of the whites. There were some exceptions. One such generous exception saved the Indian from the bloody claws of the executioners of the Spanish Inquisition.

It is logical to believe that Mexican legislation, formulated soon after the winning of national independence, should have been better adapted to the needs of all elements of the population than were the previous laws; that there should have been more flexibility in the application of the law toward people of non-European antecedents, who had therefore a different background, economically, culturally, psychologically, and linguistically. Unfortunately, since the new legislators retained the old colonial attitudes and had no real understanding of the functioning of the complex social structure in which they lived, there was little improvement in the laws. Perhaps also the ingenuousness of these legislators led them to believe that by omitting any reference to the "Indians" in the laws (this word seldom appears in any of them) the differences and distinctions which separated the indigenous peoples from the whites would automatically disappear. Then the Indians would ascend to, or be integrated into, the level of the white, thereby being assured the prerogatives and benefits which the new legislations promised. But the Indian continued to be as Indian as ever and in some ways to be even more neglected and exploited than he was during his unhappy colonial existence. The laws, derived from the best European and North American sources and embodying part of the old Spanish Colonial legislation, were highly acceptable to the eager white minority, but were illogical and unworkable—and frequently vicious—when applied to the non-European majority.

An example of this sorry state of affairs is the fact that the great reformer, Benito Juárez, the most outstanding liberal president of Mexico and a pure-blooded Indian, in the belief that this measure would raise the economic state of the Indian contributed very significantly toward the abolition of communal property. He achieved this by nationalizing the enormous riches amassed by the clergy; but at the same time he stimulated, albeit involuntarily, the growth of the great private estates. This came about when the lands, which had formerly been held communally by the Indians, were distributed among individual families. This was a measure designed to help the Indian, but since he was unaccustomed to working land in this way, and since he did not know how to manage his property efficiently, it was easy for the great landowners to acquire these individual parcels of land at very low prices and by means which were frequently reprehensible.

CONSIDERATIONS OF INDIANIST POLICY

During the nineteenth century there were few laws in Mexico which were expressly Indianist in intention; and it was well into the twentieth century when openly pro-Indian activities originated and various Indo-Iberian countries began to incorporate into their laws codes which were directly dedicated to the native elements of the population. In some American countries very few, if any, references to the Indians have been made in the laws. In countries like the United States, the aboriginal element is easily recognized and numerically small in proportion to the total population. The Indians live relatively isolated in regions which are more or less determined for them; their cultural development is markedly different from that of the majority of the population. Consequently it is easy to determine, within certain reasonable limits, who is Indian, how many Indians there are, and how best to legislate for their benefit. In a country such as Mexico, where the Indians and mestizos constitute the majority of the population and there is almost no racial prejudice, the contact between Indians, mestizos, and whites is very close. Indians frequently occupy high positions in the government, the professions, the army, and the church. Thus legislators as advanced as those who formulated the last constitution of 1917, as well as the authors of later legislative innovations beneficial to the Indian, have avoided alluding expressly to the Indian as such. It may have appeared to them that such direct mention would imply an unnecessary and even offensive discrimination. The Mexican Agrarian Law, for example, does not specifically mention Indians or mestizos by name; but, as they constitute the great majority of the rural population, the law brought to them its major benefits. It not only restored lands to those who had been dispossessed, but distributed millions of hectares to those who had never owned even the smallest parcel of land up to that time.

On the other hand, Peru, which has a social structure very similar to that of Mexico, was one of the first Indo-Iberian countries in which laws were promulgated for the betterment of the Indian populations. This was accomplished by the great Bolívar, who, for example, in the Supreme Decree of April 8, 1824, ordered:

2. In the foregoing article, lands which are in the possession of the Indians are not included. On the contrary, they belong to the Indians, who can sell or lease them by any means they desire.
3. The lands called community lands will be divided to conform to this order among those Indians that have no lands, who shall remain pro-

prietors of them as is stated in article 2; and the remainder, following article 1, shall be sold.
4. This division will be made with recognition as to the state of each shareholder, assigning always more land to the married than to the single, in such a manner that no Indian shall be without his respective lands.

Complementing the above dispositions, the Supreme Decree of July 4, 1825, prescribed, among other things, the following:

6. Each Indian, of whatever sex or age, will receive a league and a half of land in places that are rich and irrigated.
7. In places lacking irrigation and not fertile, he will receive twice the aforesaid amount of land.

Unfortunately, such redeeming proposals of the immortal Liberator remained, like the Laws of the Indies in Mexico, without effective administration.

The English crown and the American government not only had laws expressly legislated with respect to the Indians, but also made numerous treaties and agreements with them in order to regulate their mode of living within the colonies and, later, in the Republic. However, such legislation did not necessarily bring about a real improvement in the social and personal life of the North American Indian. On the contrary, the bitter situation in which they have lived until very recently is well known. Only within the last fifteen years has the United States been intensively and constructively preoccupied with the well-being of the Indian minorities. In general, the English have had a fairer policy toward the Indians of North America than the United States has had; however, within recent time, American policy has probably surpassed that of the English.

It is highly desirable that both Indianists and legislators consider the complex problems involved in laws destined to affect the Indians and discuss them jointly; but an orderly and comprehensive codification of such laws must be made in order to facilitate their study. An example of such codification is offered by the interesting publication issued by the Office of Indian Affairs, Washington, D.C., under the title *Handbook of Federal Indian Law*. The book is written by Felix S. Cohen and has a preface by Harold L. Ickes, Secretary of the Interior, and an introduction by Nathan R. Margold, attorney for the same department.

As compilation, analysis, and comparison of the Indianist laws, past and present, continues, we are able to demonstrate authoritatively those which have had effective and beneficent administration; those that have been interpreted unilaterally or erroneously; those that are written into law but ignored in practice; those that must be adjusted; and the new ones which must be elaborated before they can be considered as definitive legislation satisfying, in a realistic manner, the necessities and aspirations of the autochthonous population.

In a publication which appeared recently in the United States [2] there are certain conclusions with respect to Indianist problems that appear to us to be in part questionable and in part inadmissible. As we cannot refer to them here in full, we will comment only upon those which affirm that nationalism and Indianism are mutually incompatible and even antagonistic.

In countries such as the United States and Argentine, where the Indian populations have remained relatively isolated and numerically very small in relation to the total population, it is scarcely necessary to discuss the invalidity of this assertion. For even when these small groups attain the fullest liberties and achieve all around progress, they will not have any great effect upon the nationality of these countries; on the contrary, they will merely add color to the life of the country as a result of their peculiar values and interesting culture. But in countries such as Bolivia, Guatemala, Peru, and Mexico, where Indo-mestizo elements compose the major part of the population, the question of nationalism cannot be ignored.

We do not propose to enter upon an academic discussion of the term "nationalism" as it is used by the social sciences. We will instead limit ourselves to a brief but realistic examination of the structure, functioning, and democratic organization which the heterogeneous social groups which form these nations must have in order to enjoy a better existence than they have had up to the present. Between these countries we can observe physical, cultural, economic, psychological, and linguistic differences, as a result of which their material and intellectual necessities and aspirations are divergent and the different groups are frequently antagonistic toward one another. In consequence, justice, education, and health programs cannot be administered by any single, general method. It is necessary instead to develop many different methods for dealing with the diverse groups whose cultural development ranges from the highest to the lowest. In a people that suffer

[2] Frank Tannenbaum, "Agrarianism, Indianism, and Nationalism," *The Hispanic American Historical Review*, XXIII, No. 3 (1943), 394-423.

from such heterogeneity there cannot exist a concept of national unity, whatever definition or criteria are used to define such a nationalism. This does not mean that we advocate that the Indo-Iberian peoples should become totally homogeneous; nor that in order to acquire such a forced nationality they adopt, exclusively, the customs of Western culture, extirpating their old ways of life. Such a goal is absurd and, happily, unattainable in the greater part of the American countries. Neither do we imply that there are nowhere peoples to whom complete social homogeneity is the basis for a sound national unity. When this condition does exist it produces the most efficient social functioning that is possible in human culture. The Scandinavian countries, particularly Sweden, are examples of such national unity and are the most socially efficient nations in the modern world.

Let us consider Mexico, for example. It is one of the most representative of the countries under discussion and the one which, naturally, we know best. It has developed a most intensive and enthusiastic program conducted by the Department of Indian Affairs, the Department of Agriculture, the Director of Rural Schools, the aforementioned Inter-American Indianist Institute, and various other organizations. Furthermore, by visiting the slums of the capital, Mexico City, one can readily apprise oneself of the magnitude of the Indian problem and see that only a small beginning has been made toward the solution of that problem.

In Mexico there are approximately a million persons who can properly be classed as Indians, since they speak only a native language, show little or no physical admixture with the Europeans, and retain cultural patterns which are, in part, analogous to those of their prehispanic ancestors. These people are Mexicans only because they live within the geographical borders of that country. Actually they are more isolated and removed from Mexican nationality and more foreign to it than the true foreigners who can speak Spanish, or any of the other languages which are common among the ruling classes of the country, such as English or French. The numerous small groups that make up this million people speak languages, or dialects, different from each other, so that each group is isolated from and ignorant of his neighbors, both aboriginal and white. They are generally afraid of contacts with whites and avoid them when possible. Their interests are exclusively within the tribal group into which they are integrated. They live entirely within the realm of the mountains, forests, or plains where they were born and where they will die, and they are as remote as if they inhabited some desert island.

There are another million Mexicans who, though racially and culturally Indian, speak some sort of Spanish in addition to their aboriginal tongue. This serves them in their relations with other elements in the population, although not, of course, in relation with the monolinguals just referred to. Actually, the role that this group plays, so far as the matter of unified Mexican nationality is concerned, is not much greater than that of the groups who speak only a native idiom.

Several million inhabitants have forgotten their native languages and speak only Spanish. They continue however as Indian by race, habit, and custom. The difficulties of speech separate the people of this category from the aboriginal monolinguals cited above, but they do have frequent relationships with the bilinguals. Their material and external contacts with the rest of the population are more or less close, but they are not effectively united with them in nationality, for the nature of their psychological, cultural, and historical characteristics is different in one way or another.

Among the elements of the remaining groups—chiefly mestizos and criollos whose culture and ideas are predominantly of Western origin, though adapted through life in America, especially Mexico—there is some concept of national unity. But in spite of this, the influence of native regionalism and localism is still so pronounced, even in this group, that until recently they have persisted in attempts to set up separate local governments in various parts of the country, such as Yucatán and Oaxaca. The marked economic inequality that reigns among these four great social groups is a fundamental cause of the antagonism that divides the country. The wealth and means of production are in the hands of a minority who are in coöperation with the mestizos and criollos. This greatly reduces the possibilities of acquisition and consumption for the other three groups, so that their standard of living is low and their cultural and biological development retarded. Contributing to the complexity of the situation is the rugged nature of the country, which makes communication expensive and difficult. An inquiry into the deep causes of trouble and revolution will show that the social heterogeneity and unbalanced economy are the chief factors behind these revolutionary movements. Such upheavals are generally moderated or suppressed by means which are temporarily effective but are not satisfactory in the long run.

If we transpose these facts of the local or Mexican scene to the continental side of the picture, or at least to those countries which can properly be called Indo-Iberian, we are confronted with curious conclusions: The members of the fourth group—the people fully incorporated into Western culture and who are directly or indirectly running the country—are much the same from the Rio Grande to the extreme south of Chile; they understand each other, and their necessities, aspirations, and ideals are so similar that, were there no national boundaries to consider, they could constitute a great Ibero-American nationality. On the other hand, the Indians of these countries also might constitute a separate nationality since they have had the same background for thousands of years upon the American soil; they are very similar to one another in character and tradition; in cultural and psychological orientation they have followed the same, or similar, evolutionary steps. Because of all the things which they hold in common, they could be united into a continental Indian nationality, in spite of the differences of language and dialect that now exist among them. On the other hand, in each of these various countries a true national unity cannot come into being because the peoples of Western culture live in one world and the three remaining groups of culturally autochthonous peoples dwell in another.

Those who are preoccupied with this most pressing and important of all Mexican problems are striving to reach a solution by means of a comprehensive and resolute nationalist policy. One of the first to take up this cause was President Avila Camacho, who in advising the people has frequently recommended a drawing together and a mutual understanding among the various social groups, in order to make Mexico a great and unified country whose national significance all can comprehend and whose benefits all can enjoy.

There is no intention, we repeat, of attempting to create an absolute social homogeneity. The social distinctiveness and the historical and traditional background of none of the aforesaid four groups need be destroyed; but certain common denominators may be established which will permit these groups to come to an understanding among themselves, to coöperate for the well-being of all, and to live in as democratic a way as possible. This is the type of nationalism which, given the prevailing conditions, we desire for Mexico. It is not too unusual a situation. The Swiss are one example of a nation in which human groups of different and distinct origins have lived together peacefully and happily, although it must be admitted that the social heterogeneity in Switzerland is less accentuated than in Mexico.

Among the common denominators which will operate to promote better understanding among the groups we can cite the following, although not all are new and some have already been established in Mexico or in other countries on the continent: The monolingual autochthonous group should be taught Spanish, but without belittling their native tongues; native languages should be conserved and encouraged among the bilingual groups. All people of every group should be made literate. Basic periodicals should be widely distributed, if necessary free of charge, so that there would be no repetition of those frequent and discouraging situations in which individuals are taught to read but cannot obtain reading matter. Such publications should be adapted to the diverse abilities and culture of the people who have recently been made literate. Knowledge should be widely diffused concerning the geography of the country, its inhabitants, the democratic system of government, and the advantages that are made possible through the coöperation and interdependence among the diverse social groups and individuals who make up the country. This could be done by means of publication and the radio. The latter method could be made effective by providing numerous representative towns with receiving apparatus. Broadcasts from strategically located central stations could then be made in the native language of the particular audience whom it was desired to reach. Simple movements and migrations of people should be facilitated by permitting individuals and families to move from one region to another, with the objective of encouraging them to know, understand, and evaluate one another. At the same time, the means of communication with all of the isolated regions should be improved in order to stimulate trade, which in turn would lead to other types of contact. Measures should be taken to prevent cultural differences and degree of social advancement from becoming a sign of innate superiority or inferiority, and consequently a source of antagonism among groups. All racial discrimination should be avoided—prejudices of this kind are practically nonexistent in Mexico and some other Indo-Iberian countries. As we have said before, laws should be interpreted or modified to satisfy the distinct and peculiar desires and necessities of the diverse groups and individuals, so that they will serve as instruments of harmony in the population. The anachronistic and harmful ideas that are prevalent today, especially among the Indians, with reference to hygiene, diet, sickness, and the utilization of natural forces and resources, should be replaced by modern concepts. By these means we shall not only be able to reorient the ideas of these people, but it is hoped that the universality of the scientific approach will help in drawing them together.

We may assume, however, that this political nationalism will not be successfully achieved unless the economic condition of the Indian is also improved. We may point out a few of the means by which this can be accomplished: The policy of granting lands and of providing irrigation for lands with inadequate rainfall should be continued. Antiquated and inefficient agricultural and industrial techniques should be replaced by modern and efficient methods. Also it should be made possible for the Indian to obtain money, at very low interest, with which to obtain tools, seeds, and other necessary materials for working his land. Starvation wages should be prohibited; taxes should be lowered; and unjustified duties and arbitrary obligations abolished. Adequate systems of coöperatives or collectives should be established in order to improve production both in quantity and quality and at the same time to lower consumer prices.

When a program, such as we have briefly sketched, is put into effect in the Indo-Iberian countries, the groups that make up the population will be linked by ties of common interest and a real nationalist concept will develop. A real constitutional and organic democracy can be formed under these conditions and the government will no longer be expected to produce panaceas to alleviate all the social ills of the country. The last vestiges of separatist tendencies and the fantastic ideas of local sovereignty will be extinguished.

Under such a nationalism, the social groups that constitute the population will conserve the distinctiveness, the personality, and the essential natures that are characteristic of them. Their traditions, ethical values, religious customs, artistic expression, inner social organization, picturesque dress, healthy natural habits, all will leave their mark upon the total population, making a rich and varied culture of indescribable originality.

The reasoning and conclusions set forth above concerning legislation and nationalism lack meaning if the Indians cannot be clearly identified. At first glance the matter may appear oversimple, but, in reality, this is one of the most perplexing problems in the whole Indian question. Is a man to be considered an Indian, even though he is clearly

Indian racially, if he does not speak an aboriginal language and is totally incorporated into Western culture to the point of being able fully to satisfy his aspirations and necessities under European laws and to have true national feelings? Undoubtedly not. Also it would be illogical to regard as white those individuals who are predominantly European from a racial point of view but whose lives are regulated by ideas and cultural characteristics that are Indian. Furthermore, is the Negro who shares the Indian culture to receive the benefits of special legislature designed for the Indian? We believe so. These considerations make the conventional number of thirty million Indians for the American continent much too small an estimate.

Linguistic data, generally applied in the census, obviously cannot lead to correct estimates when they exclude a million people who do not speak a native language but are Indian racially and culturally. How can a satisfactory census be made? A physical or racial basis is not practicable because the techniques of physical anthropology do not yet permit one to distinguish between the Indian of pure blood and the mestizo in whom Indian blood is dominant. Even if this difficulty did not exist, the individual study of millions of persons would require a very long time, be very costly, and necessitate a large staff of scientifically trained census personnel. Aside from this consideration, in those countries which have large Indian populations, there is practically no race prejudice, and such knowledge would have special significance only for biologists and physical anthropologists.

The utilization of cultural data in the census is probably the most practicable way properly to identify individuals and social groups. Should this be the objective of Indianist policy, regardless of race or language? We will set forth briefly, some of the tests and propositions that have been made in this direction.

Twenty-one years ago, when the census of the valley of Teotihuacán was taken,[3] the use of cultural data was introduced for the first time. Without its aid we could not have reached any conclusions in regard to the nature of the social evolution of the valley. Nor would we have been able to improve the abnormal living conditions of the inhabitants.

From that time on, it was clear that linguistic data lacked significance. As only seven individuals out of 8,330 spoke Aztec, it could

[3] Manuel Gamio and collaborators, *The Population of the Valley of Teotihuacan* (Direccion de Talleres Graficos of Mexico, 1922); see "Introduction," p. xxvii, Plate 3.

have been assumed that all except these seven belonged to the white race and were incorporated into a European type of culture. Actually the majority were racially and culturally indigenous. This same census revealed that 5,464 persons were of Indian culture and 2,673 were of Western cultural origin. From a racial point of view, 5,657 were Indian, 2,137 mestizos, and 536 white. This last classification, because of the difficulties encountered in the racial classification of Indians and mestizos, is not claimed to be too exact.

Later, the Director General of Statistics became interested in these new aspects of the problem and incorporated cultural data into the techniques of the census of the Mexican Republic of 1940. It was then observed that while it is feasible to use forms which cover numerous cultural characteristics in a small locality numbering hundreds or thousands of inhabitants, it is not practical to fill out such forms for millions of individuals. In view of this fact, only linguistic data and a reduced number of representative cultural items were included on the forms. These cultural traits were gauged for both European and aboriginal culture types. For instance: Europeans eat white bread, sleep in beds, wear shoes, and dress in European style. Indians eat maize instead of bread, go barefoot or wear huaraches or sandals, and sleep on the floor or on a mat on the floor, or in a hammock.

In order to give a more thorough idea of this procedure, for which we feel the Office of Statistics is much to be praised, the tabulations on page 413 are offered. These tabulations were made by the Inter-American Indianist Institute and the Institute of Social Research of the National University of Mexico on the basis of the data of the 1940 census. They were first compiled in the pueblo of Tepoztlán, Morelos, Mexico, where the Inter-American Indianist Institute made an investigation of Indian personality, working with both adults and children. This study was made with the economic aid of the Viking Fund under the coördination of Dr. Oscar Lewis.

From a consideration of these characteristics, together with the linguistic data, a very acceptable generalization can be arrived at. For example, it is very probable that the individuals who speak an Indian language, wear huaraches or sandals, wear native clothing, eat maize, and sleep on the floor can be conceptualized as a type representative of all the individuals that speak only native tongues in Mexico. There are a few more than a million of these.

Census of Linguistic and Cultural Characteristics of the Pueblo of Tepoztlán, Morelos, Mexico

Characteristics	Individuals		
	M	F	Total
Eat Wheat Bread	701	745	1,446
Sleep on the floor	100	116	216
Sleep on a mat on the floor	278	289	567
Sleep in a hammock	..	..	..
Sleep in a cot or bed	323	340	663
Do Not Eat Wheat Bread	2,325	2,263	4,588
Sleep on the floor	1,025	960	1,985
Sleep on a mat on the floor	1,031	995	2,026
Sleep in a hammock	..	..	..
Sleep in a cot or bed	269	308	577
Speak Indigenous Languages or Dialects	20	9	29
Go barefooted	1	..	1
Wear huaraches and typical Indian dress	8	17	25
Wear huaraches and non-Indian dress	..	2	2
Wear shoes and typical Indian dress	..	..	..
Wear shoes and non-Indian dress	1	..	1
Speak Spanish and One or More Indigenous Languages	1,806	1,798	3,604
Go barefooted	588	1,625	2,213
Wear huaraches or sandals and typical Indian dress	919	19	938
Wear huaraches or sandals and non-Indian dress	245	53	298
Wear shoes and typical Indian dress	4	..	4
Wear shoes and non-Indian dress	50	101	151
Speak Only Spanish or a Foreign Language, or Spanish and a Nonindigenous Language	1,210	1,191	2,401
Go barefooted	742	976	1,718
Wear huaraches or sandals and typical Indian dress	179	3	181
Wear huaraches and non-Indian dress	194	25	219
Wear shoes and non-Indian dress typical	2	..	2
Wear shoes and non-Indian dress	94	187	281

It would undoubtedly be premature to assume that these very few cultural characteristics would be sufficient to classify a person as belonging to the Indian culture, when he no longer speaks an aboriginal language and even possesses many European cultural traits. Neither does it necessarily follow that a person who speaks Spanish and possesses the few European traits selected above is essentially affiliated with the European culture type, for he may have many other characteristics of an indigenous kind, principally those of intellectual disposition.

With the object of concretely valuing the degree of effectiveness with which these data and characteristics would classify individuals as to culture type in a general census, the Institute has attempted to identify all the cultural characteristics of a representative group of inhabitants within Tepoztlán. Later, the conclusions obtained will be compared with those deduced from the above cited information which the same group gave to the census of 1940.

In the article, "Need for a Standard Definition of Indian"[4] the Statistician of the U.S. Office of Indian Affairs, Mr. J. Nixon Hadley, put forth an interesting proposal concerning those individuals in the United States who would be classified as Indians. The person in question must satisfy at least three of the following conditions:

1. Enrollment with an organized tribal group or on a reservation census role. This would imply acceptance by the tribal group.
2. General recognition by members of his local community as an Indian. Such recognition would include certain individuals not enrolled with any tribal group.
3. Ability to speak an Indian language.
4. The following of such typical Indian pursuits as the manufacture of Indian arts and crafts or the use of special Indian techniques of agriculture and hunting. This and the immediately preceding criterion is strong indication of a considerable retention of Indian culture.
5. Ownership of restricted property.
6. Residence on an Indian reservation. The last two criteria would include those individuals for whom obligations have been accepted by the Office of Indian Affairs.

We believe that the interesting proposals of Mr. Hadley are well-founded inasmuch as they refer exclusively to the Indians of the United States, or perhaps to some rare groups in other countries where analogous conditions of social structure and development are found. But so far as the majority of indigenous groups of Latin America are concerned, it is truly exceptional, for instance, to find the tribal organizations or the other special characteristics which are present in the United States. Likewise, there have never been treaties between the Latin American governments and the Indians; and the native peoples do not live, nor have they ever lived, upon reservations, as is the case in

[4] In "Statistics," Journal of the Interamerican Statistical Institute, Mexico, D. F. September, 1943.

the United States. There are no specific restrictions for the Indians in the matter of property. Conditions 3 and 4 are, of course, applicable to Indian groups or individuals anywhere on the continent.

It would be convenient, as Mr. Hadley has indicated, if those persons interested in the problem would contribute ideas and suggestions toward overcoming the difficulties which today impede us in the matter of classification. It is to be hoped that the censuses made on the continent in 1949–50 will be more satisfactory than the preceding ones.

Techniques of Community Study and Analysis as Applied to Modern Civilized Societies   By CARL C. TAYLOR

LIFE in all of its aspects comes to farm people at the places where they live—in rural communities. Here is where they work, earn and consume, where they participate in institutional and agency programs, where they meet the outside world. The products they produce flow to the ends of the earth and the Great Society flows into their communities and lives, over trade channels, newspapers, telephones, and radios. When they go out to meet the outside world they most often function as representatives of their local groups and thus operate as members of their home communities. Government, commerce, institutional activities, even science and urban traits come to the American farmer through pieces of social machinery located near him. Society for the average farmer is his local community.

The rural community is probably the simplest and easiest unit of modern society in which to study society as a whole. It offers opportunities to study population in relation to natural resources, adjustments of people to natural resources and to each other, and their relationships to the current life of society. It offers opportunities to study social adjustments and maladjustments, equilibriums and disequilibriums, conflicts and integrations. It offers opportunities to study basic attitudes and value systems, public opinions and sentiments. It is a living, functioning, social structure that is geographically identifiable and easily susceptible of systematic observations which can be recorded and analyzed. Rural sociologists have for approximately forty years been making these systematic observations and analyses. The history of their accomplishments is part of the story of the development of "techniques of community study and analysis as applied to modern civilized societies."

Why did not studies of rural communities take place for three hundred years after the first rural communities were established in the

United States? Why did they begin at the end of that three hundred years? Why were sociologists' first studies of rural life in the United States community studies? Why haven't sociologists in other parts of the world studied the social aspects of agriculture at all? Answers to these questions furnish a part of the explanation of the whys and whats and even the hows of rural sociology's contributions to the science of man.

Some answers to these questions are that integral, self-contained communities probably do not study themselves because life runs smoothly in them as compared to the course of life in more complex societies. Rural life and rural communities changed a great deal in the long period between the settlement at Jamestown and the publication in 1906 of J. M. Williams's study of *An American Town*, but they changed less than other aspects or segments of American society and were thus, relatively speaking, the stable residue of a greatly changing society. Jamestown in 1940 was a lot more like Jamestown in 1640 than New York in 1940 was like New Amsterdam in 1640, because one had remained rural and the other had become urban. By around 1900, however, agriculture and rural life in the United States had definitely begun to feel the impact of the cumulative change which had been in progress from the beginning of settlement. The agricultural enterprise had become quite thoroughly a part of the price and market economy; the limits of geographic expansion had been reached; and population migration from rural to urban areas had become pronounced. The changes had created disequilibriums and maladjustments in which great masses of people were involved and with which they became concerned. Rural leaders began to talk about "rural problems." Leaders of churches, schools, and agricultural colleges, whose programs were centered in rural areas, turned their attention to the same questions, seeking to find a solution. There were also well-established research agencies which responded to this new concern with attempts to analyze the problems and the situations out of which they arose.

The report of the Theodore Roosevelt Commission on Country Life, published as a United States Senate Document in 1910, did not in its analysis mention rural communities but did discuss rural problems. It diagnosed the weaknesses of rural life in terms of lack of educational institutions and agencies, lack of transportation and communication, lack of capital, inadequate legislation and few or weak farmers' organizations. It said,

The underlying problem is to develop and maintain on our farms a civilization in full harmony with the best American ideals. To build up and retain this civilization means, first of all, that the business of agriculture must be made to yield a reasonable return to those who follow it intelligently; and life on the farm must be made permanently satisfying to intelligent, progressive people. The work before us, therefore, is nothing more or less than the *gradual rebuilding of a new agriculture and new rural life*.[1]

The Commission identified the factors and processes of changes which were disturbing the equilibrium and stability of our one-time fairly simple rural life without identifying, or at least without mentioning, the fact that it was these factors and processes which were causing the disequilibrium.

Western civilization, the American rural community a part of it, has moved so far and so fast toward the reign of the Great Society that neither the public at large nor social scientists have been much concerned with the simple units of social structure. They have in fact rather assumed that the old simple units had been dissipated and dissolved in the evolution of the Great Society. They therefore became primarily concerned with studying and measuring trends—population trends, institutional trends, trends in levels of living, and the like—not seeming to recognize clearly, or at least not being concerned with, the fact that the phenomena that could be observed in trends and could be analyzed by the use of mass statistics were always living, meaningful facts in the lives of persons living in communities; furthermore that a complete analysis of communities could and would use the same facts used for the analyses of trends, and in doing so would reveal facts that were meaningful to both the scientist and participants in local community life.

The techniques for analyzing communities and whole societies were well established by cultural anthropologists before rural sociologists began studying rural communities, but rural sociologists have made little use of them, due probably to two facts. In the first place the cultural anthropologists have very largely confined themselves to the study of primitive, or at least simple, societies and have not thus far proved that all the significant variables of modern society are the same as, or even present in, simple societies. Thus their methods if borrowed *in toto* have not appeared to be adequate for the observation and analysis of even the simplest modern society, the rural community. In the

[1] *Report of the Theodore Roosevelt Commission on Country Life* (New York, 1911), pp. 18–25. (Senate Document No. 705, 60th Cong., 2d Sess.) Italics added.

COMMUNITY STUDY AND ANALYSIS 419

second place rural social research began in an era when competence in statistical, some would say segmental, methods of research seemed to be a prime requisite to initiation into the cult of science. This fact, together with the fact that most rural social research has been done at Agricultural Experiment Stations, has driven rural sociologists to a study of social trends and current rural problems rather than rural communities and rural societies as integral social structures.

No type of social group, above the family, has a longer history in the United States than the rural community. It has changed but still remains a community, with its own identifiable locale and functioning structure. Because it has too often been studied as if it were static it is possible to see clearly the shortcomings of community analyses only by knowing the changes to which rural life has been subjected, and yet relatively little is known about the changing aspects of rural community life. That Jamestown, Plymouth, Salem, and other early colonial settlements were fairly simple, highly self-sufficient rural communities is well known. Such communities, however, early developed trade relations with Europe and later among themselves. They sometimes swarmed, so to speak, and sent some of their members to establish new communities. When the westward movement of population began many of them were disseminated. Each of the types of community which were established in one frontier area after another had a larger national society behind it, a more adequate system of transportation and communication, and a larger body of technical knowledge at its command. The communities were often composed of diverse ethnic elements, subject to new physical environments and engaged in the process of evolving different types of farming than those to which their members were previously accustomed. Before the westward expansion was completed large sections of national life had become industrialized and many newly established rural communities from the beginning of their existence practiced commercialized rather than self-sufficient farming. Furthermore, as the geographic limits of settlement were reached, population began to flow from farms to towns and cities in ever increasing numbers and the three hundred-year history of establishing new isolated rural communities began to draw to a close. American rural communities, simple in their early history, became complex.

American rural life, and consequently American rural communities have never been as stable as many peasant communities in other parts of the world and have never been as "simple" as those in primitive societies. American agriculture was somewhat commercialized from earliest settlement. Tobacco, the earliest American cash crop, was planted in the Virginia Colony in 1610 or 1611. Within two decades tobacco farmers in Virginia and Maryland were highly aware of their economic relations with world markets and in revolt against the "controllers" of the world tobacco market.[2] The steady conversion from self-sufficient farming to commercialized farming, the maladjustments and adjustments of farmers to the price and market regime, the development of market economy and of technologies of transportation and communication have thrust the farmer deeper and deeper into participation in the Great Society. This participation has not stopped with the functions of buying and selling but has come to include many other things previously a part of city life only. The rural community in this stream of change has by necessity and by choice made many new orientations to functions and processes which led far beyond local areas but has never because of this fact lost its locality orientation.

Edwards lists seven significant changes which took place in American agriculture and rural life after the end of the Colonial Period: (1) The passing of the public domain, (2) completion of the westward movement, (3) invention and mechanization, (4) extension of transportation, (5) migration of industries from farms to cities, (6) extension of markets, (7) establishment of agencies for promoting science. Johnstone describes three great types of changes in rural life as commercialization, urbanization, and technological advance.[3]

What has scientific analysis revealed about the change in the structure and functioning of rural communities and about the customs, traditions, attitudes, and value systems of those who lived or now live in rural communities under the impact of these changes? It is assumed, correctly I believe, that contacts with urban people and urban centers have led farm people and rural communities to acquire urban traits and adopt urban standards of social status; to sacrifice folkways and folklore for science; to become bookkeeping and calculating businessmen, and specialists instead of generalists in production; and machine operators instead of gardeners and husbandmen. It is also assumed that more

[2] Meyer Jacobstein. *The Tobacco Industry in the United States* (New York, 1907), p. 12; and L. C. Gray, "The Market Surplus Problem of Colonial Tobacco," *William and Mary Quarterly Historical Magazine*, 2d Ser., VII, No. 4 (1927) and VIII, No. 1 (1928).
[3] E. E. Edwards and P. H. Johnstone, "Farmers in a Changing World," *Yearbook of Agriculture* (1940), pp. 171–276, 111–70.

COMMUNITY STUDY AND ANALYSIS

frequent contacts with those outside the community have lessened contacts between neighbors and weakened local social cohesions; and that old colonial and pioneer rural neighborhoods have passed away and rural communities are passing.

Sociologists have been attempting to study rural life scientifically for more than thirty years. What techniques of analysis have they developed? What have their findings revealed to prove or disprove these assumptions? What needs yet to be done to answer all these questions? Research in or scientific analysis of rural life awaited a consciousness of developing maladjustments on the part of farm people and (or) their leaders. In the absence of that consciousness the only impulse to research in this field was the search for field laboratories in which inductive sociological studies could be made by those seeking to develop a "Science of Society." [4] The first approach to scientific studies of American rural life came from this impulse. It did not come from research men at agricultural colleges. However, such studies had not developed very far when agricultural experiment stations, which were well-established research agencies with a vast knowledge of scientific procedures, entered the field. In a relatively short time they were making the major contributions to rural social research. It was thus the rise of rural social problems, incident to the changing national economy and culture, and the existence of already well-established research institutions in agriculture that accounted for the rise and rapid development of rural sociology in the United States and thus accounts for a great volume of research in communities.

It is interesting, and probably significant, to note that although those dealing with the so-called practical aspects of American agriculture had not focused their attention on the rural community, all the earliest rural social studies were studies of communities. The drift of farm population to towns and cities, and price and market maladjustments had become matters for concern to farmers and farm leaders. President Theodore Roosevelt in his written statement to the Commission on Country Life said, "No growth of cities, no growth of wealth, can make up for the loss in either the number or the character of the farming population. . . . There is too much belief among all our people that the prizes of life lie away from the farm." [5] But the earliest critical social analyses were not of these aspects of rural life. They came at the

[4] See especially F. H. Giddings, *Inductive Sociology* (New York, 1901).
[5] *Report of the Commission on Country Life*, pp. 44-45.

hands of three of Professor Giddings's graduate students, each of whom credited at least a part of his motive to developing a science of society in which Giddings was deeply interested. Williams said, "Let us have studies of strategic communities from all parts of the country which will open up problems for discussion and eventually give us data for a sociology" [6] and Sims said, "Acknowledgments are gratefully made first of all, to Professor Franklin H. Giddings . . . from whose inspiration has come the deep interest in the science of sociology which led to this study." [7]

In his study of *An American Town* Williams described a rural area "divided into twelve school districts, each of which has long been known to the inhabitants of the town by a traditional name . . . used as designating not a civil division, but a distinct self-conscious community" [8] and traced the social dissolution of these neighborhoods and their amalgamation into the larger village community. The town had been settled in 1792, but he says that until 1835, "there was little or no contact with the outside world." [9] Some of the significant concomitants of this first change in social structure and functioning were the emigration of the artisans from the rural districts into the village center, the disappearance of small manufacturing industries from the rural districts, the centering of "cultural activities" in the village center, and social differentiation of the population, chiefly on the basis of "economic inequality." [10] A part of the process of establishing the integrity of the larger center was the role it played as intermediator between the local rural population and the outside world. Williams measured these early outside contacts by news items in the local paper, "journeys made by townsmen" to other localities,[11] and later by the number of newspapers and periodicals subscribed for by local residents and the number who left the town seeking educational opportunities and market contacts.[12] He noted that these changes not only reflected themselves in the social structure of the old locality groups but that the increase in commercialized farming and in consumer goods, secured from outside the area, aroused and satisfied new wants and induced speculative attitudes and habits.[13]

---

[6] J. M. Williams, *An American Town* (New York, 1906), p. 11.
[7] N. L. Sims, *A Hoosier Village* (New York, 1912), p. 14.
[8] Williams, *op. cit.*, p. 21.   [9] *Ibid.*, p. 43.   [10] *Ibid.*, Chap. VII.
[11] *Ibid.*, pp. 97–99.   [12] *Ibid.*, Chaps. XII and XIII.
[13] *Ibid.*, pp. 209–36. In his later expanded works, *Rural Heritage and the Expansion of Rural Life*, Williams greatly expanded his consideration of the cultural-psychological phenomena.

COMMUNITY STUDY AND ANALYSIS 423

Wilson in *Quaker Hill* and Sims in *A Hoosier Village* followed somewhat the same pattern of analysis as Williams. Wilson writes of Quaker Hill (founded in 1689) as "a community of Quakers who desired to live apart, maintain their form of religion, and possess land fertile and rich." [14] They carried on trade among themselves by means of barter; numbered among them were artisan farmers who performed local manufacturing processes. All lived in an isolated though quite self-sufficient community. Excess products—first pork and then butter and cheese—were transported by wagon to towns and villages outside Quaker Hill. When the construction of better roads and finally a railroad, in 1849, "immersed the Quakers in the world economy, the Quaker code was insufficient, retarded rather than assisted survival, and rather forbade than encouraged success." [15] The authority of the Quaker meeting broke down, "the whole character of the neighborhood changed, consumer goods from the outside began to flow in and marketable products to flow out of the local community. Gradually but surely the old community bonds disintegrated and even the leaders in the area came to be others than those who were primarily interested in the Quaker religion or followed the sanctions and taboos of the Quaker meeting."

The Hoosier Village, established by 1836, was relatively self-contained until 1869; it was without shipping facilities, "had its own wagon and blacksmith shops, tanneries, cabinet works, saw and planing mills, a grist mill, a foundry and a water mill." These were small individual enterprises that had arisen to meet a purely local demand. The railroad came in 1869 and a resulting boom transformed the town into "a substantial business center . . . the only market and shipping point for an extensive territory." In 1885 a college was established with the aid of outside capital, and in 1906 another railroad passed through the town. The village had by that time made its transition from an isolated pioneer settlement to the type of trade center of which there are now thousands in rural America. Sims traces the changes in public opinion, moral values, gossip, custom and beliefs and in political, religious, educational and economic activities; he concludes that the forces of change came from without, that "its activities have been energized and vitalized by disturbing agencies not inherent in the group itself." [16]

The techniques employed in these three early studies are best illus-

[14] W. H. Wilson, *Quaker Hill* (privately published, 1907), pp. 200-201.
[15] *Ibid.*, p. 211.   [16] N. L. Sims, *A Hoosier Village*.

trated by Williams because his analyses were the most detailed. He assembled statistical data from every local, state, and federal source available and presented them in 21 tables, 17 charts, and two maps which recorded trends, usually through three periods, 1845, 1875, and 1900, sometimes for all years. By means of these quantitative methods he precisely measured trends in population, institutional life, industrial development, poor relief, education, and all types of social participation. His qualitative data were gathered from testimony of local residents. His interpretations were his own as a trained sociologist. He later continued his observations and greatly expanded his interpretations in two additional volumes which could very well be called the first books ever written on rural social psychology.[17] Of the twenty-five chapters of *Our Rural Heritage*, eleven were on "Attitudes" and of twenty-eight chapters in *Rural Expansion*, seven were specifically on some of these same attitudes under the impact of the farmer's expanding world. A number of others dealt with social adjustments incident to participation in activities covering wider geographic areas than the local community. Very few quantitative data were presented in these two additional volumes and the only precise techniques demonstrated were frequent exact quotations classified as evidence of the correctness of the author's interpretations. Nevertheless, Williams in his three volumes quite thoroughly traversed all areas of observation essential to complete community analysis.

That these three early studies were not followed immediately by others of a similar and improved type was probably due to the fact that social agencies and institutions, especially churches and schools—or more properly stated some church and school leaders—became more quickly aware of the dynamic changes that had occurred or were occurring in American rural life than did academic social scientists. W. H. Wilson became a rural church leader and in 1912 wrote a book entitled *The Evolution of the Country Community, a Study in Religious Sociology*.[18] In his Preface to the book, Professor Giddings said:

The rural community has suffered in nearly every imaginable way from the rapid and rather crude development of our industrial civilization. The emigration of strong, ambitious men to the towns, the substitution of alien labor for the young and sturdy members of the large American families of other days, the declining birth rate and disintegration of a hearty and cheerful

[17] J. M. Williams, *Our Rural Heritage* (New York, 1925) and *The Expansion of Rural Life* (New York, 1926).
[18] Boston, New York, and Chicago, 1912.

COMMUNITY STUDY AND ANALYSIS

neighborhood life, all have worked together to create a problem of the rural neighborhood, the country school and country church unique in its difficulties, sometimes in its discouragements.[19]

Wilson remarked, "In these chapters the center of attention will be the church, regarded as an institution for building and organizing country life." [20] His reform or program motive did not keep him from making a valuable contribution to an analysis of the changing rural community but did lead him to extoll "exceptional communities," which were in fact cultural islands that had to a degree insulated themselves against many of the changes occurring in American rural life at large. His institutional or agency approach to the rural community and consequently to social problems was in a way a point of departure for a considerable number of rural social surveys during the next few years.

Sixteen rural church surveys were made and published between 1910 and 1916 under the auspices of the Board of Home Missions of the Presbyterian Church of the United States of America, of which organization Dr. Wilson was Rural Director. All of these are now out of print but while current they served to give considerable direction to methods of rural social studies. Specialized studies of rural churches were carried out in considerable numbers during the next ten or fifteen years.[21] They reached their high point in magnitude between 1920 and 1924 when Gill analyzed the 6,000 rural churches of Ohio, Morse and Brunner summarized the rural findings of the Inter-Church World Movement, and Fry made a census study of rural churches.[22] No other period, before or since, has been so productive of material on the rural church, not only in the findings of research but in magazine and periodical articles, books and pamphlets.[23] Rural school studies did not equal this record but a considerably larger number of books were writ-

[19] *Ibid.*, p. viii.   [20] *Ibid.*, p. xix.
[21] See especially C. O. Gill and G. Pinchot, *The Country Church* (New York, 1913) and *Six Thousand Country Churches* (New York, 1920); E. de S. Brunner and M. V. Brunner, *A Church and Community Survey of Pend Oreille County, Washington* (New York, 1922); E. de S. Brunner, *Churches of Distinction in Town and Country* (New York, 1923); B. Y. Landis, *Rural Church Life in the Middle West* (New York, 1922). There have been others, some of them more analytical than those mentioned, but they appeared later than the period under consideration here.
[22] Gill and Pinchot, *op. cit.* H. N. Morse and E. de S. Brunner, *The Town and Country Church in the United States* (New York, 1923); and C. L. Fry, *Diagnosing the Rural Church* (New York, 1924).
[23] See especially K. L. Butterfield, *The Country Church and the Rural Problem* (Chicago, 1911); G. A. Bricker, *The Church in Rural America* (Cincinnati, Ohio, 1919); E. L. Earp, *The Rural Church Serving the Community* (New York, 1918); P. M. Camp, *Developing Our Rural Churches* (Dayton, Ohio, 1924); W. H. Wilson, *The Farmers' Church* (New York, 1925).

ten on the rural school and its problems during this period than at any time before or since.[24]

Reform problems as stimuli to diagnosing rural life did not stop with the studies of rural agencies and institutions. Among other recognized areas of maladjustment, the three which received the greatest amount of attention in the early development of rural sociology were farm tenancy, depletion of the farm population, and farmers' local trade relations. The tide of concern about rural life problems ran so high that the American Sociological Society in 1916 dedicated the chief consideration of its annual scientific meeting to the topic "The Sociology of Rural Life." Papers were read on such topics as "Country versus City," "Folk Depletion as a Cause of Rural Decline," and "The Land Problem and Rural Welfare," all having to do with the problem approach to rural life concerns. A report analyzing the then prevalent rural surveys was presented to the Society.[25]

The techniques of the social survey were perfected to a considerable extent during this period of agency and problem research and themselves became objects for analysis. Kellogg, Aronovici, and Elmer discussed the survey as a body of techniques for urban social studies and Taylor made a systematic study of the history and development of the social survey as an instrument of science.[26] The documents expounding this methodology were all transient but nevertheless had some influence. They emphasized two important social research principles: first, that the degree of exactness which any science attains depends almost wholly upon the techniques and technologies with which that science works, and second, that the analysis of a social fact demands an understanding of the total situation of which that fact is a part.[27] The surveys themselves fell short of being scientific studies of communities chiefly because they lacked any clear conceptualization of the social object which they were seeking to analyze [28] but contributed

---

[24] E. E. Davis, *A Study of Rural Schools in Travis County, Texas* (Austin, Texas, 1916); C. E. Lively, *Some Rural Social Agencies in Ohio, 1921–31* (Columbus, Ohio, 1933; W. A. Hayes, *Community Value of the Consolidated School* (New Orleans, 1923).
[25] Publications of the American Sociological Society, Vol. XI.
[26] P. U. Kellogg, ed., *Pittsburgh Survey* (6 vols., New York, 1909–14); C. Aronovici, *Knowing One's Own Community* (Boston, 1912); M. C. Elmer, *Technique of Social Surveys* (Los Angeles, 1927); Carl C. Taylor, *The Social Survey, Its History and Method* (Columbia, Mo., 1919).
[27] Carl C. Taylor, "The Social Survey and Sociology," *American Journal of Sociology*, XXV, No. 6 (May, 1920).
[28] For special reference to what is meant here by "social object" see K. Mannheim, *Ideology and Utopia* (New York, 1936), pp. 12, 44, 77, 113, 151, 241.

definitely to methods of community analysis and stimulated community activity and consciousness.

Dr. C. J. Galpin in a way picked up where the earliest community studies left off and started a line of community research which was a great refinement of Wilson's crudely defined "rural community as an area within a team haul of a trade center." [29] In his *Social Anatomy of an Agricultural Community* [30] Galpin literally invented a new method of community analysis. He quantified community relationships in such a way as to reveal the roles played by institutions and agencies in community life and structure. His statement of the purpose of his significant analysis reflects the agency and reform orientations of the period (but his quantitative findings were in no way colored by this purpose): "Many remedies have been advanced and several well-defined movements have been started for the improvement of country conditions. . . . It was hoped that this inquiry would cast some light upon current rural problems of education, local government, and religion." He added a purpose which had been indirectly served but not primarily intended by previous community studies, that of revealing the role of local towns in the life of farm people.

A new rural and urban point of view has grown out of the attempt to answer satisfactorily the following series of questions: Is there such a thing as a rural community? If so, what are its characteristics? Can the farm population as a class be considered a community? Or can you cut out of the open country any piece, large or small, square, triangular, or irregular in shape and treat the farm families in this section as a community and plan institutions for them? . . . Has each farm a community of its own differing from that of every other? What is the social nature of the ordinary country school district? What sort of a social unit is the agricultural township? [31]

Williams, Wilson, and Sims had shown that rural communities and neighborhoods were no longer insulated against outside influences and that town-country relations were a part of rural community life. Galpin proposed to discover and carefully describe the functioning patterns within a farm and village set of relationships. He delineated "twelve trade zones" in a Wisconsin county and demonstrated that surrounding each village or city center there is an area or zone of land

---

[29] W. H. Wilson, *Evolution of the Country Community* (New York, 1912).
[30] (Madison, Wis., 1915).
[31] Galpin, *Social Anatomy of an Agricultural Community* (Univ. of Wisconsin Agricultural Experiment Station, Research Bulletin No. 34. Madison, Wis., 1915), pp. 1 and 2. Reprinted by permission of the publishers.

including farm homes that trade regularly at the center.[32] He then delineated the agency or institution operating zones within these trade areas: eleven banking zones, seven local newspaper zones, twelve milk zones, twelve village church zones, nine high school zones, four village library zones, and numerous local school districts which were "on the prevailing scale . . . of the neighborhoods." [33] He said,

"Analysis of the use of the leading institutions of each center by the farm population discloses the fact that these institutions are agencies of social service over a comparatively determinable and fixed area of land surrounding each center; that this social service is precisely the same in character as is rendered to artisans, employers, or professional persons who happen to live within the corporate limits of the city or village; moreover, the plain inference is that the inhabitants of the center are more vitally concerned in reality with the development and upkeep of their particular farm land base than with any other equal area of land in the state.[34]

He later described this set of relationships and patterns as a "rurban community."

Following this remarkable study and undoubtedly stemming in considerable part from it were a number of studies of two types; one type attempted to discover and describe the first patterns of association (outside the family) in which farmers habitually participate, the other type comprised more or less specific studies of farmers' trade relationships and trade centers.[35] Some of them followed quite closely the "social anatomy" kind of analysis. Others became more interested in what might be called lineal analysis, that is, analyses of consumption practices and trade center relations. A few of them explored the relations of farmers with persons, agencies, and so on, beyond the confines of local trade areas.[36]

Rural sociologists whose early researches began by analyzing local

[32] Galpin, op. cit., p. 6.   [33] Ibid., pp. 6–16.
[34] Ibid., pp. 16–18. Reprinted by permission of the publishers.
[35] See J. H. Kolb, Rural Primary Group (Madison, Wis., 1921); C. C. Zimmerman and Carl C. Taylor, Rural Organization (Raleigh, N.C., 1922); D. Sanderson and W. S. Thompson, The Social Areas of Otsego County (Ithaca, N.Y., 1923); E. L. Morgan and O. Howells, Rural Population Groups (Columbia, Mo., 1925); E. A. Taylor and F. R. Yoder, Rural Social Organization in Whitman County (Pullman, Wash., 1926); A. W. Hayes, Some Factors in Town and Country Relationships (New Orleans, 1922); J. H. Kolb, Service Relationships of Town and Country (Madison, Wis., 1923).
[36] The first intensive study of trade center relationships was A. W. Hayes, Some Factors in Town and Country Relationships (New Orleans, 1922). The most detailed was B. L. Melvin, Village Service Agencies (Ithaca, N.Y., 1929). There were many others.

COMMUNITY STUDY AND ANALYSIS 429

neighborhood and communities, their agencies and institutions, and who discovered that such patterns of association tended to disintegrate or at least were progressively diluted by contacts beyond the local area of farmers' residences, did not immediately advance to analyses of the relations of farm people with the Great Society. This was probably partly due to the growing influence of statistical techniques in social science research, partly to an insistence on the part of others that rural social research be "more practical," [37] and partly due to the fact that rural sociology was new and rural sociologists devoted their attention to diverse fields of interest. Rural social research therefore began to develop more in line with the statistical economic research of that time. Specialized components of rural social life, or special types of social phenomena, became the objects of field investigation. Detailed statistical analyses of the farm population, farm family levels of living, farm tenancy, and the like, ranked high among research projects. The 1920 Federal Census for the first time separately enumerates the rural-farm and rural-nonfarm population. In the next two decades a special analysis of the farm population of eight selected counties was followed by a number of studies of population composition, characteristics, and trends in a number of states or in some particular segment of the rural population.[38] Levels and standards of living studies using statistical methods of analysis were for a time the most popular projects in the field.[39]

The techniques used in these studies were primarily quantitative. Census records or elaborate field schedules furnished a sufficient volume of data to permit correlation analyses and, for a time, one who was not skilled in such techniques was scarcely considered a scientist. These studies contributed a great deal to the analysis of certain components of rural social life, through their precision in observation and analysis

[37] By being practical was meant that social research should resemble more closely the research in farm management conducted at Agricultural Experiment Stations from which research funds came.

[38] See especially such early studies as C. J. Galpin and V. B. Larson, *Farm Population of Selected Counties; Composition, Characteristics, and Occupations in Detail* (Washington, D.C., 1924); E. L. Morgan and O. Howells, *Rural Population Groups* (Columbia., Mo., 1915); W. L. Harter and R. E. Stewart, *The Population of Iowa, Its Composition and Changes* (Ames, Iowa, 1930); E. de S. Brunner, *Immigrant Farmers and Their Children* (New York, 1929).

[39] Early rural studies were E. L. Kirkpatrick, *The Standard of Life in a Typical Section of Diversified Farming* (Ithaca, N.Y., 1923); E. L. Kirkpatrick, H. W. Atwater, and I. M. Bailey, *Family Living in Farm Homes* (Washington, D.C., 1924); G. H. Von Tungeln, J. E. Thadus, and E. L. Kirkpatrick, *Cost of Living on Iowa Farms* (Ames, Iowa, 1926).

and the relating of social phenomena to important physical and economic phenomena in agriculture. Population data were related especially to land use and other economic opportunities and levels of living related especially to farm income.

While community studies by surveys and other techniques had used quantitative data in what might be called gross units—schools, churches, health, types of social participation, modal opinions and attitudes, and so on—it was only when arrays of data in greater volume than were available in the study of a single community were used that gross units could be broken down into their various components and thus analysis made of their constituent elements. In other words the contributions of well-established statistical techniques which could not be used to a very great extent in the analysis of one community could be used when segments of behavior from numerous communities became the object of analysis.

In 1926—twenty years after Williams's study of *An American Town* a national survey of rural social research furnished a static picture of the scope and methods of rural social research at that time. There were 104 rural research projects in progress—80 at Land Grant Colleges and 24 at other institutions. They were classified in the following subject matter fields: [40]

	By Land Grant Institutions	By non-Land Grant Institutions	Total
Social Organization	20	7	27
Population	16	7	23
Standard of Living	14	1	15
Youth Organizations	5	1	6
Social Psychology	6	0	6
Rural Institutions	4	1	5
Farmers' Organizations	3	0	3
Miscellaneous	12	7	19
Total	80	24	108

Forty-one, approximately 38 percent, of these studies were of organization: community, institutional or other groups. Few of them were studies of whole communities. Some were chiefly concerned with the measurement of the participation of farm families in the organized group life of their communities, some with the relations between vil-

[40] C. J. Galpin, J. H. Kolb, Dwight Sanderson, and Carl C. Taylor, *Rural Sociology Research in the United States* (Social Science Research Monograph, 1927).

lages and the surrounding farm population, some with the effects of industrial development on rural life, and some with village organization and life. Others were concerned with what might be called the functioning of rural groups themselves—locality, special interest, and youth groups. The institutional studies were of schools, churches, libraries, community buildings, and hospitals.[41] Thirty-eight were statistical studies in the fields of population and standards of living.

An analysis of research methods used in the 80 land-grant colleges studies showed that field schedules were used in 53.7 percent of them; data were compiled and analyzed statistically. In the community, institutional, and other organizational studies the two chief techniques were mapping zones of operation and statistical analyses of individual and family participation. Very little use was made of the diary or notebook, and more often than not enumerators who were not highly trained observers were employed as "schedule takers." Coöperation of participant observers—local residents—was seldom if ever sought in either gathering or interpreting facts. It was thus clear that the techniques were chiefly those of statistical analysis. In the standard-of-living studies, expenditures for the various elements in the level of living were analyzed in relation to each other and to total family income and size and composition of families. Levels of consumption and participation were practically never compared with the values or desired standards of families. Even within the community, other group and institutional studies, analyses of group relationships and cohesions were made solely by counting numbers of participations in various types of group activities.

Until very recently the tendencies revealed in the 1926–27 survey have continued. Research projects have become less episodic but have, by and large, dealt with particular types of phenomena—they have been straight-line, usually statistical, analyses of problems, situations, or trends. Only those which have been definitely tied to "locality" and those of newly constructed communities have tended to pursue analyses of relationships. Even these, with their chief focus on internal structure and relationships within locality groups, have all been short on analyses of outside relationships. They have treated rural communities somewhat as if they were cultural islands and seemed not to recognize that even greater than the significance of the expansion of the physical boundaries of rural service areas and diversity of internal relationships

[41] *Ibid.*

has been the farmer's increasing participation in the Great Society.

Galpin had initiated locality group studies in his *Social Anatomy* and had stimulated Sanderson, Kolb, Taylor, Morgan and Yoder to pursue similar studies. Sanderson alone systematically continued this line of research and during the twenty-five years following his and Warren's first study of the social areas of Otsego County, New York, he and his students developed precise techniques for delineating and mapping rural communities and neighborhoods as systems of association of individuals and families, the community as a cluster of institutional services, and as a center of common interest, and in a few studies analyzed relationships between rural areas and larger cities.[42] By their techniques rural communities, whether open country, village, or otherwise, can be located, analyzed in detail, and compared with all others. They do not in and of themselves offer methods for analyzing all the concerns of those who live within locality boundaries or even methods of *measuring* the amplitude, much less the meaningfulness, of various types of relationships.

Other community studies have gone beyond those of purely locality groups. Nelson in his studies of two communities in Utah had and used the opportunity of analyzing fixed local farm village patterns under the impact from 50 to 75 years of changing American society.[43] In a previous study the same author clearly delineated the ideological factors that predicated the whole physical pattern of Mormon communities.[44] Others studied special features of community life and structure: hospitals, libraries and fire halls; youth groups, community organizations, health and health service, special interest groups, social participation, churches, schools, coöperatives, and local governments. These were studies of segments of rural communities, and while they inadvertently served to show relationships with the Great Society their fundamental

---

[42] See especially D. Sanderson and W. S. Thompson, *The Social Areas of Otsego County, New York* (Ithaca, N.Y., 1923); H. C. Hoffsommer, *The Relation of Cities and Larger Villages to Changes in Rural Trade and Social Areas in Wayne County, New York* (Ithaca, N.Y., 1934); and E. A. Taylor, *The Relationship of Open Country Population of Genesee County, New York, to Villages and Cities* (Ithaca, N.Y., 1934). These and some 30 other studies of locality groups appeared as publications of the Cornell Agricultural Experiment Station between 1923 and 1943.

[43] Lowry Nelson, *A Social Survey of Escalante* and *The Utah Farm Village of Ephraim* (Brigham Young Univ. Studies No. 1 and No. 2, Provo, Utah, 1925 and 1928, respectively).

[44] Lowry Nelson, *The Mormon Village, a Study in Social Origins* (Provo, Utah, 1930).

COMMUNITY STUDY AND ANALYSIS

purposes were either to point to examples of good things or to analyze in detail some one factor in community life.

Three recent types of community studies do demonstrate either new or improved research techniques. Zimmerman made a typological study of communities, Loomis and others have studied newly founded rural communities and Ensminger and others have considerably refined and expanded Galpin's and Sanderson's techniques for analyses of locality groups. Zimmerman studied fifteen communities in a conceptual framework of typology and suggested the idea that local communities, like individuals, possess personalities which are expressions of both their internal structures and their large environments. His studies included communities in Asia, England, the Canadian prairie provinces, New England, the South and the Middle West. His personalization of communities by such names as "good-natured Littleville," "indecisive Hamlet," and the like may have oversimplified the analyses of individual communities but the fact that he studied all of them within a carefully formulated conceptual frame of reference constitutes his type of analysis as a much needed contribution.[45]

Loomis began the study of newly established communities shortly after a number of completely new communities had been established by the Division of Subsistence Homesteads, the Federal Emergency Relief Administration, and the Resettlement Administration. Since his first report on the study of seven of these communities this line of analysis has been continued by a number of others. The original purpose of such studies was "to set a bench mark indicating quantitatively and objectively the extent of social participation among the families" living in these communities.[46] The major contribution of this first study was the discovery and measurement of the outstanding role of informal group participation and the influence of such groups in the processes of integration and disintegration within the life and administration of the communities. Loomis showed that the exodus of families from one of these project communities was almost literally in "cliques." Those who left and those who stayed did so in whole groups composed of families which visited, exchanged work and borrowed among themselves. He used and improved J. L. Moreno's so-called sociometric techniques to describe precisely—and in some cases to

[45] C. C. Zimmerman, *The Changing Community* (New York, 1938).
[46] C. P. Loomis, *Social Relationships and Institutions in Seven New Rural Communities* (Washington, D.C., 1940).

measure the amplitude and meaning of—these informal groups.[47]

Other studies have been made of some of these and similar communities after they had been longer in existence. One was an appraisal of sixteen subsistence homesteads projects.[48] Another of ten Farm Security Administration communities (unpublished) was primarily a study of community morale and its relation to community administration.

The persistent and elaborated analyses of rural locality groups have also recently made considerable contribution by the analysis of such groups in relation to so-called "action programs," past and present. An example is *Community Organization and Agricultural Planning: Greene County, Georgia*.[49] The white settlement of Greene County was approximately completed by 1790. The social structure at that time consisted of a number of typical, simple, self-sufficient, frontier communities. In the 150 years that followed this social structure changed with changing American culture. Between 1810 and 1815 the old simple communities gave way to the emerging slave plantation organization which lasted until the Civil War. The slave plantation came and passed; commercialized agriculture, in terms of cotton produced for the market, was intensified by the increasing necessity of purchasing commercial fertilizer. Units of the state government were established in the area; schools and churches were built; road, welfare and health districts established. Recently a number of new Federal Government agricultural agencies have set up operating and administrative districts. Thus the geography and the people of the county in 1942, when the study under discussion was made, were organized into five distinct and separate kinds of administrative areas and districts, none of them coinciding with others or with the natural communities and neighborhoods of the county. There were five Farm Security Administrative districts, eight Soil Conservation districts, twelve Agricultural Adjustment Administration districts, seven local Extension Club areas, seven white school attendance areas, five county health-department clinic areas, sixteen militia districts, seven white church zones, and in addition, sixteen committees, boards, and councils composed of

---

[47] Further development of these techniques can be found in other studies by Loomis: see "Development of Planned Rural Communities," *Rural Sociology*, III (Dec., 1938); "Governmental Administration and Informal Local Groups," *Applied Anthropology*, (March, 1942); and "Informal Groupings in a Spanish-American Village," *Sociometry*, IV (Feb., 1941).
[48] R. Lord, P. H. Johnstone, et al., *A Place on Earth* (Washington, D.C., 1942).
[49] By L. Coleman (Washington, D.C., 1942).

COMMUNITY STUDY AND ANALYSIS

farmers and other local people. On the face of such facts Greene County offered a beautiful laboratory for the study of the impact of a larger number and great diversity of social structures than were represented by the local rural communities of the area. Notwithstanding, the fact that all of these social structures were imposed so to speak, on the rural people of the county, farm families still lived and functioned in communities and neighborhoods which had no administrative boundaries and which they had evolved over time to supply and satisfy their social needs and desires. The analyst with the help of the people themselves delineated and mapped these self-conscious communities and neighborhoods. There were nine white communities and thirty-eight Negro neighborhoods in the county, about which the authors made the following comment: "In the last 40 years, the community surrounding the county seat has almost doubled in size at the expense of three other communities. In 1900, neighborhoods were more important and communities less important than today. However, no white communities in Greene County have completely disappeared since 1900, nor have any new ones emerged. The neighborhood is still the most meaningful local group for rural Negroes. In the absence of strong outside ties with towns and villages, the neighborhood functions as 'their community.' " [50] The Great Society is a part of the life of Greene County but rural people still live in communities while they participate in it.[51]

An attempt to close the gaps in rural community research demands first a clear conception of what is meant by the term "rural community." Cultural anthropologists have constructed concepts as bases for their studies of simple societies. Sociologists have created dogmas which they think are useful concepts by means of which to see the integrating factors, or common denominators, in complex societies. Each of these makes its contribution but none is adequate to the task at hand. Rural sociologists, because they could literally see rural communities in terms of geography and internal patterns of relationships, have gone about analyzing these things as objects of research without an adequate conceptual framework. They have known that the geographic rural community is not a society but apparently have not

[50] *Communities and Administrative Areas of Greene County, Georgia* (Washington, D.C., 1941).
[51] For a much more elaborate study of Greene County, Georgia, see A. Raper, *Tenants of the Almighty* (New York, 1943). Raper's study was part of the study of Contemporary Rural Communities, described below.

clearly seen that to the persons living in these geographic areas society, almost in its entirety, comes to them through participation in structures, functions, and attitudes, all of which are resident and operative in the local community. Arensberg and Kimball in a study of *Family and Community* in County Clare, Irish Free State, approximated a study of contemporary communities, but these authors say in the introduction of the report of their findings that they studied "only a few of the many aspects of contemporary Irish social life" and that "the purpose of their study is not so much to characterize the communities described as it is to examine the behavior of persons living in them." [52]

The operational and realistic concept of a rural community as a societal or cultural object concerns itself with man's habits and traits and with those ideas and attitudes which he holds more or less in common with others. The "others" may be a clique of friends, members of a mutual aid neighborhood, members or participants in institutional activities, a group of persons who hold common viewpoints about world affairs or about truth itself. The groups are not communities, but all of them exist in a geographically identifiable area which for purposes of analysis is a useful object of research. This area is, for the overwhelming majority of farmers, the so-called trade area community which includes within its boundaries all the patterns of association in which rural people meet face to face and all the instruments of communication through which they know and participate in the Great Society.

The task of analyzing this community requires the use of a whole group of techniques, each appropriate to the type of phenomenon which it studies. If the phenomena are conditioned strongly by such physical facts as soils, topography, and distance, then identification and mapping of geographic zones help in the analysis. If they are value systems, the techniques of analyzing attitudes can and should be used. If they are some highly segmented but deeply significant components of life which can be better understood in terms of time or space variations, the techniques of statistics are adequate for their analysis. If they are qualitative facts, as many significant personal and social experiences are, then the only person who can reveal their meaning and influences is one who experiences them—a so-called participant observer. Com-

[52] C. M. Arensberg and S. T. Kimball, *Family and Community in Ireland* (Cambridge, Mass., 1940), pp. xxii, xxv. See also Arensberg's *The Irish Countryman* (New York, 1937).

COMMUNITY STUDY AND ANALYSIS

plete understanding requires the use of the folk knowledge of the participant observer and of the research techniques and conceptual thinking of the scientist. Folk knowledge is not science at all and "science," as Karl Pearson said, "is method." Complete analysis requires a synthesis of these two revealers of truth.

Statistical analysts have meticulously studied some of the obvious currents of and in society but certainly cannot claim thereby to have diagnosed the community or society as a whole. Rural sociologists have envisioned the rural community as a geographic whole and have pretty clearly described its social anatomy and analyzed various segments of its functioning. No one of them has, however, completely analyzed any single rural community in terms of all of its activities—those relating to family life, informal associational life (friendships), institutional and agency participation, and participation in currents of behavior and thinking of the many segments of the Great Society. No one of them ever will completely analyze it by studying its most folklike units of association and then adding them together in something labeled by them a rural community. The modern rural man lives and moves in all his functional relationships at one time and without undue ambivalence; in his family, neighborhood, geographic trade area, among his friends, and with the news of world markets and world wars coming to him with the same dispatch it does to those in the city. The science that would analyze him and his community must be as multiplex as his life. It must isolate components of his life—trends and units of behavior and association—but it must not fail to integrate the knowledge gained by such dissection and analyses into a knowledge and understanding of his life as a unity. This unity will probably not turn out to be a community at all but a moving equilibrium of diverse daily activities and a fairly stable cluster of attitudes which constitute the modal value system of the individual and of those with whom he most frequently associates. Such activities and value systems are related to and result from all his units of social participation from family circle to Great Society. Since the community is where his activities and thoughts occur and since it is an identifiable geographic area which contains all the major institutions, agencies, and instruments of communication through which his contacts flow, it furnishes the laboratory in which to study his society.

An approach to an analysis of this total situation was made when in 1939 a group of sociologists, anthropologists, and social psychologists set up a research project "to investigate the cultural, community, and social psychological factors in rural life, with special reference to those factors which facilitate or offer resistance to change, contribute to adjustments and maladjustments and to stability and instability in individual and community life." Elaborate and fairly precise procedures were laid down to guide the study: (1) collect and analyze all statistical data available on the areas; (2) identify and delineate all neighborhoods and communities in the area; (3) gather, by schedules, information on the form, nature, and extent of social participation, including formal and informal groupings, leadership, visiting relationships, and the like; (4) by means of repeated and detailed interviews of a carefully selected sample of informants, assemble information on values with respect to the following matters in particular: (a) cultural patterns having to do with land use, physical and biological phenomena, economic techniques, attitudes toward hard work, thrift, fortitude, and other virtues; (b) formal and informal organization of the local community; (c) leadership with particular reference to officers of various organizations, their role and status in the community, and with regard to other leaders, and to various classes in the community; (d) effects of commercialization on farming and farmers' attitudes, impact of mechanization on farming and farmers, and influence of urbanization.[53]

All field analysts were supposed to follow the same procedures. 1. The boundaries of the communities to be studied were to be determined by "delineation" of each community itself and all communities which bordered it. 2. All neighborhood institutional and agency "zones" of operation within the boundaries of the community were to be delineated and mapped. 3. All data available from secondary sources, statistical and historical, concerning such things as origin and changes in population, types of farm production and land use, and institutional development were to be carefully compiled. 4. From 15 to 20 "participant observers," representing the class structure of the area were to be systematically used in the gathering of qualitative information and interpretation of quantitative data. 5. Sociometric charts were to be made of patterns and association and frequencies of participation of members of the community within and outside the community. 6. Attitude studies of the seniors in the high schools and possibly of the participant observers were to be made. 7. A trained analyst was to live

[53] Unpublished manual of instructions.

COMMUNITY STUDY AND ANALYSIS

in each community for a period of from four to six months and to spend from eight to ten months on the total study.

It was discovered by experience that the time allotted was not sufficient to accomplish the complete analysis. The sociometric measurements were made in only one community and the attitude studies were made in none. The six community studies were, however, published with the recognition that they had only partially fulfilled the design and scope of analysis laid down in the manual of procedure. The chapter titles indicate the scope of their findings: "History of Settlement," "Manner, Means and Methods of Making a Living," "Community Organization and Values," "The Farmer's Expanding World," "Integration and Disintegration in Community and Individual Life." [54] These studies are being followed up by a series of others which it is hoped will, over a considerable period of time, accomplish everything and more than these studies of the culture of contemporary rural communities had intended to accomplish. The plan for a new series now in progress is as follows:

Approximately 70 of the 3,000 counties in the United States, selected by the most careful sampling techniques, are assumed to be representative of American rural life and will be used as research laboratories.

The most typical community in each of these counties is selected and studied by the best techniques thus far evolved by numerous previous community studies.

Each county and community is sampled, per geographical and class structure, and one or more local "key observers" appointed for each subarea and class.

A competent, professionally trained analyst works in two communities concurrently, carrying on an analysis of each as a whole and gathering information on measurable social trends.

A series of trend (time-series) studies are carried out in all counties and communities, noting changes in farm family levels of living, changes in mechanization, commercialization and urbanization, changes in basic attitudes, and so on.

Each field worker will, in due time, write a research monograph on each of the two counties and communities he has studied and different analysts will write a monograph, every five years, on the findings of the time series.

[54] *Culture of a Contemporary Rural Community, Rural Life Studies,* Nos. 1–6 (Washington, D.C.): No. 1, O. E. Leonard and C. P. Loomis, *El Cerrito, New Mexico* (1941); No. 2, Earl H. Bell, *Sublette, Kansas* (1942); No. 3, Kenneth MacLeish and Kimball Young, *Landaff, New Hampshire* (1942); No. 4, W. M. Kollmorgen, *The Old Order Amish of Lancaster County, Pennsylvania* (1942); No. 5, E. O. Moe and Carl C. Taylor, *Irwin, Iowa* (1942); and No. 6, Waller Wynne, *Harmony, Georgia* (1943).

In this elaborate scheme and program of research, attempts are made to use all quantitative techniques which are applicable to the type and scope of data available. Qualitative information is obtained from resident participant observers and by trained social scientists. Thus what may be described as a combination of statistical and cultural techniques is used, each to supplement the other. Quantitative data not only yield precise information on trends and precisely comparable data for all areas being studied, but furnish cues for some specific types of qualitative information needed to interpret and add meaning to facts revealed by statistics.

In order to make use of two fairly well-established types of analytical techniques two universes for analysis or objects of research are clearly recognized, the local community and the time and space behavior of certain important measurable components of social life. It is believed that only by the combined use of these two universes of observation and analysis the studies rise above the plane of "surveys" so prevalent in the early days of rural social research. The rural community as the farmer's society is the object for analysis but when the components of the community are isolated for meticulous examination the volume of data in any rural community on each component is too small to be subject to statistical analysis. Such data are acquired by "time series" carried on concurrently in all selected communities, and thus a volume of data are made available.

A secondary but tremendously important objective is accomplished by analyzing rural society in terms of the two universes just described—the objective of furnishing to each professional research worker engaged in the large over-all program a zestful research objective. Field observations of the qualitative type required in community or cultural studies require insights which only mature and competent social scientists possess. Such men cannot be expected to find professional zest in "schedule taking" for experts in time and space analyses of population, levels of living, basic attitudes, and the like. They do gather information by means of field schedules and hand over such information, from all communities, to experts in analyses of the various time series but they also use all these types of information, together with all other statistical, historical, and qualitative information in the analysis of their own object of study—the rural community. Furthermore the experts in time-series analyses furnish to the community analysts types of information about the communities which can be gained only from statistical analyses of data from all the communities.

The techniques used in each type of analysis are those that have been evolved by social scientists in the evolution of the social sciences, most of which have been described here in telling the story of the evolution of rural social research. The array of statistics on each component of rural life represented in the time series will be great enough to warrant use of all quantitative techniques of statistical analysis; and the observations of trained social scientists who have lived for months in the communities, together with those of their coöperating key observers, should furnish elaborate and acceptable qualitative information and interpretations.

The statistical techniques for analyzing the components of rural life have developed in the field of science, but many of the phenomena analyzed by them arose from relations with the Great Society which has become more and more a part of rural life. Some of these phenomena (such as trade relations) developed directly out of physical interchange between farm and urban people. Others developed out of the infiltration into rural communities of new standards of consumptions, new standards of institutional and agency services, new standards of social status, and even new attitudes and value systems. In order to adjust to commercial market changes, the modern farmer must keep his enterprise flexible both in types of products and capital investments. This conflicts with his age old stability accomplished by ecological adaptations made by himself and previous generations. Many means of communication, especially newspapers, radios, and moving pictures, make it possible for urban and rural residents to participate concurrently in things that are aspects of the total national and world culture. The secondary contacts of farm people are increasing steadily and rapidly and such contacts reach far beyond the local community. Farmers, however, live almost altogether in local rural communities. Techniques of research capable of analyzing the total behavior and meaning of their lives in local communities will therefore accomplish complete analysis of the farmer's contemporary society.

The Acquisition of New Social Habits
By JOHN DOLLARD

THANKS to his special neural equipment man is of all animals the most capable of learning.[1] He learns easily in his first contacts with the social environment and seems to have special abilities for acquiring new habits in later life. These abilities are apparently based on his capacity to stimulate others by speech and, similarly, to be stimulated by them. He is advantaged also by his capacity for thought, which seems to be a skill at placing silent sentences end to end until they suggest appropriate courses of action in the environment.

The laws of learning are apparently the same for complex as for simple organisms.[2] All learning follows this formula: The individual must be driven or excited in order to learn. He must hit upon the response which is to be learned. This response must be made in the presence of the relevant environmental and somatic cues. The connection between cues and response must be cemented by reward. In other words, the individual must "want something, sense something, do something, and get something"—there must be (1) drive, (2) cue, (3) response, and (4) reward.[3] Some responses, like sentences, have a kind of intermediate function in that they provide cues which evoke other responses. The field of psychotherapy is peculiarly dependent upon these intermediate sentence responses.

Be it noted that we are not here concerned with "therapy" but with learning. The former is a broader category and includes, for instance, environmental changes or support which are therapeutic in that they reduce discomfort but do not necessarily teach anything.

There seem to be at least five situations in which the habits of individuals may change. They are:

[1] I do not refer to "conditioning" at this point because the word tends to stress the narrow Pavlovian theory which has now been incorporated in the larger body of learning theory itself.
[2] The many and elaborate propositions in a theory of learning stem from the work of Pavlov, Thorndike, Terman, Hull, and others. They are perhaps best integrated in the work of Hull (Clark L. Hull, *Principles of Behavior*, New York, 1943).
[3] Neal E. Miller and John Dollard, *Social Learning and Imitation* (New Haven, Conn., 1941), p. 35.

(1) the situation of culture change in the society,
(2) life dilemmas in a social group,
(3) the psychiatric learning situation,
(4) the psychoanalytic learning situation,
(5) the situation of the clinical group.

Each of these situations sets up conditions in which individuals may or must learn new habits.

Anthropologists have noted the massive conservatism of culture, the apparent transmission of perfect pattern from one generation to the next. But they have also noticed that cultures do change. They change by the diffusion of patterns from without, as Western European culture was changed by the introduction of gun powder. They change by invention from within, as by the invention of the printing press. They change by the demands and imposition of conquest, as Latin speech was imposed on a large part of the Western world.

THE SITUATION OF CULTURE CHANGE

As cultures change, for whatever reason, men learn. In fact, culture change and individual learning are identical processes described at different levels of abstraction.[4] As men learn, they transmit the new learning to their children, take the new habit under the moral umbrella of the society, and sanction it for all time to their descendants. It is this moral addition to the newly acquired habit which gives it its subsequent resistance to change.

Keller has described social learning in terms of "mass trial and error."[5] When, for any reason, old habits cease to work, traumatic drives appear among the masses of men. Under the goad of pain or some other drive, men borrow, invent or accept habits different from their own. New responses are hit upon at random or are copied from prestigeful sources for imitation. They are tried out first by a few, then by the masses. If successful, they become part of the mores of the society.

Ogburn envisions the current world struggle in a somewhat similar manner.[6] The problem of government, as he sees it, is to master the forces released by modern technology. No modern national state has yet succeeded in doing so. War may be seen as an incident to this struggle, with the varying states affected proposing somewhat differ-

[4] William Graham Sumner, *Folkways* (Boston, 1906), p. 19.
[5] A. G. Keller, *Societal Evolution* (New York, 1915), Chaps. IX-XI.
[6] William F. Ogburn and Meyer F. Nimkoff, *Sociology* (Boston, 1940), pp. 192, 870-71.

ent solutions to the fundamental problem. When a solution is hit upon and the enormous potential production of machine technology is subordinated to a workable social system, the result will be a great new demand on men for learning. The new system can only be stabilized when it becomes habitual, when all the relevant skills to operate it are acquired by its members. One of the required social changes will be the abolition of war. However the change may come, whether by revolution or slow adaptation of existing patterns of organization, it can only be secured when new and appropriate habits are formed and are given the sanctity of the traditional. The rule here as elsewhere would seem to be that social change is habit change.

LIFE DILEMMAS IN A SOCIAL GROUP

Within any relatively stable social order new learning is constantly required of the component individuals. No sooner has the child firmly developed the habit of suckling than he must abandon it and learn to drink from a cup. The asexual habits of childhood must be transmuted into positive sexual behavior in the normal adult. The school imposes a new strain on the child and puts him in a measured learning competition with other children. Change from childhood to adolescence forces a new learning dilemma on the child, and much of what he learns helps him to control the mounting sex tension of this period. Leaving home, whether to get a job or to go to college, again sets up a learning situation where new habits are grafted on the old. The lack of family control permits exploration in new directions, with a resultant reconditioning of the individual. Marriage brings its new demands for adjustment, and change from one job to another, as from civilian to soldier, presents new learning dilemmas.

It is therefore far from true to suppose that no new learning occurs after early childhood. People learn wherever they are impelled to learn and free to learn, that is, in the anxiety-free areas of their lives; men will learn as long as they are in learning dilemmas, providing no barrier habits, such as anxiety, interfere. There is no reason to assume that old people cannot learn efficiently as long as relevant neural mechanisms are intact. Perhaps they have a reputation for not learning because their social situation does not create the motivations and provide the rewards for learning.

One of the most important and difficult types of learning is that imposed on an individual who is socially mobile, the individual who wishes to change his social position in his society.[7] In order to do so he must acquire the habits and attitudes of the group into which he wishes to move. To be effective, such social habits must be deeply engrained and unconscious; apparently only a training which begins in childhood establishes them adequately. The mobile individual has, at first, only marginal participation in a clique in the superordinate class. His clique sponsor may in some cases "score" his behavior, criticizing inappropriate traits and suggesting the desired traits. The clique sponsor also serves as a model. If the aspirant to mobility is perceptive, he can learn much by consciously watching and changing his behavior. The mechanism here involved is that of acquired reward value when he matches with his sponsor and acquired punishment value (red ears) when his behavior does not match. Even in the best cases the mobile individual matches only approximately, enough to remain in the new group but not enough to wipe out all perception of difference between himself and the others. Coaching and copying [8] are two stand-bys of mobility learning. Those who lack a coach or fail to learn to copy lose their marginal status in the superordinate group and must be content to bear their economic prosperity at an inferior social level. Psychiatric or psychoanalytic treatment can frequently aid a mobile individual to be more successful and adaptive in his mobility campaign. But in mobility, as in other learning, the four fundamentals apply.

Throughout life individuals continue to learn from secondary as well as from primary sources. Books and magazines suggest new responses. A radio program may drop a sentence into one's vocabulary which becomes a basis of new action. Advertisers continuously teach their names and slogans to the public. Much of this learning is of a vagrant and half-conscious type, especially when it occurs as a result of the wish to be amused. The conditions of such learning are exceedingly complex and are not now well understood. It seems reasonable to suppose that the usual variables must be operating.

As is implied by the foregoing, new learning is always provisional. A new habit unit is not necessarily permanent. Habits may disappear because the drive which excites them is no longer operative, because some competing response prevents the occurrence of the former response, because the cues which release the habit become indistinct or

---

[7] Allison Davis, Burleigh B. Gardner, and Mary R. Gardner, *Deep South* (Chicago, 1941), pp. 171–202; Allison Davis and John Dollard, *Children of Bondage* (Washington, D.C., 1940), pp. 12–15.
[8] Miller and Dollard, *Social Learning and Imitation*, Chap. X.

because the environmental reward system changes. Unrewarded habits may continue for a time but will gradually extinguish. The habits of daily life are maintained by the rewards of daily life. Let him who doubts this notice the greater difficulty in working when hungry, sexually excited, or anxious. Habits must reduce drive by leading to reward, else drive remains strong, and new responses are tried out.

PSYCHOTHERAPY

The existence of a need for psychotherapy is a kind of criticism of the society and its institutions, particularly the family institution. It implies that individuals have not been properly prepared to behave in their adult orbits. Although much attention has seemingly been given to the matter, the field of the social learning of the child is still relatively unexplored. The fact remains that many individuals survive childhood training only to find that they are ill prepared for the contingencies of adult life.

Apparently much of the decisive training of childhood is inadvertent. Parents set habits in the child without being aware that they are doing so. Some families may be quite adept at rewarding the child for his first tentatives toward speech and thus aid in his language development. Persons who converse much with a child may greatly develop his vocabulary and inadvertently aid him in learning to think, thus, in turn, contributing an element to the child's intelligence quotient. Neglect or resentment on the part of the mother may serve to confirm a homosexual character in her son, although doing so is no part of her conscious policy. Early sex training, negligently and thoughtlessly administered, may frighten a girl so that she will not marry. The existence of perverse, neurotic, and psychotic adults seems to point to factors in the culture of the family which are aberrant and destructive. Perhaps these negative aspects of the culture of childhood were once adaptive, especially those which tend to brutalize the child, thus aiding in producing soldiers for periods of warfare.

The "artificial" learning situations of psychotherapy have been devised for those who have learned such ugly lessons in early life. The normal learning situations of adult life do not teach these people what they need to know. The psychotherapist steps in to create a special kind of situation and gives the deviant individual a belated chance to learn what he might much better have learned in his own family. One

ACQUISITION OF NEW SOCIAL HABITS

of the greatest challenges to social science arises from this fact. We need a scientific culture of childhood which will eventually make adult psychotherapeutic aid needless. So far only first sketches of this new science have been drawn.

A psychiatrist has resources of many kinds: physical, chemical, electrical, psychological, and social. We shall consider his function only in so far as he attempts to teach his patient new habits. People usually come, or are brought, to the psychiatrist in some kind of crisis. Whatever the therapy, the crisis is always a behavioral one; the person cannot meet his adult responsibilities with ordinary enthusiasm or resignation. The psychiatrist is a privileged individual because of his social role as physician. The physician is the man who can control pain and give directions in the important matter of maintaining health. Hence he acquires a great anxiety-reducing power. "Just having him come into the house" makes one feel better. People tend to come to him when bearing conflict or anxiety.

In so far as he acts as psychiatrist he does not claim any special magic of theory or interpretation. He can give, or secure, sound medical advice for the patient. Since he sees so many mental problems, he tends to be sophisticated with regard to common-sense solutions to such problems. He can give an immediate reassurance against groundless fear. Very often he gives unexpected information which reduces the patient's sense of isolation or peculiarity and suggests more adaptive courses of action. Realistic information on sexual matters is apparently greatly appreciated. Many patients find it helpful to be told exactly what to do. In this case the therapist always runs the risk that should the venture turn out badly he will be blamed. The permission to act provided by information and reassurance undoubtedly furnishes just that spark which some people need to begin acting more adaptively.[9]

The psychiatrist takes justified pride in not going "deeper than needed." He smiles at the psychoanalyst who "will not direct a man to the post office until the fellow has submitted to a complete anamnesis." However, the shoe is sometimes on the other foot. The failure of a psychiatrist to recognize the deepest anxiety habits of a patient may nullify the good effect of practical and sensible suggestions for behavior and may necessitate his having continued recourse to psychiatric aid. Many psychiatrists pride themselves in making some use of psycho-

[9] Carl R. Rogers, *Counseling and Psychotherapy* (New York, 1942), pp. 18 ff.

analytic concepts and of somewhat unsystematically venturing interpretations. Indeed, there seems to be occurring in psychiatry a kind of slow drift toward the astringent models of Freudian thought.

However unsystematically, the psychiatrist functions as a teacher for those whose habits do not permit them to survive comfortably in the modern world. His reassurance, if it functions effectively, reduces anxiety so that the patient can try again under more favorable circumstances. His giving of information suggests new modes of response and gives authoritative permission to try such new modes. His instructions may force his patient at least to try behavior which may prove adaptive. He has success with many kinds of problems not yet clearly classified from a theoretical standpoint. He gives intelligent aid and care to those so severely afflicted that they must be institutionalized. But the psychiatrist's success, where he has it, must be brought about by the usual mechanisms of learning. Only new learning can bulwark the patient against a recurrence of internal stresses and lead to a tolerable state of being.

The assumption is herewith made that all cases of permanent psychotherapy are learning cases. In such cases the patient has acquired new habits which continue to mediate the ever-surging primary drives. Reassurance or instruction may help the neurotic individual, but only for the moment. In order to free himself at once from his therapist and his conflicts he must learn to reduce his own drives. He can do so only by changing his habits. Reassurance may be helpful to therapy, however, in that it may aid a person who has stopped the "trying" essential to new learning to begin it again.

THE PSYCHIATRIC LEARNING SITUATION

Psychoanalysts have given but little and incidental attention in their theory to the importance of learning, and yet I believe that psychoanalytic theory is entirely congruent with learning theory. I have often thought that much of what learning theorists emphasize is hidden behind Freud's concept of "Durcharbeitung," or working through. Freud contended that the single moment of illuminating insight in a psychoanalysis is not enough. The patient must "work through" this insight until it permeates every aspect of his life. Presumably a part of any such working through is the forming of new habits. Dr. Abram Kardiner once said to me during a control session, "The patient does not get well on the psychoanalytic couch; he gets well in life." I took this to mean that it is not the mere verbal exchange of the psychoanalytic situation which is effective, but in order to achieve a therapeutic result the patient must act in the social world outside the psychoanalysis and get rewarded for it. Some of us believe that great progress may come when the joint skills of the psychoanalyst and the learning theorist are firmly lodged under one skull. Psychoanalysis has great exploratory courage and empirical richness. Learning theory has a rigor of concept and a connection with an experimental base which might aid in the development of psychoanalysis as a social psychology.

Freudians contend that in certain areas their patients have stopped learning. The ordinary situations of adult life will not evoke the necessary new responses because the patient is biased against these situations, is unable to act in a free, exploratory manner, and is therefore unable to get rewarded for trying something new. Behaviorally viewed, neurotics may deviate in that they are unable to trust others and therefore will not take the risks of ordinary social life. A neurotic may have peculiar attitudes toward persons in authority, alternately rebelling and showing excessive submission. He may be unable to bring forward that minimal aggression which is necessary to win the respect of others. Though all social circumstances seem favorable, he may not be able to make a satisfying sex response. A neurotic may be "screwy" in that he is unable to assess his environment rationally and score it as others would score it. He may not be able to work because his attention is constantly deflected by competing drives.

If the person is neurotic the attitudes above enumerated are not transitional or situational. They are matters of long standing which have served to characterize the individual in one degree or another since his childhood. The real learning situations of adult life by which the average person is able to profit cannot teach the neurotic what he needs to know; though coöperation might advantage him, he cannot risk it. He rebels even where rebellion is disastrous. No amount of social teasing can produce the required sexual response. Such a deficit in learning ability demands a special learning situation, and that is what has been provided by Freud.

Maladaptive habits in the neurotic person have been produced in the powerful learning situations of childhood. In these situations the child is "strapped, noosed," [10] and must learn what his overburdened, neg-

[10] A. E. Housman, "Eight O'clock," in The Collected Poems of A. E. Housman (London, 1939), p. 115.

lectful, or incompetent parents teach. Of course, they do the best they can, but too often the best they can do is to produce a disordered individual.

The strong habits of the neurotic child tend to persist while he is in the family situation, and this means with most neurotics through adolescence. The habits persist, of course, because they are adaptive in the disordered culture of his family. The same forces and dilemmas which have produced the original neurotic habits usually persist, although when neurotic training has been inadvertent or unconscious on the part of the parents they may verbally deplore the result of such training. Neurotics do not change early bad habits for better ones because they do not try again the response which has been outcompeted. The barrier habit of anxiety stands between the individual and those new trials which might lead to a more adaptive self. Even when the situations of adult life seem to the casual eye only remotely analogous to those of childhood, strong anxiety responses are attached to them by the neurotic, and thereby he feels that he is still facing the immutable outlines of his childhood life. The freer environment of adult life thus assumes some of the limiting and foreboding character of the environment of the neurotic child. The problem, then, is to strip the adult environment of the fearsome quality which it has by virtue of its supposed similarity to the world of childhood and to persuade the neurotic to take this freer, adult world on its own merits. The problem is in part a discrimination problem.[11]

As Freud has emphasized, discrimination is difficult when some forces in the mental conflict are unconscious (that is, unverbalized). Verbal labeling is important because it brings the repressed or condemned trend into the mental field of sorting and evaluation. Presumably, in mental conflict we juggle sentences which raise different apprehensions of future reward or punishment. The psychoanalyst therefore tries to find and label the unconscious or unverbalized elements in the neurotic's mental field. Without such verbal aids he cannot prop-

[11] Captain N. E. Miller (Army Air Corps) and I discussed this problem several years ago. It was he who pointed out to me the possible importance of the discrimination mechanism in relation to therapy. He and I once intended, and so far as I know still do intend, to make a joint attack on the problem of psychoanalytic therapy as learning.

More recently, in 1943-44, I have been working with Professor O. H. Mowrer of Harvard University on a somewhat analogous matter—that of the mechanisms operative in social case-work therapy. Our findings and discussions concerning casework will be separately published, but I am pleasantly aware of an immediate debt to him in aiding clarification of thought on our common problem, that is, the building of a useful and workable social psychology.

erly anticipate either danger or ecstasy. He cannot score and correct his own errors, as when a neurotic might learn to say, "Oh, I'm treating So-and-So as if he were my brother; but actually he behaves quite differently." Particularly likely to suffer repression are the strong emotional drives of the individual, and thus it occurs that the neurotic can hate or love or fear without knowing that he is doing so and without being able to discriminate those who are in fact fearsome from those who are endowed with fearsomeness by his neurotic anxiety.

This labeling activity differentiates psychoanalytic therapy from mere reassurance. Reassurance may bring relief, but after it the subject cannot "talk about it"; whereas, if behavior is to be really changed, talking to oneself is quite important since thus a person can give himself the reassuring lesson over and over again.[12]

Three of the drives found by psychoanalysts to be most regularly repressed are those of sex, aggression, and fear. The sex tendencies of the child are but rarely admitted into family discourse. Labeling may occur in the childhood playgroup but is prohibited within the family group. Aggressive tendencies are likewise discouraged within the family, and the individual is given to know that he should not feel, let alone express, such tendencies. The fears of childhood are not well understood by adults and are frequently not labeled; indeed, there may be a rewarding fear-reduction in the fact that one does not "think about" fearful situations. Thus, the neurotic may come to adulthood without knowing very accurately whom he loves, fears, or hates and may as a result show behavior which is incongruous and puzzling.

Freud was not at all unaware of the great importance of "words" and used to admonish his students not to forget how important words could be. That patient is more nearly well who has sentences to cover all of his wishes, fears, and hopes. He is able to predict the future more accurately, to behave more consistently, to judge all the forces and factors in his environment more realistically. The psychoanalyst tries

[12] One of the apparent functions of verbal labeling is to make small differences in the external environment highly discrete and conspicuous. Professor C. L. Hull has pointed out that counting can make the hundredth orange highly different from the ninety-ninth, even though the addition of this orange to the mass of the ninety-nine does not make a discriminable difference to the ordinary eye. Verbal cues when added to external cues therefore can create tremendous stimulus differences to which separate responses can be attached. One's wife, for instance, can be the spit and image of one's mother in physical fact and yet be highly different as a stimulus pattern because of the addition of verbal stimuli. It is for this reason that proper labeling can have the effect of making situations of adult life seem highly different from those of childhood life and can thus prevent transfer of anxiety and other responses from the childhood to the adult situation.

to produce the right sentences for his patient (but what an art to hit upon them!), and toss them into the sentence arsenal of his patient at just the right moment. The analyst must imaginatively perceive his patient's unconscious conflict, label it appropriately and recite the resultant labeling. He must use his prestige to help his patient resist the fright that appears when condemned trends must be labeled.

Psychoanalytic therapy can occur only in an environment which is more benign than that which produced the neurosis. The analyst himself is the first sign to the patient of this benign environment. He attempts to anticipate the rewards and punishments which will actually be forthcoming should the patient change his behavior. Since the patient neurotically expects the same severity in the adult environment which was present in the environment of childhood, the analyst can legitimately represent a more lenient picture. The analyst may reasonably assert, for instance, that though the neurotic's parents seemed to indicate that sex behavior was inappropriate under all circumstances, the adult world allows it and, indeed, demands it in the married state. Though aggression may have been tabooed under all circumstances by a tyrannical father, it cannot be so effectively suppressed by a tyrannical boss. The analyst acts as a kind of predictor of the normal demands on a normal adult. He owes this skill, incidentally, to his general social training and not to his medical school or Psychoanalytic Institute.

The labeling function of the analyst has a further value. Not only does it help to redefine the situation for the subject and to aid him in discriminating the adult world from the world of childhood, but it also has the overtone of permissiveness. Any behavior which an analyst is willing to label may be thought about by the patient and considered as a course of action. The analyst may label a course of action which might later bring the patient in conflict with the realities of his social life, but he leaves this eventual decision to the patient, knowing that the pressures of social reality will lead to a rejection of dangerous trends. Although the analyst does not say, "Do this" or "Do that," it must never be forgotten that the identification of unconscious trends carries permission at least to consider putting them into action.

The analyst behaves throughout as a labeling-machine for his patient—as a kind of Rorschach ink blot; he is not injecting his own peculiarities into the situation but instead is simply producing the sentences needed to aid the patient in solving his own problems. This is the famous "screen function" of the analyst.

The new sentences provided by the psychoanalyst are merely stimuli

ACQUISITION OF NEW SOCIAL HABITS

to possible courses of overt action. Although essential to such action and critical in the process of therapy, they are not themselves the new habits which bring relief from drive pressure. Real therapy can occur only when real rewards attend the new strivings. People actually "get well" not merely by labeling their wishes to make love but by making love in fact; not only by talking to themselves about an appropriate act of resistance, but by performing it; not by merely wishing for security and imagining the acts which might bring it, but by behaving consistently over time in such a way that money or status is accumulated; not by vainly discussing with themselves the means of social mobility, but by vigorously lopping from the personality those habits which interfere with it and laboriously acquiring the new habits which facilitate it. It might be added that though a neurotic does not get well *merely* by labeling he cannot get well at all without it.

From the anthropological standpoint, the neurotic person who manages a cure develops a newer, freer personal culture in place of his older, neurotic culture. This new personal culture cannot, however, go beyond the bounds of permissiveness of the culture of his society. Within every society there is a kind of band or zone within which individual behavior may deviate. The neurotic person deviates to the side of greatest personal inhibition and lack of use of cultural resources. The healthy person deviates in the other direction. He explores fully the field of culturally permitted behavior and takes advantage of all gratifying and constructive possibilities. The mores, however, exert their inexorable control on this outer limit of deviation. It follows, therefore, that a man cannot comfortably be psychoanalyzed into committing a crime such as murder because he would be blocked by society with its electric chair and hangman's rope.

Psychoanalytic therapy has to date been almost entirely a big-city therapy. Viewed as a trait, it seems to be spreading over the urban world of the West and now is beginning a successful penetration of the smaller urban areas. Perhaps the more liberal environment of urban life tends to set up conditions that favor the effectiveness of psychoanalytic therapy by providing an adult environment which is actually less rigorous than that of childhood. Perhaps its success is also connected with the weakening of religious sanctions. At any rate, strong defenders of sectarian beliefs tend to be among the main opponents of psychoanalysis.

Nor may it be a matter of indifference that a Jewish physician invented psychoanalysis. Because of a certain degree of exclusion and isolation in our society the Jews may also have a degree of objectivity toward it which more comfortable members do not have. In the bitter-clear perception of Freud there may have been also an element of aggression toward the traditional habits of the group. This touch of aggressive insight may have enabled Freud, a child of the society, to see how social customs could set up neurotic processes in the individual. In any case, his doctrine of the neurosis constitutes a major form of cultural criticism. Freud speaks for the naïve or natural man, warns society that this man has his conditions for social life and that if these are not for the most part met, a man cannot act as a burden-bearing member of society.[13]

Testimony as to the therapeutic effect of psychoanalytic procedures does differ,[14] but it may certainly be considered a useful method of correcting bad emotional habits.[15] In some cases, not too well understood theoretically, a briefer version of the long psychoanalysis is advised.[16] In all cases apparently the processes of learning by labeling remains a standard feature.

THE SITUATION OF THE CLINICAL GROUP

Clinical groups, that is, social groups, formed and led for the purpose of exercising a therapeutic function, are distinguished by their intent from, say, the social clique which has no planned purpose to change behavior. Specially led groups in which problem children are placed are clinical groups: [17] Alcoholics Anonymous [18] is a clinical group; the Oxford Movement [19] provides a series of shifting clinical groups.

[13] Sigmund Freud, *Civilization and Its Discontents* (New York, 1930), pp. 135-36.
[14] Harold Thomas Hyman, "The Value of Psychoanalysis as a Therapeutic Procedure," *Journal of the American Medical Association*, CVII (1936), 326-29; Gerald R. Jameison and Edwin E. McNiel, "Some Unsuccessful Reactions with Psychoanalytic Therapy," *American Journal of Psychiatry*, XCV (1938-39), 1421-48.
[15] Robert P. Knight, "Evaluation of the Results of Psychoanalytic Therapy," *American Journal of Psychiatry*, XCVIII (1941-42), 437-39; *Five-Year Report, 1932-1937* (Institute for Psychoanalysis, Chicago, Illinois), pp. 31-39.
[16] Oskar Diethelm, "Brief Psychotherapy" (paper presented at the meeting of the American Neurological Association, 1944; now in press).
[17] S. R. Slavson, and others, "Group Therapy: Special Section Meeting 1943," *American Journal of Orthopsychiatry*, XIII (1943), 648-90; S. R. Slavson, "Group Therapy," *Mental Hygiene*, II (1940), 36-49.
[18] *Alcoholics Anonymous* (New York, 1939); Walter A. Thompson, "The Treatment of Chronic Alcoholism," *American Journal of Psychiatry*, XCVIII (1941-42), pp. 846-56.
[19] Irving G. Benson, *The Eight Points of the Oxford Group* (London, 1936); R. A. E. Holme, *The Oxford Group, Its Progress and Principles* (London, 1934); V. C.

While the theory of the teaching efficiency of the clinical group is not well worked out, I see no reason why it does not follow the main lines already indicated here. The final test of any therapy is acceptance of the treated individual by his group. In this sense every therapy, including psychoanalytic therapy, is a group therapy. As already emphasized, if the group does not reward the person treated, no stable changes in behavior can be anticipated.

Let us take the case of the clinical group set-up for dealing with problem children.[20] The factor of drive must be present in that the children must have some desire, conscious or unconscious, to participate with others and to be approved by them. If this desire is weak or absent, new responses cannot be elicited because a child will refuse group participation. The neutral leader of the group accepts the behavior of the maladjusted child, whatever it may be, and leaves the eventual correction of the child's behavior to the pressures exerted by the group of other children. If the child be anxious, the neutrality of the leader (that is, his lack of punishing character) permits the child to bring forth and test out his antisocial responses or irrational projections. Such lack of punishment is accepted by the child as proof of love by powerful adults.

Presumably the child at first tries out responses which are not acceptable to the other children in the group and is punished, or at least not rewarded, for these. No real integration of an individual child into the group can be secured while he is behaving in a manner contrary to the moral order of the group, and in this connection it must be remembered that the child wishes full participation and acceptance.

If deviant or neurotic responses do not "work," a child begins to score his own behavior as "good" or "bad" according to group standards. He begins to imitate and copy some preferred group member and as he does so begins to produce the responses which can be rewarded by group approval and acceptance. He learns just when what may be done. He is rewarded for inhibiting unacceptable responses and hitting upon acceptable ones by the free approval and acceptance of the other children in the group. Not least of the rewards associated with group acceptance is a marked reduction of the anxiety which burdens the lonely deviant. Most persons learn early in life that it is punishing to be the odd one. Perception of difference between one's

---

Kitchen, *I Was a Pagan* (New York, 1934); Philip Leon, *The Philosophy of Courage, or The Oxford Group Way* (London, 1939).
[20] S. R. Slavson, "Group Therapy," *Mental Hygiene*.

own behavior and that of others in one's group acquires strong anxiety value; whereas perception of sameness acquires reward value.[21] The copying of other's behavior in the group situation functions in somewhat the same way as the interpretation does in the psychoanalytic interview. The subject apparently says to himself, "What has worked for others may work for me," though it is not critical that these interstitial mental links be present. In any case, the novel behavior item must be acted out and rewarded if a new habit is to result.

In the case of psychoanalysis the individual has to hit upon new lines of behavior in the analytic interview and thereafter test them out in group life. In the case of the clinical group, this reaction of approval or disapproval is direct and immediate. In the clinical group of children, play materials are provided which enable the children to "act out" their needs and wishes. In the adult clinical group, such as that formed by Schilder[22] the leader plays the same neutral role but the subjects report verbally on their conflicts and experiences. Here again, the wish to be well is essential—the very wish which brings the person into the group. Likewise, isolation anxiety is reduced by the permissive presence of the leader and the self-revealing confessions of other members of the group. The frightened individual feels "They cannot punish me for what they have done themselves." This reduction of anxiety is one of the strong rewards for confession in such a group.

However, in the adult clinical group modeled on psychoanalytic theory the verbal elements play a much greater role. The admissions and confessions of other members of the group have somewhat the effect of a "hit and miss" series of interpretations. One member of the group may, for instance, confess to a fear of heights. A second may express a similar fear but note that he does not have this fear in an airplane where he is sure that he cannot jump out of the plane. A third may realize that he is not afraid in tall buildings which are securely glass-enclosed but is much afraid if there is nothing to prevent his jumping off. A fourth with the same fear of heights may suddenly recognize that the real problem is his own wish to jump off the high place, that is, that behind his fear of a high place is the fear of a strong suicidal wish.

This is the sort of interpretation which might be swiftly and ac-

[21] Miller and Dollard, *Social Learning and Imitation*, pp. 155-63.
[22] Paul Schilder, "The Analysis of Ideologies as a Psychotherapeutic Method, Especially in Group Treatment," *American Journal of Psychiatry*, XCIII (1936), 601.

curately made by a psychoanalyst confronted with the same data in an individual case. The further question "Why the suicidal wish?" would probably occur to the individual who had learned this much. But this question cannot be answered in the group therapeutic situation, since the leader himself does not make interpretations of behavior. If the individual must have this question answered in order to be comfortable he would have to seek more searching and systematic personal aid. Nevertheless, many people may experience considerable relief from applying such a notion to their own cases.

The behavior changes produced in a group like Alcoholics Anonymous probably follow much the same fundamental processes, although the apparent apparatus of behavior change is somewhat different. The initial step is to excite in the alcoholic a lively belief in God which probably functions in somewhat the same way as the transference to the analyst or the identification with the group leader. Belief in the loving care of God may help the alcoholic to combat the first and worst of his symptoms—his alcoholism. If he can at least temporarily stop drinking, the stage is set for the appearance of other responses.

A type of self-analysis or a "fearless moral inventory" [23] is urged upon the members of this group. It is possible that some insight may be obtained by this means. By "insight" I mean that the individual may learn to label some of his previously unknown behavior tendencies.

Since alcoholics have usually damaged others in no inconsiderable way they bear a burden of guilt about past behavior which may inhibit their attempts at a better adjustment in the future. Reducing this guilt is therefore essential. They are advised to consider the persons whom they have wronged and make such amends as are possible, thus perhaps not only reducing guilt but also putting the persons in their immediate environment in a more favorable mood toward them.

The new habits of self-study, helpfulness and, above all, avoidance of drinking are reinforced by a strong clique relationship of mutually helpful persons. Membership in Alcoholics Anonymous always places the alcoholic in a group where his behavior is at once policed to guard against backsliding and is rewarded in specific ways. In group meetings comparisons of autobiographic details can reduce the individual's isolation anxiety. New friends, sometimes socially advantageous friends, can be made. There is always a place for a member to go where a congenial companion can be found. Joint recreational projects help to

[23] Thompson, "The Treatment of Chronic Alcoholism," p. 852.

bulwark and stabilize the formerly alcoholic individual. Since it is sometimes the lack of such group approval which has driven him to drink in the first place, the presence of group support tends to reward nonalcoholic habits. Several members of Alcoholics Anonymous whom I interviewed reported a peculiar inversion of a familiar type of competition among drinkers. Instead of competing to see who had the greatest capacity to hold liquor they compete to see who can stay on the wagon the longest. Such a competition tends to make group members the innocent policemen who scrutinize one's behavior and criticize deviation from the narrow path.

The Oxford Movement,[24] though not directed to the problem of the alcoholic, apparently uses, perforce, very much the same mechanisms. Anxiety is reduced by stressing the importance of belief in Divine protection, guidance, and personal inspiration. Members take time regularly for self-analysis wherein they may hit upon a better understanding of their behavior trends. The occasional practice of the group confessional may both reduce the isolation of the lonely member and suggest to him new ways of formulating his own tendencies to act. As in Alcoholics Anonymous, guilt-reducing responses are tried out. Restitution to others for injuries done them is attempted and guilt over past misdeeds allayed. Most important of all, perhaps, is the fact that the convert coming into an Oxford Group has an opportunity to join a clique with social prestige and actual possibilities of real-world helpfulness. Group approval of the new member, even in the face of past sinfulness, is accorded but, of course, only so long as more constructive tendencies prevail in his current life.

Both Alcoholics Anonymous and the Oxford Group stress that every person has a chance to reform and that if he will but produce the adaptive responses desired the past will be forgotten and he will be taken at the value of his new behavior and rewarded therefor. And in the case of both groups there is always the possibility that the rewards for new habits will not compete successfully with those offered by the older habits of drinking and "sinful gratification." In this case, the new habits will be infirm and may extinguish entirely; thus the member becomes a "backslider."

A moment of comparison between psychoanalytic therapy and these group therapies may be in point. The psychoanalyst is superior in the precision of his labeling and the exactness of his implied suggestions

[24] Benson, *The Eight Points of the Oxford Group;* Holme, *The Oxford Group.*

for action. He is weak, so to speak, in group approval. The patient in analysis still has his group to confront and can never be sure, until he tries it out, that the psychoanalyst has correctly forecasted the reaction of this group. Group therapy, on the contrary, is superior in that it delivers immediate approval for acceptable behavior trends. It is weak, however, in that the interpretations suggested by the behavior of the imitated leader or the confessions of fellow members are accidental and lacking in precision. The group sometimes may not provide just that unit of labeling which is essential for a permanent modification of an individual's behavior.

In recent times, physical,[25] chemical,[26] surgical,[27] and electric shock[28] techniques have been used as means of changing behavior, especially in the serious mental illnesses. These devices will not be discussed here because they are not well understood theoretically. It is not clear, to me at least, how reconditioning or learning is involved. Perhaps learning is not involved and new hypotheses will have to be devised to cover the efficacy of these techniques.

MODIFICATION OF GROUP RIVALRIES

Herewith are some fragmentary propositions on the difficult and timely theme of social prejudices. No individual can be expected to change his attitude toward an ethnic group unless at the same time the group to which he belongs and is responsible simultaneously changes its attitude. No ordinary white citizen can defy caste etiquette against the Negro and prosper in a Southern community. He would be promptly isolated, to his own acute discomfort and social and professional disadvantage. A member of a group prejudiced against Jews must listen passively to invidious remarks directed against Jewish people. If he makes himself distinctive by protest he immediately puts a

---

[25] Winfred Overholser, "Physical Therapy in Psychiatric Practice," *Journal of the American Medical Association*, CXXIII (1943), 32-35; Edmund Jacobson, *Progressive Relaxation* (Chicago, 1929).
[26] R. D. Gillespie, "Narcosis Therapy: Critical Review," *Journal of Neurological Psychiatry*, II (1939), 45; H. D. Palmer and F. J. Braceland, "Six Years Experience with Narcosis Therapy in Psychiatry," *American Journal of Psychiatry*, XCIV (1937), 35-37.
[27] Gosta Rylander, *Personality Changes after Operations on the Frontal Lobes* (London, 1939).
[28] B. L. Pacella and S. E. Barrera, "Follow-Up Study of a Series of Patients Treated by Electrically Induced Convulsions and by Metrazol Convulsions," *American Journal of Psychiatry*, XCIX (1942-43), 518; Nathaniel J. Berkwitz, "Non-Convulsive Electric (Faradic) Shock Therapy of Psychoses Associated with Alcoholism, Drug Intoxication and Syphilis," *American Journal of Psychiatry*, XCIX (1942-43), 365.

"distance" between himself and other members of his subsociety. Such distance can be a very punishing affair since it brings in its train social and personal punishment. Therefore the effort to recondition individuals, one by one, to free them from anti-Negro, or anti-Semitic sentiments is likely to be futile. The real controls of individual opinion are exercised by the intimate social group to which the individual belongs, and these cannot be blithely supplanted by mere mass propaganda. This is what some observers mean when they say that "Prejudice is in the air we breathe." Prejudice is not in the air but in the social environment which punishes us when we make any other than prejudiced responses.

Prejudiced reactions exerted by individuals tend, therefore, to reduce to the rivalries and antipathies which exist between subgroups in the society.[29] Competition between social classes leads to derogatory labeling and hostility. Prejudice between castes is exhibited in epithets and restrictions on behavior. Prejudice against ethnic minorities is revealed in the scorn for them expressed by such terms as "Sheeny," "Shanty Irish," "Wop," "Polack," and the like.

There seems to be little general social concern about competition between social classes and there is no visible effort to reduce it. But prejudice against the Negro caste and the ethnic minority can be so vigorous and violent as to provoke continued conflict in the consciences of members of the American in-group. Let us take as a case in point the chronic anti-Semitism of Western European societies. While this form of prejudice may be relatively weak in the United States, it is nevertheless still a social fact. We must note first that this prejudice has an historical basis. It is a kind of culture pattern rooted in theological controversy and in the dispersed nationalism of the Jew. It is an inheritance from our European sources of culture diffusion.

The Jew coming into American society is likely to be highly visible because of his dietary habits, which preclude ordinary social participation at meals, and because of various religious customs, such as the observance of a day of rest on Saturday. Thanks partly to their enforced isolation from Christian culture during centuries past, Jews have also formed a community of sentiment and a kind of defensive-

[29] The point of view in this section is based upon the forthcoming volume by W. L. Warner and Leo Srole, *The Social Systems of American Ethnic Groups* (The Yankee City Series, Volume III, Yale University Press; in press). It is further based on the general point of view which has been originated by Professor Warner and was expressed in Volumes I and II of the Yankee City Series.

aggressive alliance which tends at once to make them conspicuous and strange in American society. Thanks also to their schooling in a European urban environment, many Jews are likely to be successful in the urban occupations in this country and thus attain that element of visibility which comes from success in economic competition.[30] In times of fullness and peace when the American structure is functioning at its best as an open-class structure, there is little tendency to utilize the Jew as a target of social aggression. When, however, the system begins to freeze or when particular subsections of the society are disadvantaged, a kind of internal aggression arises. Since it is dangerous to express this aggression against the power-holders within the society, it is very likely to be displaced on some convenient target. This is perhaps the case today. The penalties of war are being differentially assessed against different social segments. The white-collar group seems to be taking a relative beating. Its renunciations are not being differentially rewarded. Its hope of security is being reduced; its fear of tumbling back into a lower-class status is heightened. As a result, the white-collar class is a group very likely to produce marked social aggression.

In such a case, hostility probably tends to flow through the permissive outlets which already exist. If some hostility is permitted against Jews in normal times and if exceptional circumstances occur which generate great fear and hostility in a subgroup, such hostility may flow through the existing channels of least resistance. Any forms of hostile behavior against the social order, such as riot or revolution, evoke punishment signals which compete with the aggressive responses. In the case of aggression against the Jew or the Negro, however, these punishment signals are relatively weak. For this reason there is a basis for our common alarm at the possible rise of strong anti-Semitic or anti-Negro feelings. One obvious counsel to give to an ethnic group in danger of becoming the target of displaced aggression is to reduce its conspicuousness in every way possible. Such a process has indeed been going on in this country. Many Jews are today not differentiated from other Americans in regard to food or essential religious habits. A change of this kind cannot occur quickly, but the attempt of the Jew to integrate himself into American life has already brought about this change to a considerable degree. The reduction of stimulus visibility of the Jew is advised on the ground that you cannot hate a man as a representative of a group stereotype unless you can recognize who he is.

[30] Warner and Srole, *op. cit.*

It is the sad fate of the Negro that reduction in such visibility is impossible for him.

Sanctions against manifestations of anti-Semitism are useful and must be continued, although they, in turn, have the disadvantage of calling wide public attention to the ethnic group in whose behalf they are invoked. Such sanctions can be particularly important when they are not merely matters of law and police regulation but matters of convention and intimate control of sentiment. The existence of sanctions of a police or economic sort may be effective in that they prevent overt manifestations of group aggression and avert crowdlike summation of such hostilities. They are ineffectual in that they do not get at the latent, informal bases of control.

It should be helpful for those in the favored group to have as much rewarding personal contact as possible with the prejudiced-against group. Such contacts in childhood gangs, in school or business, can at least create a proper ambivalence in those belonging to groups with strong prejudices. A familiar example of this ambivalence is the remark by a gentile, "Some of my best friends are Jews." Although Jews often and properly resent this type of statement they should note that it does contain a strong positive element. If the positive tendencies toward Jewish friends can be made strong enough by rewarding contacts, they decrease expressions of hostility. After all, one cannot be hostile against some of one's "best friends." When social contact between groups helps, this is the way it must function; it must be rewarding contact. Mere looking at a person belonging to a minority group, mere awareness of his existence, may serve only to identify the victim of prejudice more clearly. Since for most children teachers represent a prestigeful group in the society, propaganda against anti-Semitism by teachers may be useful. The difficulty, of course, is in getting the teachers to conduct such propaganda when as individuals they may be members of groups which are anti-Semitic. Since public school teachers are largely lower-middle class people, this is indeed a very difficult condition to meet. If the children are subject to counterteaching in their families or cliques, it will be very difficult for the teacher to lodge effective unprejudiced opinions in her pupils. Only when the teacher is supported by the home and the play-group of children can her doctrines have much effect.

Perhaps the most positive mechanism, if it could be managed, would be the example and influence of leaders at the top of our society. If they

ACQUISITION OF NEW SOCIAL HABITS

consistently oppose anti-Semitism privately as well as publicly the problem might really be seriously affected. But do they? Are Jews as Jews admitted to the top cliques and intimate symbolic associations? Is intermarriage not opposed on the highest as well as the lowest social levels? Do law firms and banks not continue a subtle policy of discrimination? Are Jews not rationed in the colleges and universities of highest symbolic significance? I think the answer to every one of these questions would reveal that anti-Semitism, perhaps of an indirect kind, is a matter of fact among the social leaders of America. Since only they can apply the most stringent, informal sanctions against anti-Semitic beliefs, the outlook is not good for making anti-Semitism unconventional. At the present time only occasional dissenters are willing to pay the price in social isolation and can thus afford to be informally and intimately defiant of anti-Semitic prejudices. Perhaps the leaders of our society will renounce the incidental benefits which the "scapegoat" mechanism may have for them; perhaps they will recognize the dangers of irrational aggression to them and to the social system as a whole; perhaps they will still more seriously make the attempt to reduce factors promoting internal friction and aggression. In this case we may hope that they will also put their powerful taboos on the phenomena of race and ethnic prejudice.

I do not see any ready hope for control of the mass phenomenon of anti-Semitism by reconditioning the individual, but he who wishes to put his force against this vicious form of displaced aggression may consider this advice: Do what you can to keep the American system an open-class system. Keep the public schools at a high level so that the talented may have a chance to improve their skills and better their social positions. Keep a liberal administration in power which will find the means to give to the masses the benefits of our present productive capacity. In particular, have concern for the goals and frustrations of the white-collar workers who are rivalrous toward all competitors and especially those successful and visible competitors, the Jews.

But if the Jews remain conspicuous, if social cleavages occur, if aggression is thus generated, if suppression fails, if social leaders do not taboo prejudice, then anti-Semitism and other antiethnic movements are inevitable. Against such massive processes one cannot work very effectively by the indirect means of books, radio or periodicals. What counts is the private behavior of the group members in intimate situations. As long as these social forces tend to reward anti-Semitic expressions and feelings, all other attempts to extirpate them are bound to be ineffectual. In a group so disposed, even an intimate knowledge of unconscious sources of anti-Semitism will only serve to transmute an individual from a strongly prejudiced potential leader to a more or less passive follower.

Individuals can be reconditioned when the social and personal circumstances are favorable to the formation of new habits. The search for effective therapies, therefore, is a search for the conditions which will generate new and desired habits. Dangerous prejudice reactions can best be dealt with by controlling the social conditions which produce aggression.

Communications Research and International Coöperation

By PAUL F. LAZARSFELD *and* GENEVIEVE KNUPFER

IN THE LAST hundred years the world has become much smaller because of the rapid development of communications. We may expect a continuation of this trend after the war, for technological progress in communications is continuing. The fact that people all over the world are being drawn closer together creates an urgent problem, since nothing could be more erroneous than the assumption that being close necessarily means being friendly. The facilitation of communications causes an increase in the intensity of interaction between people but does not determine the quality of their relationships. There may be more coöperation or more conflict. The control of conflict, especially armed conflict, becomes, therefore, increasingly imperative for human survival. How can communications help us to cope with the dangers communications have aggravated? By communication we mean the conveyance of symbols by radio, print, or film. We know that these media are powerful devices for influencing public opinion. A single film can change the hair-do of a large proportion of the young girls in a country. The radio determines what songs are popular in every dance hall of the land. A few articles in popular magazines can bring a man to national prominence. The influence of mass media is particularly effective in the presentation and popularization of concrete symbols. It is our thesis that in the international field, too, mass media will be most effective when they focus upon a positive program of action. Such a focus can only be a world organization of nations, an international authority. The contribution of these media to international coöperation will only be effective if we conceive it frankly in terms of a public relations program for an international authority and apply to it all the knowledge we have acquired of popularization efforts in private and domestic areas.

A similar restatement of the problem suggests itself from still another point of view. In the past, the two main approaches to promoting international cooperation have been to teach people to know and understand other nations and to make them hate war. But it has turned out that this was not enough. We are not fighting the Japanese because they wear kimonos and sit on the floor. In fact, people who know and understand each other well may be able to wage war the more effectively. As for the hatred of war, the last few years have shown us that unwillingness to go to war on the part of some nations may operate merely to encourage aggression on the part of others. The social and psychological forces impelling rivalry between nations are too strong to be controlled by a vague allegiance to "all men everywhere," or to the ideal of "international cooperation." It seems that a concrete international authority is needed around which people can build up new identifications and supranational loyalties.

Once such a development has started, the media of mass communication can be used to build up something like an educational campaign the purpose of which is to make the international authority (hereafter symbolized as IA) accepted as part of everyday thinking, to give it prestige, to see that as many people as possible are intimately acquainted with its functions. The promotion of respect and sympathy among nations finds its place in this scheme because people cannot accept equality with other nations before international law unless they have learned some respect and sympathy for them.

The presentation of such a program depends, of course, on the particular psychological situation in each country and among different groups in each country. We know in general what some of the favorable and unfavorable attitudes will be. The desire for peace is strong and the experience of this war will make people eager to avoid another. The ideal of unity has a long tradition in liberal thought as well as in Christianity. On the other hand, the belief in the right of national sovereignty is also strong, especially among the more powerful nations, and the history of the first League of Nations is not one to inspire confidence. Internationalism has an unpleasant sound to various groups who associate it with Communism, Imperialism, or Judaism. The attitudes and prejudices of each audience must be determined and taken into consideration.

Obviously, the content of the program must also be guided by actual world conditions. If opposition to the creation of any kind of IA proves so strong that not even a rudimentary world authority comes into being after the war, educators who seek to popularize the idea of international coöperation may well have to begin their work by using a weaker symbol than the IA in order to secure support for a preliminary and tentative kind of world association. If, on the other hand, a forceful and democratic IA does actually come into being, our educational program will resolve itself into the simpler task of informing people of its functions and winning support for its activities. More likely, some kind of IA will exist but will be full of weaknesses and perhaps injustices. An important element of our program will then be an effort to make the individuals of various nations see that these weaknesses do not negate the value of the IA, to win support for a stronger IA, and perhaps to suggest ways in which the IA can be strengthened. It would be rather difficult to attempt to foresee more specifically what such a campaign would consist of. But it is possible and useful to speculate on what agencies will be involved in running it and what problems they will meet in their use of media of mass communication. Three different types of organizations will probably be concerned. First, there will almost certainly be a number of private associations similar to the Women's International League for Peace and Freedom, the Foreign Policy Association, and the Free World Association which will support the IA and which at the same time will try to offer wholesome and constructive criticism of its policies. For convenience, we will call such associations "Friends of the IA." Second, the various national governments may be active in using communications for the promotion of international coöperation. Third, the IA itself will undoubtedly have some educational or propaganda committee such as the Intellectual Coöperation Organization of the League of Nations.[1]

Friends of the IA. Such groups are often able to marshal public opinion and bring pressure to bear quite effectively. (For example, the American League of Decency—a Catholic organization formed to eliminate "obscenity" from American movies—has, for example, exerted considerable influence on the content and presentation of United States films.) In order to get a hearing these groups first must have access to radio and other media of mass communication. Their access to radio time will depend partly on the quality of their programs and the size of the audiences they can reach. Here they can benefit by the experience of educators with the problem of audiences. It has been

[1] The Intellectual Cooperation Organization of the League of Nations forms one of the League's four technical organizations; the others are Health, Communications and Transit, and Economic and Financial.

found that people are more likely to listen to serious broadcasts when such listening is suggested to them by organizations in which they trust. A great part of the listeners to serious broadcasts in the United States are members of the Y.M.C.A., of farm organizations or of parent-teachers organizations, where listening is made part of the duties of the conscientious member. At the same time local organizations are held together more easily when one of their national leaders has a regular radio program which becomes the nucleus for weekly meetings all over the country. The use of such listening groups to strengthen organizations and at the same time to build up audiences for serious programs has long been recognized as an outstanding device by people active in adult education. In Great Britain, Sweden, Canada, and America many thousands of people are organized in such listener groups. For the Friends of the IA a study of these experiences will be very useful.

But as long as the group is weak it may have a hard time getting such public hearings; in that case, some additional help from a central source may be necessary. A bold reminder from a spokesman for the IA would usually find a willing ear with officials of networks and broadcasting corporations holding public charters and therefore sensitive to reminders that they are supposed to act in the public interest.[2] Newspapers are less centralized and are usually less subject to public regulation, but their space is open to news and news can be made. Visits from prominent leaders in the IA or awards given to the local friends of the IA could well be the starting point for a campaign to direct attention to the activities of the group. The progress of frequency modulation will be helpful to the development of serious broadcasting programs. For technical reasons FM broadcasting makes possible a much larger number of local stations than can be operated in ordinary broadcasting. When there are numerous local stations, there will be more chance to satisfy the tastes of minorities and to try out programs which may not be immediately popular.

National governments. National governments have often engaged in promoting good relations with other countries, traditionally by diplo-

---

[2] This is not to say that those in control of broadcasting would necessarily be antagonistic to the IA. They may in fact start educational campaigns in its favor on their own initiative. A precedent for this type of campaign may be established by CBS, which is planning a series of broadcasts to be entitled the Versailles Series, designed to inform the American public on the reasons for the failure of the Wilsonian ideal. See *Variety*, July 5, 1944, p. 1.

matic representation. As public opinion becomes more important and includes a larger proportion of the population, other methods, designed to reach larger audiences, become necessary. Public relations experts are employed. The aid of the press is enlisted. For example, the French newspaper *Le Temps* with the encouragement of the British foreign office published a special edition on the British Empire in July, 1939, on the occasion of the visit to France of the British sovereigns. Before the present World War international broadcasting was infrequent; but it has become a regular activity of all countries, and is in most cases controlled by the government of a country from which the broadcasting is sent. Even the United States Government has entered the field since the war began and now broadcasts about 500 hours a week in thirty languages to practically all countries of the world. Such broadcasts will probably remain as a regular and important institution in most countries. From an administrative point of view they will present two problems.

In the first place, in countries where the domestic broadcasting is done by private corporations should the foreign broadcasting also be done by private industry or by the government or by a combination of the two? The United States, for whom this question will become urgent, will find itself in an interesting conflict between two basic principles. We consider foreign affairs a prerogative of the Federal Government, but at the same time we consider freedom of communications an inalienable right of the private citizen. The solution of the conflict will be a major legislative problem of the near future.[3]

The second administrative problem is what access should one government have to the eyes and ears of the people in another country? Printed material and films can be held up at the border, but radio programs from neighboring countries cannot be stopped. As long as one country tries merely to extoll its own virtues, the situation is simple. However, when it comes to endorsement of the activities of the IA, difficult problems may arise. Governments that are in disagreement with the policy of the IA would not like to have their own citizens pitted against their official policy. Here new problems of international law and regulations somewhat similar to those governing the Red Cross or to the disarmament agreements will have to be worked out.

[3] For discussion of problems in the administration of international cable radio and telephone facilities, see an article on "U.S. and World Communications" in *Fortune Magazine*, May, 1944.

The International Authority. The IA itself will undoubtedly have some educational or propaganda committee. It is to be hoped that this will conduct a vigorous program for the promotion of international coöperation. Two main lines of approach may be envisaged: an attempt can be made to influence the existing flow of communications or an independent program can be set up. A beginning was made in both these areas by the League of Nations. An illustration of the first approach is provided by several resolutions on textbook revision which were adopted by the League. A resolution adopted in 1925 outlined a procedure for textbook revision to be initiated by the national committees of the Intellectual Coöperation Organization whenever they found that a foreign text intended for use in schools conveyed "wrong impressions leading to an essential misunderstanding" concerning their own countries. In 1932 the resolution was extended to include not only history texts but texts on the history of civilization, geography, civics and morals, as well as anthologies and readers. Criteria for the examination of school manuals were proposed at the Paris meeting of the Moral Education Congress in 1930. Objectivity and impartiality in the treatment of other nations were advocated and it was also urged that contemporary histories give instruction about the League and that they support international law. Little was actually accomplished but a sound idea was launched.

Some independent use of communications for promoting international coöperation was also carried on by the League. A committee on Arts and Letters organized "conversations" between representatives of world thought on such questions as the future of European thought, art and the state, the training of modern man. Each "conversation" was published. Studies on international relations, on teaching international coöperation, on the educational role of broadcasting and of the press were also made and published. It will be noted that the chief communications medium used by the League was the printing of books. As an independent source of communications the League did not make use of modern mass communications. The possibilities still to be developed here are many: the IA might have its own radio broadcasts, its own press service, it might publish a daily newspaper as well as several magazines, and it might produce films. Only by means of radio can the IA be really independent of other powers in control of communications media. Of course, it will have to obtain allocation of wave lengths by international agreement, but aside from that it can broadcast directly to the listener in any country. Any publication or film, on the other hand, will need active coöperation on the part of the national government in order to reach its audience.

Even if the IA had its own transmitter, however, and could broadcast its own radio programs, problems in dealing with other powers would arise. In countries where reception from that transmitter was difficult the IA would want to have its programs relayed locally from point-to-point transmission,[4] a practice which is becoming increasingly widespread. In such a case arrangements would of course have to be made with local stations and the IA would become dependent on the agent in control; in some countries this would be the national government, in others private corporations. It would probably be inadvisable, however, for the IA to rely exclusively on point-to-point broadcasting, since such broadcasting can be barred from the nationals of any country by their government.

Much depends, then, in considering a program for promoting international coöperation, on what the IA will be allowed to do and will be furnished the necessary funds to do. Since all the money to support it will have to come from the different nations, the national governments themselves will be able to decide the character and scope of the promotion program. The different national governments as well as private organizations will be able to threaten the IA program either by political pressure or by controlling communications media. We cannot foresee how such problems will be handled or what the balance of power will be.

We now have the picture of a number of agencies which will be concerned with using media of mass communication for the express purpose of gaining popular support for their way of looking at things and for the program of the International Authority. What help can we expect from the social scientists? The answer lies in a discipline of communications research which has developed only recently from three roots. The social scientists, themselves, in their quest for objective indices of social behavior have become interested in mass media. To increase understanding of the new immigrant population, Robert E. Park studied the foreign language press.[5] Hornell Hart, when called

---

[4] Point-to-point transmission is narrow-beam broadcasting suitable for rebroadcasting but not for reception by the average receiving set.
[5] Robert E. Park, *The Immigrant Press and Its Control* (New York, 1922).

upon to examine recent social trends in public attitudes took recourse to an elaborate study of magazines.[6] When Raymond V. Bowers looked for an index from which to study cultural diffusion he chose the number of radio amateurs in different parts of the country.[7] These are just a few examples and do not include the more informal use which anthropologists have always made of recorded documents.

The second root stems from the activities of American business. When large nation-wide concerns developed they had to find ways of keeping in contact with their consumers as objects of advertising as well as of their public relations policies. At least a thousand million dollars a year are spent this way and it is therefore not surprising that the business organization tried to collect all available knowledge on the working and effectiveness of mass media.

The third root springs from the soil of changes in the world political situation. Everywhere the importance of central governments has increased. In the Fascist countries the dictators sought additional means to keep their peoples in line. In democratic countries where increasing economic and international difficulties forced a central government into stronger leadership, governments sought ways to assure the participation of the people. Therefore an increasing amount of public money was spent investigating what could be done with the media of mass communication.

These three roots merged finally in a discipline of communications research which has now taken on rather standardized forms. The formula that in this area we study "what is said, by whom, to whom, and with what effect" via radio, print, or film has been suggested. Accordingly, the whole field can be divided into four sections:

a Audience analysis (to whom is the communication addressed?);
b Content analysis (what is being said?);
c Response analysis (with what effect?);
d Analysis of social control (who is saying it?).

The purpose of the rest of this paper is to review briefly the techniques prevailing and some of the results obtained in this new field of research. Hardly anything is yet known on an international plane but

[6] Hornell Hart, "Changing Social Attitudes and Interests," in *Recent Social Trends in the United States* (New York, 1933).
[7] Raymond V. Bowers, "The Direction of Intra-Societal Diffusion," *American Sociological Review* (Dec., 1907) and "Differential Intensity of Intra-Societal Diffusion," *American Sociological Review*, III (1938), 21–31.

STUDYING THE AUDIENCE

we have tried to stress the implications for a future field of international communications research.

Any agency seeking to influence public opinion must reckon with the potential audience. No audience, no effects. Where communication is free the audience is self-selective. Those who choose to listen or read, do so because they expect satisfactions, and those who would be heard must shape their messages accordingly. This applies to those who would promote international coöperation as much as to those who advertise to sell toothpaste. Basically, what each would like to know about the audience is the same. Because the questions arise in a different setting, they take a slightly different form. However when it comes to methods of audience research, much can be borrowed from American experience.

By audience we mean, of course, people who are reached by mass media; newspapers, magazines, pamphlets, movies, or radio programs. Incidentally, even the seemingly elementary matter of establishing the size of an audience involves a number of difficult problems. For example, the *Saturday Evening Post* and *Life Magazine* have approximately the same circulation—that is, the same number of copies of each are sold. But *Life* has at least twice as many readers, because a single copy is more often passed along to a number of people. Furthermore, the audience of both magazines is a shifting one. The composition of the audience changes from issue to issue. There is a similar problem in connection with radio programs. Fairly reliable methods have been developed to determine by periodic surveys how many people listen to a given program at a given time. A very successful educational program may reach only five percent of the adult population at a given time, whereas one of the popular comedians commands an audience of about one third of all sets in the country. Important speeches of the President have ratings as high as 60 percent and over. But from one day to the next the audience may change, and within a period of a month, two or three times as many people may have listened to one installment of a series as listen to an isolated broadcast. When it comes to the measurement of film audiences, box office reports on movie attendance should be, theoretically, the simplest counting index, but unfortunately these are never published; they are considered trade secrets, partly because they are an important weapon in the perpetual controversies between producers, distributors, and exhibitors of films.

We do not want to go into the technicalities of these audience measurement devices here, but rather to look at some of the more general results which may be derived from an analysis of their findings.[8]

Availability of communications. The audience reached by communications is chiefly determined by how easily the latter are available. This can be shown in many ways. For instance, experiments have been made in which students were asked to list the kind of books they were most interested in. The books were then set up on different levels of availability. Some could be obtained in the students' dormitory; others were in a general reading room; another group could be found in the library; and some of the books were issued only with special permits. According to this experiment the actual reading of the students followed much more closely the pattern of availability than the personal preferences that had previously been expressed.

Corresponding observations have been made extensively in the field of radio. People acquire certain listening habits in regard to time as well as to station. Consequently they are much more likely to listen to a program which is on at an habitual listening time than to one of their favorite programs if it comes at an unaccustomed time; this can be shown by a study of audience reactions if, in an experimental situation, several of the programs are given in succession. This fact is further illustrated by the varying audiences which the same program attracts at different times. The great importance of broadcasting at the time when people are available has led to some of the first international audience studies, conducted by the British Broadcasting Corporation among others. For example, mealtimes vary widely from one country to another and are closely related to people's listening habits. Even within America, broadcasters must take into careful account the different living habits of urban and rural populations.

Self-selection of audiences. After availability, one of the most important factors is the tendency of all audiences to listen to or read only

[8] All these techniques are so new that in most cases one must go to original studies in order to know the details of their operation. In the field of radio there is now a general presentation, which, however, is considerably biased in the direction of a specific method in which the authors are themselves commercially engaged: Chappell and Hooper, *Audience Measurement*, New York, 1944. Many of the major magazine studies are concentrated in the hands of the Magazine Audience Group (the chairman is Theodore H. Brown of the Harvard University School of Business from whom material can be obtained). The best source for newspaper research is the Advertising Research Foundation in New York City.

those communications with which they agree. A good opportunity to test this fact is furnished by political campaigns in democratic countries where all parties have an equal chance to promote their case. It has been found in the United States that Republicans will usually expose themselves to Republican speeches and read Republican newspapers and that Democrats have the same preference for the propaganda output of their own party.

This tendency becomes a real handicap in many fields of civic education. A group of agencies some time ago organized a series of broadcasts to promote tolerance. The idea was to show that all the various groups of immigrants in this country have greatly contributed to its cultural development; therefore no group should be prejudiced against any other. However, audience studies showed that when the Italians were praised Italian immigrants were most likely to listen, and when the contributions of Negroes were presented the audience structure was slanted toward the colored groups in the population. Thus it appeared very doubtful whether the program could actually promote tolerance, since, in each case, the program reached largely those people who did not "need" its message.

In this connection the movies occupy a special place. It is easy to turn off a radio program or to skip an article in a magazine, but one is less likely to leave before the moving picture is over. Therefore the insertion of short educational films between the major features may in the long run prove to be one of the most powerful devices for social education in the domestic as well as in the international field.

Cultural level of the program. A third factor which plays an outstanding role is what may be called the cultural level of the program in its relation to the audience structure. A few examples will show what is meant here. The musical programs on the American radio can be classified on several levels of seriousness; on the highest level one would have classical music, on the lowest level current popular song hits. Studies have shown that the average education and even the average income of the audience declines proportionately with the seriousness of the preferred musical fare. This is true also of dramatic programs: the more serious the problems dealt with, the less likely are the lower educated strata of the population to listen. This is true of all other media, and the pertinent observations are often very striking. It has been shown that the average price of dresses worn by women parallels the seriousness of the newspapers they read, the New

York *Times* ranking at one extreme and one of the tabloids at the other.[9]

The unwillingness of people on the lower income and educational levels to listen to serious broadcasts has been one of the great disappointments which the radio has brought to the educators and reformers. About twenty years ago, when it became clear that the radio would reach into every home, it was generally hoped that at last cultural messages would go everywhere. All the people who had been denied extensive formal education and for whom therefore reading was more difficult would now have a chance to further their education by listening to the radio. It turned out however that the lack of conceptual training which hampered their reading also made them unwilling to listen to serious subject matter, so educational radio still goes mainly to people who are already educated.[10] This same difficulty in reaching mass audiences will obviously be an important problem for international communications.

Incidentally, there is an interesting tie-up between audience structure and the pattern of control. The problem of getting an audience for serious broadcasts is more difficult in countries with commercial broadcasting than in those where radio is government-owned. In America, where the networks have to compete for mass audiences because their success depends upon the amount of goods their advertising sells, the broadcasters have a tendency to play up to the desires of the population—to serve as entertainers and not as "educators." In England, the government urges a greater number of serious broadcasts upon the BBC, and as a result people are not so strongly conditioned to exclude serious subject matter from their listening. Here a new field of comparative communications research opens up: we shall soon want to know how much serious subject matter people in different countries are willing to accept. This is partly a matter of the literacy of the country—in the broadest sense—and partly a question of conditioning. It is well known, for example, that European newspapers are much more concerned with political subject matters than are newspapers in America. Possibly it is easier in Europe than in America to interest broad groups in the discussion of international issues.

Stratification of audiences. Men are more interested than women

---

[9] See Paul Lazarsfeld, "The Daily Newspaper and Its Competitors," *Annals of the American Academy* (Jan., 1942), p. 34.
[10] Paul F. Lazarsfeld, *Radio and the Printed Page* (New York, 1940).

in current events. This is true of their reading as well as their listening habits. In general, American women prefer love stories and men prefer tales of adventure. This probably holds true for most other countries, but other findings of American audience research seem to be more characteristic of this country alone. For instance, it was found that younger people in America are much less interested in politics than are older people. Many observations lead one to believe that the opposite may be true in Europe. Farmers in this country are more interested in serious subject matter than industrial workers on the same educational level. This probably is a result of the national composition of these two occupational groups as well as of peculiarities of the American educational system. Because of such international differences we cannot always draw conclusions about other countries from the results of research in the United States.

Because of the commercial, competitive character of American radio, audience research has developed widely in this country. England has followed suit, although on a much narrower plane. Recently our Good Neighbor policy has led to some audience research in South America, but the results are not known. Judging by incidental observations of travelers, Russia has conducted some researches in the same field. But, in general, the field outside of America is a matter for future investigation.

The case of backward areas. In the preceding discussion we have assumed that communication facilities existed and that the problem was how best to use them in order to capture audiences. But there are vast areas in the world where the population has little or no access to books, magazines, and radios. In some areas in China, for example, the population is so isolated from the outside world that crowds gather around simple exhibits of year-old news photographs, which are sent around the country by representatives of the Office of War Information. Even within Europe there are enormous differences in the distribution of radios. The number of radio homes in Sweden and Denmark is over 200 per thousand inhabitants, higher than the figure for the United States; whereas in Rumania and Spain there are fewer than 20 per thousand inhabitants.[11]

In the case of backward areas, we need to investigate the more primitive and informal communications media that may exist. In southeastern Europe, in many instances,

---

[11] Arno Huth, *Radio Today* (New York, 1942), p. 156.

old established calendars, some of them appearing for over 100 years, together with a prayer book, were the main sources of printed information. In addition the opinion of leaders, clergymen, teachers, doctors, veterinarians, leaders of farm and trade organizations exerted an influence far beyond the importance of the established media. No wonder the Germans ruthlessly exterminated these carriers of information. The Sunday Church services, the Sunday morning walk on Main Street, the meeting in local gymnastic, singing or veteran societies played an important part as opinion centers.[12]

The development of backward areas presents interesting opportunities generally for any promotion program. Moreover, the development of communications facilities in all countries will be in the interests of the IA. For, although an increase in mass communications in general does not, as we have pointed out, necessarily make for coöperation, yet it does afford a necessary prerequisite to any broad educational program. A study of the spread of radio ownership in rural areas of the United States, for example, indicates that people in hitherto isolated areas who acquire a radio acquire with it an added interest in the affairs of the larger world.[13] Furthermore if an organization pioneers in the building up of communications in backward areas, it is apt to gain a special influence over content, even though it must operate within the limits of formal agreements with local and national governments. When the Nazi party brought movies to remote village communities, the party endeared itself in this way to millions of country people by giving them their first film service.[14] Similarly, where books and magazines are scarce people are eager to accept almost any kind of printed material, especially if it is of an informative character, no matter what the source. Such for example has been the experience of Allied propagandists in Middle Eastern countries.

Mobile units can also be useful where communication facilities are poor. The mobile broadcasting and projection units used by the OWI to reach Arab villagers are a case in point. This field has also been exploited by the Nazis. "In some conquered territories the Reich Film Chamber has organized armies of mobile cinemas, sending them far and wide, for example, through Poland and occupied Russia. . . .

[12] Karl Ettinger, "Communications Facilities in South-Eastern Europe." Unpublished paper available at the Bureau of Applied Social Research, Columbia University.
[13] William S. Robins on "Radio Comes to the Farmer," in *Radio Research 1941*, ed. by Paul F. Lazarsfeld and Frank Stanton (New York, 1941), p. 238.
[14] Derrick Sington and Arthur Weidenfeld, *The Goebbels Experiment* (New Haven, Conn., 1943), p. 48.

The film-van service does not regard it as beneath its dignity to arrange performances even for tiny audiences consisting of two or three German settler families." [15]

STUDYING THE CONTENT

Content analysis is the study of the communication itself—what is said in the pamphlet, film or radio program and how it is said. Agencies interested in promoting international coöperation will need to analyze the content not only of the material which they themselves produce but also, more generally, of what is being said to their audiences by others.

In studying their own output, the agencies will hope chiefly to discern possible responses to the content. Are statements credible? Will they be received favorably? Are they likely to induce the desired action? In other words, the analysis of one's own communications serves to check how information policies and plans are actually being carried out in practice. In studying what others are saying, the aim of the agencies will be to find out whether or not the content has any bearing on international coöperation, and if so, what sorts of things are being said about it. Such studies may be particularly useful in spotting unfavorable propaganda, thus enabling the agencies to employ appropriate countermeasures. Content analysis may also serve a broader purpose by indicating something of the cultural values and the communications preferences of the audience.

The techniques of content analysis may vary from an impressionistic appraisal of the communication to an elaborate quantitative analysis.[16] The impressions of a single critic about a film, a pamphlet, or a radio program may be valuable in providing a fresh point of view. The critic may have a perspective to which the producers themselves are blind because of their complete concern with their own activities and purposes. However, it is only by the development of more systematic procedures that content analysis can attain its full usefulness. Methods must be found which permit a description of the content in terms that are both objective and meaningful for purposes at hand. A systematic content analysis requires the development of standardized categories of description. By these we mean categories which have been so defined that each individual statement can be properly placed in one or another

[15] Sington and Weidenfeld, *op. cit.*, p. 85.
[16] Douglas Waples, *What Reading Does to People* (Chicago, 1941), Appendix on "Content Analysis."

of the categories. The classificatory scheme used in any study is neither a matter of caprice nor of rigid custom. It depends, rather, on the analyst's hypotheses as to what is potentially significant in the material he is studying.[17]

One classification system which has found popularity in propaganda studies is based on weakness-strength and morality-immorality dimensions. This system involves a twelvefold classification: statements may refer either to the enemy or to the self; they may impute either weakness or strength, or they may be neutral in this respect; and they may impute either morality, immorality, or be neutral in respect to this characteristic. Although, of course, all combinations of these three elements are possible, actual content analyses indicate that when talking about the enemy his weakness and immorality are most frequently emphasized while, when talking of the self, stress is usually placed on strength and morality.[18]

In some cases, a more simple system of classification may be adequate. A study of Communist propaganda in the United States showed that the slogans used in Chicago could be classified as either "positive" or "negative." During the periods of the "united front," when the Communist Party sought to coöperate with liberal groups in this country, their slogans were positive in that they stressed the common goals of workingmen. In other periods, when the Communists sought revolutionary change, their slogans were revealed to be negative—to focus mainly on the vilification of the common enemy, capitalism.[19]

No matter what the system of classification used, an additional "dimension of emphasis" must be defined. In other words, an adequate content analysis must make statements concerning the relative importance, in terms of emphasis, of the various themes defined by the categories. In some studies, emphasis may be appraised by counting the amount of space or time devoted to a theme. Thus, for instance, we would count news items pertaining to a specific subject, references to a given theme, and so on. In other cases, however, more elaborate techniques will be needed. Newspapers, for example, give emphasis to different items by means of headlines and by placing them in prominent

---

[17] Hans Speier and Margaret Otis, "German Radio Propaganda to France during the Battle of France," in *Radio Research 1942–1943*, ed. by P. F. Lazarsfeld and F. Stanton (New York, 1944), p. 209.
[18] For an example of the use of this scheme of classification, see *ibid.*, p. 240.
[19] Harold D. Lasswell and Dorothy Blumenthal, *World Revolutionary Propaganda, a Chicago Study* (New York, 1939), p. 121.

positions on the page. Measures of these less obvious means of emphasis must be standardized.

Any international communications research organization then, will have the widest latitude in selecting the technique of content analysis most appropriate to the purposes of the investigation under consideration. We can do no more here than discuss the different functions of content analysis and the methods used in achieving these purposes.

In the first place, it will be to the interest of the agencies of international communications—the IA itself, the national governments, or private organizations—to study what is being said by the other agencies. Two different purposes in such studies can be distinguished. Content analyses are never carried out for their own sake, but always to permit inferences about other phases of communication. First of all we may want to infer the influences which are being brought to bear upon the audience, whether with conscious or unconscious intent. Or, secondly, we may want to make inferences about the audience itself, about its preferences and attitudes.

Inferences about how the audience is being influenced. The proposal by the League of Nations that it study textbooks in order to detect material harmful to international understanding is typical of this kind of investigation.

A more recent research of this same type is the study of foreign language broadcasts which originate in local American stations.[20] Here the purpose was to determine whether or not these programs influenced their audiences in a manner harmful to the wartime interests of the United States. Systematic content analyses revealed that, from a political point of view, the programs held little danger. The advertisements heard on these programs, on the other hand, had highly nationalistic implications. The character of these appeals is quite likely to make the immigrant's adjustment to his new American environment more difficult. If reform is needed, then it must start with the sponsors of the program, and not as previously believed, with the station managers.

In order to detect these propaganda influences, various tests have been devised by Harold Lasswell.[21] These can be briefly summarized:

The Presentation Test is an examination of the amount of favorable

[20] Rudolf Arnheim and Martha C. Bayne, "Foreign Language Broadcasts over Local American Stations" in *Radio Research 1941*, ed. by P. F. Lazarsfeld and F. Stanton (New York, 1941), pp. 3 ff.
[21] Harold D. Lasswell, "Communications Research and Politics" in *Print, Radio and Film in a Democracy*, ed. by D. Waples (Chicago, 1941), pp. 106–10.

and unfavorable treatment given to different symbols and propositions in the contents of a given channel of communication.

The Test of Distortion examines whether or not statements are modified in a direction favorable to one side of the controversy. This may be detected by noting that statements favorable to the "other" side are consistently eliminated or nullified by opposing statements, while propositions favorable to one's "own" side are not so distorted.

The Parallel Test involves a comparison of the content of a given channel of communication with that of a known propaganda source. If they vary together, the inference is that they are subject to the same control. This test has two forms:

a) *The consistency test*, an examination of the content in terms of whether or not it is consistent with recognized propaganda aims;

b) *The distinctiveness test*, an analysis in terms of vocabulary. The vocabulary associated with the different world ideologies, for instance, is quite distinctive and can be identified by means of content analysis.

The Source Test relies on the assumption that, if a medium of communication makes use of sources popular with a known propaganda group, it may be under the latter's control. This is especially true when alternative sources are ignored. A variation of this is the Concealed Source Test which is applied when the communication fails to disclose the source of its information or bias.

So far, the content studies which we have discussed have focused on the intents and policies of those who control the channels of communication. The assumption has been that content is regulated by those who control the media, and that, therefore, any proposal for the modification of content must be addressed to the controlling organizations. One might also venture the hypothesis, however, that it is the preferences and attitudes of the audience which determine the content and effectiveness of communications. If we proceed on this assumption, then, it is by "counter-propaganda," rather than by pressures on controlling agencies, that we modify propaganda influences. Here content studies would serve to indicate what techniques of persuasion are most effective with different audiences.

It is impossible to anticipate all of the different influence studies which agencies interested in fostering international coöperation may want to undertake. But it is clear that content analyses of the types we have outlined here will form a basis of any such investigations.

Inferring audience attitudes from content. Wherever communications are relatively free, it can be assumed that their content reflects in part the tastes and interests of the audience. Newspapers would not be sold and commercial radio programs would not be listened to if people were not in basic agreement with what is said. In this sense content studies constitute a basic technique of sociological and psychological research. If we want to know whether religious interest has increased or decreased in recent years, we find out whether a larger or smaller number of articles on religious topics or leaders has been published in mass magazines. And, if anthropologists want to know whether two tribes differ in the amount of aggression prevailing in their cultures, they often compare the content of the folklore of the two societies. Similar studies in the international field are easily thought of. What is the stereotype of the Bulgarian in popular Greek literature? Do Croat newspapers point out the nationality of criminals if they are Serbs? If two countries coöperate in building a channel, do the newspapers of each country tend to overemphasize the achievements of its conationals?

As we shall see presently, the idea of a barometer of international tension [22] should be developed. Growing international animosities may be detected through the use of public opinion polls before the tensions become too dangerous. Content analysis of local mass media can also contribute to such a barometer by collecting all complaints, accusations, and innuendo which are aired in the press and on the radio.

The directors of such studies will find an interesting precedent in some studies conducted by the American government at the beginning of the war. The regional press was carefully examined to find all unfavorable references to the different rationing programs which had been inaugurated. The data thus collected were remarkably sensitive to changing attitudes: originally the press in the Southwest, an area rich in oil and gasoline, had been violently opposed to gasoline rationing. When the Baruch report was made public, and when the surprisingly large number of military uses for oil and gasoline was explained, however, the attitude of the Southwestern press underwent an overnight change.

In studying one's own output, the chief aim, as we have pointed out, is to anticipate possible responses of the audience. It often happens, for

[22] The idea of a barometer of international tension was suggested to the authors by Stuart C. Dodd. For a study of public opinion on this subject in the United States, see *The Public Looks at World Organization,* University of Denver, National Opinion Research Center, Report No. 19.

example, that authors and producers overlook the presence of emphases and juxtapositions detrimental to their aims. Any agencies interested in promoting international coöperation, then, must continually check the content of their products to see that it conforms to the information policies of the agencies.

Several illustrations of the types of analysis we mean will serve to clarify their purposes and their values. The first type of study centers about thematic analysis. In a pamphlet concerning Negroes, for instance, there were two main themes: the gains and achievements of Negroes in a democracy, and the deprivations which Hitler's victory would bring. According to a count of paragraphs and captions in this pamphlet the first theme received 84 percent of the emphasis, while only 16 percent was accorded the second. From this analysis, then, we should expect that readers of the pamphlet would have a feeling of pride in the achievements of Negroes, but that these feelings would not be canalized into aggression against the Nazis. Studies of reader reactions confirmed the hypothesis. This is a particularly pertinent example, because it parallels the kind of trouble which may be encountered by promoters of the IA. Suppose that a film were made showing the dangers of aggression and stressing that these must be guarded against by international coöperation. Suppose, furthermore, that the film used examples from the history of Nazism to illustrate its themes. Unless the themes are well integrated and properly emphasized, the effect of such a document might be simply to foster a desire for revenge against these particular aggressors or their compatriots and descendants.

A second type of study deals with the symbol analysis of one's own output. In terms of what is the enemy presented? How is the self identified? By what symbols is the international coöperation presented to the audience? Obviously, the types of symbols will play a large part in determining the effects of any communication. An example of this kind of investigation is provided by a radio series of moral programs. A content analysis of the scripts of this series showed that the "personification stereotype" was used extensively in referring to the enemy: approximately 25 percent of all symbols denoting the enemy referred to Hitler, Mussolini, Goering, and so on. On the other hand, only 4 percent of the references to the United Nations and only 11 percent of those to the United States made use of such personifications. This use of simplified personalized stereotypes may lead to effects not desired by the producer. Since the enemy is presented as consisting essentially of a small band of evil men, the implication may well be that, once these are destroyed, all will be well. This kind of personification proves to be all too acceptable to listeners, since it accords with common simplistic ideas. For example, a parallel notion is that we must fight crime primarily by punishing criminals rather than by preventive measures.

A third type of content analysis of one's own communications attempts to relate the known effects of a document to specific parts of the content. For example, it was planned to show a documentary film to European audiences on how the United States Government had coped with housing problems in a war-boom town. It was thought that American prestige abroad would be increased by showing that our great war effort had created considerable problems that were being solved in a progressive way. But a large part of the test audiences, when questioned on their reactions to the film, were more impressed with the poor conditions of life in America than with anything else. The impression made by such books as *The Grapes of Wrath*—which was very popular in Europe—was confirmed by the film. The analyst's problem was to discover what could have led to such a reaction. A preliminary content analysis suggested that the scenes of new housing and improved conditions were very much briefer than the scenes showing the need for the changes. In part this was perhaps due to the fact that the film, intended for domestic audiences, emphasized the need for government housing on the assumption that Americans required convincing on this point, whereas a European audience would not need to be convinced. Moreover, there was no continuity between the two phases of the town's history: the same family was not followed, nor the same house or street, and perhaps the audience was not able to trace the changes clearly enough.

STUDYING THE EFFECTS OF COMMUNICATIONS

In every field of communication there comes a moment when the people concerned with it begin to wonder whether they could not acquire some more systematic evidence as to the effect of their efforts. They usually have a limited budget and therefore have to make decisions as to how the funds at their disposal should be spent. They also notice that some of their communications products are likely to "go over big" while others "fall flat." Some evince a certain readiness to accept the more scientific test procedures. But this does not hold true for all; the first generation of communications producers usually feel that it is a matter of their own intuition, that no outsider can possibly know their business as well as they do and that, in any case, art cannot be approached by statistical tables. But slowly new people come in, and an alliance develops between the younger administrators and the research experts which opens the door for more scientific procedures.

Three main types of tests can be applied to films, radio programs, pamphlets, and the like. One of these is the *post facto* test. If a program has been under way for a certain length of time one can try to learn whether it is successful or not. The result of this type of test, of course, can only be used for doing better the next time. The second type is really a part of the first—public opinion polls—and the third, the pre-test, is made before the communication is sent out. Obviously the third test has to be made on a small scale and with expediency, because research should not delay administrative action too long; but for practical purposes this procedure is the most important one.

Pre-tests. The classical procedure which belongs here is a controlled experiment in which two so-called matched groups are selected as representative of the people we want to influence. Both contain the same number of men and women, have similar educational and age distribution, and so on. One group is exposed to the communication in question and the other is not. The objective of the communication is to increase receptiveness to the idea of international organization. Therefore both groups will be given a certain test which measures their attitude to the IA or some parts of its program or procedures. If, after the program has been presented, the exposed group shows a more favorable attitude than the unexposed, the communication is considered successful, provided that all statistical precautions have been taken. The organization of such controlled experiments is not exactly easy and therefore only where people are readily accessible as in schools and in the army have these tests been widely used.

Not many general results can be reported from such studies. By and large it was found that greater effect is produced upon knowledge than upon beliefs and emotional attitudes, and that certain combinations of presentations are more successful than others. Giving a lecture first and then showing a film leads to greater changes than if the order were reversed. A combination of reading and listening is more successful than either of the two alone. A short lecture ending in a group discussion is more impressive than if the whole time is used by the speaker. People of low educational levels are more easily influenced than people on higher educational levels.

The value of controlled experiments is greatest when they are linked together with a long-range research program. Step by step we can find out who is influenced and who is not, under which conditions the influence is greatest, how long it lasts, and so on. For practical purposes, however, controlled experiments have a number of drawbacks. The results can sometimes be misleading: we know that "in real life" people dislike to listen to ideas with which they do not agree and we also know that less well educated people dislike to listen to serious subject matters. What good does it do us, therefore, to learn that our opponents or less well educated people are greatly influenced in an experimental situation if we know that actually they won't listen to us anyway? It is also difficult "to design an experiment which will give the cumulative effect of say a year's exposure to a given medium of communication. . . . [Yet] there is a good basis for the belief that it is in just this way that communications have their principal effect." [23]

Finally, controlled experiments test the over-all effects but reveal little about the specific feature of the communication which provoked them—the very question with which a script writer and the producer are most concerned. This is the reason why recently a more direct type of pre-test has developed. Its essence consists of having people read or listen to the product we want to test and then to have very detailed interviews with them as to what they experienced when they read or listened. The procedure largely consists in encouraging introspection in the other fellow and its justification comes from the fact which one discovers in the process of such interviews—that different people react to the same product in varied and unexpected ways.

Take for example, the instructions which the American government put out at the time when the first ration books were distributed. It was assumed that since most people have had experience with postage stamps, an analogy might profitably be used in the instructions. Who would have anticipated from the vantage point of his armchair that this simple analogy would elicit comments such as these: "I didn't realize that you had to mail them." Or, "There doesn't seem to be any place to stick them." Another example is taken from a film which showed the

[23] Samuel Stouffer, "A Sociologist Looks at Communications Research," in *Radio, Print and Film in a Democracy* (Chicago, 1940), pp. 141-42.

reconstruction of Naples after its conquest by the United Nations. The plight of the Italian people was vividly pictured: they had no water, food, or shelter. When interviewed, several people declared, quite spontaneously, that these poor people could not possibly have been the dangerous Fascists of which they had heard so much. The picture, in other words, had an unexpected and possibly undesirable political effect. The same thing happened to a doctor on a radio program who meant to warn his audience not to turn to quacks when they needed an X-ray examination. He made the danger of quacks so vivid that in the end quite a number of people decided they would not want an X-ray picture taken even by a licensed doctor because the whole business sounded so hazardous.

A special technique, known as the "focused interview," has been developed to discover reactions of this kind. The appropriate procedure consists first in having people read or listen to the message and as they listen or read to indicate points at which they experience strongly positive or negative reactions. Then the interviewer goes back to these critical points for more details about the nature of the reactions and to find out as concretely as possible what it was in the text or the picture which created them.

It can easily be seen that broadcasts on international topics bring about many of the difficulties mentioned above. We might easily praise the IA as a democratic way of handling problems to an audience taught to believe that the democratic is the *wrong* way. We might praise the public achievement of women to an audience convinced that the place of women is at home. It would not promote international good will if we were to tell an American audience south of the Mason-Dixon line how well all the races in parts of the French Empire get along together. And no Austrian would be won over by a good will program if the speaker had a Prussian accent. The way to avoid such difficulties is to have small groups of nationals of different countries available to which the communications would be presented first. A few such focused interviews would usually iron out most of the serious difficulties.

Post-facto tests. The other method of measuring the effect of communications is to test a sustained promotional effort as it is being carried through. The idea of the procedure is to keep a sample of the population to which the campaign is directed under continuous observation.[24]

[24] P. F. Lazarsfeld, B. Berelson, and H. Gaudet, *How the Voter Makes Up His Mind* (New York, 1944).

With this method one has to reinterview the same people several times and to find out (a) whether they have been reached by the promotional program and (b) how they feel about the issues under discussion.

The answers to (a) will tell us how good the coverage of the whole effort is. If we find that only a few people know about the radio program or have read one of the pamphlets being studied, we will then try to find out what is wrong with the distribution methods. On the other hand, if people have been exposed to the material of the campaign and yet do not listen to or read it, there is obviously something wrong with the message itself and it becomes necessary to conduct the kind of content test mentioned above.

Knowledge of (b)—public opinion on the campaign issues themselves—helps us answer a number of questions: Are the people reached by the campaign those who agree with it anyhow? Are we reaching those whom we want to convert? And if so, does their attitude change in the desired direction? What are the characteristics of the people who change as compared to those who are reached but remain impervious to the campaign message?

When, in the course of such a study, people are found who have changed their attitude over a period of time it is especially useful to ask in detail how the change came about. Moreover, a campaign is usually carried through many channels. Such interviews will permit an evaluation of the relative effectiveness of the media whether newspapers, radio, or personal contacts. The results, of course, will vary from case to case and from country to country. To illustrate the whole procedure, in a study made during the presidential campaign of 1940, it was found that the main effect of the campaign was not to win people over from one party to another, but to activate their political predispositions. The campaign made people more aware of the social groups to which they belonged, and while they had not been greatly interested in politics, they now decided to vote for the candidate preferred by the more articulate people of their own group. Newspapers and other printed materials played the smallest role in bringing about campaign results. Radio was somewhat more effective. But by far the most important kind of communication was personal contact. The majority of the women and a surprisingly great number of politically not-so-interested men did not hesitate to report that they had formed their vote intention under the influence of a particular person (or persons) in their social group. Such a result has obvious implications for the way a campaign budget can be profitably spent.

In the international field this technique of tracing the actual effects of campaigns will be still more important. Very often we will deal with a country where little is known about the prevailing communication habits. The quickest way to get a preliminary picture will be to look for people who have recently formed opinions on international issues. By getting their story as to *how* this opinion was formed we get the quickest idea of what channels reach them most successfully. As a matter of fact it will often be useful to use such technique on a variety of issues. We can set up a panel of farmers and study those who have recently acquired new ideas about how to improve their crops; we can study housewives who have changed the brands of some common merchandise; we might try to trace how people first got wind of a new story or rumor. All this will help us to learn what the psychological networks of communication in a given country are. In other words, *post-facto* tests are a useful form of communications research though the facts we are tracing are not necessarily those which we have created ourselves.

International public opinion polls. Part of the method just outlined implies the taking of regular polls. We have mentioned some of the administrative problems which this task encompasses. There are also certain new difficulties to be faced once these polls are employed on an international scale. There is first the problem of sampling. It is difficult enough to compare the stratification of a small Midwestern town with New York City; much greater difficulties will arise in setting up status standards for different countries. A university professor in a European city will definitely belong with the upper class whereas in America he has only middle class status. The status of the village teacher is probably higher in Europe than in America and, moreover, the European teacher is likely to be a man and the American a woman. To this must be added the problem of nationality; in Yugoslavia, for example, the status of a trader differs according to whether he is a Greek, a Moslem, or a Serb.

A second problem arises when we think of the wording of the questions. Even where one language prevails, slight differences in terminology change the frequency distribution of the answers. In a Republican area more people approve of "daylight-saving time" than "Roosevelt's plan introducing daylight saving time." The word "politics" has a bad connotation in America but not in France or Germany. The word "leader" is used in this country in a perfunctory manner whereas it certainly has a high emotional connotation in Germany. The translation of questions from one language to another so that answers can be compared productively will not be without difficulty. The development of an international language would of course immensely facilitate this problem as well as many others in international communication. The popularization of such a language seems unlikely, however, in the near future. Over three hundred international languages have been invented since the seventeenth century, but none has achieved wide acceptance. Basic English appears to be the most promising step in this direction, but it is likely to be hampered by the fact that it may be associated with British imperialism or with Anglo-American domination.[25]

In addition to these problems inherent in an international polling system—none of which is insuperable—there will arise the problem of "public opinion" of the public opinion polls. In the United States, Congress has usually been antagonistic to such polls, viewing them as a usurpation of the prerogative of elected officials to express the opinions of their constituents. This opposition will undoubtedly be met on a larger scale on the international level; delegates may not only object to "interference" with their "rights" but also protest such objective methods, if they want to conceal the real opinions of their peoples.

Nevertheless, if the IA is to function on a democratic basis, it will be important to conduct such polls—especially in countries where democratic processes are imperfect—in order to test the claims of rival parties to popular support. To the extent that opposition is based on the devious ambition of politicians, the only solution will be to gain the active support of those who are genuinely devoted to international coöperation and democratic processes. To the extent that opposition stems, as some of it may, from a suspicion of the integrity of the research itself, it can be met by building up an independent, international polling organization in which high standards of professional prestige and ethics obtain. Such an organization would, of course, have to be financially independent and profoundly watchful of its own integrity.

[25] For a discussion of the potentialities of Basic English by an enthusiast, see C. K. Ogden, "Will Basic English Become the Second Language?" *Public Opinion Quarterly*, VIII (1944), 3–9.

STUDYING THE ORGANIZATION AND CONTROL

There can be no doubt that studies of the control and organization of media of communication will play an important role in international communications. Just as international coöperation cannot be created out of thin air, so international communications cannot venture onto thin ice. Whatever organizations are created must operate, to a considerable extent at least, within existing national systems of control. At the same time, any organization for international communications must be self-conscious at least to the extent of studying its own structure. No special research techniques have been evolved for such a study. Several investigations of the control of intranational communications, however, will show the type of problems to be faced by the communications branch of the IA, and will also indicate what kinds of research such an organization will have to conduct.

One type of study deals with the "flow of decisions" through an organization. What happens to an idea, document, or product once it has left the hands of its producers? Is its acceptance left to its audience, or is it "foisted" upon the public by the industry? Is any idea or document permitted to circulate freely, or must it receive the stamp of approval from the organization which controls the medium in question?

The motion picture industry in America is an extreme case of a "closed system" of communication. It is so organized that it has achieved a minimum of dependence on audience reaction: it has so to speak, created to its own concepts concerning public tastes in movies.[26] And, one of the firm convictions of the motion picture industry is that the public dislikes controversial material.[27] In dealing with films, then, the IA would not only have to contend with possibly unfavorable reactions to its material, but it would also face the problem of combating the attitude that "the industry knows best what should or should not be said." The problem will be made easier by certain recent developments in the field of documentary films. First, there has been a great development of nontheatrical audiences; there are now approximately 18,000 projectors in use in our educational institutions alone. Secondly, the public and the film industry both have been educated to a more

[26] Donald Slesinger, "The Film and Public Opinion," in *Radio, Print and Film in a Democracy* (Chicago, 1940), p. 86.
[27] *Ibid.*, p. 83.

favorable attitude towards documentaries because of the widespread use of "fact films" for wartime training and morale building.[28]

In other countries, particularly those in southeastern Europe, different economic conditions have led to a more flexible organization of media control. In many of these countries, the advertising business is virtually unknown. Instead, newspapers have been subsidized by paper manufacturers, printing press owners, by the government, or by political parties. The high editorial costs of such independent publications made the publishers more willing to accept handouts, fairly indiscriminately, from domestic or foreign political agencies. Within such an organization of the media, the problem of the IA would be that of maintaining its own propaganda in the forefront. It must make sure that it receives as large an audience as do opposing views. The first type of study, then, will show the IA how it can make use of existing channels of communication most successfully. It will indicate from where communications policies come, how they can be modified, and how new ones can be inaugurated.

The second type of control study, investigations of the personnel of the organization, will be conducted within the IA itself. It is well known that the type of people employed in any communications medium has a considerable influence on the product. If the educator propagandizes, his document may be completely factual and completely ineffective; if the dramatist acts as producer, the validity of the statement may sometimes be sacrificed to its effectiveness. Studies of the personnel of any organization, then, will define its social role fairly accurately and will also indicate that as the social role changes so do the members. For example, as the American weekly newspaper became less an outlet for printers and more an organ of editorial opinion, professionally trained personnel replaced the amateurs.[29] In the motion picture industry, the introduction of sound brought more and more Broadway actors to Hollywood. And they, with their strong tradition of unionization, soon changed the whole relationship between actors and producers.[30] Changes in the functions of the Washington offices of large newspapers have also brought a corresponding change in personnel. For many years, this was the sinecure of the organization, given as a courtesy to older newspaper men who had served their papers

[28] Arthur L. Mayer, "Facts into Film," *Public Opinion Quarterly*, VIII (1944), 206-25.
[29] Raymond Lawrence, "Kansas Publishers, a Professional Analysis," *Journalism Quarterly* (Dec., 1938).
[30] Murray Ross, *Stars and Strikes* (New York, 1941).

faithfully for several decades. The increasing importance of Washington as the site of national and international history, however, has encouraged the newspapers to replace the older men with especially able and well-trained correspondents.[31]

We cannot tell what the personnel of the IA's department of education and promotion will be. Undoubtedly the personnel will bring more training in mass communications, in propaganda, in advertising, and radio than did members of such earlier organizations as the Internation Cooperation Organization. And, just as probably, this influx of specialized technicians will preëmpt the places of many distinguished intellectuals who were found in those earlier organizations. Personnel will be important to the IA in another connection. Not only its activities in different countries but also its public relations will be affected by the character of its representatives. The influence of American diplomatic personnel, for example, is clearly seen in American foreign policy. Men of independent fortunes are usually sent to important diplomatic posts, partly because the expenses of the positions are larger than the salaries provided and partly because the posts are frequently regarded as suitable rewards for men who have contributed generously to the campaign funds of the party in power. As a result, American diplomats are likely to associate exclusively with the upper class in the country to which they are assigned, and to represent the monied interests. If the IA is to inspire confidence among the liberal and leftist groups which will have assumed power in some countries, it will have to avoid selecting its representatives from among aristocrats and bankers.

International communications will play an increasingly decisive role in the postwar world—either for good or for evil, either to maintain peace or to stimulate war. If the media are controlled by agencies sympathetic to International Authority, they can be made to serve the interests of coöperation. They can have a large share in promoting intergroup understanding, in obscuring intergroup differences, in counteracting divisive propaganda. These same media, if controlled by organizations inimical or indifferent to the principles of an IA, can only nourish and accelerate the development of further aggressions. They will, in this case, serve the cause of chauvinistic nationalism.

And control of the media will go to those who use them most effectively. To them will go the power of decision, the power of prescrip-

[31] L. C. Rosten, *The Washington Correspondents* (New York, 1942).

tion, and the power of direction. This, then, presents a challenge to those who are interested in fostering international coöperation. To use the media of communications most effectively they must determine what avenues of access are open to them; they must remove the art of producing effective propaganda from the realms of instinct and guess work; they must anticipate and recognize propaganda which is antagonistic to their own purposes. None of these problems can be solved except through systematic communications research. None of them can be approached except by a rigorous discipline. If the promoters of the IA accept this challenge, if they attempt to control the media of communications through achieving a high degree of effectiveness, science will have become the tool of social progress.

Nationalism, Internationalism, and the War By GRAYSON KIRK

OF ALL human institutions, war is the most supremely destructive. Its toll in shattered buildings and mangled bodies is apparent to all, but the horror which these arouse should not cause one to overlook its equally profound effects upon the institutions of international intercourse. In some ways these effects are at least as significant as those which are more obvious. For one thing, they may last longer. A blasted city or countryside can be restored so that within a few years the scars of war will virtually have disappeared. And the fecundity of the human race quickly replaces those who have fallen on the battlefield. But the institutions of international society are more fragile than the buildings which are blasted to rubble, and their reconstitution may require a longer time than that needed to fill the gaps in the soldiers' ranks.

This comment should not be taken to mean that the sword merely cuts through the fabric of international society, leaving nothing but remnants behind. Actually, while it destroys the old patterns, it creates new ones as it goes. Thus, when the war is over the total complex of international institutions will consist of some which have survived almost unscathed, some which will have been modified and changed, and some which will have emerged during, and as a result of, the war. In the midst of a war it is difficult to forecast accurately what all these changes will be, but it is obvious that they will be numerous and fundamental, and it is possible to single out some of the trends which are likely to influence the final result.

The disruptive and destructive effects are always the most obvious, for institutions built on the basis of the hopeful internationalism of peacetime years are the first to suffer when war comes. Of these, one of the major casualties is always international law. Men have labored persistently for centuries to develop a code of principles designed to regularize international intercourse even in time of war, but the historian of modern times can find no instance of war in which each party

NATIONALISM, INTERNATIONALISM, AND WAR

has not been charged by the other with gross violations of the code. This breakdown, or at least the substantial nonobservance of the code, has had the effect in the popular mind of discrediting the whole attempt to build a body of principles and rules to govern nations in their relations with each other. Why, it is asked, should people take seriously the attempt to construct a system of international law when it fails to meet the major emergencies in which it would be most useful? The reply, that even a partial observance of the code is an improvement over the past, is not satisfactory to people who are accustomed to think of law in municipal terms.

Somewhat parenthetically, it should be pointed out that the nonobservance of the laws of war is due about as much to the changing character of war itself as to the inherent tendency of man to violate rules whose only sanction is that of public opinion. The changes in the technique of warfare are seldom widely apparent until the actual outbreak of conflict, and then it is too late to change the rules to meet the new situation. Thus, during the first World War, it soon became clear that the accepted rules of contraband—which drew a distinction between absolute contraband, conditional contraband, and noncontraband—were no longer applicable, now that war was becoming "total" in character. The decline of the principle of neutrality during the present war provides another illustration of this point.

A second internationalist growth which suffers during war is somewhat less tangible. This is the general belief in the existence of a world community in which each nation assumes certain obligations with respect to its conduct and in turn asserts certain prerogatives which derive from its status of independence and its willingness to observe certain principles in its dealing with others. This sense of the unity of the nations as members of a single global community, even though that community is not organized politically in a way comparable to groups of individuals, grows steadily during times of peace. It is based upon the view that, wholly apart from the rules of international law, there are common standards of international conduct or morality which nations can be expected to follow in their dealings with each other. It is based on the assumptions of fair play, a decent respect for the rights of others, a willingness to curb the excesses of international rivalry, and the observance of reasonable standards on the part of the state toward its own citizens. Americans especially, seeing the world shrink physically before their eyes, have been as interested in spreading this gospel of international morality as they have been uninterested in the development of effective means to enforce its observance.

War destroys this picture. The enemy, by resorting to war, has shown that he has rejected this doctrine of world community and international morality, lock, stock and barrel. The necessary intellectual readjustment thereupon takes place, and the result is a new picture, one which divides the world into the group of those who do believe in these principles and are prepared to fight for them (oneself and one's allies), those who deny them and are prepared to destroy them if they can (the enemy), and those who accept them but not as a fighting faith (the neutrals). Thus, the world is no longer a unity but it is composed of three distinct communities. And these new lines of cleavage persist after the war until the solidarity of the allies is destroyed and a reconciliation with the enemy has been effected. Slowly, and almost unconsciously the principle of world community reasserts itself—to be shattered again by another war.

At the organizational level the impact of war either destroys or it impairs the activities of the existing institutions and agencies which have been established to handle the international relations of the member states. Since in a major war the handling of nearly all international matters is profoundly changed there is scarcely a single international agency which can carry on its work much as if the war did not exist. Almost the sole exception is perhaps the International Red Cross. The others pass into a state of suspended animation. Their funds may be cut off, and their scope of authority and activity is narrowly circumscribed. Many are compelled by force of circumstances to move their headquarters. For example, the League of Nations now maintains a skeleton staff in Geneva, but its economic intelligence activities have been moved to Princeton, and the International Labor Office is in Montreal.

In times of peace one of the most marked signs of the growth of internationalism is the multiplication of private or semipublic international societies, congresses, conferences, and the like. During the decade from 1920 to 1930 more than 1,800 meetings of these unofficial international organizations were held. War causes an almost complete cessation of such activities, and those which do "carry on" do so largely in order to keep the organization alive until its normal activities can be resumed in the future. And even this attenuated existence is confined to one or the other set of belligerents and a scattering support from neutral states. In all belligerent states the concentration of energies upon the prosecution of the war is so complete that there is no time for continuing any of the ordinary activities of the transnational world. Organized internationalism, as it existed before the outbreak of hostilities, comes to a full stop.

In the realm of international economic affairs, a war such as the present one has equally far-reaching consequences. The belligerents make every effort to interfere with each other's foreign trade. Through blockades, blacklisting of neutral traders, preclusive buying of neutral exports valuable to the enemy, and every other device which human ingenuity can contrive, the old trade channels are sealed off. Moreover, each belligerent is compelled to reorient its own industrial plant to war production, and it continues to export only those goods which must be sold in order to provide needed exchange for the importation of war materials, or which are necessary in order to maintain satisfactory relations with allies or wavering neutrals. During the present war virtually all international trade is being conducted directly by the governments concerned and the sphere of the private trader has been reduced to insignificance. Shipping is commandeered, currencies are rigidly managed, and international credits are made available only for political reasons or for carrying on activities which will be useful to the war effort of the creditor.

The basis of the prewar international trading system is destroyed also by the necessary changes in the economic activity of the belligerent states. Cut off from normal supplies of rubber and tin, the United States has constructed giganitc synthetic rubber plants at home, and it has engaged in immense new tin-producing activities in South America. Britain, facing a food shortage, took heroic steps to intensify production at home. Perforce, economic nationalism is given a tremendous stimulus because countries must try to produce at home what they have formerly procured from abroad. This same situation is true among the neutrals as well, with the result that industrialism grows in the hitherto nonindustrialized states, and agricultural production is increased in the industrialized states.

The end of the war does not bring a return to the *status quo ante bellum*. New vested interest groups have been created in each country, and they attempt to protect themselves by monopolizing as much of the home market as possible. In this drive for import restriction, the producer groups are supported by all those who, fearful of another war in the future, contend that the state must remain in as self-sufficient a condition as possible even at the expense of the national standard of living. Thus, the fight over the future of synthetic rubber in this country has already begun. In the agricultural field the net result is overproduction, which becomes apparent as soon as the war is over and the devastated areas are tilled once more. The agricultural depression of the twenties, which was shared by most of the raw-materials producing areas of the world, is still too fresh in mind to require any extended discussion in this connection.

A further stimulus to new trade controls at the end of a war derives from the international financial position of many belligerents. If they have bought heavily from abroad during the war, or if they have need for extensive capital imports in order to finance their reconstruction and rehabilitation, they will be faced with an inescapable need for a highly favorable trade balance in order to maintain the stability of their position. The alternative is either drastic import restriction or the maintenance of rigid governmental controls over foreign exchange. At the end of this war, in the absence of other palliatives, many countries will probably have to follow both courses.

Thus if the experience of the last war and the trends during the present war offer any basis for generalization, it is obvious that a major and prolonged war has a catastrophic effect upon preëxisting international financial and trading arrangements. Though wisdom and accumulated experience may bring new solutions and new policies, no return to the prewar system is possible.

These disruptive effects of war upon international law and organization, upon international economic relations, and upon internationalism (in the sense of belief in a world community) are matched to some extent by the effects of war upon the basis of nationalism in the participating states. In general it is clear that war tends to intensify nationalism. No other activity of the state demands the same cohesion, the same unity of effort, the same single-mindedness of purpose. In the history of nationalism war has been the greatest contributory factor. Through the existence of a common enemy, and the requirement of immense sacrifices in order to try to triumph over that enemy, a sense of group unity is achieved which cannot be attained by any peacetime activities of the state. In nearly all states war is closely and inseparably associated with the birth of nationalism, and each recurring war rejuvenates and fortifies this strongest of all the group bonds of modern life.

This does not mean that each war raises the nationalism of the participating states to a new high plateau. It does, however, raise the sentiment of nationalism to a higher peak than before, and the degree of decline thereafter depends upon the political and economic aftermath. While there is an inevitable reaction when, faced with the perplexing problems of the after-war period, many question the necessity of the war and the motives of their former leaders, this relapse is generally brief. Following a defeat, the relapse tends to be greater because of the discouragement and the hardships of the new era, but, because the pendulum swings very far in the direction of disintegration and disillusionment, it may also swing back all the more quickly and forcefully. The experience of Germany since Versailles is the most striking example of this tendency in modern times, but other illustrations, such as the resurgence of Turkey after the treaty of Sèvres, come quickly to mind.

At the same time, and despite what has been said above about the way in which war destroys existing international beliefs and institutions, it also lays a basis for a new growth of internationalism. Shocked by the basic irreconcilability between the pretensions of civilization and the savagery of war, men are always spurred on in time of war to try to devise methods to prevent its recurrence. In former years, solution was usually sought in a policy of territorial aggrandizement, an increase in military strength, and in all the other elements of fortified national power. Time, however, has brought some change in this point of view because it is extremely difficult to show that when a nation arms heavily it frees itself thereby from the danger of involvement in war. Historically, the heavily armed nations have been involved in war about as frequently, to say the least, as those with lesser armaments. An armed status should go far to insure victory, once the battle is engaged, but it has not prevented war.

This lesson has become so obvious that, while people still are led in time of war to demand a greater postwar military establishment as insurance against the future, they are conscious of the fragmentary and inadequate character of this solution. The other possibility, which may be considered either as an alternative or as a supplement to a great military establishment and a strong strategic position, is that of trying to assure the future peace by some form of international coöperative action. Thus, during the First World War the League of Nations took form, and, as will be discussed later, an even greater drive in this direction is taking place during the present conflict.

It is not difficult to see why this drive for some closer form of international organization should be given special impetus during time of war. There is a desire to justify the sacrifices which have been made, and there is an understandably strong feeling that this can best be done by clinching the victory with an arrangement which will provide what is hopefully called a "lasting" or an "enduring" peace. The politicians cater to this deep human sentiment by providing assurances for a permanent peace, and their rotund phrases, which are discounted when applied to domestic issues, are taken literally in matters relating to foreign policy. In this way the desire to attempt some form of international coöperative action develops out of the horror and weariness of war; it is taken up and given articulate form by the leaders, and the ground is prepared for a new attempt at internationalism. In time of peace, the public is satisfied with the *status quo* and looks sourly at proposals of this kind, but in time of war there is a willingness to admit the mistakes of the past and to undertake to explore new paths to security. Moreover, if the war is being fought in alliance, a kind of *de facto* international organization is already in existence. The first hurdle has been jumped because there was no alternative, the second one—permanent organization—therefore appears less formidable.

To sum up, the impact of war tends to destroy many, if not most, of the existing forms and ideologies of previous internationalism. Though nationalism is tremendously fortified, there is also a new willingness, even a strong desire, to undertake new forms of international collaboration. And both of these seemingly contrary trends are manifestations of the same urge for the achievement of peace and security. Both represent a determination to profit from the mistakes of the past in order to build a better future when "Hope creates from its own wreck the thing it contemplates."

The effects of the present war in influencing trends toward nationalism can best be examined by observing what appears to be happening in certain of the leading belligerent states. These may be too incomplete to warrant widespread generalization, but they tend to bear out the general conclusions indicated above. They are illustrative and significant if not conclusive.

The case of the Soviet Union is particularly striking. Originally, the Soviet authorities attempted to construct a political unit which would be devoid of the traditional nationalistic sentiments of the bourgeois

NATIONALISM, INTERNATIONALISM, AND WAR

capitalist states. The cultural differences of the various national groups within the U.S.S.R. were carefully preserved. The traditional agencies of unity—the church, a common language, and so on—were discarded, and an effort was made to tie together the various groups within the Union solely through the acceptance of a common economic credo as implemented and guarded by the Communist Party and its ancillary organizations. This was a logical outcome of the doctrine of the indispensability of the world revolution as a preliminary step toward international organization of all national groups on the same basis of loyalty to the Communist doctrine.

The victory of Stalin over the Trotskyites paved the way for the abandonment of this view. Thereafter it was no longer believed that a communist state could not exist in a capitalist world. While suspicion of the noncommunist world remained strong, interest was focused upon the strengthening of the Soviet Union in the belief that its example would do more to advance the cause than the zealous encouragement of world revolutionary propaganda elsewhere. Also, the Nazi triumph in Germany was recognized to be a powerful object lesson in the folly of refusing support to noncommunist democratic forces in the capitalist states. The Comintern line was changed, and thus a first step toward international coöperation was taken.

So it happened that before the present war the way had been cleared, to some extent at least, for the development of orthodox nationalism in the Soviet Union. The events of the war have brought about an acceleration of this trend to a striking degree. In a sense, the last aspect of the old view disappeared when the Comintern was dissolved in May, 1943. Many recent developments have pointed the way toward the return of the Soviet Union to the more familiar manifestations of nationalism. In December, 1943, the *Internationale*, the hymn of world revolution written by Eugene Pottier in France in 1871, was abandoned as the Soviet national anthem. It was replaced by a "Hymn of the Soviet Union" with a familiar patriotic appeal. The chorus of the new anthem is as follows:

> Long may she live our motherland,
> Long may her flag be over us
> Flag of the Soviets, our trust and our pride,
> Ride through the storm victorious.
> Lead us to visions glorious—
> Flag of a people in friendship allied,

The use of the term "Russia" has become more frequent than in earlier years, and it appears that there has been an increased publication of volumes of patriotic poems and collections of patriotic excerpts from Russian writers of the Czarist as well as the postrevolution period.[1] At the same time there has been a distinct reversal of the past policy of hostility against the church. In September, 1943, the rights and privileges of the Russian Orthodox Church were largely restored, and the aging Metropolitan Sergius, who had held the remnants of the church together during the long period of official persecution, was officially installed as the Patriarch of all Russia. While no change was made in the constitutional provision of freedom for religious and antireligious activities, it was evident that a fundamental change in governmental policy had occurred. This was borne out by the subsequent announcement of the projected creation of a series of religious schools for the training of priests, a new *Journal of the Orthodox Church and Moscow Patriarchy*, and other indications of a rapprochement which would set up a separation of church and state along familiar Western patterns. While this change in religious policy was partially motivated, in all probability, by the desire to remove barriers against fuller cooperation with the Western powers, it can scarcely fail to be an important milestone in the development of stronger Russian nationalism. That the church will be patriotic in its teachings has been shown by the substantial funds which the church had already raised, long before the change in its status, for the prosecution of the war effort.

As yet it is too soon to judge how far Russian nationalism will be affected by the decision of the Supreme Soviet in February, 1944, to enlarge the sphere of autonomy of the sixteen constituent republics by giving to each larger powers with respect to foreign affairs and the constitution of Red Army units. However, to the extent that this decentralization is actually carried out in practice it will verify the assumption that the change was a reflection of the strengthened solidarity of the units of the Union produced by the effects of the war. Clearly, this administrative change would not have been made if it had been felt that it would detract from, rather than add to, the sense of nationalistic solidarity of the peoples of the U.S.S.R.

In short, it appears that the ordeal of the war against Nazi Germany is having in the Soviet Union the familiar effect of strengthening the

[1] For example, "Fatherland: a Collection of Points of View of Russian Writers about the Fatherland" (published in Russian, Moscow, 1943).

sense of national unity, and of stimulating patriotism on a nationalistic rather than a class basis. The blend of the old and the new is well illustrated by Premier Stalin's statement on the twenty-sixth anniversary of the October Revolution. Hailing the war achievement, he said,

> All the peoples of the Soviet Union have risen up as one to defend their motherland, rightly considering the present patriotic war the common cause of all working people irrespective of nationality or religion. . . . The friendship of the peoples of our country has stood all the hardships and trials of war and has become tempered still further in the common struggle of all the Soviet people against the Fascist invaders.

The probable effects of the war upon nationalism in China are necessarily less obvious. All that can be said at the present time is that the effects of the war should provide the background for the growth of Chinese nationalism to a much greater degree than at any previous time. Industrialization has been stimulated, internal communications will have been improved, and some improvement will have been made in solving the basic problem of illiteracy. If the differences between the Chungking government and the Chinese Communists can be solved so that there will be a single central authority commanding the loyalty of all China, there should be a growth of strong Chinese nationalism. One evidence of this tendency, which is already at hand, is the increasing determination of the Chinese Government after the war to take a strong position with respect to the continuance of Western political influences in the Far East. It is becoming increasingly clear that, to the extent of its ability, the Chinese Government will insist upon the termination of the last vestiges of these controls, and will go to great lengths to see to it that, in all future relations between the East and the West, China will be dealt with as a fully sovereign power. Some steps have already been taken in this direction—for example, the relinquishment of all extraterritorial rights by Great Britain and the United States in May, 1943—and it is probable that these gains in the political sphere will be accompanied by comparable attempts to solve such territorial problems as the status of Hong Kong.

Since victory will, as promised by the Cairo conference, increase the territory of China by the restoration of Manchuria and Formosa, it would seem as if all these developments, taken together, would favor the growth of a spirit of nationalism to match the new status of equality, already conceded as a courtesy measure, as one of the four "superpowers." The conditions are favorable and the war experience should speed up the process to a marked degree. The possibility, however, of continued political disunity and instability remains a serious problem, as there is little evidence that the end of the war will find the present Chungking regime in a position of strength comparable in any way to that of her major allies.

In the United States and Great Britain the most obvious effect of the war will be the stimulation of nationalistic pride by the success of a great war effort. The British will take an understandable and legitimate satisfaction in the fact that their perseverance through the grim days of 1940 was ultimately crowned by complete victory. It is equally obvious that, in the United States, there will be patriotic pride through contemplating in retrospect the magnitude of the war effort, the speed with which an unprepared nation girded itself for a global war, and the completeness of the success which its armed forces achieved over the enemy. Victory will mean that, in each country, there will be renewed confidence in the fundamental soundness of its political and social institutions, and an institutional loyalty of this kind is an indispensable basis for vigorous nationalism. Dunkirk and El Alamein, Tarawa and the battle of Normandy will take their places in British and American history as new evidences of patriotic achievement.

In a comparable way the tribulations of the occupied countries of Europe will feed the nationalistic pride of the peoples concerned. Sufferings as well as victories have their part in the lore of nationalism, and suffering which is crowned with eventual victory as the justification for resistance is one of the most potent of all. If there is doubt on this score, one need only remember the potent symbolism of Valley Forge in American history. After the war, the occupied countries will each have dozens of similar examples to be recalled for the patriotic edification of future generations.

Not only the war effort, but the war settlements as well, may serve to stimulate nationalism. If past wars conducted in alliance are any guide to the future peace settlement, it is not to be anticipated that the victors will see eye to eye on all matters which must be dealt with. Nationalism is not only fed by pride in achievement; it is also supported by disagreements with other nations. Thus if Britain, Russia and the United States "fall out" over the peace, the suspicion and distrust engendered in each with respect to the others will favor the growth of belligerent nationalism. Confident of the justice and reasonableness of its own position, each state will read the worst motives into the opposition of the others—and this is the stuff on which the narrowest and most reprehensible nationalism feeds most greedily.

Since territorial compromises are inevitable in the peace-making process, some states—chiefly the smaller ones—will fail to have their claims satisfied. Whether a defeated state is forced to cede part of its territory to the victors or a victor state fails to get the territory which it feels rightfully belongs to it, the resultant irredentism becomes a focal point for nationalist agitation. Alsace-Lorraine was such a symbol for France in the years from 1871 to 1918. Hitlerian propaganda made skillful use of the territorial losses sustained by the Reich in the Versailles settlement. If, for example, at the end of the present war the Poles lose some of their eastern territory to the Soviet Union and are not compensated by other territorial gains at the expense of Germany, a similar situation will exist. In general, any territorial loss or any failure to gain territory which is regarded as properly belonging to the demanding state will set up a pattern of symbolism which fosters an intransigent nationalism. Unless a country disappears entirely—for example, Austria-Hungary after 1918—a forced detachment of territory remains as an object of agitation. Transylvania, the Dobrudja, Bessarabia, the Polish Corridor—all these were subjects of continual agitation after the 1919 settlement. Can one doubt that they contributed to the nationalistic feelings of Hungary, Bulgaria, the Soviet Union, and Germany? It is too much to expect that similar situations will not be produced by the settlements of the present war.

The intensity and duration of a nationalist reaction produced by dissatisfaction with the war settlements depends a great deal upon the economic situation of the postwar period. While in each dissatisfied state numerous individuals and groups will persist indefinitely in carrying on agitation about the losses, the popularity of the appeal as a nationalist symbol will be heightened greatly by economic hardship. Prior to the onset of the depression in Germany, the territorial losses of Versailles, while by no means forgotten, did not have overpowering symbolic potency. After the depression, the Nazis were skillful in developing and gaining popular acceptance of the view that the hardships of the time were due in large part to the injustices of the treaty settlement. In such an atmosphere the popularity of the *Lebensraum* doctrine as a panacea for all ills, real and fancied, was assured. Only general prosperity can blunt the cutting edge of a nationalistic reaction which is sharpened by a sense of injustice concerning the peace arrangements.

Because of its global character and the number of participating states, the present war has produced an unprecedented growth of international organizations and arrangements. While many of these will disappear from view shortly after the end of hostilities, others may be continued for some time thereafter, and they may, in this way, be important steps toward the postwar development of new international organization and new manifestations of internationalism. Since these wartime innovations are *ad hoc* in the strictest sense of the term, it follows that in almost every case they have been set up solely with a view to the prosecution of the war and not with any intention that the organization in question is to be a permanent mechanism.

The "United Nations" itself is merely an unorganized wartime coalition of nations bound together by their signatures to the Declaration of January 1, 1942. Each signatory is obligated to "employ its full resources, military or economic, against those members of the tripartite pact and its adherents with which such government is at war." It agreed also to coöperate with the other signatory states in all war matters and "not to make a separate armistice or peace with the enemies." At the political level this is the sum and substance of the United Nations organization. From time to time prominent citizens and groups in many countries have stressed the desirability of creating a United Nations Council or some similar agency which would provide a mechanism whereby the member states collectively could determine policies with respect to the war and the war settlements. The proponents of this view have argued that such a step would provide a means of maintaining better solidarity through the period of peacemaking and in the interim or transition period before the establishment of some general international organization to replace the old League of Nations. Thus far, however, the opposition has been too strong for such a step. Governments busy with waging war have an understandable aversion to any step which might slow up the process of decision making. Also, there is a troublesome problem regarding the status of some of the so-called "Governments-in-Exile" and the ability of their leaders to speak for the states which they purport to represent.

It is understandable that the chief pressure at the official level for the creation of such a United Nations organization has come from the smaller states because they tend to see in such a development a means of safeguarding themselves against excessive domination by the larger powers. The latter have as yet shown only moderate interest in projects relating to the organization of the United Nations. As will be discussed later, they have made some commitments concerning postwar international organization but it is clear that they have no intention of going very far in this direction until after the end of hostilities.

Space does not permit an extended examination of the merits and disadvantages of this view. Undoubtedly, there is merit in the contention that the early organization of the United Nations would capitalize upon the fact that during the period of hostilities states and peoples may be more willing to engage in international undertakings of this kind than at a later time when there is no longer a binding tie in the shape of a common enemy. On the other hand, it is true that it might be difficult to set up such an organization at a time when speed of decision is important and when those states carrying the brunt of the war must be free to exercise their full authority unimpeded by their lesser colleagues. To one attempting to chart the trends toward internationalism during the war, the chief matter of importance is the fact that the desire to set up such an organization seems to be persistent and widespread.

At the technical level, two United Nations organizations have been created recently. These are the United Nations Relief and Rehabilitation Administration and the Interim Food Commission. In each case the establishment of the organization was preceded by a conference of the representatives of all the United Nations. The conference on food and agricultural problems, held at Hot Springs, Va., in May, 1943, brought about a decision to create a permanent organization to deal with the food production and requirements of the member states, the efficient distribution of food exports, the promotion of higher nutritional standards, and consideration of the necessary commercial and financial arrangements to enable states to procure their needed food imports and to market their exportable surpluses. The Interim Commission was established to prepare the constitutional charter for a permanent organization, and to undertake certain preliminary and exploratory activities. A second Conference is to place the organization on a permanent basis.

The organization for relief and rehabilitation has already been fully established. In this case, agreement upon a fundamental charter had been reached by international negotiation before the conference was called. One interesting feature of this charter is the way in which the special position of the largest states has been combined with the principle of state equality. This has been accomplished by providing that while most features of the agreement can be changed by a two-thirds vote, a vote to change the status of the Director General or to change the composition of the Central Committee (which consists of the American, Chinese, Russian, and British representatives) requires the approval of all members of the Central Committee.

The relief and rehabilitation agency is by its nature a short-time organization, whose activities will draw to a close after the first problems of urgent post-hostilities need have been met. Therefore, the only new, broadly international organization of a permanent character created during the present war is the one dealing with the important, but relatively nonpolitical, matters of food and agriculture. Thus, to date, the net development in tangible terms is not impressive.

A far different picture is presented when one turns to examine the various international agencies which have been established as a direct part of the prosecution of the war. In this case, the general picture is that of a number of organizations each of which has a limited membership and specific restricted functions.

At the technical level the most numerous are the American-British Combined Boards and other agencies set up to facilitate the collaboration of the two powers in the war effort. The Combined Chiefs of Staff is an organization of the highest military authorities of the two countries. Acting as a kind of board of directors, it has supervision over a variety of special committees dealing with intelligence, meteorological information, military transportation, and the like. A Combined Food Board, consisting of the United States, Britain, and Canada, undertakes to marshal and distribute available food supplies in the way best calculated to advance allied needs. A Combined Raw Materials Board, confined to the United States and Britain, performs a similar function with respect to industrial war materials needed for war purposes. At the next stage, that of processing, there is an American-British Combined Production and Resources Board. The transportation stage is likewise dealt with by a Combined Shipping Adjustment Board.

Closely allied with these is the Middle East Supply Center, a coordinating agency established at Cairo by Britain in 1941. It is now an Anglo-American agency with an organization both in Egypt and in London; its functions are largely those of planning in the fields of supply and its primary purpose is to conserve shipping facilities in the interests of efficiency.

In this hemisphere, the United States and Canada, following the Ogdensburg Agreement of 1940, set up a Permanent Joint Board on Defense and a Joint Economic Committee. Both now deal with the problems of coördinating the economic and the military aspects of the respective war efforts of the two countries. Similar in character in the military field is the Joint Mexican–United States Defense Commission, established in January, 1942, and a Joint Brazil–United States Defense Commission which was organized in August, 1942. More representative in character is the Inter-American Defense Board, set up in accordance with a resolution of the Meeting of the Foreign Ministers of the American republics at Rio in January, 1942. Its function is to make recommendations to the several governments concerning matters of importance to the defense of the Western Hemisphere. It operates under the general auspices of the Pan American Union.

At the political level there has been a greater dependency on *ad hoc* consultation. Nonetheless, certain agencies have been created. Among these are the Emergency Advisory Committee for Political Defense for the Western Hemisphere, authorized by the Rio Conference. It consists of representatives of Argentina, Brazil, Chile, the United States, Mexico, Uruguay, and Venezuela, but the Committee is authorized to represent and to act in the names of all the members of the Inter-American organization. Representatives of the governments at war with Japan constitute a Pacific War Council, with its headquarters in Washington, but there is no great evidence that this organization has a great deal of vitality in terms of actual joint-policy making.

The establishment of organized political coöperation with the Soviet Union was not accomplished until after the Moscow Conference in October, 1943. Thereafter, there was set up a European Advisory Commission, with headquarters in London. It consists of representatives of Britain, the United States, and the Soviet Union. While its authorized functions are those of study and recommendation to the three governments on matters relating to the peace settlements in Europe, it has developed into a useful agency for the coördination of policies, and it may well prove of great importance in preparing the way for a common policy with respect to many of these thorny questions. Comparatively little information is available to the public concerning its current activities.

The coördination of Allied policy with respect to Italy has been provided by the establishment of an Advisory Commission which includes British, Russian, and American representatives as well as a representative from the French Committee of National Liberation. Provision was also made for the eventual inclusion of Greek and Yugoslav representatives. Its sphere of activity is limited to nonmilitary matters. It, too, has operated in an atmosphere of considerable secrecy.

Both technical and political aspects are involved in the problem of punishing war criminals. In January, 1942, the governments-in-exile in London signed a joint declaration committing themselves to a policy of postwar punishment for Axis individuals guilty of acts of criminal violence in violation of the 1907 Hague Convention. Subsequently, most of the United Nations have adhered to this declaration or have made similar statements of policy. In London, a United Nations Commission for the Investigation of War Crimes has been set up. Not all the states with an announced policy toward the punishment of war crimes have participated in the work of this Commission, but it has met regularly and usefully over a period of many months.

In addition to the developments of an organizational nature, sketched above, numerous other efforts to seek common solutions to problems of international interest have been, or are being, made by the various groups of the Allied governments. Thus, conversations between Britain and the United States concerning postwar civilian air transport regulation have already been held, and it is probable that, in the near future, the matter will be considered on a more broadly international basis. International currency and monetary problems were considered at an international conference held at Bretton Woods, N.H., in July, 1944. The United States extended invitations to the British, Russian, and Chinese governments to a conference in August, 1944, on the basic problems of a postwar general international organization. Presumably, if agreement among these states is secured concerning the general features and framework of such an organization, representatives of other nations will be invited to a subsequent conference on the subject.

Behind the organizations already established and these projected conferences, there are the commitments which have been undertaken by the various governments. Reference has already been made to the obligation of the United Nations Declaration to wage war and to conclude peace on a collaborative basis. This is the only general commitment entered into by all these states in common. More important, perhaps, as an indication of the probable future trends toward internationalism are the special commitments undertaken jointly by Britain, the Soviet Union, and the United States. Particular importance naturally attaches to the policies of these three states because, at the end of the war, they will have a near monopoly on the world's military power, and they will possess the potentials of power—industrial plant, raw materials, strategic position—to an unprecedented extent. By their industrial and military development in recent years they have raised the level of great-power status higher than it has ever been in history, so high, in fact, that the near-great states have been hopelessly outdistanced. Consequently, this unique situation has placed these states in a position of particular effectiveness for the enforcement of such policies as they can agree upon.

First of all, how far do the "Big Three" plan to go in creating a general international organization? What kind of an organization do they envisage? What powers is it to have? Is it to be another agency for the coördination of the policies of sovereign member states, or an organization to which the members will delegate a considerable amount of actual decision making? Is organization to be regional or world-wide? Is the peace to be kept by an "international police force" which will restrain aggression among the nations much as the blue-coated policeman does among individuals? The answers to these questions will determine how far the war is likely to bring about a relatively greater increase of nationalism or of internationalism.

The Atlantic Charter, of August, 1941, referred to this problem only in a general statement to the effect that there must be after the war "a wider and permanent system of general security." A second equally vague statement was contained in the Anglo-Soviet twenty-year treaty of alliance concluded in May, 1942. In this document the parties recorded their "desire to unite with other like-minded States in adopting proposals for common action to preserve peace and resist aggression in the postwar period," and they agreed that their own bilateral assistance arrangements should, by mutual agreement, be superseded when such general arrangements had been made.

The next—and at time of writing, the last—commitment of an official character is the Moscow Declaration of October 30, 1943. The four signatories—Britain, Russia, the United States, and China—"recognize the necessity of establishing at the earliest practicable date a general international organization, based on the principle of the sovereign equality of all peace-loving States, and open to membership by all such States, large and small, for the maintenance of international peace and security." In the period prior to the establishment of such an organization the four states pledged themselves to "consult with one another and as occasion requires with other members of the United Nations with a view to joint action on behalf of the community of nations." In order to pave the way for the development of an effective international organization, the four states further agree that "after the termination of hostilities they will not employ their military forces within the territories of other States except for the purposes envisaged in this declaration and after joint consultation."

This agreement, and subsequent statements by Secretary Hull, Foreign Secretary Eden, and, more recently, by President Roosevelt, indicate the present view accepted by the "superpowers." First, they are not contemplating a superstate which would infringe the sovereignty of the members. This point is clear. The Moscow Declaration, for example, refers to "the principle of sovereign equality," and President Roosevelt in his statement of June 15, 1944, said flatly that "we are not thinking of a superstate with its own police forces and other paraphernalia of coercive power."

As to the type of organization, the American view—according to President Roosevelt—is that there should be a broadly representative body responsible "for promoting and facilitating international coöperation, through such agencies as may be found necessary to consider and deal with the problems of world relations." This general body would elect a smaller council which would include the "four major nations and a suitable number of other nations" and would deal with peaceful settlement of disputes "and with the prevention of threats to the peace or breaches of the peace." To implement the decisions of this council, there should be

effective agreement and arrangements through which the nations would maintain, according to their capacities, adequate forces to meet the needs of preventing war and of making impossible deliberate preparation for war, and to have such forces available for joint action when necessary.[2]

For the present inquiry the important point is whether or not the proposed organization is merely to be an agency for international coöperation or whether it will, as an organization, have effective power to deal with problems of international security. An inference, at least, in the latter direction is contained in a statement by the prime ministers

[2] The quotations in the above paragraph are all taken from President Roosevelt's statement released to the press, June 15, 1944.

of the British Dominions, issued in May, 1944, at the conclusion of their conference in London, and signed also by Winston Churchill. These British Commonwealth leaders said, "We affirm that after the war a world organization to maintain peace and security should be set up and endowed with the necessary power and authority to prevent aggression and violence." Actually, of course, there is no halfway ground. Either we are to have a powerful organization, as the prime ministers have indicated, or we are to have another League of Nations in which the power of decision concerning collaboration for security purposes is to remain as before fully in the hands of the individual states. The former would constitute a tremendous step in the direction of international government. The latter, being essentially consultative, would not. On the contrary, it would leave the way open for a strengthened nationalism.

It is true that even a consultative organization might be a first step in the direction of a growing internationalism, and participation in it would be a step in this direction as far as the United States is concerned. But there is another aspect of the problem that has an important bearing on the subject. This is the fact that a kind of deception being practiced today may have weighty consequences in the future. It is well illustrated by the Connally Resolution adopted by the United States Senate in November, 1943. This statement of policy proposed "That the United States, acting through its constitutional processes, join with free and sovereign nations in the establishment and maintenance of international authority with power to prevent aggression and to preserve the peace of the world." In other words, people are being led to believe that they can maintain full sovereignty in the traditional sense of the term, but that, at the same time, they can set up an international organization with sufficient power to prevent the disturbance of the future peace.

Obviously, the two are incompatible. And if, as President Roosevelt's statement indicates, the plan is to set up a merely consultative organization, we will not have an organization inherently powerful enough to meet any important crises. Each nation will still be free to exercise its ultimate right of deciding, in a given situation, whether it will or will not support the proposed action against an aggressor. Such decisions, inevitably, will be taken in the light of what are considered to be the highest national interests, and these may not always lead to the support of the organization. It was so with the League of Nations and it will be so with any future organization which is in essence merely consultative in character.

The point is that if this should occur, and if the organization should not manifest the strength and solidarity expected of it, there would be a strong probability of a sharp nationalistic reaction in many countries. If, for example, the United States should support the taking of strong measures against a state which seemed to be threatening world peace, and if either Britain or Russia should prove uncoöperative, old suspicions would be aroused again and extreme nationalism would be strengthened immensely. Once more it would be said that neither the British nor the Russians could be trusted, that each was selfish in the narrowest sense of the term, and that we should rely in the future only on ourselves for our future security. If the American people were made to realize that such differences were inherent in the type of organization which had been created, no such striking reaction would be likely to occur.

The price to be paid for anything approaching absolute security is great. It would involve the creation of a true superstate, the establishment of a powerful international force, and the concomitant disarmament of the member states down to a level where they would be unable to resist this force. Unquestionably, neither the American people nor those of any of the other great powers are prepared to make such sacrifices at the present time. But it would be the part of wisdom to make these issues more clear than they have been up to the present time. In any event, the outcome will affect the trends in these countries toward nationalism.

If we are to assume the probable creation of a general consultative international organization, then future nationalistic trends will be affected by some of the international relationships which will exist behind this façade. There is, for example, the problem of regional relationships. The United States will undoubtedly insist upon preserving and even expanding the Inter-American system. It is increasingly clear that Soviet Russia will assert a special interest in the small states on her western frontier. As evidence of this, reference may be made to the Soviet opposition to the creation of an Eastern European federation of some sort, a step which was undoubtedly motivated by the fear that such a federal grouping would be anti-Soviet in orientation.[3] If one may judge from existing trends, the Soviet policy is not only to pre-

[3] New York *Times*, Nov. 17, 1943.

vent the development of unfriendly regimes on her frontiers; it is also designed to bring about the existence of a pro-Soviet regime in these states. The refusal to deal with the obviously anti-Soviet, Polish government-in-exile is a good illustration of this point. Another may be found in the mutual assistance pact signed between Czechoslovakia and the U.S.S.R. in December, 1943. Finally, it may be noted, that according to current press reports, one of the Russian peace terms demanded of Finland is that Finnish policy shall be oriented favorably toward Soviet Russia.

This does not mean necessarily that Russia is looking ahead to a peace settlement which will facilitate the gradual expansion of Soviet influence throughout Central Europe. It may mean merely that as a part of a future security policy the Soviet Union wishes to have beyond her own frontiers a protective shield of small states which, though independent, will be pro-Soviet in general policy and will look to Moscow for aid and perhaps protection in case of need. If so, it would be a policy motivated from substantially the same considerations that have led the United States to interest itself in the political orientation of the regimes of the small Caribbean states situated uncomfortably close to the Panama Canal.

On the other hand, one should not overlook the possibility that such a policy might be interpreted, especially in the United States, as an indication of Russian desire to extend the domination of the Kremlin gradually throughout Europe. If such should be the view taken by the American people, it would have a chilling effect upon Soviet-American relations. The Russians might well feel that what they would regard as a wholly inconsistent attitude on our part was in reality merely another evidence of our desire to do what we could to confine and cramp the development of the U.S.S.R. On both sides there might be a distinctly nationalistic reaction which would have the effect of increasing the hostility of the two peoples against each other.

If, unhappily, such should be the case, then the British would be placed in a difficult position because they might be compelled to make the choice between continuing their special alliance arrangements with the Soviet Union or choosing to rely upon American support and reinforcing it by such arrangements as they could make with France and the other states of Western Europe. Undoubtedly, Downing Street would do all in its power to avert such a dilemma, for the net result would be the creation either of an American-British, anti-Soviet bloc or of a Soviet-British bloc which would further alienate the United States.

Aside from the complication of Russian policy, there are many opportunities for postwar friction between the United States and Great Britain. While these will not, in all probability, be grave enough to threaten the essential solidarity of interests which both peoples have recognized in time of crisis in the past, they may be sufficiently irritating to prevent the two countries from establishing the full and satisfactory coöperation requisite for any substantial growth of postwar internationalism. These potential irritants are well known. The United States and Britain may fail to work out any solution to the problem of postwar air-transport arrangements. British policy may not be willing, at the time of the peace settlements, to go as far as American opinion thinks desirable in granting an increased measure of autonomy, or even independence, to certain portions of the Empire. American opinion may not be satisfied with the British contribution to the war in the Pacific after the war in Europe has been brought to a close. There may be sharp disagreement over the final settlement of the wartime financial arrangements between the two countries. There may be acrimonious controversy over respective trade and commercial policies. The net result of these and many other possibilities of friction may be that the United States will turn toward nationalism rather than internationalism, and Britain may turn toward the Continent and Russia.

France presents another problem. If the present policy of the United States, toward France, acquiesced in by Britain and Russia, remains unchanged until the French government is firmly reëstablished on French soil, it may well be that the French, seeking that equality of status in great-power councils which the present policy of the "Big Three" does not seem to contemplate, will try to place themselves at the head of all the smaller states of Europe which are unhappy over the prospects of too much domination by these great powers. The success already achieved by the De Gaullist group in securing recognition from many of these smaller states is an indication that this possibility is by no means to be discounted. If, in such circumstances, France is still excluded or treated as a less-than-great power, or even if France is admitted belatedly and grudgingly into the charmed circle, the end result is obviously one which would conduce toward nationalist rivalry and suspicion rather than toward any internationalist collaboration.

A broader aspect of this problem deserves some attention. This is the delicate adjustment of large-power relations with the smaller powers in the postwar period. Thus far, the smaller members of the United Nations have been generally excluded from great-power councils, and the Moscow Declaration seems to forecast a continuation of this arrangement through the transition period before the establishment of the general international organization. It is clear—and understandable—that these smaller states are not happy over the prospect of great-power action, even though taken ostensibly "on behalf of the community of nations," unless the smaller states are regularly consulted in some organized and prearranged fashion. If the great states refuse to make any such arrangements, and if the creation of a permanent organization is delayed until some time long after the peace settlements have been made, it will be difficult to prevent a natural growth of nationalistic bitterness among these lesser states.

Moreover, the same problem will be encountered in setting up a permanent organization. The great powers, on whom the primary burden of the maintenance of peace must inevitably rest, will undoubtedly take the view that, in so far as security matters are concerned, they must have authority commensurate with this responsibility. Any arrangement that placed upon the great powers the obligation to carry out measures determined by other states would be unworkable. In the United States, it would revive such fears of international organization as might easily prevent American membership. On the other hand, if the smaller powers are not given some share in decision making, they will feel that they have placed themselves fully at the mercy of their larger neighbors. This is perhaps the most delicate problem of all. There seems to be no easy or completely satisfactory solution for it. No matter which way the balance is shifted, there is a prospect of such dissatisfaction as will jeopardize that full collaboration of large and small which is needed if internationalism rather than narrow nationalism and traditional power politics is to be the dominant feature of the postwar world.

All of this is but another way of saying that the sky is far from cloudless. There can be no assurance that the victory won on the battlefield will bring about either a lasting peace or any automatic assurance that the international politics of the future will differ markedly from those of the past. In a world filled with many small states, a few of medium size, and a very few with surpassing power, the development of satisfactory international collaboration is by definition a most difficult and delicate task. It will require, above all, the close and continuous collaboration of those on whom leadership must fall. This collaboration must somehow achieve a synthesis between the legitimate safeguarding of essential national interests and the furtherance of the welfare of those who cannot protect themselves. This is not a matter which can be determined in a single conference, nor in a single constitutional charter however skillfully contrived. It will depend upon patient and far-sighted statesmanship, which will build gradually but surely toward a distant goal. The stakes are great because history has demonstrated the impossibility of localizing conflict in the modern world. The millennium, however, is not at hand.

Index

Acculturation, 89 f., 135 ff., 205, 443; among American Indians, 282 ff., 399; borrowings in, 179, 209; colonial, 382, 393 f.; diffusion studies, 147; sociopsychological aspects of, 171-200; discovery and invention, 150 ff., 173, 208 f.; and dominant interests, 108, 164 ff., 208 ff.; in economy, 173; induced by force, 192 ff.; institutional approach to, 157 ff.; processes of, 143-70; psychological approach to, 163 ff.; resistances to, 179 ff.; and specialization of skills, 180
Adaptation, processes of, 107, 175 ff.
Adult education, use of listening groups, 468
Africa, 383n; British anthropological studies, 376; oil, 233; population problem, 265; see also East Africa; West Africa; South Africa
Agencies, international cessation of activities, 498; established as part of prosecution of war, 510
Agricultural Experiment Station, 419, 421
Agriculture, 214 ff., 263, 420; land-use pattern (chart), 250; and population, 259 ff. (see also Farm population); seven changes in, 420; and world food supply, 250 ff., 259 f.
Air transport regulation, 512
Alcoholics, clinical groups, 454, 457, 458
Alorese culture, 115 ff., 120
Alsace-Lorraine, 362
Aluminum, 245
American-British Combined Production and Resources Board, 510
American League of Decency, 467
American life, technology as cultural focus of, 167
American Sociological Society, Papers, 426
American Town, An (Williams), 417, 422, 430
Ammon, on race mixture, 46
Anthropology, collaboration with other disciplines, 12 ff., 17, 108 ff.; contributions to colonial administration, 380 ff.; definition, 3 f.; divisions of, 5 f.; physical, and race classification, 22
Anthropologists, war work of, 379
Anti-Semitism, *see under* Jews

Anxiety drives, 193 ff., 197 f.; reduction of, 455, 457, 458
Applied Anthropology, Society for, 378
Archeology, 8 f.
Aracaunian Indians, 289, 297
Arensberg, C. M., and S. T. Kimball, 436
Argentina, Indians, 296 f.; natural resources, 224 ff.
Army, intelligence tests, 29, 69 ff.; rejections for nutritional deficiencies, 261
Arnheim, Rudolf, and Martha C. Bayne, 481n
Aronovici, C., 426
Arsenian, C., 73n
Artist, as cultural inventor, 155
Ashley Montagu, M. F., on race, 43, 47
Asia, population problem, 265 f.; see also China; Far East; Japan
Assimilation, colonial problem of, 328 f., 336; policy of minorities, 358 ff.
Atlantic Charter, re colonies, 341
Atwater, H. W., and I. M. Bailey, 429n
Audience, radio, 473-79; attitudes, 482; how influenced, 481
Australia, 226, 261; anthropological work, 396; National Research Council, 377; native culture, 30; population problem, 265
Automobile, effect on American culture, 207 f.
Avila Camacho, 408
Aymara Indians, 297

Bailey, I. M., H. W. Atwater and, 429n
Barber, B., 198n
Barnett, H. G., 186n, 198
Barrera, S. E., B. L. Pacella and, 459n
Barstow Memorial Foundation, 378
Basic personality structure, 107 ff.
Bauxite, 245
Bayne, Martha C., Rudolf Arnheim and, 481n
Beaglehole, E., on the anthropological approach to colonial problems, 380 f.; on Hawaiian culture, 184n, 190; and P. Beaglehole, 383n
Bear ceremonialism, 161
Behavior, cultural, 91 f., 93 f., 97, 126, 177 f.; habitual character of, 131 f., 442-64

INDEX

Behaviorism, 141*n*, 162
Belgian Congo, 334 f.
Belgium, Institut Colonial International, 378; minority groups in, 353
Bell, Earl H., 439*n*
Benedict, Ruth, 108*n*
Bennett, J., 145
Benson, Irving G., 454*n*, 458*n*
Berelson, B., *et al.*, 488*n*
Berkwitz, Nathaniel J., 459*n*
Bernard, *Instinct*, 126
Beyer, H. O., work in the Philippines, 378
Bidney, David, 106, 175
Biological processes, cultural forms of, 88 f.
Birth rate, 264 ff.
Black, J. D., 261, 262
Blood groups, 45
Blumenbach, 41*n*
Blumenthal, Albert, 106
Blumenthal, Dorothy, H. D. Lasswell and, 480*n*
Boas, Franz, 86; on Alaskan needlecases, 143; on descendants of immigrants, 22 f., 57 ff.; diffusion studies, 147; on half-breed Indians, 27; early view on racial differentiation, 66
Body size, increase in, 23 f.
Boers, 26 f.
Bolivia, Indians, 300
Bounty (ship), 27
Bowers, Raymond V., 472
Bowles, physical records of Harvard students, 23
Braceland, F. J., H. D. Palmer and, 459*n*
Brazil, Negroes in, 277; and U.S. Defense Commission, 511
Bretton Woods conference, 512
Bricker, G. A., 425*n*
Brigham, C. C., intelligence tests, 29, 70
British Empire, resources, 224 ff.
Britt, S. H., 54*n*
Brown, G. G., 378; and A. M. B. Hutt, 383*n*
Brown, P. E., on land use, 260
Brown, Theodore H., 474*n*
Brunner, E. de S., 429*n*; and M. V. Brunner, 425*n*; H. N. Morse and, 425*n*
Burma, 322
Butterfield, K. L., 425*n*

Camp, P. M., 425*n*
Canada, 261; Indians in, 189 f., 296; natural resources, 225 ff.
Canberra Agreement, 373

Carr, E. H., 367
Carr-Saunders, A. M., 270*n*
Caste system, 208 f., 369; colonial, 308, 311, 318, 320, 324, 329, 332 f., 336
Castle, *re* miscegenation, 26
Cattle complex, 161 f.
Caucasus, minority problem, 371
Central America, Indians in, 282 ff., 302 f.
Cephalic index, 57 f.
Ceylon, 322
Chaco Indians, 297 f.
Chamberlain, H. S., 65
Chappell, and Hooper, 474*n*
Childhood, 447, 449
Children, intelligence of Negro and white, compared, 74 f.; problem, clinical group set-up for dealing with, 455; treatment of, in primitive societies, 111, 115, 119 f., 135
China, exterritorial rights, 505; natural resources, 225 ff. *passim;* population problem, 266
Chinese students, personality tests, 76
Chinnery, E. W. P., 377
Chou, S. K., and C. Y. Mi, 76
Christensen, R. P., 266; on land use, 262
Christianity, cultural impact of, 170, 190 f., 196, 285, 390
Churchill, Winston, 274, 515
Cinemas, *see* Moving pictures
City dwelling, effect of, 215 f., 420 f.
Civilization, and innate ability, 30; effect of environment upon, 34; *re* racial degrees of, 30; *see also* Culture
Classification, racial, 20 ff., 38 f., 50, 52; by physical characteristics, 29, 39 ff., 47 ff., 50 ff., 67, 263 ff.; *see also* Differentiation, racial
Clifford, Hugh, 313
Climate, effect of, 35 f.
Clinical group situation, 454-59; verbal elements, 456
Coal, 227 ff.; production (table), 231; reserves (table), 230, 231; world resources, 230 ff.
Cohen, Felix S., 404
Coleman, L., 434*n*
Collier, John, 15
Colombia, Indians, 303
Colonial administration, 15, 187 f.; applied anthropology in, 373-98; color line, 308, 311, 318, 320, 324, 329, 332 f.; causes of ill feeling, 374; and culture, 101; economic status, 309 f., 315 f., 325, 329, 337, 386 f.; education, 311, 316 ff., 321, 326 f.,

332, 391; and firearms, 194 f.; government, 308 f., 312 ff., 321 ff., 325, 327, 332, 388 f.; labor, 316, 325, 334, 344, 387; second World War and, 374; social sciences in, 386; social services, 311, 316, 321, 322, 336, 342, 386, 390; training of personnel, 397
Colonies, advantages of, 337 ff.; area and distribution, 306 f.; evolution in, 319 ff.; industrial development, 344; international coöperation, 341 f.; native populations, 310; *see also* Colonial administration
Color line, *see* Caste system
Comanche Indians, 113 f., 119
Combined Boards, 510
Commission on Country Life, 417, 421
Communication, radio, 465 ff.
Communications research, and international coöperation, 465-95; audience, 473-79; content, 479-85; organization and control, 492-95; tests, 486 ff.
Communism, 220, 503
Community, basic personality of, 122; study of, 416-41; rural: West's study of, 117 f.
Community Organization and Agricultural Planning: Greene County Georgia (Coleman), 434
Conditioning, cultural, 89 f.; *see also* Acculturation; Culture
Connally Resolution, 515
Contraception, and birth rates, 271 ff.
Coon, C. S., 50n, 54n; *re* Jews as race, 54
Cossacks and Tungus, 181, 185 f.
Cranial index, 55
Criollo, 290
Cross-cultural similarities, list of, 124
Crossing, in monkeys, 40n
Cultural-historical school, 148
Culture, changes in, *see* Acculturation; concept of, 78-106; definitions, 78 ff., 203; diffusion of, 109, 147 ff., 167 ff., 174; family organization in, 140; environment and, 90 ff.; focus point in, 108, 164 ff., 208 ff.; historical approach to study of, 145 ff., 174; institutions as dynamic units of, 107 f.; laws of growth and decay, 95; nonhistorical approach to, 149 f.; organization of, 206 f.; survival values, 86; theory of racial contributions to, 65; universal aspects, 123-42, 144 ff., 174
Cuvier, 54
Czechoslovakia, relations with Russia, 517

Dahlberg, G., 46; on racial differentiation, 418; *re* species, 40
Dart, *re* Cuvier's findings, 54
Davis, Allison, 61; and John Dollard, 445n; B. B. Gardner, and M. R. Gardner, 445n
Davis, E. E., 426n
Designs for living, 97 f.
Determinism, cultural, 94, 153
Devereux, George, on American Indians, 195; and E. M. Loeb, 188
Dewey, John, 176
Dictatorship, and colonial government, 314
Diet, 14 f., 85
Dietary standards, 261 f.
Diethelm, Oskar, 454n
Dietrich, J. H., 278
Differentiation, racial, 22; genetic theory of, 42; by intelligence, 29 f., 63 ff., 276 f.; physiological, 31, 41, 64, 65 f.; psychological, 66; *see also* Classification, racial
Disarmament, 516
Discovery, 151 ff., 153 ff., 173
Discrimination, racial, *see* Race prejudice; Segregation
Disease, racial tolerance or susceptibility to, 16, 26, 31 f.; cultural diffusion of, 31, 195
Distributional school, 147
Dixon, R. B., 151 f.
Division of Subsistence Homesteads, 433
Dobzhansky, T., 40, 41
Dodd, Stuart C., 483n
Dollard, John, 82, 106, 123n; Acquisition of New Social Habits, 442-64; Allison Davis and, 445n; N. E. Miller and, 106, 183n, 197n, 442n, 445n, 456n
Dominant interests, *see* Focus, cultural
Drives, 183 f., 186, 204 ff.; anxiety, 193 ff., 197 f.; stimulation and satisfaction of, 130
DuBois, Cora, on Alorese culture, 115
Dutch Ashkenazim Jews, 57
Dutch East Indies, *see* Netherlands Indies

Earp, E. L., 425n
East, E. M., 276n
East Africa, 186; cattle in culture of, 161 f.
Eastern European federation, Soviet opposition to, 516
Eating, cultural aspects of, 85, 128, 164, 184, 186, 196
Ecuador, Indians, 301
Eden, Anthony, 514

Education, as a social need, 134 f.; colonial problem of, 311, 316 ff., 321, 326 f., 332, 391
Edwards, E. E., and Johnstone, P. H., 420*n*
Egyptian culture, 148
Eiselen, *re* missions in South Africa, 191
Elkin, A. P., 396
Elliott-Smith, G., 148
Elmer, M. C., 426
Endocrine glands, and racial differentiation, 32 f.
Energy resources, 227 ff.
England, government urges serious broadcasts, 476; population, 274 f.
English diffusionist school, 147 f.
Ensminger, 433
Environment, effect on culture, 90 ff., 112; on the individual, 23 f., 34 f.; and population problems, 268 f.
Eskimo, 296
Ethnology, 8, 10 ff.
Ettinger, Karl, 478*n*
Europe, oil reserves, 233 ff.; population problem, 263 ff.
European Advisory Commission, 511
European culture, attempts to organize, 220; impact of, 150 ff., 192 f.; influence on American Indians, 283 ff., 399
Europe, colonization by, 307, 350; migrations, 171, 188; racial classification of, 20; spread of disease by, 31, 195
Evolution of the Country Community ... (Wilson), 424
Exterritorial rights in China, 505

Family and Community ... (Arensberg and Kimball), 436
Family organization, 140 f., 179
Far East, agriculture, 251; myth of racial inferiority, 312; Western political influences in, 505
Farm population, 416 ff.
Fascism, 220, 223
Fashions, analysis of changes in, 158 f.
Fear, repression of, 451
Federal Emergency Relief Administration, 433
Federation, colonial, 343 f.
Field, H., 53*n*
Fijian Frontier (Thompson), 383*n*
Finland, relations with Russia, 517
Fire, 213
Firearms, acquisition and use of, by native peoples, 194 f., 312
Firth, R., 149

Fishberg, 58
Fischer, study of the Rehobother Bastards, 26 f.
Focus, cultural, 108, 164 ff., 208 ff.
Folk tales, diffusion of, 156
Food economy, 214 ff., 263
Food habits, 128, 164, 184, 186, 196
Food supply, world, 248 ff., 259 f.; and culture, 112; Hot Springs conference, 509
Force, as means of inducing cultural change, 192 ff.
Ford, Clellan S., 106, 123*n*; definition of culture, 81
Foreign language broadcasts, 481
Foreign Ministers of the American republics, Meeting, 511
Fortune, R., 149
Foy, W., 148
France, 261, 518; colonial policy, 328 ff., 378; secessionist minorities, 362
Frank, L. K., 106; on the use of cultural patterns, 98 f.
French Canadians, 277
French Committee of National Liberation, 511
Freud, 108, 109, 141, 451, 454; concept of working through, 448; discrimination mechanism, 450
Friedl, Ernestine, study of the Ojibwa, 117 f.
Friends of the IA, *see under* International authority
Fry, C. L., 425*n*

Galpin, C. J., 427, 432, 433; quoted, 428; and V. B. Larson, 429*n*; J. H. Kolb, Dwight Sanderson, and C. C. Taylor, 429*n*
Gamio, Manuel, Some Considerations of Indianist Policy, 399-415
Gardner, Burleigh B., *et al.*, 445*n*
Gardner Mary R., *et al.*, 445*n*
Garth, intelligence studies, 29
Gaudet, H., *et al.*, 488*n*
Genetic variation, 22, 24 f., 42
German diffusionist school, 147
German "historical" school, 174
Germany, 224 ff. *passim*, 261, 312; colonial administration and anthropology, 378; natural resources, 222 f.; secessionist minorities, 362
Giddings, Franklin H., 421*n*, 422; quoted, 424 f.
Gilfillan, S. C., 153
Gill, C. O., and G. Pinchot, 425
Gillen, John, on the anxiety drive, 198

INDEX 525

Gillespie, R. D., 459n
Gist, N., analysis of secret societies, 160
Gobineau, de, 65
Goldenweiser, A. A., 145; on cultural accident, 169
Goldschmidt, R., 39n; and Mayr, re species, 39
Good Neighbor policy, 477
Government, 443; colonial, see Colonial administration
Governments-in-Exile, 508
Graeber, J., and S. H. Britt, 54n
Graebner, Fritz, 148
Grant, Madison, 26
Gray, L. C., 420n
Great Britain, 261; colonial administration, 309, 318 ff., 341, 375 ff.; effect of war, 506; natural resources, 224 ff.; U.S. and, 518
Greece, 211
Greene County, Ga., 434
Gregory, W. K., re variation, 43
Groups, modification of rivalries, 459-64; new vested interests, 499; see also Clinical group
Group therapies, comparison between psychoanalytic therapy and, 458
Groves, W. C., 396
Guam, study of education, 378
Guam and Its People, 383n
Guaraní, 290, 298
Guatemala, 181 f.
Guilt, reducing feeling of, in alcoholics, 457, 458
Guthe, C. E., 57

Habit formation, 131, 137, 442-64
Hadley, J. Nixon, 414
Hailey, Lord, colonial policy, 341
Haldane, J. B. S., 269, 276
Hallowell, A. I., on bear ceremonialism, 156; Sociopsychological Aspects of Acculturation, 171-200
Harrison, H. S., 151
Hart, Hornell, 471, 472n
Harter, W. L., and R. E. Stewart, 429n
Harvard Univ., physical records of students, 23
Hawaii, 58 f.; Beaglehole re, 184n, 190
Hayes, A. W., 426n, 428n
Hershey, General, re nutritional deficiencies, 261
Herskovits, Melville J., 175n, 190; Processes of Cultural Change, 143-70
Hirsch, N. D. M., study of cephalic index, 57

Hoffsommer, H. C., 432n
Hogbin, H. I., 383n; re the Solomon Islands, 191, 193, 197; and C. Wedgwood, 396n
Holme, R. A. E., 454n, 458n
Holmes, S. J., 268n, 277n
Hooper, Chappell and, 474n
Hoosier Village, A (Sims), 423
Horowitz, E. L., 63n
Hot Springs Conference on food and agricultural problems, 509
Hottentots, 26 f.
Housman, A. E., 449n
Howells, O., E. L. Morgan and, 428n, 429n
Howells, W. W., 50
Hsü, E. H., 76n
Hull, Clark, 123n, 442n, 451n
Hull, Cordell, 514
Hunter, M., 383n
Huntington, studies of optimal environment, 34
Hurgronje, Snouck, on the East Indies, 317 f.
Hu Shih, 278n
Hyman, Harold Thomas, 454n
Huth, Arno, 477n
Hutt, A. M. B., 383n
Huxley, J., on race, 45
"Hymn of the Soviet Union," 503

IA, see International authority
Ickes, Harold L., 404
Identification, with the dominant group, 196
Imitation, in social learning, 184 f., 456
Immigrants, descendants of, 22 f., 57 ff.
Impulse, see Drives
Inbreeding, 42
Incas, 42n
India, 321, 322 f., minority problem, 363; Nilgiri tribes, 180
Indians, American, 27, 86, 117 ff., 187, 210; classification of, 90, 410 ff.; cultural changes among, 282 ff.; disease, 31, 195; effect of European culture, 283 ff., 399; emotional tests of, 75 f.; and firearms, 194; folk tales, 156 f.; food habits, 196; government policy, 294 f., 399-415; Indianist movements, 288 ff.; intelligence studies of, 29, 73; language and acculturation, 407, 409, 411; legislation, concerning, 400, 402 ff.; maize culture, 155 f.; as a minority group, 284 f., 293 f., 403; national institutes, 400; and nation-

INDEX

Indians, American (*Continued*)
alism, 405; population trends, 290 ff., (table), 292; racial attitudes, 293 f.; religion, 190; status, 399 f.; trade with, 189

Indian Tribe in Transition (Majumbar), 383n

Individual, cultural role, 98 f., 153

Indo-China, 330

Inferiority, racial, false theory of, 312 f., 369

Instinct, and cultural behavior, theory of, 126 f.

Institute of Pacific Relations, 378

Institutions, dynamic units in culture, 107; international, effects of war upon, 496; primary and secondary, 111; social, Sumner and Keller on, 127

Intelligence, civilization and, 30; and environment, 71 f.; and race, 29 f., 30, 63, 68 ff., 276 f.

Intelligence: Its Nature and Nurture, 72n

Intelligence tests, 29, 276 f.; army, 69 ff.; problem of representative samples, 73 f.; in study of racial psychology, 68 ff.

Inter-American Defense Board, 511

Interim Food Commission, 509

Intermarriage, *see* Miscegenation

International authority, 466 ff.; Friends of the IA, 467 ff., 493; interest of national governments in, 467; personnel, 493; promotion of coöperation by national governments, 467, 468, 470; types of organizations concerned, 467

International coöperation, and communications research, 465-95; promotion of, 470, 473

Internationale, 503

International Institute of African Languages and Cultures, 376

Internationalism, 466; nationalism, and the war, 496-520; war lays basis for a new, 501

International law, one of major casualties of war, 496

International organization, postwar, 512 ff.

International Red Cross, 498

Inventions, 151 ff., 153 ff., 173, 208 f.

Iranian Plateau Race, 53n

Iron, 241 ff.

Isolation, 49, 67, 173; anxiety, 455 ff.; of Indians in Mexico, 406; of minorities, 350, 359, 369; racial, 42; *see also* Segregation

Italian-Americans, 91

Italy, 261, 363; coördination of Allied policy *re*, 511; natural resources, 224 ff. *passim*

Jacobs, M., *re* Jews as race, 54
Jacobson, Edmund, 459n
Jacobstein, Meyer, 420n
Jamieson, E., and P. Sandiford, 73n
Jameison, Gerald R., and E. E. McNiel, 454n
Japan, 169; coal production, 230 f.; colonial policy, 308, 335 f., 351; cultural borrowings, 188; industrial achievements, 312; population problem, 265
Japanese-Americans, 91
Jessup North Pacific Expedition, 147
Jews, 57; in medieval Europe, 355; as minority, 360, 361; no Jewish race, 53 f.; objective attitude toward society, 454; prejudice against, 459 ff.; sanctions and propaganda against anti-Semitism, 462; tuberculosis among, 32
Johnstone, P. H., E. E. Edwards and, 420n; R. Lord, *et al.*, 434n
Juárez, Benito, 402

Kappers, C. U. A., 57
Kardiner, A., 112n, 448; Concept of Basic Personality Structure, 107-22
Keesing, Felix M., 383n; Applied Anthropology in Colonial Administration, 373-98; on guns in Melanasia, 195, 197n; and M. Keesing, 383n
Keith, Sir Arthur, endocrine origin of racial differences, 32 f.; *re* plasticity, 59
Keller, Albert G., 123n, 127, 443n
Kellogg, Charles E., on increased crop yields, 262
Kellogg, P. U., 426
Kelly, W. H., *see* Kluckhohn
Kennedy, Raymond, The Colonial Crisis and the Future, 306-46; on colonial acculturation, 187 f.
Kimball, S. T., C. M. Arensberg and, 436
Kinsey, A. C., definition of species, 39
Kirk, Grayson, Nationalism, Internationalism, and the War, 496-520
Kirkpatrick, E. L., 429n
Kiser, L. K., 267n
Kitchen, V. C., 455n
Klein, W., 57
Klineberg, Otto, 71n; intelligence studies, 29 f., 71; Racial Psychology, 63-77
Kluckhohn, Clyde, and W. H. Kelly, Concept of Culture, 78-106
Kluckhohn, Florence, 78n

INDEX

Knight, Robert P., 454n
Knupfer, Genevieve, see Lazarsfeld
Kolb, J. H., 428n; et al., 429n
Kollmorgen, W. M., 439n
Kretschmer, Ernst, 66
Kroeber, A. L., 147; analysis of fashions, 159, 163
Krogman, Wilton M., 49n; The Concept of Race, 38-62

Labeling, learning by, 451, 454
Labor, in colonial policy, 316, 325, 334, 344, 387; supply and population problems, 279
Ladino, 290
Land Grant Colleges, 430; research methods, 431
Landis, B. Y., 425n
Land-use, 259 f.; chart, 250
Language, 179, 185 f.; and culture, 100; and Indian acculturation, 407, 409, 411; international, 491; linguistic "drift," 168; and mental tests, 73
Lanier, L. H., 71
Larson, V. B., C. J. Galpin and, 429n
Lasswell, Harold D., 481; and Dorothy Blumenthal, 480n
Lawrence, Raymond, 493n
"Laws of the Indies," 401, 404
Lazarsfeld, Paul F., 476n; and B. Berelson, and H. Gaudet, 488n; and Genevieve Knupfer, Communications Research and International Coöperation, 465-95; and Frank Stanton, 478n, 480n
League of Nations, 466, 498, 501; textbook revision by Intellectual Coöperation Organization, 470
Learning, formula for, 442; habit and, 137 f.; as means of power, 197; in old age, 444; psychotherapy and, 446; social, 443
Learning process, 80 f., 109, 126 f., 163 f., 175, 177, 182 f., 451, 454; psychiatric learning situation, 448-54
Lebzelter, Viktor, 53n
Lee, Dorothy, 100 f., 106
Leonard, O. E., and C. P. Loomis, 439n
Lindgren, Ethel J., on culture contacts, 181, 185 f.
Linguistics, 7
Linguistic "drift," 168
Linnaeus, 39
Linton, Ralph, 49, 106, 112, 113, 123n, 165, 175n; Aim and Scope of Anthropology, 3-18; on elaboration of cultures, 86; on nativistic movements, 198, 199; Present World Conditions in Cultural Perspective, 201-21; re Tanala and Marquesans, 110
Lively, C. E., 426n
Loeb, E. M., 188
Loomis, C. P., 433, 434n; O. E. Leonard and, 439n
Lord, R., P. H. Johnstone, et al., 434n
Lorimer, F., E. Winston, and L. K. Kiser, 267n
Lotsy, J. B., re species, 40
Lyell, uniformitarianism, 172

MacLeish, Kenneth, and Kimball Young, 439n
McNiel, Edwin E., Gerald R. Jameison and, 454n
Mair, L. P., 383n, 392
Maize culture, 155 f.
Majumbar, D. N., 383n
Malaria, tolerance for, of West African Negroes, 16
Malaya, 313, 321, 343
Malinowski, Bronislaw, 106, 123n, 127, 149, 376, 384
Malthus, T. R., 259, 275
Man, and society, 19-37, 174 f.; differentiation, as basis of race classification, 28 f.; genetic constitution, 42, 268 f.; increase in physical size, 23 f.; physical differences, 41
Mandelbaum, D. G., on Nilgiri tribes, 180
Mannheim, K., 426
Mansfeld, F. W., 273n
Maoris, renaissance movement, 377; "taihoa policy," 396
Maori People Today, The (Sutherland), 383n
Marett, J. R. de la H., 43n; definition of race, 43
Marquesans, 110, 112, 115
Martin, study of stature of army recruits, 23
Mayer, Arthur L., 493n
Mayr, F., 39n; re species, 39, 40
Mead, Margaret, 14, 101
Melanesia, 149, 150; introduction of weapons, 195, 197n
Melvin, B. L., 428n
Mental defectives, 269 f.
Mental tests, see Intelligence tests
Mestizos, 300; in Mexico, 403, 407, 412

Metabolism, 65; and racial differentiation, 31
Mexico, Indians, in, 301 f., 401 ff., 406; and U.S. Defense Commission, 511
Meyerhoff, H. A., Present State of World Resources, 222-57
Mi, C. Y., 76
Middle East Supply Center, 510
Miller, Neal E., 450n; and John Dollard, 106, 183n, 197n, 442n, 445n, 456n
Mills, study of bodily development, 24; re effect of climate upon metabolism, 31
Mineral resources, 240 ff.
Minority, 77, 347 ff.; American Indians as, 284 f., 293 f., 403; assimilation policy, 358 ff.; attitudes of, 348 f.; cultural renaissance, 356 f.; declaration re, 357; defined, 347; emergence of, 364 f.; exchange of populations, 372; and dominant group, 196, 352 ff., 359 ff.; isolation, 350, 359, 369; Jews as, 360, 361; militant, 362 f., 366; and nationalism, 366 ff.; pluralistic, 354 ff.; rights of, 354, 356, 367; secularism and, 368 f.; secessionist, 361 f., 366; social status, 276 f., 348
Miscegenation, 26 f., 42, 44 f., 324, 333 f.
Missionaries, role in acculturation, 188, 190 f., 382, 390 f.
Moral Education Congress, 470
Morant, G. M., re Cuvier's findings, 54; and O. Samson, 58
Moreno, J. L., 433
Morgan, E. L., and O. Howells, 428n, 429n
Morgan, Lewis H., 125
Morse, H. N., and E. de S. Brunner, 425n
Moscow Declaration of Oct. 30, 1943, 513, 519
Moving pictures, 473 ff.
Mulatto, 26
Mumford, Lewis, 121
Murdock, George P., 106; Common Denominator of Cultures, 123-42
Murray, Sir Hubert, 377
Mutation, 42
Myrdal, Gunnar, on concept of race, 64, 71n
Mythology, as cultural mirror, 154, 156

Nationalism, 466; American Indians and, 405 ff.; in China, 505; internationalism, and the war, 496-520; and minorities, 366; and population growth, 274 f.; in Russia, 502 ff.; territorial loss and, 507; see also Nativist movements
National Research Council, 14
National Socialism, see Nazis
Native cultures, and colonial policy, 323, 329, 382 ff.; preservation of, 392; see also Acculturation; Primitive Societies
Native peoples, as minorities, 349; myths re character and capacity, 387; see also Culture; Race
Nativistic movements, 198 f., 394; Amermerican Indians, 288 ff.; Maori renaissance, 377
Natural gas, 236
Natural resources, see World resources
Nauru island, 383
Navaho Indians, 86, 291
Nazis, 222, 312, 478
Needs, satisfaction of, 203 ff.
Negro, and disease, 16, 26, 32; intelligence tests, 29, 62 f., 69, 74 f., 276 f.; minority status, 353, 358; population problem, 265; racial attitudes toward, 293, 459, 460; in South America, 297
Nelson, Lowery, 432
Netherlands Indies, administration, 187 f., 309, 315, 317, 324 ff., 375
"Neuroticism," in Chinese students, 76
Neurotic person, 449, 452, 453
Neurotic symptoms, and the practices of primitive people, 109
New Guinea, 377; introduction of firearms, 195; *The Making of Modern New Guinea* (Reed), 383n; Reed on, 189, 195, 197
Newman, study of twins, 29
Newspapers, see Press
New Zealand, 261, 377
Ngata, Sir Apirana, on colonial administration, 374
Niebuhr, Reinhold, 103
Nilgiri tribes, cultural changes among, 180, 187
Nimkoff, Meyer F., W. F. Ogburn and, 443n
Nonliterate peoples, 171, 177, 193
Nordenskiöld, E., 147
Nordic, 26
North Pacific Expedition, 147
Nutritional standards, 261 f.

Oberholzer, Emil, 117
Oberhummer, E., 39n
O'Connell, Cardinal, 278
Odum, H. W., on concept of race, 64
Ogburn, W. F., and D. Thomas, 153; and M. F. Nimkoff, 443
Ogden, C. K., 491n
Ogdensburg Agreement, 511
Oil, 228 ff.

INDEX 529

Ojibwa Indians, 117 ff.
Old age, 88; learning in, 444
Ontario Indians, 73
Ortega y Gasset, 83
Os Inca, 42n
Otis, Margaret, Hans Speier and, 480n
Overholser, Winfred, 459n
OWI, 478
Oxford Group, 458
Oxford Movement, 454, 458

Pacella, B. L., and S. E. Barrera, 459n
Pacific Relations, Institute of, 378
Pacific War Council, 511
Pai, T., S. M. Sung, and E. H. Hsü, 76n
Palmer, H. D., and F. J. Braceland, 459n
Pan American Union, 511
Pangai (Beaglehole), 383n
Papua, 377, 380, 395
Paraguay, Indians in, 298
Pareto, 121
Park, Robert E., 471
Pavlov, 442n
Peace, maintaining postwar, 515; terms, 506, 507
Pearl, Raymond, 271, 272, 273, 278; on population growth, 259
Pearson, Karl, 437; and Tippet, study of cephalic index, 57 f.
Pei-sung Tang, 266
Perry, W., 148
Personality, concept, and the social sciences, 107 ff.
Personality psychology, contributions of, 13 f.
Personality tests, 76; *see also* Intelligence tests
Peterson, J., and L. H. Lanier, study of Negro intelligence, 71
Peterson, William, study of weather and function, 31
Peru, Indians in, 298 ff., 403 f.
Philippines, 375; American policy toward, 330 ff.; *Taming Philippine Headhunters* (Keesing), 383n
Physical characteristics, in racial classification, 29, 31, 39 ff., 44 f., 47 ff., 50 ff., 64, 65 f., 67
Pierson, E., 277
Pinchot, G., C. O. Gill and, 425n
Pitt, William, 275
Plains Indians, 160, 161, 196; Sun Dance, 145n, 147, 155
Plasticity, 24, 59
Poland, minorities, 351, 363; government-in-exile, 517

Police force, international, 513, 516
Polynesians, 209; disease among, 31, 32
Population, 258-81; effect of race mixture on, 29; American Indian, 290 ff.; growth and distribution, 274 ff., 424; and labor supply, 279
Portellus, intelligence studies, 29
Portugal, colonial policy, 334
Pottier, Eugene, 503
Poverty, and birth rate, 278 f.
Power, development of, 217 ff.
Prejudice, racial, 28, 312 f., 369, 461; social, 459 ff.
President, ratings of speeches, 473
Press, and the IA, 468 f.; change in attitude of Southwestern, 483; interest in political and international issues, 476; in southeastern Europe, 493; Washington correspondents, 493
Pressey X-O test, 75
Priestly, H. J., 187n
Prime ministers, British, *re* world organization, 515
Primitive societies, study of, 10 ff., 108; use of tools and fire, 213 f.; *see also* Acculturation; Native peoples
Propaganda, 480 f.
Psychiatric learning situation, 448-54
Psychiatry, drift toward model of Freudian thought, 448
Psychoanalysis, drift of psychiatry toward, 448; and the learning theory, 449; in the study of culture, 108 ff.
Psychoanalytic Therapy, 452 f., 458
Psychology, racial, 63-77; and the color line, 312 f.; technique in the study of culture, 108 ff.
Psychotherapy, 446, 451
Public opinion, devices for influencing, 465; increasing importance of, 469; polls, 483, 486, 490, 491
Pueblo Indians, 296
Puerto Rico, 271

Quaker Hill (Wilson), 423

Race, classification, 20 ff., 29, 38 ff., 47 ff., 50 ff., 67; concept of, 7, 38-62; definition of, 38, 49, 64; differential birth rates, 270; inferiority, 312 f., 369; and intelligence, 29 f., 276 f.; major stocks, 50 f., 263 ff.
Race "mixture," *see* Miscegenation
Race prejudice, 28, 312 f., 369, 459, 461; *see also* Miscegenation

Radio, and IA, 467 ff.; foreign language broadcasts, 481; international broadcasting, 469; musical and dramatic programs, 475; serious broadcasts, 476
Radio listening groups, 468
Raper, A., 435n
Redfield, Robert, 106; on the concept of race, 60; on culture contacts, 181 f.
Reed, S. W., re effect of trade on native culture, 189; on New Guinea, 189, 195, 197, 383n
Regional relationships, postwar, 516
Rehobother Bastards, 26 f.
Reich Film Chamber, use of mobile cinemas, 478
Religious systems, in primitive cultures, 111, 138, 165 ff., 169, 170, 190 f., 386, 390; and psychoanalytic therapy, 453
Resettlement Administration, 433
Rhodes–Livingstone Institute of Central African Studies, 376
Richardson, J., and A. L. Kroeber, analysis of fashions, 159, 163
Robbins, William S., 478n
Rogers, Carl R., 447n
Roheim, Geza, 106
Roman Catholic Church, 190; attitude toward birth control, 273, 278
Roosevelt, Franklin D., 514, 515
Rorschach test, 76, 117 f.
Ross, Murray, 493n
Rosten, L. C., 494n
Rural church surveys, 425
Rural community, 416 ff.; analysis, 427, 437 ff.; concepts of, 435; new orientations, 420; plan for new series of studies, 439
Rural Expansion (Williams), 424
Rural school studies, 425n
Rural social research, 416 ff.
Russia, *see* U.S.S.R.
Russian Orthodox Church, 504
Rylander, Gosta, 459n

Samoa, 378; *Modern Samoa* (Keesing), 383n
Samson, O., 58
Sandiford, P., 73n
Sanderson, Dwight, 432, 433; and W. S. Thompson, 428n, 432n; *et al.*, 429n
Sapir, Edward, 106, 168
Sax, Karl, Population Problems, 258-81
Schapera, I., 170, 383n; on culture contacts, 190; South African research, 376
Schilder, Paul, 456
Schmidt, W., 148

Schweizinger, G., 268n
Schwidetzky, J., re cranial index, 55
Scientific method, 218 f.
Screen function of psychoanalyst, 452
Secret societies, 160
Secularism, impact of, on the minorities problem, 368
Segregation, colonial problem of, 308, 318, 320 f.; of minorities, 353 f.; *see also* Isolation
Selection, 42; biological, 27 f.; cultural, 95
Self-determination, cultural, 393 ff.; national, 366 ff.
Self-government, colonial, 308, 313, 322 f., 336 f., 399 ff.
Self-sufficiency, national, and natural resources, 222 ff., 420
Sergius, Metropolitan, 504
Sexual behavior, 128 f., 140, 461
Shapiro, H. L., Society and Biological Man, 19-37; cephalic index of Japanese in Hawaii, 58
Shelden, W. H., Work on link between constitution and psychology, 66 f.; S. S. Stevens, and W. B. Tucker, 66n
Sikh culture, 117 f.
Similarities, cultural, 123-42, 144 ff., 174; list of, 124
Simmons, Leo, 106; on culture, 82
Simpson, G. G., re variation, 43
Sims, N. L., 422, 423, 427
Sington, Derrick, and Arthur Weidenfeld, 478n, 479n
Skin color, 67 f.
Skull, *see* Cephalic index; Cranial index
Slavson, S. R., 454n, 455n; and others, 454n
Slesinger, Donald, 492n
Smith, Marian W., study of Sikh culture, 117 f.
Snyder, L. L., 46
Social behavior, acquisition of new, 442-64; drives as a basis of, 127 ff.
"Social heredity," 82
Social learning, *see* Learning
Social needs, 134
Social prejudices, *see under* Prejudice
Social research, rural, evolution of, 416-41
Social sciences, and anthropology, 12 ff., 17, 108 ff.; demands upon, in present crisis, 202, 447
Social services, status in the colonial system, 311, 316, 321, 322, 336, 342, 386, 390
Society, and biological man, 19-37; distinguished from culture, 79 f.; life dilemmas in, 444-48; parallels between social and biological phenomenon, 202 f.; *see*

INDEX

also Culture; Native culture; Primitive peoples
Sociologists, rural, 416, 418, 419, 421
"Sociology of Rural Life, The," 426
Solomon Islands, Western culture and, 191, 193, 197
Somatology, 6
South Africa, Institute of Race Relations, 376; missionaries in, 191; *Reaction to Conquest* (Hunter), 383n; *South Africa Western Civilization and the Natives of* (Schapera), 383n
South America, Indians in, 282 ff., 296 ff.; oil, 232
South Pacific, Congress on, 376
South Seas in the Modern World (Keesing), 383n
Soviet Union, *see* U.S.S.R.
Spain, colonies, 335, 401; cultural influence on American Indians, 285 ff.
Species, definitions of, 39 f.
Speier, Hans, and Margaret Otis, 480n
Spencer, 125
Spengler, 121
Spier, L., 147, 155
Srole, Leo, W. L. Warner and, 460n, 461n
Stalin, Joseph, 503; on minorities, 371 f.; quoted, 505
Stanton, Frank, P. F. Lazarsfeld and, 478n, 480n
Stein, M. R., study of racial differences in teeth, 16
Stern, Bernhard J., 153, 371n
Stevens, S. S., 66n
Steward, Julian H., The Changing American Indian, 282-305
Stewart, R. E., W. L. Harter and, 429n
Stouffer, Samuel, 487n
Subsistence Homestead, Division of, 433
Sudeten, 362, 372
Sumner, William Graham, 443n; and Keller, division of social institutions, 127
Sun Dance, 145n, 147, 155
Sung, S. M., 76n
Survival value of cultural aspects, 86
Sutherland, I. G., 383n

Tanala, 110, 112 f., 115, 119 f.
Tannenbaum, Frank, 405n
Tax, Sol, on Guatemalan culture, 182
Taylor, Carl C., 426, 428n, 439n; Techniques of Community Study and Analysis as applied to Modern Civilized Societies, 416-41; *et al.*, 429n
Taylor, E. A., 432n; and F. R. Yoder, 428n

Technology, 210 f.; as American cultural focus, 167
Teeth, Stein's study of racial differences in, 16
Terman, 442n
Textbook revision, 470
Thadus, J. E., *et al.*, 429n
Theodore Roosevelt Commission on Country Life, 417, 421
Thomas, D., 153
Thompson, L., 378, 383n
Thompson, W. S., on land use, 260; D. Sanderson and, 428n, 432n
Thompson, Walter A., 454n, 457n
Thorndike, 442n
Thurnwald, R. C., on social contact in East Africa, 186
Thurston Neurotic Inventory, use in China, 76
Tippet and Pearson, study of cephalic index, 57 f.
Tobacco, 420
Toynbee, 121
Trade, effects of war upon, 499
Traders, effect on native cultures, 188 f.
Trade zones delineated, 427
Tropics, agriculture, 251
Tucker, W. B., 66n
Tungus and Cossacks, 181, 185 f.
Tylor, 125

Uniformitarianism, 172
U.S.S.R., 502 ff.; anthropology applied in colonial problems, 378; autonomy of constituent republics, 504; economic specialization, 224; mineral resources, 244; minority problem, 370 f.; natural resources, 224 ff.; and Poland, 517; and U.S., geographical analogy, 226; opposition to an Eastern European federation, 516; organized political coöperation with, 503, 511; policy toward church, 504; policy toward frontier states, 517; Soviet-American relations, 517
United Nations, organization, 508; declaration *re* war and peace, 512
United Nations Commission for the Investigation of War Crimes, 512
United Nations Relief and Rehabilitation Administration, 509
United States, colonial policy, 330 ff., 375, 378 f.; and Britain, 518; Government broadcasting, 469; minerals, 240 ff.; minority groups, 347, 353, 358 ff., 369 f., 403 f.; natural resources, 225 ff.; nutri-

INDEX

United States (*Continued*)
  tional standards, 261; prestige among colonial peoples, 331; test scores of various ethnic groups, 68 f.; and U.S.S.R., 226, 517; *see also* Indians, American
Uruguay, natural resources, 225 ff., *passim*

Variation, genetic, and environment, 22, 24 f.; studies of, 42 f.
Veblen, Thorstein, 152
Venezuela, Indians, 297 f.
Versailles, Treaty of, 366, 368
Vollenhoven, C. van, 375
Von Tungeln, G. H., J. E. Thadus, and E. L. Kirkpatrick, 429n

Waples, Douglas, 479n, 481n
War, abolition of, 444; control of, 465; nationalism, internationalism, and the, 496-520; penalties against different social segments, 461
War Crimes, United Nations Commission for the Investigation of, 512
Warner, W. L., and Leo Srole, 460n, 461n
Warren, 432
Washington, George, 217
Water power, 236 f.; distribution (table), 238; utilization (table), 239
Weather, physiological effects of, 31
Wedgwood, C., 396n
Weidenfeld, Arthur, Derrick Sington and, 478n, 479n
Weidenreich, F., 42n
Wellman, B. L., study of intelligence and environment, 72
West, James, study of Plainville, 117 f.
West Africa, cultures of, 165 ff.; maize culture, 156; Negro tolerance for malaria, 16
Western Civilization and the Natives of South Africa (Schapera), 383n
Western culture, 393; and Am. Inds., 406; changes in, 199; colonial diffusion of, 345; impact, 219 f., 221, 388 f.
White-collar workers, 461, 463
White race, dominant status of, 351
Whiting, John, 123n
Williams, F. E., 377
Williams, J. M., 417, 422, 427, 430; measurement of population trends, 424
Wilson, W. H., 423, 424, 425n, 427
Wilson, Woodrow, on national self-determination, 367
Winston, E., 267n
Wirth, Louis, Minority Groups, 347-72
Wissler, C., 125; on maize culture, 155
Witty, P. A., and M. A. Jenkins, 75n
World authority, *see* International authority
World War, second, impact on colonial problems, 378, 379
World resources, 222-57; energy, 227-40; minerals, 240-48; food, 248-54, 260; land-use pattern (chart), 250
World revolution, 503
Wynne, Waller, 439n

Yerkes, R. M., 69n
Yoder, F. R., E. A. Taylor and, 428n
Young, Kimball, Kenneth MacLeish and, 439n

Zinn, Earl, 123n
Zimmerman, C. C., 428n, 433
Zionism, 361